Tragic Pleasures

✳

Frontis. Lysippides Painter (manner of). Attic black-figure type A zone cup, ca. 520 B.C.E. Collection of the J. Paul Getty Museum, Malibu, California.

Tragic Pleasures

*ARISTOTLE ON PLOT
AND EMOTION*

*

Elizabeth S. Belfiore

PRINCETON UNIVERSITY PRESS

PRINCETON, NEW JERSEY

Copyright © 1992 by Princeton University Press
Published by Princeton University Press, 41 William Street,
Princeton, New Jersey 08540
In the United Kingdom Princeton University Press, Oxford
All Rights Reserved

Library of Congress Cataloguing-in-Publication Data

Belfiore, Elizabeth S , 1944–
Tragic pleasures Aristotle on plot and emotion / Elizabeth S Belfiore
p cm
Includes bibliographical references and index
ISBN 0-691-06899-2 (alk paper)
1 Tragedy—Greek influences 2 Aristotle Poetics 3 Poetics
4 Aristotle—Aesthetics 5 Aristotle—Influence I Title
PN1899 G74B45 1992
808 2—dc20   91-42103   CIP

This book has been composed in Linotron Garamond

Princeton University Press books are
printed on acid-free paper, and meet the guidelines
for permanence and durability of the Committee
on Production Guidelines for Book Longevity
of the Council on Library Resources

Printed in the United States of America

1   3   5   7   9   10   8   6   4   2

FOR PETER

✱

Would it give you pleasure to see bitter sights?

—Euripides, *Bacchae*

We take pleasure contemplating the most accurately made
images of things that themselves give us pain to see, such as
the shapes of the most despised animals and of corpses. The
cause of this is that learning is most pleasant not only to
philosophers, but to others in the same way,
though they have only a small share in this.

—Aristotle, *Poetics*

*

❋ *Contents* ❋

* Acknowledgments *

THIS BOOK could not have been written without the help of many individuals, who read drafts, discussed relevant issues, and gave encouragement. I am particularly indebted to Helen Bacon, David Balme, Peter Belfiore, Christopher Carey, David Charles, Norman Dahl, David Depew, Patricia Easterling, Marcia Eaton, Montgomery Furth, Eugene Garver, Leon Golden, Allan Gotthelf, Richard Janko, Richard Kraut, Sandra Peterson, Deborah Roberts, George Sheets, Charles Young, and the readers and editors of Princeton University Press.

Research for this book was supported by a fellowship from the American Council of Learned Societies, with funding from the National Endowment for the Humanities (1987–1988), and by a Single-Quarter Leave from the University of Minnesota (1989). Funding from the National Endowment for the Humanities allowed me to attend the 1988 Summer Institute on Aristotle's Metaphysics, Ethics, and Biology, where I learned a great deal about Aristotle from individuals too numerous to mention. I would like to thank the organizers of this institute: John Cooper, Michael Frede, and Allan Gotthelf.

Earlier versions of parts of this book have been published previously. "A Medicine to Produce *Aidōs*" (in chapter 1) is, in part, a shortened version of "Wine and *Catharsis* of the Emotions in Plato's *Laws*," CQ 36 (1986): 421–37, reprinted by permission of Oxford University Press. Chapters 2 and 7 reproduce, with some revisions, material from "Pleasure, Tragedy, and Aristotelian Psychology," CQ 35 (1985): 349–61, reprinted by permission of Oxford University Press. An earlier version of "Plot and *Ēthos* in the Greek Tragedies" (in chapter 3) was published in "Aristotle's Concept of *Praxis* in the *Poetics*," CJ 79 (1983–1984): 110–24, reprinted by permission of the Classical Association of the Middle West and South. "Peripeteia" (in chapter 5) is reprinted, with minor revisions, from "*Peripeteia* as Discontinuous Action: Aristotle, *Poetics* 11.1452a22–29," CP 83 (1988): 183–94, copyright © 1988 by The University of Chicago.

* *Abbreviations* *

ANCIENT WORKS

Aristotle

Ath. Pol.	*Athenian Constitution*
Cat.	*Categories*
DA	*De anima*
DMA	*De motu animalium*
EE	*Eudemian Ethics*
EN	*Nicomachean Ethics*
GC	*Generation and Corruption*
GA	*Generation of Animals*
HA	*History of Animals*
Meta.	*Metaphysics*
Meteor.	*Meteorologica*
MM	*Magna moralia*
PA	*Parts of Animals*
Phy.	*Physics*
Po.	*Poetics*
Pol.	*Politics*
Post. An.	*Posterior Analytics*
Pr. An.	*Prior Analytics*
Prob.	*Problems*
Rhet.	*Rhetoric*

Other Ancient Works

Eum.	Aeschylus, *Eumenides*
Il.	Homer, *Iliad*
IT	Euripides, *Iphigenia in Tauris*
LB	Aeschylus, *Libation Bearers*
Od.	Homer, *Odyssey*
OT	Sophocles, *Oedipus the King*
Prot.	Plato, *Protagoras*
Rep.	Plato, *Republic*
Soph.	Plato, *Sophist*
Sym.	Plato, *Symposium*
Tim.	Plato, *Timaeus*

MODERN WORKS

Bekker	Bekker, *Aristotelis opera*
Bonitz	Bonitz, *Index Aristotelicus*
DK	Diels and Kranz, *Fragmente der Vorsokratiker*
Gauthier and Jolif	Gauthier and Jolif, *Aristote*
Ibycus	Ibycus Scholarly Computer
Kuhner-Gerth	*Ausfuhrliche Grammatik*
Littré	Littré, *Oeuvres complètes d'Hippocrate*
LSJ	Liddell, Scott, and Jones, *Greek-English Lexicon*

JOURNALS

AJP	*American Journal of Philology*
BJA	*British Journal of Aesthetics*
CJ	*Classical Journal*
CJP	*Canadian Journal of Philosophy*
CP	*Classical Philology*
CQ	*Classical Quarterly*
CR	*Classical Review*
G&R	*Greece and Rome*
GRBS	*Greek, Roman, and Byzantine Studies*
HSCP	*Harvard Studies in Classical Philology*
JAAC	*Journal of Aesthetics and Art Criticism*
JHS	*Journal of Hellenic Studies*
MH	*Museum Helveticum*
PR	*Philosophical Review*
REG	*Revue des études grecques*
RhM	*Rheinisches Museum fur Philologie*
TAPA	*Transactions of the American Philological Association*

Tragic Pleasures

*

* Introduction *

THIS BOOK is a study of the ways in which, according to Aristotle, the tragic plot arouses emotion in the audience. As the *Poetics* repeatedly states, the plot has the function (*ergon*) of arousing the emotions of pity and fear, and of producing pleasure and katharsis by this means. If tragedy is "imitation of action . . . by means of pity and fear accomplishing the katharsis of such emotions" (*Po.* 1449b24–28), it is, specifically, plot, "the first principle, and, as it were, the soul of tragedy" (1450a38), that imitates action (1450a3–4). In Aristotle's view, once we understand the structure of the plot we will also understand how tragedy affects the audience as it does. His chief contribution to aesthetic theory is a careful analysis of this plot structure in terms of its nature and function. This emphasis on plot helps explain why the *Poetics* does not contain a detailed discussion of the nature of the emotional responses to tragedy. Moreover, Aristotle would have expected his contemporaries to be aware of traditional views about these responses, many of which he shared.

Modern readers, however, necessarily study the *Poetics* not only outside its cultural context, but also in the foreign contexts of our own very different culture and of a long tradition of interpretation. Modern concepts of "the tragic flaw," "the unities," "purgation," "purification," "climax and denouement," the "tragic hero," and "aesthetic emotion," as well as a host of scholars from antiquity to the present, all condition and complicate our reading of this text. To see it clearly we must make a conscious effort to place the *Poetics* once again in its own philosophical and cultural context. I have attempted to do this in several ways.

First, I have tried to be aware of and to question the critical tradition and the biases of modern scholars. For example, twentieth-century scholars hold, almost universally, that katharsis is homeopathic: they believe that pity and fear, the emotions aroused by tragedy, accomplish a "purgation" or "purification" or "clarification" of similar emotions. This homeopathic interpretation is, however, merely assumed rather than explained and argued for. Only after we are aware of this and other biases, assumptions, and prejudices can we begin to consider the merits of a particular interpretation.

Second, I have tried to study the *Poetics* as an important philosophical text that can best be understood in the context of Aristotle's other philosophical works. While scholars of the *Poetics* often refer to selected passages

3

from such texts as Aristotle's *Rhetoric* and *Nicomachean Ethics*, they have, for the most part, neglected a great deal of relevant information contained not only in these sources, but also in the psychological treatises, the *Politics*, and the physical, metaphysical, and biological works. In these other works, we find more detailed information about such crucial concepts as imitation, necessity, and probability, as well as about kinship (*philia*) and the cognitive and physical components of emotional responses. Aristotle's biological treatises are of particular interest, for they help us understand what the philosopher means when he compares tragedy to a living thing. Moreover, Aristotle's frequent references in these writings to a process of katharsis can help clarify his elusive concept of tragic katharsis. I have tried to be cautious and judicious in using these other sources in interpreting the *Poetics*. Whenever possible, I have drawn on ideas in other works only when statements in the *Poetics* itself appear to justify this procedure. For example, the frequent biological analogies in the *Poetics* justify an appeal to biological concepts found elsewhere, especially since these concepts are consistent with and help us understand the *Poetics* as a whole. In some cases, notably that of katharsis, the *Poetics* tells us so little that we must rely almost exclusively on Aristotle's views in other sources. In these instances I have attempted to give an account that is plausible, coherent, and consistent with the philosopher's views generally. While many will undoubtedly disagree with my use of specific passages in other texts, few, I think, will deny that Aristotle's own writings are the best source we have for views that are expressed elliptically and obscurely in the *Poetics*.

Third, because Aristotle's views on tragic emotion were so much a part of the Greek literary, philosophical, and social tradition, I have tried, to the necessarily limited extent possible here, to study the *Poetics* in this broader context. Other Greek philosophers, before and after Aristotle, provide important information about ideas that may have influenced him, and about his possible influence on others. Greek medical theories are another important source, since Aristotle, the son of a physician, made frequent use of medical theory in his ethical and biological works. The Greek tragedies provide still another source of helpful information. It is also illuminating to look more broadly at the ideas held in Greek society as a whole about the emotions of pity and fear and about the related shame emotions. The Greeks were very much aware of the need for a certain kind of fear to control the aggressive and competitive tendencies of their society. In lyric poetry, in tragedy, and in philosophy, it is a common theme that fear of wrongdoing is a necessary antidote to a natural desire to act aggressively and shamelessly. A study of some examples of this theme illuminates why Aristotle believed tragic fear to be beneficial. Seen in the context of these and other aspects of Greek culture, Aristotle's ideas about tragic emotion and katharsis appear less mysterious and less original, but also more intelligible and more plausible, than is often supposed.

The dangers of the broad approach adopted here are, of course, great. It is clearly impossible for one book to do justice to so many difficult and controversial subjects. Moreover, I am not an expert on many of the topics I discuss, and have undoubtedly made mistakes. I believe, however, that the benefits of this approach justify the risks. For too long scholars have tended to study the *Poetics* as a kind of sacred text, in isolation from almost everything except the long and involved tradition of interpretation itself. It is time we began to look at the *Poetics* as an integral part of Aristotle's philosophy as a whole, and as a part of, and response to, the literary and philosophical traditions of a living society, many aspects of which are still accessible to us. I will have accomplished what I set out to do if I can suggest some new ways of looking at old problems, and make some mistakes that are worth correcting. In addition, I hope this book will contribute to the search, in which a number of scholars are now engaged, for a fruitful way of combining philosophical analysis with literary, philological, and historical studies.

While this book is primarily addressed to specialists in classics and in ancient philosophy, I have made every effort to make it accessible to the educated general reader as well. Although some sections are unavoidably technical, I have tried to make the main ideas clear to those who prefer to skip the details. Most Greek (except in a few technical passages) is translated or transliterated, and a glossary provides the English equivalents of frequently occurring Greek words. I have also taken the liberty of transliterating Greek words when quoting other writers.

Unless otherwise indicated, all translations are my own, and are intended to be accurate rather than fluent and idiomatic. In reporting the views of ancient writers, as well as in translating, I have not attempted to "correct" sexist language and points of view; to do so would be to misrepresent historical fact. For example, it is misleading to use "she" or "he or she" in discussions of Aristotle's ideas about courage. The Greek word ἀνδρεία (courage) is etymologically connected with ἀνήρ (man), and courage was thought, by Aristotle and his fellow Greeks, to be primarily a male virtue. I use the English masculine except where a gender-neutral term is clearly appropriate (e.g., to translate ἄνθρωπος [human being] in cases where this term clearly refers to both sexes).

PART I

THE GREEK BACKGROUND

*

The Gorgon at the Feast

WHEN ARISTOTLE defines tragedy as ' imitation by means of pity and fear accomplishing the katharsis of such emotions" (*Po* 6 1449b24–28), he notoriously fails to explain tragic emotion and katharsis Nevertheless, his views on aesthetic emotion are rooted in certain traditional Greek beliefs of which his readers would have been aware For one thing, Aristotle and his fellow Greeks of the fifth and fourth centuries B C E shared beliefs about the benefits of fear

It is a commonplace in Greek thought that a certain kind of fear is essential to a well-ordered society

> ἔσθ' ὅπου τὸ δεινὸν εὖ
> καὶ φρενῶν ἐπίσκοπον
> δεῖ μένειν καθήμενον

> There is a place where the terrible is good,
> and must remain established,
> an overseer of thoughts

> (Aeschylus, *Eum* 517–19)

This beneficial fear, which preserves law and custom, prevents civil strife, and averts shameless crimes against kin, is the fear of wrongdoing and the respect for parents, gods, and custom that the Greeks called *aischunē* or *aidōs* (shame, respect) Aristotle follows Greek tradition in characterizing *aidōs* in negative terms as an emotion that restrains people from wrongdoing (*EN* 1128b18), or as "avoidance of blame" (*EN* 1116a29) [1] Because this beneficial fear averts evil, it has a function that can be called apotropaic The highly competitive and aggressive Greek male society made this kind of fear especially desirable Particularly at feasts, festivals, and symposia (drinking parties), all of which involved drinking, celebrating, and competition, disruptive strife among friends (*philoi*) was always a danger Even peaceful, well-ordered symposia included many competitive, aggressive elements contests in words and music, obscene, insulting iambic po-

---

[1] Aristotle s views are discussed in chap 6

etry [2] It is significant that the Greeks used the same word, *eris* (strife), for competition within a society of friends and for strife among enemies [3] Critias, using a word cognate with *eris*, calls the poetry of Anacreon a "rouser" or "provoker of symposia" (*sumposiōn erethisma* frag 8 Diehl)

One function of tragedy was to provide the kind of beneficial fear that helped prevent strife among friends This function of tragedy would have been particularly clear in the context of the City Dionysia, the festival of the wine god that included dramatic competitions In an expression similar to that of Critias just quoted, Aristophanes refers to the "provokers of choruses" (*chorōn erethismata*) that take place in this spring festival of Dionysus [4] The competitive performance of tragedies was preceded by a revel (*kōmos*) and followed by a satyr play representing the more shameless aspects of Dionysus [5] This festival of Dionysus was so conducive to the arousal of shameless emotions and to acts of violence that a special assembly was held afterward to consider the violations of good order that had taken place [6] Within this setting, as in Greek society as a whole, tragedy was indeed an "overseer of thoughts," providing a necessary beneficial fear as an antidote to shamelessness

Aristotle's views on tragic fear and tragic katharsis must be understood in the context of these traditional views about beneficial fear and the function of tragedy Tragic fear, according to Aristotle, is aroused not by what is merely painful and destructive, but by deeds of violence among kin (*philoi Po* 1453b19–22) Unlike fear of physical pain, fear connected with harm to *philoi* is beneficial, preventing wrongdoing and encouraging respect for society and religion It averts evil by restraining the shameless emotions that destroy families and societies Aristotle adapts and uses for his own philosophical purposes traditional beliefs about the apotropaic and political functions of fear in casting out and purging the shameless emotions

Because Aristotle's views were influenced by Greek traditional beliefs

---

[2] On the symposium, see Murray, *Sympotica* Pellizer gives good accounts of aggression and quarrels in symposia in Zuffa, and of the control of passion and aggression within the symposium in Sympotic Entertainments, in Murray, 177–83

[3] See esp Hesiod, *Works and Days* 11–26, and the other examples given in LSJ

[4] *Clouds* 309–12 See Dover s note on 311 in *Clouds*

[5] Although the order of events in the City Dionysia is not known for certain, it is likely that the *kōmos*, a revel the details of which are not known, took place before the tragedies were presented The evidence for the *kōmos* is discussed in Pickard-Cambridge, *Dramatic Festivals*, 63–66

[6] Ibid , 68–70 On festivals and aggression, see also Parker, *Miasma*, 154–60, esp 159

concerning beneficial, apotropaic fear, it is essential to begin by looking briefly at a few aspects of this tradition. In this chapter, I focus first on one neglected image that can tell us much about Greek views on beneficial fear: that of the Gorgon at the feast. In particular, I examine two literary uses of this theme, one by Pindar (*Pythian* 12) and one by Aeschylus (*Eumenides*). I then discuss Plato's views on wine and on beneficial fear in the *Laws*.

GORGON AND GORGONEION

In Greek thought, the Gorgon is associated with fear and strife. This is apparent, for example, in "Hesiod," *Shield of Heracles*. One of the figures represented on the shield is Perseus, who holds the head of the Gorgon Medusa in a bag as he flees in terror from the other Gorgons, who pursue him. From the pursuing Gorgons' belts hang serpents, gnashing their teeth in rage and glaring savagely. Fear (*Phobos*) is in motion on the heads of the Gorgons (216–37). Fear also occupies the center of the shield. Like a Gorgon, Fear has a glance like fire. On Fear's brow is Strife (*Eris*), who takes away the wits of men (144–50). Although the Gorgon's glance does not turn people to stone in the *Shield*, this ability, prominent in other accounts, is surely to be connected with her fear-inspiring qualities, for extreme fear paralyzes.[7]

In the Perseus myth, Perseus must not look at the Gorgon Medusa as he kills her, in order to avoid being turned to stone. Once "tamed," however, the Gorgon and the gorgoneion (the severed head of the monster) have the apotropaic function of averting evil, and as such they are common devices on shields and temples.[8] As an apotropaic gorgoneion, the Gorgon's head

[7] Aristotle (frag. 153) states that the effect of the Gorgon's head is *kataplēxis*, an extreme kind of fear that prevents one from acting or speaking (*MM* 1193a4–6). In Plato, *Sym.* 198c, Socrates punningly pretends to fear that the Gorgon's head of Agathon's Gorgianic rhetoric might turn him to stony speechlessness. "Aristotle" lists paralysis of the tongue as one effect of fear (*Prob.* 947b35). The Gorgon's power to paralyze and kill should also be connected with that of the evil eye, on which see Deonna, *Symbolisme*, 153–58, and Phinney, "Perseus," 447–50.

[8] In Homer, for example, the shield of Agamemnon has a Gorgon on it (*Il.* 11.36–37), as does the *aigis* of Athena (*Il* 5.741–42). For further examples and discussions of this kind of "terrible" shield device, see Chase, *Shield Devices*, 28–29. The best-known example of a temple Gorgon is that of the temple of Artemis in Corcyra. While there is much dispute about the origin and nature of the Gorgon and gorgoneion, most scholars agree that they have a generally apotropaic function. Among the many interesting studies of the Gorgon

retains its ability to produce fear, but this ability is used against the enemies of civilization, to avert harm. After cutting it off, Perseus gives the head of Medusa to Athena, who wears it on her *aigis* (goatskin shield) to terrify her enemies.[9] The Perseus myth, then, shows how paralyzing, destructive terror can become beneficial when redirected away from oneself and one's enemies.

One use of the gorgoneion, however, is at first sight rather puzzling. In the black-figure drinking cup reproduced in the frontispiece, a central gorgoneion is surrounded by six symposiasts, who drink or hold musical instruments.[10] While the gorgoneion on the shield serves to avert an obvious danger, it is less clear why this terrifying monster should appear at a peaceful symposium. What dangers need to be averted here? Or is the gorgoneion in the cup a purely decorative motif?[11]

We know from ample literary documentation that discord and strife among friends were common at drinking parties Theognis, for example, frequently advises moderation in drinking to guard against this danger. Immoderate drinking, strife, and lack of shame (*aidōs*) are closely connected:

> Whoever exceeds the measure in drink, no longer is that man
> in control of his own tongue or thought,

are Bessig, "Gorgo", Croon, "*Mask*", Feldman, ' Gorgo", Howe [Feldman], "Origin ', Floren, *Studien*, Krauskopf and Dahlinger, "Gorgo' , Napier, *Masks*, 83–134, Niese, "Gorgo , and Riccioni, 'Origine "

[9] A good brief survey of the myth in art and literature is given by Phinney, 'Perseus "

[10] I am indebted to Kenneth Hamma, Associate Curator for Antiquities at the Getty Museum, for information concerning this cup This theme is also represented in a black-figure cup, the "Bomford cup," now in the Ashmolean Museum, Oxford (Oxford 1974 344), discussed by Boardman, "Curious Eye Cup," and illustrated in his *Vases*, fig 177 See also Napier, *Masks*, 175–79, on the Gorgon of the Bomford cup Other examples of central gorgoneia in cups are given by Lissarrague, *Aesthetics*, figs 5 and 33, and by Schauenburg, "Zu attisch-schwarzfigurigen Schalen mit Innenfriesen ' I am indebted to Kenneth Hamma for the last reference

[11] Apotropaic motifs (gorgoneia, eyes) appear frequently on drinking cups Napier, *Masks*, 175, argues against seeing these as mere fill-ins, but does not suggest a specific reason why they appear so frequently on drinking cups other than their general connection with Dionysiac motifs Deonna, *Symbolisme*, 183–96, discusses the use of the apotropaic eye, and writes that the eyes on cups serve to "neutralize the evil that could contaminate their contents" (187) Krauskopf and Dahlinger, ' Gorgo," 322, connect the gorgoneia on vessels and other useful objects with an original, apotropaic function, calling particular attention to an eye cup on which the pupils are gorgoneia (pl 43) As far as I know, however, the specific interpretation for which I argue has never been suggested

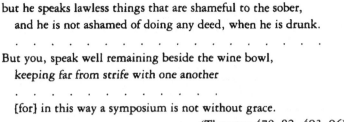

but he speaks lawless things that are shameful to the sober,
and he is not ashamed of doing any deed, when he is drunk.

. . . .

But you, speak well remaining beside the wine bowl,
keeping far from strife with one another

. . . .

[for] in this way a symposium is not without grace.

(Theognis 479–82, 493–96)[12]

A symposium was intended to promote peace and friendship. Plutarch writes that the goal of the symposium is "to bring about, by means of pleasure, the increase or production of *philia* [friendship] among those present."[13] Wine drinking, however, especially among the highly competitive Greek aristocrats, could also lead to unguarded remarks and acts, to insult and injury. The "peace [that] loves the symposium" (Pindar, *Nemean* 9.48) represents a triumph over disorder, strife, and *hubris* (violence).[14] Because constant vigilance was needed to create and maintain peace, warnings like those of Theognis are an important part of sympotic poetry. Just as a good symposiarch (master of the symposium) mixes wine and water in the proper proportions, so the poet must mix pleasure and restraint.

The gorgoneion among the symposiasts in the drinking cup can be seen as a visual analogue of Theognis's poetic warnings. It is an apotropaic device against the dangers of shameless "strife with one another," and is used to inspire the beneficial fear of wrongdoing that was particularly needed on just such festive occasions. Just as the gorgoneion on the shield averts the dangers of war, so the gorgoneion in the cup averts the dangers of strife among friends. The combination represented in the cup, of gorgoneion and sympotic revelers, is a good visual symbol of the mixture of wine with water, of pleasure with restraint, that must be maintained at the symposium. Thus, the gorgoneion in the wine cup is a symbol of apotropaic fear used as an antidote to shameless revelry, to create a mixture

[12] See also Theognis 467–78, 211–12, 837–40, 873–76. On the symposium and moderation in Theognis, see Levine, "Symposium." The association of drunkenness and shamelessness goes back as far as Homer. George Sheets called my attention to *Il.* 1, where Achilles says that Agamemnon is "shameless" (158, cf. 149), "drunken" (225), and "most greedy" (122).

[13] Plutarch, *Quaestiones convivales* 621c, quoted by Vetta, *Poesia*, xxxv n. 55

[14] On this theme in sympotic poetry and in Pindar, see Slater, "Peace," and Dickie, "Hēsychia." See also Pellizer, "Zuffa," on aggression in the Greek symposium.

that is healthful and beneficial to the individual's body and soul, and to the society of which he is a part

PINDAR

This interpretation of the symbolism of the gorgoneion at the symposium can help us understand a puzzling literary Gorgon that of Pindar's *Pythian* 12 [15] While this poem celebrates Midas's victory in an *aulos* contest, [16] most of it concerns the myth of Perseus and Polydektes, the king of the island of Seriphos, who raped Perseus's mother Danae In retaliation, Perseus brings the head of the Gorgon Medusa as his contribution to an *eranos* (a feast to which everyone contributes) [17] With Athena's help, Perseus first steals the eye shared by the three daughters of Phorcus, the eye that helps him find the Gorgons Facing away from the Gorgon Medusa to avoid being turned to stone, Perseus beheads her and returns to Seriphos, where he uses the head to turn Polydektes and the islanders to stone After recounting this story in Pindar's typical elliptical fashion, the poem describes Athena's invention of the *aulos* in imitation of the crying of the Gorgon Euryalos Pindar begins the poem by stating that Midas has conquered all of Greece in the art invented by Pallas Athena,

> the craft that once
> Pallas Athena invented, weaving
> the wretched lament of the bold Gorgons,
>
> which Perseus heard with painful labor poured out
> from beneath the maidens' unapproachable snaky heads,
> when once he destroyed the third part of the sisters,
> bringing fate to Seriphos in the sea and to her people
> Indeed he blinded the oracular race of Phorcus,
> and he made bitter to Polydektes the feast,
> and the lasting slavery and compulsory bed of his mother,
> stripping off the head of fair-cheeked Medusa,

[15] This poem has received relatively little attention The best study is that of Kohnken *Funktion*, 117–53

[16] The *aulos* was a wind instrument with a vibrating reed that most closely resembled the modern clarinet flute is a misleading translation

[17] On *eranos* in Pindar, see Slater, Doubts, 200, and n 40, which refers to the discussion of the technical term *eranos* by Vondeling, Eranos

he, the son of Danae, who, we say, was born
from a shower of gold. But when the maiden [Athena]
had drawn the beloved man out of these toils,
she crafted the many-voiced song of the *aulos*,
so that she might imitate with instruments
the loud-sounding wail approaching her from the ravenous jaws of
　　Euryale.
The goddess invented it. But having invented it
for mortal men to have,
she called it the many-headed tune,
the fair-famed wooer to the contests that arouse the people,

a tune that crowds through the thin bronze and the reeds
that grow beside the city, fair in dances, of the Graces
in the holy ground of the nymph of Kaphisos, to be faithful witnesses
　　of the dancers
If there is any happiness among humans, it does not shine forth
　　without labor

　　　　　　　　　　　　　　　　　　　(*Pythian* 12.6–29)[18]

The presence of the Gorgon in this poem has troubled commentators.
Why does Pindar stress Athena's invention of beautiful *aulos* music in imitation of the wails made by a grotesque *Gorgon* at the death of her sister?
Interpretations of the poem have not really explained the specific connection between *aulos* music and Gorgons.[19] This connection is clearer, however, if we see a parallel between the *aulos* music and the gorgoneion
Athena wears on her *aigis*. In the Perseus myth, Athena's divine craft allows her to use the terrifying and destructive Gorgon's head for beneficent,
apotropaic purposes, by making it the gorgoneion of her *aigis*.[20] In a similar way, in *Pythian* 12, Athena uses the ugly, terrifying wail of the Gor-

---

[18] I translate the text of Bowra, *Pindari carmina*

[19] Kohnken, *Funktion*, 117–20, criticizes views that Athena's invention represents "creation from suffering," and "life from death" (Dolin, "Interpretations," 48, Kohnken, 120
n 15, quotes from the summary in *HSCP* 71 [1966] 315), or "cosmic harmony " (Schlesinger, "Pindar," 283, quoted by Kohnken, 118), or "the nature of art, which is to transform what is ugly and distressing into what is exalting and enlivening" (Bowra, *Pindar*,
293, quoted by Kohnken, 118) Yet Kohnken's own explanation (esp 147–53), which
refers in general terms to victory after toil, simply ignores, like those he criticizes, the
question of the Gorgons' relevance any kind of labor or distress would serve equally well

[20] On Athena's connection with the Gorgon and with the gorgoneion of the *aigis* see
Cook, "The Aigis and Gorgoneion of Athena," *Zeus* 3 837–65

gon for beneficent purposes when she imitates it with beautiful *aulos* music that celebrates victory.[21] In this poem, instead of weaving the gorgoneion into her garment, Athena weaves the wail of the Gorgon into *aulos* music (7–8).

This parallel between imitative music and the gorgoneion of the *aigis* is especially meaningful because of the function music serves in Pindar. *Aulos* music, like the victory ode itself, represents pain and toil in their positive aspects, as victory and good fortune. The relationship between happiness, or good fortune, and labor expressed in *Pythian* 12 28–29 ("If there is any happiness among humans, it does not shine forth without labor") is, as Adolf Köhnken points out in *Die Funktion des Mythos bei Pindar*, the same as that between *aulos* music and its function as celebrator of victory through toil (147). Neither victory nor music changes the essential nature of painful toil, but each represents its pleasant and beneficial aspects. Pindar writes in *Nemean* 8, "By means of song, a man makes even labor painless" (49–50). Similarly, in *Pythian* 12, Athena weaves the threnody of the unapproachable heads (9) into an imitation that is a "song of many heads" (23), and gives it to mortals to serve as a wooer (24) to contests. Even though remembered toil is sweet and painless, painful toil is necessary to victory, and the memory of painful toil is essential to the peaceful celebration of victory. In this way, the many-headed song is like the still-powerful and snake-haired, but now beneficial, apotropaic gorgoneion of the *aigis*.

The Gorgon in *Pythian* 12, then, represents the painful elements, the mortal limits, that are an essential part of human good fortune, and that must be remembered if we are to enjoy good fortune without *hubris* and injury.[22] The need to remember mortal limits is particularly great in moments of supreme happiness, such as victory, and at feasts and symposia. Both victory and the symposium are especially conducive to shameless, insolent acts and words, to a lack of the moderation necessary for the peaceful enjoyment of human happiness.[23] It is significant that *Pythian* 12 uses sympotic themes and images to help make the point that toil is necessary to human happiness. The Gorgon's head appears in the midst of a communal feast (*eranos*: 14). While an *eranos* is not exactly the same as a

[21] See Köhnken, *Funktion*, 140–43, on the *aulos* as celebrator of victory

[22] The need to remember mortality is a common theme in Pindar. See, for example, *Nemean* 11 13–16 (cited by Köhnken, *Funktion*, 149) "If someone having good fortune will surpass another in beauty, / and shows strength by victory in contests, / let him remember that he clothes mortal limbs, / and that last of all he will be clad in earth

[23] On this idea, see Crotty, *Song*, 83–84, and Dickie, *"Hēsychia,"* 88–91

symposium, the connection is close. In Plato's *Symposium* 177c5, for example, the speeches given by the symposiasts are said to constitute an *eranos* for Eros.[24] The *aulos* itself is associated with the symposium, as is the crown (5). The wail of the Gorgon that is imitated by Athena's *aulos* music is said to be "poured out" (λειβόμενον. 10), the term used to refer to the libation of wine. This metaphor is especially significant when one considers that Pindar calls his own song a "musical drink amidst the Aeolian breath of the *auloi*" in *Nemean* 3.79.[25] The victory ode is like the wine drunk in moderation at a peaceful victory celebration.

> Peace loves the symposium. The newly flourishing glory of victory
>   increases with soft song
> The voice becomes bold beside the mixing bowl
> Let someone mix it, sweet prophet of the revel,
> and distribute in silver cups
> the mighty child of the vine
>
> *(Nemean 9.48–52)*

"Peace" (*hēsuchia*) in Pindar, as Matthew Dickie argues, is "a restraining of the impulses that are induced by prosperity and the good things of life and which, if unchecked, lead to *hubris*," in the symposium and in life in general. *Hēsuchia* has the function of "enabling men to live harmoniously with each other."[26] Thus, the "peace" that "loves the symposium" is like the restraint and respect (*aidōs*) that prevents *hubris* and strife with one's fellows in Theognis.[27]

The Gorgon at the feast in *Pythian* 12 represents "peace," restraint, and *aidōs* in good fortune in a number of ways. It represents the toil and labor that produce good fortune, and the victory song that celebrates good fortune while warning of the need to remember mortal limits. It also represents the need for restraint in moments of victory, feasting, and drinking. The Gorgon at the feast has, in short, an apotropaic function similar to that of the gorgoneia in drinking cups and on Athena's *aigis*. Because Pindar's Gorgon serves to remind us of mortal limits, especially in the midst of victory and feasting, it helps avert the evils to which this very happiness

[24] Note also that Socrates' pun on the Gorgon's head of Gorgianic rhetoric that almost turned him to stone occurs exactly in the middle of the *Symposium* (198c) This Gorgon in the *Symposium* is a verbal analogue of the gorgoneion in the drinking cup

[25] This and other passages are cited by Crotty, *Song*, 83, in a good discussion of the parallels between victory ode and symposium in Pindar

[26] Dickie, "*Hēsychia*," 90, 91

[27] On *aidōs* in Pindar, see Walsh, *Varieties*, 57–58

can lead. Its destructive, fear-inspiring powers become, within the poem, beneficent and apotropaic

In *Pythian* 10.46–48 the Gorgon's head also serves as a reminder of mortal limits. Pindar first describes Perseus's visit to the feasts of the Hyperboreans (29–46) and then mentions that Perseus killed the Gorgon and brought its head to Seriphos Whatever the connection may be between the Hyperborean episode and that of the Gorgon,[28] it is clear that the juxtaposition within the poem of feasting and Gorgon slaying serves to mark a contrast between mortal Perseus and the Hyperboreans Kohnken argues in *Funktion* that the Hyperboreans are immortals (though not gods) who enjoy a permanent state of the happiness that can be enjoyed only temporarily by mortal victors like Perseus and the athletes Pindar celebrates. The happiness of the Hyperboreans takes the form of "continual feasts" (34), while Perseus's enjoyment is limited to a single occasion (31).[29] While the Hyperboreans are free from sickness, old age, and toil (41–44), Perseus is a bringer of death (ἔπεφνεν 46, θάνατον 48)[30] In Kohnken's view, then, Perseus, in his role as Gorgon-slayer, is himself a kind of memento mori at the immortal feast of the Hyperboreans. As in *Pythian* 12, the Gorgon slain by Perseus is a reminder of mortal limits, and it is associated with feasting within the movement of the poem

In connecting the Gorgon's wail with *aulos* music, *Pythian* 12 also makes an explicit statement about the nature of poetry The idea that song makes pain and toil beautiful and pleasant is, of course, an old one In *Iliad* 6, for example, Helen laments that Hector must undergo much toil (355) because of herself and Paris

> us two, on whom Zeus set a vile destiny, so that hereafter
> we shall be made into things of song for the men of the future
>
> (357–58 Lattimore)

In *Pythian* 12, however, Pindar uses the verb "imitate" (*mimēsait*. 21) to express this traditional idea. This is one of the earliest extant occurrences of this verb and cognates in connection with artistic creation,[31] and as such

---

[28] The nature of this connection has long puzzled scholars For example, Burton, *Pythian Odes*, 9, remarks that there is no connection between the Hyperborean episode and that of the Gorgon slaying For a summary of various opinions about the connection, see Barkhuizen, "Text Analysis,' 18–19

[29] Kohnken, *Funktion*, 154–87 The contrast between the continual feasts and the single occasion is made on 160 and in n 23

[30] Kohnken notes the contrast ibid , 172–73 and 179–81

[31] Schlesinger, "Pindar," 278, writes that this is the earliest occurrence of the verb in

it is highly significant. In Pindar's poem, imitation does not create a new reality, but instead gives meaning and order to human life by showing us the beautiful and beneficent aspects of what appears ugly and painful The *aulos* music is beautiful and pleasant in itself, and it is at the same time an imitation of what is ugly and painful. the scream of a monster.[32] This concept of imitation is remarkably similar to that of the *Poetics*. "We take pleasure contemplating the most accurately made images of things that themselves give us pain to see, such as the shapes of the most despised animals and of corpses" (1448b10–12).[33]

Pythian 12 is an important source for Pindar's views on poetry. It is the earliest evidence for a concept of imitation that is in some respects much like that of Aristotle. Moreover, in implicitly connecting imitative song with the apotropaic gorgoneion of the *aigis* and with the apotropaic motifs of the symposium, Pindar implies that imitation itself has an apotropaic function. By reminding us of mortal limits and thus inspiring us with the fear of wrongdoing, imitation helps avert the evils too often associated with victory and good fortune. Pindar thus represents his own poetry as a kind of gorgoneion at the feast. a pleasurable celebration of toil, and a salutary reminder of it in the midst of the good fortune of victory.

EUMENIDES

Pindar's image of the Gorgon at the feast has a parallel in Aeschylus's *Eumenides*. The Erinyes (Furies) in this play are closely connected with the Gorgon in both appearance and nature. Moreover, their two aspects—as hated, destructive powers and as revered, positive forces that keep wrongdoing from the city—parallel the two aspects of the Gorgon as terrible monster and as beneficent, apotropaic gorgoneion. Furthermore, just as Pindar in *Pythian* 12 connects the gorgoneion with the art of poetry, so Aeschylus's use of the Gorgon-Erinyes theme suggests that he viewed tragedy as a kind of gorgoneion at the Festival of Dionysus.

this connection However, the verb is used in connection with choruses in the *Delian Hymn to Apollo*, 163, which is certainly earlier Else lists and discusses occurrences of *mimeisthai* and cognates through the fifth century B C E in "Imitation ' See also Gentili, *Poesia*, chap 4

[32] The myth that Perseus beheaded Medusa while looking at her reflection in his shield may also be connected with the idea of imitation However, Phinney, "Perseus," 453–63, finds no evidence that this variant was current as early as the fifth century B C E

[33] The parallel is noted by Schlesinger, "Pindar," 281 I discuss Aristotle's views on pleasure and imitation below, see chap 2 ("Imitation")

The Erinyes were associated with the Gorgon in Greek thought generally,[34] and this connection is particularly close in Aeschylus In the *Libation Bearers*, Orestes says the Furies are Gorgons twined about with snakes (1048–50), and that they have blood dripping from their eyes (1058). He himself is compared by the Chorus to Perseus.[35] We do not see the Erinyes in the *Libation Bearers*, but in the *Eumenides* they make up the highly visible Chorus. While we have no certain evidence for the appearance of the members of this Chorus, the hypothesis that they looked much like Gorgons is supported by a number of suggestive facts. Benedikt Niese, noting that Aeschylus brought the Gorgons onto the stage in his *Phorcides*, suggests they were the pattern for the Erinyes of the *Eumenides*,[36] and A.J.N.W. Prag notes that the "foot-bending Erinys" of Aeschylus's *Seven against Thebes* (791) recalls the knee-running Gorgon of archaic vases.[37] Moreover, visual representations influenced by Aeschylus's play show Erinyes with some Gorgon-like aspects. The snakes they wear or carry are associated with Gorgons, and Prag calls attention to one red-figure vase on which an Erinys raises a foot in a pose that recalls the archaic knee-running Gorgon.[38] Even differences may be significant. While the Erinyes are represented in the visual arts as women rather than as terrifying monsters, the Gorgon also had a "beautiful," more human type. Prag argues in her *Oresteia*, moreover, that the representation of the Erinyes as women was influenced by Aeschylus's portrayal of them as beneficent (48). Again, Haiganuch Sarian suggests that portrayals of Erinyes as winged may be more influenced by Aeschylus's comparison of the Erinyes to (winged) Gorgons and Harpies than to his explicit denial that they are winged (*Eum* 51).[39] The hypothesis that the Erinyes looked like Gorgons is also supported by the text of the play, and by the visual and dramatic impact a Gorgon-like Chorus would have had

[34] See Dietrich, *Death*, 141–45

[35] *LB* 831–37 The text is unfortunately corrupt, but the comparison is clear whether or not we accept Kirchhoff's emendation at 835, followed by Page, *Aeschyli* Γοργοῦς λυγρᾶς The connection between Orestes and Perseus in the *Oresteia* is noted by Sider, "Stagecraft," 23–24, and Moreau, "Oeil, 56–58, who also notes many other references in Aeschylus to terrifying eyes and Gorgons See also, on the Perseus-Orestes theme in Aeschylus and in Euripides' *Electra*, O'Brien, ' Orestes , Sheppard, Electra, 140, and Headlam, "Notes, 99–100

[36] Niese, "Gorgo," 1642

[37] Prag, *Oresteia*, 48

[38] Ibid , 48–49 and pl 31a (ca 440 B C E)

[39] Sarian, ' Erinys," 841 This article reproduces numerous illustrations of the *Oresteia* See also the illustrations of the *Eumenides* on several vases published by Trendall and Webster, *Illustrations*, 45–49

In the *Eumenides*, we hear about the Erinyes before we see them. The Priestess says that the members of the Chorus of Erinyes are Gorgon-like women:

> I call them not women but Gorgons,
> or rather, I don't liken them to Gorgon figures
> I once saw painted [Harpies]
> carrying Phineus's meal away

(48–51)

While the Erinyes are unlike Gorgons in being wingless (51), they share the Gorgons' most distinctive feature: terrifying eyes. The Priestess says that the Erinyes' eyes drip disgustingly (54) [40] They are "terrible to see with the eyes" (34), and they have "fearful faces" (990). The Priestess, after seeing them, is so terrified (38) that she cannot stand up, but must crawl on all fours (36–38). The first line she speaks after seeing them (34) contains the word "terrible" (*deina*) twice. Fear, especially the extreme, paralyzing fear called *ekplēxis* or *kataplēxis*, is the principal emotional effect produced by the Gorgon. Aristotle (frag. 153) states that the Gorgon's head produces *kataplēxis*, and in Plato's *Symposium* (198b5), Socrates says he was struck with *ekplēxis* by the "Gorgon's head" of Agathon's Gorgianic rhetoric. [41] It is significant, then, that the Chorus of the *Eumenides* is said to have aroused *ekplēxis* in the audience, and that this effect was generally associated with Aeschylus. [42] The evidence indicates that the Erinyes looked much like Gorgons, had the emotional effects that Gorgons did, and might well have been represented as such on stage. [43]

The role of Athena in the *Eumenides* provides additional evidence for the view that the Erinyes resembled Gorgons. If Orestes is a Perseus figure in the *Libation Bearers*, Athena in the *Eumenides* plays a role similar to the one she has in the Perseus myth. she helps a mortal hero and uses for constructive purposes a power that can also be destructive. This parallel would have

---

[40] ἐκ δ' ὀμμάτων λείβουσι δυσφιλῆ λίβα Sommerstein, *Eumenides*, notes the similarity between this line and *LB* 1058 κἀξ ὀμμάτων στάζουσιν αἷμα δυσφιλές

[41] On *ekplēxis*, see further below, chap 6

[42] The entrance of the Chorus of the *Eumenides*, according to the *Vita Aeschyli* 9 (Pollux 4 110, see Page, *Aeschyli*, 332 10–13), aroused such *ekplēxis* that children fainted and pregnant women miscarried In the debate between Aeschylus and Euripides in Aristophanes' *Frogs*, Euripides contrasts himself with Aeschylus, saying that he (Euripides) did not arouse *ekplēxis* in the audience (962)

[43] Sider, "Stagecraft," 23–24, argues that the Erinyes looked like Gorgons Maxwell-Stuart, "Appearance," argues unconvincingly that they looked like bats

been brought out in the staging. An *aigis*, complete with gorgoneion, was undoubtedly part of the goddess's costume, and David Sider suggests that, at 403–4, Athena calls attention to the gorgoneion on her *aigis* by stretching out her arms as she addresses the Erinyes.[44] This scene would have been most effective if the Erinyes wore Gorgon masks.

Giving the Chorus Gorgon masks would also have solved a problem connected with staging. The masks must be terrifying at the beginning of the play, as we know from the Priestess's statements (34–63), but also compatible with the representation of the Erinyes as forces for good at the end of the play. There is no indication that the members of the Chorus did, or could have, changed their masks, and line 990 ("fearful faces") clearly indicates that the masks remained terrifying.[45] What better solution to this problem than to give them Gorgon masks that change, in the perception of the audience, into apotropaic gorgoneia, like the gorgoneion on Athena's *aigis*?[46] Gorgon masks that can be perceived as either evil and destructive or beneficent and apotropaic would also be consistent with the costuming. Instead of changing costume after they yielded to Athena's persuasion, the members of the Chorus put red robes over the black ones they had been wearing (1028).[47]

The ambiguous Gorgon mask, moreover, is a good visual symbol of the ambiguous nature and function of the Erinyes. Contrary to a common misconception, they do not change their names in the course of the play: the word "Eumenides" does not occur in our text.[48] Their function, like their names, remains unchanged. From the beginning, the Erinyes are concerned with offenses against a god, a *xenos* (host or guest), or a blood-

---

[44] Sider, "Stagecraft," 22

[45] This point is made by Macleod, "Clothing," 41–43, and by Taplin, *Tragedy*, 85, and *Stagecraft*, 413.

[46] In this interpretation, the masks of the Chorus in the *Eumenides* have the same kind of ambiguity that Foley attributes to Dionysus's smiling mask in Euripides' *Bacchae* This mask, she writes, is perceived by audience and characters as both benign and destructive "One mask represents two meanings in a manner that captures the central irony of the dramatic action" ("Masque," 128). I am indebted to Helen Bacon for calling my attention to this parallel

[47] The view that no change of costume was involved is now generally accepted See Taplin, *Tragedy* and *Stagecraft*, and Macleod, "Clothing." Tarkow, "Thematic Implications," 163–65, has some good remarks on the significance of the donning of additional robes.

[48] Brown, "Eumenides," 267–76, argues that the common view that the Erinyes are renamed has no basis in our text. He notes (275) that Athena refers to them as Erinyes at line 950. See also Sommerstein, *Eumenides*, 11–12, 281, and Macleod, "Clothing," 41

relative (270–71, 545–48). They allot good and evil to humans, punishing those who do wrong, while allowing those who have pure hands to flourish (312–20). At the end of the play, the Erinyes retain their function of allotting reward and punishment (953–55). They remain concerned with the household (895) and with marriage and children (835). At 916–1020, they call down blessings of peace and prosperity on Athens, praying for the increase of crops, flocks, and people (916–67), that the citizens may love and hate with one mind (985–86), and that civil war may be averted (976–83; cf. 862–63).[49] Throughout the play, they are goddesses concerned with protecting *philia* relationships.[50]

The Erinyes punish those who violate *philia* relationships because they are, as Robert Parker writes, "animate agents of pollution who embody the anger of one slain by a kinsman."[51] The connection of the Erinyes and their living human agents with anger is especially clear in the *Oresteia*, where the "child-avenging Wrath" (*Mēnis: Agamemnon* 155) that awaits Agamemnon's return is the same as the "Erinyes bred in the race" (1190) of whom Cassandra speaks.[52] Throughout the *Eumenides*, the Erinyes are characterized as angry spirits.[53] Because they are angry with those who pollute, the Erinyes can inspire a maddening, destructive fear caused by the consciousness of pollution. This fear results from wrongdoing. However, the fear inspired by the Erinyes can also be a positive force that prevents pollution and wrath.

In the *Eumenides*, the Erinyes remain the same but our perception of them changes; we are aware first of the negative aspects of the fear inspired by their wrath at pollution, and later of the positive aspects of fear, which can prevent wrongdoing and wrath. In the first part of the play, their "binding song" causes fear that maddens and paralyzes:

[49] On the blessings prayed for by the Erinyes, see Sommerstein, *Eumenides*, on 916–1020.

[50] On the function of the Erinyes as guardians of harmony in family and city, see Said, "Concorde "

[51] Parker, *Miasma*, 107. He discusses at length (106–10) the connection between pollution and anger While the connection of the Erinyes with anger is undeniable, it is less certain that their name is derived from a word meaning "anger." On the disputed etymology, see Dietrich, *Death*, 96–98.

[52] These translations are from Fraenkel, *Agamemnon* See his excellent commentary on the connection between these two passages, on *Agamemnon* 154ff. (μίμνει), and on 1190. I am indebted to Helen Bacon for calling my attention to the connection of the Erinyes of the *Oresteia* with anger.

[53] See, for example, μῆνις (314), κότος (501), θυμοῦσθαι (733), βαρύκοτος (780), μένος, κότον (840).

> Over the victim
> this is the song, frenzied,
> mad, mind-destroying
> chant of Erinyes
> binding the wits
>
> (328–32)

This maddening fear is a punishment for those who, like Orestes, have shed kindred blood.[54] At the end of the play, however, after their persuasion by Athena, we are more fully conscious of the Erinyes' power to inspire the good fear that prevents kin from harming one another "reverence [*sebas*] . . and inborn fear of wrongdoing" (690–91). Fear of wrongdoing is necessary for the preservation of the city, as Athena states when she advises the citizens to establish the Council of the Areopagus as an object of reverence:

> Do not cast the terrible entirely out of the city
> For what mortal who fears nothing is just?
> If you justly stand in fear of such an object of reverence,
> you would have a defense for the land and salvation for the city
> such as no other human possesses
>
> (698–702)

This "reverence" (*sebas*. 700, or *aidōs*. 548, 705, 710) is the fear of wrongdoing that will avert internal strife (862–63), and its consequences. the wrath of the Erinyes and of their living human agents. This fear is what the Erinyes have in mind when they speak of "the terrible [that is] good" and that is an "overseer of thoughts" (517–19) From the fear of wrongdoing inspired by the "fearful faces" of the Erinyes will come "a great advantage to the citizens" (990–91). This is the "divine fear" that Plato praises in the *Laws* (671d2) [55]

The first two plays of the trilogy are dominated by fear resulting from wrongdoing. This fear is aroused by a series of kin murders. In the *Agamemnon*, the Watchman tells us that fear (*phobos*) prevents him from sleeping (14), and the Chorus tells of the "fearful treachery" (154–55) that

---

[54] On madness and the Erinyes, cf 'mad women' (μαιναδων 500), and in the *LB* "madness" (λύσσα 288) and 'disturbance in the mind' (1056)

[55] On the functions of fear in the *Eumenides*, see Romilly, *Crainte*, 107–14 Other good remarks on this subject are those of Macleod, 'Politics," 31–32, Solmsen, *Hesiod*, 209–11, Sommerstein, *Eumenides*, 87, and Vourveris, "ΘΕΙΟΣ ΦΟΒΟΣ ' The connection between Aeschylus's beneficial fear and that of Plato's *Laws* is noted by Romilly (112–13), Solmsen (209 n 115), and Vourveris

remains at home awaiting Agamemnon's return. After Agamemnon enters the house, the Chorus sings a long threnody of fear in response to Cassandra's descriptions of the feast of Thyestes and her prophecies of the murder of Agamemnon. The Chorus says that fear flutters in the heart (975–77), and mentions the "threnody of the Erinyes" (991). Its responses to Cassandra's prophecy show increasing terror. At 1135 and 1152 it is frightened by her prophecies. At 1164 it is "stricken" (*peplēgmai*), and at 1243 it says "I shuddered and fear holds me." At 1306 it asks who will turn fear aside. All these fears are aroused by Agamemnon's murder by his wife, who, in anger at his murder of their daughter Iphigenia, sacrifices him to the Erinys (1432–33).

In the *Libation Bearers* also, fear is aroused by kin murder, as Orestes kills his mother, Clytemnestra. The play opens with an account of the fear aroused in Clytemnestra by her dream (35; cf. 523–25, 535, 547, 929). The Chorus is afraid to speak (46). At 55–59, it says that Clytemnestra and Aigisthus arouse fear, but not reverence (*sebas*). Orestes is also afraid. Before the matricide he is threatened by his father's Furies (283) and with "madness and vain terror in the nights" (288), and after the murder of Clytemnestra Orestes is seized with fear sent by the Erinyes (1024). The Chorus tells him not to fear (1052), but he cannot free himself from the "disturbance in the mind" (1056).

In the *Eumenides*, we first see the negative aspects of the fear inspired by the Erinyes, who hunt Orestes down in anger at his murder of Clytemnestra. They terrify the Priestess (34–38), who views them as completely loathsome, saying that their garments make them offensive to gods and humans (55–56). According to Apollo, they are complete outcasts with whom no god, human, or even wild beast associates (69–70), and they are "hated by men and the Olympian gods" (73). Dishonored by all alike, the Erinyes are seen as forces of evil (71–72), and the maddening terror inspired by their wrath at pollution reduces human beings, like the Priestess, to the condition of animals, who go on all fours (37).

In the course of the play, however, the Erinyes' status changes as they receive due honor and reverence. The fear they inspire in those who honor them is the positive kind, that which prevents wrongdoing and thus averts the Erinyes' wrath. We first see a change away from maddening fear taking place in Orestes. He has now undergone ritual katharsis (280–89, 445–52) and is protected by Apollo, who tells him to feel no fear (88). Indeed, in the *Eumenides*, Orestes never expresses the destructive kind of fear produced by the Erinyes in the *Libation Bearers*. He is now unaffected by their binding song (328–33), which attempts to produce the emotional disturbance he experienced at the end of the *Libation Bearers*. Orestes's ritual katharsis, then, is paralleled by an emotional katharsis that relieves him from the maddening terror caused by kin-murder During the persuasion of the Erinyes, as they are given honor by Athena and her people (e.g., 868–69), the change from destructive fear to reverence is completed when the Erinyes arouse this emotion not in Orestes, who has no further role after his trial, but in the Athenians. By revering (*eusebountes*. 1019) the Erinyes, the Athenians will avoid the harm to kin that is punished with maddening fear of the kind Orestes suffered in the *Libation Bearers*. At the end of the *Eumenides*, the Erinyes remain wrathful spirits whose "hateful anger" (937) utterly destroys evil people (932–37)—that is, those who dishonor them and do not fear their anger until it is too late. In coming to honor them, however, the Athenians have undergone an emotional experience like that of Orestes, as destructive terror caused by the Erinyes' anger at pollution becomes the fear of wrongdoing that prevents pollution and anger.

Aeschylus uses the image of the Gorgon-Erinys just as Pindar uses that of the Gorgon-gorgoneion. as a symbol of something that can be perceived as either destructive and evil or good and necessary to an orderly society. Moreover, like Pindar, Aeschylus implicitly connects this image with poetry. His play suggests that the transformation in the audience of maddening terror caused by wrongdoing into beneficial reverence is to be connected with the power of art to change our perceptions Aeschylus does this in the second half of the *Eumenides* by leading us, implicitly, to reflect on tragedy itself.

As the play progresses, it becomes increasingly relevant to fifth-century Athens. The Athenians in whom reverence has replaced maddening terror are characters in Aeschylus's play, represented by a second Chorus of "escorts" (*propompoi*), which accompanies the Chorus of the Erinyes in the final procession.[56] However, this second Chorus is also closely related to the actual Athenians in the audience, for while the first two plays dealt with a past that was purely mythological, the *Eumenides* connects the past with the fifth-century present. The allusions to the Areopagus and the prayers of blessing for Athens help the audience relate the action of the play to the real world of everyday Athens [57] The Erinyes in this play are not merely

[56] The identity of this second Chorus has been the subject of much dispute Taplin, *Stagecraft*, 410–11, and *Tragedy*, 39, identifies it with the jurors of the trial scene More compelling are Sommerstein's arguments that they are instead the women and girls who are cult-servants of Athena Polias (*Eumenides*, 276–78, 282–83)

[57] This does not mean, however, that the significance of the play is confined to fifth-

mythological characters without relevance for fifth-century Athenians; they would also have been connected by the audience with the actual guardians of contemporary Athens, thought to dwell in a cave under the Areopagus. In addition, the blessings for which they pray are fully realized only at the time Aeschylus wrote his play. In particular, the final procession of the play, in which the second Chorus and others participate,[58] closely resembles the historical Panathenaic Procession in which *metics* (resident aliens) clothed in red were escorted by torchlight.[59] In the staging of the dramatic procession, moreover, audience and actors are as closely interrelated as anywhere in Greek tragedy. The "escorts" of the second Chorus are citizen-actors representing themselves,[60] who honor the Erinyes in their own persons. Those whom they address with the words "keep religious silence, countrymen" (1035; cf. 1038) include, implicitly, the Athenians in the audience.[61] The audience members are present at and participating in a real rite in honor of Dionysus, watching in respectful silence at the command of this Chorus and, at last, perhaps actually giving ritual cries themselves at the command "raise the cry" (1043, 1047).[62]

Above all, Aeschylus draws the audience into the play emotionally. Athena's address to the jury that begins "Attic people" (681) also persuades the members of the audience. They, the posterity referred to at 683 and 708, must also feel "reverence [*sebas*] . . . and inborn fear of wrongdoing" (690–91); they also must "respect their oath" (710) and not "cast

---

century Athens. As Macleod points out, the contemporary allusions in the play have a universalizing tendency rather than a narrowly historical and topical focus. "Politics," 27–28 See also Easterling, who cautions against making too close a connection between dramatic and real-life ritual in "Tragedy and Ritual," esp 98–101 on the *Eumenides*

[58] On the composition of the procession, see Sommerstein, *Eumenides*, 276–78.

[59] This connection was first pointed out by Headlam, "Last Scene," and is now accepted by many scholars Goheen, "Aspects," 123, notes that the color red is also a "prophylactic symbol." The color of the robes thus has the same apotropaic function as the Gorgon-gorgoneion masks

[60] Sommerstein, *Eumenides*, 272, seems to imply that they were the actual cult-servants of Athena, although he is not explicit on this point They were in any case nonprofessional Athenians, for, according to Nagy, at the City Dionysia, "poetry was performed by professional actors while song was performed by the nonprofessional chorus". *Pindar's Homer*, 405, cf. 85.

[61] Bain, "Audience Address," and Taplin, *Stagecraft*, 129–34 and 394–95, give compelling reasons against the view that the audience in Greek tragedy is ever addressed "directly (as opposed to implicitly)" (Taplin, 131). However, Taplin does not rule out the kind of implicit address that I believe this final scene includes

[62] Stanford, *Emotions*, 162, suggests that the audience joined in these cries On the noisiness of audiences, see Pickard-Cambridge, *Dramatic Festivals*, 272–73.

the terrible entirely out of the city" (698).[63] The arousal of reverence in the audience continues in the persuasion scene. A necessary condition for Athena's persuasion of the Erinyes is the reverence and good fear of their wrath felt by the Athenians who honor them in the play But the same emotion must be aroused in the Athenian audience members if they are to perceive the Erinyes as benign rather than maleficent. Only to the extent that Aeschylus succeeds in arousing this beneficial fear of shameless wrongdoing in each of the Athenians in the audience do the Erinyes change, in their perception, from Gorgons to apotropaic gorgoneia, from objects of maddening terror to revered goddesses. This change does not take place in the appearance, names, or specific powers of the Erinyes, but depends instead on the way in which they are perceived by human beings. As their perception changes, the audience members experience an emotional katharsis in some respects like that undergone by Orestes in the play, in which fear resulting from pollution is cast out and replaced by reverence and respect, which prevent pollution and wrath. If Aeschylus succeeds in drawing the audience into the play in this way, he has created an extraordinarily effective drama that at the same time serves a serious social and religious purpose.

There are some indications in the *Eumenides* that Aeschylus sees this transformation of terror resulting from wrongdoing into reverence and respect as a function of his own art form. He writes. "From their fearful faces [*phoberōn . . . prosōpōn*], / I see great advantage for these citizens" (990–91). *Prosōpon* means "mask" as well as "face," and "the fearful *prosōpa*" that bring advantage to the citizens are, implicitly, the masks of tragedy as well as the faces of the Erinyes in the play Moreover, the events represented in the play would have reminded the audience of the festival of the City Dionysia in many ways. The final procession of the play not only recalls the historical Panathenaic Procession, it also resembles the processions that took place at the Dionysian Festival in which the members of the audience were themselves participating. In the *eisagōgē* (bringing-in) of this festival, a torchlight procession escorted the statue of Dionysus Eleuthereus to the very theater in which the *Eumenides* was being performed. In the *pompē*, another procession that took place during the City Dionysia, *metics* wore red robes, and the *choregoi* (producers) walked dressed in fine costumes [64] Moreover, Orestes' trial in the play is similar to the

---

[63] Taplin, *Stagecraft*, 394–95, notes that, while Athena does not directly address the audience at 681–710, her words are also meant for the posterity mentioned in these lines

[64] On these processions, see Pickard-Cambridge, *Dramatic Festivals*, 59–62

process by which the plays were judged at the Dionysia. The trial in the play begins with a trumpet blast (566–69); a trumpet also announced each event in the competition of the Dionysia.[65] The judges at Orestes' trial vote with ballots (709) and take an oath that they are exhorted to "respect" (680, 710). While this is primarily an allusion to legal practice, we should not forget that plays were judged at the Dionysia in a similar fashion. The judges were selected by an archon who drew names from urns present in the theater at the beginning of the dramatic contest, and the selected judges voted by casting their ballots into an urn. They, like the judges in the play, were told to keep their oaths.[66] The actual voting urns that were used in the dramatic contest might, then, have been used as props in Aeschylus's trial scene; in any case, the audience might well have been reminded of them. Finally, the celebration of the greatness of Athens at the end of Aeschylus's play would have reminded the Athenian audience of the celebration of their city at the City Dionysia. The sons of fallen war heroes were honored at this festival, as were those who had served the state. Shortly after the *Oresteia* was produced, the allies of Athens brought tribute to this festival.[67] In the City Dionysia, as well as in the Panathenaia, citizens, *metics*, women, and children joined in a common purpose.[68]

There is reason to believe that Aeschylus, like Euripides in the *Bacchae*,[69] is implicitly making a statement about the nature of tragedy and the Dionysia in the last half of the *Eumenides*. The "fearful *prosōpa*" that are a "great advantage for these citizens" are not only the faces of the Erinyes in the play but also the masks of tragedy that arouse the good fear of wrongdoing. The *Eumenides*, in which the Erinyes come to be perceived as benign goddesses, revered by the Athenians, is also a kind of practical demonstration of the benefits of tragedy. By representing shameful deeds, father sacrificing daughter, wife murdering husband, and son killing

[65] Ibid., 67.

[66] Ibid., 95–98.

[67] As Goldhill points out in "Great Dionysia," 104, this ceremony could not have taken place before the transfer of the treasury from Delos to Athens (454 B.C.E.); it would thus not have been part of the Dionysia of 458, when the *Oresteia* was produced. It is, however, an important indication of the nature of this civic festival.

[68] On the Dionysia as a celebration of Athens' glory in which everyone participated, see Pickard-Cambridge, *Dramatic Festivals*, 58–59. The question of whether or not women attended the plays is discussed on 263–65. On the relationship between tragedy and the Dionysia as celebration of the polis, see Winkler, "Ephebes' Song," and Goldhill, "Great Dionysia," who has some excellent remarks on "the range and complexity of relations between the tragic texts and the civic ideology of the preplay ceremonies" (118).

[69] See Foley, "Masque."

mother, tragedy arouses in the audience terror (*ekplēxis*) resulting from polluting kin-murders Within the dramatic, imitative context, however, this emotion is transformed into reverence and fear of wrongdoing that prevents strife among kin In this way, tragedy itself is a gorgoneion at the Dionysian festival

If this analysis is correct, the Gorgon-Erinyes of the *Eumenides* have the same function as the sympotic Gorgons discussed earlier They are reminders of the dangers of internal strife that are particularly great at festivals of the wine god, and they are used to arouse reverence and respect, which restrain aggression against *philoi* The City Dionysia is, like the symposium, a celebration of the wine god, at which participants drink freely [70] While both symposium and dramatic festival aim at preserving and creating *philia*, both also create an atmosphere conducive to the violation of *philia* In both, a warning against wrongdoing is particularly necessary and appropriate It is the function of tragedy, Aeschylus's trilogy suggests, to provide this warning through the arousal of terror caused by shameful wrongdoing and pollution, and through its kathartic transformation into reverence and respect

A MEDICINE TO PRODUCE *AIDŌS*

If Aristotle's views on the benefits of tragic fear were influenced in a general way by Greek beliefs about the symposium and tragedy, there is reason to believe he was more specifically influenced by Plato's views on wine, the symposium, and education expressed in books 1 and 2 of the *Laws* [71] In these books, Plato's psychological theories give clarification and philosophical support to the idea that fear can be an antidote to shamelessness and aggression against *philoi* These psychological theories are also of interest because of their connection with the medical "principle of opposites," according to which opposites cure opposites Aristotle's psychology was also influenced by this allopathic medical principle In addition, Plato's views on wine and the symposium are of interest because of their aesthetic implications Plato believes that the emotions associated with Dionysus, god of wine and the theater, are beneficial and necessary elements in the human soul, and he advocates their arousal in a controlled environ-

---

[70] See Stanford, *Emotions*, 13, and Pickard-Cambridge, *Dramatic Festivals*, 272

[71] I discussed this topic in detail in Belfiore, Wine Here, I summarize the main points of that article and present some new material on *aidōs*

ment that has many aesthetic characteristics These ideas influenced Aristotle's views on tragic katharsis

In *Laws* 1 and 2, Plato advocates the use of wine in symposia in order to strengthen, temporarily, the desires and emotions opposed to reason Plato is certainly aware of the shocking and paradoxical aspects of this idea, for the Athenian in this dialogue notes that wine affects people like "anger, lust, *hubris*, ignorance, greed, and cowardice," and "everything that drives us out of our minds with the intoxication of pleasure" (*Laws* 1 649d4–7) Nevertheless, these very qualities, the Athenian argues, make wine useful in giving older people training in resisting pleasure and desire, a test of dispositions (649d7–e2), and a safeguard for correct education (2 652b3–653a3) Wine is good for older people, Plato believes, because it intensifies emotion and weakens reason, giving adults the malleable dispositions of young children (1 645d5–646a5) that are conducive to education For these reasons, wine is a medicine to produce *aidōs* in the soul (2 672d7–9)

These ideas are more comprehensible within the context of the views on education and excellence expressed in the *Laws* *Laws* 2 653a5–c4 defines *paideia* (education) as the production of that part of excellence—correctly trained pleasures and pains—of which children are capable before they are able to reason This training is given largely by music and dance By nature, Plato writes at 653d7–654a5, all young animals cry out and move about as though dancing with pleasure However, the gods have given to humans alone the pleasant perception of order and harmony in these movements, and they use this perception to move us in dances (*chorous*), which derive their name from the word for pleasure (*charas*) If children are trained in good music, Plato believes, they will take pleasure in what is good (654c4–d3) Even the elements in the soul that are opposed to reason (antirational elements) are important in early education [72] At 672b–d, when Plato again discusses the origin of music and dance in the young child's natural desire to move about, he explicitly characterizes these movements as disordered and mad, he indicates, moreover, that these mad, antirational qualities are valuable in themselves Mad movement, he states in a reference to the earlier discussion at 653c–654a, is the source of music and gymnastics "In that time in which it has not yet acquired the wisdom proper to it, every animal is mad, and makes disordered noises, and as

---

[72] On the importance of psychic elements other than reason in Plato s late dialogues, and in the *Laws* in particular, see Dodds, *Greeks*, chap 7, North, *Sophrosyne*, 186–96, and Tecuşan, *Logos Sympotikos*

soon as it becomes active, it also makes disordered leaps. Let us remember that we said these are the sources of music and gymnastics" (672c2–7).

The natural, antirational dispositions of the young contribute to well-ordered souls because of the opposition of these tendencies to reason. A metaphor Plato uses in *Laws* 6 clarifies his views on education. He writes that "a city should be mixed like a wine bowl, in which mad wine boils when poured in, but when it is punished by another sober god [sc., water] and joins in a good combination, it makes a good and measured drink" (773c8–d4). In this metaphor, excellence is a good psychic mixture (*krasis*) of opposites, just as the beverage drunk at symposia is a proportionate mixture of wine and water. This *krasis* is not complete harmony; rather, it involves conflict. Wine is in itself "mad," but it is moderated by water, which "punishes" it. Wine is the primary element in the mixture. It is poured first into the bowl, and it gives its name to the mixture, which retains the essential "mad" quality of the unmixed wine. Water does not change wine and then coexist peacefully with the other liquid, it continually combats wine. Similarly, in the education of the young, a "mad" element, the tendency to make disordered cries and movements, must be mixed by a wise teacher in proper proportions with a "sober" element, the perception of order and harmony and obedience to the law, to produce music and dance. Just as the good and measured drink remains wine, so dance remains movement when excellence is produced in children. excellence is madness successfully combated

Plato's view that antirational emotion is valuable in itself depends on his view, in the *Laws*, that *sōphrosunē* (temperance) involves constant strife.[73] In the *Republic*, Plato views *sōphrosunē* idealistically as complete harmony in the soul (442c10–d1, cf. 432a7–9). In the *Laws*, however, Plato is much more convinced that this is an unattainable ideal. He still believes that the best condition for individuals and cities is complete health and harmony that has never been weakened by sickness or internal strife, and that a restoration to health and harmony is only second best. It would be foolish, Plato writes, "if someone should think that a sick body that has received medical purgation [katharsis] is in the best possible condition, and should give no thought to the body that has no need at all for a purge," or should have similar ideas about the happiness of a city or individual (628d2–e1). However, in this as in other respects, the *Laws* is concerned with second best. It therefore treats *sōphrosunē* not only as a state

---

[73] On Plato's concept of *sōphrosunē* in the *Laws*, see E Barker, *Theory*, 343–45, North, *Sophrosyne*, 186–96, Stalley, *Introduction*, 54–56, and Hall, *Plato*, 187–215

of health after sickness has been cured, but also as a somewhat precarious condition in which there is a constant need for rehabilitation. Accordingly, the concept of strife is much more important in the ethical theory of the *Laws* than in that of the idealistic *Republic*. Courage is defined in the *Laws* as "*combat* against fears and pains, and also against desires and pleasures" (633c8–d3). Only the soul that successfully combats the cowardice within itself can be completely courageous. Similarly, only someone who has to struggle continually against pleasure and desire can become perfect in *sōphrosunē*, defined not as harmony and agreement, but as "victory over oneself."[74]

A particularly important emotion in this conflict theory of excellence is the *aidōs* or *aischunē* (shame or respect) that wine helps produce in older people.[75] In *Laws* 1.646e–647b, Plato distinguishes two kinds of fear. "we fear evils, when we expect them to occur" (646e7–8), and "we often fear opinion, believing that we will be thought to be evil if we do or say anything that is not good" (646e10–11).[76] The first kind of fear, associated with cowardice (647c10), is the ordinary fear of physical pain that prevents courageous acts. The second kind of fear Plato calls *aischunē* (647a2) or *aidōs* (647a10) interchangeably. He says it is the opposite of *anaideia* (shamelessness. 647a10), and that it opposes both the first kind of fear and pains and pleasures: "Now I spoke of these two fears, one of which opposes pains and the other kinds of fears, and also opposes most of the greatest pleasures" (647a4–6).

Because it opposes both pleasure and pain, *aidōs* is conducive to the development of both courage and *sōphrosunē*. Since it opposes fear of physical pain, *aidōs* is said (647b3–7) to have many benefits, including the victory and safety in war that come equally from courage with respect to enemies and from "fear of friends concerning the bad kind of shame" (647b7). Since it opposes pleasure, *aidōs* is also a preparation for the excellence of *sōphrosunē*.[77] Without fighting shameless pleasures and desires,

---

[74] The phrase "victory over oneself" occurs at *Laws* 626e2–3, 634a9–b1, and 647c9, where it is clear that *sōphrosunē* is in question O'Brien, *Socratic Paradoxes*, 183, writes that courage in the *Laws* is needed by a "soul in which strong emotions imply some danger of disorder " England, *Laws*, on 626c6–d2, notes that Plato begins by describing life as a fight, and (on 630a5) that he treats *sōphrosunē* as a fight against oneself

[75] On *aidōs* in the *Laws*, see Schopsdau, "Tapferkeit," and the works cited above, n 55

[76] In *Euthyphro* 12b, Plato makes a similar distinction between *deos*, or fear of sickness, poverty, and other such evils, and *aidōs*, or fear of a bad reputation

[77] In the *Charmides* (160e–161b), Socrates rejects Charmides' definition of *sōphrosunē* as *aidōs*, on the grounds that the former is *agathon* (good), while the latter is "no more good

Plato writes, no one can become completely temperate (*sōphrōn*: 647d3–7). This resistance to shamelessness is part of the training in pleasure and pain, discussed in *Laws* 2.653a–c, that constitutes the first education of children, teaching them to love and hate correctly. It produces the "first excellence of children" (653b2), which they acquire before they are capable of reason. This is preparatory to the "entire excellence" (653b6) that is attained only after people have acquired *phronēsis* (wisdom: 653a7). Because *aidōs* consists in opposition to both pain and pleasure, the natural, fiery, antirational desires of the young are, paradoxically, necessary to its production, for they provide the shameless opponent without which combat against shamelessness cannot take place.

Aidōs in the *Laws* is not perfect excellence, but it is nevertheless a kind of excellence that people who are to be part of a community must be capable from childhood of acquiring. It is a "political excellence," just as *aidōs* and *aischunē* are in other Platonic dialogues. Through its connection with the courage needed by all male citizens, the *aidōs* of the *Laws* is conceptually related to the "citizens' courage" of the *Republic* (4.430c2–3), which consists in the "preservation of true and lawful opinion concerning what is terrible and what is not" (430b2–3). Plato contrasts this kind of courage with the pseudocourage that develops even without education and is "bestial and slavish" (430b6–9), and with the finer kind of courage based on knowledge.[78] Plato has a high regard for "citizens' courage" in the *Republic*. It is the only courage of which most people are capable, and it is essential to *sōphrosunē* in the state, the harmony of ruler and ruled. It is inculcated by the early musical education that provides training in pleasure and pain. While Plato does not use the term *aidōs* in the *Republic* 4 discussion of citizens' courage, in the *Protagoras aidōs* is explicitly characterized as political, for it is said to make *philia* possible in the first place. According to Protagoras (322b–323a), Zeus gave "political craft" to all human beings to prevent destruction of the human race. This is a craft based on *aidōs* and justice, which provide "the order of cities, and the bonds that produce *philia*" (322c3). Zeus says: "There could never be cities if only a few had a share of it [sc., 'political craft'], as is the case with the other crafts. And set it down as a law from me that the person who is not able to share in *aidōs* and justice must be killed, as a sickness of the city" (*Prot.* 322d2–5). Again, in Plato's *Symposium*, Phaedrus expresses tradi-

than bad" (161a11–b2). In the *Laws* also, *aidōs* is not identical with *sōphrosunē*, though it plays a very important role in the development of this excellence.

[78] Knowledge (*epistēmē*) is not discussed until after book 4. On "political courage" in *Rep.* 4, see Adam, *Republic*, on 430c

34

tional Greek views when he praises *"aischunē* with respect to shameful things, and love of honor with respect to fine things. For without these it is not possible for a city or an individual to do great and fine things" (178d1–4). *Aidōs* in the *Laws* also has this political function. It is the less than perfect but supremely important excellence that is necessary to *philia*.[79]

Plato's theory that wine can be a medicine to produce *aidōs* depends on the view that *aidōs* and *sōphrosunē* involve conflict, but it is also indebted to Greek medical theory. The ethical theories of the *Laws* are similar in some respects to the medical theory of Alcmaeon, who viewed physical health as *isonomia* (equilibrium) between opposing *dunameis* (powers) within the body. The absence of opposition created by the *monarchia* of one overmastering "power" destroys this balance, creating sickness. The Hippocratic corpus holds a similar view of health as a proportionate *krasis* of opposites.[80] This view of health readily led many physicians to believe that disease can be treated by the allopathic principle of opposites. If one power is too strong, the opposing power can be used to counterbalance it, thus recreating equilibrium and restoring health. For example, a hot drug, such as wine, can be used to cure diseases caused by excessive cold.[81] Plato's statements in the *Timaeus*, a work greatly influenced by medical theory, show that he adhered to this principle of opposites. "Kinds that are identical or similar cannot work [act] any change in one another, nor can they suffer anything from what is identical and in the same condition."[82]

Plato is clearly indebted to these medical theories in the *Laws*. Since *sōphrosunē* and *aidōs* in this dialogue are a constantly renewed combat against shamelessness, Plato views the psychic health to which they contribute as an equilibrium of opposites. Moreover, it is apparent from the details of Plato's theories on the benefits of wine that psychic qualities are closely related to physical qualities: wine is a medicine for both body and soul.

[79] Schopsdau, "Tapferkeit," 110, calls attention to the connection between *aidōs* and *philia* that is evident at 1 647b7, where Plato defines the good kind of fear as "fear of friends concerning bad shame," and at 3 699c1–6, where he states that *aidōs* produces *philia*.

[80] On Alcmaeon and Greek medical thought, see Tracy, *Mean*, 22–76, esp 22–24. On *isonomia*, *krasis*, and the balance of opposites in Greek medical thought and cosmology, see Vlastos, "Equality," and MacKinney, "Concept." Tracy, 77–156, argues that Plato's physiological and psychological theories have a similar basis.

[81] On the principle of opposites, see chaps 8 and 9.

[82] *Tim* 57a3–5, translated by Solmsen, *System*, 357 (brackets in original). Solmsen also cites *Lysis* 214e3–215a1. On *Tim* 57a, see also Taylor, *Timaeus*, 388–89.

Plato believes that the child is moist and warm, while older people are cold and dry [83] The natural heat of young people makes them malleable and educable because it contributes to their mad, antirational tendencies By the same token, this heat makes wine drinking dangerous for the young, since wine intensifies their fiery, shameless dispositions (*Laws* 2 666a3–8) On the other hand, people become more timid, as well as colder, as they age Older people become slack and out of practice (653c7–9) in combating shamelessness, and they become too ashamed to take part in the songs they must sing (665d8–e3) Wine makes these people "less ashamed" (666c4), because it restores, temporarily, the fiery, shameless desires in which they have become deficient [84] Dionysus provides, Plato writes, "the initiation rite and play of the old, which he gave to the human race in the form of wine, [85] a medicine [*pharmakon*] as a remedy for the austerity of old age, so that we might become young again, and so that through forgetfulness of despondency the hard character of our soul might become softer, like iron put into fire, and so made more easy to mold" (*Laws* 666b4–c2) Just as a medical purge (*pharmakoposia Laws* 646c4) temporarily weakens the body in order to produce the conditions necessary for greater permanent health and strength, so wine temporarily increases the vicious tendencies of the soul, providing the conditions required for greater permanent health and excellence By restoring to older people the fiery disposition of the young, wine helps renew the combat that excellence requires Under the direction of a wise and sober symposiarch this combat can be successful, just as battles can be won only when calm and rational generals lead soldiers who are in the grip of disturbing emotions (*Laws* 671d–e) Wine, used properly, preserves and increases *philia* in the symposia (640c10–d2, 671e5–672a3), where, above all, there is danger of enmity and strife (640c1–2, 671a4–6) Thus, in the symposia of the *Laws*, older people renew and practice their ability to fight shamelessness with "the best   fear   which we have called *aidōs* and *aischunē*, a divine fear" (671d1–3) Wine, Plato concludes, was not given as a punishment to make us mad, but, on the contrary, as a "medicine for the production of *aidōs* in the soul, and of health and strength in the body ' (672d5–9)

Although Plato does not use the word "katharsis" in this connection, his symposia have an effect on the soul that is closely analogous to that of an allopathic medical katharsis on the body At 628c9–e1, Plato compares an unhealthy city and an unhealthy soul to bodies in need of "medical

---

[83] See Bertier, *Mnésithee*, 66–67, 121, Bertier cites *Laws* 2 666a2–c3 and 7 789e2–3

[84] Plato indicates that wine increases shameless desires at *Laws* 645d6–646a2 and 649d4–7

[85] Reading τòν οἶνον at b6, with Burnet

katharsis" (628d2). The reestablishment of health in this soul, which helps produce the kind of *sōphrosunē* in question in the *Laws*, is, then, a kind of psychic katharsis. Plato also indicates that wine acts like a drug for the soul in helping produce *aidōs* and *sōphrosunē* when he compares the effects of a "fear drug," analogous to wine, to the effects of a medicine (*pharmakoposia*: 646c3–8), and when he explicitly calls wine a medicine (*pharmakon*: 2.672d7–9). The psychic katharsis produced by wine is allopathic, being effected by means of opposites. The artificial arousal of shamelessness strengthens the ability of the soul to combat both pleasure and the bad kind of fear with *aidōs*, the opposing (*enantios*: 647a4) good kind of fear. Plato's discussion of the "fear drug" analogous to wine also indicates that psychic katharsis is allopathic. When we want to make people fearless, Plato writes at 647c3–5, we lead them into fears, in accord with the law. This process involves combat between two opposite (*enantia*: 646e4) kinds of fear: fear of a bad reputation (*aidōs*) and fear of the enemy (646e4–647b7). On the other hand, Plato writes, when we want to make people feel the good kind of fear (*aischunē*, fear of a bad reputation), we lead them to shamelessness (lack of fear of doing wrong) and make them practice fighting against it (647c7–9). In this case also, two opposites, fear of a bad reputation and lack of this fear, are in combat. Thus, the artificial arousal of fear by a fear drug helps strengthen people permanently in courage, and the arousal of shamelessness by wine helps purge them of vice and helps produce *sōphrosunē*. Both processes are allopathic.

Plato's views on the benefits of wine are clearly indebted to Greek medical theory, according to which wine was allopathic and kathartic.[86] He also uses medical theories—that of *krasis* of opposites, and that of cure by means of opposites—to account for ethical habituation, in accord with his beliefs about the interconnection of body and soul. The physical deficiency of old age makes the body cold, hard, and dry. Wine counteracts these physical deficiencies and thus acts as a physical purge, driving out excess cold, dryness, and hardness. But wine affects the soul as well as the body, for Plato holds in the *Laws*, as he does at *Timaeus* 86b–87b, that a physical excess or deficiency can produce psychic disorder. The physical dryness, hardness, and coldness of the old people of the *Laws* produces the psychic disorder of despondency (*dusthumia*). Wine helps remedy this disorder by making the soul more fiery and liquid, creating a temporary "viciousness," and also making the soul more malleable, more ready to accept another's

[86] When used as a medical purge, wine had the allopathic function mentioned in "Aristotle," *Prob.* 1.2, discussed in chap. 9. On the kathartic properties of wine, see also Mnesitheus, frag. 45 (Athenaeus 11.484a), and "Hippocrates," *Regimen* 2.52, Littré 6:554 "Wine is hot and dry, and it has something kathartic from its matter."

control.[87] In this process of emotional katharsis, the soul is first purged of excessive shame and despondency and then strengthened in *aidōs* by the symposiarch's training In this way, wine helps reestablish psychic health and equilibrium, and helps recreate *sōphrosunē*

If Greek medicine provides much of the theoretical basis for the psychology of *Laws* 1 and 2, the Greek festivals of Dionysus, the god of beneficial madness, provide much of the background for the institution of the symposium in these books. For one thing, Dionysus in the *Laws* is the god of the theater as well as the god of wine, and the symposia of Plato's *Laws* are, in many respects, theatrical events as well as medical treatments Staid old people temporarily take on the personae of mad young children in order to play their roles as members of the Chorus of Dionysus (665a–666c), and to renew their education through song and dance Everyday rules are suspended, and emotions are aroused that are alien to the cold and timid dispositions of older people In sum, those very events occur for which Plato blames the drama in *Republic* 10 There, poets are criticized for falsely claiming to educate us (606e) and to provide a safe and pleasant special situation in which we can indulge our shameless emotions without real-life consequences Because the symposia of the *Laws* are in many ways aesthetic situations in which aesthetic emotions are aroused, Plato would seem more favorably disposed toward the god of drama he so mistrusted in the *Republic* Nevertheless, the *Laws* stops short of providing the apology for imitative poetry asked for in *Republic* 10 (607d) Most tragic poetry is no more welcome in the second-best state of the *Laws* than in the ideal state of the *Republic*, because Plato continued to believe that a poet who is not also a philosopher or a servant of the laws cannot arouse emotions correctly

Even though Plato's new psychology did not lead him to recall the banished poets, it could have helped open this possibility to Aristotle We know that Aristotle read the *Laws* very carefully, referring to this work repeatedly in his *Politics* At *Politics* 1274b11–15, he particularly mentions Plato's views on drinking [88] Aristotle would have found Plato's psychological theories attractive in a number of ways The *Laws* stresses the importance of psychic elements other than reason, as do Aristotle's own psychological and ethical works [89] Plato's views also assume an Aristotelian

---

[87] See Tracy, *Mean*, 126–32, for an excellent discussion of the medical basis for Plato s prescription of wine as a remedy for the *dusthumia* of old age

[88] This passage was bracketed by Newman, *Politics*, but not by Dreizehnter and many others Morrow includes it (148) in Comments, his thorough examination of Aristotle s debt to the *Laws*

[89] Fortenbaugh, *Emotion*, 23, argues that the *Laws* seems to be working towards a psy-

distinction between temporary emotional states (*pathē*) and permanent dispositions (*hexeis*).[90] The theories of the *Laws* take into account, in a very Aristotelian way, observed phenomena, "what people say," customs and practices, and traditional accounts of the physical and psychological effects of wine and emotion. Moreover, Plato's views on *aidōs* closely resemble those held by Aristotle. Finally, wine in the *Laws* produces many of the same effects tragedy does in the *Poetics*. Both arouse emotions temporarily and artificially, in pleasant, harmless, and socially controlled circumstances. Both contribute to an emotional education.

The most intriguing possibility, however, is that the *Laws* directly influenced Aristotle's views on tragic katharsis. As we have seen, Plato's symposia provide what may be called an allopathic katharsis of the emotions, one that takes place in a situation that is in many ways aesthetic. While Plato himself is concerned with arousing the (hot) emotions opposite to the tragic emotions of (cold) fear and pity, his ideas could easily be applied to tragedy. Plato is concerned with older people, who are excessively cold and sober. His psychological theory, however, is equally applicable to young people, who are excessively hot, shameless, and aggressive; in their case also, psychic equilibrium could be restored by the application of an opposing excess. A cold drug that produces a fear of wrongdoing could help correct their excessive heat. Tragedy itself might be just such a drug. This, as we will see below, is Aristotle's view.

In this chapter I have examined some Greek beliefs about the benefits of fear of wrongdoing. In symposia, festivals, and poetry, *aidōs* has the apotropaic, political function of averting shameless strife among *philoi*. In the visual arts, the gorgoneion in the drinking cup has a similar apotropaic function. The traditional idea that fear of wrongdoing can be an antidote to shamelessness and strife among *philoi* is given philosophical support and clarification by the psychological theories of Plato's *Laws*. There is reason to believe that Aristotle was influenced by Greek traditional views, and in particular by the Platonic psychology of the *Laws*, in formulating his own theory of tragic emotion and katharsis.[91]

---

chology that Aristotle ultimately made his own and exploited within his political and ethical writings "

[90] See, for example, *EN* 2 5

[91] I am indebted to Christopher Carey for criticisms of an earlier draft of the material on Pindar, to Helen Bacon, Patricia Easterling, and Richard Kuhn for criticisms of the *Eumenides* section, and to George Sheets for reading a draft of the entire chapter

PART II

PLOT: THE SOUL OF TRAGEDY

*

*

I‌T WILL be more evident, in parts III and IV, how deeply Aristotle's views on tragic emotion are rooted in the Greek literary and philosophical traditions that were examined in part I. Before we can begin to consider this topic, however, we must understand Aristotle's views on the nature of the tragic plot whose function it is to arouse the tragic emotions. Accordingly, part II studies, first, two fundamentally important concepts necessary to an understanding of Aristotle's views on the nature of the plot: imitation and *philia* (chapter 2). Next, chapter 3 looks closely at the reasons why Aristotle believes plot to be *the* essential part of tragedy, and why, in particular, he thinks plot is so much more important than "character." Chapter 4 discusses the basic principles that govern plot structure: necessity and probability. Finally, chapter 5 examines each of the three parts of the tragic plot—*pathos* (a painful or destructive event), *peripeteia* (reversal), and recognition—and discusses the criteria for good and bad plots given in *Poetics* 13 and 14.

Philia and Tragic Imitation

T<small>WO FUNDAMENTAL CONCEPTS</small> underlie Aristotle's views on plot structure and emotional arousal. *philia* and imitation. I begin with a study of these concepts because of their intrinsic importance and because it is easy to confuse them with very different modern ideas.

Although *philia* can be translated as "kinship," "friendship," or "love," the Greek phenomenon has in fact no equivalent in twentieth-century Western civilization. For one thing, kinship no longer has the primary importance for us that it did for Aristotle and his contemporaries. Aristotle writes in the *Politics* that the person who, like Homer's lover of war, is ἀφρήτωρ, ἀθέμιστος, ἀνέστιος ("without phratry, without *themis*, without hearth") is not really human at all.[1] If these qualities, all closely connected with kinship, characterize the nonhuman, we today are hardly human by Greek standards. We no longer have kinship-based "brotherhoods" (phratries). Nothing in our language corresponds to the Greek *themis*, the unwritten law of custom and tradition, governing, in particular, behavior toward kin, and sanctioned by ancestors, the gods, and society as a whole. We also lack any equivalent of the ancient hearth, which was the social and religious center of family life and the physical center of the many common tasks in which family members engaged. sheltering, cooking, socializing children, praying, receiving guests It requires, then, a constant effort of the imagination for us to read the Greek tragedies, which are so deeply concerned with *philia* relationships, and the *Poetics*, in which this concern is taken for granted.

Imitation is another potentially confusing concept, especially since Plato's ideas on imitative craft tend to be more familiar to us than do those of Aristotle. For Plato, an imitation is "third from the truth," a copy that has an inferior relationship to a model or an original, and to imitate is to engage in an activity that is derivative, second-rate, peripheral to the important business of life.[2] Aristotle's views are quite different. Far from being peripheral and second-rate, imitation, in his view, is one of the activities that is most essential to our being human. Through imitation

---

[1] *Il* 9 63, quoted by Aristotle, *Pol* 1 1253a5

[2] On Plato's views, expressed chiefly in *Rep* 10, see Belfiore, "Accusation "

we learn about the world and our place in it, and we take a distinctively human pleasure in doing so. Tragic imitation has an especially close connection with our nature as human beings, for tragedy deals with the *philia* relationships that make us human. Thus, tragedy imitates, and teaches us about, ourselves. Imitation is not entertainment, or play, or relaxation after the serious business of life; rather, in Aristotle's view, it is itself part of the serious business of life. Imitation is one of the activities that constitute the *diagōgē* in *scholē* (*Pol.* 8.1338a21–22) for the sake of which all other activities, such as war or moneymaking, are done (*Pol.* 8.1334a2–10; cf. 8.2 and 8.4). *Diagōgē*, in this context, is not "amusement," or "pastime," but "rational activity," a way of living, of conducting one's life according to certain principles.[3] Similarly, *scholē* is not "leisure" in the sense of idleness, but the freedom from necessary occupations that allows a person to practice excellence.

Philia and imitation are fundamental to Aristotle's more specific views on tragedy. For this reason, many of the ideas addressed in this chapter in a preliminary and introductory way will be discussed in more detail below. Aristotle's views on imitation can only be fully understood in the context of his ideas on necessity and probability, on the organization of the plot as a whole, and on each of the parts of the plot that make up the whole. Moreover, the role of *philia* in Aristotle's theory of tragedy only becomes fully clear through an examination of the subject matter of tragedy and of the specific emotional responses aroused by tragedy. The following remarks will serve in part as an outline to be filled in as the book progresses.

IMITATION

Tragedy produces the emotional effects it does because it is a particular kind of imitation. "Tragedy is imitation of action . . . by means of pity and fear accomplishing the katharsis of such emotions" (*Po.* 6.1449b24–28).[4] More specifically, "the plot is the imitation of the action" (1450a3–

---

[3] Compare Plato, *Rep* 344e1–2 "Do you think it is a small matter to try to define the conduct [*diagōgē*] of an entire life, how each of us might conduct life [*diagomenos*] so as to live the best life?"

[4] Among the relatively recent studies of Aristotelian and Greek concepts of imitation are those of Dupont-Roc, "Mimesis," Gentili, *Poesia*, chap 4, Lallot, "*Mimesis*", Else, "Imitation" and *Plato*, chap 5, 74–88, Halliwell, *Aristotle's Poetics*, chap 4, 109–37, Koller, *Mimesis*, and Sörbom, *Mimesis and Art* Also very helpful, though they do not deal directly with Aristotle, are the discussions of the concepts of imitation and representation in Gombrich, *Art*, and Goodman, *Languages*

4) In *Poetics* 14, Aristotle again states that imitation of action (the plot, or the "organization of the events") produces audience reactions "Since the poet should produce the pleasure that comes from pity and fear by means of imitation, it is clear that this should be put into the events" (1453b11–14) Aristotle's view is that the tragic poet makes a plot, an imitation of a certain kind of action, and that this plot produces pity, fear, pleasure, and katharsis

Tragedy is one of many kinds of imitation Aristotle begins the *Poetics* thus "Concerning the poetic craft itself and its kinds " (1447a1) All these kinds of poetic crafts—music, dance, painting, and drama—are imitations (*mimēseis* 1447a16) made by people who "make images" (1447a19) They differ from one another in medium, in manner of imitation, or in objects imitated, the last include "characters, emotions, and actions" (1447a28) Tragedy is the kind of imitation that imitates "serious" or "noble" action (*praxeōs spoudaias* 1449b24) done by people "better than those of today" (1448a16–18), in rhythm, song, and meter (1447b24–27), and in the manner of enactment rather than by narration (1448a19–29)

Imitation is not merely an aesthetic concept, in Aristotle's view, but an essential part of human nature

> It seems that there are two causes of poetry as a whole, and that these are natural causes For to imitate is inherent from their childhood in human beings, who differ from other living things in being most imitative, and in learning their first lessons by means of imitation, and all take pleasure in imitations A sign of this is what happens in fact For we take pleasure contemplating the most accurately made images of things that themselves give us pain to see, such as the shapes of the most despised animals and of corpses The cause of this is that learning is most pleasant not only to philosophers, but to others in the same way, though they have only a small share in this For this reason, people take pleasure seeing images, because it happens that while they contemplate they learn and reason what each thing is for example, that this is that For if someone has not happened to see something previously, the imitation will not give pleasure as an imitation but because of the workmanship, or the color, or for some other reason (*Po* 4 1448b4–19)

This passage tells us that the capacity to imitate differentiates humans from other living things in several ways This capacity is "inherent in" (*sumphuton*) humans, humans are "most imitative," learn by means of imitation, and take pleasure in imitations.[5] The emphasis on learning throughout this passage is significant Aristotle believes that imitation is a distinctive characteristic of humans because it is an activity of the rational part of the soul (that with which we "reason" *sullogizesthai*, 1448b16), which other living things lack Moreover, "the function [*ergon*] of a human being is activity of the soul in accord with reason, or not without reason" (*EN* 1098a7–8), and happiness, the good for a human being, depends on function (*EN* 1097b22–28) Through the activity of imitating (*to mimeisthai* 1448b5, *mimēseōs* 1448b8), and through taking pleasure in the products of imitation (*mimēmasi* 1448b9), then, we perform the distinctively human function on which our happiness depends This means that the imitative crafts, for Aristotle, are not merely play and entertainment, they are closely connected with the end of human life, that for the sake of which all else is done They are therefore among the most serious activities.

This view of the importance of imitation in human life is supported by Aristotle's views in the *Politics* on music, the most important and comprehensive of the imitative crafts Aristotle believes that "war is for the sake of peace, business for the sake of leisure [*scholē*], and necessary and useful things for the sake of the fine."[6] Aristotle argues that music is one of the most important of those leisure activities for the sake of which the other activities are done. It is an end in itself, a *diagōgē*, a "rational activity" in leisure for a free human being It is not necessary or useful for moneymaking, housekeeping, or political activity, or for health and strength, but is a fine and liberal activity, an end in itself (8. 1338a9–32) [7]

[5] Cf *Rhet* 1371b4–10 and 'Aristotle," *Prob* 956a14, on learning by means of imitation Both learning from and taking pleasure in imitation are clearly part of human nature in *Po* 4, however we interpret the "two causes' that are said to generate the poetic craft in 1448b4–5 On the "two causes," see Else, *Argument*, 127–31, and Dupont-Roc and Lallot, *Poetique*, 164–67

[6] *Pol* 7 1333a35–36 See also the other formulations of this principle cited by Solmsen, "Leisure,' 210 n 70 *EN* 10 1177b4ff , *Pol* 1334a14ff , 1337b30ff On music and leisure in the *Pol* , see also Stocks, "*Scholē*", Carnes Lord, *Education*, and Depew, "Politics '

[7] While music and the other imitative crafts may be practiced by professionals, who are concerned with moneymaking, this is not the sort of thing Aristotle has in mind Carnes Lord's discussion of ' serious leisure' (*Education*, 55–57) is of interest in this connection Aristotle's views on the educational uses of music and on its *relative* value in leisure activity are much debated Solmsen , ' Leisure," 216, believes that music has an ethical rather than an intellectual effect, and so cannot be the highest human leisure activity Lord, *Education*, holds a similar view (62–66) Depew, "Politics," opposes this view, arguing that music is a stimulus to contemplation The account of imitation in *Po* 4 supports this interpretation

47

In spite of its importance, Aristotle's concept of imitation (mimesis) is elusive, for he nowhere gives the kind of detailed theoretical account that Plato gives in the *Republic*.[8] Nevertheless, the *Poetics*, especially chapter 4, and some relevant passages in other works indicate that Aristotle did have definite views on the characteristics of imitations that serve to distinguish them from nonimitations. A study of these characteristics can help us understand the cognitive and emotional responses human beings have to imitations. An imitation of the kind discussed in the *Poetics* would seem to have four main distinguishing characteristics: (1) it *represents* the object imitated—that is, it stands for, refers to, or symbolizes this object;[9] (2) it is *produced* by the act of imitating; (3) it is *similar* to the object imitated; and (4) it has a *theoretical* rather than a practical function.

Representation

In *Poetics* 4.1448b15–19, quoted above, Aristotle tells us that there are two ways of viewing an imitation or an image (*eikōn*).[10] He distinguishes viewing an imitation (or an image) "as an imitation" (ἠ μίμημα)—that is, as what we would call a representation—from viewing it in a nonrepresentational way, as an object with certain intrinsic properties of "workmanship" or color. To enjoy something as an imitation we must previously have seen the object imitated, so as to be able to conclude that there is a certain asymmetrical relationship, "that *this* is *that*" (ὅτι οὗτος ἐκεῖνος), between the imitation and that of which it is the imitation, the perceptible object we have seen before.[11] This kind of pleasure does not come from observing or learning about properties intrinsic to the object, but from learning about its relationship to some other object.

A passage in Aristotle's *On Memory* helps clarify this distinction between viewing an image as "of something else," that is, as a representation, and viewing it only as an object with intrinsic properties of its own. After

[8] On Plato's views, see Belfiore, "Theory '

[9] I follow Goodman's characterization of representation in *Languages*, 5

[10] The terms *mimēma* and *eikōn* are used interchangeably in *Po* 4 At 1448b11 and 1448b15, Aristotle uses the term *eikonas*, *mimēma(si)* occurs at 1448b9 and 1448b18 See also 1447a19 *mimountai   apeikazontes* I discussed the cognitive responses we have to imitations in Belfiore, "Pleasure " While a few paragraphs of the earlier article are reproduced here with little change, I have modified my earlier views considerably

[11] For a good survey and discussion of the controversy over the meaning of οὗτος (this) and ἐκεῖνος (that), and of the problem of what we learn from imitations, see Gallop, "Animals," and Sifakis, "Learning " I discuss the kind of learning involved below in "*Theōria*," and in chap 7 ("Tragedy and Rhetoric') and chap 10

stating that perception makes an impression in the soul that is like a picture (450a27–30), Aristotle explains that when we remember something we are aware of this impression not "as a thing in itself," but "as of something else"

> The animal drawn on a panel is both an animal and an image This thing, while being one and the same, is both, but the being of the two is not the same, and it is possible to contemplate it both as an animal and as an image In the same way one must suppose the appearance in us to be both an object of contemplation in itself, and to be an appearance of another thing [12] As something in itself [ἦ καθ' αὐτὸ], it is an object of contemplation or an appearance. But inasmuch as it is of another thing [ἦ ἄλλου] it is like an image and a reminder (450b21–27)

A portrait of Coriscus (the example Aristotle gives just after this passage) is both something in itself and an image of Coriscus, and it may be viewed in either of these ways. [13]

According to *On Memory*, an image reminds us of the object of which it is the image. This is similar to the account in *Poetics* 4, which holds that only when we have previously seen the object imitated can we learn about the relationship between imitation (or image) and object imitated (1448b15–19). An imitation, then, has an asymmetrical, representational aspect because it is "of another" (ἦ ἄλλου), a reminder, something from which we can learn about something else. There is, however, one important difference between the imitation in the *Poetics* and the image in *On Memory*. the image is a portrait of an individual, Coriscus, while the imitations in the *Poetics* are not imitations of individuals. *Poetics* 9 distinguishes poetry—that is, imitation—from history on just this basis. Poetry speaks of "the universal," of "what kinds of things it happens that a certain kind of person says or does according to probability or necessity," while history "speaks of the particular," for example, "what Alcibiades did or experienced" (1451b6–11). [14] An account of the life of Alcibiades is not imitation but history. It would seem to follow, then, that a portrait,

[12] I follow Bekker, and G R T Ross, *De sensu*, in reading θεώρημα καὶ ἄλλου φάντασμα at 450b25 W D Ross, *Parva naturalia*, omits θεώρημα and brackets φάντασμα

[13] Good accounts of the ideas expressed in this passage are given by Wedin, *Mind*, 138–41 (although I disagree with him about the meaning of θεώρημα), and Modrak, *Perception*, 121–30 and 167–71

[14] Poetry is said to be a kind of imitation at 1 1447a13–16, while the poet is said to be a poet because he imitates at 9 1451b28–29 (cf 1 1447b13–16) It would seem that poetry "speaks of the universal" because it is imitation

which is more like history than poetry, is not an imitation according to the criterion of *Poetics* 9. It is hard to say, however, whether Aristotle would have accepted this conclusion.[15]

Aristotelian imitations or images thus have an asymmetrical, representational relationship to something else, of which they remind us In *On Memory* 450b21–27, Aristotle characterizes this relationship as one in which an imitation is "of another" in that its "being" is relational. "The being of the two is not the same, and it is possible to contemplate it both as an animal and as an image." Thus, if something is an imitation or image of Coriscus, being "of Coriscus" is essential to "the being" of the image, while, of course, being "of an image" is not essential to "the being" of Coriscus. As I will argue below ("Production"), "the being" of something depends on its function. In the *On Memory* passage, then, the function of an image depends on its being viewed (that is, functioning) in a certain way

Nevertheless, Aristotle does not fully explain what it is for an image or imitation to be "of another." He does not adequately account for what we would call today the representational aspect of an image Is an image "of another" in the way in which a name is a symbol and a sign of something else by convention and not by nature?[16] Or is an image "of another" in the way in which a part is of a whole, and a natural slave is of a master (*Pol* 1 1254a8–17)? "The master," Aristotle writes, "is only the master of the slave, but he is not of him [sc., the slave]. The slave, however, is not only the slave of the master, but he is also entirely of him [sc , the master]." This is so because the natural slave is "a human being who is by nature not of himself but of another" (1.1254a11–15) That is, it is part of "the being" of a natural slave qua human being to be "of another," but this is not true of a natural master.[17] An Aristotelian image does not appear to be "of another" in either of these ways Like the slave, an image has an asymmetrical relationship to something else. being "of another" is part of "the being" of the image, while this is not true of that of which it is the

[15] Rorty, "Psychology," makes the intriguing suggestion that a portrait might show what kind of man Pericles is by picking out certain features that remain constant over time and through changes of mood I am indebted to her for allowing me to read a draft of this article

[16] See *De interpretatione* 1–2, esp 16a19–20, 26–28 On this difficult passage, see Ackrill, *Categories*, 113–14 He notes that there are ' grave weaknesses in Aristotle s theory of meaning" (113)

[17] Contrast the *reciprocal* πρός τι relationship of master and slave (qua master and slave) discussed in *Cat* 7 6b28–30, cf 6a36–37

image. Nevertheless, the slave is not the imitation or image of the master. The image is not "of another" in the way in which a name is, either. Unlike the purely conventional name, an image is similar to that which it imitates, and similarity, in Aristotle's view, is not purely conventional.

An Aristotelian image comes closest to being "of another" in the way in which a rhetorical example is "of another."[18] In *Rhetoric* 1.2.19, Aristotle explains that one thing is an example of another if it is related to it "as part to part, like to like, when both are under the same kind, but the one is better known than the other" (1357b28–30).[19] An example is used in certain kinds of rhetorical arguments. If, Aristotle writes, a rhetorician wants to show that Dionysius, who asks for a guard, is plotting a tyranny, he might do so by choosing better-known examples that are "under the same universal" (1357b35–36)—that is, instances of the same universal. In this case, the universal is "the man plotting a tyranny asks for a guard" (1357b36), and well-known examples are Pisistratus and Theagenes. These well-known tyrants may be used as examples of Dionysius (1357b34).

The rhetorical example is like an imitation or image in several ways. It is similar ("like to like") to that of which it is an example, just as an imitation is similar to that of which it is the imitation. Moreover, the example, like the imitation, stands for something else. As we have just seen, imitation involves, among other things, an asymmetrical, representational relationship in which being "of another" is essential to "the being" of an image or imitation, but being "of an image" is not essential to "the being" of the other thing. This would also appear to be true of the example, for being "[an example] of Dionysius" is essential to the being of Pisistratus, qua example. In spite of these similarities, however, an example is not an imitation or an image. Aristotle's discussion of a story used as an example helps make the differences clearer.

Aristotle tells us that the rhetorician might use a story as an example in arguing that a particular man is plotting a tyranny. Such a story is that of the horse and the stag told by Stesichorus, when the people of Himera had chosen Phalaris as dictator and were about to give him a guard (*Rhet.* 2.20.1393b8–23). In the story, a horse, wishing to punish a stag, allows a man to put a bridle on him and to mount him armed with javelins. As a result, the horse is enslaved. This story recounts an instance of the universal that "the man plotting a tyranny asks to 'mount' another with arms,"

---

[18] I am indebted to Eugene Garver for some good discussions of rhetorical examples.
[19] See Grimaldi, *Rhetoric I*, 69, for some good remarks on this passage.

that is, asks for a bodyguard. Stesichorus, according to Aristotle, makes a practical application. "So you also see that in wishing to punish your enemies you do not suffer what the horse did. You already have the bridle, having chosen a general as dictator. If you give him a guard and allow him to mount you, you will at that time be the slaves of Phalaris" (1393b19–23). The example leads us to see that Phalaris, another particular individual of the same kind (an instance of the same universal), is in fact aiming at a tyranny. This story is an example (παράδειγμα) because it is used to point out (δεικνύναι) another particular that falls under the same universal and that is of immediate, practical interest

While the man in this story is used as an example of Phalaris, the story is obviously not an imitation of the actions of Phalaris. It appears, then, that an imitation is not "of another" in the way in which an example is "of another."[20] The nature of this difference, however, is not immediately obvious, especially when we consider that the same story is an imitation of the actions of the horse and the stag. What is it that makes this same story an example of Phalaris and an imitation of the horse and the stag? As we will see below ("*Theōria*"), Aristotle's view that being "of another" depends on function can explain the difference. Aristotle did not see, however, that this insight into the nature of representation is not compatible with an imitative theory of art, which cannot, in itself, give an adequate explanation of the different ways of being "of another." As modern philosophers have argued, the representational aspects of art depend on context and function, and cannot be explained in terms of imitation. This point is made by E. H. Gombrich in discussing a couch made by a sculptor. "Must it always be true that the sculptor's couch is a representation? If we mean by this term that it must refer to something else, that it is a sign, then this will surely depend on the context. Put a real couch into a shop window and you thereby turn it into a sign."[21] In failing to give an adequate ac-

[20] Eden, *Fiction*, fails to make this important theoretical distinction when she writes that a tragedy is an example or paradigm (70) While a tragedy *contains* examples, as I will argue in chap 7 ("Tragedy and Rhetoric"), it is itself an imitation rather than an example Some good discussions of the differences between rhetoric and imitation are those of Weinberg, *History*, 350–52, and "Formal Analysis", Howell, "Aristotle ' and "Rhetoric and Poetics " According to Howell, in using a story as an example, the rhetorician makes a nonmimetic use of an imitation ("Aristotle, ' 333), for "poetry is mimetic, and rhetoric non-mimetic" (327) While this is an excellent point, neither Howell nor Weinberg adequately distinguishes, in theoretical terms, imitations from nonimitations

[21] Gombrich, *Art*, 98 See also Goodman, *Languages*, esp 6–10, who argues that 'representation [is not] a matter of imitation" (10)

count of the representational aspects of art, Aristotle's theory shares the defects inherent in all imitative theories of art. Nevertheless, his views are in other respects remarkably insightful

Production. Tragedy Imitates Nature

Aristotle's theory that "craft imitates nature" illuminates some of the most significant aspects of his concept of tragic imitation. The craft of tragic imitation, like all crafts, resembles the natural process that produces a biological organism. Tragic imitation, however, is a particularly good example of a craft that imitates nature. Aristotle's frequent biological analogies in the *Poetics* show that tragedy is an artifact that has more in common with living things than do most other artifacts. For one thing, the plot of tragedy is analogous to the soul (1450a38), the internal principle of motion in living things. A study of imitation in the *Poetics* must take into account this biological analogy [22]

Mimesis, an act of "making" (*poiēsis*), is a process of imitating.[23] In this process, the poet makes the plot and the actor enacts it (*Po.* 1449b31) Mimesis, however, is not primarily an act of the poet, but of the poet's craft within the plot The plot is a change (*metabasis* 1452a16, *metaballein* 1451a14) from beginning, to middle, to end, it is a process (*kinēsis*) of imitating an action (*mimēsis praxeōs* 1449b24). It is a product of a certain kind, an imitation (*mimēma*), in part because it is produced by this process. In the *Topics*, Aristotle states the general rule that "an *eikōn* is something that comes to be by means of imitation" (140a14–15) The term *eikōn* means here "the product of an act of imitation." In the *Poetics*, the term *mimēma* also has this meaning, and, as noted above, the terms *mimēma* and *eikōn* are used interchangeably in *Poetics* 4

If the plot is itself a process of imitating a particular kind of process (an action), imitation is, more generally, a process in which craft (*technē*) imitates the process of nature (*phusis*). In a number of passages, Aristotle writes that "craft imitates nature "[24] He means that both processes have an end (*telos*), something "for the sake of which" all the successive stages of the process are done

[22] Gallop, "Animals," gives an account of Aristotle s biological analogy that is excellent in many respects, although I do not agree with him on certain points

[23] See Else, *Argument*, 1–13, on this idea

[24] This is stated at *Phy* 194a21–22 and 199a15–17, and *Meteor* 381b6, cf *Protrepticus* 13 2–3, 14 1–2, 23 3

In all those things in which there is some end, for the sake of this the earlier, successive things are done As it is done, so it is by nature, and as it is by nature, so each thing is done, if nothing impedes It is done for the sake of something, and it is therefore by nature for the sake of something For example, if a house were among those things that come to be by nature, it would come to be as it does now by means of craft   In general, in some cases, craft completes what nature is not able to finish working up, and in other cases it imitates [nature] So that if things produced in accordance with craft are for the sake of something, it is clear that things produced in accordance with nature are also For the relationship of the later to the earlier [stages of production] is similar in the things produced in accordance with craft and the things produced in accordance with nature (*Phy* 199a8–20)[25]

Immediately before this passage, Aristotle opposes processes that occur with regularity to those that occur by chance. "All things that are by nature come to be in this way either always or for the most part, but none of the things that come to be by chance and of their own accord do so" (*Phy.* 198b35–36). Here, Aristotle uses the expression "always or for the most part" to refer to the regular way in which things happen when they are "for the sake of something" instead of occurring "by chance." According to Aristotle, natural processes occurring "always or for the most part" occur "for the sake of an end." He argues that, of the two possibilities—that natural processes occur "by coincidence" (that is, by chance or of their own accord), or that they occur "for the sake of something"—the second is clearly correct (199a4–5).[26] Both natural and craft processes, then, occur with regularity ("always or for the most part") for the sake of an end

Just as natural objects come to be "always or for the most part," so in the process of the tragic plot, events must come to be according to the rule of probability or necessity (e.g., *Po.* 1451a36–38). Only plots that follow this rule will be one, whole, and complete, with parts put together so that none can be added or removed without changing the whole (1451a30–35). A plot that proceeds according to probability or necessity is one that "speaks of the universal" rather than of the particular. "Poetry speaks more of the universal, history of the particular. The universal is what kinds of

[25] Cf *Protrepticus* 14 1–2 "If, then, art imitates nature, it is from nature that the arts have derived the characteristic that all their products come into being for the sake of something " I quote the translation of J Barnes and G Lawrence, in Barnes, *Oxford Translation*, 2405

[26] On this argument, see Waterlow, *Nature*, 74–81 She points out (75 n 25) that "by coincidence," "by chance," and "by spontaneity" (that is, of their own accord) are synonyms in this passage

things it happens that a certain kind of person says or does according to probability or necessity" (1451b6–9). The particular plot that "speaks of the universal" is an instance of a universal, just as the individual natural object belongs to a certain class of things that occur "either always or for the most part."[27]

If the process of imitation in the crafts is like a natural process, in which everything is done for the sake of an end, it follows that the product of the act of imitating will have an organized structure, a *sustasis*, like that of a natural product. It is important to note, however, that Aristotle's analogy between tragedy and living things is less than exact in respect to the process-product distinction. In nature, the process by means of which a living thing develops is different from the product, the completed living thing. This is also true of the craft of house building, Aristotle's example in *Physics* 199a8–20, quoted above. In the case of tragedy, however, the plot is both the process of imitating and the product produced by imitating. By keeping in mind this difference between living things and tragedy, we can avoid confusion as we examine further Aristotle's views on the ways in which the structures of craft products are similar to those of living things. *Parts of Animals* 1.5 gives additional information about this similarity:

> It remains to speak of the nature of living things, passing over, so far as is possible, neither what is more despised nor what is more esteemed. For even in those that are not pleasing to the senses, when contemplated, the nature that crafted them gives immense pleasure in the same way[28] to those who are able to gain knowledge of the causes and are philosophers by nature. For it would be unreasonable and strange if we should take pleasure contemplating the images of these things because at the same time we contemplate the craft that made them, for example, painting or sculpture, but did not love more the contemplation of the things themselves organized by nature, at least if we are able to see the causes. And so one should not be childishly disgusted at the examination of the more despised living things. For in all natural objects there is something marvelous. (*PA* 1.5.645a5–17)

In this passage, Aristotle connects the structure of both living things and craft products with causation. To contemplate the "craft that made" something is to understand the "causes." These are the final causes, that for the sake of which as an end (*telos*) each part and the whole exist (ἕνεκά

---

[27] The relationship between the rule of "probability or necessity" in tragedy and that of "always or for the most part" in nature is discussed in chap. 4 ("Necessity and Probability").

[28] At 645a8 I read ὁμοίως with the MSS and Balme, *De partibus animalium*.

τινος [του] 645a24, 645b15, οὗ ενεχα τελους 645a25) In the *Parts of Animals*, as in the *Physics*, this final cause is opposed to chance (645a23–24) The final cause, moreover, is the activity of the soul of a living thing, and this activity is the function (*ergon*) of the living thing

> Since every instrument is for the sake of something, and each of the parts of the body is for the sake of something, and what they are for the sake of is an action, it is clear that the whole body also is organized for the sake of a complex action Sawing has not come to be for the sake of the saw, but the saw for the sake of sawing For sawing is a kind of using So that the body also is in some way for the sake of the soul, and the parts [of the body] are [for the sake of] the functions to which each is [suited] by nature (*PA* 645b14–20)

That the soul is the functioning of the living thing is also clear from *Parts of Animals* 641a18–21 "When soul has gone there is no longer an animal, nor does any of its parts remain the same except in shape alone, like those turned to stone in the fable "[29]

These passages help us understand Aristotle's comparison of the structure of tragedy to the structure of living things Tragedy imitates nature because the plot resembles a biological organism in having an intelligible structure that is organized for the sake of an end, its function Aristotle writes that "the plot is the first principle and, as it were, the soul of tragedy" (*Po* 1450a38–39) Because the plot is itself a kind of process or movement, tragedy is analogous to a living thing with a nature of its own that "has within it a principle of movement and rest" (*Phy* 192b13–14) Aristotle uses the biological term *sustasis* to refer to the organized structure of the tragedy This word and its cognates are used in the biological works of the action of the semen in "setting" the menstrual fluid in the first stage of the reproductive process A L Peck suggests that a possible translation would be ' organiz[ation] [30] This translation also makes excellent sense in the *Poetics*, for in this work, the plot is said to be the organization of

---

[29] Balme s translation Balme has some excellent remarks on Aristotle s view that soul is the functioning of a living thing The soul is the living organism s capability It is neither an entity independent of body, nor a function of the constituents of the body, but exists only when these constituents are organized in a living animal or plant (*De partibus animalium*, 71), As the *form* of the body, the soul is the animal s being (*ousia*) considered in abstraction from flesh and bones It is the animal s functioning including its ability to function (at times when it is not actually functioning) (90)

[30] Peck, *Generation of Animals*, lxii See his discussion of *sunistanai* and its cognates as technical, biological terms, lxi–lxii As Allan Gotthelf pointed out to me, the translation

the events" (*sustasis tōn pragmatōn*) and the poet is said to "organize plots" or "events" (*sunistanai tous muthous, ta pragmata*).[31] The term Aristotle uses for the "parts" of tragedy, *moria*, is also biological.[32]

Aristotle's biological analogy illuminates his views on the end and function of tragedy. In *Poetics* 6, he writes that the plot is the end of tragedy (1450a22), and that the poet who makes plots will best produce "that which is the *ergon* of tragedy" (1450a30–31). Elsewhere, however, Aristotle identifies emotional arousal and pleasure, rather than plot, with the *telos* and *ergon* of tragedy (1460b24–26, 1462a18–b1, 1462b12–15). The biological analogy helps reconcile these accounts by clarifying the relationship between plot and pleasure. Aristotle writes that "it is necessary to organize [epic] plots, just like tragic plots, so that they are dramatic, and about one whole and complete action having a beginnning, and middle, and end, so that like one whole living thing it [sc., the epic] might produce its proper pleasure" (1459a18–21). The plot is itself a process, an action, and its activity is the *ergon* of tragedy.[33] Just as the activity of the soul is the *ergon* and *telos* of a living thing, so the functioning of the plot in arousing the "proper pleasure" is the *ergon* and *telos* of tragedy.

Specifically, the final cause (*telos* or *ergon*) of tragedy is the functioning of the plot to produce pleasure and katharsis by means of pity and fear. In *Poetics* 13, after saying he is going to discuss "whence will be the *ergon* of tragedy" (1452b29), Aristotle states (1452b32–33) that the best tragedy should be "imitative of fearful and pitiable things, for this is proper to this kind of imitation." He goes on to consider which kinds of plots best arouse pity and fear. However, the *ergon* or *telos* of tragedy is not the mere arousal of pity and fear, but the production of the pleasure belonging to tragedy:

"organize" has the disadvantage of implying that previously existing pieces are put into order, which is not what happens in reproduction. Nevertheless, the biological connotations of the term "organize" seem to me to outweigh these disadvantages.

[31] The nominal form *sustasis* and its cognates are used in connection with the tragic plot at *Po.* 1450a15, 1450a32, 1450b22, 1452a19, 1453a3, 1453a23, 1453a31 (twice), 1453b2, 1454a14, 1454a34, 1459b17, 1459b21, and 1460a3. *Sustēma* occurs at 1456a12 The verbal or participial forms occur at 1447a9, 1450a37, 1450b32, 1450b35, 1451a29, 1451a32, 1451b12, 1452b29, 1453b4, 1455a22, 1459a18, 1459b14, 1460a28, 1460a34, and 1462b10.

[32] Gallop, "Animals," calls attention to this On *morion* as a biological term, see Peck, *Generation of Animals*, xlvii

[33] As Bonitz points out (s.v. ἔργον), there is a certain process-product ambiguity in Aristotle's use of the term *ergon*. In the *Poetics*, the *ergon* of tragedy is a process, an action (1450a22–23, with 1450a18), as is the *ergon* of a human being in *EN* 1097b26 and 1098a7.

57

that which comes "from pity and fear by means of imitation" (1453b11–13) This is also clear from 1459a20–21 "so that like one whole animal it might produce its proper pleasure," and from 1462b12–15, where Aristotle states that the *ergon* of the craft of epic and tragic imitation is to produce a certain kind of pleasure, and that tragedy accomplishes this *telos* better than epic This pleasure, moreover, is closely connected with katharsis, which is mentioned in the definition of tragedy "Tragedy is imitation . . . by means of pity and fear accomplishing katharsis" (1449b24–28). In the definition of tragedy, then, katharsis is the *telos* of tragedy, and this *telos* is said elsewhere to be the pleasure that comes from pity and fear by means of imitation [34]

In biological structures, the soul is the functioning of the body and its parts, and the body is organized in a particular way for the sake of this functioning (*PA* 641a18–21 and 645b14–20) Similarly, in tragedies, the plot structure, which is analogous to the soul of living things (1450a38), is the functioning of its parts to accomplish its *ergon* the production of pleasure and katharsis from pity and fear [35] Plot structure and emotional arousal are thus as intimately connected as the soul and the functioning of the parts of an animal In an animal, "the soul *is* the working of the muscles, the perceiving through sense organs, the nourishing and growing It is not merely a resultant of such working "[36] Similarly, the plot structure *is* the working of the parts of the plot to produce the proper pleasure of tragedy that which comes from pity and fear by means of imitation To understand the plot, the "organization of the events,' is to understand how tragedy "by means of pity and fear accomplishes katharsis" and the "proper pleasure" of tragedy

This essential connection between plot and emotion helps explain why Aristotle stresses the importance of the plot, and why he continually appeals to the principle that tragedy should arouse pity and fear when he discusses the plot and its parts At 1452a1–4 he says that events that occur "contrary to expectation, because of one another" are desirable because "the imitation is not only of a complete action, but also of pitiable and fearful events." Each of the three parts of the plot also arouses pity and fear Aristotle writes that the best *peripeteia* and recognition "will have pity or fear," and he states that "tragedy is assumed to be an imitation of these

[34] On pleasure, katharsis, pity, and fear, see further below, chap 8 (The Definition of Tragedy) and chap 10
[35] Note, however, that the biological analogy is less than exact in one respect, for it is not clear what, in the case of tragedy, would correspond to the body of a living thing
[36] Balme, *De partibus animalium*, 90

kinds of actions" (1452a36–b1). Recognition is also said to arouse *ekplēxis*, another term for tragic emotion, at 1455a16–17.[37] Because recognition and *peripeteia* arouse pity and fear, the complex plot is better than the simple one. Again, the third part of the plot, the *pathos*, is "a destructive or painful action" (1452b11–12), and it is also pitiable and fearful, as Aristotle indicates at 1453b11–22. In chapters 13 and 14, Aristotle discusses principles of plot construction that are essential to the *ergon* of tragedy: the accomplishment of pleasure and katharsis by means of pity and fear. He opens his discussion by making explicit the connection between plot structure and *ergon*. Chapter 13 begins, "What one should aim at and what one should guard against in organizing plots, and whence will be the *ergon* of tragedy, should be stated next in order after the things just now discussed" (1452b28–30). A tragic plot should be "imitative of fearful and pitiable things, for this is proper to this kind of imitation" (1452b32–33). He then lists good and bad ways of constructing plots. In chapter 14, he writes: "Since the poet should produce the pleasure that comes from pity and fear by means of imitation, it is clear that this should be put into the events [of the plot]" (1453b11–14). Here also, Aristotle classifies plots according to how well they accomplish the *ergon* of tragedy: "Let us determine what kinds of happenings appear terrible or pitiable" (1453b14–15).

Other important aspects of Aristotle's biological analogy emerge when we compare tragedies and other kinds of artifacts. In some ways, tragedy is more like a living thing with a nature of its own than like a typical artifact. Aristotle even writes that tragedy as a genre has acquired "its own nature" (*phusin: Po.* 1449a14–15). Things that exist "by nature," such as animals and their parts, plants, and primary bodies, have within themselves "a principle of motion and rest" (*Phy.* 192b8–15; 193b3–5). Because the plot of tragedy is analogous to the soul, or internal principle of motion, of a living thing, tragedy is unlike artifacts such as beds and garments that have nothing analogous to this internal principle of motion (*Phy.* 192b16–19).[38] In that tragedy does not reproduce itself, however, it is more like an artifact than like a living thing (see *Phy.* 193b8–12). In this respect, the *ergon* of tragedy is more like that of artifacts than of living things, for, as the *Generation of Animals* tells us, the primary *ergon* of plants

[37] On *ekplēxis*, see chap. 6.
[38] For a good discussion of Aristotle's concept of "nature" and of his views on what things have natures, see Waterlow, *Nature*, chaps. 1 and 2. The problem of whether tragedies have natures is similar in some ways to the problem she discusses (50ff.) of whether self-moving automata would have natures. Kullmann, "Mensch," 434–41, gives good arguments against viewing the city and tragedy as true substances with their own natures.

and animals is reproduction (717a21–22, 731a24–26, 735a15–19). The *ergon* of tragedy, unlike that of living things, has an external reference: tragedy arouses emotion in human beings. Moreover, tragedy has a kind of "nature" that is causally dependent on, and functions in relation to, another nature: that of human beings. *Poetics* 4 makes this clear: "It seems that there are two causes of poetry as a whole, and that these are natural [*phusikai*] causes. For to imitate is inherent in the nature [*sumphuton*] of human beings" (*Po.* 1448b4–6). There is, in this respect, a close parallel between tragedy and the city, which is also said to exist "by nature" (*Pol.* 1.1252b30, 1253a2), and to depend on human nature: "The human being is by nature [*phusei*] a political animal" (*Pol.* 1253a2–3). We may conclude, then, that tragedies are more like living things than other artifacts in having something analogous to an internal principle of motion, a soul. Tragedies, however, resemble other artifacts and differ from living things in that they lack the *ergon* of generating other tragedies. It is instead the function of tragedy to produce emotional reactions of a certain kind in human beings.

The soul of tragedy, its plot structure, is to be understood in terms of its *ergon*: the arousal of (the katharsis and pleasure that come from) pity and fear in human beings. To understand the plot and its parts it is necessary to understand how they contribute to this *ergon*. Further, to understand this is to grasp the intelligible beauty inherent in the structure of tragedy. Aristotle's biological analogy also helps us understand this principle.

It is function (final cause) that gives beauty to a living thing: "In all [living things] there is something natural and beautiful. For that which is not by chance, but for the sake of something, is above all in the products [*ergois*] of nature. The end for the sake of which they have been organized or come to be has a place among the beautiful" (*PA* 645a22–26). The beauty in question here is intelligible beauty, as opposed to the perceptible beauty of colors and shapes. Shortly before this passage, Aristotle contrasts color and shape with the intelligible function that determines what a living thing is: "If, now," he writes, "each living thing and its parts is [what it is] because of its shape and its color, Democritus would speak correctly" (*PA* 640b29–31). Aristotle, however, rejects Democritus's view that a human being is known by color and shape, arguing that "a dead person has the same form of shape [as a living person], but nevertheless is not a human being" (*PA* 640b33–35), since neither corpse nor stone hand can perform "its own *ergon*" (641a1–2). The idea that function defines being is also stated in *Politics* 1 1253a23 "All things are defined by their function and power"

The products of nature are beautiful because of their function, and not because of their colors and shapes, the same is true of the products of human craft In *Poetics* 1450b34–37, Aristotle writes that in the case of "a living thing and of everything that is organized out of parts," "beauty consists in size and arrangement"[39] To enjoy the beauty of a craft product is to understand it as an organized structure, instead of merely seeing it as color and shape More specifically, to enjoy a tragedy properly, we must understand its structure and not merely take pleasure in sights ("spectacle") or sounds (words and music)

It is tempting to see an allusion to this distinction between intelligible beauty dependent on structure, and perceptible beauty dependent on color and shape, in *Poetics* 4 1448b17–19 "For if someone has not happened to see something previously, the imitation will not give pleasure as an imitation, but because of the workmanship [ἀπεργασιαν], or the color, or for some other reason" Aristotle might mean by "workmanship" the kind of craft process that, like a natural process, proceeds for the sake of an end and gives something an intelligible structure The noun (ἀπ)εργασια (working-up) and cognates are used in Aristotle's other works to refer to natural, and especially biological, processes [40] To enjoy the workmanship of an imitation might be to enjoy it as an understandable structure as opposed to enjoying its perceptible colors and shapes This may well be reading too much into one word, Aristotle might simply be using "workmanship" to refer to sensible qualities other than color But whether or not Aristotle's term *workmanship* refers to this way of viewing a craft product, his biological analogies in the *Poetics* leave no doubt that the response to imitations as intelligible structures is important

The preceding analysis is meant to suggest how viewing imitations as intelligible structures differs from viewing them as representations Aristotle's theory that "craft imitates nature" commits him to the view that imitations are similar to other things Imitations are produced by a craft process that is similar to the natural process by means of which living things come to be This similarity is one between the two processes, in

---

[39] Size is defined in terms of the principle of probability or necessity at 1451a11–15 The arrangement (τάξις) of parts allows a tragedy to accomplish its function as one whole, according to probability or necessity (see 1451a30–35) On arrangement and the connection between *Po* 1450b34–37 and *PA* 645a23, see Dupont-Roc and Lallot, *Poétique*, 212–13 Cf *Pol* 1326a29–34 for the principle that beauty consists in size and order

[40] For example, *GA* 728a26–29, 765b15–16, 765b28–34, *Phy* 2 199a15–17

each of which the prior stages stand in a definite relationship to the later stages.[41] The products of craft are also similar to those of nature in that both are organizations (*sustaseis*) in which everything is for the sake of an end. Moreover, the tragic plot is structurally similar to the action it imitates.[42] It is not, however, in virtue of similarity that tragic imitations *represent* either the universal of which they "speak," of which they are instances, or the particular actions they imitate. To view them as intelligible processes and organized structures is to view them as objects with certain intrinsic properties and not as representations.

The foregoing discussion also implies that when we view an imitation "as an imitation" (ἧ μίμημα: 1448b18), we have three different but complementary responses. First, we see it as a particular, sensible object with pleasing "colors and shapes" (or in the case of tragedy, painful sights and sounds) of its own. For example, we see the man on the stage addressed as "Oedipus" as an individual who speaks certain words, and who has blinded, bleeding eyes. We must see the imitation in this way before we are able to view it in a second way: as an organized structure with beginning, middle, and end proceeding according to probability or necessity. When we grasp this, we will see the actions of the stage Oedipus as those of someone with "great good reputation and good fortune" (*Po.* 1453a10) who arrives at bad fortune by a probable or necessary sequence of events. We will, that is, see the actions of Oedipus as those of someone who is "such as to suffer," who is a member of the class of those who are "such as to suffer."[43] These two responses correspond in some respects to what Richard Wollheim calls the "twofoldness" of "seeing-in"—of seeing, for example, a boy in a stained wall. We see a wall with colored marks on it, and we also see a boy (an organized structure) in the marks on the wall. These are, Wollheim argues, "two aspects of a single experience" that should not be confused with representation, to which they are prior "logically and historically."[44]

In Aristotle's theory, as in Wollheim's, to see something as a particular, sensible object and to see it as an organized structure, an instance of a

[41] That similarity is involved is clear from *Phy.* 199a18–20 ("is similar": ὁμοίως . . . ἔχει), quoted above, and from *Meteor.* 381b6–7: "For craft imitates nature, since indeed the concoction of the nourishment in the body is like [ὁμοία] boiling."
[42] See, for example, *Po.* 1452a12–14: "Of plots, some are simple and others complex. For the actions of which the plots are imitations are in themselves of such kinds."
[43] This phrase, τοιοῦτοί εἰσιν οἷοι παθεῖν, is that of *Rhet.* 2.5.1383a9, a passage discussed in chap. 7 ("Tragedy and Rhetoric").
[44] Wollheim, *Painting*, 46–47. I owe this reference to Marcia Eaton.

universal, is not the same thing as seeing it in a third way, as an imitation that represents. To see the actions of Oedipus in Sophocles' play as an instance of a universal, we do not need to reason "that this is [an imitation of] that" thing, which we have "seen before" (*Po.* 1448b17). To see the actions of Oedipus-in-the-play as those of someone who is such as to suffer is to see these actions as an instance of a universal without necessarily understanding that the play represents anything. Similarly, to see Callias as a human being (Aristotle's example in *Post. An.* 2.19.100a15–b1) is to see him as an instance of a universal without seeing him as a representation of anything. *On Memory* 450a21–27 (discussed above, in "Representation") provides a good example of this kind of nonrepresentational way of viewing a painting as an intelligible structure (Wollheim's "seeing-in"). To view the animal drawn on a panel as a thing in itself and not as an image is to view it neither as an abstract shape nor as a portrait of, for example, Fido, but "as an animal"—that is, as an animal-shape that does not represent anything.[45] Just as Wollheim notes that "seeing-in" is prior to representation, so in Aristotle's view we must see a painting or a play as an organized structure in itself (a "this") before we can see it as a representational imitation, recognizing "that this is that." Poetic imitation differs from history in being an organized structure that "speaks of" the universal of which it is an instance. What this structure represents, however, is not the universal, but something we have seen before.

Similarity

Aristotle held that imitations are similar to that which they imitate in that they have the same kind of intelligible structure. More generally, the process of imitation is similar to a natural process, since "craft imitates nature."[46] However, the wide range of objects that are said in the *Poetics* to be imitated makes it very difficult to be more specific about the ways in which imitations are similar to objects imitated. Among these objects are characters, emotions, actions (1447a28); speech (1459a12); people who are better than, worse than, or like us (1448a4–5); and "things as they were or are, or as people say and think they are, or as they should be"

---

[45] I discussed this point in more detail in Belfiore, "Pleasure," 351–52. On the idea of a nonabstract image that does not represent, see, in addition to Wollheim, *Painting*, 46–47, Gombrich, "Meditations," and Goodman, *Languages*, 21–26.

[46] See above, esp. notes 41 and 42. That Aristotle was committed to the concept of similarity is noted by Sorabji, *Aristotle on Memory*, 2–7, and Butcher, *Aristotle's Theory*, 124–25, who cites Teichmuller, *Aristotelische Forschungen* 2.145–54.

(1460b10–11). In one particularly difficult passage, Aristotle writes that the imitator who puts horns on a doe errs less than the one who paints "unimitatively" (ἀμιμήτως: 1460b32)[47] Another problem concerns the apparent contradiction between *Poetics* 3, where the use of narrative is said to be an integral part of one manner of imitation, and 24.1460a5–9, where Aristotle writes that the poet who uses narrative "is not an imitator in this respect."

In spite of these difficulties, it is possible to make one further generalization about the ways in which imitations are similar to objects imitated, according to Aristotle. *Poetics* 4, taken in conjunction with a passage in the *Politics*, indicates that the sensible qualities of imitation and object imitated produce similarly painful or pleasurable sensations

In *Poetics* 4, Aristotle distinguishes between the pain that we have in *seeing* (ὁρῶμεν. 1448b10, προεωρακώς 1448b17) objects themselves and the pleasure we get in *contemplating* (θεωροῦντες 1448b11, θεωροῦντας. 1448b16) images of them. The pleasure of contemplation comes from grasping a relationship between image and object imitated It depends on the representational aspect of the imitation "It happens that while they contemplate they learn and reason what each thing is. for example, that this is that" (1448b16–17, cf. *Rhet.* 1.1371b4–10)

In the *Politics*, Aristotle writes that the pain and pleasure we get from seeing the objects imitated is the same as that which we get from seeing their imitations. "The habit of feeling pain and pleasure at things that are similar is near to feeling the same way toward the reality For example, if someone takes pleasure viewing[48] the image of something for no other reason than because of its shape, this person's view of the thing of which it is an image will necessarily be pleasant also" (*Pol.* 1340a23–28). This passage has been thought to contradict *Poetics* 4.[49] It is important to note, however, that the *Politics* passage is not a statement of a general rule that we derive the same pain or pleasure from imitations and from objects imitated. What it says is that we react in the same way to an object imitated and to an imitation only if we view the imitation as something with in-

[47] A textual variant is κακομιμήτως Rosenmeyer, "Design," 234–36, defends the reading ἀμιμήτως, interpreted as "something that is not   imitative of empirical reality (234)

[48] θεώμενος I translate θεωρία and its cognates as "view(ing)" throughout this passage, because here Aristotle clearly uses the term to refer to perception rather than to contemplation note αἰσθητῶν, "perceptible objects," at 1340a28

[49] See, for example, Golden, "Purgation, 475–76 I argued against this view in Belfiore, "Pleasure," 353–54 See also Wagner, ' Katharsis, 72–73

trinsic properties of its own and not as an image: "If someone takes pleasure viewing the image of something *for no other reason* than because of its
shape," which is "similar" to the shape of the object imitated, they will
give the same pleasure. The *Politics* passage refers to the kind of pleasure
people get when they view an imitation only as something with intrinsic,
nonrepresentational properties. *Poetics* 4, however, distinguishes this pleasure from that of enjoying something "as an imitation," that is, as a representation. While the example given in the *Politics* is one of feeling pleasure, the passage also states that the same account can be given of feeling
pain (1340a23). Presumably, then, if we take pleasure in viewing something with a beautiful shape as a thing in its own right, we will feel pain
in viewing something with an ugly shape as a thing in its own right. We
will get the same pain from seeing imitations of the shapes (*Po.* 1448b12)
of corpses and of despised animals that we get from seeing these objects
themselves.

There are, then, three kinds of similarity relationships between imitations and objects imitated. First, there is a similarity between mimetic
process and natural process. Second, there is a structural similarity between imitation and object imitated. Finally, there is a similarity that is
"aesthetic" in the etymological sense (*aisthēsis*: perception).

An examination of Aristotle's views on three characteristics of imitations—representation, production, and similarity—shows that, in spite of
the difficulties inherent in an imitative theory of art, his account is remarkably useful and informative. By distinguishing viewing something as
a (representational) imitation from viewing it as a thing in itself, with
intrinsic properties of its own, Aristotle can explain aesthetic responses
without recourse to a theory of special "aesthetic emotions" that differ
from painful "real-life" emotions in being pleasurable.[50] It is possible, in
his view, to explain how we derive both pain and pleasure from the same
image. As a thing in its own right, an imitation of a corpse will have an
ugly shape and color that give pain to those who perceive it with their
senses. It will also give pleasure, viewed as an organized structure, an
instance of a universal. Moreover, viewed as a (representational) imitation
of something else, the image will give the intellectual pleasure that comes
from learning and from contemplating relationships. Not only are these
three responses compatible, but the painful response to ugly colors and
shapes (or, in the case of tragedy, sounds and sights) is a prerequisite for

[50] On "aesthetic emotions," see chap. 7.

65

the two pleasurable ones. We cannot contemplate something as a (representational) imitation until we have first seen it as a thing in its own right, with perceptible shapes and colors and with an intelligible organized structure. Because these three responses differ in this way, there is no need to posit a particular kind of "aesthetic emotion" to explain the pleasurable reactions we have to imitations of things that give us pain in real life. Imitations of these things also give us real pain when viewed in one way. However, they give us pleasure when viewed in another way. All these responses are necessary to our appreciation of something as an imitation. The painful responses are not overwhelmed by the pleasurable responses, but contribute to them in a way that will be discussed in chapter 10.

Aristotle's concept of imitation is remarkable in another way also. Although he does not adequately account for what we today call the representational aspect of images, passages in his works allow us to draw significant inferences about his views on the functions of imitations and of nonimitations. This brings us to the last characteristic of imitations: they are used in *theōria*.

Theōria

Aristotle's imitative theory of art cannot, in itself, give an adequate account of the representational aspects of art, which depend on context and function. Nevertheless, Aristotle's views on dreams and on contemplation (*theōria*) indicate that he understood the significance of context and function in determining responses to different kinds of objects. These views have important implications for his concept of imitation.

We do not take practical action in response to objects in certain circumstances because we realize that these are not situations that require this kind of action. This is true of the dreamer who knows that the dream is not real, or the sick person who does not run from the monster, knowing that it is a product of delirium. This insight about dreams also helps us understand the importance of context in aesthetic and rhetorical situations. In the case of the story of the horse and the stag (discussed above, in "Representation"), we do not respond by trying to give aid to the horse, because we realize that this is just a story. This is true whether the story functions as a rhetorical example or as an imitation.

Aristotle's views on contemplation also imply that, in his view, context and function help determine our different responses to a story used as an example and to the same story used solely as an imitation. The story used by the rhetorician as an example has a primarily practical function, for it is used to induce us to act in a certain way. On the other hand, the story used by the poet as an imitation has a purely theoretical function. *Poetics* 4 contrasts *theōria* of images as imitations with seeing images as objects having certain shapes and colors. We see ugly shapes and colors, but by means of *theōria* we learn and reason about a representational relationship between the imitation and the object imitated. *Theōria* is nonpractical. *Theōria* alone, Aristotle writes in *Nicomachean Ethics* 10.1177b1–4, "is loved [ἀγαπᾶσθαι] for itself. For nothing results from it except contemplating, but from practical things we acquire something, to a greater or lesser degree, in addition to the action." The story used as an imitation by the poet is an object of contemplation of this sort, of use only for its own sake.

In making an object of contemplation, the poet differs from both the historian and the rhetorician. The historian "speaks of the particular" (*Po.* 1451b6–11)—for example, of what Alcibiades or Oedipus did or experienced. Unlike the historian, both the poet and the rhetorician who uses a story as a rhetorical example "speak of the universal," for both make a story that is a particular instance of a universal, and both lead us to see it as an instance of a universal. They lead us, for example, to see the horse and the stag as certain kinds of beings who say and do certain kinds of things. The rhetorician has an immediate, practical goal, leading us to apply the story to a particular situation, that of Phalaris the dictator, in which practical action is required. The poet, unlike the rhetorician, does not have a practical, immediate goal, but leads us to contemplate for its own sake the universal as a representational imitation of things we have seen before, without any particular, practical goal. The poet leads us to enjoy an imitation as an imitation, for its own sake, and to discover for ourselves, by recollection, that the organized structure of the imitation reflects that of things we have previously perceived with our senses. He has no further practical goal.

Imitation has the unique function of leading us to contemplate, for their own sake, objects that also arouse us emotionally. In its theoretical function, imitation resembles philosophy, which, like poetry and rhetoric, deals with classes (*Rhet.* 1.2.11).[51] Philosophy, however, does not arouse emotion, for it does not present us with particular instances of universals, which alone arouse emotion.[52] Because imitation presents us with in-

[51] Rhetoric and dialectic both deal with a class, τὸ τοιοῖσδε (*Rhet.* 1356b28–34). On this passage, see Cope, *Introduction*, 155–56. Poetry also deals with a class, τῷ ποίῳ (*Po.* 1451b8).

[52] See, for example, *Rhet.* 2.2.1378a34–35: "It is necessary for the angry person always

stances of universals, it shares with rhetoric the ability to arouse emotion. Imitation leads us to contemplate the relationship between representations that are, in themselves, capable of arousing emotion, and objects we have perceived previously that arouse the same emotions. In this way, imitation teaches us about the objects of perception that arouse emotion, and leads us to understand them intellectually and emotionally.[53]

A further look at the parallel between *Poetics* 4 and *Parts of Animals* 1.5.645a5–17 (quoted above, in "Production") can clarify the kind of theoretical pleasure we get from enjoying imitations as imitations, for their own sake. In *Poetics* 4, Aristotle writes that the kind of pleasure we get from recognizing the relationship between imitation and object imitated comes from learning and reasoning that "this is that." The imitation teaches us about the object imitated, which we have seen before. If we are philosophical, we will, as Aristotle urges us to do in *Parts of Animals* 1.5, come to view even ugly natural objects with pleasure, because the human workmanship that organizes the structure of the imitation will help us understand better the natural "workmanship" that structures the object imitated. Through its theoretical function, imitation leads us to contemplate natural objects as intelligible organized structures (*sustaseis*) like craft products, instead of seeing them merely as beautiful and pleasant or painful and ugly colors and shapes.

In *Parts of Animals* 1.5, Aristotle uses the strongly positive word ἀγαπῶμεν, "we love," to characterize the philosophical response to contemplation of organized living structures. The verb ἀγαπᾶν is a synonym of τιμᾶν (to honor, value, esteem) and of χαρίζεσθαι (to take pleasure in).[54] The love of the philosopher is thus diametrically opposed to the disgust and displeasure of the childish people who despise some natural objects: to these childish people, some animals are "more despised" or

---

to be angry at some particular individual [τῶν καθ' ἕκαστόν τινι], at Cleon, for example, and not at a human being." Baldry, "Interpretation," 42, makes the point that the poet, unlike the philosopher, "expresses the universal . . . through the individual and the particular." On the differences among philosophy, history, and rhetoric, Deborah Roberts called my attention to Philip Sidney's *Apology for Poetry* (1595)

[53] Goodman, *Languages*, 248, writes that "in aesthetic experience the *emotions function cognitively*. The work of art is apprehended through the feelings as well as through the senses" (emphasis in original). On the cognitive role of the emotions in aesthetics and ethics, see also Taplin, *Tragedy*, 169–71, Nussbaum, *Fragility*, esp. 45–47, 307–9, and 378–94, and "Fictions," and Sherman, *Fabric*, 44–50, 165–74 I discuss the cognitive role of the emotions at greater length in the second half of this book

[54] See Bonitz, s.v. ἀγαπᾶν, who cites *Cat.* 14b6, *EN* 1179a27 (τιμᾶν), and *EN* 1168b33 (χαρίζεσθαι). Cf. *EN* 1177b1–4, where ἀγαπᾶσθαι is associated with contemplation.

"dishonored" (ἀτιμοτέρων), and such as to displease the senses (τοῖς μὴ κεχαρισμένοις . πρὸς τὴν αἴσθησιν). The contemplation of the philosopher transforms these negative reactions into the opposite, positive reaction of love. This transformation of disgust and displeasure can be mediated by imitation. If seeing a relationship between imitation and the object imitated teaches us and gives us pleasure, not only with respect to the imitation but also with respect to the object imitated, imitation transforms disgust and displeasure into love. It does so not by changing the object imitated (cleaning it up, adding or subtracting), but by leading us to view it in a new way. It does not eliminate the pain ugly objects give to our senses, for this pain inevitably accompanies the perceptions that are necessary before we can understand. Instead, seeing a relationship between imitation and object imitated provides a new, higher, more philosophical viewpoint of *theōria*, one that transcends the perceptions of the senses. In this way, imitation appeals to and strengthens the highest and best aspects of our human nature. This is part of Aristotle's answer to Plato. Through its formal structure, its *sustasis*, tragedy affords us a deeper understanding of what gives pain to our senses, leading us away from the narrow, sensual point of view from which we can perceive only physical pain and pleasure, toward the philosophical pleasure of contemplation.[55]

For Aristotle, the goal of all contemplation is not to gain knowledge of abstract Forms, but to know ourselves. In *Parts of Animals* 1 5, he connects the study of living things with this self-knowledge. "If someone has gotten the opinion that contemplation concerning other living things is to be despised, he should think the same thing about [contemplation concerning] himself also. For it is not possible to look without much disgust at the things out of which humankind is organized, such as blood, flesh, bones, veins, and these kinds of parts" (*PA* 645a26–30). Alan Code points out that, in Aristotle's view, all human contemplation, even "first philosophy" (metaphysics), is really the study of ourselves. "We are by nature systematic understanders," and first philosophy "is the systematic understanding of what it is to be a systematic understander, and hence is a form of self-knowledge. The ultimate goal of First Philosophy is to systematically understand our nature as systematic understanders."[56] Code's word "systematic" is well chosen. We understand systematically, and thus know

---

[55] On this topic see Gallop, "Animals," 166–67 Deborah Roberts called my attention to Wordsworth, who compares the poet "who looks at the world in the spirit of love" to the scientist "However painful may be the objects with which the Anatomist's knowledge is connected, he feels that his knowledge is pleasure" "*Preface*" 1 140

[56] Code, "Aporematic Approach," 1–2

ourselves, through contemplation of the natural "systems" (or "structures". *sustēmata, sustaseis*) in nature that are imitated in craft products.

If all knowledge is a form of self-knowledge, we can learn about ourselves from all kinds of imitations. painting and sculpture are the examples
given in *Parts of Animals* 1.5.645a5–17 Tragedy, however, is particularly
well suited to teach us about ourselves, for it deals very directly with our
nature as human beings, as animals whose nature it is to function within
philia relationships. This aspect of tragedy is the subject of the next section.

PHILIA

"When the *pathē* [destructive or painful events] take place within *philia*
relationships, for example when brother kills or is about to kill brother,
or son father, or mother son, or son mother, or does something else of this
sort, this is to be sought [by the poet]" (*Po.* 1453b19–22). *Philia* is of
primary importance in Aristotle's theory of tragedy. Because the individual parts of the plot and the plot structure as a whole involve *philia*, it
determines in large part the emotional responses of the audience. Aristotle's views on the importance of *philia* in tragedy reflect the practice of
dramatists, the beliefs of Greek society as a whole, and his own philosophical views, expressed in the ethical works and in the *Politics* Before we can
understand its significance, however, it is essential to understand what
philia is.

In the *Poetics*, *philia* retains its traditional sense to a much greater extent
than it does in Aristotle's ethical works. Although *philia* can mean "friendship" or "love," it is primarily, in Greek thought, an objective relationship of mutual obligations and claims The closest *philoi* are blood kin.
However, *philia* also includes other relationships, especially those of marriage and of host and guest (*xenia*).[57] *Philia* does not necessarily involve
"friendly" feelings. It is expressed, instead, in actual behavior that benefits
another. Arthur Adkins writes that the verb *philein* refers to "an *act* which
creates or maintains a co-operative relationship, and *it need not be accompa-*

[57] On the importance of *philia* in Greek thought, see Blundell, *Helping*, 26–59 (with
extensive bibliography) On kinship *philia*, see Dirlmeier, "*Philos*," 7–21, and on *xenia*,
see Herman, *Ritualised Friendship* Marriage is in many ways an especially close form of the
xenia relationship See, for example, *Eum* 660–61 "She [the mother], like a *xenē* for a *xenos*
guards the offspring ' (As Rose notes, *Commentary*, 273, the *xenos* in this passage is the
father, not the offspring)

nied by any friendly feeling at all. it is the action which is all-important."[58] As we will see, this fact has significant implications for tragedy, in which action is of primary importance.

Although *philia* does not necessarily imply affection or "friendly feelings," it does have an essential connection with the emotion of *aidōs*. Gustave Glotz notes, "Constantly, in Homer, *philos* is joined with *aidoios*. The compound expressions *philos te aidoios te, aidōs kai philotēs, aidesthai kai philein* [dear and respected, respect and love, to respect and to love] are used of the same people, and indicate the same relationships as the words *aidoios, aidōs, aidesthai*. Relatives and in-laws, servants and friends, all those who are united by the reciprocal duties of *aidōs* are called *philoi*."[59] Thus, a *philos* can be defined as a human being toward whom one feels *aidōs*, and who feels *aidōs* in return.[60] Those who "respect" one another by

[58] Adkins, "Friendship," 36, emphasis in original Cf Glotz, *Solidarité* "*Philotēs* [friendship] is an external phenomenon, a social state' (139), and Benveniste, *Vocabulaire*, who notes that *philotēs* can be "a solemn agreement in which the sentiment of 'friendship,' in the ordinary sense, has no part' (1 342) Benveniste's account of *philia*, however, depends so heavily on that of Glotz that the latter should be given credit for much of what is often attributed to Benveniste see below, n 60

[59] Glotz, *Solidarité*, 138 "Continuellement, dans Homere, φίλος est joint à αἰδοῖος Les expressions composées φίλος τε αἰδοῖος τε, αἰδὼς καὶ φιλότης, αἴδεσθαι καὶ φιλεῖν s emploient pour les mêmes personnes, désignent les mêmes relations que les mots αἰδοῖος, αἰδώς, αἴδεσθαι Parents et alliés, domestiques et amis, tous ceux qu'unissent des devoirs réciproques d'αἰδώς sont appelés φίλοι "

[60] Benveniste, *Vocabulaire* 1 341, notes that "*aidós* clarifies the proper meaning of *philos* ' This insight should probably be attributed to Glotz (*Solidarité*), however, for Benveniste's account is so far indebted to that of Glotz as to repeat, nearly word for word and without quotation marks, a number of Glotz's phrases For example, Glotz's statement quoted above (n 59) is repeated by Benveniste 'C est ainsi qu'il y a liaison constante, chez Homère, entre *phílos* et le concept de *aidós* Des expressions comme φίλος τε αἰδοῖός τε αἰδὼς καὶ φιλότης, αἰδεῖσθαι καὶ φιλεῖν montrent, de toute évidence, une connexion étroite" (340), "Tous deux [*aidōs* and *philos*] s'emploient pour les mêmes personnes, tous deux désignent en somme des relations de même type Parents, alliés, domestiques, amis, tous ceux qui sont unis entre eux par des devoirs réciproques d'*aidós* sont appelés *phíloi*" (341) Other examples of Benveniste's indebtedness are Glotz, 139–40 "accomplir les actes positifs qu'impose le pacte d'hospitalité," repeated by Benveniste, 344 "l'accomplissement des actes positifs qu'implique le pacte d'hospitalité mutuelle," Glotz, 141–42 "Sur le point d'engager avec Achille son duel suprême, Hector propose de convenir que le cadavre du vaincu ne sera pas livré aux bêtes,' and Benveniste, 343 "Quand Hector et Achille vont s'affronter pour un duel suprême, Hector propose de convenir que le corps du vaincu ne sera pas livré aux bêtes " Benveniste claims in his "avant-propos" that he does not give a bibliography because his own work is too original to require one "Nous ne voyons guère de travaux antérieurs auxquels nous aurions pu confronter nos propres raisonnements Tout ce que nous disons provient d'études de première main sur les faits

fulfilling specific social obligations of mutual aid and protection are *philoi*. people united in a social community with a common function. Failure to fulfill these obligations marks someone as shameless (*anaidēs*. without *aidōs*), and arouses extreme horror in others. Plato's Protagoras reflects the common Greek viewpoint in stating that *aidōs* and justice are the basis for the "bonds of *philia*" (*Prot*. 322c2–3) and for the "political excellence" (323a7) in which all who belong to a human society must share. The person who is without *aidōs* and justice, Zeus states in Protagoras's story, must be killed as a disease of the polis (322d2–5) As I will argue below, this connection between *philia* and *aidōs* is important for an understanding of the tragic emotions.

Aristotle's *Poetics* clearly uses the term *philia* in the popular and traditional sense, in which blood kinship is of central importance. Gerald Else argues convincingly that *philia* in the *Poetics* is not "love" or "friendship" but *"the objective state* of being *philoi*, 'dear ones' by virtue of blood ties."[61] He points out (415) that the *philoi* listed in *Poetics* 1453b20–21 (quoted above) are all blood kin (brothers, parents, children), and that, in the plots Aristotle discusses, harm of *philos* by *philos* is a central theme Examples of good stories in *Poetics* 13 are those "about Alcmeon, and Oedipus, and Orestes, and Meleagros, and Thyestes, and Telephus, and others who happened to suffer or do terrible things" (*Po*. 13.1453a20–22).[62] In all these plots, Else points out, someone harms or is on the point of harming a blood relative. Aristotle's examples of plots in chapter 14 support Else's view. Aristotle mentions Orestes' murder of his mother, Clytemnestra, Alcmeon's murder of his mother, Eryphile, Medea's murder of her children, the story of Oedipus's parricide and incest, and Haemon's threat to his father in Sophocles' *Antigone*. He also mentions Euripides' *Iphigeneia in Tauris*, in which sister is about to sacrifice brother, as well as Merope, who is about to kill her son, and another mother who is about to betray her son in a play (unknown to us) called *Helle* The importance of kinship in the *Poetics* is also shown by Aristotle's use of other kinship terms in addition to *philia*. tragedy concerns "families" (γενῶν. 1453a11, γένη. 1454a10) and "houses" (οἰκίας 1453a19, 1454a12)

---

utilisés" (1 12) Yet his unacknowledged indebtedness to other scholars in the two volumes of *Vocabulaire* is noted by at least two reviewers A M Davies, *CR* 22 (1972) 378, and O Szemerényi, *JHS* 92 (1972) 217

[61] Else, *Argument*, 349, emphasis in original He also discusses *philia* at 349–52, 391–98, and 414–15

[62] Else discusses the plots of these plays ibid , 391–98 See also Gudeman, *Aristoteles*, 257–58, for a list of tragedies, including the fragments, in which *philos* harms *philos*

Else's interpretation of *philia* as "blood kinship," however, excludes one important category of *philoi*: spouses. Yet the marriage relationship creates important ties of *philia* among those who are not necessarily related by blood, and spouse murder is an important theme in a number of plays. Surely Clytemnestra's murder of Agamemnon should be counted as an instance of *philos* harming *philos*.[63] It makes sense, then, to include spouses among the *philoi* Aristotle has in mind when he writes that *philos* harms or is about to harm *philos* in the best plot, even though he does not explicitly mention this kind of *philia*.

Philia in the sense of blood or marriage relationship is of central importance in the Greek tragedies themselves and in Aristotle's account of them in the *Poetics*.[64] Harm of *philos* by *philos* is a central *pathos* (destructive or painful event: 1452b11–12) in many of the extant tragedies [65] The *Poetics* takes this into account in making *philia* an essential element in the plot structure. The plot, or imitation of action, arouses pity and fear largely because the actions imitated concern *philoi*. Aristotle makes this clear in chapter 14:

> Now of necessity these kinds of actions must be those of *philoi* toward one another, or of enemies, or of neutrals If enemy acts or is about to act against enemy, it is not at all pitiable, except with respect to the *pathos* itself Nor [is it pitiable] if [those involved] are neutrals But when the *pathē* take place within *philia* relationships, for example when brother kills or is about to kill brother, or son father, or mother son, or son mother, or does something else of this sort, this is to be sought [by the poet]. (1453b15–22)

In this passage, Aristotle sharply distinguishes *pathē* that are merely destructive or painful, such as the murder of enemy by enemy, from destructive or painful *pathē* that take place between *philoi*. While both kinds of *pathē* arouse pity and fear, only those between *philoi* do so in a properly tragic way. This is a very strong claim, as the context shows. Just before *Poetics* 14.1453b15–22, Aristotle states that the poet must seek to produce the "proper pleasure" of tragedy, that which comes "from pity and fear by means of imitation" (1453b10–13), and that this must be put into the

[63] Gudeman, *Aristoteles*, 258, lists, within one category (no 7) of plays in which *philos* harms *philos*, a number of plays in which wife kills husband, although he notes (257) that Aristotle does not explicitly mention this category

[64] On the importance of *philia* in the *Poetics* and the tragedies, see Else, *Argument* (see n 61), Vickers, *Tragedy*, 230–43, Goldhill, *Reading*, chap 4, and Blundell, *Helping*

[65] Gudeman, *Aristoteles*, 257–58, lists fifteen extant tragedies in which *philos* harms *philos*

73

plot, the "organization of the events" (1453b2, 1453b13). He then considers what kinds of happenings appear terrible or pitiable (1453b14–15), and he concludes, at 1453b15–22, that these are *pathē* that occur within a *philia* relationship. Thus, harm (actual or imminent) of *philos* by *philos* is essential to the production of the proper pleasure of tragedy. The examples given in the rest of *Poetics* 14 of actual plots in which *philos* harms or is about to harm *philos* show that Aristotle's views reflect the practice of dramatists. For Aristotle, the Greek tragedies are about *philia* relationships, and our emotional response to them depends on this fact.

This idea governs Aristotle's views on the plot as a whole and on the individual parts of the plot. All the essential elements of the plot structure involve *philia*. The principle of necessity or probability, which governs the plot structure as a whole, from beginning to middle to end, is to be understood in large part in terms of the *philia* relationships necessary to human nature. Again, good and bad fortune, the end points between which the tragic action moves (1451a13–14), also depend on *philia* relationships. There can be no good fortune without *philoi*, and bad fortune includes the loss or misfortune of *philoi*. This is a traditional Greek belief, and it is a view Aristotle frequently expresses in his other works. In Aristotle's view, as in that of his fellow Greeks, Oedipus is pitiable less because he suffers blindness and exile than because he has irrevocably lost all the *philia* relationships that make him part of the human community.

The three parts of the plot—*pathos*, recognition, and *peripeteia*—are all defined in terms of, or depend for their emotional effects on, *philia*. The *pathos* that best arouses pity and fear is, as we have seen in 1453b15–22, harm, actual or imminent, of *philos* by *philos*. Recognition is defined in terms of *philia*: "Recognition, just as the word also indicates, is a change from ignorance to knowledge, either to *philia* or to enmity, of those defined with respect to good or bad fortune" (1452a29–32). In *Poetics* 14, the second-best kind of plot is said to be one in which someone does a terrible deed and then recognizes *philia* (1453b31), and the best plot is said to be one in which recognition (of *philia*) prevents a terrible act from taking place (1454a4–9). While *philia* does not enter into the definition of the third part of the plot, *peripeteia*, Aristotle is careful to tell us that the best recognition occurs at the same time as *peripeteia* (1452a32–33). *Philia* is also important in *peripeteia* because *peripeteia* is a change of the action from good to bad or from bad to good fortune (1452a22–23), and *philia* is important to good fortune. These three parts of the plot, in all of which *philia* is of central importance, help determine whether the plot as a whole is good or bad. The presence of *peripeteia*, recognition, or both distinguishes the better type of plot, the complex one, from the inferior simple plot (*Po.* 10). Recognition also helps distinguish good complex plots from bad ones, for the best complex plots, according to *Poetics* 14, are those in which recognition occurs in time to prevent the *pathos*, the next best are those in which recognition takes place after the *pathos*.

Because *philia* enters into the plot structure in these ways, it is essential to the function of the plot, the production of pleasure and katharsis from pity and fear The audience experiences tragic pity and fear in response to certain actions *because* these actions threaten *philia*. *Philia* thus helps determine the nature of the tragic emotions, of the "proper pleasure" of tragedy, and of katharsis. Because tragic pity and fear are aroused specifically by threats to *philia*, these emotions differ in some important ways from the fear and pity aroused by other kinds of evils.

The importance of *philia* within Aristotle's theory of tragedy can be better appreciated in the context of his philosophical views on *philia*.[66] One important source for these views is the *Politics*, where Aristotle is much concerned, as he is in the *Poetics*, with kinship *philia* Another source is Aristotle's ethical works, even though here, as in the *Rhetoric*, his interest is not primarily in kinship *philia*. In *Rhetoric* 2.4.1381b33–34, Aristotle lists kinship as one of several kinds of *philia*. In *Nicomachean Ethics* 8 3, Aristotle discusses three kinds of *philia*: those based on utility, pleasure, and excellence Family relationships, those between parents and children, siblings, and spouses (*EN* 8.12), can involve all three kinds of *philia* (1162a7–14, 1162a24–26). One of Aristotle's chief concerns in the *Nicomachean Ethics* is with *philia* based on excellence, a relationship between two people who are not necessarily blood kin Since in the ethical works, however, *philia* in a broader sense is closely related to kinship *philia*, Aristotle's views on *philia* in these works as well as in the *Politics* can help us understand the role of *philia* in tragedy

That *philia* is central to Aristotle's philosophy is shown by his devoting more space to this topic than to any other single subject, in both the *Nicomachean Ethics* and the *Eudemian Ethics*.[67] *Philoi* are essential to good for-

---

[66] This important subject is now beginning to receive the attention it deserves Among relatively recent informative studies are those of Annas, ' Plato and Aristotle", Cooper, 'Forms," "Fortune," and "Friendship', Fortenbaugh, "Aristotle's Analysis", Fraisse, "*Autarkeia* et *Philia* , Irwin, *Principles*, chap 18, Kraut, *Aristotle*, esp chap 2, Nussbaum, *Fragility*, chap 12, Price, *Love*, Sherman, *Fabric*, chap 4, and Voelke, *Rapports*

[67] About one-fifth of each work is concerned with *philia* books 8 and 9 of the *Nicomachean Ethics* and book 7 of the *Eudemian Ethics* This point is made by Cooper, "Forms," 619

tune. According to *Nicomachean Ethics* 1169b9–10, *philoi* "are held to be the greatest of external goods," and Aristotle lists *philoi* among the "parts" of happiness in *Rhetoric* 1.5.1360b27. At *Eudemian Ethics* 1234b32–33, he writes that "we take the *philos* to be among the greatest of good things, and lack of *philoi* and isolation to be most terrible." Moreover, Aristotle begins his discussion of *philia* in *Nicomachean Ethics* 8 by stating that it is "most necessary to life. For no one would choose to live without *philoi*, though having all other good things" (1155a4–6) It is "necessary" because the human being is a *philial* animal, one that forms, in the first place, the primary *philia* relationship between male and female for the purpose of reproduction: "The human being is by nature more a coupling animal than a political one, inasmuch as the household is more necessary than and prior to the polis, and reproduction is more common to animals" (*EN* 1162a17–19). The permanent, reproductive *philia* relationship is the nucleus of the household. "The human being is not only a political but also a householding animal [and] the human being is an animal that lives in a community with those who are kin by nature. . . . For the household is a kind of *philia*" (*EE* 1242a22–28; cf. *EN* 1155a16–22). Aristotle believes that the polis is made up of and depends on the *philia* relationships of the household. "In the household first of all are the first principles and beginnings, and the springs of *philia*, and of government, and of justice" (*EE* 1242a40–b1).

Politics 1.2 discusses in more detail the way in which *philia* relationships make up the polis. The primary unit is the household, based in large part on the union of male and female. "It is necessary, first, for those to couple who cannot exist without each other, for example, female and male for the sake of generation" (*Pol.* 1252a26–28). Several households in turn make up a village, and several villages a polis. Aristotle argues that the polis exists "by nature" because it is the end (*telos*) of the "first communities," that is, households and villages, which exist "by nature" "And so every polis exists by nature, if indeed the first communities do also. For it is the end of these, and nature is the end" (1252b30–32). Aristotle concludes by characterizing the human being as a "political animal"

> From these things, then, it is clear that the polis is among those things that exist by nature, and that the human being is by nature a political animal, and that the person who is without a polis, by nature and not by chance, is either base or superior to a human being—like the person reviled by Homer "without kin, without established custom, without hearth"—for he is by

nature like this and at the same time a lover of war, like an isolated piece in the game of draughts *(Pol* 1253a1–7)[68]

"Political animal" in this passage is often taken to mean "animal that lives in a polis," the social organization that is the culmination of a historical development that begins with scattered households. Wolfgang Kullmann argues convincingly, however, that the fundamental sense of "political animal" is biological rather than historical.[69] Kullmann cites *History of Animals* 487b33ff. as evidence for a biological interpretation of "political animal". "Political animals are those for whom there is something one and common that is the function [*ergon*] of all of them" (488a7–8). Among these "political animals" are bees, wasps, ants, and cranes, as well as human beings.[70] In this passage, "political" clearly does not mean "living in a polis," but has a biological sense. Kullman argues that a biological interpretation is appropriate in all the occurrences of "political [animal]" in Aristotle, including that in *Politics* 1.2.[71] According to Aristotle, Kullmann writes, human beings have a biologically based desire to "live together" (συζῆν), one they share in part with herding animals, which are capable of merely living Humans, however, are especially "political," for their rational capacities give them the ability to "live well" (εὖ ζῆν) that is expressed in the specifically human forms of living together the household and the polis [72] Thus, humans and other animals are "political," in *Politics* 1 2 and elsewhere, because of biologically based impulses (and, in the case of humans, rational capacities) conducive to living together, and not merely because they happen to live in an actual, historical polis. While David Depew bases the political nature of humans more specifically than does Kullmann on their ability to use language and reason, he also believes that "political animal" has a primarily biological sense, arguing that hu-

[68] Vernant writes that the game Aristotle has in mind is one called "polis," in which the squares represented cities (' Ambiguity," 118 n 123) See also Vernant's perceptive comments (107) on the applicability of the *Politics* passage to the case of Oedipus

[69] Kullmann, 'Mensch " He is followed by Irwin, *Principles*, 401 and 616 n 17 The "biological ' interpretation is also supported by Depew, "Contradiction?" The historical' view is argued for by Keyt, "Three Fundamental Theorems ' Mulgan, "Doctrine" (followed by Roberts, "Political,' 191 n 11), holds that 'political animal" has different senses in different passages I am indebted to David Depew for good discussions of this topic

[70] Kullmann, ' Mensch," 431–32 He writes that the "common function" in which cranes engage is migration to the south

[71] Mulgan, 'Doctrine, lists the eight relevant passages (1) *HA* 487b33–488a13, (2) *EE* 1242a21–26, (3) *EN* 1162a16–19, (4) *EN* 1169b17–19, (5) *EN* 1097b8–12, (6) *Pol* 1278b17–21, (7) *Pol* 1253a1–2, (8) *Pol* 1253a7–9

[72] Kullmann, "Mensch," esp 427–34 See also Irwin, *Principles*, 399–402

mans, like other political animals, are "political" because each human being contributes, through "functional role division," to "something one
and common that is the function of all of them" (*HA* 488a7–8).[73] According to John Cooper, humans are political in a strong sense because the
polis exhibits the highest and most complex form of functional role division.[74]

Thus, it appears that human beings are "political animals" because they
are living things whose nature it is to function within a community,
through the *philia* relationships of family and polis.[75] They are "political"
in the same way in which they are *philia*l: because they engage in the
mutual duties that maintain the cooperative relationships of people who
contribute to a common function. Aristotle's further remarks in *Politics*
1.2 support this interpretation, because they connect the idea of being
human with that of having a function as part of a community:

> All things are defined by their function and power, so that if they are no
> longer such as to perform their function, they cannot be said to be the same
> things, except homonymously. Now it is clear that the polis is by nature,
> and is prior to each individual. For if each individual when separated is not
> self-sufficient, he will be like other parts in relation to the whole. And the
> person who is not able to participate in a community, or who needs nothing
> because of self-sufficiency, is no part of a polis, so that he is either a wild
> animal or a god. And so the impulse toward this sort of community is pres-
> ent in all {humans} by nature. (*Pol.* 1253a23–30)

What Aristotle means is that to function as a human being is, first and
most fundamentally, to participate in the *philia* relationships of the human
community. These are primarily kinship relations and, by an extension
that is "natural" in a strong sense, the "political" relationships of the
broader community. The person who loses these relationships no longer
functions as a human being.

This account of what it is to be a "political animal" helps us understand
Aristotle's views on the nature of *philia*. If human political animals contribute to a common function through role division, they do so by partic-

---

[73] Depew, "Contradiction?" 4; on language, see esp. 8. Roberts, "Political," 193–200,
also stresses the importance of "differentiated functions" that are "part of a larger common
function" (197) in Aristotle's political theory. See also Sherman, *Fabric*, 147, who calls
attention to Aristotle's views on the division of labor in the household.

[74] Cooper, "Political Animals," 225–27.

[75] See Irwin, *Principles*, chaps. 18–21, for a discussion of human nature and the human
function in connection with *philia* and the polis.

ıpating ın *phılıa* relatıonshıps. In the tradıtıonal Greek concept of *phılıa*, as we have seen, mutual oblıgatıon ıs of prımary ımportance. In Arıstotle's concept of *phılıa* also, the ıdea of sharıng a common functıon ıs central. Wıthın the household, husband and wıfe play dıfferent roles ın the common functıon of reproductıon, and each contrıbutes, ın dıfferent ways, to the acquısıtıon and preparatıon of food, clothıng, and other necessıtıes of lıfe. Other *phıloı*, such as hosts and guests, offer mutual aıd and protectıon, and so share the functıon of preservıng lıfe. Moreover, each cıtızen of a polıs contrıbutes to the materıal or socıal functıonıng of the polıs. Just as the common functıon of all saılors on a shıp ıs the preservatıon of the shıp, so the preservatıon of the state ıs the common functıon of all cıtızens (*Pol.* 3.1276b26–29) Indeed, each of Arıstotle's three kınds of *phılıa* ıs characterızed by a dıfferent common functıon. the productıon of utılıty, pleasure, or excellence Arıstotle's requırement (*EN* 1171b29–1172a15) that *phıloı* should "lıve together" ıs explaıned ın thıs way. Only by lıvıng together can *phıloı* engage ın the common functıon, whether ıt be drınkıng, playıng at dıce, exercısıng, huntıng, or phılosophızıng (1172a3–5), that they strıve for because of an ımpulse that ıs ın part bıologıcally based.[76]

Arıstotle's vıew that "lack of *phıloı* and ısolatıon [ıs] most terrıble" (*EE* 1234b32–33) has, then, a fırm phılosophıcal basıs ın hıs vıews on the nature of human beıngs These phılosophıcal vıews help explaın why tragedy, as ımıtatıon of pıtıable and fearful actıon, ıs essentıally concerned wıth *phılıa*. Loss of *phıloı* or harm to them ıs, because of our nature as "polıtıcal" and *phılıa*l anımals, the most terrıble and pıtıable thıng humans can suffer.

As an ımıtatıve craft that deals wıth *phılıa*, tragedy not only arouses pıty and fear; ıt ıs also partıcularly useful for educatıon As *Poetıcs* 4 tells us, humans dıffer from other anımals ın "learnıng theır fırst lessons through ımıtatıon" (1448b7–8). We learn more about these "fırst lessons" ın Arıstotle's other works. Educatıon as a whole ıs an ımıtatıve process, through whıch the chıld comes to resemble ıts *phıloı* Nancy Sherman argues that Arıstotle, ın *Polıtıcs* 2, prefers educatıon wıthın the famıly to Plato's communıstıc, publıc educatıon ın large part because the ındıvıdual, affectıve relatıonshıp between parent and chıld helps make the parent a good model for emulatıon [77] Moreover, as A. W. Prıce poınts out,

[76] See Cooper s dıscussıon of the "shared actıvıtıes ın whıch frıends engage ın "Frıendshıp,' 302–10
[77] Sherman, *Fabrıc*, 151–53

through education the child ceases to be a part of its parents (*EN* 1134b11) and becomes "another self" (*EN* 1161b27–29), a fully grown "copy of its parents," with a relation to them that is "partly biological, partly moral."[78]

The account in *Politics* 7.1336a28–b35 shows the importance of imitation in early education. Children's games should be imitations (*mimēseis*) of their later serious pursuits (1336a33–34). Children also learn by means of the imitative crafts. painting and sculpture, which are said to be "imitation of actions" (*praxeōn mimēsin*. 1336b16), the theater (1336b20–21), and stories (1336a30). Because children learn especially well from the examples of those with whom they associate, they should have little to do with slaves, and with those who speak or do disgraceful things (1336a39–b12). Although Aristotle does not use the term "imitation" in connection with learning by example, the concept is clearly relevant

Education through imitation continues throughout adulthood, as the *Nicomachean Ethics* indicates. The adult *philoi* who live together and engage in a common activity (*EN* 9.1171b29–1172a15) can be said to imitate one another in two ways. they act like one another in contributing to a common function, and they imitate one another by coming to resemble each other in character. By *philia* with base friends, people become vicious, "likening themselves to one another" (1172a9–10) The *philia* of decent people, on the other hand, is itself decent and increases with this association. Decent people "become better when they act on and correct one another For they take impressions [ἀπομάττονται] from one another of the characteristics that please them" (*EN* 1172a11–13). This taking of impressions, or molding, occurs even in friendships based on excellence. Sherman explains that each of the friends who express excellence "in ways that are distinct yet complementary" emulates the good qualities the other friend has to a greater degree.[79] Thus, *philia* among adult friends involves role division in a shared function. The friend becomes "another self" (*EN* 9.9.1170b6–7) in part because friends imitate each other's characters in this way. The *philoi* who imitate one another also gain self-knowledge. According to the *Magna moralia*, a *philos* is "another self" through whom we come to know ourselves.

> It is both most difficult, as some wise people have said, to know oneself, and most pleasant (for it is pleasant to know oneself), but we ourselves are not able to see ourselves by [looking at] ourselves   . Thus, just as when we

[78] Price, *Love*, 164–65
[79] Sherman, *Fabric*, 141–42

wish to see our own faces, we see them by looking into a mirror, similarly when we want to know ourselves, we could know ourselves by looking at a friend. For the friend is, as we say, another self. Now if it is pleasant to know oneself, and it is not possible to know this without another, a friend, the self-sufficient man would need *philia* in order to know himself. (*MM* 1213a13–26)[80]

In many respects, tragedy, the imitation of human action, can provide the same kind of education through imitation that *philoi* can. When viewing tragedy, we engage in an imitative process that is similar to the process in which a friend imitates and learns from a friend who is "another self." Like an older, more experienced, and practically wise friend, tragedy provides us with examples to imitate.[81] And like a friend, tragedy imitates us, and thus provides us with a mirror in which we can come to know ourselves. If the craft of imitation as a whole teaches us about things we have seen before (*Po.* 4), the craft of tragic imitation teaches us specifically about ourselves as human beings, for it is imitation of human action. Because it imitates actions within *philia* relationships, tragedy imitates what is most essential to human nature, and it teaches us to know our essential nature as humans. Moreover, as we learn what it is to be human, we function as human beings, taking pleasure in learning, which is the highest and most human of activities. Thus, if a *philos* teaches us to know ourselves as individuals with characters of certain kinds, tragedy teaches us to know ourselves as human beings. This knowledge is most difficult. and most pleasant.

This chapter has examined two important concepts: imitation and *philia*. While Aristotle does not give a detailed theoretical account of imitation, the *Poetics*, together with relevant passages in other works, indicates that, in his view, imitations have four distinct characteristics. First, an imitation represents the object it imitates. To view something as an imitation is to understand "that this is that": that there is an asymmetrical relation-

---

[80] The authenticity of the *Magna moralia* has been defended by Dirlmeier, *Magna moralia* (see esp. 146–47, 185), and Cooper, "*Magna moralia*." Whether or not the entire work is Aristotelian, the mirror passage is certainly in accord with Aristotelian ideas. Cf. *EN* 9.9.1170b6–7, quoted in the previous paragraph, and the parallel passages in Aristotle and other writers noted by Dirlmeier, *Magna moralia*, 467–71. On the *Magna moralia* passage and self-knowledge, see Voelke, *Rapports*, 35–37; Nussbaum, *Fragility*, 364–65, and Cooper, "Friendship," 295–302.

[81] On the role of tragedy as teacher, see chap. 6 ("*Aidōs*, Excellence, and Habituation") and chap. 10.

ship between the imitation and the object imitated Second, imitations are produced by the process of imitating Like a natural process, the process of imitating has an end for the sake of which everything is done, and it produces something that has an organized structure, a *sustasis* Third, imitations are similar to that which they imitate Their structure resembles that of the object imitated, and they give the same "aesthetic" (sensible) pleasure or pain Fourth, imitations used solely as imitations are objects of contemplation (*theōria*) for their own sake They do not, like rhetorical examples, have a further, practical use

Philia is also of great importance for an understanding of Aristotle's views on tragedy In Aristotle's theory, and in the practice of the tragedians, Greek tragedy is centrally concerned with *philia* in the sense of kinship by blood or marriage In the *Poetics*, *philia* is of fundamental importance in the plot structure as a whole, and in each of the three parts of the plot Aristotle's philosophical views on *philia* help us understand why this is so In his account, *philia* relationships are essential to being human because we are political animals whose nature it is to live in a community of *philoi Philoi* are most necessary to good fortune, and loss of *philoi* is most pitiable and terrible Thus, tragedy, because it imitates actions within *philia* relationships, teaches us about our nature as human beings An understanding of imitation and *philia* is fundamental to an analysis of Aristotle's views on plot structure and emotional arousal [82]

[82] I am indebted to Marcia Eaton for her criticisms of an earlier draft of Imitation, and to David Depew for his criticisms of the section on political animals

✳ CHAPTER 3 ✳

Plot and Character

ARISTOTLE has a number of reasons for making plot rather than character (*ēthos, ēthē*) central to his theory of tragedy [1] These have to do with his concept of the nature of tragedy as imitation of action, with his desire to counter Plato's attacks on poetry, and with his views on the development of tragedy. Accordingly, Aristotle makes a clear theoretical distinction between plot and *ēthos*, and he denies that *ēthos* is essential to tragedy. Although a number of serious theoretical difficulties arise when this distinction is made, it is important for an understanding of Aristotle's views on the tragic plot, and it is useful for an analysis of the plots of the Greek tragedies.

THE PLOT-CHARACTER DISTINCTION

Plot is of primary importance in tragedy because, in the first place, tragedy imitates actions (1449b24, 1449b36), as opposed to other objects, such as characters and emotions (1447a28). Of the six "qualitative parts" of tragedy—plot, character, speech, thought, spectacle, and song (1450a8–10)—it is plot, defined as "the composition of the events" (1450a4–5), that imitates action (1450a3–4). Aristotle is careful to distinguish between the plot, which is an *imitation of* action, and "the actions of which the plots are imitations" (1452a13) His terminology reflects this distinction, for he uses the terms "plot" (*muthos*) and "organization (composition) of the events" (*sustasis*. 1450a15, or *sunthesis tōn pragmatōn*. 1450a15) to refer to the imitation of action, and the term "action" (*praxis*) to refer to the action imitated. [2] Aristotle insists that tragedy is imitation of action,

---

[1] One problem in Aristotle's account is that of his often confusing use of the singular (*ēthos*) and plural (*ēthē*) Aristotle calls the qualitative part of tragedy either (*ta) ēthē* (e g , 1450a5, 1450a9, 1450a39), or (*to) ēthos* (e g , 1450a14) Because this distinction is not of great importance here, I use the English "character" to translate both singular and plural

[2] This distinction between *praxis* and *muthos* (*sustasis pragmatōn*) is noted by J Jones, *Aristotle*, 24 According to Dupont-Roc and Lallot, *Poétique*, 219, Aristotle distinguishes, in *Po* 8, between the many *praxeis* (which, they say, make up "brute reality") of one individual, and the one, unified *praxis*, which is a kind of first-order representation created

as opposed to imitation of *ēthos*: "They [sc., poets and actors] do not act in order to imitate the *ēthē*, but they include the *ēthē* along with the actions; so that the events and the plot are the end of tragedy, and the end is the most important of all" (1450a20–23); "tragedy is imitation not of human beings but of actions and [the events] of a life" (1450a16–17); "it is imitation of action, and because of this [sc., action] above all [it is imitation] of those acting" (1450b3–4). Plot is not only the most important, it is the only essential part of tragedy. Character is strictly secondary: "the organization . . . of the events . . . is the first and most important part of tragedy" (1450b22–23); "the first principle and as it were the soul of tragedy is the plot; second is the *ēthē*" (1450a38–39); "it is right to distinguish tragedies that are the same or different on the basis of nothing other than the plot" (1456a7–8); "without [imitation of] action there could be no tragedy; without *ēthē* there could. The tragedies of most of the new poets

by a poet who selects and orders the many *praxeis* This is a misunderstanding. When the poet chooses to imitate one unified *praxis* from among many *praxeis*, he does not thereby imitate and represent, but instead grasps one intelligible structure in order to imitate it In so doing, he resembles the philosopher who understands the causes of the objects he perceives. (See *PA* 1.5.645a5–17.) Aristotle's use of *pragmata* and of the nominal forms of *praxis* is remarkably consistent (I leave the verbal forms out of consideration because they do not allow for the kind of distinction in question) The plural *pragmata* occurs seventeen times in the *Poetics*, and it always refers to the events that make up the "organization of the events" (the plot), which is an imitation of action On eight occasions (1450a15, 1450a33, 1450a37, 1450b22, 1451a33, 1453b3, 1453b14, and 1454a34) it occurs within the phrase *sustasis (sunthesis) tōn pragmatōn*, or a close variant, and at 1450a4–5 the *muthos* is defined as the *sunthesin tōn pragmatōn* On the other eight occasions (1450a22, 1451b22, 1453b5, 1453b13, 1454b7, 1455a17, 1456a20, and 1456b2) *ta pragmata* are the events that make up the *sustasis tōn pragmatōn*—the plot (Note the phrase *ta pragmata kai ho muthos*. "the events, that is, the plot" at 1450a22.) The singular *pragma* occurs twice, at 1450b35 and at 1451a10 It means simply "thing," and does not refer to the plot or to an event in the plot. *Praxis*, on the other hand, refers to an action of which the plot is an imitation, or to actions in life generally. The noun *praxis* occurs a total of thirty-five times On fourteen occasions, *praxis* occurs in conjunction with *mimēsis* or *mimeisthai* 1447a28, 1448b25, 1449b24, 1449b36, 1450a4, 1450a17, 1450b3, 1450b24, 1451a31, 1451b29, 1452a2, 1452a13, 1452b1, and 1462b11 Three times it occurs in a variant of the phrase *sunistanai* (or *poiein*) *peri praxin* 1451a28, 1459a19, and 1459b1 On fourteen occasions, Aristotle uses *praxis* to refer to an action in life generally. 1450a1, 1450a2, 1450a18 (twice), 1450a20, 1450a22, 1451a18, 1451a19, 1451b33, 1452a14, 1452a37, 1453b16, 1459a22, and 1462b8. In three difficult passages (1452b11, 1453b27, and 1454a18) *praxis* is used of an event in the plot. At 1452b11, for example, the *pathos*, a part of the plot, is defined as "a destructive or painful *praxis*." In these passages, I believe, Aristotle uses *praxis* as the singular of *pragmata* in order to avoid the vague singular of *pragmata* (events of the plot). *pragma*, which means "thing." In another difficult case, 1450a24, I take *praxeōs* to be short for "imitation of *praxeōs*."

are without *ēthos*, and in general there are many such poets" (1450a23–26).

Because tragedy is imitation of action and not of character, it is the plot structure rather than *ēthos* that accomplishes the function of tragedy. "Ethical speeches," writes Aristotle, will not accomplish "that which is the function of tragedy" as well as the plot and "the organization of events" will (1450a29–33). This idea is expressed graphically in Aristotle's comparison of plot to a white outline drawing and of *ēthos* to coloring that fills in the drawing. "It is much like the case of painting. For if someone should smear on the most beautiful colors at random, this would not give pleasure in the same way as an image drawn in white" (1450a39–b3). *Ēthos* is a kind of coloring that fills in the plot, which is a kind of outline.[3]

Aristotle has several reasons for insisting that plot is more important than character For one thing, this gives him two ways of countering Plato's attack on tragedy. If it is plot rather than *ēthos* that is essential, tragedy can be shown to be the product of a craft, and not, as Plato insists in book 10 of the *Republic*, the creation of ignorant imitators of images. Plot, unlike *ēthos*, has a natural order—beginning, middle, and end—that gives tragedy a definite structure of its own, with well-defined laws that can be studied and taught.

Aristotle also wants to insist that plot is more important than *ēthos* because this allows him to counter Plato's contention that tragedy is ethically base. Unlike Plato, Aristotle believes that tragedy has the function of arousing fear and pity rather than praise or blame As a general rule, praise and blame depend on a judgment about *ēthos*, for we praise and blame someone for a choice (*prohairesis*) that leads to action.[4] Because *ēthos* in tragedy is an indication of what kind of choice a person makes (1450b8–10), someone in a tragedy with an exceptionally excellent or vicious *ēthos* is also praiseworthy or blameworthy. Praise and blame, however, interfere with the tragic responses of pity and fear, as is clear from 1453a4–10 Pity is felt for someone who is *not* blameworthy, the person "suffering undeserved bad fortune," whose bad fortune is not the result of "baseness and

---

[3] On *ēthos* in painting, see Keuls, *Plato*, 95–107

[4] The excellence of an action is not intrinsic to it, but depends on the ethical qualities of the agent, and especially on the excellence of the agent's choice (*EN* 1105a28–33) Aristotle discusses praise and blame in *Rhet* 1 9 See esp 1367b21–23 "Since praise is for actions, and it is proper to the *spoudaios* [to act] according to choice, one should try to show that someone acts according to choice " On choice in connection with *ēthos*, see also *EN* 1111b4–6, *Rhet* 1417a15–21, and *Po* 1461a4–9, discussed below In *EN* 1114a23–29, pity rather than blame is said to be felt for what is not in our power

depravity." Fear is felt for someone "like us," and not so "outstanding in ethical excellence and justice" as to evoke praise rather than fear. Thus, if someone in a tragedy is characterized by the ethical extremes of excellence or vice, this tends to interfere with the tragic responses of pity and fear, and must be excluded from the best tragedy.[5]

By stressing plot and excluding from tragedy the ethical extremes that are praised or blamed, Aristotle is able to counter Plato's charge that the poets are "imitators of images of excellence" (*Rep.* 10.600e5)—that is, of what is not truly excellent but only appears excellent to the ignorant.[6] These false images of excellence are imitations of *ēthos*. Plato explicitly states that the poet imitates *ēthos* at 604e1–3. "The complaining [*ēthos*] gives rise to much and varied imitation, but the wise and quiet *ēthos* . . . is not easy to imitate." In other ways also, Plato's account of imitation in the *Republic* consistently stresses *ēthos*. In his characterization of imitation at *Republic* 10.603c4–7, Plato's emphasis is on human beings and ethical responses, not on actions: "We say that the imitative craft imitates human beings doing compulsory or voluntary actions, and as a result of acting thinking that they have fared well or ill, and in all these cases experiencing pain or pleasure." The account of imitation in book 3 of the *Republic* also stresses character. The reference ("we say") in the passage just quoted is to 3.399a5–c4, where Plato allows into his ideal state music that imitates the speech of a courageous man doing the compulsory actions of war (399a6) or of a man doing in a temperate way (399b8) the voluntary actions of peace (399b3–4). In Plato's view, not only is an imitation of a base *ēthos* ethically base in itself, it also appeals to a base part of the soul and produces base effects (10.603b4). In particular, this kind of imitation makes us praise (605e6, 606b3) what we would be ashamed to do.[7]

Aristotle believes that tragedy does not have these pernicious ethical effects in large part because it does not imitate *ēthos*. Aristotle's definition of tragedy in *Poetics* 6 ("tragedy is imitation of action") is a significant rephrasing of Plato's characterization in *Republic* 10.603c ("the imitative craft imitates human beings doing compulsory or voluntary actions"). Ar-

[5] Similar points are made by Halliwell, *Aristotle's Poetics*, 179, Heath, *Poetics*, 81–82, and Stinton, "*Hamartia*," 229 For an example in lyric poetry of the incompatibility of pity and praise, see Simonides 531 3 the dead at Thermopylae receive praise instead of pity (ὁ δ' οἶκτος ἔπαινος)

[6] On Plato's views in the *Republic*, see Belfiore, "Accusation "

[7] Plato states that tragedy and epic evoke praise, sympathy, and pity (*Rep* 605d4, 605e6, 606b3) Aristotle, however, separates the arousal of pity by tragedy and epic from the evocation of praise by another poetic genre the encomium

ıstotle explicitly opposes Plato's view at 1450a16–17. "Tragedy is imitation not of human beings but of actions " Because tragedy does not lead
us to praise what is base, it cannot deceive us about excellence While
tragedy does, in Aristotle's view, have ethical effects, these effects differ
from the ones Plato condemns, and they depend on the audience's reactions to the plot structure.[8] The audience cannot, in Aristotle's view, react
to the plot in the right way if it is primarily concerned with praiseworthy
or blameworthy character.

Aristotle also wants to distinguish plot from *ēthos* for teleological reasons. In his account of the "evolution" of tragedy and comedy in *Poetics* 4,
he distinguishes genres that evoke praise and blame (hymns and encomia)
from those that arouse fear and pity (epic and tragedy), or laughter (comedy).[9] Early in the development of poetry, some poets "imitated fine actions and those of such people," creating hymns and encomia, while others
imitated the actions of inferior people (*phauloi*), making *psogoi*. invective,
or blame poetry (1448b24–27). Gradually, true comedy developed, as
"the laughable" replaced invective (1448b37). An important stage was
reached when Crates abandoned the iambic form and composed stories and
plots universally (1449b7–9)—that is, according to the principle of probability or necessity.[10] In this development of comedy, plot takes the place
of the "ethical" invective or iambic element While Aristotle does not tell
us explicitly what, in tragedy, corresponds to the development of comedy
from "blame" to the "laughable," it is reasonable to suppose that tragedy
also developed away from ethical concerns toward imitation of action—
from praise poetry to plot-centered poetry Some of Aristotle's remarks in
Poetics 6 confirm this view The "first poets," he writes, were better at
making *ēthos* than at creating plots (1450a35–38) On the other hand, the
tragedies of many of the "new poets" are "characterless" (*aētheis*. 1450a25)
There is reason to believe that tragedy of the fourth century B.C.E. did in
fact became increasingly concerned with intrigue, complicated plots, and
adventures, a characteristic shared by some of the late plays of Euripides [11]
The kind of tragedy Aristotle praises is between these two extremes im-

---

[8] On the ethical effects of tragedy, see chaps 6 and 10

[9] The question of whether this evolution is purely teleological or in part temporal need
not concern us here A good account of the role of praise and blame in Aristotle s account
is that of Nagy, *Best*, 253–64 See also Schutrumpf, *Bedeutung*, 74–80, and Else, *Argument*,
135–49 For a discussion of the development of comedy from blame poetry, see Janko,
Comedy, 242–50

[10] On Crates' innovation, see the perceptive remarks of Heath, "Comedy," 348–52

[11] See Xanthakis-Karamanos, *Studies*, chap 1, 3–34

itation of action is primary, but *ēthos* is an important secondary part of tragedy that is carefully kept from dominating and interfering with the plot.

For the reasons just discussed, Aristotle's repeated assertions that plot is essential to tragedy while *ēthos* is secondary should be taken literally. The plot structure, like the soul of a living thing, is what is essential to tragedy: that by means of which it accomplishes its function of producing pleasure and katharsis from pity and fear. *Ēthos*, while important, is not essential to tragedy in this way.[12]

The *Poetics* adopts a very different perspective from that of Aristotle's ethical works. In the *Poetics*, good and bad fortune are connected with plot and not with *ēthos*. The plot is a change from good to bad fortune, or vice versa (1451a13–14). *Ēthos*, on the other hand, is defined as "that which indicates choice [*prohairesis*]" (1450b8–9), and is distinct from plot. This means that plot and the good and bad fortune between which it moves do not in themselves have anything to do with choice, which is peculiar to *ēthos*. It is easy to be confused about this, for plot is imitation of action. In the ethical works, of course, people act, in the full sense, only when they choose; "the origin of action is choice" (*EN* 1139a31), and actions themselves are qualified in large part according to the ethical choice the agent makes (*EN* 1105a28–33). The *Poetics*, while admitting that this is true of actions in real-life situations, correctly sees that plot, *imitation of* action, is different. A poet who creates a dramatic *imitation of* action may not give us all the information relevant to ethical judgments about real-life actions.[13]

This distinction between real-life actions and dramatic imitations of action helps clarify Aristotle's meaning in *Poetics* 6:

[12] I argued for a strict interpretation of Aristotle's statements that *ēthos* is not essential to tragedy in Belfiore, "*Praxis*," a view I still hold, though I now believe this distinction is problematic for reasons discussed below ("Problems") The strict interpretation is also supported by Catherine Lord, "Character"; Janko, *Comedy*, 229–31, who cites *Po* 1450a12: οὐκ ὀλίγοι αὐτῶν, and Heath, *Poetics*, 118–19. Halliwell, *Aristotle's Poetics*, 149–64, has some good remarks on the plot-character distinction, though I disagree with much of what he says about action.

[13] On this difference between the ethical works and the *Poetics*, see Dupont-Roc and Lallot, *Poétique*, 196. The *Poetics*, they say, "reverses the perspective of the *Ethics*. It is no longer the agent but the *action* that is in the foreground here." However, they incorrectly conclude that, in the *Poetics*, agents are ethically qualified because actions are. "and *because* this action must be qualified in ethical terms, the agents must also be so qualified" (emphasis in original).

Since it [sc , tragedy] is imitation of action, and [this action] is acted by certain people acting, who must necessarily be qualified according to *ēthos* and thought (for because of these we say that actions also are qualified—there are by nature two causes of actions thought and *ēthos*—and according to these [sc , actions] all people succeed or fail) The plot, then, is the imitation of action I mean by plot here the composition of the events, and by *ēthē* that according to which we say that those acting are qualified. (1449b36–1450a6)[14]

Here, Aristotle states the general rule that, in real-life situations, action is caused by *ēthos* and thought, which qualify agents [15] He goes on, however, to make it clear that the plot, an imitation of action, is a part of tragedy distinct from *ēthos*, according to which the agents of the *dramatic action* are qualified. When *ēthos* is not added by the poet, there is no way to tell what the causes of the *dramatic* action are. In that case, the events of the plot are, to use Aristotle's own metaphor (1450a39–b3), ethically colorless. An act of killing, for example, is neither a heroic defense of one's country nor vicious treachery, if *ēthos* is not added by the poet.[16]

The passage just quoted also clarifies Aristotle's statements in *Poetics* 2.

Since the imitators imitate people acting, and it is necessary that these be either noble [*spoudaioi*] or inferior [*phauloi*] (for *ēthē* almost always correspond to these [categories] alone, for all *ēthē* differ in baseness [*kakia*] or excellence [*aretē*]), [they imitate people acting who are] either better than we are, or worse than we are, or such as we are   Tragedy is distinguished from comedy by means of this difference, the one tries to imitate people worse, the other better than those of today. (1448a1–5, 1448a16–18)

While this passage might appear to assert that tragedy imitates *people* with certain *ēthē*, the *Poetics* 6 passage just quoted (1449b36–1450a6) shows that this is not really Aristotle's view. In *Poetics* 2, Aristotle is speaking loosely, in a way that he is careful to avoid once he makes the technical distinction between plot and *ēthos* in chapter 6. He then makes it clear that what he really means is that the *action imitated* is done by agents, and that

[14] At 1450a1–2, I do not follow Kassel in bracketing πεφυκεν   ἦθος

[15] I cannot discuss *dianoia*, "thought," here A good account of *ēthos* and thought is that of Else, *Plato*, chap 8, 116–24, who argues cogently that thought is "nonmoral" while *ēthos* is "moral " On *ēthos* and *dianoia*, see also Fortenbaugh, "Modo," and Blundell, *Helping*, 16–25

[16] See Belfiore, "*Praxis*," for arguments against the view that the word *praxis* in the *Poetics* has the technical sense of deliberate action by a rational agent that the term often has in Aristotle's ethical works

these agents are necessarily ethically qualified. This is not true of the actions done by the agents of the *dramatic* action, the events of the plot: these events are not necessarily qualified by *ēthos* as a part of tragedy.

A similar distinction between tragedy and real life is relevant to an understanding of a difficult passage in *Poetics* 6: "Tragedy is imitation not of human beings but of actions and [the events] of a life. Both happiness and unhappiness [*eudaimonia kai kakodaimonia*] lie in action, and the end is some action, not a quality. People are qualified in a certain way according to their *ēthē*, but according to their actions they are happy or the opposite" (1450a16–20). In this passage, Aristotle makes a conceptual distinction between action and happiness on the one hand and *ēthos* and quality on the other. In real life, of course, *ēthos* is a cause of action and of happiness. Tragedy, however, imitates action, and represents a movement between good fortune and bad fortune, without necessarily representing the person moving between good and bad fortune as having certain ethical qualities. In 1450a17–20 ("Both . . . opposite"), bracketed by Kassel,[17] Aristotle makes general statements about life.[18] This is why he uses the strongly ethical term *eudaimonia* (happiness) instead of the more colorless *eutuchia* (good fortune), which is used to refer to one end point of the tragic change at 1451a13–14 and 1455b27–28.[19]

It is also important to read a passage in *Poetics* 25 with the distinction between tragedy and real life in mind:

> In deciding whether something was well or not well said or done by a person, one must not only consider the point by looking at whether the thing itself that was said or done was noble or inferior [*spoudaion ē phaulon*], but one must also look at the agent or speaker, to whom, or when, or with what he acted or spoke, or for the sake of what, for example, to bring about a greater good, or to prevent a greater evil. (1461a4–9)

While this passage makes the general statement that the qualities of actions are not inherent in them, but depend on the qualities of the agents,

---

[17] The passage is defended by Janko, *Poetics I*, 86, and Horn, "Begrundung."

[18] Else, *Argument*, 255, notes that almost all interpreters agree on this point.

[19] Halliwell, *Aristotle's Poetics*, 202–8, has some good remarks on the relationship between *eudaimonia* and *eutuchia* in Aristotle's thought, and I now agree with him (203 n. 2) that my earlier view (Belfiore, "Praxis," 115–16), that *eudaimonia* is equivalent to *eutuchia* in 1450a16–20, was incorrect. I do not, however, agree with Halliwell's view (203–4) that Aristotle's use of *eudaimonia* in this passage implies that tragic action has ethical dimensions.

it does not state that we can always determine what these qualities are. In tragedy, it is not always possible, even in theory, to tell what the qualities of the agents of the dramatic action are.

Because Aristotle makes a strict distinction between plot and *ēthos*, and insists that plot is essential to tragedy while *ēthos* is not, his views on the nature of tragedy differ radically from those of many modern readers and scholars, for whom character is the center of interest. Martha Nussbaum, for example, writes, "The great tragic plots explore the gap between our goodness and our good living, between what we are (our character, intentions, aspirations, values) and how humanly well we manage to live."[20] Not only is this character-centered view of tragedy opposed to Aristotle's plot-centered theory, but it can also lead to misunderstandings about the Greek tragedies themselves. For one thing, a bias in favor of character has often led scholars to attempt to find a "psychological realism" in Greek drama that the dramatic conventions of this genre did not allow and that the extant tragedies do not display. The inappropriateness of the view that agents in drama are psychological entities much like their real-life counterparts is now widely recognized, as scholars from Tycho von Wilamowitz to Thomas Rosenmeyer have argued against the idea of "a constant dramatic personality existing independently of the sequence of scenes in which the playwright develops the action."[21] Such questions as what thoughts Aeschylus's Agamemnon has as he walks on the carpet or what sort of father he is are out of place, unless specific passages in the play invite us to ask them.[22] There are, as John Jones remarks, no further realities lying behind the masks.[23]

A second and less well recognized consequence of the modern character-centered view of tragedy is the tendency of many scholars to see Aristotelian character as an integral part of plot or action. Lionel Pearson, for example, states that "it is by representing people's actions that one shows

[20] Nussbaum, *Fragility*, 382. For other expressions of this view, see Belfiore, "Iphigenia."

[21] Rosenmeyer, *Art*, 211, summarizing the view of T. von Wilamowitz-Moellendorff, which is expressed in *Die dramatische Technik des Sophokles*.

[22] Dodds, "Misunderstanding," 21, puts it neatly. "*What is not mentioned in the play does not exist*" (emphasis in original).

[23] J. Jones, *Aristotle*, 45 My account of modern opinions is an oversimplification of varied and complex views. Good summaries of the controversy about character in Greek drama are given by Easterling, "Presentation of Character" and "Character," 83–89; and by Goldhill, *Reading*, 168–72.

what kind of people they are "[24] According to John Jones, Aristotle has a concept of "characterful action" in which "the human self is present in its acts."[25] Stephen Halliwell's statement that "we must be able to identify it [sc., Aristotelian character] as a specific dimension of the action" is quoted with approval by Simon Goldhill.[26] To incorporate *ethos* into action in this way is to misunderstand a fundamental premise of the *Poetics*. Tragedy is imitation of action, as distinct from *ethos*, and for this reason it has the function of producing pleasure and katharsis from pity and fear.

While the nature of and motivation for Aristotle's distinction between plot and character are clear enough, there are, nevertheless, some serious philosophical difficulties connected with this distinction. Before we can understand how these difficulties arise we must first study in more detail Aristotle's concept of *ethos* in the *Poetics*

ĒTHOS

Aristotle's views on *ethos*, and on related matters such as the noble (*spoudaios*) person and the decent (*epieikēs*) person, are extraordinarily difficult to grasp. Not only does he fail to explain his views clearly and in detail, but he is also inconsistent in a number of ways. Unfortunately, the scholarly controversies surrounding these issues have often only added to the confusion. A greater degree of clarity can be obtained, however, if we pay close attention to two important principles The first principle has just been discussed: drama is not ethics, and this difference must be kept constantly in mind as we study "ethical" concepts in the *Poetics*. Second, as we will now see, Aristotle uses *ethos* in two different senses in the *Poetics*.

The first section of this chapter was concerned with *ethos* primarily as one of the six qualitative parts of tragedy, second in importance to plot. *Ethos* and *ēthē* in this sense are technical terms, defined in chapter 6 along with the other six qualitative parts of tragedy "I mean   this by   . the *ēthē*. that according to which we say that those acting are qualified" (1450a5–6)[27] After this definition, *ethos* is frequently used in the technical

[24] Pearson, "Characterization," 79–80

[25] J Jones, *Aristotle*, 33

[26] Halliwell, *Aristotle's Poetics*, 152, quoted by Goldhill, ' Character,' 119 For another example, see Dupont-Roc and Lallot, *Poetique*, 196, translated above, n 13

[27] The phrase "I mean   this by (λέγω γὰρ   τοῦτον 1450a5) introduces the definitions of "character" and "thought (1450a5–7), as well as the definition of "plot As Else notes (*Argument*, 244), the statements about character and thought at 1450a5–7

sense to refer to a part of tragedy or epic.[28] However, Aristotle also uses *ēthos* in a nontechnical sense, to refer to character generally. *Ēthos* has this nontechnical sense in the *Poetics* before it is defined as a technical term.[29] The term is also occasionally used in a nontechnical sense after the definition in chapter 6. For example, when Aristotle writes that poets and actors "do not act so as to imitate the *ēthē*" (1450a20–21), he cannot mean that they do not imitate *ēthos* as a part of tragedy; he must instead be using the term in a nontechnical sense. Again, at 1460a10–11, when Aristotle writes of an "*ēthos* that is not without *ēthos*," he is obviously using *ēthos* in two different senses, at least one of which must be different from the technical sense defined in chapter 6.[30] On the other hand, in many passages after the definition of *ēthos* it is very difficult to decide whether Aristotle is using the term in the technical sense. At 1450a21–22, for example, Aristotle writes, "they include the *ēthē* on account of the actions [that they imitate]": τὰ ἤθη συμπεριλανβάνουσιν διὰ τὰς πράξεις. Here, it is impossible to be certain whether the *ēthē* that are included in the tragedy are *ēthē* in the technical sense of one of the parts of the tragedy, or in the nontechnical sense of noble or inferior characters of people whose actions are imitated.[31]

In spite of these difficulties, however, the *Poetics'* concept of *ēthos* in the technical sense is in many respects clear and useful. Moreover, close attention to the question of whether *ēthos* is used in a technical sense in a given passage helps us understand Aristotle's views on plot as well as *ēthos*.

---

are "definitions of specific and technical meanings which the two words are to have *as 'parts' of tragedy*—a status which is not necessarily the same as they have in life at large" (emphasis in original).

[28] *Ēthos* has this technical sense, for example, at 1450a9, 1450a14, 1450a36, 1450a39, 1450b8, 1450b10, 1454a16, 1454a17, 1454a33, and 1460b5.

[29] That is, at 1447a28, 1448a2, 1448a3, 1448b24, 1449b38, and 1450a2.

[30] There is no need to delete the first occurrence of *ēthos* here, as many have suggested (e.g., according to Schutrumpf [*Bedeutung*, 94], Castelvetro, Reiz, Susemihl, and Gomperz, Janko, *Poetics I*, on 1460a11, also advocates deletion). On this passage, see further below, "*Ēthos* as Part of Tragedy."

[31] An informative discussion of the meaning of the term συμπεριλανβάνειν is given by Pearson, "Characterization," 81–83. Pearson argues that the verb means "acquires," "picks up," "gathers in," or "involves," and that 1450a21 should be interpreted to mean that "the actions of a dramatic personage imply or involve character-development" (82). This interpretation, however, tends to confuse character with action in a way inconsistent with Aristotle's explicit statements. Aristotle means instead that *ēthē* are included in the tragedy, when they are included, because agents happen to have *ēthē* (1449a36–1450a3). On the idea of imitation of the actions of people with noble or inferior characters, see below, "The *Spoudaioi*."

Ēthos *as Part of Tragedy*

Ēthos (*ēthē*) in the technical sense is the second most important of the six qualitative parts of tragedy. I argue in this subsection that *ēthos* in this sense refers specifically to something within a particular passage in a tragedy (or within all such passages collectively) that indicates what kind of choice is made by an agent of a dramatic action. A passage that "has *ēthos*" may, for example, be one of the "ethical speeches" mentioned at 1450a29. These would include "the lament of Odysseus" and the "speech of Melanippe," which, at 1454a30–31, are said to be examples of *ēthos* [32]

In a number of passages Aristotle tells us that *ēthos* in the technical sense indicates what kind of choice someone makes. In his discussion of the six qualitative parts of tragedy, Aristotle states that the *ēthē* are what qualify the agents of a dramatic action. "I mean this by . . the *ēthē*: that according to which we say that those acting are qualified [*poious*]" (6.1450a5–6). Aristotle's word *poious* (qualified, of a certain sort) belongs to the vocabulary of ethics, and often means "character." [33] Aristotle is more specific when he rephrases the definition of *ēthos* in the technical sense later in chapter 6: "*Ēthos* is that which indicates choice [*prohairesis*], of whatever sort, for which reason those speeches do not have *ēthos* in which there is nothing at all that the speaker chooses or avoids" (1450b8–10) [34] Aristotle again states that *ēthos* indicates choice at 15.1454a17–19 "It will have *ēthos* if, as was said, the speech or action makes clear what sort of choice is made." In the ethical works, a *prohairesis* is, in Irwin's words, a "decision, which is a desire to do something here and now, the action that deliberation has shown to be the action required to achieve the end," and correct *prohairesis* "is necessary for virtue of character, and expresses a person's virtue." [35] *Prohairesis* has a similar sense in ordinary Greek. A *prohairesis* is a choice that indicates someone's motives, purposes, principles, or policies. [36]

A number of passages in the *Poetics* make the most sense if *ēthos* is interpreted narrowly as an indication of choice Aristotle classifies the *Odyssey*

---

[32] Keuls, *Plato*, 97–98, has some good remarks on *ēthē* (in one sense) as 'passages in the dialogue which reveal individual character" (97) I would qualify this statement slightly, however, for *ēthos* is not a passage, but an indication of choice within a passage

[33] See Irwin, *Ethics*, 390 " 'character often translates *poios*

[34] I omit the phrase bracketed by Kassel ἐν οἷς   φεύγει (1450b9–10)

[35] Irwin, *Ethics*, 392–93

[36] See LSJ, s v προαίρεσις

as "ethical" (1459b15), because this epic deals with Odysseus the *polutropos* (*Od.* 1.1), the "versatile man," who constantly chooses how to act in different situations. Aristotle's examples in *Poetics* 15 also support the view that *ēthos* in the technical sense is an indication of what kind of choice someone makes. Two of these examples are taken from extant tragedies. First, Menelaos in Euripides' *Orestes* is given as an example of "unnecessary evil of *ēthos*" (1454a28–29). In Euripides' play, Menelaos, in his speech at 682–715, makes it clear that he chooses not to help Orestes because of selfish love of gain. This speech, then, "has *ēthos*," in that it contains indications of the kind of choice Menelaos makes Second, Iphigenia in Euripides' *Iphigenia in Aulis* is said to be an example of an inconsistent *ēthos*, "for the suppliant is not at all like the later [girl]" (1454a32–33).[37] The speeches that have *ēthos* in this play would, then, be those in which Iphigenia seeks to avoid death by supplicating her father (1211–52), and those in which, inconsistently, she chooses to sacrifice herself (e.g , 1374–1401) All of these speeches "have *ēthos*" in that they contain indications of the kind of choice Iphigenia makes

When Aristotle writes that an action as well as a speech can make clear what sort of choice someone makes (1454a18), he means that attendant circumstances can give ethical "color" to an action While he does not give examples of actions that do this, examples are easily found in the tragedies. In Euripides' *Electra*, Orestes' motives in murdering Clytemnestra and Aigisthus are shown by the circumstances attending his actions, as well as by his speeches Orestes kills Aigisthus during a sacrifice, and he kills Clytemnestra while she is preparing for a sacrifice. Passages in which these actions take place "have *ēthos*" because they contain indications that Orestes chooses to kill in a way that is offensive to the gods and to human custom. An interesting parallel to this kind of *ēthos* is provided by an example given by Jerome Pollitt of *ēthos* in painting A painting of Polygnotus was said to depict Ajax swearing at an altar while Cassandra sat holding the image of Athena to which she clung as a suppliant when Ajax dragged her away.[38] Here also, attendant circumstances clearly show that Ajax's act is impious

The foregoing analysis helps us interpret two problematic passages in which *ēthos* might be taken to mean dramatis persona It provides support for the view that *ēthos* never has this meaning in the *Poetics*, as some have

---

[37] On the meaning of *ēthos* in these two examples, see further below, this subsection
[38] Pollitt, *Ancient View*, 188

thought.[39] As B. R. Rees points out, the Greek for what we call a dramatic "character" is "mask" (*prosōpon*) and not *ēthos* [40]

In the first of these problematic passages (15.1454a28–32), Aristotle states that Menelaos and Iphigenia are examples of *ēthē* of certain kinds. Because Menelaos and Iphigenia are not people whose actions are imitated but "Menelaos in the *Orestes*" and "Iphigenia in Aulis" [sc., in Euripides' *Iphigenia in Aulis*], *ēthos* might be taken to mean dramatis persona here. However, later in the same sentence, specific passages are given as examples of *ēthos*: "the lament of Odysseus" and "the speech of Melanippe." Can *ēthos* mean dramatis persona in the first part of this sentence and "specific passages" in the second half? While the sentence is awkward at best, it is least difficult if we take *ēthos* to refer throughout to indications of choice within specific passages. In this interpretation, "Menelaos" would be short for "the indications of choice within Menelaos's speeches,"[41] and "the lament of Odysseus" would be short for "the indications of choice within the lament of Odysseus" The comparison Aristotle makes between plot and *ēthos* immediately after this puzzling sentence supports the view that *ēthos* refers to indications of choice within specific passages throughout this sentence. Aristotle writes. "One should always seek either necessity or probability in the *ēthē* just as in the organization of the events, so that [one should represent] a person of a certain kind saying or doing things of a certain kind according to either necessity or probability, and this should come after that either by necessity or by probability" (1454a33–36). If the plot as a whole is made up of a number of individual events (things said or done), similarly the *ēthē* as a whole are made up of a number of indications of choice within specific passages. Each of these passages individually "has *ēthos*."

Another passage that might seem to favor the view that *ēthos* can mean dramatis persona is 1460a10–11 Aristotle states that Homer "at once brings on a man or a woman or some other *ēthos*, and none without *ēthos* but having *ēthos*" (εὐθὺς εἰσάγει ἄνδρα ἢ γυναῖκα ἢ ἄλλο τι ἦθος, καὶ οὐδέν' ἀήθη ἀλλ' ἔχοντα ἦθος) This difficult passage is phrased in a deliberately paradoxical way. Clearly, if there can be *ēthos* without *ēthos*, the term must be used in two different senses Here, the distinction between a technical and a nontechnical sense of *ēthos* can be helpful. In the

[39] The view that *ēthos* means dramatis persona is defended by, among others, Else, *Argument*, 456–57

[40] Rees, "Plot,' 192 Schutrumpf, *Bedeutung*, 93–99, gives some good arguments against the view that *ēthos* means dramatis persona in the *Poetics*

[41] Cf Else, *Argument*, 466

second and third occurrences of *ēthos* ("none without *ēthos* but having *ēthos*")
the term is used in the technical sense, to refer to one of the qualitative
parts of epic. The first occurrence of *ēthos*, on the other hand, does not have
this technical sense, nor does it mean dramatis persona. Instead, it refers
to the character (in a broad sense that can include such qualities as gender)
of the person whose actions are imitated.

Some parallel passages support this interpretation of 1460a10–11. At
1454a26–28 Aristotle writes "For if the one furnishing the imitation
[ὁ τὴν μίμησιν παρέχων] is someone inconsistent and this sort of *ēthos* has
been added [τοιοῦτον ἦθος ὑποτεθῇ], nevertheless, it should be consistently inconsistent." Aristotle uses similar language at 1455b12–13,
where he writes that after setting out the plot, the poet should "add [ὑπο-
θέντα] the names and episodize."[42] To "add" *ēthos* or "names" in this way
is not to supply dramatis personae, but to set it down as a premise that
the person whose actions are imitated, the one who "furnishes the imitation," has certain individual qualities; it is, for example, to set down that
the actions imitated are those of Iphigenia, who is inconsistent. The poet
then creates *ēthos* in the technical sense, in the form of consistent indications, within specific passages, that she chooses inconsistently. Similarly,
at 1460a10–11, the *ēthos* that Homer "brings on" is that of the person—
for example, Agamemnon or Helen—who "furnishes the imitation" because his or her actions are imitated by the plot. Homer then adds *ēthos* in
the technical sense to his imitation of the actions of this person. "none
without *ēthos* but having *ēthos*." Another parallel to 1460a10–11 is *Rhetoric*
1417b7.[43] Aristotle writes that the rhetorician "at once brings himself on
also, qualified in a certain way" (εὐθῦς εἴσαγει καὶ σεαυτὸν ποιόν τινα).
Here, the rhetorician ("himself") corresponds to the person whose actions
are imitated by the poet. The rhetorician gives himself certain ethical
qualities (he makes himself *poios*), just as the poet adds *ēthos* in the technical sense to his imitation of the actions of the person who "furnishes the
imitation."

In the *Poetics*, *ēthos* as a part of tragedy is always an indication of choice,
and never includes a broader set of "characteristic peculiarities," as *ēthos*
sometimes does in the *Rhetoric*. In *Rhetoric* 3.16, *ēthos* has two important
senses: (1) ἕν μέν, "that which indicates choice" (1417a17), and (2) ἄλλα

---

[42] House, *Poetics*, 54, suggests the translation "episodise." Aristotle also writes that
names should be 'added" at 1451b10 (ἐπιτιθεμένη) and at 1451b13 (ὑποτιθέασιν). On
the meaning of these terms, see Else, *Argument*, 307–8 and n 25. On 1455b12–13, see
chap 4 ("Plausibility, Plot, and Episode').

[43] This parallel passage was called to my attention by Schutrumpf, *Bedeutung*, 95.

ἠθικά, traits that "accompany each character." For example, talking while walking is a trait that belongs to a boorish character (1417a21–23). *Ēthos* in this second, broader sense includes characterizations of age, sex, and nationality, as well as disposition (*Rhet.* 3.7.1408a25–29).[44] The analysis of *Poetics* 1460a10–11 just given, however, does not support the view that merely to represent someone as a man or a woman is to add *ēthos* as a part of tragedy. Nor does 1454a17–25 support this view. Here, *ēthos* is an indication of choice that qualifies someone as a *good* woman, man, or slave; it is not merely the representation of someone as a man, woman, or slave.

A passage in *Poetics* 15 presents greater difficulties. Samuel Bassett argues that the "wrathful" and "easygoing" *ēthē* mentioned in this chapter are "characteristic peculiarities."[45] According to Aristotle,

> since tragedy is imitation of those better than we are, [the poet] should imitate good portrait-painters. For they also make their subjects like by giving them their individual shape, but paint them more beautiful. In the same way the poet [should] also, in imitating people who are wrathful or easygoing or have other such qualities with respect to their *ēthē*, make them such [τοιούτους] as that, but decent. For example, Homer [made] Achilles stubborn and good. (1454b8–15)[46]

If the poet in this passage makes someone in his play "such as" the character of the person whose actions are imitated, he clearly does so by adding *ēthos* as a part of his tragedy. There is, however, no reason why this *ēthos* cannot indicate choice, as *ēthos* is said to do at the beginning of chapter 15 (1454a17–19). Homer's Achilles is shown to be wrathful in those speeches in the *Iliad* in which he chooses to revile Agamemnon and to keep from the fighting rather than accepting the loss of Briseis without complaint. He is shown to be stubborn by his decision to play the lyre instead of fighting, by those speeches in which he rejects the gifts offered by Agamemnon, and by those in which he repeatedly asserts his decision to cease fighting.[47]

---

[44] The phrase "characteristic peculiarities" is that of Cope, *Rhetoric* 3:193. This discussion, together with his *Introduction*, 113, connects *ēthos* in the second sense in 3.16 with *ēthos* in 3.7. In *Introduction* (112–13), Cope indicates that *ēthos* as a part of tragedy can have this broader sense in the *Poetics*. A similar view is held by Bassett, "Hē de Odusseian," 6–7.

[45] Bassett, "Hē de Odusseian."

[46] The text of this last sentence is hopelessly corrupt, but its general sense is clear.

[47] Achilles is shown making a decision at *Il.* 1.188–89 ("his heart . . . was divided between two opinions") about whether to attack Agamemnon. After Athena's intervention, he decides to avoid attacking Agamemnon, but to keep out of the fighting (1.239–

Aristotle's restriction of *ēthos* in the technical sense to indications of choice implies that *ēthos* must qualify someone as base or excellent in a sense that is at least in part "moral."[48] Aristotle's use of terms with some "moral" connotations in connection with *ēthos* as a part of tragedy supports this view. In chapter 15, Aristotle uses the terms "good" (*chrēston*: 1454a19), "evil" (*ponērias*. 1454a28), and "courageous" (1454a22) in giving examples of *ēthos* as a part of tragedy In chapter 13, two of the terms that characterize the dramatic agent who moves between good and bad fortune have primarily "moral" connotations. "justice" and "depravity" (*mochthērian*. 1453a8–9) These qualities would be indicated by *ēthos* in the technical sense.

Aristotle's strict separation of plot and *ēthos* has two further consequences It implies that whatever belongs to the plot does not in itself have the "moral" qualities that are given by *ēthos* alone. In particular, because good fortune and bad fortune (*eutuchia* and *dustuchia*), the end points between which the tragic plot moves (1451a13–14, 1453a13–14), belong to plot and not to *ēthos*, good and bad fortune do not have the "moral" qualities that *ēthos* alone confers. The separation of plot and *ēthos* also implies, conversely, that *ēthos* in the technical sense does not in itself indicate good or bad fortune. In the *Poetics*, then, *ēthos* in the technical sense differs from *ēthos* in *Rhetoric* 2 12, where *ēthē* are said to differ in "fortunes" (*tuchas*. 1388b32)—that is, in "noble birth, and wealth, and power, and the opposites of these, and, in general, in good and bad fortune [*eutuchian kai dustuchian*]" (1389a1–2).

If this is so, the good fortune that marks one of the end points of the tragic change must be primarily social and material good fortune. prosperity, high status, good reputation. This view of tragic good fortune makes sense for a number of reasons. Aristotle tells us that tragedy should imitate the actions of the *spoudaioi* (1448a27)—the socially superior "nobles," "those with great good reputation and good fortune," and "illustrious men" (1453a10–12). Aristotle's theory is in accord with the facts, for tragedy and epic do in fact imitate the actions of those who are "fortunate" in a social sense. kings and heroes.[49] Oedipus himself (before his discovery,

<hr/>

44, 297–99) It is again clear what kind of choice Achilles makes throughout *Il* 9 He plays the lyre at 186–89, at 356 he says he does not wish to fight Hector, and at 345 he says "He will not persuade me,' after giving his reasons for this choice

[48] Pace Keuls, *Plato*, 97 n 28 Because no Greek term corresponds to the English "moral,' I place this word in quotation marks On the "moral" and "nonmoral" distinction, see below, "Problems "

[49] See Halliwell, *Aristotle's Poetics*, 166–67 and 202–8, on the social and material con-

but after the parricide and incest) is called *eudaimōn* (that is, *eutuchēs*, "fortunate") by Euripides [50] Moreover, *eudaimonia*, "happiness," in the ordinary Greek sense, depends, like *eutuchia*, in large part on objective prosperity and social status [51] Even in Aristotle's ethical works, *eudaimonia*, a word with much stronger "moral" connotations than *eutuchia*, includes external goods such as wealth and social status that are necessary for the full exercise of excellence [52] We may conclude, then, that the people whose actions are imitated by tragedy are "fortunate" in a primarily material and social sense that does not include the "moral" qualities that are given by *ēthos* as a part of tragedy However, the people whose actions are imitated by tragedy do have *ēthos* in a nontechnical sense, for they are the *spoudaioi*

The Spoudaioi

In *Poetics* 2, Aristotle uses the term *ēthē* in discussing the objects imitated by tragedy and comedy "The imitators imitate people acting, and it is necessary that these be either noble [*spoudaioi*] or inferior [*phauloi*] (for *ēthē* almost always correspond to these [categories] alone, for all *ēthē* differ in baseness [*kakia*] or excellence [*aretē*])" (1448a1–4) Here, *ēthē* does not have the technical sense of one of the parts of tragedy, for this sense is not defined until *Poetics* 6 Instead, the term refers to the characters of the people whose actions are imitated These characters are "base" or "excellent" in a sense that is in large part social, for they "correspond to" the *spoudaioi* and the *phauloi*, those who are socially fortunate (the *agathoi*) or unfortunate [53] Tragedy and epic deal with the "nobles" (*spoudaioi* 1448a2,

notations of good fortune in the *Poetics* For a good discussion of the fact that Greek tragedy deals with great families, see Lattimore, Legend That misfortunes of great families arouse more emotion is a commonplace in tragedy Lattimore cites Euripides, *Hippolytus* 1465–66 and *Helen* 1678–79 (190 n 8)

[50] Euripides, *Antigone* frag , quoted in Aristophanes, *Frogs* 1182, 1187 (Nauck, *Fragmenta*, frag 157, 158) This use of *eudaimōn* as a synonym for *eutuchēs* is noted by Sheppard, *Oedipus Tyrannus*, xxix and n 2 Aristotle himself notes that the two words are often taken to be synonymous (*EE* 1214a25)

[51] See Adkins, *Merit*, 254 and n 12, and 257–58 The data collected by Heer, *Makar*, also supports this view

[52] See, for example, *EN* 1099a31-b8, 1100b22–1101a22, 1178b33–1179a9, *Rhet* 1360b14–30, and *Pol* 1323b40–1324a2 On *eudaimonia* and external goods, see J M Cooper, Fortune

[53] Else, *Argument*, 71–79, shows the importance of social qualities in Aristotle s concepts of *spoudaios* and *phaulos* He points out (76–77) that the term *spoudaios*, like *aretē*, charac-

1448a27, 1449b9–10), who are the agents of the "noble-and-serious"[54] (*spoudaiai*) actions imitated by these two closely related genres (1448b34, 1449b24). These are the people with "great good reputation and good fortune" whom Aristotle mentions in *Poetics* 13 (1453a10). Comedy, on the other hand, imitates the actions of socially "inferior" people (1448a16–18). These two classes differ in *ēthos* in large part because they differ in good and bad fortune, one way in which *ēthē* are said to differ in *Rhetoric* 1388b32–1389a2. *Ēthē* in the nontechnical sense used in *Poetics* 2, then, includes broader and more social qualities of people in general, while *ēthos* in the technical sense refers narrowly to indications of choice within a tragedy.

A conceptual distinction between the ethical qualities that characterize the *spoudaioi* and those indicated by *ēthos* as part of tragedy is apparent in Aristotle's characterization of the best agent of the dramatic action in *Poetics* 13: "The person between these is therefore left. This sort of person is one who is not outstanding in excellence and justice, and who does not change to bad fortune because of baseness and depravity, but because of some error; [he is one] of those with great good reputation and good fortune, such as Oedipus and Thyestes and illustrious men from such families" (1453a7–12). Here, the person with "great good reputation and good fortune" is one of the kings and heroes whose actions are among the "traditional stories" imitated by tragedy (1453b22–23). This person is *spoudaios* in a primarily social sense, and has an excellent *ēthos* corresponding to his or her social class. On the other hand, outstanding "justice" and "depravity" in this passage are characteristics closely connected with choice, with "morality." The conjunction of "excellence" with "justice," and of "baseness" with "depravity," suggests that all four terms have a "moral" sense here. All indicate characteristics that would be added to a tragedy by *ēthos* in the technical sense.

The *spoudaia ēthē* of the people whose actions are imitated are important to tragedy as a genre. When Aristotle defines tragedy as "imitation of a

---

terizes the heroic, aristocratic class. Else also notes that *spoudaios* includes "moral" qualities, on which see further below, "Problems." Gellrich, *Tragedy*, 126–62, also notes that *spoudaios* in the *Poetics* combines traditional social qualities with "moral" qualities. It is thus a mistake to give *spoudaios* too narrowly "moral" an interpretation, as do Schutrumpf, *Bedeutung*, 57–63 (criticized by Rees in his review of *Bedeutung*, 51, and praised by Golden, in his review, 286), Golden, "Serious," and Held, "*Spoudaios*," esp. 171.

[54] This translation, while awkward, takes into account that the Greek term *spoudaios*, like the English "noble," has both social and "moral" connotations, and that it also means "serious" as opposed to "laughable" or "trivial."

spoudaia action" (1449b24), he means one done by a *spoudaios* person
Tragedy differs in this respect from comedy, which deals with "the laughable" (1449a34), and is an imitation of the actions of the socially "inferior"
(*phauloi*. 1448a2, *cheirous* 1448a16–18, 1448b24–27, 1449a32) [55] More
specifically, a *spoudaios* person is someone capable of the good fortune that
is one of the end points of the tragic plot. This view is supported by *Nicomachean Ethics* 1177a1–11, where Aristotle writes that *spoudaia* rather
than laughable things contribute to the *eudaimonia* of which a slave is not
capable.[56] Since tragedy represents a change between good and bad fortune, it imitates actions that are *spoudaiai* in the sense of "serious," and it
does so because it imitates the actions of the *spoudaioi*, the "nobles," people
with the excellent *ēthē* that characterize those who are fortunate in a social
sense. kings and heroes. The actions imitated by comedy, in contrast, are
those of the *phauloi*, who have base *ēthē* that characterize people who are
capable of neither great good nor great bad fortune

This way of distinguishing tragedy from comedy might appear inconsistent with the view that *ēthos* is not essential to tragedy Aristotle states
in *Poetics* 2 that drama imitates the actions of people who are *spoudaioi* or
inferior, and he indicates that these people differ in having excellent or
base *ēthē* (1448a1–4) Yet in chapter 6 he states that there can be tragedies
without *ēthos* (1450a23–26), and in chapter 13 he characterizes the ideal
dramatic agent as someone who is not outstanding in excellence or justice,
and who does not fall because of baseness and depravity (1453a7–12). We
might then ask how a tragedy can imitate the actions of a *spoudaios*, someone who has an excellent *ēthos*, without including *ēthos* in some way Moreover, it might be objected, if the *spoudaia* qualities of actions depend on
the ethical qualities of the agents, Aristotle's distinction between plot and
ēthos must be less strict than I have indicated

While the difficulties just noted are real and serious, they cannot be
solved by conflating plot and *ēthos*. As I have argued, both Aristotle's explicit statements and his theory of drama require a strict separation of these
two parts of tragedy. Moreover, Aristotle's narrow definition of *ēthos* in the
technical sense provides a partial solution, although it cannot completely
prevent inconsistency. A tragedy can, in his view, imitate the actions of
the *spoudaioi* simply by representing the social and material good fortune

[55] See Golden, "Serious," 284–85, on the dependence of genre distinctions on character
[56] Else calls attention to this passage in *Argument*, 241 n 73, where he notes that the
phaulos class "never arrives at either real happiness or its opposite ' See also *EN* 1100b27,
where Aristotle writes that the use of the good things given by fortune is ' fine and *spoudaia* "

102

that is one end point of the tragic plot. Such a tragedy would not necessarily have *ēthos* in the technical sense, for it would not necessarily include indications of ("moral") choice.

PROBLEMS

The difficulties just noted arise because certain features of Aristotle's ethical theory are not entirely consistent with his dramatic theory. His distinction between plot and *ēthos* in the *Poetics* depends in part on a conceptual distinction between social excellence and "moral" excellence involving choice. Because the ethical theory on which the *Poetics* is based does not fully recognize this distinction, however, Aristotle cannot consistently restrict *ēthos* in the technical sense to indications of "moral" qualities, nor can he completely restrict the qualities of the *spoudaioi* to social qualities.

As Adkins notes, Aristotelian excellence includes both the "competitive" excellences of tradition, for which success and prosperity are all-important, and the "cooperative" excellences, such as justice and *sōphrosunē*.[57] According to the *Rhetoric*, "*Aretē* is thought to be the power of getting and keeping good things and the power of conferring many and great benefits" (1366a36–38). Its "parts" include what the *Nicomachean Ethics* calls "ethical excellences"—justice, courage, and *sōphrosunē*—and the intellectual excellences of *phronēsis* (practical wisdom) and wisdom (1366b1–3).[58] However, according to the *Rhetoric*, these are excellences not so much because they are good in themselves or good for their possessors, as because they are useful to others: "Of necessity, the greatest excellences are those which are most useful to others, if excellence is the power of conferring benefits" (1366b3–5). This concept of excellence is very close to the Homeric "competitive" concept, according to which *aretē* is the power of benefiting *philoi* and harming enemies.[59] However, it also includes the "co-

[57] See Adkins, "Aristotle," whose analysis of the combination of "competitive" and "cooperative" excellences in Aristotle's thought is very useful for an understanding of some of the difficulties in the *Poetics*. See also Nussbaum, *Fragility*, 378–94, who discusses a tension between moral excellence and good fortune in connection with the *Poetics* and tragedy. I disagree with many of their conclusions, however

[58] The distinction between "ethical" and "intellectual" excellence is made, for example, at *EN* 1103a14–18

[59] This popular view is reflected in Meno's definition of male excellence in Plato, *Meno* 71e For other examples, see Blundell, *Helping*

operative," "moral" excellences of justice and *sōphrosunē*. Moreover, as I argued above ("*Ēthos* as Part of Tragedy"), *eudaimonia* (happiness) includes external goods as well as "moral goods," even in Aristotle's ethical works The two value systems are inextricably mixed in Aristotle's concept of excellence, especially in works that, like the *Rhetoric* and the *Poetics*, tend to adopt more popular ethical perspectives than do his ethical treatises

This mixed ethical theory is not entirely compatible with a theory of tragedy that depends in part on a strict distinction of the kind Aristotle makes between plot and *ēthos* If the plot moves between good and bad fortune, and if excellence in a mixed social and "moral" sense is necessary to good fortune, plot must also in some way involve "moral" excellence of the kind that, according to Aristotle's theory of tragedy, is given by *ēthos* alone.

A problem of this kind is apparent in a number of passages in the *Poetics*. For example, in 1453a7–9, as I argued above ("The *Spoudaioi*"), Aristotle writes that the best agent of the dramatic action should not be outstanding in the "moral" qualities of excellence (*aretē*) and justice, or baseness and depravity. These are qualities associated with choice, with *ēthos* in the technical sense. Aristotle also writes that tragedy should represent this person, who is not outstanding in excellence, changing from good to bad fortune (1453a9). This disjunction between excellence and good fortune, however, is problematic in view of 1448a1–4, where the *spoudaioi*, the fortunate people whose actions are imitated by tragedy, are those who have an *ēthos* characterized by *aretē*. If excellence is a quality that characterizes both the socially fortunate and the "morally" superior, it is hard to see how someone can be very fortunate without having outstanding *aretē*

Aristotle could avoid inconsistency if *aretē* meant "moral" excellence at 1453a8, where it is a quality indicated by *ēthos* in the technical sense, and "social" excellence at 1448a3, where it is a quality connected with *ēthos* in a nontechnical sense. Aristotle does seem to be trying to define *aretē* in strictly "moral" terms at 1453a7–9, for he links it with the more narrowly "moral" terms "justice" and "depravity" (*mochthēria*) in this passage, and he adds the further qualification "outstanding."[60] These qualifications do not entirely resolve the difficulty, however, for in Greek thought, the *spoudaioi* are those who are "outstanding in *aretē*," in a mixed social and "moral" sense that Aristotle himself in large part accepts.[61] The difficulty

---

[60] Cf the conjunction "excellence and justice' in *Pol* 1309a36, used to indicate a different kind of excellence from that more closely connected with helping friends at 1310b9–12 See Newman, *Politics*, on 1310b11

[61] Vahlen, *Beitrage*, 267–68, has some excellent remarks on the interconnections among

would remain even if we followed Alfred Gudeman in bracketing the phrase about *arete* at 1448a3–4.[62]

Aristotle's use of the term *spoudaios* at 1461a4–9 (quoted above) is also an indication of a conceptual inconsistency. He writes that in considering whether something said or done was *spoudaion*, one should consider the agent's "purpose" (οὗ ἕνεκεν), a concept very close to that of "choice" (*prohairesis*).[63] However, if having good "purpose" or "choice" is one important characteristic of a *spoudaia* action, and if tragedy as a genre is defined as "imitation of a *spoudaia* action," then *ethos* in the technical sense, an indication of choice, would seem, contrary to Aristotle's explicit denial, to be essential to tragedy as a genre.

A conflict similar to that between the requirements that the dramatic agent be *spoudaios* and not outstanding in excellence is also evident in Aristotle's account of the "decent person" (*epieikes*) in *Poetics* 13 and 15. Chapter 13 states that two kinds of people should not be agents of a dramatic action. "decent men" (*epieikeis*. 1452b34) who change from good to bad fortune, and "depraved" (1452b36) or "very bad" (*sphodra poneros*: 1453a1) people. The context shows that *epieikes* must mean "outstanding in excellence" here. The best agent of the dramatic action, Aristotle writes, is "the in-between man". "The man between these is therefore left" (1453a7). This man does not excel in *arete* or justice, and does not change to bad fortune because of baseness or depravity (1453a8–9). He is, therefore, between the "depraved" or "very bad" person mentioned at 1452b36 and 1453a1, and another man who is "outstanding in excellence." Because the phrase "between *these*" (τούτων. 1453a7) indicates that the man who has outstanding excellence has been mentioned previously, he can only be one of the *epieikeis* of 1452b34. In chapter 13, then, *epieikes* means "outstanding in excellence," and Aristotle holds that this kind of person should not be the agent of a dramatic action.[64]

---

the terms *spoudaios*, *epieikes*, and *chrestos* in the *Poetics*, and in Aristotle's thought generally He notes that Aristotle states (sc , in *Cat* 10b5–9) that the *spoudaios* is so called because he has *arete*, and that *spoudaios* carries with it the whole range of meanings of *arete* (268) See also D W Lucas, *Poetics*, 63, who calls attention to *Pol* 1324a12–13, where *spoudaios* is used as an adjective of *arete*, and to *EN* 1145b8–10 On this latter passage see Nagy, *Best*, 254, who notes that Aristotle uses *spoudaios* and *phaulos* as synonyms for "praiseworthy" and "blameworthy" (*EN* 1145b9) Again, in the *Rhetoric*, *epieikeis* (1378a13) and *spoudaioi* (1378a16) are used as adjectives of *arete* (1378a9)

[62] See Gudeman, *Aristoteles*, ad loc , and critical note

[63] Cf *Rhet* 1367b21–23, where *prohairesis* is connected with the *spoudaios*

[64] The view that *epieikes* means "outstanding in excellence" in *Po* 13 is held, among others, by Halliwell, *Aristotle's Poetics*, 219 and n 24, and Stinton, "*Hamartia*," 237

Chapter 15, on the other hand, *recommends* making the agents of the dramatic action *epieikeis*. At 1454b8–15, Aristotle writes that, since tragedy is an imitation of people "better than we are," the poet should make people "such as" those he imitates, but *epieikeis*, like a good portrait-painter who makes people "like" but "more beautiful." This passage appears to contradict chapter 13, which denies that the *epieikeis* (those who are outstanding in excellence and justice) are good agents of a dramatic action The inconsistency can be accounted for if Aristotle has a mixed social and "moral" concept of *epieikēs*, a concept that leads him to use the term in two different senses. In this view, *epieikēs* does not mean "outstanding in excellence" in *Poetics* 15, but is a close synonym of *spoudaios*. In the corrupt next line (1454b14), in fact, *agathos* (good), a term with strong social connotations, is substituted for *epieikēs*.

A puzzling mixture of "moral" and "social" qualities also characterizes Aristotle's concept of the person "like" us In *Poetics* 13 1453a5, "like" seems to mean "like" the human average in respect to "moral" qualities, for Aristotle goes on to say that the best agent of the dramatic action has qualities between those of excellence and justice on the one hand and baseness and depravity on the other. "Like" appears to have the same sense in *Poetics* 15.1454a24, where it is a quality indicated by *ēthos* in the technical sense. However, "like" has a social sense in *Poetics* 2 1448a6, where people who are "like" (that is, like us. 1448a4) are opposed both to those who are "better" than we are in a social sense (the *spoudaioi* whose actions tragedy imitates) and to those "worse" than we are, the socially inferior *phauloi* whose actions comedy imitates (1448a1–6, 1448a16–18). Aristotle may be attempting to resolve this difficulty at 13 1453a16–17, where he writes that tragedy should imitate the actions of "either a person such as has been mentioned {sc., the in-between person], or of someone better rather than worse."

Aristotle's concept of someone who suffers undeserved bad fortune (*ton anaxion dustuchounta*. 1453a4) also involves a problematic fusion of "moral" and social qualities. *Poetics* 13 tells us that someone who "does not deserve to suffer bad fortune" is, in the first place, someone who does not change to bad fortune because of baseness or depravity But surely Aristotle also has in mind the person whose bad fortune is not to be expected (*axioō*) because of his or her high social rank (*axiōma*).[65] *Rhetoric* 2 5

[65] *Axioō* means "expect" as well as "deserve," according to LSJ Aristotle writes that we pity those who are "like" us in *axiōmata*, "social positions,' at *Rhet* 2 8 1386a25 On the mixed social and "moral" qualities included in the concept of *axia* (worth) in Aristotle's thought, see Newman, *Politics*, on 1278a20 and 1310b33 Many scholars agree that the

makes it clear that external good fortune was thought by Aristotle and his fellow Greeks to make bad fortune unlikely. "Those who are and are thought to be in great good fortune do not think they could suffer anything" (1382b35–1383a1). The same idea is expressed in 2.8: "If they think they have all good things, it is clear that they also think they cannot suffer anything evil" (1385b22–23).

The difficulties just discussed cannot be resolved completely, for they stem from a tension between Aristotle's ethical and dramatic theories. Aristotle's dramatic theory requires a strict separation of the social qualities associated with plot and the "moral" qualities associated with *ēthos*. In his view, the function of tragedy is to arouse pity and fear rather than praise and blame. He therefore defines tragedy as "imitation of action," as a movement between good and bad fortune in a sense that is primarily social and material rather than "moral." Aristotle excludes "moral" elements from tragedy because "moral" judgments lead us to praise or blame and thus interfere with the tragic emotions. In Aristotle's ethical theory, however, good fortune and the excellence necessary to it include both social and "moral" goods. This ethical theory to some extent prevents Aristotle from separating "moral" and social qualities as his dramatic theory requires.

Nevertheless, the inconsistencies to which this conflict gives rise are not fatal to the practical application to most tragedies of the criteria by means of which Aristotle distinguishes plot and *ēthos*. On the contrary, his distinction between plot, a movement between good and bad fortune, and *ēthos*, an indication of choice within a specific passage, reflects a distinction inherent in many of the plays themselves.

Plot and *Ēthos* in the Greek Tragedies

Two plot outlines in the *Poetics* support the interpretation of the plot-character distinction argued for above.[66] In distinguishing plot from episode, Aristotle gives an outline of the plot of the *Odyssey* and of Euripides'

---

phrase *ton anaxion dustuchounta* has social connotations See, for example, Heath, *Poetics*, 82–83, with notes Adkins, "Aristotle," 91–101, provides an excellent discussion of the social and "moral" connotations of this expression, though I do not agree with him about the discrepancy between Aristotle's views and those of the fifth century B C E

[66] An earlier version of the material in this section was included in Belfiore, "*Praxis*"

Iphigenia in Tauris [67] The "universal" (1455b2–3) of "the Iphigenia," the plot common to Euripides' and Polyidos's versions of the story, is as follows

> A certain girl after being sacrificed and disappearing from the view of those sacrificing her was settled in another land where the custom was to sacrifice strangers to the goddess, and she came to hold that priesthood A while later, it happened that the brother of the priestess arrived The fact that the oracle commanded him to go there, for some reason that is outside the universal, and his purpose [in going], are outside the plot [68] He arrived, was seized, and when about to be sacrificed, he made himself known, either as Euripides or as Polyidos wrote it, saying, as was plausible, that not only his sister but he also had to be sacrificed Thence is salvation (17 1455b3–12)

This plot outline explicitly excludes any indication of choice "That the oracle commanded him to go there, for some reason that is outside the universal, and his purpose [in going], are outside the plot "

Aristotle's outline of the "story" (*logos*) of the *Odyssey*—its plot—also excludes *ēthos*

> The story of the *Odyssey* is not long A certain man is away from home for many years, carefully watched by Poseidon and alone Moreover, things at home are in such a state that his possessions are wasted by the suitors and his son is plotted against He himself arrives, storm-tossed, and making himself recognized by some, attacks and is himself saved while he destroys his enemies This is what is proper [to the story] the rest is episode (17 1455b16–23)

In this example also, *ēthos* is conspicuous by its absence Odysseus the versatile is simply "a man," while his villainous enemies are just "the suitors "

An excellent way of further illustrating and testing the interpretation of Aristotle's distinction between plot and *ēthos* argued for above is to apply it to three plays with the same basic plot Aeschylus's *Libation Bearers*, Sophocles' *Electra*, and Euripides' *Electra* If we base an outline of the plot common to all three plays on Aristotle's examples of the *Odyssey* and the

---

[67] On the plot-episode distinction, see chap 4 (Plausibility, Plot, and Episode) The importance of these two plot outlines for an understanding of Aristotle s view that there can be tragedy without *ethos* is noted by Catherine Lord, Character, 59 I discuss Aristotle s views on the *Iphigenia* plot in Belfiore, Iphigenia

[68] I adapt Janko s translation (*Poetics I*) of 1455b7–8 (τὸ δ' ὅτι   μῦθου), which makes excellent sense of the text, without the need for bracketing διὰ   καθόλου, with Kassel

Iphigenia in Tauris plots, we will get something like this. "A woman has killed her husband, and now rules in his stead, along with her lover, who helped in the killing. She has, by her dead husband, a daughter, and a son, living in exile. The son returns from exile, makes himself known to his sister, and kills his mother and her lover."

This plot, common to each of the plays, tells us absolutely nothing about the "moral" quality of the act of Orestes in killing his mother. In fact, the plot is such that we cannot in principle determine this quality from his act alone. As a general rule, it is right to avenge one's father, and as a general rule, it is wrong to kill one's mother. However, the act of avenging one's father by killing one's mother presents ethical difficulties. Each play solves this dilemma in a different way, by attributing different motives and qualities to the agent, that is, by the use of *ēthos*.

In a passage early in the *Libation Bearers*, Orestes gives his reasons for choosing to commit matricide. They are the oracle, grief for his father, and the loss of his patrimony, which, he says, entails the servitude of the very men who sacked Troy (297–305). Of these, all praiseworthy motives, the oracle is by far the most important. When about to act, Orestes hesitates and asks Pylades, "What shall I do?" Pylades answers, "What of the oracle? Count all human beings as enemies except the god." Orestes answers, "You are right," and does the deed (899–904) These passages have *ēthos* in Aristotle's technical sense, for they indicate why something was chosen. Orestes' act is shown by the poet's use of *ēthos* to be justified, and it is vindicated by the gods in the *Eumenides*.

The motives of Orestes in Sophocles' *Electra* are very different. He also gives them in a speech early in the play. the desire to win fame, the desire to destroy his enemies, and the desire to regain his patrimony (59–72). He does *not* give as reasons an oracle, love of his father, or the desire to free his land from tyranny. We conclude (and other "ethical" speeches in the play bear this out) that Orestes' motives in this play do not justify matricide.

In Euripides' *Electra*, Orestes' motives in committing the murders are shown not by speech so much as by the circumstances attending his actions. Orestes kills Aigisthus during a sacrifice, and he kills Clytemnestra while she is preparing for a sacrifice. He brings Aigisthus's corpse to Electra and asks her to maltreat it as she wishes (895–99). He doubts the oracle (971) but does the deed anyway. All this shows a lack of concern for the gods and for human standards of decency. Such a man can have no motive for matricide that can justify the act. This is in fact what the Dioscuri tell Orestes: "She has received justice, but you did not act justly" (1244).

These examples show that Aristotle's distinction between plot and *ēthos* is, in spite of the theoretical difficulties noted above, useful for an analysis of the Greek tragedies themselves. The three plays analyzed here do seem to have plots that imitate an action without intrinsic "moral" qualities. The act is, in each case, given a different ethical "color" by *ēthos*, an indication of what kind of choice someone makes. This distinction will be useful for the studies, with which the next chapter is concerned, of the way in which the tragic plot moves between the end points of good and bad fortune, and of how plot differs from episode.

This chapter has discussed Aristotle's reasons for insisting that plot is more important than character (*ēthos*), and for making a strict distinction between these two qualitative parts of tragedy. Tragedy, he believes, arouses pity and fear in response to the movement of the plot between good and bad fortune in a primarily social and material sense. This emotional response is incompatible with praise or blame, which are responses to character.

Aristotle's views on *ēthos* are problematic for several reasons, however. First, he sometimes uses the term *ēthos*, "character," in the *Poetics* broadly and nontechnically to refer to character in a primarily social sense. The *spoudaioi* whose actions are imitated by tragedy have *ēthē* that are excellent in a social sense. However, Aristotle also uses *ēthos* in a technical sense to refer to one of the six qualitative parts of tragedy. *Ēthos* used thus is an indication of what kind of choice a dramatic agent makes. Other difficulties are created by Aristotle's failure to make an entirely clear and consistent distinction between the "moral" qualities indicated by *ēthos* in the technical sense and the social qualities connected with plot and good fortune. Nevertheless, these difficulties do not prevent Aristotle's distinction between plot and *ēthos* from being of great practical use as a tool for analyzing the plots of the actual Greek tragedies.

CHAPTER 4

Necessity, Probability and Plausibility

NECESSITY AND PROBABILITY

THE MOST IMPORTANT structural principle governing the tragic plot is that the events that make it up should follow one another "according to probability or necessity" (*kata to eikos ē to anagkaion*).[1] Each of the three parts of the plot must follow this rule Aristotle explicitly states that the two parts of a complex plot, recognition and *peripeteia*, should come about "by necessity or probability" (1452a18–20, 1452a24). It is clear that the third part of the plot, the *pathos*, should also come about "by necessity or probability," for *Poetics* 14, where Aristotle discusses kinds of *pathē*, begins with the statement that the fearful and the pitiable should come "from the organization of the events itself" (1453b2–3)—that is, from the plot structure (1453b4). That this means "according to probability or necessity" is shown by the parallel statement at 1452a18–20 "These things [sc., recognition and *peripeteia*] should come about from the organization of the plot itself, so that it happens that they come to be by necessity or probability as a result of what went before."

The principle of necessity or probability governs the tragedy as a whole, as well as each of the three parts of the plot. In his definition, Aristotle states that tragedy is an imitation of a "complete" (*teleias* 6.1449b25) action. He repeats this definition in *Poetics* 7. "We have assumed that tragedy is imitation of a *complete* and *whole* action" (1450b23–24). He then explains that a *whole* action is one that proceeds from beginning to middle to end according to probability or necessity (1450b26–31, cf. 23.1459a19–20). This action will begin at good fortune and end at bad fortune, or vice versa (7.1451a12–14). It will have order (7.1450b37), and it will be *one* and *whole*, because none of its parts can be changed or removed without changing the whole (9.1451b30–35). Aristotle's phrasing in these passages shows that the terms "one," "whole," and "complete" are used synonymously, to characterize an action that moves, according to

---

[1] The phrase *kata to eikos ē to anagkaion*, or a close variant thereof, is used in connection with the events of the plot at 1451a12–13, 1451a27–28, 1451a38, 1451b9, 1451b35, 1452a20, 1452a24, 1454a34, 1454a35, and 1454a36

necessity or probability, from beginning (good or bad fortune) to end (bad or good fortune).[2] A plot that is not one, whole, and complete is defective in one or more ways. It may be "episodic," lacking organization according to necessity or probability (1451b33–35), it may be "double," having one ending for good people and another for bad (1453a31–33), it may imitate more than one action (1451a16–19). Character as well as plot should follow the principle of necessity or probability (1454a33–36). It is this principle of necessity or probability in plot and character that distinguishes poetry from history. Poetry speaks of "the universal," that is, "what kinds of things it happens that a certain kind of person says or does according to probability or necessity" (1451b8–9).

Although the *Poetics* makes it clear that the principle of necessity or probability is extremely important, Aristotle does not define or explain either "necessity" (*to anagkaion*) or "probability" (*to eikos*) in this work. To understand these concepts, it will be helpful to begin by analyzing the role necessity and probability play in individual passages in the *Poetics*, taking into consideration Aristotle's statements about these concepts elsewhere.

The principle of "necessity or probability" is introduced in the definitions of "beginning," "middle," and "end" in *Poetics* 7.

> The beginning is that which is not itself after something else by necessity, but after it something else is or comes to be by nature [*pephuken*] The end, on the contrary, is that which is itself after something else by nature, either by necessity or for the most part, but after this there is nothing else The middle is that which is itself after something else, and after it there is something else (1450b27–31)

Although the term "probability" (*to eikos*) does not appear in this passage, Aristotle substitutes the equivalent expression "for the most part."[3] Here,

---

[2] Pace Gudeman, *Aristoteles*, 191–92 The terms one" and "whole" are close synonyms in *Meta* 1023b26–28, while at 1024a1–3 a whole is said to be something that has a beginning, middle, and end, and the order of whose parts makes a difference W D Ross, *Metaphysics*, on 1023b26, notes that the definition of "whole" here is equivalent to the definition of *teleion* (complete) given at 1021b12–13 Clark, *Man*, 50, gives a good definition of "whole" "A whole is something complete, perfect without addition and dependent for that perfection upon its arrangement "

[3] On the equivalence of *to eikos* and what happens ' for the most part (ὡς ἐπὶ τὸ πολυ) in Aristotle's thought, see the passages cited by Sorabji, *Necessity*, 55 n 36 *Pr An* 2 27 70a5, and *Rhet* 1 2 1357a34, 2 25 1402b16, and 1403a1 (that is, Kassel s 1402b35–36) See also Dupont-Roc and Lallot, *Poétique*, 211–12, and Goldschmidt, *Temps physique*, 248 On Aristotle's concept of 'for the most part, ' see Sainte-Croix, "History, ' 47–50

he uses the three expressions "necessity," "by nature," and "for the most part": the beginning is that which does not follow something else *by necessity*, and after which something else *by nature* is or comes to be; the end is that which is *by nature* after something else either *by necessity* or *for the most part*; the middle is that which comes after something else [by necessity or for the most part], and after which something else comes in this way These three expressions have interconnected meanings.

Other passages in the *Poetics* help us understand what Aristotle means when he writes, in *Poetics* 7 and 15.1454a36, that one thing comes after another by necessity or probability. In *Poetics* 9 1452a4–6, Aristotle contrasts events that occur "because of each other" (*di' allēla*) with those that happen "of themselves and by chance." He also contrasts what happens "because of" something else with what happens merely "after" something else in *Poetics* 10: "These things [sc., recognition and *peripeteia*] should come about from the organization of the plot itself, so that it happens that they come about by necessity or probability as a result of what went before. It makes a great difference whether this comes about because of this or after this" (1452a18–21). These passages tell us that events that follow one another by necessity or probability occur "because of" and not merely "after" other events, that is, they are efficiently caused by other events. The events linked to one another by efficient causation make up the whole process of change (*metabasis*: 1452a16) that constitutes the tragic plot. The concept of efficient causation is also relevant to an understanding of Aristotle's views on the two divisions of the tragic plot, the *desis*, "complication," and the *lusis*, "solution"[4] When Aristotle writes that the *lusis* is that part of the tragedy "from the beginning of the change [*metabaseōs*] to the end" (18.1455b28–29), we should remember that, in other works, he defines the efficient cause as "the beginning of the change [*metabolē*]."[5]

The structural principle of probability or necessity is further elucidated by the parallels between tragedy and natural processes discussed in chapter 2. Natural processes occur "always or for the most part", that is, they occur with regularity and not by chance. Similarly, the events of a tragic "organization" (*sustasis*) occur "by necessity," "by nature," or "for the most part" rather than by chance. The tragic plot also resembles a biological *sustasis* in having an intelligible structure that is organized for the sake of an end, its function. Thus the events of the plot are not only the efficient

---

[4] In translating *lusis* as "solution" I follow Janko, *Poetics I*

[5] For example, *Phy* 194b29–30 and *Meta* 1013a29–30 Cf *Post An* 94a22, where the efficient cause is defined as "that which begins a process "

causes of one another; they also occur for the sake of an end, the function and final cause of tragedy. Final and efficient cause work together in tragedy, as they do in natural processes.

Just as Aristotle's use of the expressions "by nature" and "for the most part" is more understandable in the context of the analogy between tragic and biological *sustaseis*, so his use of the term "necessity" in the *Poetics* is less puzzling when placed in this biological context.

"Necessity" is a strong word to use, especially of events that are the efficient causes of one another. Aristotle does not generally use it to characterize actions, for action is something that "can be otherwise," and is thus not "necessary."[6] Aristotle makes this point in the *Rhetoric*: "Few [of the premises] that make up rhetorical syllogisms are necessary (for most of the things with which judgments and considerations deal can be otherwise; people deliberate and consider about the things they do, and things done are all of this kind, and practically none of these things is from necessity)" (*Rhet.* 1357a22–27). If this is Aristotle's view, we might well wonder why he insists that in the tragic plot, an imitation of action, events should proceed according to "necessity." Commentators often tacitly assume that the concept of necessity is not really in question here in any meaningful way, for, after all, Aristotle writes of *probability or necessity*."[7] If the term "necessity" served no real function in the *Poetics*, however, Aristotle could easily have omitted it altogether. It is important to explore why, in most cases, he does use *to anagkaion* along with *to eikos*, or the equivalent phrase "for the most part," when he refers to the principle that governs the plot structure.[8]

Aristotle's definitions of three senses of "necessary" (*anagkaion*) in the "dictionary" of *Metaphysics* 5.5 help us understand what "necessity" means in the *Poetics*. "Necessary" means (1) that without which it is not possible to live, or for the good to be or come to be (1015a20–26); (2) the compulsory, or force (1015a26–33); (3) that which cannot be otherwise (1015a33–b9). The third sense is clearly not relevant to the *Poetics*, for the human actions with which tragedy deals can be otherwise, as *Rhetoric*

---

[6] For exceptions, see Sorabji, *Necessity*, 238.

[7] Some representative comments are those of Else, "Aristotle so carefully uses the double formula 'according to probability or necessity' throughout the *Poetics*; for necessity can never be absolute in the sublunar world" (*Argument*, 305), and Halliwell: "Necessity [is] an ideal though scarcely attainable standard" (*Aristotle's Poetics*, 106). That necessity in the *Poetics* is "hypothetical" is noted, all too briefly, by House, *Poetics*, 61, Gallop, "Animals," 153, and Gellrich, *Tragedy*, 112.

[8] Some exceptions that prove the rule are discussed in the next section.

1357a22–27 states. On the other hand, tragedy does deal with what is necessary in the sense of compulsory. In fact, Aristotle gives an instructive example from tragedy in discussing the second definition: "As Sophocles also says, 'but force makes it necessary for me to do this' " (1015a30–31).[9] "This," what Electra is compelled to do in Sophocles' play, is her lamentation (254–55). In her speech at 254–309, Electra discusses the bad fortune that compels her to lament: her own ill-treatment, her father's murder, her mother's and Aigisthus's triumph, the absence of Orestes. These circumstances are the *necessary* conditions within which her lamentation and indeed all her actions take place. Her speech concludes with this very point: "But in evil circumstances / there is great necessity to practice evils" (308–9). "Necessity" in the sense of "compulsion or force" is clearly relevant to this and other tragic plots, in which actions take place under certain unavoidable circumstances.

It is the first sense of "necessary," however, the one connected with the nature (*phusis*) of a living thing, that is of most interest. The "necessary" in this sense is "that without which, as contributing cause, it is not possible to live (for example breathing and food are necessary to a living thing, for it cannot exist without these), and things without which it is not possible for the good to be or come to be" (1015a20–23). Aristotle also discusses this "hypothetical necessity" in a number of other passages. For example, in *On Sleep* 455b26–28, he writes: "I mean the necessity that depends on a hypothesis, that if a living thing is to exist having its own nature, by necessity something must belong to it, and if these things belong, others [must also] belong."[10] The kind of necessity that belongs to living things is, unlike the kind of necessity that "cannot be otherwise," compatible with, rather than opposed to, what happens "for the most part."[11] That which is "by nature" is not only "for the most part,"[12] but

---

[9] The reference is to *Electra* 256, as W. D. Ross notes, *Metaphysics*, on 1015a30.

[10] This passage is cited ibid., on 1015a20ff., among a number of other passages concerning "hypothetical necessity". *Phy.* 199b34, *PA* 639b24, 642a9. See also *Meta.* 1072b12. For some recent discussions of the highly controversial topic of "hypothetical necessity," see Balme, *De partibus animalium*, 76–84 and "Teleology and Necessity", Sorabji, *Necessity*, 143–54, Charles, "Hypothetical Necessity", Gotthelf, "Aristotle's Conception", J M Cooper, "Hypothetical Necessity"

[11] Nonhypothetical necessity and what happens "for the most part" are opposed, for example, in *Meta.* 1026b27–30, *Pr. An.* 32b5–6, and *Rhet.* 1357a31–32

[12] In a number of the passages cited by Sorabji, *Necessity*, 50 n. 20, "for the most part" and "nature" are linked: *GA* 727b29–30, 770b9–13, 777a19–21, *PA* 663b28–29, *Pr. An* 25b14, 32b4–13.

can also be "by (hypothetical) necessity." Aristotle explains this idea in the *Prior Analytics*:

> ['The possible" means] in one sense that which comes to be for the most part
> and falls short of necessity, for example, that a human being turns grey or
> grows or wastes away, or in general what belongs by nature [*to pephukos*] (For
> this is not continually necessary, because a human being does not always
> exist, but if a human being exists it is, either by necessity or for the most
> part) (*Pr An* 32b5–10)

In this passage, Aristotle distinguishes the kind of necessity that applies
to eternal things, which cannot be otherwise, from that which applies to
living things, just as he did in *Metaphysics* 5.5. Although living things
"can be otherwise," so that nothing can belong to them "by necessity" in
one sense of the term, things can belong to them in another sense of "necessity" because of the nature they have as living things. What happens
according to this kind of "necessity" can also happen "for the most part."

Aristotle links "by nature," "for the most part," and "by necessity" in
Poetics 7, just as he does in the *Prior Analytics* passage just quoted In the
definition of the beginning, middle, and end (1450b27–31), the expression "by nature" (*pephuken*) links the two concepts of "by necessity" and
"for the most part": "The end   is that which is itself after something
else by nature, either by necessity or for the most part." Events that occur
"by necessity" or "for the most part" are, that is, events that occur "by
nature," in *Poetics* 7, just as is the case in *Prior Analytics* 32b5–10. Because
"for the most part" is equivalent to *to eikos* in *Poetics* 7,[13] Aristotle's expression "according to probability or necessity" in the *Poetics* refers to
things that happen by nature It is a formula like the others Aristotle uses
to refer to things that happen by nature· "always or for the most part"
(*Phy.* 198b34–36, *Rhet.* 1369a35–36), "by necessity or for the most part"
(*Pr. An.* 32b5–10), and "in all cases or for the most part" (*PA* 663b28–
29).

The events of the tragic plot occur "by nature," "for the most part," or
"by (hypothetical) necessity" because tragedy is a *sustasis*, like that of a
living thing, organized for the sake of an end. The nature of the tragic
sustasis, however, depends on human nature in two ways. First, the end
and function of tragedy is to produce certain effects in human beings.
Second, because tragedy imitates human action, the events that constitute
the tragic plot occur according to the necessity of *human* nature. According

[13] See above, n 3

to *Rhetoric* 1.10, human actions that are due to necessity are caused either by force or by nature (1368b32–36),[14] and what happens by nature happens "either always or for the most part" (1369a35–b2). Those human actions that are due to the necessity of nature surely include those that allow us to live in accord with our physical or "political" nature. In book 1 of the *Politics*, Aristotle makes it clear that the necessity of human nature leads, in the first place, to the reproductive union of male and female: "It is necessary, first, for those to couple who cannot exist without each other, for example, female and male for the sake of generation. And this is not by choice, but just as in other animals and plants, the striving to leave behind another such as oneself is natural" (1252a26–30).[15] From this primary association develop the household and the polis, something that exists by nature, as the end of human life. the polis "comes into being for the sake of living, and exists for the sake of living well. And so every polis exists by nature, if indeed the first communities do also. For it is the end of these, and nature is the end" (1252b29–32).

In Aristotle's view, then, many human actions are "necessary" in the first sense defined in *Metaphysics* 1015a20–23: "that without which . . . it is not possible to live . . and that without which it is not possible for the good to be or come to be." Actions that are necessary in this sense include activities that preserve the physical nature of humans, such as eating, drinking, sleeping, and reproducing. They also include activities, such as those that create and preserve "political" relationships, that are necessary for a good human life. All these activities are due to "nature" and "necessity," and are not, like the actions about which people deliberate (*Rhet* 1357a22–27), due to choice. As *Politics* 1252a26–30 states, coupling occurs by nature and not by choice. It is likely that Aristotle also considered acts done because of certain emotions to be "necessary," for he writes of acts due "to anger and other emotions that are necessary or natural to humans" (*EN* 1135b21–22).

Aristotle's views on tragedy make good sense if "necessity" in the *Poetics* is connected with human nature in this way. In *Poetics* 9, Aristotle defines the "universal" (*to katholou*) in terms of necessity or probability: "The universal is what kinds of things it happens that a certain kind of person says or does according to probability or necessity" (1451b8–9). The universal

---

[14] See Cope's note (*Introduction*, 218–33) on the discussion in *Rhet* 1 10 of the various causes of action Cf *EN* 1112a30–33, and the other passages cited by Grimaldi, *Rhetoric I*, on 1368b32–1369a2

[15] See also Plato, *Rep* 5 458d, who contrasts a "natural" or "erotic" necessity with a "geometric necessity"

with respect to human actions must concern, in the first place, what all human beings have in common if they function as human beings at all. The *Politics* tells us that to be human is to participate in *philia* and "political" relationships. A human being, in Aristotle's view, is essentially a "political animal," and being "political" begins with and is based on *philia* relationships. Any threat to these relationships is a threat to our humanity, and so best arouses pity and fear. It is no accident, then, that tragedy is concerned with *philia* relationships and with threats to them This general principle helps explain why the specific events that make up a tragic plot occur according to probability or necessity. Because *philia* relationships are necessary to human life, harm of *philos* by *philos* will by necessity lead to bad fortune, at least once it becomes known This is what happens in the plot of *Oedipus the King*. Moreover, because it is against human nature for *philos* to harm *philos* deliberately, recognition of *philia* will by necessity lead people to try to avert such a terrible event (*pathos*), so as to enjoy the good fortune that necessarily results from benefiting *philoi* and preserving (*sōtēria* 17.1455b12) them [16] This is what happens in *Iphigenia in Tauris*. In these two best plots, then, one event follows another by the necessity of human nature

Ēthos, the second most important of the six qualitative parts of tragedy, must also follow the principle of necessity or probability. "One should always seek either necessity or probability in the *ēthē* just as in the organization of the events, so that [one should represent] a person of a certain kind saying or doing things of a certain kind according to either necessity or probability, and this should come after that either by necessity or by probability" (1454a33–36). This requirement also is to be understood in terms of human nature. *ēthos* is an indication of the kinds of choices made by a human being with a certain *individual* nature in a given set of circumstances. Aristotle's definition of "the universal" in *Poetics* 9 includes this kind of necessity also. "a certain kind of person."[17]

What happens according to "necessity" in the *Poetics*, then, happens by (human) nature. Because things that happen by nature do not happen with

---

[16] The term *sōtēria*, used in *Po* 17 to refer to the final "rescue' in the Iphigenia plot, is frequently used in Greek literature of preservation of *philoi* See Blundell, *Helping*, 32–33

[17] Note, however, that "the universal" in *Po* 9, which includes the kind of necessity connected with *ēthos*, differs from "the universal" in the narrower sense of "plot,' that which the poet is said to "set out in universal form" (*ektithesthai katholou* 1455b1) in *Po* 17 In the plot outlines given as examples in *Po* 17, *ēthos* is omitted, for the choices Orestes makes are not included in the plot outline of 'the Iphigenia " However, his *philia* relationship to Iphigenia ("brother" 1455b6) is part of the universal that constitutes the plot

complete regularity, however, Aristotle frequently uses the expression "according to *probability or* necessity" in the *Poetics*, just as he uses expressions like "always or for the most part" in other works, to refer to what happens by nature "Necessity" in the *Poetics* also refers to what is forced or compelled, for the events of a tragic plot are constrained by certain unavoidable external circumstances In the plot of *Iphigenia in Tauris*, for example, Iphigenia is compelled to serve as priestess in a rite that includes human sacrifice These two aspects of "necessity" are, however, not really distinct in the *Poetics* one event of the plot causes another by the necessity of human nature, constrained by external circumstances

Although I have been discussing necessity in the *Poetics* in terms of Aristotle's philosophical views, his concept is far from narrowly philosophical It is in fact remarkably similar to the concept of necessity that Martin Ostwald attributes to Thucydides, in an account that makes him appear to be more poet than historian [18] Ostwald argues convincingly that the kind of necessity that leads, in Thucydides' history, to wars and other important human actions is produced by a combination of external factors and universal human motives, the most powerful of which are fear, prestige, and self-interest [19] The Peloponnesian War, for example, was made necessary by the growth of the Athenian empire, combined with the fear this produced in the Spartans "The Athenians   becoming great and causing fear in the Lacedaimonians made it necessary [*anagkasai*] for them to go to war "[20] Similarly, the Aristotelian tragic plot deals with the kind of necessity produced by the motivation proper to human nature (hypothetical necessity) in a given set of circumstances (force)

PLAUSIBILITY, PLOT, AND EPISODE

I have been translating *to eikos* as "probability" when it is used in conjunction with "necessity" to characterize the sequence of events that make up the plot structure In this context, *to eikos* refers to what happens "for the most part," and the entire phrase "according to the *eikos* or necessity" refers to what happens "by nature"—that is, always or for the most part While

[18] The view that Thucydides is more poet than historian is held, for example, by Sainte-Croix, History See also the description of Thucydides narrative technique given by J de Romilly, *Histoire et raison chez Thucydide*, 47–48 (quoted by Ostwald, *Anagkē*, 44)

[19] Ostwald, *Anagkē* Ostwald cites Thucydides 1 75 3 and 1 76 2 for the motives of fear, prestige, and self-interest (29)

[20] Thucydides 1 23 6, discussed ibid , 1–5

eikos in this sense is nearly always accompanied by "necessity," in one passage a variant of *eikos* alone is used to refer to what happens according to probability or necessity. At 9 1451b13, Aristotle writes of those "organizing the plot by means of *eikota* " Here, the *eikota* are the universal (*ta katholou*: 1451b7); they are what happens according to probability or necessity (1451b6–9).[21]

Another sense of *eikos*, however, is relevant to an understanding of certain other passages in the *Poetics* in which *eikos* occurs without "necessity." *Eikos* can mean "plausible" instead of "probable" when it is used to refer to what is *apparently* "for the most part." *Eikos* in this sense can refer to what is apparently true as opposed to what is really so This idea emerges from *Rhetoric* 1402b14–16. conclusions drawn from what is *eikos* are drawn from what is "for the most part, either really or apparently " The two senses of *eikos* are of course closely related, for things tend to be plausible and believable when they really happen "for the most part," that is, "according to probability." On the other hand, the unusual also occurs regularly. In two passages, the *Poetics* mentions the paradox that "it is *eikos* that some things should happen even contrary to the *eikos*" (1456a24–25, cf 1461b15). Here, Aristotle may be punning on the two senses of *eikos*. it is probable and plausible that some things should happen "contrary to probability."

Plausibility, whether expressed by *eikos* or by another term, such as *pithanon* (believable), is an important concept in Aristotle's theory of tragedy. Tragedians, Aristotle writes, keep the names of actual historical figures because "the possible is believable [*pithanon*], for we do not believe the things that have not happened to be possible, but it is clear that the things that have happened are possible" (9.1451b16–18) Ideally, events in a tragic plot are both possible and plausible, but plausibility is more important. At 1460a26–27 Aristotle writes that the poet "should choose impossible and *eikota* [plausible] things rather than possible and unbelievable [*apithana*] things." Here, *eikota* is a synonym for "believable." In a parallel passage, in fact, Aristotle uses "believable" (*pithanon*) instead of *eikota*: the poet should prefer "the believable and impossible" to the "unbelievable and possible" (1461b11–12).

The conceptual distinction between "plausibility" and "probability" is especially important for an understanding of Aristotle's views on plot and episode. While the events that make up the plot itself must be "probable

---

[21] This point is made by Heath, "Comedy," 351 n 28

[*eikos*] or necessary," those that make up the episodes need only be *eikos* in the sense of "plausible."

Aristotle sometimes uses the term "episode" in the technical sense of "act" between choral odes, one of the quantitative parts of tragedy. "Episode" in this sense is to be connected with the entrance (*epeisodion*) of an actor.[22] Aristotle also uses "episode" in another sense (or senses, as some believe), to contrast a certain part of tragedy or epic with the plot. "Episode" is used in this sense in *Poetics* 17.1455b1, where the poet is said to first set out stories in universal form, that is, to outline the plot, and then to "episodize" (*epeisodioun*: cf. 1455b13), and in *Poetics* 23 (1459a35–37), where the (epic) poet is said to "interrupt" (διαλαμβάνει) the poem with episodes. These uses of "episode" and cognates have aroused a great deal of controversy. Some take these episodes to be "nonessential added scenes." Others have argued that they have an essential role in the dramatic action, without, however, giving an adequate account of how the episodes can play this role and still be meaningfully distinct from the events of the plot.[23] Although Malcolm Heath falls into this second category, arguing that dramatic episodes are segments of the plot, his account of *epeisodioun* in *Poetics* 17 is very helpful. According to Heath, *epeisodioun* means to supply "circumstantial details appropriate to the persons involved."[24] This view is correct provided we stipulate that episodes are merely plausible, while the events of the plot itself are probable or necessary. A study of Aristotle's concepts of necessity, probability, and plausibility in connection with his statements about episodes and the episodic, in the *Poetics* and in other works, supports this view.

[22] On "episode" in this sense, see Nickau, "Epeisodion," 160, who cites *Po.* 12.1452b16, 12 1452b20, and 18.1456a31.

[23] "Non-essential added scenes" is Else's phrase, *Argument*, 326 n. 85. The view that episodes are "nonessential" was opposed by Gilbert, "*Epeisodion*," who takes "episode" to mean "any action that is a subordinate but necessary component of the integral action of the play" (64). Nickau (followed, in the main, by Friedrich, "*Epeisodion*," argues that the episodes are necessary to the whole, and that to "episodize" is to work out "the realization of *all* of the particulars of the action" ("die Ausführung *aller* Einzelheiten der Handlung": 163). Nickau's interpretation has the advantage of giving the episodes a real dramatic function and of taking into account Aristotle's statement that they should be "appropriate" (*oikeia*. 1455b13) It tends, however, to blur the distinction between plot and episode, and, as Nickau admits (165–66), it does not apply to *epeisodiōdeis* in 1451b33. Heath, *Poetics*, 101, who follows Nickau's account of "episode" in *Po.* 17, nevertheless has justified difficulties in reconciling this account with Aristotle's statement at 1459a35–37 that episodes "interrupt" the poem. On "episode," see also Heath, *Unity*, 49–55, who distinguishes between epic and dramatic episodes.

[24] Heath, *Unity*, 52.

The distinction between plot and episode is made in *Poetics* 17, where Aristotle writes that the poet should first "set out in universal form" (*ek-tithesthai katholou*: 1455b1; cf. *to katholou*: 1455b2) the Iphigenia story, and then "episodize" (*epeisodioun*: 1455b1, cf. 1455b12–13). In *Poetics* 17, *to katholou*, "the universal," is equivalent to *to muthos*, "the plot." This equivalence is indicated by Aristotle's definition of "the universal" in *Poetics* 9 in terms of "probability or necessity," the same principle that is said to govern the "organization of the events," or plot, in *Poetics* 7.[25] The universal is the entire sequence of necessary or probable events that constitute the tragic change from beginning to middle to end. It includes, but is not limited to, the three parts of the plot: *pathos*, recognition, and *peripeteia*. If this is the universal, it is reasonable to infer that the "episodes" that are opposed to it in *Poetics* 17 occur according to something less than probability or necessity. This view is confirmed by Aristotle's statement at 9.1451b33–35 that "episodic" (*epeisodiōdeis*) plots are those in which the "episodes" occur after one another, but not by probability or necessity.

Aristotle also uses the term "episodic" (*epeisodiōdēs*) in two passages in the *Metaphysics*. At 1075b37–1076a2, Aristotle criticizes those who give different first principles (*archai*) for different things because these people "make the being of the whole episodic, for nothing contributes [*sumballe-tai*] to anything else by being or not being." The same point is made at 1090b19–20, where, significantly, Aristotle compares nature to a tragedy: "It does not appear from the phenomena that nature is episodic, like a bad tragedy." In these passages, Aristotle denies that nature is "episodic," as it would be if there were many first principles, and if each thing did not "contribute" (*sumballetai*: 1076a2; cf. *sumballesthai*: 1090b15) to the others by its being. Because it is not in fact "episodic," but is governed by one first principle according to which everything contributes to everything else, nature, in Aristotle's view, is like a tragedy that imitates one whole action, whose parts cannot be changed or removed without making a difference to the whole (*Po.* 8.1451a30–35). A tragedy of this kind, like nature, is governed by one first principle (*archē*), its "soul" (6.1450a38–39), that is, by a plot in which events succeed one another according to necessity or probability. The *Metaphysics* passages, then, support the view that what is "episodic" lacks the kind of unity given by probability or necessity.

[25] The arguments of Dupont-Roc and Lallot, *Poétique*, 285–86, against this view are not convincing.

An episode can, however, be *eikos* in the sense of "plausible."[26] The distinction between necessary or probable plot and plausible episode can be best understood by looking at Aristotle's specific examples

In *Poetics* 17 (1455b3–12), Aristotle sets out "the universal" of "the Iphigenia," that is, the plot common to Euripides' and Polyidos's versions of the story (quoted in chapter 3). It is helpful to divide this plot outline into beginning, middle, and end.[27] The beginning is the situation from which the other events follow by necessity or probability, but which does not itself follow anything else in this way. The beginning of this plot consists in, first, the external circumstances that constrain the action of the story. a certain girl was supposedly sacrificed, but actually came to a foreign land, it is the law to sacrifice strangers to a goddess in this land, and the girl holds this priesthood (1455b3–8). Second, the arrival of the girl's brother (ἐλθών 1455b8) is part of the beginning, because it makes the following events necessary, but does not itself follow other events by probability or necessity. As we saw in chapter 3, the brother's purpose in going is excluded from the plot outline because this would be part of *ēthos* rather than plot. Aristotle also explicitly excludes from "the universal" anything that makes the beginning itself probable or necessary. the oracle of the god, he writes, is "outside the universal" (1455b7–8). If the arrival of the brother did follow anything else "by probability or necessity," it would, of course, not be a beginning. The arrival of the brother, we should note, is the only part of the beginning represented in the stage action in Euripides' play.

The beginning causes the events that constitute the middle to occur by necessity or probability. These events are the capture of the brother, his being about to be sacrificed by his sister, and the recognitions that occur together with *peripeteia*. The brother's arrival and the other circumstances that constitute the beginning lead by probability or necessity to his capture (ληφθείς) and to his being "about to be sacrificed" (θύεσθαι μέλλων. 1455b9) by his sister. It is the law to sacrifice foreigners, and the sister is compelled to be the instrument of this law. Moreover, because the brother believes his sister to be dead, he cannot suspect that the priestess is actually his sister. Furthermore, human nature, constrained by these circumstances, makes it probable or necessary that recognition will occur (ἀνεγνώ-

---

[26] According to Tsagarakis, Porphyry connects episodes with "the believable," a synonym for "the plausible" "Every episode is used by the poet for the sake of either the believable or the useful" (*Quaestionum Homericarum ad Iliadem {Odysseam} pertinentium reliquiae*, ed H Schrader, 30), quoted in Greek by Tsagarakis, "*Katachrēsis*," 305

[27] I discuss this plot outline in more detail in Belfiore, "Iphigenia '

ϱισεν. 1455b9). Given human nature, *philia* relationships are uppermost in the thoughts of a person who is about to die and who has time to reflect on this circumstance. The revelation of these thoughts, in a way that leads to recognition, is, then, probable or necessary, unless another event (which would be part of a different plot, and therefore of a different tragedy) occurs to prevent recognition. Although Aristotle does not explicitly mention a *peripeteia*, a "change to the opposite of the things done," in this plot outline, his statement at 1455b12 ("thence is salvation") shows that a *peripeteia* in fact takes place together with the recognition, for the recognition marks the beginning of the change to the good fortune of salvation. Indeed, recognition and reunion with *philoi* is itself good fortune. The *peripeteia* follows the recognition by probability or necessity, for *philoi* in such a situation will naturally, if they recognize one another, do all they can to avoid harming each other and to give aid instead

Finally, the events of the middle make the end, the good fortune of salvation, probable or necessary ("thence is salvation" 1455b12), for it is probable or necessary that people who do all they can to escape will succeed, if nothing prevents them—unless another event, which is not part of *this* plot, occurs to make another *peripeteia* necessary or probable.

These necessary or probable events that make up the plot are distinct from the episodes After outlining "the universal   of the Iphigenia," Aristotle writes (1455b12–15). "After this, adding[28] the names, [the poet should] 'episodize ' The episodes should be appropriate, for example, in the case of Orestes, the madness by means of which he was captured, and the salvation by means of the purification." These episodes are, as Heath writes, "circumstantial details appropriate to the persons involved."[29] That is, while the escape ("salvation") itself is part of the universal, the purification is a circumstance appropriate to Orestes the matricide, whose name has now been added. Similarly, the capture itself is part of the plot, while the madness by means of which it takes place is a circumstantial detail appropriate to Orestes, who is pursued by his mother's Furies.

[28] On ὑποθέντα, see chap 3, n 42

[29] Heath, *Unity*, 52 In Heath's view, οικεια means "appropriate to the *persons*" whose names are set down by the poet (1455b12–13) This view is also defended by Bywater, *Aristotle on the Art*, 246, Rostagni, *Poetica*, 101–2, and Else, *Argument*, 511 Others take οικεια to mean "appropriate to the story" D W Lucas, *Poetics*, on 1455b13, and Gudeman, *Aristoteles*, 311 Both views have some validity, for, while οικεια in this passage refers primarily to persons, the episodes, like the persons themselves, must be appropriate to a universal in which a certain kind of person says and does certain kinds of things according to probability or necessity (1451b8–9)

The particular means by which capture and salvation are brought about in the play are explicitly called episodes, but it is less clear what we are to make of Aristotle's two examples of ways in which recognition is brought about. Orestes "recognizes," or "makes himself known,"[30] Aristotle writes, "either as Euripides or as Polyidos wrote it, saying, as was *eikos*, that not only his sister but he also had to be sacrificed" (1455b9–11) Recognition itself is clearly part of the plot, but are these two ways of bringing about recognition part of the universal (the plot), or are they episodes?

Although these examples are included in the outline of the universal in such a way as to make them appear, at first, to be parts of it, there are some compelling objections to this view. There is, first, a logical objection. Aristotle calls his plot outline "the universal . . . of the Iphigenia" (1455b2–3). However, if the two mutually exclusive ways of bringing about recognition are both parts of a plot, they must be parts of two different plots (see 1451a30–35), and of two different universals.

A second objection to taking Aristotle's examples to be parts of the plot emerges from additional information given in *Poetics* 16. While the *Poetics* 17 outline mentions both Euripides and Polyidos, it stresses Polyidos's way of bringing about recognition, stating that it takes place by means of Orestes' speech. In *Poetics* 16 this same speech of Orestes is cited as an example of an inferior way of bringing about recognition. "by reasoning" (1455a4–8). *Poetics* 17 is not explicit enough about Euripides' way of bringing about recognition to allow us to be certain which of the two recognitions in the *Iphigenia in Tauris* he has in mind. that of Orestes by Iphigenia or that of Iphigenia by Orestes (both mentioned at 11. 1452b5–8). Of these, the recognition of Orestes by Iphigenia is placed in *Poetics* 16 in the inferior category of recognitions brought about by means of things "made up by the poet." Orestes is recognized because "he says what the poet, but not the plot, requires" (16. 1454b30–35). It is unlikely that these two inferior ways of bringing about recognition—Euripides' way of bringing about the recognition of Orestes by Iphigenia, and Polyidos's way of bringing about recognition "through reasoning"—form part of a probable or necessary plot structure, though they might well be episodes. However, the means by which Euripides brings about the recognition of Iphigenia by Orestes might be thought to form part of the plot. This way of bringing about the recognition, by means of the letters Iphigenia sends,

---

[30] The active form of the verb ἀνεγνώρισεν presents problems at 1455b9, as it does elsewhere in the *Poetics* See chap 5 ("Recognition"), esp n 61

is given as an example of the best way of bringing about recognition in
Poetics 16, one that comes "from the events themselves" (1455a16–19). If
"from the events themselves" means "by probability or necessity" in this
passage, Iphigenia's sending of the letters would be part of a probable or
necessary plot structure in *Poetics* 16.[31] Even so, however, we could not
conclude that the examples given in *Poetics* 17 are part of the plot, for there
Aristotle stresses Polyidos's inferior way of bringing about recognition "by
reasoning," which is opposed, in *Poetics* 16, to the way of bringing about
recognition "from the events themselves."

While there are serious objections to the view that the ways of bringing
about recognition cited in *Poetics* 17 form part of the plot, they can plausibly be seen as two episodes belonging to different versions by different
playwrights of the same Iphigenia plot.[32] Each is a particular method of
bringing about the same event (recognition) in the same plot, that is, in
the same tragedy (18.1456a7–9). The recognition itself follows by probability or necessity from Orestes' capture. However, the methods of bringing it about are plausible rather than necessary or probable, for different
episodes can and do bring about the same event equally well.[33] Moreover,
people in the circumstances in which Iphigenia and Orestes find themselves do not send letters or reason as Orestes does about their sisters "by
nature" or "for the most part," although both events are plausible in the
plays in which they occur.

Instead of being parts of the plot, Euripides' and Polyidos's ways of
bringing about recognition are episodes that supply circumstantial details
appropriate to Orestes and Iphigenia. In Euripides' *Iphigenia in Tauris*,
Iphigenia gives the letter to Orestes, saying:

> Tell Orestes, son of Agamemnon:
> "She who was slaughtered at Aulis sends this,
> living Iphigenia, but to those in Argos, dead."
>
> (769–71)

---

[31] The meaning of the phrase "from the events themselves" is discussed below.

[32] The identity of Polyidos is problematic, since he is called a sophist at 16.1455a6, and
we know of no tragedian of that name. However, as Else notes (*Argument*, 509–10), ἐποίη-
σεν ("made") in 1455b10 clearly marks him as a dramatist in *Po.* 17; cf. Gallavotti, *Aristotele*, 164.

[33] Nickau, "Epeisodion," 162, makes the point that other plausible episodes could also
have been used, but he does not see that this conflicts with his view that the episodes are
"necessary" ("nötig").

While these and other details given by Euripides' Iphigenia are appropriate to the individuals involved and to the story, they are not probable or necessary In Polyidos's version of the Iphigenia story, the recognition occurs because Orestes says that his sister was sacrificed, and it is his lot also to be sacrificed (*Po* 16 1455a8) This speech is appropriate to Orestes, for he alone has such a sister, but it is no more probable or necessary than another speech

If Aristotle's examples in *Poetics* 17 are of episodes that bring about the recognitions, *eikos*, when used of Orestes' speech at 1455b10, means "plausible" rather than "probable " It is suggestive (if not conclusive, for *eikos* alone means "probable or necessary" at 9 1451b13), that *eikos* at 1455b10 occurs without its frequent companion, "necessity " This same speech of Orestes is also said to be *eikos*, again without "necessity," at 16 1455a7 Moreover, Iphigenia's desire to send a letter to her brother is said to be *eikos* at 16 1455a18–19, and not "*eikos* or necessary "

Additional linguistic evidence also suggests that the Euripides and Polyidos examples are episodes Aristotle uses the word *dia* (by means of) in connection with what are explicitly called episodes in *Poetics* 17 "the madness by means of which [*di' hēs*] he was captured and the salvation by means of [*dia*] purification" (1455b14–15) Significantly, the different methods of bringing about recognition are also referred to throughout *Poetics* 16 as the "means by which" (*dia*) recognition is brought about At 1454b32 Iphigenia's letter is said to be "the means by which" (*dia*) she is recognized, and at 1455a16–19 Iphigenia's recognition by Orestes is said to be brought about "by means [*di'*] of *eikota* "[34] As Else points out, the discussion of recognition in *Poetics* 16 "adds nothing on the connection of *anagnorisis* [recognition] with the structure of the complex plot or on its emotional function, but limits itself strictly to studying the *techniques* of recognition," "the *methods* for the recognition of persons "[35] The word *dia* in *Poetics* 16, then, is used to refer to the methods of bringing about recognition, just as it is used in *Poetics* 17 to refer to the methods of bringing about capture and salvation that are explicitly called episodes These methods of bringing about recognition can plausibly be seen as different ways of supplying appropriate circumstantial details This is true of even the best method of bringing about recognition, that "from the events

[34] The word *dia* is also used in this way at 16 1454b21, 1454b25, 1454b26, 1454b32, and 1454b37
[35] Else, *Argument*, 484 (emphasis in original)

themselves" (1455a16–19). The recognition itself is a part of the plot that comes about "from the organization itself of the plot . . . either by necessity or according to probability" (1452a18–20). The best method of bringing about the recognition, however, does not come about in this way, but "from the events themselves . . by means of plausible things [*di' eikotōn*]" (1455a16–17). That is, the best method of bringing about recognition is an "appropriate" episode (1455b13) in which the persons involved say what the plot requires (see 1454b34–35)

The same distinction between necessary or probable plot and plausible episode can be applied to Aristotle's outline (17. 1455b16–23, quoted in chapter 3) of the "story" (*logos*) of the *Odyssey*—that is, its plot [36] What belongs to the plot, the probable or necessary sequence of events, is (1) the beginning. a man's return home after a long absence to find suitors threatening his household; (2) the middle: the recognitions (e.g., Odysseus's recognition by Telemachus, the Nurse, and Penelope), and his attack on the suitors, and (3) the end. his salvation from the dangers that surround him at home, and the suitors' destruction. "The rest is episode." Among the episodes are the ways in which the recognitions are brought about (for example, the tokens of the scar and the bed), and the way in which salvation is achieved (the bow, the locking up of the suitors) These episodes are plausible, but they are not necessary or probable.

The foregoing analysis of plot and episode illuminates Aristotle's account of the complication and the solution. These views are integral to his theory of plot structure.[37] After distinguishing plot and episode in *Poetics* 17, Aristotle discusses in *Poetics* 18 the division of the plot into the complication and the solution. Like the beginning, middle, and end, the *desis* (complication) and the *lusis* (solution) are divisions of the probable and necessary sequence of events that make up the plot. Their importance is apparent from Aristotle's statement (1456a7–9) that the same tragedy is one that has the same plot, that is, the same "tying up" (*plokē*, here used as an equivalent of "complication"), and solution Aristotle defines "complication" and "solution" at the beginning of *Poetics* 18

Of every tragedy one [part] is the complication and the other the solution The things outside [*exōthen*] and often some of those inside are the compli-

[36] Kassel, *De arte poetica* ("Index Graecus, s v λογος) correctly notes that λογος (story) is equivalent to μῦθος (plot) at 1455b17 Dupont-Roc and Lallot, *Poétique*, incorrectly distinguish the two (180, 286)
[37] Pace Else, *Argument*, 517–22

cation; the rest is the solution. By "complication" I mean the [tragedy] from the beginning until the last part from which it changes to good or bad fortune. By "solution" I mean the [tragedy] from the beginning of the change until the end. Just as in the *Lynceus* of Theodectus, the complication consists in the things done before [*ta propepragmena*] and the capture of the child and again the [   ] of them. The solution is that part from the accusation of murder until the end. (1455b24–32)

This passage presents a number of problems. Even if the textual difficulty at 1455b31 could be resolved, Aristotle's example would be of limited usefulness in the absence of Theodectes' *Lynceus*.[38] A more tractable difficulty concerns the meaning of "the things done before" (*ta propepragmena*: 1455b30) and the things "outside" (1455b25). Both the "things done before" and the things "outside" are said to be part of the complication, and it is reasonable to suppose that these expressions refer to the same events. However, because these events are part of the complication, and therefore part of the plot, they cannot be "outside" in the same sense as that in which the oracle in the Iphigenia story in *Poetics* 17 is "outside" (1455b7–8), for the oracle is "outside" "the universal" and "the plot"; that is, it is not part of the plot.[39] Instead, the "things done before" and those "outside" the plot in *Poetics* 18 must be events such as the sacrifice at Aulis and Iphigenia's settlement in a foreign land, which are mentioned in the outline of the Iphigenia plot. These are "outside" the action represented on stage, but they are part of the beginning of the plot, because the other events follow them by necessity or probability.

In spite of these difficulties, it is not hard to use Aristotle's unusually clear definitions of "complication" and "solution" in analyzing specific plays. The complication includes at least some of the beginning, and the solution includes the end, of the plot. How much of the beginning and middle are part of the complication and how much part of the solution will vary a great deal from play to play, but will depend in part on whether

[38] The reading δήλωσις, preserved by the Arabic translation and favored by Else, *Argument* (521), Gudeman, *Aristoteles*, and Janko, *Poetics I*, is a promising way of filling the gap. Kassel, *De arte poetica*, does not explain why he finds the testimony of the translation "incertissimum." For some speculative reconstructions of the *Lynceus*, see Else, *Argument*, 521–22, and Xanthakis-Karamanos, *Studies*, 53–54.

[39] Aristotle's use of the term "outside" (*exō*) is confusing. He also uses it at 1460a29, writing that Oedipus's ignorance of how Laius died is *exō tou mutheumatos*. This must mean much what it does at 1455b7–8. not a part of the plot at all. *Exō (tēs tragōdias, tou dramatos)* at 1454b3 and 1454b7 has this sense also.

the plot is complex (having recognition, *peripeteia*, or both) or simple (lacking both). In a simple plot, the action moves continuously in one direction, that of the change Accordingly, the beginning of the change, the point at which the solution begins, will be either in the "things done before," which are "outside" the action represented on stage, or in that part of the beginning that is represented on stage in tragedy or narrated in epic For example, in the *Iliad*, which has a simple plot (1459b14), the beginning of the change is the quarrel in book 1 between Agamemnon and Achilles Everything after this is the solution In a complex plot, on the other hand, a change in direction is marked by *peripeteia*, recognition, or both, and the solution will begin at this point In this case, the solution begins somewhere in the middle of the play In Sophocles' *Oedipus the King*, the "beginning of the change," the point "from which it changes" (ἐξ οὗ μεταβαίνει 1455b27) to bad fortune, occurs in the scene where the Corinthian messenger sets in motion the events that make recognition and bad fortune probable or necessary Aristotle in fact tells us (11 1452a22–26) that a *peripeteia*, a "change to the opposite," takes place in this scene While *peripeteia* is not itself the tragic change, as I will argue in chapter 5, it often marks the beginning of this change

In the Iphigenia plot, as in that of the *Oedipus*, the solution begins at that point in the play at which *peripeteia* and recognition coincide [40] Until the recognition, Orestes appears to be headed toward bad fortune, and just before the recognition, in Aristotle's plot outline, he is said to be "about to be sacrificed " Aristotle explicitly indicates the beginning of the change in this plot, stating "thence [sc , from the recognition] is salvation" (ἐντεῦθεν ἡ σωτηρία 1455b12) This recognition is the beginning of the solution, the point "from which it changes" (ἐξ οὗ μεταβαινει 1455b27) Aristotle's outline of the *Odyssey* plot also suggests that the solution coincides with a recognition "being recognized by some and attacking, he himself was saved" (1455b21–22)

The solution, then, follows by necessity or probability from the complication, just as the events of the plot that make up the middle and end follow from the preceding events by necessity or probability The complication-solution division, however, is not simply a logical one, as is the beginning-middle-end division It marks the structural and emotional fo-

---

[40] Pace Else, who locates the beginning of the solution in both plays in or just after the prologue (*Argument*, 520), and Bywater (*Aristotle on the Art*, 248) who, without explanation, locates that of the *Iphigenia* at line 391, and that of the *Oedipus* in the opening scene On this point, see further below, chap 5 (*Peripeteia*), esp n 40

cal point of the tragedy, the height of good fortune or the depth of bad fortune from which the tragic change begins.[41]

This concludes the study of Aristotle's views on the plot as a whole. The plot is a necessary or probable sequence of events, and it is distinct from both *ēthos* and episode. I have argued that actions that occur "according to probability [*to eikos*] or necessity" are those that occur "for the most part" and according to a "hypothetical necessity," or because of compulsion. They do not occur according to the kind of necessity that characterizes things that "cannot be otherwise." Necessary human actions are those that occur according to the necessity of human nature, constrained by external circumstances. I have also argued that *eikos* sometimes means "plausible" rather than "probable" in the *Poetics*. In particular, episodes are not "probable (*eikos*) or necessary," as are the events of the plot, but merely "plausible" (*eikos*), for other episodes could bring about the events of the plot equally well.

It is now time to look more closely at the three parts of the plot: *pathos*, recognition, and *peripeteia*. In the first section of chapter 5 these parts will be studied individually, while the second section will consider how these parts help, in combination, to produce different kinds of plots.

[41] In *Po*. 15.1454a37-b2, the term *lusis* does not have the technical sense of part of a tragedy, but instead has its ordinary sense of "solution of difficulties," the meaning it has in *Po*. 25 (1460b6). At 1454a37-b2, Aristotle writes "It is clear that the *luseis* of plots should come about from the plot itself, and not, as in the *Medea*, from the machine, and in the *Iliad* the things concerning the sailing away." *Lusis* in the technical sense of the part of tragedy from the beginning of the change until the end is not introduced until *Po*. 18 Moreover, the technical sense would not be appropriate in *Po*. 15 Here, Aristotle states that the *lusis* should come about "from" (*ex*) the plot itself and not "from" (*apo*) the machine, as it does in the *Medea*. However, the machine is used to allow Medea to escape after she has taken vengeance on Jason, and not at the beginning of the change, which occurs when Creon grants Medea a day's grace. In Aristotle's other example of an improperly contrived *lusis*, the sailing away in *Il* 2 has nothing at all to do with the beginning of the change. The machine of the *Medea* is, however, a *lusis* in the sense of a solution of difficulties in the story This is also true of the intervention of Athena, used in *Il*. 2 to stop the Greeks from running away. In each case, the plot has reached an impasse that is resolved not by probability or necessity but by divine intervention

131

* CHAPTER 5 *

Parts and Wholes

THE PARTS OF THE PLOT

*P*OETICS 11 (1452b9–13) tells us that there are three parts of a tragic plot. *pathos* (a destructive or painful action), *peripeteia* (reversal), and recognition. All plots, both simple and complex, have a *pathos*,[1] while only complex plots have *peripeteia*, recognition, or both (10.1452a14–18). In order to understand Aristotle's views on *pathos*, *peripeteia*, and recognition, it is essential, in the first place, to understand their role as parts of the organized structure of the plot that contribute to its function. the production of pleasure and katharsis from pity and fear.

The plot arouses pity and fear because, first, it is a movement or change, (*metaballein*. 1451a14, *metabasis* 1452a16) between the end points of good and bad fortune, according to probability or necessity. This change as a whole arouses pity and fear, and each of the parts of the plot contributes in its own way to this function. A *pathos* arouses fear and pity because, as a destructive or painful action, it obviously involves bad fortune Recognition and *peripeteia* also arouse pity and fear because they lead to good or bad fortune: "This kind of recognition and *peripeteia* will have either pity or fear . . . since bad and good fortune will also follow from these kinds of things" (1452a38–b3).

The plot and its parts also arouse pity and fear because they represent unexpected suffering. After discussing, in *Poetics* 7–9, the principle of probability or necessity that governs the plot, Aristotle introduces this new topic at the end of *Poetics* 9: "Since the imitation is not only of a complete action, but also of fearful and pitiable things, these things come to be most of all when they come to be contrary to expectation, because of one another" (*para tēn doxan di' allēla*. 1452a1–4). Things that happen "because of one another" happen according to the principle of probability or necessity discussed in *Poetics* 7–9. "Contrary to expectation," on the other hand, introduces a new idea that will be important in the discussion

---

[1] This is clear from Aristotle s unqualified statement at 1452b9–10 that *pathos* is one of the three parts of the plot, and from his exhaustive (1453b36) classification in *Po* 14 of plots according to the kind of *pathos* they have

of *peripeteia* and recognition in *Poetics* 10 and 11. Before we can understand the role of the unexpected in the arousal of pity and fear, however, we must explore what Aristotle means by "contrary to expectation."

According to some commentators, the unexpected is simply a "surprise."[2] But Aristotle surely has something more significant and more specific in mind than a mere "surprise." In the *Rhetoric*, he also discusses the role of the unexpected in arousing emotion:

> When it is better for people to be afraid, it is necessary [sc , for the rhetorician] to put them in such a state [as to believe] that they are such as to suffer, for others who are greater have also suffered And [it is necessary] to show people who are like [those in the audience] suffering or having suffered, and by means of those from whom they did not think [to suffer] this, and things they did not think to suffer, and at a time when they did not think to suffer (2.5.1383a8–12)

Pity, like fear, is aroused by sufferings from an unexpected source. it is pitiable for "some evil to come whence it was fitting for one to get something good" (*Rhet.* 2.8.1386a11–12).[3] According to the *Rhetoric*, fear and pity are aroused at the spectacle of the sufferings of those who do not themselves expect to suffer as they do, and whose objective situation also makes their suffering unlikely, in the opinion of others. This concept of "the unexpected" helps us understand Aristotle's views in the *Poetics*. The best agents of the dramatic action, discussed in *Poetics* 13 and 14, suffer unexpectedly in just the ways mentioned in the *Rhetoric*. They do not deserve to suffer in part because they are at the height of good fortune and good reputation (*Po.* 13.1453a10),[4] that is, they suffer "things they did not think to suffer, and at a time when they did not think to suffer," because good fortune seemed assured. Moreover, when they suffer at the hands of their own *philoi* (*Po.* 14.1453b19–22), they suffer "by means of those from whom they did not think to suffer." Sufferings of this kind arouse pity, and they arouse fear because they show us that, since even those who appear least likely to suffer in fact do suffer, we also, a fortiori, are likely to suffer.[5]

---

[2] The word "surprise" is used, for example, by Golden-Hardison, *Aristotle's Poetics*, 163, D W Lucas, *Poetics*, 133, and Bywater, *Aristotle on the Art*, on 1452a3

[3] This passage is cited by Bywater, *Aristotle on the Art*, 223, on 1453b18, who notes that harm by *philoi* is least expected and most pitiable Other relevant passages were quoted in chap 3 ("Problems") *Rhet* 1382b35–1383a1, 1385b22–23

[4] See chap 3 ("Problems ') on this view of unmerited suffering (*ton anaxion dustuchounta*)

[5] These ideas are discussed in more detail in chap 7 ("Tragedy and Rhetoric ')

Thus, Aristotle's statement that pity and fear are aroused when events occur "contrary to expectation because of one another" sums up two fundamental principles in the *Poetics*. The tragic plot as a whole and each of its parts individually arouse pity and fear at the suffering, according to probability or necessity, of someone in circumstances in which this is least to be expected. The best tragic *pathos* arouses pity and fear because it is an action in which *philos* harms *philos* (14 1453b14–22), and *philoi* are those who are least expected to harm one another. As we will see, recognition and *peripeteia* also arouse pity and fear because they occur "contrary to expectation," because of other events. Thus, all three parts of the plot contribute to the lesson tragedy teaches the audience. that human suffering is in fact likely even when it appears unexpected These two principles must be kept in mind throughout this chapter, as I first examine each of the three parts separately and then (in "Good and Bad Plots") study how the three parts work in combination to make good or bad plots

Pathos

Aristotle's views on the tragic *pathos* have suffered undeserved neglect by scholars. Rees's comment, made in 1972, that *pathos* had received very little attention in the scholarly literature is still pertinent today [6] For example, Dupont-Roc and Lallot characterize the *pathos*, in the single paragraph they devote to it, as "a sort of intrusion of spectacle into the story,"[7] and Halliwell remarks that "*pathos* in itself is of minor importance."[8] Correctly understood, however, the *pathos* is centrally important to Aristotle's theory of tragedy. That this is so is apparent not only because *pathos* is part of every plot, simple and complex, but also from Aristotle's account of comedy. While the tragic *pathos* is "a destructive or painful event," comedy deals with just the opposite "the laughable," that is, "an error and ugliness that is painless and not destructive" (1449a35) [9]

Aristotle defines *pathos* in *Poetics* 11.1452b11–13 "The *pathos* is a destructive or painful action [*praxis*], for example, deaths in the open, great pain, and wounds, and all things of this kind." The definition tells us,

---

[6] Rees, "*Pathos*," 1–3 Since Rees, the most helpful discussion of *pathos* is that of Moles, "Notes, 82–87

[7] Dupont-Roc and Lallot, *Poétique*, 234

[8] Halliwell, *Aristotle's Poetics*, 223 n 30 See also *Poetics of Aristotle*, 120, where Halliwell disagrees with Vickers's view (*Tragedy*, 60), that *pathos* is "indispensable " (Halliwell neglects to mention that Vickers is quoting Else, *Argument*, 229)

[9] On this distinction between comedy and tragedy, see Heath, "Comedy,' 352–53

first, that a *pathos* is a *praxis*, one of the *pragmata* (events) that make up the plot, the "organization of the events" (*sustasis pragmatōn*) [10] This means that a *pathos* is not a "scene of suffering," as some have argued [11] The definition also tells us that the *pathos* is a (physically) painful or destructive event As such, it must arouse pity and fear Aristotle uses vocabulary similar to that of the *Poetics* 11 definition of *pathos* when he defines fear as "pain or disturbance [resulting] from the expectation of an imminent destructive or painful evil" (*Rhet* 2 5 1382a21–22), and pity as "pain at an apparent destructive or painful evil   when it appears near" (2 8 1385b13–16) The appearance of an imminent (*mellōn* 1453b18) destructive or painful evil (a *pathos*) arouses pity and fear in tragedy, as it does in real life

It is difficult to say whether a tragedy can have more than one *pathos*, as it can have more than one recognition (e g , 1452a7–8 "another recognition") While many tragedies do in fact have several destructive or painful events, Aristotle's examples in *Poetics* 14 suggest that, in most cases, only one *pathos* is of such central importance to the plot as to count as one of its three parts For example, in Euripides' *Medea*, the deaths of Creon and his daughter are destructive and painful events, but Aristotle considers only Medea's murder of her children in classifying this play as one in which someone acts with knowledge (1453b28–29) The example of Haimon's attempted murder of Creon in Sophocles' *Antigone* (1453b37–1454a2) further complicates the issue The context leads us to believe that this is a central *pathos*, like Medea's child-murder Yet this event is not actually of great importance in the play, moreover, Aristotle remarks that this kind of plot is "without *pathos* "[12] We may tentatively conclude, then, that while a tragedy can have several destructive or painful events in its episodes, in most cases there is only one centrally important *pathos* that is one of the three parts of the plot

One major problem in Aristotle's brief discussion of *pathos* in *Poetics* 11 is the meaning of the phrase ἐν τῷ φανερῷ θάνατοι "deaths in the open" (1452b12) Rees argues convincingly that this refers not only to events that take place on stage, but also to deaths that take place offstage and are then visually presented to the audience by means of the *ekkuklēma*, the

---

[10] This is one of the few instances in the *Poetics* in which *praxis* is used to refer to an event in the plot, instead of to an action imitated by the plot It is used here as the singular of *pragmata* See chap 3, n 2

[11] ' Scene of suffering is Butcher s translation (*Aristotle's Theory*) Cf Bremer, *Hamartia*, 6–7 (quoted by Rees, *Pathos*, 2)

[12] On this passage, see further below, this subsection

theatrical machine used to display interior scenes.[13] While in Rees's view, deaths vividly described by messengers and others are not included among events "in the open" (10), there are nevertheless good reasons for including such events. A death described by a messenger is brought "before the eyes" and made so "vivid" (ἐναργής) by means of language that it also is "in the open."

Several passages in the *Rhetoric* and the *Poetics* support the view that "in the open" means "before the eyes" or "vivid" in a primarily rhetorical, rather than literal, sense. In *Rhetoric* 2.8, Aristotle discusses the use of dramatic techniques to enhance emotional arousal: "Of necessity, those who contribute to the effect with gestures, and voice, and appearance,[14] and the actor's art generally are more pitiable. For they make the evil appear near by placing it before our eyes" (1386a31–34). Language as well as visual effects can place things "before the eyes." In *Rhetoric* 3.11.1411b21–26, Aristotle states that metaphors place things "before the eyes" and explains that this means to make them "vivid." *Poetics* 17.1455a22–25 holds a view similar to that of *Rhetoric* 2.8, stating that the poet "should organize plots and contribute to the effect with speech, placing [the events] as much as possible before his eyes," so that he might see them "most vividly," and "as though he himself were in the presence of the things done." In these passages, something that happens "before the eyes" is, as Cope notes, "a vivid, graphic, striking representation."[15] Moreover, when things happen "before our eyes" they "appear near" (*Rhet.* 2.8.1386a31–34), and events that "appear near" or "imminent" arouse fear (1382a21–22) and pity (1385b13–16). In the *Poetics* also, things that are "imminent" or "about to occur" (*mellon*: 1453b18) arouse pity and fear. The poet, like the rhetorician, can arouse pity and fear by placing evils "before the eyes," thus making them "appear near." The descriptions of deaths given by messengers in tragedy are in fact vivid representations in words that arouse pity and fear by placing evils "before the eyes" of the audience and making them "appear near." They are "in the open" not because they are presented to the audience visually, but because they are brought vividly "before the eyes" by means of words.[16] Events "in the

[13] Rees, "*Pathos*," 9, who indicates that he is following a suggestion of Gudeman, *Aristoteles*, 227ff Rees gives a good survey of the controversy about the meaning of "in the open," 6–11

[14] Reading αἰσθήσει, with Kassel, *Ars rhetorica*

[15] Cope, *Rhetoric* 2 105, citing these parallel passages in the *Rhetoric* and the *Poetics* See also Eden, *Fiction*, 71–73

[16] Note the conjunction of "in the open" and "in the eyes" at *Rhet* 2 6 1384a35, and of "open" and "vivid" at *EN* 1095a22

open," then, are those vividly presented to us, whether directly on stage, or indirectly by speech, so as to appear near or imminent and thus arouse fear and pity. The murder of Laius in Sophocles' *Oedipus* is a death "in the open" in this sense, even though it takes place before the action represented on stage. It is vividly described by Oedipus himself at 798–813.

The best tragic *pathos* is not an event that is merely (physically) destructive or painful, as the definition in *Poetics* 11 might lead us to believe. In *Poetics* 14, Aristotle begins the discussion of good and bad plots by asking "which occurrences appear terrible or pitiable" (1453b14–15), and he goes on to say that actions in which enemies or neutrals harm one another do not arouse pity and fear "except in respect to the *pathos* itself" (1453b18). Here, *pathos* refers to a (physically) painful or destructive event, especially a death (1453b19–22), just as it did in *Poetics* 11. Here, however, Aristotle states that a *pathos* that is *merely* painful or destructive does not best arouse tragic pity and fear. These emotions are best aroused when the *pathos* takes place between *philoi*. In chapter 2, I presented reasons why Aristotle would want to add this qualification. Because *philia* is essential to our identity as humans, a *pathos* between *philoi* is especially terrible and pitiable. Moreover, while a *pathos* between *philoi* necessarily leads to unqualified bad fortune, one between enemies may lead to a heroic end, in which death is mitigated by glory (*kleos*). This is true in Euripides' *Alcestis*, for example, where enemy (Death) harms enemy (Alcestis), who, however, gains *kleos* and saves her household.[17]

Aristotle's statement that the best *pathos* is one between *philoi* also has important implications for his views on the development of tragedy, and on the distinction between the genres of tragedy and epic. While harm of *philos* by *philos* is a common theme in the extant tragedies, epic deals with *pathē* among such enemies as Achilles and Hector, or Odysseus and the suitors.[18] This difference appears significant when we remember that tragedy developed from epic (*Po.* 4, especially 1449a2–5). Aristotle's remarks in *Poetics* 13 and 14 also indicate that use of the best *pathos* occurs late in the development of tragedy. "At first," writes Aristotle, "poets told any chance stories, but now the best tragedies are composed about few houses, [those in which people] happened to suffer or do terrible things" (13.1453a17–22). These "few houses" include those of Oedipus and Orestes (1453a20), in which *philos* harmed *philos*. Again, at 14.1454a10–13,

---

[17] On Alcestis's glory as a perfect victim, and her desire to save her household, see Burnett, *Catastrophe*, 22–37.

[18] This difference between tragedy and epic is noted by Seaford, "Sacrifice," 87–88. On the theme of *philos* harming *philos* in Greek tragedy, see chap. 2 ("*Philia*").

Aristotle writes that chance discoveries were responsible for finding out which plots are best, and that poets "are compelled to have recourse to those houses in which these kinds of *pathē* occurred." These best *pathē* were said earlier in *Poetics* 14 to be those in which *philos* harms *philos*.

Aristotle's remarks about the function of tragedy and epic support the view that tragedy developed into a genre distinct from epic in part because it discovered how *pathos* can best arouse pity and fear. Tragedy and epic both have the function of producing pleasure from pity and fear, but tragedy accomplishes it better. If tragedy is superior to epic, Aristotle writes, in accomplishing "the function of the craft (for they [sc., tragedy and epic] should not produce any chance pleasure, but that which has been stated), it is clear that [tragedy] will be superior and achieve its end more than epic" (26.1462b12–15). The reference ("that which has been stated") is to *Poetics* 14.1453b10–14: "One should not seek [to produce] every kind of pleasure from tragedy, but that which is proper to it. Since the poet should produce pleasure from pity and fear by means of imitation, it is clear that this should be put into the events." This passage immediately precedes Aristotle's statement that a *pathos* in which *philos* harms *philos* best arouses pity and fear.

Poetics 14 not only tells us that the best *pathos* is one in which *philos* harms *philos*; it also states that an action need not actually occur to count as a *pathos*.[19] It may instead be only *mellon*, "about to occur": "When the *pathē* come about within *philia* relationships, for example [when] son kills or is about to kill mother . . ." (1453b19–21; cf. "neither acting nor about to act": 1453b17–18). In fact, a *pathos* that does not actually occur would appear preferable, at least in some respects, for Aristotle says the best plot is one like that of Euripides' *Iphigenia in Tauris*, in which sister is about to kill brother, but does not do so because recognition intervenes (1454a4–9). It is easy to see why a *pathos* that is only "about to occur" arouses pity and fear as well as, or even better than, a *pathos* that does occur.[20] Fear is aroused by the expectation of a destructive or painful evil that is *mellon* (imminent or about to occur: *Rhet.* 2.5.1382a21–22), and pity is aroused when an evil "appears near" (2.8.1385b13–16).

It is, however, more difficult to reconcile the idea that an action need not actually occur to count as a *pathos* with Aristotle's statements later in *Poetics* 14 (1453b37–1454a2). Aristotle condemns the plot in which some-

---

[19] This point is made by Bremer, *Hamartia*, 7.

[20] Moles, "Notes," 86, discusses this issue. See also Stinton, "*Hamartia*," 253–54, and the other works cited by Moles, 84 n. 1.

one is "about to" (*mellēsai*) act with knowledge and then does not act as "revolting" (*miaron*) and "not tragic," for, he writes, it is "without *pathos*" (*apathes*: 1453b39). Aristotle's example is Sophocles' *Antigone*, in which Haimon attempts to strike his father Creon but misses. In this passage, Aristotle appears to be saying that an action that is only "about to occur," but that does not occur, is not a *pathos* at all. Aristotle's two accounts of an action that is about to occur cannot be entirely reconciled. Nevertheless, Aristotle's views on this subject become clearer if we focus on a crucial difference between the action in the *Iphigenia in Tauris* that is "about to occur" and that of Haimon in the *Antigone*.

In the *Iphigenia*, sister is about to put brother to death, but does not do so because she recognizes him. In the *Antigone*, on the other hand, son is about to kill father, with knowledge of what he is about to do, but he does not do this deed; instead, in Sophocles' play, he draws his sword and misses (ἤμπλακ': 1234). In the *Iphigenia* plot, recognition prevents the occurrence of an action by necessity or probability, for a *philos* who recognizes a *philos* will, by necessity or probability, give aid instead of harming. In the *Antigone*, however, chance alone prevents the murder from occurring, and something that is prevented from occurring by mere chance cannot be part of the probable or necessary sequence of events that make up the tragic plot.[21]

Aristotle's distinction between what will occur (*to esomenon*) and what is about to occur (*to mellon*) in *On Divination in Sleep* illuminates why this is so:

> That many dreams have no fulfilment is not strange, for it is so too with many bodily symptoms and weather-signs, e.g., those of rain or wind. For if another movement occurs more influential than that from which, while the event [is] still future [*mellousēs*], the given sign was derived, the event does not take place. So, of the things which ought to be accomplished by human agency, many, though well-planned, are by the operation of other principles [*archas*] more powerful brought to nought. For, speaking generally, that which was going to happen [*to esomenon*] is not in every case what now is happening; nor is that which will in fact happen identical with that which is going to happen [*to mellon*]. Still, however, we must hold that the beginnings from which, as we said, no consummation follows, are indeed

[21] Cf. Moles, "Notes," 87, who writes that in the *Iphigenia* plot, "the *pathos* at least seems to be a real possibility, whereas in the case of the former [sc., the *Antigone*], though the idea of the *pathos* is indeed broached, nothing is made of it—there is no tension, and the agent simply fails to carry his plan out."

beginnings [*archas*], and these constitute natural signs of certain events, even though the events do not come to pass (*On Divination in Sleep* 463b22–31)[22]

In this passage, "natural signs" indicate what "is about to occur" (*to mellon*), even though that of which they are signs will not occur if a more powerful movement, something other than chance, prevents this Aristotle's view that signs are "beginnings" (*archai*) for things that are ' about to occur," but that will not occur if prevented by a more powerful movement, is of particular interest in connection with tragedy In *Poetics* 7, Aristotle defines a "beginning" (*archē*) as something after which "something else by nature is or comes to be" (1450b27–28) A beginning is something after which something else occurs by probability or by (hypothetical) necessity It is reasonable to suppose, then, that an event in tragedy that does not in fact take place really is "about to occur' if it would have followed from another event (its "beginning") by probability or necessity had it not been prevented from occurring by a more powerful force This interpretation of "about to occur" is supported by *Rhetoric* 2 19 1392b24–1393a5, where Aristotle connects what is "about to occur" with what is *eikos*, necessary, or "for the most part "

The sacrifice of brother by sister in the *Iphigenia in Tauris* is ' about to occur" because the events that precede the sacrifice make this probable or necessary unless something more powerful intervenes Recognition is a more powerful force of this kind, for it is more probable that sister will aid brother than that priestess will sacrifice victim On the other hand, when mere chance prevents the occurrence of a *pathos* in which *philos* knowingly harms *philos*, this event is not really "about to occur " If such a *pathos* can be prevented by mere chance, and not by a more powerful force, its actual occurrence would also have been due to chance and not to probability or necessity This kind of action is certainly the worst kind for tragedy It is "revolting" (*miaron*) for *philos* knowingly to threaten *philos* Moreover, something that is not really "about to happen" does not effectively arouse pity and fear In the *Iphigenia* plot, then, imminent evil is averted, in the *Antigone*, however, the appearance itself of imminent evil turns out to be deceptive This explains why Aristotle says that Haimon's thwarted attack is "without *pathos* "

While Aristotle's use of the terms *mellēsai*, *pathos*, and *apathes* in *Poetics* 14 is undeniably problematic, a good account can be given of why he praises one kind of plot in which someone is about to act but does not do

---

[22] Translation by J I Beare in Barnes, *Oxford Translation*, bracketed words added Cf *GC* 2 337b3–9

so, while condemning another kind of plot in which this also happens. This account gives us reason to believe that an action in a tragedy is a *pathos* when it really is about to occur, by probability or necessity, but is prevented by recognition.

The preceding analysis also implies that, in *Poetics* 14, *mellein*, "to be about to," should not be translated as "to intend," as is often done.[23] Intentions can and do enter into an account of what it means for an event to be "about to occur." For example, since human actions are in part defined by the intentions of the agent, things that are "well planned" (as in the *On Divination in Sleep* passage quoted above) are also "about to occur" in the relevant sense. Nevertheless, in the *Poetics* action is distinct from *ēthos*, so it is not always possible to tell what someone's choices, motives, or intentions are. "To intend" is seriously misleading, since it imports an alien psychological emphasis into the *Poetics*.

Peripeteia

Since the best tragic plot—the "complex" plot—has recognition, *peripeteia*, or both, *peripeteia* is of obvious importance in Aristotle's theory of drama.[24] It has, however, received relatively little attention from scholars, and discussion of it has often been hampered by a lack of clarity about basic concepts. Specifically, the long-standing debate about whether *peripeteia* is a "reversal of fortune" or a "reversal of intention" has been marked by the failure of both sides adequately to define their terms.[25] Turner, for example, correctly notes that "reversal of intention" is ambiguous, since it can mean either "change of purpose" or "frustration of an unchanged purpose." Yet he concludes that only a "very vague" interpretation could embrace all Aristotle's examples of *peripeteia*: "being in a situation which

[23] This is the translation given by, for example, Butcher, *Aristotle's Theory*, D W Lucas, *Poetics*, on 1453b18, Else, *Argument*, and Golden-Hardison, *Aristotle's Poetics* J Jones, *Aristotle*, 48–50, correctly notes that this translation is misleading

[24] This subsection is a slightly revised version of Belfiore, "*Peripeteia*"

[25] For "reversal of intention,' see Lock, 'Use", F L Lucas, "Reverse", and House, *Poetics*, 96 For "reversal of fortune," see Bywater, *Aristotle on the Art*, 198–99, Else, *Argument*, 343–45, and Turner, "Reverse" Although Vahlen, *Beitrage*, 34–35, is often identified with "reversal of intention," it should be noted that Vahlen did not use the German equivalent of this phrase Rather, he wrote that *peripeteia* is "was man tat oder tut zu einem bestimmten Zweck, das aber nicht diesen sondern den gerade entgegengesetzten zur Folge hat" (34) It is entirely possible that his meaning has been distorted by some of his followers

may be expected to lead to the development indicated."[26] Not only is this too imprecise, it is also not clear how Turner's "expectation" is to be distinguished from the "intention" of his opponents. Such confusion is understandable, since the *Poetics* itself gives little explicit information about *peripeteia*. The approach I adopt here should, however, make possible a new clarity and precision.

Aristotle's introductory statement about complex plots invites us to consider *peripeteia* in the light of a subject about which he has a great deal to say elsewhere: action. At *Poetics* 10.1452a12–14, he states. "Of plots some are simple and others complex. For the actions of which plots are imitations are in themselves of such kinds." If actions as well as plots can be complex, involving recognition or *peripeteia* or both, Aristotle's views on actions and other processes (for example, locomotion and qualitative alteration) should be relevant to his concept of tragic *peripeteia*.[27]

Aristotle's brief remarks in *Poetics* 11 support this hypothesis. Aristotle defines *peripeteia* and gives two rather puzzling examples:

> *Peripeteia* is the change to the opposite of the things done, as was said, and this [occurs], as we say, according to probability or necessity For example, in the *Oedipus*, [the messenger,] coming to cheer Oedipus, and [intending] to free him from his fear concerning his mother, by showing him who he was, did the opposite. And in the *Lynceus*, the one being led away to be put to death and Danaus following to kill [him], it happened as a result of the things done that the one [Danaus] was put to death and the other [Lynceus] was saved. (1452a22–29)

On the most natural reading of the Greek, *peripeteia* involves actions as well as motives and beliefs.[28] *Peripeteia* is defined as a "change . . of the things done," and the result of the action is stressed in Aristotle's examples: the messenger "did the opposite" and "it happened as a result of the things done."[29] That *peripeteia* should also be connected with belief and

---

[26] Turner, "Reverse," 207–8

[27] I am particularly indebted to Charles, *Action*, a study that makes clear the relevance of Aristotle's theory of *kinēsis* (movement, process) in the *Physics* to his theory of action in the ethical works

[28] "Fortune" and "intention" are often assumed to be mutually exclusive, an exception is Glanville, "Note," 75, who does not, however, adequately discuss Aristotle's theories

[29] I do not agree with D W Lucas, *Poetics*, 128, that "the things done" is ambiguous because it can mean either "the course of events" or "what the characters are trying to achieve " The phrase simply refers to the events that "occur as a result of the organization itself of the plot," discussed in the previous paragraph, at 1452a18–20 Aristotle's phrase "as was said" (1452a23) tells us as much

motive is indicated by Aristotle's use of ὡς and the future participle (ὡς εὐφρανῶν, ὡς ἀποθανούμενος, and ὡς ἀποκτενῶν: "to cheer," "to be put to death," "to kill"), a construction normally used to indicate an agent's purpose or beliefs.

Although Aristotle has a great deal to say about actions, processes, and intentions in his other works, studies of *peripeteia* have largely ignored this important material. I argue that Aristotle's views on action provide the philosophical basis for a detailed account of *peripeteia* that takes both "fortune" and "intention" into consideration. *Peripeteia* is the specific kind of discontinuous action that occurs when the action of an agent is prevented from achieving its intended result and instead arrives at an opposite actual result. The exact meaning of this statement will become clear through a study of Aristotle's examples of *peripeteia* in conjunction with his accounts of involuntary and discontinuous actions.

Two passages in Aristotle's ethical works give a good account of the kind of involuntary action *peripeteia* involves:

> The voluntary seems to be the opposite of the involuntary; and [acting] with knowledge of who [it is] or with what [it is done] or for the sake of what (for sometimes one knows that it is one's father but [does] not [think one is acting] to kill but to save [him]—as the daughters of Pelias did—or knows that this is drink but [thinks] that it is a love-charm or wine, when it was hemlock) seems to be the opposite of [acting] in ignorance of who [it is] and with what [it is done] and what [the act is], through ignorance and not accidentally. (*EE* 1225b1–6)

> The person who is ignorant of one of these things acts involuntarily. Perhaps it is not bad to set down what and how many these are: who [the agent is] and what [the act is], and concerning what, or in what circumstances [the act is done], and sometimes with what, for example with what instrument, and for the sake of what, such as for safety. . . . Giving someone drink for safety, one might kill [the person]. (*EN* 1111a2–14)

Both passages include among involuntary actions those done in ignorance of the actual result, the *hou heneka* ("that for the sake of which"). In such cases the agent does something voluntarily in order to produce a given result, but a different result occurs. For example, when Pelias's daughters voluntarily boil their father in the mistaken belief that this will restore the old man's youth, they do not act "to kill" (ἵνα ἀποκτείνῃ) but "to save" (ἵνα σώσῃ). Because the actual result is not intended, the action should be regarded as involuntary under a description that includes this result: "boiling in order to kill." The *Rhetoric* discusses this kind of action in less technical terms:

> [In justifying oneself] it is possible to offer the intended result [*to hou heneka*] in compensation [for the actual result],[30] [claiming] that one intended not to injure but [to do] this [other thing] instead of what one is accused of doing, and [the victim] happened to be injured. [One might say:] "It would be right to hate [me], if I did it so that this [result] would come about." (*Rhet.* 1416a17–20)

Aristotle's expression "for the sake of which" (*hou heneka* or *heneka tinos*) is potentially confusing. In the passages from the *Eudemian Ethics* and the *Nicomachean Ethics* quoted above, it denotes the actual result of an action.[31] In the *Rhetoric*, however, it denotes the intended result of an action, as it does also at *Poetics* 1461a4–9 ("One must consider . . . for what purpose [*hou heneka*]" the agent acts), and at *Nicomachean Ethics* 1139b1–2 ("Everyone who does something does it for some purpose [*heneka tou*]"). To avoid confusion, I distinguish between these two uses of the expression by translating one as "actual result" and the other as "intended result." *Hou heneka* can also refer to the final cause of processes other than actions.

Aristotle's examples in *Poetics* 11 show that *peripeteia* involves the kind of involuntary action we have been considering: that done in ignorance of the actual result. When the messenger in Sophocles' *Oedipus the King* tells Oedipus that Polybus is dead, Oedipus's joy and good fortune is the intended result (ὡς εὐφρανῶν τὸν Οἰδίπουν: "to cheer Oedipus"). The actual result—Oedipus's misery and bad fortune—is very different: "he did the opposite." The example from the *Lynceus* also concerns involuntary action done in ignorance of the actual result. When Danaus follows Lynceus, the latter's death is the result Danaus intends (ἀκολουθῶν ὡς ἀποκτενῶν: "following to kill"), but Danaus's action produces a different actual result: Lynceus's salvation and his own death.[32] In this example, Aristotle uses ὡς with the future participle to characterize the experience of the subject of the passive verb, Lynceus (ὁ μὲν ἀγόμενος ὡς ἀποθανούμενος). This phrase has created needless confusion. As O. J. Schrier points out, ἀποθνῄσκω serves as the passive of ἀποκτείνω, as it often does elsewhere, and the intention is that of the agent, Danaus, who is leading Lynceus

---

[30] The Greek phrase is ἀντικαταλλάττεσθαι τὸ οὗ ἕνεκα. On the meaning of this verb see Cope, *Rhetoric* 3:180.

[31] See Woods, *Eudemian Ethics*, 146–47.

[32] This much is clear from Aristotle's own words; for a reconstruction of the plot, see Xanthakis-Karamanos, *Studies*, 53–54.

away to put him to death [33] We can understand ὑπο Δαναοῦ, "by Danaus," and translate it thus "the one [Lynceus] being led away to be put to death [by Danaus] "[34]

Even though an intended result enters into the account of *peripeteia*, it is misleading to translate it as "reversal of intention " *Peripeteia* is a part of the plot (1452b9–10 "these are two parts of the plot, *peripeteia* and recognition"), and the plot is an imitation of action, not of *ēthos* Intention of a certain narrowly defined kind enters into the account only because *peripeteia* includes a voluntary action, and the intended result of a voluntary action is an essential property of this action For example, when someone piles bricks one atop the other, we need to know what his or her intentions are before we can decide whether to call this action "building" or "playing "[35] This principle also applies to the actions with "morally" qualified goals discussed in the ethical works At *Nicomachean Ethics* 1115b22, Aristotle states that "each thing is defined by its *telos*" for example, a brave man acts "for the sake of the good" (1115b23), and it is this end that makes his actions brave In *peripeteia*, however, there is no question of a "morally" qualified action "Moral" qualities are added by *ēthos*, and *peripeteia* is a part of the plot The intention that enters into an account of *peripeteia* has nothing to do with choice (*prohairesis*), with "morally" qualified purposes and motives, but is narrowly limited to intention to produce good or bad fortune Intention is relevant only insofar as it affects the *direction* of the tragic action, as it moves toward good or bad fortune

Aristotle's account of *peripeteia* differs in another way from his account in the ethical works of involuntary actions done in ignorance of the actual result In *peripeteia* the actual result does not simply differ from the intended result, it is the opposite of the intended result *peripeteia* is "the change to the opposite of the things done " What this means is clear from Aristotle's examples in the *Lynceus*, death and salvation are opposites, in *Oedipus the King* the action that is intended to cheer and produce good fortune instead produces misery and bad fortune, while an action that is intended to free someone from fear of bad fortune instead increases fear and leads to bad fortune

[33] Schrier, *Peripeteia*, 102 It is a mistake to interpret the passage as implying anything about Lynceus s expectations (see D W Lucas, *Poetics*, 129, and Turner, Reverse, 208) or those of the audience (see Else, *Argument*, 346–48)

[34] Cf *Po* 13 1453a38–39 and 14 1453b23–25, where ἀποθνῃσκω is used with ὑπο

[35] Charles, *Action*, 5–108 and 252, makes it clear that intended results are essential properties of actions, just as ends are essential properties of processes The example of building is based on *Phy* 201a10–19, cited by Charles (16)

Because an action does not achieve its intended result in *peripeteia*, *peripeteia* must be discontinuous action of the kind Aristotle discusses elsewhere. Indeed, in the *Poetics* itself Aristotle indicates that *peripeteia* is discontinuous action when he states that a simple plot is an imitation of an action that is "continuous [συνεχοῦς] and one," such that the "change occurs without *peripeteia* or recognition" (10 1452a15–16) In complex plots, this passage implies, recognition and *peripeteia* break up the continuity of action.

Although several scholars have connected *peripeteia* with discontinuous action,[36] the connection has not been worked out in detail, nor has its importance been appreciated. To understand fully Aristotle's view of *peripeteia* as discontinuous action it is necessary to examine his views on continuous processes (*kinēseis*).

For Aristotle, *kinēsis* includes qualitative alteration, locomotion, and quantitative change. It can also include actions, as is clear from *Eudemian Ethics* 1220b26–27. "*Kinēsis* is continuous, and action is *kinēsis*." Accordingly, Aristotle's account of *kinēseis* (processes) in the *Physics* and elsewhere should bear on his account of actions in the *Poetics*. As David Charles notes. "In the *Physics*, the account of processes is applied explicitly to actions teaching, learning (III 3), walking (V 4), building, doctoring, jumping (III 1). Aristotle himself assumes that in giving an account of processes he has provided an ontology of actions."[37]

Each Aristotelian *kinēsis* is continuous only if it reaches its end point without hindrance. In *Physics* 8 8, Aristotle distinguishes continuous from discontinuous motion along a straight line. "Everything in motion moves continuously if it is turned aside by nothing and if it arrives at that place toward which it was originally set in motion For example, [something moves continuously from A to B] if it arrives at B [from A], and was in motion toward B not only when it came near to B, but as soon as it began to move" (*Phy.* 264a9–13) If, however, the moving thing goes back to A immediately upon reaching B, it cannot be said to move continuously. "It is clear that the thing in motion [back and forth] along a straight and finite line is not in motion continuously. For it turns back, and that which turns back along a straight line moves with opposite motions" (261b31–34) Other kinds of *kinēseis* also are continuous or discontinuous depending on whether or not they reach their end point without impediment Aristotle

---

[36] See Turner, "Reverse," 208, who cites L Potts, *Aristotle on the Art of Fiction*, 81, Glanville, "Note," 73 (citing an unpublished paper of F Cornford) and 75, and Garvie, "Aeschylus," 63–64

[37] Charles, *Action*, 63

often calls the end point of changes other than locomotion the *hou heneka* ("that for the sake of which"), using the expression to refer to the final cause, or, in the case of actions, as we saw above, the intended result For example, Aristotle writes in *Parts of Animals* 641b23–25 "Everywhere we say that this is for the sake of this, wherever there appears some end toward which the *kinēsis* proceeds when nothing impedes", and in *Physics* 194a29–30 he states "When a *kinēsis* is continuous and there is some end of the *kinēsis*, this last thing is also the *hou heneka* "[38]

Aristotle's distinction between continuous and discontinuous *kinēsis* illuminates both the kind of action that *peripeteia* itself is and the role of *peripeteia* in the larger dramatic action of which it is a part First, *peripeteia*, as a part of the tragic plot, is itself a discontinuous action It is a *kinēsis* proceeding toward an end point (the resulting good or bad fortune intended by the agent) that it is prevented from reaching, like the discontinuous motion back and forth along a straight line discussed in *Physics* 261b31–34, *peripeteia* includes a "turning back "

The discontinuous action of *peripeteia* is also part of a discontinuous plot A plot, whether simple or complex, is a "composition of events" (*Po* 1450a5), a series of "things that happen successively" (1451a13 ἐφεξῆς γιγνομένων)[39] This series of events constitutes the imitation of action a change of someone from bad to good fortune, or from good to bad fortune Each of the events, including the "things done" (1452a22) that make up the *peripeteia*, contributes to this change, whether or not the person who changes is the active agent of each of them For example, the "things done" that constitute the *peripeteia* of *Oedipus the King* are done by the messenger, but they contribute to the composition of events, the plot, in which Oedipus proceeds from good to bad fortune This first step in the revelation of Oedipus's identity is a necessary part of the sequence of events that culminates in his bad fortune In a simple plot the motion is continuous, each of the individual "things done" representing a segment of a straight line from A to B In complex plots with *peripeteia*, however, motion between A and B is prevented from continuing along a straight line, and is instead made to change direction one or more times When the

[38] I follow Charlton, *Physics*, 48, in reading τοῦτο ἔσχατον at 194a30 The two passages quoted here are cited by Charles, *Action*, 252 He also cites (108) two other passages that contain an and nothing impedes clause DMA 701a16–17 and 702a15–16

[39] In *Phy* 8 259a16–20, τὸ ἐφεξῆς, successive, is opposed to τὸ συνεχές, continuous While the two terms are not opposed in the *Poetics*, it is possible that ἐφεξῆς is used at 1451a13 as a technical term for the genus that includes both simple (continuous) action and complex (discontinuous) action

peripeteia of the *Oedipus* occurs, for example, the action has been proceeding from Oedipus's good fortune (A) to his bad fortune (B). The "things done" by the messenger at first proceed toward his intended result of cheering Oedipus, and thus turn this action back toward (A). Oedipus's good fortune. Prevented from attaining this result, however, the messenger's action then turns back and moves in the opposite direction, toward Oedipus's bad fortune (B).[40] As a consequence, the action imitated by the plot moves from A to B in a "complex" or "plaited" (πεπλέγμενος) line that doubles back on itself. Thus, as "the change to the opposite of the things done" by the messenger, the *peripeteia* is also part of the movement between good and bad fortune that constitutes the tragic plot itself At *Poetics* 11.1452a39–b3, Aristotle makes explicit this contribution of *peripeteia* to the tragic plot as a whole when he connects bad fortune and good fortune with *peripeteia* and recognition.[41]

This analysis of *peripeteia* in terms of discontinuous action helps us understand how it differs from the tragic process of change (*metabasis*) that is essential to all plots, whether simple or complex, as Aristotle states at *Poetics* 10.1452a14–18. The tragic change is the whole movement of the plot between the two end points of good and bad fortune (1451a12–14), whereas *peripeteia* is a change in direction within the movement between these two end points. Moreover, there is only one tragic change in each play. There can, however, be several *peripeteiai*: although Aristotle never explicitly states this, it is suggested by his use of the plural at, for example, 24.1459b10, and by the close association between *peripeteia* and recognition, which Aristotle does say can occur more than once in a single play (11.1452b3–8, 16.1454b26–28). Further, in the tragic change there is not necessarily an opposition between intended result and actual result, as there is in *peripeteia*. Thus, *peripeteia* should not be identified with a tragic change of an especially sudden kind.[42] While Johannes Vahlen's

[40] In this view, the action of the *Oedipus* twice begins to change from good to bad fortune once before the events represented onstage, and once again at the *peripeteia* Because the second change is so much more marked and definite, however, it constitutes the 'beginning of the change" at which the play's solution begins On 'solution,' see chap 4 ("Plausibility, Plot, and Episode")

[41] Vahlen and Else each see only part of the truth Else, *Argument*, 344, correctly writes that in the definition of *peripeteia* "τῶν πραττομένων [the things done] are simply *the events of the play as it moves along*" (emphasis in original) Some of these individual "things done" that make up the plot, however, are also actions done by an agent "for a definite goal," as Vahlen writes, *Beitrage*, 34

[42] For "sudden change," see Bywater, *Aristotle on the Art*, 198–99, and Else, *Argument*, 345 Halliwell, *Aristotle's Poetics*, 211, also appears to identify *peripeteia* with the tragic

view that *peripeteia* is the means by which the tragic change takes place is nearer the truth,[43] it is more accurate to say that a *peripeteia* can mark that point within the whole movement of the plot (the tragic change) at which the solution begins. The solution is not the beginning of the whole movement of the plot, but the point at which the end of good or bad fortune begins to follow other events, by probability or necessity (*Po.* 18.1455b24–29).

This account of *peripeteia* allows us to understand the significance of Aristotle's phrase "as was said" in his definition of *peripeteia* (1452a23). It refers to the passage in *Poetics* 10 where simple and complex plots were distinguished on the basis of their continuity or lack of continuity. *peripeteia* is "the change to the opposite of the things done, as was said [sc., when we denied that complex plots are imitations of continuous actions and implied that they therefore involve the discontinuity produced by a change in direction]." This explanation of "as was said" is preferable to the view that it refers to the phrase "contrary to expectation, because of one another" (9.1452a4).[44] The passage in *Poetics* 10 is nearer; moreover, it is the passage in which Aristotle first distinguishes simple and complex plots. The phrase "contrary to expectation," on the other hand, occurs in a discussion of simple plots. the paragraph at 9.1451b33 begins with "of simple plots," and there is no mention of complex plots until the beginning of the next chapter, at 10.1452a12.[45] Moreover, "contrary to expectation" refers to a broad class of unexpected events, not only to those involved in *peripeteia*.

Two important points, then, have emerged from a study of Aristotle's theory of actions and *kinēseis*. First, *peripeteia* is the kind of discontinuous action that occurs when the action of an agent is prevented from achieving its intended result (that is, good or bad fortune) and produces instead the opposite actual result. Second, *peripeteia* is the "turning back" that helps constitute the discontinuous action of the complex plot. This account fits the examples of *peripeteia* that Aristotle gives in the *Poetics* and elsewhere.

Of the two examples given in *Poetics* 11, only the one drawn from *Oe-*

---

change when he writes that in a complex plot "the change will form a critical element or section within the play's structure "

[43] Vahlen, *Beitrage*, 34

[44] For the latter view, see Dupont-Roc and Lallot, *Poétique*, 231, Glanville, "Note," 73–78, Halliwell, *Aristotle's Poetics*, 213 n 16, Kamerbeek, "Note," 279, and D W Lucas, "Pity," 52–55 For a survey of other suggestions, see Allan, "Peripeteia," 338–41

[45] Else, *Argument*, 323–24, argued that chap 10 should begin at 1452a1 "Since not only " I see no problem with the traditional chapter division

dipus the King requires further discussion. This is a vexed passage, since the most natural reading of the Greek—taking both εὐφρανῶν and ἀπαλλάξων with ἐλθών ("by coming to cheer Oedipus . . . and to free him from his fear")—does not accord with our text of the play. The messenger in the *Oedipus* does not arrive with the intention of freeing Oedipus from a fear about which he knows nothing. This difficulty can be resolved, however, if we follow W. J. Verdenius in taking ἀπαλλάξων (independent of ὡς) to refer to a later stage in the conversation.[46] Halliwell's translation expresses this idea: "The person comes to bring Oedipus happiness, and intends to free him from his fear about his mother, but he produces the opposite effect, by revealing Oedipus's identity."[47]

Aristotle's statement, though somewhat less precise than we would like, is entirely consistent with the events of Sophocles' play. The *peripeteia* takes place in the messenger scene.[48] In this scene the ultimate result intended by the messenger is his own good fortune (1005–6): "Indeed I came for this reason most of all, to get some benefit when you return to your house." The messenger intends to bring about this ultimate result by way of an intermediate result: cheering Oedipus with the announcement of his good fortune in becoming king of Corinth (934–40). Because only this intermediate result is important for the plot in which Oedipus changes from good to bad fortune, only this result is mentioned by Aristotle: "coming to cheer Oedipus." The messenger intends to cheer Oedipus by announcing that Polybus is dead (942). This announcement, however, produces an actual result that is the opposite of the intended result, for it sets in motion, according to probability or necessity, a chain of events culminating in the terrible revelation of Oedipus's parentage, and so in Oedipus's bad fortune. After learning that his supposed father Polybus is dead, Oedipus rejoices because he thinks that the oracle about his parricide has proved false (964–72). He still refuses to go to Corinth, however, for fear of committing incest with his supposed mother Merope (1007–13). To free him from this fear (1014), the messenger reveals to Oedipus that

---

[46] Verdenius, "Arist. *Poet.* 1452a25." This view is also held by Halliwell, *Aristotle's Poetics*, 212 n. 15. I cannot see why D. W. Lucas, *Poetics*, 129, and Schrier, "*Peripeteia*," 106, claim that Verdenius's separation of ἀπαλλάξων from ἐλθὼν ὡς εὐφρανῶν makes the sentence "obscure." For surveys of the dispute about the text of this passage, see Allan, "Peripeteia," and Schrier, "*Peripeteia*." My present interpretation differs from the views expressed in Belfiore, *Peripeteia*, 190–91, on which Deborah Roberts gave me helpful criticisms.

[47] Halliwell, *Poetics of Aristotle*, 42.

[48] *OT* 911–1085. I disagree with Bywater, *Aristotle on the Art*, 200–201, who argues that *peripeteia* takes place in the following scene (1110–85).

he is not the son of Polybus (1016). This first step in the revelation of Oedipus's identity turns the movement of the action back toward Oedipus's bad fortune, as is apparent when Jocasta exits, calling him "wretched" (1068, 1071). This *peripeteia* involves a sequence of events in which actions intended to achieve certain results actually produce the opposite results. Instead of cheering Oedipus and bringing him good fortune, the messenger's announcement of Polybus's death brings to his mind the fear of incest, and instead of removing that fear, the messenger's revelation that Oedipus is not Polybus's son increases Oedipus's fear, and leads to his bad fortune.

We can now turn to Aristotle's other examples of *peripeteia*. At *Poetics* 16.1454b29–30, Aristotle praises *Odyssey* 19 317–490, in which the nurse's recognition of Odysseus comes about *ek peripeteias*, "from a *peripeteia*." As D W Lucas notes, *ek* (from) does not indicate the cause of recognition but the manner of its introduction into the story.[49] An examination of Homer's passage shows that this is indeed a case in which the actual result is the opposite of the intended result. Odysseus asks the old nurse to wash his feet, with (as she realizes) the intention of avoiding as much as possible the "outrage and many shameful deeds" of the young maidservants, which might endanger him.[50] Instead, because this action leads to his recognition by the nurse, Odysseus risks facing what he had tried to avoid. The nurse's recognition nearly causes her to reveal his presence to his enemies, a revelation that could have led to the greatest outrage of all, his own death. For this reason, when the nurse recognizes him and attempts to betray his presence, Odysseus says to her, "Mother, why do you wish to destroy me?" (482).

At *Poetics* 18.1456a19–23, Aristotle writes. "In *peripeteiai* and in simple [organizations of] events they aim at the effects they wish wonderfully, for this is tragic and *philanthropon*. This happens when the clever but evil man is deceived, like Sisyphus, and the brave but unjust man is defeated." The text of this passage is problematic, and it is not clear whether the examples are intended to illustrate *peripeteia*, the wonderful in simple plots, the tragic, or the *philanthropon*.[51] The best that can be said is that the examples

---

[49] D W Lucas, *Poetics*, 168 There is no need to accept the view of Bywater, *Aristotle on the Art*, 235, Gudeman, *Aristoteles*, 293, and Lock, "Use," 253, that *peripeteia* does not have a technical sense here

[50] *Od* 19 373–74 On Odysseus's intention, cf Turner, "Reverse," 213, though his view of the nature of this *peripeteia* differs from mine

[51] On the *philanthropon*, see below, "*Poetics* 13 " Because the meaning of this word is much disputed, I leave it untranslated

could well illustrate *peripeteia*. A clever but evil Sisyphus might perform an action with the intended result of deceiving, but instead produce the opposite result: his own deception. A brave but unjust man might attack with the intention of winning, but produce instead his own defeat. As in the example drawn from the *Lynceus* at *Poetics* 11, something (we are not told what) would prevent these actions from achieving their intended results.

At *Poetics* 24.1459b14, the *Iliad* is classified as "simple." This epic in fact has no *peripeteia*, for there is no opposition between actual result and intended result in the "things done" that constitute the plot, the imitation of Achilles' change from good to bad fortune. Achilles regrets his refusal to fight the Trojans, for this has the unexpected consequence of Patroclus's death. This is not *peripeteia*, however, for Achilles' action did not have his friend's safety as its intended result. Again, when Achilles lends Patroclus his armor, this is followed by his friend's death. This is not *peripeteia* either, for Achilles' action was intended not to save Patroclus but to drive the Trojans back from the ships and to win glory for Achilles himself (*Il.* 16.84), which in fact does happen. Finally, although Achilles' killing of Hector will lead to his own death, this is by no means *peripeteia*, for in killing Hector Achilles does not intend to prevent his own death, which he well knows must follow.[52]

Although it has received a kind of notoriety in the literature, *History of Animals* 590b13–19 is a red herring.[53] Aristotle writes that "crayfish master even big fish, and a *peripeteia* happens to some of these [τούτων]. For octopuses master crayfish." Aristotle writes that crayfish master congers, which in turn eat octopuses. Unfortunately, it is impossible to decide which fish is subject to *peripeteia*, for we cannot determine the referent of τούτων. Grammatically, we would expect it to refer to the nearer subject, the big fish.[54] Logically, however, it would seem to refer to the crayfish, who are mastered by larger fish in the example immediately following "for."[55] David Balme offers the best explanation of Aristotle's use of *peri-*

[52] Cf. Turner, "Reverse," 209. A different interpretation is given by Halliwell, *Aristotle's Poetics*, 264 n. 18, who believes that the *Iliad* does have *peripeteia*, citing R. Rutherford, "Tragic Form and Feeling in the *Iliad*," 146.

[53] This passage is frequently cited as evidence for one or another view of *peripeteia*. See, for example, Allan, "Peripeteia," 349 n. 8, Butcher, *Aristotle's Theory*, 331 n. 2, Bywater, *Aristotle on the Art*, 198, and F. L. Lucas, "Reverse," 100–101.

[54] This is Allan's view, "Peripeteia," 349 n. 8.

[55] The passage is taken this way by Louis, *Histoire des animaux*, and, as Allan, "Peripe-

peteia in this passage the reference of τούτων is general ("some of these [fish], as follows"), and Aristotle is simply making a joke in characterizing what happens to fish in terms of poetic *peripeteia*.[56]

Finally, at *Rhetoric* 1371b10–11 Aristotle states that "*peripeteiai* and [*kai*] being barely saved from dangers" are pleasant. Ingram Bywater, citing this passage in support of the view that *peripeteia* means "a sudden change of fortune," apparently takes *kai* to mean "that is" (198). While this is possible, *kai* could merely be linking two distinct possibilities. In any case, the passage does not support the view that *tragic peripeteia* is a tragic change of an especially sudden kind.

The preceding study of Aristotle's views on action and *kinēsis*, allows us to conclude that Vahlen's statement was substantially correct, so far as it went. *peripeteia* does indeed involve "what someone did or does for a definite goal, but which does not result in this, but in the exact opposite."[57] However, an understanding of Aristotle's philosophy of action allows us to be more precise than Vahlen, and to avoid the inaccuracy of those who translate *peripeteia* as "reversal of intention." *Peripeteia* is the kind of discontinuous action that occurs when the action of an agent is prevented from achieving its intended result, and instead arrives at an opposite actual result. *Peripeteia* breaks up the simple plot's linear motion between the end points of the tragic change and forces it to turn back. Thus, *peripeteia* is neither a "reversal of intention" nor a "reversal of fortune," but a turning back of the action from its straight course.

Recognition

Aristotle defines recognition (*anagnōrisis*) in *Poetics* 11 immediately after the discussion of *peripeteia*:[58]

Recognition, just as the word also indicates, is a change from ignorance to knowledge, either to *philia* or to enmity of those defined with respect to good fortune or bad fortune [59] The best recognition is that which occurs together

---

teia," notes at 349 n 8, by D'A W Thompson, *Oxford Translation*, now in Barnes's revised edition

[56] Balme suggested this to me

[57] Vahlen, *Beitrage*, 34

[58] On recognition, see the studies of Perrin, "Recognition", L Cooper, *Comedy*, 290–305, Philippart, "Théorie", Dworacki, "Anagnorismos", Vuillemin, "Reconnaissance", and Cave, *Recognitions*, 27–83

[59] Else defends translating ὡρισμένων (1452a32) as "defined" in *Argument*, 351–52 For

with *peripeteia*, as happens in the *Oedipus*. There are other recognitions as
well: for they can occur, in the manner stated,[60] with respect to inanimate
and chance things, and it is possible to recognize if someone did or did not
do something. But that which is most [a part] of the plot and of the action
is the recognition stated This kind of recognition and *peripeteia* will have
either pity or fear (of which actions tragedy has been assumed to be an imitation), since bad or good fortune will also result from such things Since
recognition is recognition of certain people, some [recognitions] are only of
one person by another, when it is clear who the other is, at other times both
must recognize [each other]. (11.1452a29–b5)

Recognition is again discussed in *Poetics* 16, where Aristotle lists and gives
examples of different ways in which it is brought about.

It is clear from these accounts that recognition, like *peripeteia*, is a
change (*metabolē*: 1452a31) and that it can be produced in various ways. In
other respects, however, interpretation is very difficult. It is far from obvious what Aristotle means when he writes that this change is one "from
ignorance to knowledge, either to *philia* or to enmity [*ē eis philian ē eis
echthran*]," and how this kind of change contributes to the whole tragic
change between good and bad fortune. Even the meaning of the verb *anagnōrizein* is problematic, for in several passages in the *Poetics* (1454b32,
1455b9, 1455b21) the ordinary active meaning "to recognize" does not
make good sense. Yet there are also objections to interpreting it as "to
make [oneself] known."[61]

The whole of *Poetics* 16 is notoriously difficult. Aristotle lists several
ways in which recognition can be brought about, four of which are enu-
merated in the text. These are recognitions (1) "by means of signs"
(1454b21), (2) "made up by the poet" (1454b30–31), (3) "by means of
memory" (1454b37), and (4) "from reasoning" (1455a4). Aristotle also

---

a parallel, see *OT* 1082–83 οἱ δὲ συγγενεῖς/μῆνές με μικρὸν καὶ μέγαν διώρισαν—"The
kindred months have defined me as small and great "

[60] "In the manner stated' (1452a35) is Janko's translation in *Poetics 1*, reading συμ-
βαίνειν instead of συμβαίνει with Kassel, *De arte poetica* This reading is also adopted by
Dupont-Roc and Lallot, *Poétique* According to Gudeman s apparatus in *Aristoteles*, συμ-
βαίνειν is the reading of Parisinus 2040

[61] The interpretation "to make [oneself] known" was proposed by Vahlen, in the works
cited by D W Lucas, *Poetics*, 169 *Sitzb K Preuss Ak Berlin* (1898) 258–69 = *Ges
phil Schr* 2 498ff , and *Beitrage*, 275 Objections to Vahlen's view are raised by Else,
Argument, 508–10, and Lucas, 169, who also notes (182) that the construction with τινάς
in 1455b21 is difficult even if we accept Vahlen's interpretation Lucas proposes (169) that
anagnōrizein can mean "have an *anagnorisis* "

mentions, without numbering them, recognition "from false inference" (*paralogismos*: 1455a13), and recognition "from the events themselves" (1455a16–17). While there is general agreement that this last way of bringing about recognition is a separate category, recognition "from *paralogismos*" is more controversial Most scholars believe that it is merely a subcategory of the fourth way of bringing about recognition, that "from reasoning." These people hold that *Poetics* 16 lists only five separate ways of bringing about recognition. Others, however, place recognition "from *paralogismos*" in a category of its own, believing that Aristotle lists six ways of bringing about recognition in *Poetics* 16.[62] Other difficulties concern the distinctions among the different categories and examples given. B. Perrin writes that all Aristotle's categories involve "reasoning" and that the recognition of Orestes by Electra in Aeschylus's *Libation Bearers*, listed by Aristotle as a recognition "by reasoning" (1455a4–6), also involves the use of tokens. Accordingly, he argues that three of the categories in *Poetics* 16 are not exclusive.[63]

The three kinds of recognition listed in *Poetics* 11—of persons, of inanimate objects, and of someone having or not having done something—are also problematic. Gudeman, D W. Lucas, and Perrin take Oedipus's recognition to be a recognition that he did something [64] Else, on the other hand, criticizes Gudeman's "curious obtusity," and argues that Oedipus's recognition is without doubt recognition of a person.[65]

Nor is it clear what the difference is between recognition "to *philia*" and recognition "to enmity." Roselyne Dupont-Roc and Jean Lallot write that recognition is "the discovery of the fact . . . that he [sc , the hero] is united to a certain other person by an objective relationship, socially defined as positive (*philia*) or negative (*ekhthra*) as in the case of Oedipus, who 'recognizes the *philia*' that unites him to his father (chap. 14, 53b31)."[66] Else, like Dupont-Roc and Lallot, believes that recognition "to *philia*" is recognition of "*the objective state of being philoi*, 'dear ones' by virtue of blood ties," and he also classifies Oedipus's recognition as one "to

---

[62] Among those who believe there are six categories are L Cooper, *Comedy*, 293–94, and Philippart, "Théorie," 176–77 What Aristotle means by *paralogismos* presents problems of its own in *Po* 16 and in 24 1460a18–26 On this topic, see Cooper, 290–305, Cave, *Recognitions*, 39–46, Gallavotti, "Paralogismi", and Vuillemin, "Paralogisme "

[63] Perrin, "Recognition,' 387, 403

[64] Gudeman, *Aristoteles*, 224, D W Lucas, *Poetics*, 132, Perrin, "Recognition," 403

[65] Else, *Argument*, 353, and n 29

[66] Dupont-Roc and Lallot, *Poétique*, 233

philia."[67] This account implies that "to recognize *philia*" (*anagnōrisai tēn philian*: 14.1453b31) is the same as recognition "to *philia*" (*eis philian*: 11.1452a31). However, if recognition "to *philia*" is recognition that a blood tie exists, what is recognition "to enmity"? Else classifies Clytemnestra's recognition of her son Orestes (in Sophocles' *Electra*) as a recognition "to enmity," because she recognizes "that he who was naturally *philos* is now her enemy" (*Argument*, 350). According to this reasoning, however, a good case could also be made for classifying Oedipus's recognition as one "to enmity," instead of "to *philia*," as Else argues. Oedipus learns that it is his father and his mother to whom he has done evil; he learns that he has acted as enemy to his *philoi*. As Teiresias tells him, "You do not know that you are an enemy to your own, below and above the earth" (*OT* 415–16).

Finally, it is not always easy to recognize an Aristotelian recognition when we see one. Aristotle explicitly states that the *Iliad* is a simple plot (24.1459b14), one without recognition or *peripeteia*. Yet does not Achilles first treat his *philoi*, the Greeks, as enemies, and then change back so as to become their *philos*?

Aristotle does not give us enough clear and unambiguous information to allow us to solve all these and other difficulties connected with recognition. We can nevertheless arrive at some important conclusions. Aristotle explicitly tells us that a tragedy can have more than one recognition (1452b3–8; 1454b26–28). We can also distinguish between the recognition itself and ways of bringing about the recognition. Because recognition is one of the three parts of the plot, it is itself part of a probable or necessary sequence of events, and it contributes to the arousal of pity and fear "from the organization itself of the events" (1453b2–3). On the other hand, the recognition is brought about by means of a "plausible" (*eikos*) episode. *Poetics* 16, as Else noted, is concerned with these "techniques" or "methods" of bringing about recognition, and not with recognition as part of the plot itself.[68] We need not be concerned with this difficult chapter, then, in trying to understand the role of recognition in the plot itself. In *Poetics* 14, however, Aristotle's brief account of plot types gives us valuable information about the role of recognition in the plot. This chapter gives us a better understanding of the connection between recognition and *philia* than does *Poetics* 11. Aristotle tells us that in the best plots, those in which *philos* harms or is about to harm *philos*, recognition is recognition "of phi-

---

[67] Else, *Argument*, 349.
[68] Ibid., 484.

lia" (anagnōrisai tēn philian. 14 1453b31).[69] The "change from ignorance to knowledge" mentioned in *Poetics* 11 turns out, in *Poetics* 14, to be a change from ignorance to knowledge of a *philia* relationship. The later chapter also shows us that, although a play may have several recognitions, one recognition is often of central importance. that which precedes or follows a *pathos* in which *philos* harms or is about to harm *philos.*

As part of the plot, recognition is connected with good and bad fortune. *Poetics* 11 states that recognition occurs between "those defined with respect to good or bad fortune" (1452a31–32), and that the best recognition leads to good or bad fortune (1452a38–b3), in a way that is not made clear Aristotle's examples of good plots in *Poetics* 14 help clarify these views. In the best plot type (χράτιστον 1454a4), that of the *Iphigenia in Tauris*, recognition prevents a *pathos* in which *philos* harms *philos.* In this plot recognition leads, by necessity or probability, to good fortune. In the second-best type (βέλτιον 1454a2), that of *Oedipus the King*, recognition occurs after a *pathos* of this sort. In this plot recognition leads, by necessity or probability, to bad fortune.[70] In the best plots, recognition results either in the good fortune of reunion with and aid to *philoi*, or in the bad fortune of discovering that one has harmed a *philos.* This connection between recognition and *philia* explains why, in Aristotle's view, recognition is so intimately connected with good and bad fortune, pity and fear (1452a38–b3, cf 14.1454a4 recognition is *ekplēktikon*, productive of the tragic emotion *ekplēxis*) Since *philoi* are the greatest of external goods, our relationship with them is most essential to good and bad fortune. To recognize and so become able to benefit *philoi* is the greatest of good fortune, while discovering that one has harmed *philoi* is the worst of bad fortune

If recognition is connected in these ways with *philia* and with good fortune, it involves more than mere identification Recognition is not simply an act of acquiring the knowledge that one is related to someone; it involves *acting* as a *philos* or as an enemy [71] This conclusion makes sense, from Aristotle's account of plot and action generally, we would expect recognition to have consequences for action rather than being concerned with knowledge for its own sake

It appears that *philia*, in the *Poetics* as in Greek thought generally, is connected with doing good to someone As we saw above (chapter 2),

---

[69] This is not the same thing as recognition 'to *philia*" (11 1452a31), as I will argue

[70] On necessity and probability in these two plays, see chap 4 ("Necessity and Probability")

[71] Winkler makes a similar point in "Oscar "

philia is not primarily an emotion ("love," as S H Butcher translates the term in *Po* 11), but a formal relationship, with specific rights and obligations, especially between relatives But *philia* is not, as Else would have it, merely an objective state of being related The relationship must be acknowledged and acted on by those involved, for *philia* implies active good service or an acknowledged obligation to do good service Aristotle writes in the *Nicomachean Ethics* that *philoi* "must have goodwill and wish good things for each other, with each other's knowledge "[72] According to Adkins, "*philein* is to do useful services for a man   *philein* is an *act* which creates or maintains a co-operative relationship "[73] To be in a *philia* relationship is to help one's friends, and to be in a relationship of enmity is to harm one's enemies [74] Thus, while recognition of persons is always, in the *Poetics*, recognition "of *philia*," recognition that an objective *philia* relationship exists, recognition "to *philia* or to enmity" is a change from ignorance to knowledge that concerns or affects one's *actions* as *philos* or enemy Recognition "to *philia*" typically involves the start of the active doing of good services to someone within an acknowledged *philia* relationship Recognition "to enmity," on the other hand, is often a discovery that one is or has been in a state of enmity, in which one does or tries to do harmful actions In both cases, to be part of a tragic plot, recognition must result in action that changes the direction of the plot or contributes to its ongoing movement

Some specific examples from tragedy illustrate what recognition "to *philia*" or "to enmity" involves In Aeschylus's *Libation Bearers*, Orestes recognizes that the woman he sees is his sister as early as line 16 What most moves us, however, is the real "recognition scene" beginning at 212, in which Orestes reveals himself to Electra, and brother and sister acknowledge the mutual obligations and rights that their *philia* relationship entails They do this by pledging loyalty to their father and enmity to their mother The delay before this recognition creates suspense, and is needed to allow brother and sister time to learn that each is a true *philos* of their father and an enemy of their mother Electra's speech and actions at 84–151 show the listening Orestes that this is true of her Moreover, when Electra discovers Orestes' hair (164–211) she learns not merely that her brother has returned, but, more important, that he is a true *philos* [75] By

[72] *EN* 1156a3–5, cf *EE* 1236a14–15

[73] Adkins, Friendship, 36, emphasis in original

[74] On this idea and its importance in tragedy and in Greek thought generally, see Blundell, *Helping*

[75] At 219, Orestes says, Do not search for anyone who is more a *philos* [*mallon philon*] than I am

158

leaving his hair on his father's grave, Orestes declares himself to be a *philos* of his father and an enemy of his mother he shows his readiness to help his father's *philoi* and to harm his mother and her *philoi*. Only after each has received these proofs of *philia* do brother and sister embrace and pledge future mutual services. This recognition occurs together with *peripeteia*, marking the beginning of the change from bad to good fortune.

The same play has a good example of a recognition "to enmity." Clytemnestra's recognition of Orestes is instantaneous. "I understand the riddle" (887). What she understands is not simply that the stranger is her son, but that her son is her enemy because he has killed Aigisthus, he who is "most a *philos*" to her (*philtat'* 893), and because he is a danger to her also. She in turn at once acts as the enemy of Orestes, calling for an ax (889). This recognition provides an additional impulse in the direction in which the action is already moving, heightening the pity and fear that had already been aroused at the prospect of the matricide. Other examples of recognition "to enmity" are given by Else. Clytemnestra's recognition (in Sophocles' *Electra*) that her son has come to kill her, and Jason's recognition (in Euripides' *Medea*) that his wife has become his enemy, having killed their sons.[76] All of these involve recognition that a relative has *acted* as an enemy by doing or being about to do harm

If we take recognition "to *philia* or to enmity" to involve *acting* as *philos* or enemy, many instances of recognition are easier to interpret For example, if enmity involves *doing* something harmful, Oedipus's recognition is not "to *philia*" but "to enmity." What he recognizes is that he has done harm to *philoi*—that, as Teiresias says (*OT* 415–16), he is an enemy to his own. Again, though Achilles' attitude toward his fellow Greeks changes in the course of the *Iliad*, these changes are not recognitions, for Achilles has never directly harmed the Greeks. He quarrels in words with Agamemnon, but Homer goes out of his way to emphasize that Achilles does not draw his sword (*Il.* 1.210–11). He is never, therefore, in a state of enmity with the Greeks. More controversially, Xerxes' realization that by attacking the Greeks he has become "an evil to his race and fatherland" (Aeschylus, *Persians*, 931–33) is in some ways very similar to Oedipus's recognition Both Oedipus and Xerxes acted in ignorance of the harm their deeds did to their *philoi*, and later recognized this. Seen in this way, the *Persians* has a complex plot with a structure much like that of the *Oedipus*.[77] Furthermore, if recognition "to *philia*" involves doing good to a relative,

[76] Else, *Argument*, 350

[77] This play is usually cited as an obvious example of the simple plot see, e g , Garvie, "Aeschylus," 67

a recognition "to *philia*" occurs at the end of Euripides' *Hippolytus* Here, Theseus realizes that his son has, all along, done him good services, and is in dying prepared to do further service by acquitting his father of blood guilt (1449)

The foregoing discussion of recognition, *philia*, and good or bad fortune clarifies the relationship between recognition and *peripeteia* "The best recognition," Aristotle writes, "is that which occurs together with *peripeteia*, as happens in the *Oedipus*" (11. 1452a32–33) "Together" here indicates a temporal and causal relationship within the plot structure. For example, in the *Oedipus*, the messenger's action has unintended consequences that result, by probability or necessity, in the revelation of Oedipus's identity (recognition). This result necessarily involves Oedipus's bad fortune, as he discovers that he has harmed his *philoi*, instead of the result (good fortune) intended by the messenger. Thus, *peripeteia* occurs In the best plot of *Poetics* 14, that of the *Iphigenia in Tauris*, recognition of brother and sister averts the imminent *pathos* that would have led to bad fortune, and instead leads, by necessity or probability, to a change (*peripeteia*) in the direction of the action to good fortune and benefit to *philoi* [78]

Good and Bad Plots

In *Poetics* 13 and 14, Aristotle turns from the discussion of the three separate parts of the plot that occupied *Poetics* 10 and 11 to a consideration of the plot as a whole composed of these parts Aristotle begins *Poetics* 13 with the premise that the function of tragedy is the arousal of pity and fear

> What should be aimed at and what should be guarded against in organizing plots, and whence will be the function of tragedy, should be stated next in order after what has just been said Since it is necessary for the composition of the most beautiful tragedy to be not simple but complex, and for it to be an imitation of pitiable and fearful things (for this is proper to this kind of imitation), in the first place (1452b28–33)

Aristotle then considers which kinds of plots best accomplish this function Although he uses one set of criteria for good plots in *Poetics* 13 and a

[78] An excellent modern example of the combination of *peripeteia* and recognition occurs in Thomas Hardy s *Mayor of Casterbridge*, chap 19, where Henchard discovers that Elizabeth is not his daughter

different set in *Poetics* 14, these two accounts are more consistent with one another than is often thought

Poetics *13 Changes and Characters*

After the short introduction quoted above, *Poetics* 13 gives a list of the possible combinations of what I shall call "change types" and "character types " Since a tragic plot is a movement or change (*metabasis*) between the end points of good and bad fortune, there are two possible kinds of change that which begins in good fortune and ends in bad fortune, and that which begins in bad fortune and ends in good fortune Three possible "character types," that is, kind of qualities indicated by *ēthos* in the technical sense of a part of tragedy, are also mentioned in *Poetics* 13 These are the characters of "decent" (*epieikeis* 1452b34) people, people "outstanding in excellence and justice" (1453a8),[79] "evil people" (*mochthērous* 1452b36, cf *sphodra ponēron* 1453a1), and the "in-between man" (1453a7) In *Poetics* 13, Aristotle discusses the different possible combinations of these three character types with the two possible change types Although there are in fact six logically possible combinations, Aristotle lists only four combinations in *Poetics* 13 [80] In the list below, the combinations not explicitly mentioned by Aristotle are bracketed, as are my own comments and examples Because Aristotle does not rank all these combinations, they are listed below in logical rather than hierarchical order

1 Someone outstanding in excellence changes from good to bad fortune This is *miaron* (revolting), but not pitiable or fearful (1452b34–36) [Example Aeschylus's Prometheus]

[2 Someone outstanding in excellence changes from bad to good fortune This arouses admiration, inimical to pity and fear Example Euripides' Alcestis]

3 An evil person changes from good to bad fortune This has the *philanthropon* but neither pity nor fear (1453a1–4) [Example the suitors of the "double plot" of the *Odyssey* (1453a30–33)]

4 An evil person changes from bad to good fortune This is most untragic of all, for it is not *philanthropon*, pitiable, or fearful (1452b36–1453a1) [Example Euripides' Medea]

[79] On *epieikēs*, see chap 3 (Problems)

[80] These possible combinations are discussed and variously analyzed by, for example, Dupont-Roc and Lallot, *Poetique*, 240–45, Else, *Argument*, 367–75, and Halliwell, *Aristotle s Poetics*, 218–22

5   An in-between person changes from good to bad fortune, because of
hamartia, "error" (1453a7–10) This is the best tragedy according to [the
principles of] craft" (1453a22–23) [Example Sophocles' Oedipus
(1453a11)]

   {6   An in-between person changes from bad to good fortune Examples
   Orestes and Iphigenia in Euripides' *Iphigenia in Tauris*]

Of these logical possibilities, (2) on the list above is nowhere mentioned
in the *Poetics* While (6) is not listed in *Poetics* 13, the *Iphigenia in Tauris*
plot that is praised in *Poetics* 14 appears in fact to have this very combination

In *Poetics* 13, Aristotle writes that the best plot is (5) on the list above,
and that the "most untragic" is (4) Since he praises (6) in *Poetics* 14, we
may tentatively rank this combination as second-best The remaining
three combinations are all defective, and Aristotle is not concerned with
ranking them If we want to do so, (3) should probably be ranked first of
the three, since it at least has "the *philanthropon*," followed by (2), and
then (1), which is said to be *miaron* This gives us the following tentative
ranking of the six combinations, from best to worst (5), (6), (3), (2), (1),
(4)

   Some brief explanation of the examples given in the list above is in order
here It is very difficult to find an example of (1) in the extant plays The
best candidate is Prometheus, in Aeschylus's *Prometheus Bound*, a god who
suffers bad fortune That Aristotle believed gods as a class to be outstanding in excellence is clear from his remarks in *Politics* 3, where he discusses
the ostracism of someone who is "so outstanding in excess of excellence"
(1284a3–4) as to be "like a god among human beings" (1284a10–11) I
take Euripides' Alcestis to be an example of (2), for she is outstanding in
excellence (see, e g , *Alcestis* 83–84, 993), and she attains the good fortune
of salvation and glory after initial bad fortune This kind of plot is more
likely to arouse admiration than pity and fear Aristotle gives us an example of (3) when he cites the *Odyssey* as an example of a "double plot," in
which the "better people" have opposite ends from the "worse people"
(1453a30–33) The "worse people," who come to a bad end, are clearly
the suitors Euripides' Medea is a good example of (4) Medea is said to
kill her children with knowledge at 1453b28–29, and the kind of person
who would do this is surely evil [81] Oedipus is given as an example of (5),

[81] However justified Medea s anger is, Aristotle would certainly classify her child-murder among the acts, like the matricide committed by Alcmeon in Euripides play, that a
person would die rather than be compelled to commit (*EN* 1110a26–29)

at 1453a11.[82] I take Orestes and Iphigenia in the *Iphigenia in Tauris* to be examples of (6). This play moves from bad to good fortune, and Iphigenia and Orestes are neither evil nor exceptionally good.

Aristotle's reasons for rejecting combinations (1) through (4) are, for the most part, explicit and understandable. We can reconstruct his reasoning as follows. A good tragedy arouses pity and fear (1452b32). But the defective types (1) through (4) do not do this (1452b35–36; 1453a1; 1453a3–4). This is because (γάρ: 1453a4) pity concerns the person who suffers unmerited bad fortune, and fear concerns the person "like" us (1453a4–7).[83] There are, then, three requirements for the arousal of pity and fear: a person who does not deserve to suffer, bad fortune, and a person "like" us. The first two requirements are necessary for pity, and the third is necessary for fear. It is clear that the exceptionally good and evil people in all four defective types are not "like" us, and so cannot arouse fear. It is also clear, in three of the proscribed cases, that pity cannot be aroused. In (2) and (4), the passage from bad to good fortune excludes pity for at least a large part of the tragedy, and in (3), an evil person who suffers does not arouse pity because the first requirement (unmerited suffering) is not met.

One problem presented by (3) and (4) is the meaning of "the *philanthropon*." This puzzling expression occurs in only one other passage in the *Poetics*: "In *peripeteiai* and in simple [organizations of] events, they achieve what they wish wonderfully, for this is tragic and *philanthropon*. This occurs when the clever but evil man is deceived, as Sisyphus is, and the brave but unjust man is defeated" (18.1456a19–23). Most interpretations of "the *philanthropon*" fall into two categories: "poetic justice" or the "moral sense," and "sympathy" or "humanity."[84] Christopher Carey, however, has convincingly demonstrated that these interpretations are inadequate. The *philanthropon*, he argues, is not an emotion but a quality of the plot that produces an agreeable, pleasing effect on the audience. It is the opposite of the *miaron* (1452b36).[85] Because the *philanthropon* is neither a tragic emotion, like pity and fear, nor an essential part of the plot structure, it need not detain us further.

[82] Oedipus and Thyestes are examples (οἷον: 1453a11) of the in-between person as well as of "those with great good reputation and good fortune," pace G.M.A. Grube, who argued that they are examples of the latter only. *The Greek and Roman Critics*, 80 n. 3, cited and criticized by Moles, "Notes," 77–78.

[83] On "unmerited good fortune" and "like us," see chap. 3 ("Problems")

[84] See the bibliographical survey given by Carey, "Philanthropy," 133. In addition to Carey's important article, see Lamberton, *"Philanthropia,"* and Moles, *"Philanthropia."*

[85] Carey, "Philanthropy," 137.

This brings us to a consideration of (1) on the list of change and character combinations Aristotle's rejection of this plot is puzzling in one way, for the exceptionally good person who suffers bad fortune might seem to us to be a subject ideally calculated to arouse pity (though not fear, since this person is not "like" us) In Aristotle's view, however, an exceptionally good person is the subject of praise rather than pity [86] It is more difficult to understand why Aristotle writes that (1) is "not pitiable or fearful, but *miaron*" (1452b35–36) Because Aristotle does not explain what he means, any account of *miaron* in this passage must be somewhat speculative However, some helpful information is provided by Parker's analysis of the ordinary Greek sense of this word In a broad sense, *miaros* means "disgusting" or "shameless," and in a narrower sense it means "defiled" or "polluted " *Miaros* in this narrow sense refers to a dangerous and contagious condition that makes a person ritually impure, the opposite of *katharos* (pure) [87] In the *Poetics* also, I shall argue, *miaron* means "shameful" and "disgusting," and it is opposed to tragic (rather than ritual) katharsis It is not itself an emotion, however, like "the *philanthropon*," "the *miaron*" refers to a quality of a plot that has an effect of a certain kind on the audience [88] By opposing and preventing pity and fear, the *miaron* opposes and prevents *katharsis*

The *miaron* is connected with shameful events in two passages in *Poetics* 14 At 1453b37–1454a2, Aristotle states that a plot in which someone attacks a *philos* with knowledge, as Haimon does in Sophocles' *Antigone*, has the *miaron* Again, at 1454a2–4, Aristotle writes that a plot in which someone harms a *philos* without knowledge of *philia* does not have the *miaron* It appears from these two passages that a plot in which someone attacks a *philos* with knowledge has the *miaron* Harm of *philos* by *philos*, whether or not it is done with knowledge, is *miaron* in the ordinary Greek sense of "shameful" or "polluted " In the *Poetics* passages, however, a more narrowly "moral" sense of "shameful" would be appropriate To harm a *philos with knowledge* is *miaron* in the sense of "morally" shameful, lacking the *aidōs* necessary to life in society Such an act arouses neither pity nor fear, but disgust, revulsion, and anger A plot in which an event of this kind occurs has the *miaron*, and arouses emotions that oppose and prevent

[86] See chap 3 (The Plot-Character Distinction)

[87] Parker, *Miasma*, 3–5 Cf Moulinier, *Pur*, index verborum, s v μιαρός Else, *Argument*, 424–27, notes the importance of the opposition between *miaros* and *katharos* for an understanding of the *miaron* in tragedy, although I disagree with his views on these concepts

[88] Carey, Philanthropy, 137, has this view of the *miaron*

pity and fear. In so doing, it opposes and prevents the pleasure and katharsis that come from pity and fear.

Aristotle's use of the term *miaron* in *Poetics* 13 is much more problematic. When he writes that a plot is *miaron* in which an *epieikēs* goes from
good to bad fortune, Aristotle cannot be using the word in quite the same
way he does in *Poetics* 14. The unfortunate *epieikēs* (that is, the person who
excels in "moral" excellence), is not doing anything "morally" shameful.
There are also good reasons for rejecting the view of some scholars that the
downfall of an exceptionally good person is *miaron* because it arouses
"moral outrage" or creates "ethical confusion."[89] First, Aristotle does not
express outrage or confusion in the ethical works when he discusses, for
example, the *eudaimōn* (happy) person who suffers the fate of Priam (*EN*
1100a4–9, 1101a6–8). Second, this view incorrectly assumes that Aristotle characterizes the downfall itself as *miaron*, and fails to take into account that Aristotle is discussing tragic plots rather than real-life actions
in *Poetics* 13.

A better interpretation views the *miaron* in *Poetics* 13 as a quality of the
plot that imitates the passage to bad fortune of an exceptionally good person, and it also preserves the connection this term has in ordinary Greek
with the shameful. Because tragedy is the imitation of pitiable and fearful
action, to make the downfall of an exceptionally good person the subject
of a tragedy is to represent such an event as pitiable and fearful. If Aristotle
agreed with Plato that this kind of representation has a shameful element,
one that arouses disgust and revulsion rather than pity, he might well have
called it *miaron*.

Plato believes that the *epieikēs* does not think death is an evil, and is not
given to excessive grief (*Rep.* 3.387d5–e8). Moreover, when Plato's Socrates drinks the hemlock, he is, according to Phaedo, *eudaimōn* rather than
pitiable (*Phaedo* 58e1–59a1). Plato stresses this point at the end of the
Phaedo, where Socrates forbids his companions to weep.[90] Again, in the
Apology, Plato's Socrates explains why he does not produce "pitiable dramas" (35b7) in court, as do those defendants who weep, plead, and bring
forward children and friends "so as to be pitied as much as possible"
(34c4). If those who "excel in wisdom, courage, or any other excellence"
should do such things, says Socrates, this would be shameful (35a1–3).
Just as he condemns real-life "pitiable dramas" as shameful, so Plato also

[89] For "moral outrage," see Stinton, "*Hamartia*," 238 and n. 2; for "ethical confusion,"
see Adkins, "Aristotle," 99.

[90] *Phaedo* 117c–e. On the *Phaedo* as a "philosophical tragedy," see Raphael, *Paradox*,
82–86, who calls attention to *Phaedo* 58e–59a

condemns those presented by tragedy and epic When these imitations lead us to "praise and pity" the man who "claims to be good," but who "grieves out of season" (*Rep.* 10.606b2–3), they lead us to approve what we ourselves would be ashamed to do (605e5), and what a good person would be ashamed to imitate (3 396d6).

Although Aristotle places a much higher value on external goods, he agrees with Plato that the exceptionally good person can never be altogether pitiable: "The *eudaimōn*," he writes, "would never become wretched, but he would certainly not be blessed, if he met with the misfortunes of Priam" (*EN* 1101a6–8). Aristotle also agrees with Plato that the good person will not grieve excessively over bad fortune (*EN* 1124a14–16). Thus, in Aristotle's view, to represent an exceptionally good person as wretched and pitiable, to show this person weeping and wailing, is ethically false. It is likely that Aristotle, like Plato, found such a representation offensive. If he did, he might well have believed that a plot of this kind has a shameful (*miaron*) element, which arouses revulsion and disgust, antithetical to pity and katharsis

It remains to be seen why Aristotle believes that the in-between person ([5] and [6] on the list above) is the best dramatic agent. The in-between person is characterized as someone who is *not* outstandingly excellent or vicious, and as someone whose bad fortune is due to *hamartia*.[91] Aristotle requires that the in-between person not be outstanding in excellence or vice because he believes tragedy is the imitation of pitiable and fearful action rather than the imitation of praiseworthy or blameworthy *ēthos*. Aristotle's requirement that bad fortune be due to *hamartia* also depends, in large part, on this view of tragedy. *Hamartia* accounts for a change, according to probability or necessity, from good to bad fortune, yet it does not interfere with the emotional responses of pity and fear.[92] In *Poetics* 13 (1453a8–10), Aristotle lists two reasons why bad fortune may be probable or necessary, rather than the result of mere chance vice (*kakia, mochthēria*) and *hamartia*. Aristotle excludes vice because it is the cause of *deserved* bad fortune. *Hamartia*, on the other hand, can explain how bad fortune is both undeserved and probable or necessary *Hamartia* is itself made necessary or probable by the constraints of human nature, and it in turn makes bad

---

[91] Some recent studies of *hamartia* are those of Adkins, "Aristotle", Bremer, *Hamartia*, Dawe, "Reflections", Halliwell, *Aristotle's Poetics*, 215–22, Moles, "Notes , Radt, ' Poetik", Said, *Faute*, Stinton, "Hamartia", and Sorabji, *Necessity*, 295–98

[92] A similar point is made by Stinton, "Hamartia, ' 229, and Heath, *Poetics*, 81–82 On the connection between *hamartia* and probability or necessity, see the perceptive remarks of Janko, *Poetics I*, 102

fortune necessary or probable. Thucydides expresses a common point of view when he states that people "are all by nature liable to *hamartia*, both in private and in public affairs."[93] If *hamartia* is part of human nature, people who commit *hamartia* are like us in having a very human characteristic.

Is it possible to be more precise about what tragic *hamartia* involves? A clue to Aristotle's concept of tragic *hamartia* is provided by *Nicomachean Ethics* 5.8. Aristotle seems to have Oedipus's case in mind when he writes, in distinguishing voluntary from involuntary acts at 1135a28–30, that "it is possible for the person struck to be one's father, and [for the striker] to know that it is a human being or some bystander, but to be ignorant that it is his father." It is less obvious, however, that *hamartia* in the *Poetics* should, as some have argued,[94] be identified with a specific kind of involuntary act discussed in this chapter of the *Nicomachean Ethics*: a *hamartēma*.

The issue is complicated by the fact that, as Richard Sorabji points out, Aristotle uses *hamartēma* in two senses in *Nicomachean Ethics* 5.8. At 1135b18, *hamartēma* is used in what Sorabji calls a "specific sense." *Hamartēma* also has a generic sense, at 1135b12, where it refers to the genus of harms done in ignorance. This genus includes *hamartēma* in the specific sense.[95]

A *hamartēma* in the specific sense is one of three kinds of "harms" (*blabai*: 1135b11). One kind of harm, an *adikēma* (injustice), is harm done with knowledge. This category includes acts done without prior deliberation because of anger or other emotions, as well as acts done by choice because of vice (1135b19–25). The two other kinds of "harms" are both done "in ignorance" (1135b12). One is a "mischance" (*atuchēma*), which takes place "when the harm occurs contrary to reasonable expectation [*paralogōs*]," and when the origin of the action is outside the agent (1135b16–19). The other kind of harm done in ignorance is a *hamartēma* in the specific sense. This is something that occurs "not contrary to reasonable ex-

---

[93] Thucydides, 3.45 3, quoted by Said, *Faute*, 140–41.

[94] See, for example, Bremer, *Hamartia*, 18–20, Dupont-Roc and Lallot, *Poétique*, 245, Bywater, *Aristotle on the Art*, 215, and the works cited by Sorabji, *Necessity*, 295 n. 26.

[95] Sorabji, *Necessity*, 297 Sorabji's analysis of *hamartia* in the *Poetics* was in many respects anticipated by D W. Lucas, *Poetics*, 301–2, who did not, however, work out the ethical details so carefully. Sorabji (297 n. 37, citing Stinton, "*Hamartia*," 230–31) also calls attention to a third usage at 1135b22, where the verb *hamartanein* refers to the doing of injustices with knowledge, because of certain emotions but not because of vice (1135b23–25). This third usage is of less interest because, as I argue below, *hamartia* in the *Poetics* is closely connected with ignorance.

pectation but without vice . . . when the origin of the cause is in the agent" (1135b17–19).

Sorabji argues that Oedipus's killing of Laius is not a *hamartēma* in the specific sense, which, unlike an *atuchēma*, involves negligence (*Necessity*, 297). A *hamartēma* in the specific sense is culpable, for it is "not contrary to reasonable expectation," and the cause of the action is in the agent (279). Because the parricide was contrary to reasonable expectation, Sorabji argues, Oedipus's act is not a *hamartēma* in the specific sense, but an *atuchēma* (297). However, if Oedipus's act is not a *hamartēma* in this specific sense, it is a *hamartēma* in the *generic* sense in which the term is used at 1135b12, where it refers to "the genus which includes both *atuchēma* and *hamartēma* in the specific sense" (297). A *hamartēma* in this generic sense is harm done "in ignorance   when one does not do what one supposed, or to whom or with what or for the sake of what" (*EN* 1135b12–13).

Sorabji's insight, that a tragic *hamartia* is due to ignorance, unlike an "injustice" committed "with knowledge," is in the main correct. However, his view that both nonculpable *atuchēmata* and culpable *hamartēmata* can be tragic *hamartiai* does not accurately reflect Aristotle's ideas.[96] The view that *hamartia* can involve culpability is in conflict with Aristotle's statement in *Poetics* 13 that tragedy represents bad fortune caused by *hamartia* and not by vice. On the other hand, there are advantages to the view that a *hamartia* is an act done in ignorance, a nonculpable factual error, as opposed to vice.[97] Looked at this way, *hamartia* can be a genuine alternative to vice, and it can also be an action that is part of the plot, as opposed to *ēthos*. Thus, while nonculpable tragic *hamartia* cannot be identified with *hamartēma* in either sense used in *Nicomachean Ethics* 5 8, it resembles a (generic) *hamartēma* in being an action (πρᾶξη 1135b13) done in ignorance of "what, or to whom, or with what, or for the sake of what" one acts (*EN* 1135b13).

If a tragic *hamartia* is an action done in ignorance of any of the things just mentioned, it is, as Humphry House writes, "a specific error which a

---

[96] Sorabji, *Necessity*, 296–97 and n 29 This broad view of *hamartia* has now gained wide acceptance Heath writes that *hamartia* includes "a range of moral errors with mitigating circumstances" (*Poetics*, 81 n 71) He cites Stinton, "*Hamartia*," Moles, 'Notes,' and Sorabji See also Halliwell, *Aristotle's Poetics*, 221

[97] The view that a *hamartia* is a nonculpable factual error is the "orthodox" view against which Stinton argues in "*Hamartia*" Those who hold the factual-error view include Bremer, *Hamartia*, 20, D W Lucas, *Poetics*, 299–307, Dodds, "Misunderstanding", Else, *Argument*, 379–85, House, *Poetics*, 94–96, and Bywater, *Aristotle on the Art*, 215

man makes or commits."[98] For example, Oedipus's *hamartiai* are his acts of killing Laius and marrying Jocasta in ignorance of their identity. In Sophocles' *Trachiniai*, Deianeira's *hamartia* in giving the poisoned shirt to Heracles is done in ignorance of what the poison is.[99] In Sophocles' *Ajax*, Ajax's *hamartia* in killing the herds is done in ignorance of what the herds are. In Aeschylus's *Persians*, Xerxes' *hamartia* in attacking Greece is done in ignorance of the result (defeat). This kind of ignorance is most important. In fact, because tragic *hamartia* is the cause of a change from good to bad fortune, ignorance of the actual result is always involved, even if other kinds of ignorance are also in question. For example, Oedipus's act is done in ignorance that the man he strikes is Laius, but it is also done in ignorance of the more remote consequence of this act: his own eventual change to bad fortune.

Because a *hamartia* is an action, and because it can be due to ignorance of such a variety of things, it cannot simply be a mistake in the identity of a *philos* that is then discovered in recognition. Nor need it be part of a complex plot.[100] A *hamartia* can lead directly to a *peripeteia*, as it does, for example, when Deianeira gives the poisoned shirt to Heracles. *Hamartia* can also, as in *Oedipus the King*, be followed by recognition and *peripeteia*. However, a *hamartia* might, in principle, also cause downfall within a simple plot, although examples in the tragedies are hard to find. Perhaps the best example is Aeschylus's *Prometheus Bound*, in which Prometheus's change to bad fortune is frequently said to be due to *hamartia*,[101] but where no change in direction of the action occurs. Because this play does not represent the downfall of an in-between person, however, it is hard to say how Aristotle would have regarded this *hamartia*.

Aristotle's statement that the change from good to bad fortune should be brought about by a "great *hamartia*" (1453a15–16) is, as Dupont-Roc and Lallot note, to be connected with his view that tragedy concerns people "in great good reputation and good fortune" (1453a10). The magnitude of the change to bad fortune brought about by *hamartia* corresponds to the greatness of the initial good fortune.[102] Thus, a "great *hamartia*" is one capable of bringing about this change. As Aristotle states in the *Politics*, even "small *hamartiai*" can injure bodies and ships that are in poor

---

[98] House, *Poetics*, 94.

[99] This and other examples are given by Bremer, *Hamartia*, 18.

[100] These views were defended by Else, *Argument*, 379–85.

[101] See Said, *Faute*, 96–107.

[102] Dupont-Roc and Lallot, *Poétique*, 247.

condition, but those in good condition can withstand "more *hamartiai*" (1320b33–39).

A *hamartia*, then, is an action due to ignorance of the actual result, and, in some cases, to ignorance of various other kinds as well. Ignorance of the actual result, as noted above, is also involved in *peripeteia*. *Peripeteia*, however, may be caused by someone else in the play, while a *hamartia* is always an error of the person whose change from good to bad fortune is represented. A *hamartia* is an action that is not vicious but that results in the agent's "missing the mark" (*hamartanein*), and so leads by necessity or probability to bad fortune. *Hamartia* explains why bad fortune occurs. It allows us to see bad fortune as a necessary part of human nature, and not due to chance or to vice. It serves, therefore, as a link in the chain of a necessary or probable sequence of events, without interfering with the tragic responses of pity and fear.

Poetics 14. Pathos *and Recognition*

Poetics 14, like *Poetics* 13, is concerned with how plot can best arouse pity and fear. At 1453b11–14 Aristotle writes: "Since the poet must produce the pleasure that comes from pity and fear by means of imitation, it is clear that this must be put into the events." However, while *Poetics* 13 was concerned with good and bad combinations of change and character types, *Poetics* 14 discusses good and bad combinations of a *pathos* with the knowledge or ignorance of the agent.

Aristotle begins by discussing the kinds of *pathē*[103] that will best arouse pity and fear: "Let us determine what kinds of happenings appear terrible or pitiable" (1453b14–15). First, he gives an exhaustive list ("of necessity these kinds of actions must be either   or" 1453b15–17) of the possible kinds of *pathē*, classified according to the kind of relationship between the people involved. *Pathē* may occur between *philoi*, neutrals, or enemies. Aristotle then rejects, as not pitiable (1453b17) or fearful,[104] *pathē* that occur between neutrals or enemies. The best plot is that in which *philos* kills or is about to kill *philos* (1453b19–22). In the rest of the chapter, Aristotle is concerned only with this best kind of *pathos*.

[103] That the actions in question are indeed *pathē* is clear because they fit the definition of *pathos* in *Po* 11 ("a destructive or painful action"), and from Aristotle's use of the word *pathos* at 1453b18.

[104] "Fearful" should be understood here, although it is not mentioned along with "pitiable", both emotional effects are mentioned at 1453b14–15, where *deina* (terrible) is substituted for *phobera* (fearful).

170

A *pathos* between *philoi* may occur in a number of different ways, some of which Aristotle lists at 1453b27–36. He then writes: "And it cannot happen in any way besides these. For it is necessary for people to act, or not to act, and [to do this] either with knowledge, or without knowledge" (1453b36–37). This statement lists two sets of alternatives. First, a *pathos* may either actually occur, or be about to occur (*mellon*)[105] without actually occurring. Second, it may be a *pathos* between *philoi* who either know or do not know of their relationship. That knowledge or ignorance means knowledge or ignorance of *philia* is clear from the statement that people may act in ignorance and later recognize *philia* (1453b30–31), and from Aristotle's examples, in all of which knowledge or ignorance of *philia* is in question. If these two sets of alternatives are combined—*pathos* occurring/ *pathos* about to occur but not occurring, and knowledge/ignorance—there are four logical possibilities. I list them in the order in which Aristotle ranks them, from worst to best:

I.

1. A *pathos* is about to occur, with knowledge, but does not occur.
2. A *pathos* occurs, with knowledge.
3. A *pathos* occurs, in ignorance.
4. A *pathos* is about to occur, in ignorance, but does not occur.

There are two difficulties in Aristotle's exposition of these possible combinations. First, there is a textual problem. In Kassel's text, Aristotle lists only three of these four possibilities at 1453b27–36: (2) through (4) on the list above. Moreover, he says that the last possibility he lists in this passage is "the third" (1453b34), immediately before stating that these are the only possibilities (1453b36–37, quoted above). It is clear, however, that a mention of (1) has dropped out of our text, for Aristotle goes on to say, at 1453b37–38: "Of these, the worst is to be about to act with knowledge and not to act."[106]

Another puzzling feature in Aristotle's exposition is that, in giving examples of plots that involve ignorance ([3] and [4] on the list above), Aristotle adds another element that is not included on his exhaustive list of ways in which an action may be accomplished: recognition. He appears to assume that ignorance is followed by recognition, either before or after

[105] On "about to occur" see above, "*Pathos*."

[106] Gudeman, *Aristoteles*, restores ἔστι δὲ μὴ πρᾶξαι εἰδότας after Μήδειαν (1453b29). While this creates problems for τρίτον (1453b34), some such restoration is certainly necessary. See Else, *Argument*, 418–19, for a discussion of the textual problems.

the *pathos* occurs.[107] Thus, in giving Sophocles' *Oedipus the King* as an example of (3), Aristotle writes that in this plot people act in ignorance, "and then later recognize *philia*" (1453b30–31), and in outlining (4) (of which the plot of Euripides' *Iphigenia in Tauris* is given as an example at 1454a7), he writes that in this plot people are about to act in ignorance, but recognize [sc., *philia*] before acting (1453b34–36) A moment's reflection will show that Aristotle is correct in assuming that ignorance is followed by recognition. Ignorance may be of interest for its own sake in a psychological drama, but it contributes nothing, in itself, to the necessary or probable sequence of events that makes up an Aristotelian tragic plot, an imitation of action. The movement of this plot is affected only when recognition follows ignorance We should, then, rephrase the characterizations of (3) and (4) given in list I above The amended list of possibilities then reads.

II

1 A *pathos* is about to occur, with knowledge, but does not occur

2 A *pathos* occurs, with knowledge

3 A *pathos* occurs, in ignorance, and then recognition takes place

4. A *pathos* is about to occur, in ignorance, recognition takes place, and the *pathos* does not occur

We are now in a better position to understand why Aristotle prefers some of these types of plots to others. He disapproves of (1) and (2), those that involve knowledge. He states (1453b37–39) that (1) is the worst possible type because (γάρ) it has the *miaron*, and is "without *pathos*"—that is, a *pathos* is not really "about to occur." The statement that a type (3) plot does *not* have the *miaron* (1454a3–4) suggests that a type (2) plot has the *miaron*, because someone harms a *philos* with knowledge [108] This suggests, then, that (2) is the second-worst type because it, like (1), has the *miaron*, although it has the advantage of having a *pathos* The kind of plot in which someone acts with knowledge is also, of course, a plot without recognition. Unless *peripeteia* occurs without recognition, in a way that is not mentioned in *Poetics* 14, this plot will be of the inferior, simple type.

Plot types (3) and (4), those that involve ignorance and recognition, are the best. Aristotle states that (3) is "better" because (γάρ) it lacks the *miaron* and it has recognition (1454a2–4). He then states that (4) is "best,"

---

[107] This feature of Aristotle's exposition is noted by Else, *Argument*, 419, and Dupont-Roc and Lallot, *Poétique*, 256 "Ignorance always implies a recognition that comes afterwards "

[108] On "without *pathos*" see above, "*Pathos*,' and on the *miaron*, see ' *Poetics* 13 "

without giving a reason (1454a4–9). His reason might be that in (4) alone, recognition is *necessarily* coincident with *peripeteia*. Only in this plot does recognition necessarily prevent bad fortune from occurring, causing a *peripeteia* that turns the action back toward good fortune. In (3), on the other hand, recognition after the *pathos* makes an unhappy ending necessary.[109] Here, recognition *may* be coincident with *peripeteia* (as it is in *Oedipus the King*), but this is not a necessary quality of this plot type, as it is of (4). It depends, instead, on the skill of the poet. For example, Hippolytus in Euripides' play goes from good to bad fortune, harmed by his father. Recognition occurs after the *pathos*, but there is no coincident *peripeteia*: Hippolytus is dying, and no return to good fortune is possible.

It appears, then, that Aristotle ranks the four plot types according to their use of the three parts of the plot: *pathos*, recognition, and *peripeteia*. If we add an account of this feature to the list of plot types given above, it will be clear what criteria Aristotle uses to rank these types. List III is an expanded and annotated version of list II, giving the types, once again in order from worst to best, with my comments in brackets:

III.

1. A *pathos* is about to occur, with knowledge, but does not occur. Example: Haimon's attack on Creon in the *Antigone* (1453b37–1454a2). [This plot *lacks pathos*.][110]

2. A *pathos* occurs, with knowledge. Example: *Medea* (1453b27–29). [This is a *simple plot, with pathos*.]

3. A *pathos* occurs, in ignorance, and then recognition takes place. Example: *Oedipus the King* (1453b29–34). [This is a *complex plot, with pathos and recognition*; it ends in bad fortune.]

4. A *pathos* is about to occur, in ignorance; recognition takes place, and the *pathos* does not occur. Example: *Iphigenia in Tauris* (1453b34–36; 1454a4–9). [This is a *complex plot, with pathos, in which recognition is coincident with peripeteia*; it ends in good fortune.]

In *Poetics* 14, then, Aristotle ranks plot types according to the criterion of good use of the three parts of the plot. The best plot type is complex

[109] See chap. 4 ("Necessity and Probability") on happy and unhappy endings. On Aristotle's admiration for a plot of type (3), the *Iphigenia in Tauris*, see Winkler, "Oscar," and Belfiore, "Iphigenia."

[110] It is unlikely that Aristotle thinks this minor incident is central to the plot, and that Sophocles' *Antigone* is an example of (1). However, a play in which this incident were central would be of this type.

(13. 1452b31–32), and has recognition coincident with *peripeteia* (11. 1452a32–33); (4) has all these characteristics.

This view of Aristotle's criteria for ranking plot types not only makes sense of the hierarchy in *Poetics* 14; it also suggests a possible way of reconciling *Poetics* 13 and 14. In *Poetics* 14, (4) (the *Iphigenia* plot) is called "best" (1454a4), while (3) (the *Oedipus* plot) is only second-best (1454a2). In *Poetics* 13, on the other hand, "Oedipus" is twice listed among the examples of good subjects of the "best tragedies" (1453a23), those with unhappy endings (1453a25–26). Thus (3), the plot that is only second-best in *Poetics* 14, would appear to be best in *Poetics* 13. Scholars have long been puzzled by this apparent inconsistency.[111] The criterion of good use of the three parts of the plot, however, suggests that Aristotle may well have preferred (3) (the *Oedipus* plot type) in absolute terms, provided it is skillfully constructed so as to contain a *peripeteia* coincident with a recognition.

It is interesting to note that the plot of *Oedipus the King* in particular (though not all plots of this type) uses all the three parts of the plot in the best way, just as does (4). It is complex, and, in 11. 1452a33, it is given as an example of a plot in which recognition is coincident with *peripeteia*. *Oedipus the King* has the additional advantage of an unhappy ending. This play, then, combines the advantages of (4) with those of (3): it is a particularly skillful example of (3). In (4), on the other hand, the best combination of recognition and *peripeteia* is given in a sort of recipe: *pathos* about to occur, in ignorance, recognition, *peripeteia*. Although the best, unhappy, ending is not possible in (4), no special skill is needed by poets who follow this formula in arousing pity and fear "from the organization itself of the events" (14. 1453b2). The poet who is a master of his craft, however, may succeed in combining the advantages of (3) with those of (4) in a plot like that of *Oedipus the King* (3).

Some indication that this view is correct is provided by Aristotle's statement about plots with unhappy endings in *Poetics* 13: "The best tragedy according to [the principles of] craft [κατὰ τὴν τέχνην] is made from this organization [of events]" (1453a22–23). These tragedies, Aristotle continues, "appear most tragic, if they succeed" (1453a27–28).[112] In *Poetics*

---

[111] A good survey of the controversy is given by Moles, "Notes," 82–83

[112] Else, *Argument*, 403, following Duntzer, *Rettung der aristotelischen Poetik*, 159, explains ἂν κατορθωθῶσιν (1453a28) as "if they succeed   in following the rules laid down by the art " This view is also held by D W Lucas, *Poetics*, 147, Bywater, *Aristotle on the Art*, 217, and Gudeman, *Aristoteles*, 248 Radt's arguments against this interpretation are not convincing "*Poetik*," 281–82

14, on the other hand, after praising the *Iphigenia* plot type, Aristotle writes: "For this reason, as was said before, tragedies are not about many families. For seeking not by craft but by chance [οὐκ ἀπὸ τέχνης ἀλλ' ἀπὸ τύχης] they discovered how to contrive this sort of thing in plots" (1454a9–11). This statement is very similar to that of *Poetics* 13: "For at first, the poets recounted the stories they chanced upon [τοὺς τυχόντας μύθους], but now the best tragedies are composed about few families" (1453a17–19). Nevertheless, Aristotle's phrasing is significantly different in the two passages. In *Poetics* 13 he opposes an earlier stage (πρῶτον μέν), at which chance determined plot types, to the present (νῦν δὲ) practice of making the best plots "according to craft." In *Poetics* 14, on the other hand, Aristotle merely states that good plot types were found "not by craft but by chance." There is no indication here that craft has replaced chance, in leading poets to prefer plot (4), with its happy ending.

While this slight difference in phrasing is not the best kind of evidence, especially in a work with as many textual problems as the *Poetics*, it does help support an interpretation that reconciles *Poetics* 13 with *Poetics* 14, on the basis of Aristotle's own criteria. Because the evidence is not conclusive, however, I offer this interpretation as a plausible suggestion only. In the following chapters, I take *Iphigenia in Tauris* and *Oedipus the King* to be examples of the two best plots, without ranking them.

In the first half of chapter 5 I studied each of the three parts of the tragic plot: *pathos*, *peripeteia*, and recognition. The *pathos*, a destructive or painful event, is an essential part of every tragedy, and the best kind of *pathos* takes place between *philoi*. An event need not actually occur to count as a *pathos*. It need only be "about to occur" (*mellon*), in that it would have followed from another event, by probability or necessity, if it had not been prevented from occurring by a more powerful force, such as recognition, and not by mere chance. A *peripeteia*, or reversal, is a discontinuous action that occurs when the action of an agent is prevented from achieving its intended result and arrives instead at an opposite actual result. Because it causes the action of a plot to move in a "complex" (πεπλέγμενος) line that doubles back on itself, *peripeteia* is part of complex plots only. In the best plots, *peripeteia* occurs together with recognition, the other part that belongs only to complex plots. Recognition is a change that affects the movement of the plot from ignorance to knowledge of a *philia* relationship. Recognition "to *philia*" involves acknowledgment that a relative is a *philos* by doing good to this person, while recognition "to enmity" involves harming, or recognizing that one has harmed, a relative.

In the second half of chapter 5 I examined Aristotle's views on what makes plots as a whole good or bad. In *Poetics* 13, Aristotle discusses good and bad combinations of character types with the tragic change from good to bad or bad to good fortune. He prefers a play like *Oedipus the King*, in which a person between the extremes of outstanding excellence and vice changes from good to bad fortune. The in-between person is the best subject for tragedy because his or her actions arouse pity and fear rather than praise or blame. In the best tragedy, the in-between person changes to bad fortune because of a *hamartia*, a nonculpable action done in ignorance of the actual result. In *Poetics* 14, Aristotle ranks plots according to how well they use the three parts of the plot. Here, Aristotle prefers a plot, like that of the *Iphigenia*, in which recognition prevents *pathos* and leads to good fortune. The *Oedipus* plot type, which was praised in *Poetics* 13, is now only second-best. This apparent contradiction can be resolved if we take Aristotle to prefer, in absolute terms, a plot with an unhappy ending in which recognition, coincident with *peripeteia*, occurs after the *pathos*. While this *Oedipus* type of plot is best "according to the principles of craft," the *Iphigenia* type provides an easily followed formula, in which recognition is coincident with *peripeteia*.

Chapter 5 concludes part II, in which I have studied Aristotle's theory of plot structure from the general principles governing the entire plot to the three parts of the plot, separately and in combination. In Aristotle's view, the plot is a *sustasis* of events that is very strongly analogous to a biological *sustasis*. The plot, like the soul of a living thing, is organized according to definite principles for the sake of an end (*telos*) that is its function (*ergon*). The function of the tragic plot is to arouse pity and fear in an audience, and by this means to produce pleasure and katharsis. The second half of this book addresses these emotional effects in detail.

PART III

PITY AND FEAR

*

＊

ARISTOTLE'S biological, psychological, ethical, and rhetorical works have much to say about the emotions. In applying these accounts to the special case of tragic emotion, however, some important differences must be kept in mind. While Aristotle held that the pain or pleasure we experience in response to imitations is in many respects the same as the pain or pleasure we experience in response to the objects imitated, he did not believe we experience the same *emotional* responses in both cases. An emotion involves beliefs and desires as well as physiological responses, and it leads, typically, to specific actions. Imitations, viewed as imitations, clearly lead to different beliefs, desires, and actions. We do not, for example, usually run screaming from a stage monster in the belief that it is about to attack. Specifically, Aristotle's tragic pity and fear differ in a number of ways from the fear (*phobos*) and pity he discusses elsewhere. Pity and fear almost always go together in the *Poetics*, while in the *Rhetoric* the terrible is said to "knock out" pity (2.8.1386a22–23). Again, in *Rhetoric* 2.5, fear is said to be felt at the *phantasia* (appearance or expectation) of imminent danger to ourselves. Tragic fear, on the other hand, is felt "concerning someone similar" to us (*Po.* 1453a4–7). In watching the *Oedipus*, for example, we do not *fear Oedipus*, nor do we fear that we ourselves will discover that we have committed parricide and incest. Instead, we feel fear for ourselves in response to another's sufferings in a way that we do not in typical real-life situations. Yet another difference is that fear is typically aroused directly by particular dangers, while tragic fear is aroused in some other way, in response to "the universal" expressed by poetry. Finally, tragic fear and fear in typical real-life situations are aroused by different kinds of evils. Real-life fear is typically aroused by the *phantasia* of imminent destructive or painful evils (*Rhet.* 2.5.1382a21–22). The *Poetics* (1453b17–22), however, tells us that tragic fear is best aroused not by a merely destructive or painful action (a *pathos*), but by a *pathos* between *philoi*.

Used judiciously, however, Aristotle's detailed accounts of the emotions in his other works help us gain a better understanding of tragic emotion, about which the *Poetics* says so little. Aristotle's other works tell us a great deal about fear aroused in a variety of circumstances, from fear of physical danger (*phobos*) to the shame emotions concerned with fear of disgrace: *aischunē* and *aidōs*. Although the shame emotions are not usually taken into account in studies of the tragic emotions, they are of particular interest for the *Poetics*, in which *philia* is so important. Because pity is a specifically human emotion, which other animals do not experience, Aristotle's biological and psychological works have a good deal less to say about pity than about fear. Pity is discussed in detail in the *Rhetoric*, however, where it is defined in relation to fear, on which it is causally and conceptually dependent.

Part III will take all this material into account, studying a broad range of pity and fear emotions experienced in a variety of circumstances, from typical real-life cases of physical danger to aesthetic, rhetorical, and ethical situations. Chapter 6 deals primarily with Aristotle's works other than the *Poetics*. The first section discusses Aristotle's views on the cognitive and physiological aspects of fear of physical danger (*phobos*), and of pity for others in physical danger. The next section studies these aspects of another kind of fear—shame, or fear of disgrace—and discusses the essential role *aidōs* plays in ethical education. Chapter 6 concludes with an examination of two fear emotions closely associated with poetry and rhetoric: *kataplēxis* and *ekplēxis*. Chapter 7 turns to a consideration of pity and fear in the *Poetics*. This chapter also examines Aristotle's views on how emotion leads to flight or pursuit in typical cases, and on why this does not happen in aesthetic cases. After this study, part IV will consider how emotions function within tragedy to produce katharsis.

Fear, Pity, and Shame in Aristotle's Philosophy

PITY, FEAR, AND PHYSICAL DANGER

ACCORDING to the *De anima*, emotions (*pathē*) are "form in matter" (λόγοι ἔνυλοι: 403a25). That is, they involve a combination of physiological and cognitive responses.[1] For example, anger is "a movement of a body of a certain kind, or of a part or capacity of a body, because of something, and for the sake of something [ὑπὸ τοῦδε ἔνεκα τοῦδε]" (403a26–27). It thus has physical matter ("movement of a body of a certain kind") and cognitive form (the movement occurs "because of something," and "for the sake of something").

The matter of an emotion consists in the physiological responses of heating and expansion, or chilling and contraction. For example, the matter of anger is "boiling of the blood and heat around the heart" (*DA* 403a31–b1).[2] The form of an emotion includes two kinds of cognitive responses. Anger includes a goal-directed desire: it is "a desire to give pain in return" (*DA* 403a30), or "a desire accompanied by pain for what appears [*phaino-menēs*] {to us} to be revenge" (*Rhet.* 1378a31–32). This desire is the final cause, that for the sake of which the blood boils. The other part of the form is the efficient cause, that because of which this movement occurs. According to the *Rhetoric*, anger is aroused "because of what appears [*phai-nomenēn*] {to us} to be a slight on the part of someone not fitted {to slight} anything concerning us or those belonging to us" (2.2.1378a32–33).[3]

---

[1] While the following formulation is an oversimplification, I believe it is useful as an explanatory model Some of the difficulties involved in giving a single uniform account of Aristotle's views on the emotions are discussed further below, this section See also Rorty, "Aristotle", Fortenbaugh, *Emotion*, 79–83, and Charles's cautionary note in *Action*, 178 n. 15 Aristotle's views on *phantasia* involve notorious difficulties of their own, which I cannot discuss here On this topic, see Modrak, *Perception*, 81–110, Nussbaum, *De motu anima-lium*, 221–69, Schofield, "Imagination", and Wedin, *Mind*.

[2] Cf *PA* 650b35–651a2, quoted by Hicks, *De anima*, on 403a31

[3] I depart from Kassel, *Ars rhetorica*, in following the reading of A. τοῦ ὀλιγωρεῖν μὴ προσήκοντος, interpreted as Grimaldi suggests (*Rhetoric II*, ad loc) Modrak, *Perception*, 195 n 74, points out that the *De anima* definition of anger is an abbreviated version of the more complete definitions in the *Rhetoric*, and in *Topics* 156a30–33.

Both the final and the efficient cause of an emotion such as anger involve cognitive responses in that both involve *phantasia*, something that appears [*phainetai*] to us in a certain way, something that we see as an object of pursuit or avoidance.[4] In the case of anger, we have the *phantasia* that giving pain to someone is revenge, and that a person unfit to do so has slighted us. That emotions have cognitive aspects is also indicated by Aristotle's statement in the *Rhetoric* that the emotions affect our judgments (1378a20–21).[5]

Phantasia of an object, whether or not the object is actually perceived, causes the heating or chilling that is the matter of an emotion.

> But in the animal the same part has the capacity to become both larger and smaller and to change its shape, as the parts expand because of heat and contract again because of cold, and alter Alteration is caused by *phantasiai* and sense-perceptions and ideas For sense-perceptions are at once a kind of alteration and *phantasia* and thinking have the power of the actual things For it turns out that the form conceived of the warm or cold or pleasant or fearful is like the actual thing itself That is why we shudder and are frightened just thinking of something All these are affections [*pathē*] and alterations (*DMA* 701b13–23)[6]

> Now the origin of motion is, as we have said, the object of pursuit or avoidance in the sphere of action Of necessity the thought and *phantasia* of these are accompanied by heating and chilling For the painful is avoided and the pleasant pursued, and ⟨the thought and *phantasia* of⟩ the painful and the pleasant are nearly always accompanied by chilling and heating (although we do not notice this when it happens in a small part) This is clear from the passions [*pathēmata*] For feelings of confidence, fears, sexual excitement, and other bodily affections, painful and pleasant, are accompanied by heating or

[4] Nussbaum's view that *phantasia* involves "seeing as" (*De motu animalium*, 230–31) is relatively noncontroversial, provided we limit it to the case of seeing something as an object of pursuit or avoidance. For example, Schofield, who disagrees with Nussbaum in many respects, connects *phantasia* with the thought or 'something like thought" of a "desirable object" ("Imagination,' 110), and with "see[ing] something as a man' (113)

[5] On this passage, see Leighton, "Emotions ' For additional evidence that Aristotelian emotions have cognitive aspects see Fortenbaugh, *Emotion*

[6] Here and in the next passage I quote Nussbaum's translations from *De motu animalium* I omit her brackets around "warm or cold or" in 701b20 There are no textual reasons to doubt this phrase, and it belongs here as an indication that pleasure and pain are correlated with heat and cold A "warm" object is something that gives pleasure, and causes physiological heating and expansion, while a "cold' object is one that gives pain, and causes chilling and contraction

chilling, in some cases of a part, in others of the whole body. (*DMA* 701b33–702a5)

These passages not only tell us that "just thinking" of an object of pursuit or avoidance has physiological effects, causing heating or chilling (the matter of the emotions); they also tell us that pleasure and pain are correlated with these physiological responses. This latter idea is expressed at 702a2–5, and at 701b20–22: "For it turns out that the form conceived of the warm or cold or pleasant or fearful is like the actual thing itself."[7] Fear ("we shudder and are frightened": 701b22) is clearly an example of a painful emotion, characterized by chilling and contraction at the physiological level.[8] Pleasure, on the other hand, is correlated with heat and expansion.[9] Examples of pleasurable emotions are "confidence" and "sexual excitement" (702a2–3), which latter causes an erection (*DMA* 703b4–8, *DA* 432b30–433a1). Aristotle's remarks about the characteristics of young people in *Rhetoric* 2.12 indicate that here also he associated pleasure and its pursuit with heat. The young tend to be ruled by appetite, especially sexual appetite (1389a3–6), and by spirit and anger (1389a9–10). They are full of hope and confidence, and they lack fear (1389a26–29). Aristotle connects these pleasure-seeking characteristics with heat; in a passage reminiscent of Plato's *Laws*, he writes that "the young are as thoroughly warmed by nature as drinkers are by wine" (*Rhet.* 1389a19–20). Spirit (*thumos*) in particular produces heat (*PA* 650b35).

Thus, as a general rule, Aristotelian emotions involve either pleasure and heat, or pain and cold. In the *Rhetoric* and the ethical works, Aristotle usually characterizes the emotions in terms of pleasure and pain rather than heat or cold: "I mean by the emotions desire, anger, fear . . . and in general all those [affections] accompanied by pleasure and pain" (*EN* 1105b21–23). *Rhetoric* 1378a21–22 uses similar language in characterizing the emotions as "all those [affections] accompanied by pain or pleasure."[10] Is this simply another way of characterizing the matter of the emotions? The passages discussed above offer some support for making this connection. Unfortunately, however, the absence of a discussion of

[7] On this passage, see previous note

[8] That the subjective experience of fear is correlated with physiological cold is also clear from "Aristotle," *Prob.* 954b14–15 "If it [sc., the bile] is too hot, fear brings it to a moderate [temperature], and makes one self-possessed and unemotional."

[9] See also *Pol* 1340a42–b4, and Newman, *Politics*, on 1340a42

[10] See also *EN* 1104b14–15 and *EE* 1220b12–14. In stating that emotion is "accompanied by pleasure and pain," Aristotle means that pleasure and pain are part of the emotion, according to Leighton, "Emotions," 155–57 See also his "*Eudemian Ethics*"

the emotions in physiological terms in the *Rhetoric* and ethical works makes it hard to be certain of Aristotle's views

In other respects also, Aristotle did not always trouble to work out in detail the implications of his general rules about the emotions and the application of these rules to particular cases In the *Rhetoric*, for example, the statement that the emotion of hate is "not with pain" (1382a12–13) is hard to reconcile with the characterization of emotion in general as something accompanied by pain or pleasure (*Rhet* 1378a21–22) And is the view that hate is without pain consistent with the statement in *De anima* 403a16–19 that hate is one of the *pathē* that is always accompanied by some affection of the body? Aristotle's views are not clear Again, though anger is a painful emotion (*Rhet* 1378a31), its matter is hot, according to the *De anima* However, anger is not merely painful, it is also accompanied by a kind of pleasure, due to the anticipation of revenge (*Rhet* 1378b1–2)

Aristotle's views on the paradigmatic case of fear (*phobos*), with which we are chiefly concerned, are among the most consistent and clearly defined This emotion is cold and painful, and it is opposed to hot, aggressive, pleasure-seeking emotions, especially those of anger, confidence, and sexual desire

In Aristotle's works other than the *Poetics*, *phobos* usually refers to fear of physical pain or death Like all emotions, *phobos* has what the *De anima* calls matter and form Numerous passages in Aristotle's biological and psychological works indicate that fear is a painful emotion, the matter of which is a chilling and contraction in the region of the heart This in turn produces other involuntary physical reactions such as a pounding of the heart, trembling, and pallor [11] "Aristotle," in *Problems* 27, agrees in these respects with the accounts given in the genuine works, and adds other, specific physical reactions loose bowels due to the escape of heat downward (947b27–29), a rapid and punctuated beating of the heart (947b29–31), thirst, dry mouth, and paralysis of the tongue (947b34–35), trembling of voice, hands, and lower lip (948a35–36), silence (948b21–22), and contraction of the genitals, which occurs "because fear comes from without" and "flight is in the opposite direction" (948b10–12)

The form of fear, like that of anger, has an efficient and a final cause *Rhetoric* 2 5 1382a21–22 defines *phobos* as follows "Let fear be pain and

[11] See *On Respiration* 479b19ff and 480a13ff , *Prob* 888a12ff and 902b37–39, *PA* 650b27ff and 692a23–24, cited by Nussbaum, *De motu animalium*, 350, 355 See also *Prob* 954b13–14 and *Rhet* 1389b32 On the physical aspects of fear and pity in Aristotle and other Greek writers, see Flashar, Grundlagen

disturbance [resulting] from the *phantasia* of imminent [*mellontos*] destructive or painful evil."[12] Thus, the efficient cause of fear is a *phantasia*: it arises "from the *phantasia* of an imminent evil." In the *Rhetoric* definition, *phantasia* is a synonym for "expectation" (*prosdokia*), which is substituted for it at *Rhetoric* 2.5.1382b30–31. "Fear is with the expectation of suffering some destructive *pathos*." In the *Nicomachean Ethics* also, "expectation" enters into the definition of fear: "They define fear as the expectation of evil" (1115a9).

While in the *Rhetoric* and the *De anima* Aristotle does not specify what desire fear involves (its final cause), he does write in *Rhetoric* 2.5.1383a5–8 that "fear makes people deliberate," and that they do not fear where there is no hope of safety. This tells us, somewhat indirectly, that the desire included in the form of fear is that of seeking safety. This emotion, then, like anger, is goal-directed.[13]

The kind of fear with which the *Rhetoric* deals is fear of physical pain or death: "destructive or painful evil." Aristotle is quite explicit about this, writing at the beginning of his discussion of fear in *Rhetoric* 2.5 that "people do not fear all evils, for example, that one will be unjust or slow-witted, but all those evils that can cause great pains or destructions" (1382a22–24). He stresses this point at 1382a28–30. "Those kinds of things are fearful which appear to have a great power to destroy, or cause harm that brings great pain." In *Rhetoric* 2.5, then, Aristotle, like Plato,[14] explicitly distinguishes fear of physical pain or death from fear of other evils. Most often, Aristotle uses the term *phobos* to refer to fear of physically destructive or painful evils, while using the terms *aidōs* and *aischunē* to refer to fear of an evil reputation.

An exception, in which Aristotle uses the term *phobos* in a broader sense, to refer to the expectation of any kind of evil, including that of an evil reputation, is a passage in *Nicomachean Ethics* 3:

> They define *phobos* as "expectation of evil." Indeed we fear all evils, for example, a bad reputation, poverty, sickness, friendlessness, death, but the courageous person is not thought to be concerned with all of these. For it is even necessary and fine to fear some of these, a bad reputation, for example,

---

[12] Cf *EE* 1229b13–16 "Fearful things   are those that appear productive of destructive pain, when they appear near and not far off "

[13] On fear and anger as "practical," "goal-directed" emotions, see Fortenbaugh, *Emotion*, 79–81, and "Emotion and Moral Virtue," 164–67

[14] *Laws* 1 646e–647b, discussed in chap 1 ("A Medicine to Produce *Aidōs*")

and not to fear them is shameful He who fears [them] is decent and *aidēmōn*,
he who does not fear [them] is shameless (*EN* 1115a9–14)

This passage is an important indication that *phobos* does not always refer exclusively to painful and destructive evils. In *Poetics* 14, in fact, Aristotle holds that merely painful and destructive *pathē* do not best arouse tragic *phobos* (1453b17–22).

Aristotle's concept of pity, in his works other than the *Poetics*, is much like that of the Greek tradition. In Greek thought generally, pity (*eleos*, *oiktos*) has the physical manifestations of weeping and groaning.[15] *Eleein* in Homer, unlike the English "to pity," is primarily to do an action rather than to feel a certain way. For example, to pity a friend fallen in war is to seek revenge.[16] In later times also, the orator has a very practical aim in awakening the pity of the judges.[17] A primary way in which orators seek to arouse pity is to appeal to the vulnerability of the audience.[18] Pity is most deeply felt if great misfortune follows previous great good fortune, and it is often accompanied by a judgment that the person pitied did not deserve misfortune.[19] Pity is closely associated with *aidōs* from Homer on, and, like *aidōs*, it inhibits aggressive action toward its objects. To feel pity is to be part of the human community Aidōs, however, is concerned with what is higher and more general, while pity is concerned with the individual and the particular.[20] For example, Hecuba, pleading with her son not to fight the Greeks, bares her breasts, the symbol of motherhood, asking for *aidōs* for them and pity for herself (*Il.* 22.82–83) Hector responds that he has *aidōs* for the Trojans (22.105)[21] While Aristotle is, as we will see, much indebted to this Greek tradition, his classification of *eleos* as an emotion represents a development away from Homer's more objective concept.[22]

[15] On the physical manifestations of pity, see Flashar, "Grundlagen "

[16] Burkert, "Mitleidsbegriff," 69, cites *Il* 5 561, 610, 17 346, 352 On the practical, active aspect of pity in Homer, see Burkert's discussion, esp 69–72, followed by Pohlenz, "Furcht," 52

[17] See Pohlenz, "Furcht," 58, and Dover, *Morality*, 195–97

[18] For a good discussion of this topic, see Stevens, "Commonplaces, ' esp 4

[19] On these points, see Dover, *Morality*, 196–97

[20] These points are made by Burkert, "Mitleidsbegriff, ' 38, 70–72, 89–90, 94–106, 114, cf Erffa, *Aidos*, 10

[21] See Burkert, "Mitleidsbegriff," 89

[22] See ibid , 147–48, Burkert notes that the fact that the gods in the *Iliad* pity without being in danger themselves shows that *eleos* in this work is not an emotion, as it is in Aristotle, but a personal power

As we would expect, Aristotle's psychological and biological works tell us a great deal less about pity than about fear: pity is a distinctively human emotion, which the other animals do not usually feel.[23] Aristotle's most detailed discussion of pity is that of *Rhetoric* 2.8. This account, though brief, is particularly useful because it shows that pity is conceptually and causally dependent on *phobos*.

Although Aristotle nowhere explicitly tells us what the matter of pity is, he does tell us that pity is painful (*Rhet.* 2.8.1385b13). Pity is associated with weeping in his works; this is probably an indication that its matter is moist.[24] *Rhetoric* 1386a19–21 appears to indicate that weeping is a manifestation of pity that distinguishes it from fear: "Amasis, as they say, did not weep over his son being led away to death, but he did so over his friend begging. For the latter is pitiable, the former terrible." We can infer that pity is a cold emotion from the fact that it is painful, and that it frequently accompanies the cold emotion of fear, in terms of which it is defined in *Rhetoric* 2.8 (quoted below). Moreover, the discussion of the characteristics of old age in *Rhetoric* 2.13 clearly shows that pity, like fear, is a cold emotion, opposed to the hot, aggressive emotions that characterize the young. The old have characteristics opposite to those of the young (1389b30), who are discussed in 2.12; "they are chilled while the others [sc., the young] are hot" (1389b30–31). This explains why old age tends to be cowardly: "fear is a kind of chill" (1389b32). In contrast to the young, the old have few and weak desires, and weak spirit (1390a11–13), and they tend to lack hope (1390a7). Because they are weak and think that they are near to suffering all evils, the old tend to pity and to weep (1390a19–22). Aristotle notes that while the young also tend to feel pity, they do so for different reasons: love of humanity (1390a20) and the belief that everyone is good (1389b8–9). The pity of the young depends on the cognitive aspects of this emotion, while that of the old results from their own physical weakness (1390a21) and coldness.

Aristotle does not explicitly state what the desire (final cause) involved in the form of pity is, in the *Rhetoric* or in the *Poetics*, and it is somewhat difficult to determine what it might be. While we often try to help people

[23] A computer search indicates that Aristotle uses *eleos* and its cognates in connection with animals in only one passage, in which he writes that dolphins act "as though" (oĩov) pitying: *HA* 631a19. This passage is noted by Fortenbaugh, "Animals," 153.

[24] On pity and weeping, Schadewaldt, "Furcht," 142 n. 2, cites *HA* 608b8[–9], and "Aristotle," *Physiognomonics* 808a33[–35]. According to Flashar, "Grundlagen," 36, weeping is caused, in Greek medical theory, by excess moisture, and *eleos* is associated with moisture in "Aristotle," *Virtues and Vices* 1250b31ff. (38).

we pity, we also pity people who cannot be helped—for example, those who suffer death or old age (*Rhet.* 2.8.1386a7–9). Partly for this reason, William Fortenbaugh believes that pity is less "practical" than fear.[25] While it is true that, in some cases, there is no particular action we can take when we feel pity, this emotion is surely essentially connected with a desire to help the person we pity. Though our taking action may be impeded by a judgment that there is no action we can take (as can also happen in the case of fear), we desire to give help if we can. In the Greek tradition, to pity is to take a definite action, and even corpses can be pitied. That pity has a practical goal in the *Rhetoric* also is obvious from its inclusion among the emotions that cause people to change their judgments (1378a20–22). The rhetorician arouses pity in order to persuade people to act in a definite way.

The efficient cause of pity is in most respects the same as that of *phobos*. *phantasia* of an imminent physically painful or destructive evil. This is clear from the definitions in the *Rhetoric*. *Rhetoric* 2.5.1382a21–22 defines fear as "pain and disturbance [resulting] from the *phantasia* of imminent destructive or painful evil." Pity is defined in *Rhetoric* 2.8.1385b13–16: "Let pity be pain at an apparent [*phainomenō*] destructive or painful evil of someone who does not deserve to get it, that one could expect oneself, or someone belonging to oneself, to suffer, and this, when it appears [*phainetai*] near." It is important to note that this definition of pity indicates that fear (the expectation of suffering evil), rather than pity, is felt not only for oneself, but also for those "belonging to oneself," for example "parents or children or wives" (1385b28–29, 1386a17–19). One's *philoi* are a part of oneself. In other passages also, the *Rhetoric* states that fear and pity are aroused by the same evils when they happen to different people. "Those things are fearful which are pitiable when they happen to, or are about to happen to, others" (1382b26–27), "Things that people fear for themselves arouse pity when they happen to others" (1386a27–28).

The two emotions also differ in other important ways. For one thing, pity, unlike fear, is felt for past and present as well as future evils, especially when these are vividly present before our eyes (*Rhet.* 1386a28–34).[26] Again, while we do not fear what we do not expect to happen, pity is aroused by unexpected evils. Evils are pitiable when "something evil

---

[25] Fortenbaugh, *Emotion*, 82–83 However, Engberg-Pedersen, *Aristotle's Theory*, 140, argues that pity "contains an attitude towards action," and Leighton, 'Emotions,' 145 and 169 n 4, writes that, while Aristotle does not explicitly tell us the aim of emotions like pity and indignation, "it is part of the larger concept of these emotions"

[26] On this passage, see chap 5 ("*Pathos*")

comes whence it was fitting for something good to come" (*Rhet.* 1386a11–
12). Pity also differs from fear in that it involves a judgment that someone
does not deserve to suffer. Moreover, the definition of pity is conceptually
dependent on the concept of fear. One pities others for things "which one
could expect to suffer [προσδοκήσειεν ἂν παθεῖν] oneself" (1385b14–15).
While fear is not dependent on another emotional state, pity for others
cannot arise unless we expect that we ourselves could suffer the same
things—that is, unless we fear that such things could happen to us also.
Pity, unlike fear, involves thinking of two people: oneself and another.
Finally, the potential optative in the definition of pity, "one *could expect* to
suffer," indicates that pity involves a judgment of a different kind from
that involved in the typical cases of fear of immediate and perceptible
dangers. For example, we fear that our city and *philoi* will be destroyed by
the enemy now at our gates. On the other hand, we pity others who have
lost city and *philoi* in war only if we think this *could* happen to us, even
though no enemy is now attacking us. Pity, then, differs from fear in
involving more complex judgments about what kinds of things could happen to us, and about how we are similar to others. While fear may require
only a grasp of a particular situation, pity requires an understanding of
universals. In chapter 7 I will examine to what extent the account of pity
in the *Poetics* agrees with that of the *Rhetoric*.

FEAR OF DISGRACE: *AIDŌS* AND *AISCHUNĒ*

The shame emotions (*aidōs* and *aischunē*) are not explicitly mentioned in
the *Poetics*, nor have scholars studied them in connection with this work.
Nevertheless, the concept of shame is highly relevant to an understanding
of Aristotle's views on tragedy. Shame, or fear of wrongdoing, produces
and preserves *philia* in Greek society, and tragedy, in Aristotle's view, is
about *philia*. Tragedy also provides an important kind of ethical and emotional education, for it teaches us about our nature as political animals.
Aidōs, as I argue below, has a necessary explanatory role in Aristotle's elliptical account of the acquisition of ethical excellence. Aristotle's views
on *aidōs* also help us give a plausible account of the nature of the emotional
education provided by tragic katharsis by means of pity and fear. Before
we can appreciate the importance of the concept of shame in the *Poetics*,
however, we must understand the views on shame expressed in Aristotle's

189

other works. A fairly lengthy discussion is necessary here because this topic has received relatively little scholarly attention.[27]

Aristotle's views on the shame emotions present many difficulties, however. Those who have studied Aristotle's accounts of shame have sometimes concluded, with some justification, that they are confused or inconsistent.[28] This is particularly true of *aidōs*. Aristotle sometimes writes that it is a *pathos* (EN 4.9.1128b11), and, like the *pathē*, it would seem to have both matter and form.[29] On the other hand, *aidōs*, like the excellences, is frequently said to be a *mesotēs* (mean state),[30] and, in at least one passage (EN 3.8.1116a27–28), *aidōs* appears to be called an excellence In other passages, however (e.g., EN 4.9), *aidōs* is distinguished from true excellence and is said to be praiseworthy only under certain conditions Many of these inconsistencies, I shall argue, are more terminological than conceptual. I also contend that Aristotle's views are more understandable in the context of Greek traditional ideas about shame, which he shared to a great extent.

Aristotle and the Greek Tradition

Carl von Erffa's study of the concept of *aidōs* from Homer to Democritus shows the wide range of social affections and activities it involves [31] According to Erffa, the concept of *aidōs* is closely related to those of *aischunē* (*Aidos*, 21–23) and *deos*, "fear" (28–29). Thucydides' Pericles, for example, states that *deos* and *aischunē* enforce obedience to the written and unwritten laws, using the term *deos* where we might expect *aidōs* [32] In Homer, neglect of *aidōs* often brings fear of anger (28) *Aidōs*, however, is not the same as fear, but is instead "Ehrfurcht" ("respect-fear". 28–29).

In Homer, *aidōs* is the most important ethical concept (52) It originates

---

[27] Among those who discuss Aristotle's views on shame are Burnyeat, "Learning", Fortenbaugh, "Mean-Dispositions', Gauthier and Jolif, 2 1 320–24, Grimaldi, *Rhetoric II*, 105–7, and Stark, *Aristotelesstudien*, 64–86

[28] For example, Stark, *Aristotelesstudien*, believes that Aristotle s views on *aidōs* change and develop, Fortenbaugh, ' Mean-Dispositions,' believes that Aristotle's treatment of the "mean-dispositions" in general is unsatisfactory in many ways

[29] While the ethical works do not use the matter-form terminology of the *De anima*, in these works also the emotions have physical and cognitive aspects

[30] For example, at *EE* 3 7 1233b26 I follow Young in translating *mesotēs* as "mean state" and *meson* as "intermediate" "Temperance," 522 n 4

[31] Erffa, *Aidos* See also, on Greek concepts of *aidōs* and related shame emotions, Dover, *Morality*, 226–42, on *aidōs* in connection with *sōphrosunē*, see North, *Sophrosyne*

[32] Erffa, *Aidos*, 188–90, quoting Thucydides 2 37 3

in and depends on the society of human beings, as opposed to animals or gods. *Aidōs* is what distinguishes humans from beasts such as lions (*Il.* 24.41–44), or savages such as Polyphemus (*Aidos*, 36). It concerns the gods only in that they demand *aidōs* for guests or suppliants (13–14, 24, 28). In particular, Erffa argues, *aidōs* is closely bound up with the duties of the Homeric aristocrats, the *agathoi*, whose first duty is battle courage. It is therefore especially important in war. When Homer's heroes stand by one another, instead of running in fear, they are said to "have *aidōs* for one another" (*aideisthai allēlous*).[33] *Aidōs* is felt toward one's social superiors: elders, parents, and kings (10–12) As the opposite of boldness, it may be equivalent to bashfulness, especially in the case of a young person like Telemachus (17) But *aidōs* is also felt for those who are weaker: suppliants and *xenoi* (hosts and guests). It has a very strong connection with pity, though *aidōs* tends to be felt for what is higher and superior, while pity is felt for what is weaker and inferior.[34]

As the polis developed, Erffa shows, *aidōs* became more "political." In Aeschylus, it has close connections with justice (104). In Sophocles' *Ajax* (1073–76), *aidōs* is associated with fear (*deos* and *phobos*) as a preserver of state and army, and is the opposite of *hubris* (*Aidos*, 109). In Euripides, *aidōs* is connected with friendship (133–34) and with *aretē* (160–62). According to Democritus, education in literature, music, and gymnastics has the goal of producing *aidōs*.[35]

Erffa's study, then, brings out the social and political nature of *aidōs* as something that holds society together and prevents wrongdoing. While Erffa stresses the "positive, motivating" power of *aidōs*,[36] others stress the negative, restraining power of *aidōs*, with which chapter 1 was primarily concerned. For example, Walter Burkert notes the "inhibiting function" that *aidōs* shares with *eleos*.[37]

Another aspect of the traditional Greek concept of *aidōs* is also of interest. In ordinary Greek usage, *aidōs* can refer to an occurrent *pathos*, which, on any given occasion, may be appropriate or inappropriate, or to a praise-

[33] For example, *Il* 5 530, quoted by Erffa, *Aidos*, 4, cf 36–37, and Gauthier and Jolif, 2 1 102

[34] Erffa, *Aidos*, 10, citing *Il* 22 82–84, cf 28 See also above, "Pity, Fear, and Physical Danger," and n 20

[35] Erffa, *Aidos*, 198, quoting Democritus B 179

[36] "Etwas   Positives, Antreibendes" Erffa, *Aidos*, 5

[37] "Hemmungskunktion' Burkert, "Mitleidsbegriff," 71 See also North, *Sophrosyne*, 6, and Parker, *Miasma*, 189–90

worthy or blameworthy dispositional state with respect to this *pathos*.[38] For example, in *Odyssey* 3 14, *aidōs* is clearly an undesirable occurrent *pathos*, for Athena tells Telemachus that he should not feel it, but that he must instead ask Nestor for news of his father Telemachus, however, replies that a young man cannot help feeling *aidōs* when speaking to an older man (3.24). On the other hand, *aidōs* is a desirable occurrent *pathos* in the passage from the *Iliad* quoted by Aristotle at *Eudemian Ethics* 1230a19. "*aidōs* seized Hector."[39] That *aidōs* can also be more like a praiseworthy dispositional state is shown, for example, by Hesiod's elevating it to a divinity (*Works and Days* 200). *Aidōs* can also be a blameworthy dispositional state. In a well-known passage in Euripides' *Hippolytus*, Phaedra speaks of good and bad *aidōs* in terms that are most appropriate to dispositional states: "*aidōs*, two in kind, the one not bad, / the other a burden to households" (385–86).[40]

A study of Aristotle's accounts of *aidōs* and *aischunē* shows that for him also, *aidōs* is sometimes an occurrent *pathos* and sometimes a dispositional mean state. It is, moreover, a "political" fear, like that of tradition, with the ability both to motivate and to restrain. In one passage, Aristotle, like Euripides' Phaedra, implies that there are two kinds of *aidōs*, writing of "true *aidōs*, the free person's fear" (*Pol.* 1331a40–b1).[41] Aristotle departs most sharply from tradition, however, in distinguishing *aidōs* from excellence in the strict sense. The most important and detailed accounts of the shame emotions are given in Aristotle's *Rhetoric*, *Nicomachean Ethics*, and *Eudemian Ethics*. These three works are studied in turn in the following subsections.

Rhetoric

In the *Rhetoric*, Aristotle's emphasis is on *aischunē*, to which he devotes an entire chapter (2.6). He includes *aischunē* among the *pathē*, and defines it as "pain and disturbance concerning those evils that appear to bring dis-

[38] I use the term "occurrent" to refer to an actually occurring emotion, in accord with the modern distinction between occurrent and dispositional emotional states (see, e g , Lyons, *Emotion*, 53–54) It should be noted, however, that Aristotle himself distinguishes among emotions (*pathē*), capacities (*dunameis*), and dispositions (*hexeis*), instead of between occurrent and dispositional states

[39] This line does not occur in our text of Homer see Dirlmeier, *Eudemische Ethik*, 321, citing Bonitz, 507b52–508a1

[40] For parallel passages reflecting this traditional "ambivalence of *aidōs*," see Barrett, *Hippolytos*, 230

[41] On this passage, see Newman, *Politics*, ad loc

grace, whether they are present, or past, or future" (1383b13–15). Thus, like *phobos* (*Rhet.* 1382a21–22), *aischunē* is "pain and disturbance concerning evils." However, while *phobos* is concerned with evils that are destructive or painful, *aischunē* is concerned with evils that appear to bring disgrace. Moreover, while *phobos* is concerned only with future evils, those with which *aischunē* is concerned may be past, present, or future. *Aischunē* in the *Rhetoric* is felt for both voluntary and involuntary acts (1384a20–21), and even for things done by one's ancestors (1385a1–2). Young people are especially prone to feel *aischunē* "for they do not at all have a grasp of other fine things, but have been educated only by convention" (1389a29–31). Nevertheless, *aischunē* is not solely dependent on convention, for Aristotle contrasts things shameful "in truth" with things shameful "by convention" (1384b26–27).

Aidōs is seldom mentioned in the *Rhetoric*. The nominal forms of *aidōs* appear only three times, in quotations. At 1367a9–14, Aristotle quotes Sappho's reply to Alcaeus. When he said, "I wish to say something to you, but shame [*aidōs*] prevents me," Sappho answered, "but if you had a desire for what is honourable and good, and if your tongue were not stirring up something evil to say, shame [*aidōs*] would not cover your eyes."[42] This quotation is of interest because it expresses the traditional idea, shared by Aristotle's ethical works, that *aidōs* prevents one from acting on a base desire, and thus involves conflicting impulses. This is not true of *aischunē* in the *Rhetoric*, however, which can be felt for involuntary acts that are not objects of desire.

Nicomachean Ethics

Aristotle's main concern in the *Nicomachean Ethics* is with *aidōs* rather than *aischunē*. He defines *aidōs* in 4.9. "It is not suitable to speak of *aidōs* as of an excellence. For it is more like a *pathos* than a disposition. It is defined, in any case, as a fear of disgrace" (1128b10–12). This brief definition indicates that *aidōs* is better characterized as an occurrent *pathos* than as a more enduring praiseworthy emotional mean state. The mean state with respect to *aidōs* is in fact nameless in the *Nicomachean Ethics*, although the person characterized by it is said to be *aidēmōn* (4.9.1128b17). The *aidēmōn*, Aristotle writes at 2.7.1108a30–35, is intermediate between the

---

[42] Sappho, frag 137, Lobel and Page, *Fragmenta* I quote Campbell's translation from *Greek Lyric* The third occurrence of *aidōs* in the *Rhetoric* is at 1384a36, where Aristotle quotes the proverb "*aidōs* is in the eyes"

shameless person, who feels *aidōs* too little or not at all, and the person characterized by excessive shame, the *kataplēx*, who feels it with respect to everything.

The definition in 4.9 also allows us to make some plausible inferences. First, if *aidōs* is a *pathos*, it has physical aspects (matter) and cognitive aspects (form), like the *pathē* of the *De anima*. Indeed, Aristotle goes on to say that *aidōs* has physical manifestations, making people turn red (4.9.1128b13–15). We can also make some inferences about the form of *aidōs*. If *aidōs* is a kind of *phobos*, it is caused by the *phantasia* of future evils, unlike *aischunē* in the *Rhetoric*, which concerns past and present as well as future evils. However, *aidōs* is more like *aischunē* than like *phobos* in being concerned with evils that bring disgrace.

If *aidōs* is a kind of *phobos*, we can also infer that it includes a desire to seek safety from its own particular evils: those that bring disgrace. If this is so, Fortenbaugh is wrong to conclude that Aristotle's shame emotions are not "practical" and "goal-directed."[43] The fuller account of the *Magna moralia* helps bring out the kinds of desires *aidōs* includes. The *aidēmōn* "will do and say the right things, on the right occasions, and at the right times" (1193a10). The actions and desires of this person will thus lead him to avoid disgrace in the best way. The inference that *aidōs* in the *Nicomachean Ethics* includes a desire to avoid disgrace is borne out by the definition of *aidōs* as φυγὴν ὀνείδους, "avoidance of blame," at *Nicomachean Ethics* 3.8.1116a29, discussed below. It is true that excessive fear of disgrace, *kataplēxis*, may result in paralysis: the *kataplēx* may be unable to act at all, as *Magna moralia* 1193a6 tells us. This does not mean, however, that fear of disgrace is itself characterized by lack of a goal, but that excessive emotion may prevent the goal-directed action typically associated with this emotion. In other cases also, excessive emotion might well prevent action: excessive *phobos* might prevent flight, and excessive anger might cause uncoordinated movements that effectively prevent attack.[44] It appears, then, that *aidōs* is goal-directed, and that one part of its form is the desire to seek safety from evils that bring disgrace.

After defining *aidōs* in 4.9, Aristotle discusses it further:

> The emotion is not suited to every age, but to youth. For we think that young people should be *aidēmones* because they live by emotion and commit

[43] Fortenbaugh, "Mean-Dispositions," 224; cf. Leighton, "Emotions," 149.

[44] At the physiological level, something like this, in a less extreme form, must happen when anger "because of the heat and swiftness of its nature" rushes out to revenge without properly hearing reason (*EN* 1149a25–32). I am indebted to Norman Dahl for some good discussions of this point.

many errors, but are prevented by *aidōs*. And we praise those young people who are *aidēmones*, but no one would praise an older person because he tends to feel *aischunē*; for we think that he should do nothing for which one feels *aischunē*. For *aischunē* is not characteristic of a decent person, if it comes from base acts (for these kinds of things should not be done; it makes no difference if some acts are shameful [*aischra*] in truth and others according to opinion; neither kind should be done, so that one should not feel *aischunē*), and it is characteristic of a base person to be the kind who does something shameful [*aischrōn*]. It would be strange to be the kind of person who feels *aischunē* if he does something of this kind, and who thinks he is decent for this reason. For *aidōs* is felt for what is voluntary, and the decent person will never do base acts voluntarily. But [it might be argued that] *aidōs* is a decent thing on a hypothesis: for if one should do [something base], one would feel *aischunē*. But this is not possible in the case of the excellences. And if shamelessness [*anaischuntia*], that is, not being ashamed [*aideisthai*] to do shameful things [*aischra*], is base, that does not make the person who is ashamed [*aischunesthai*] of doing such things any more decent. Neither is self-control excellence, but something mixed. (1128b15–34)

This difficult passage provides further evidence that *aidōs* is more concerned with future than with past or present evils. At 1128b18, the *aidōs* that prevents people from erring is clearly fear of future disgrace. On the other hand, Aristotle tends to use *aischunē* rather than *aidōs* in this passage when a present or past action is in question. At 1128b21 and 1128b22, *aischunē*, and not *aidōs*, is said to result from doing (πράττειν) base acts, and 1128b24–25, οὐδέτερα . . . πρακτέα, ὥστ᾽ οὐκ αἰσχυντέον ("neither kind should be done, so that one should not feel *aischunē*") clearly indicates that *aischunē* results from things actually done. The same is true of the conditionals at 1128b26–27 and 1128b30: "If one should do [something base], one would feel *aischunē*." It is also important to note the different constructions used at 1128b32–33. The verb αἰδεῖσθαι, "to feel *aidōs*," is used with the infinitive: τὸ μὴ αἰδεῖσθαι τὰ αἰσχρὰ πράττειν ("not being ashamed *to do* shameful things"). On the other hand, the verb αἰσχύνεσθαι, "to feel *aischunē*," is used with the participle: τὰ τοιαῦτα πράττοντα αἰσχύνεσθαι ("ashamed *of doing* such things"). These two verbs with the infinitive mean "*I am ashamed to* do something which I have refrained from doing up to the present time and may never do," but with the participle they mean "*I am ashamed of* doing something which I do."[45]

195

Thus, while *aidōs* and *aischunē* cannot always be distinguished in this passage (e.g., at 1128b13, 1128b19–20, 1128b29–30), the definition of *aidōs* as a kind of fear at the beginning of 4.9 and the differences in usage just noted suggest that *aidōs* tends to be more concerned with future evils than does *aischunē*.[46]

Nicomachean Ethics 4.9 also tells us that *aidōs* is praiseworthy, but only in the young (1128b15–20), and that it involves conflict, just as it does in the Sappho quotation in *Rhetoric* 1.9 (quoted above). *Aidōs*, itself a *pathos*, can prevent (*kōluesthai*) young people, "who live by *pathos*," from erring (*EN* 1128b17–18). That is, in the *aidēmōn*, one *pathos* consistently opposes and overcomes another. That conflict is essential to the concept of *aidōs* in 4.9 is also shown by the fact that Aristotle compares it to *egkrateia*, "self-control," at 1128b33–34.[47] While *egkrateia* involves conflict between reason and desire (*EN* 1102b14–18), *aidōs* involves conflict between *pathos* and *pathos*. People do not feel *aidōs* at all unless they have a desire to do something base and are capable of acting on this desire. Because older people should not have base desires at all, *aidōs* is not praiseworthy in them. If *aidōs* is felt in the presence of a contrary *pathos*, we can understand why Aristotle says that it is felt for voluntary acts: we can only be said to *desire* to do acts that are voluntary. *Aidōs* in *Nicomachean Ethics* 4.9, then, differs from *aischunē* in the *Rhetoric* not only in being more concerned with future evils, but also in being felt only for voluntary acts, and in involving conflict. *Aischunē* in the *Rhetoric* need not involve conflict, because it can be felt for involuntary acts, which we do not desire to do.

Two passages in the *Nicomachean Ethics*, however, might appear to express a more positive view of *aidōs*, one inconsistent with the account of 4.9. In 3.6.1115a9–14, quoted above ("Pity, Fear, and Physical Danger"), Aristotle writes that fear of disgrace is "fine," and he states that the person with this fear is "decent" (*epieikēs*) and *aidēmōn*. However, 4.9 (1128b29–33) stresses the difference between "decency" and *aidōs*. This

and Urmson), for example, blurs it completely "not to be ashamed of doing base actions to be ashamed of doing such actions'

[46] While Gauthier and Jolif note passages in which *aidōs* concerns future errors, being "l'appréhension d'une faute qu'on n'a pas faite," they incorrectly assert that *aidōs* primarily concerns past errors "la honte et le repentir d'une faute *d'ores et deja commise*' (2 1 321, emphasis in original) Partly for this reason, they hold the erroneous view that Aristotle's concepts of *aidōs* and *aischunē* are "identical" (322, on 1128b11–13), cf Cope, *Rhetoric*, 2 71, Grimaldi, *Rhetoric II*, 107

[47] Dahl, *Reason*, 196–98, has a good discussion of Aristotle's use of the verb *kōluō* (prevent) in connection with conflict of motives in ethical situations See also Charles, *Action*, 129–30

discrepancy is easily explained: in 3.6 Aristotle has not yet made the technical distinctions, with which 4.9 is concerned, between *aidōs* and excellence in the strict sense.

It is harder to reconcile 4.9 with the account of *aidōs* given in 3.8:

[True] courage is something of this kind, but five other things are also said to be courage. First is political courage. For it is most like [true courage] For citizens are thought to endure dangers because of penalties imposed by the law, and blame, and because of honors And for this reason people are thought to be most courageous where cowards are held in dishonor, and courageous men are honored. Homer writes poems about men of this kind, for example Diomedes, and Hector [who says]. "Polydamas will first reproach me" [*Il.* 22 100], and Diomedes [who says]. "For Hector will sometime say, speaking among the Trojans, 'The son of Tydeus from me   ' " This [sc , political courage] is most like the courage discussed first [sc , true courage], since it comes to be because of excellence, for [it comes to be] because of *aidōs* and because of desire for the fine (that is, from [desire for] honor and from avoidance of blame, which is shameful) [δι' αἰδῶ γὰρ καὶ διὰ καλοῦ ὄρεξιν (τιμῆς γὰρ καὶ φυγὴν ὀνείδους, αἰσχροῦ ὄντος)] One might perhaps place in this category those who are compelled by their rulers. But these are inferior, inasmuch as they do not do it because of *aidōs* but because of fear [*phobos*], and out of avoidance not of the shameful [*aischron*] but of the painful. (1116a15–32)[48]

This passage, stating that political courage "comes to be because of excellence, for it comes to be because of *aidōs*," appears to contradict 4.9, which denies that *aidōs* is an excellence. This apparent contradiction arises not because *aidōs* has a more popular, nontechnical sense in 3.8 than it does in 4.9,[49] but because "excellence" (*aretē*: 1116a28) does not have the technical, Aristotelian sense in 3.8. True courage is the excellence that "endures as it ought to and according to reason for the sake of the fine" (*EN* 1115b12–13). It "chooses and endures because this is fine (*kalon*) and because it is base (*aischron*) not to" (1116a11–12).[50] The courageous per-

---

[48] The quotation at 1116a25–26 is from *Il* 8 148–49 Line 149 continues φοβευμενος ἱκετο νῆας ("running in fear arrived at the ships") I see no need to follow Bywater, *Ethica Nicomachea*, in bracketing "Diomedes" at 1116a24 For reasons discussed below, my punctuation of 1116a28–29 (τιμῆς   ὄντος) differs from that of Bywater, who places only τιμῆς γάρ in parentheses

[49] This is the explanation given by Gauthier and Jolif, 2 1 321–22

[50] In this passage, *aischron* means "base," because it is opposed to the *kalon*, and causes avoidance in the truly courageous person At 3 8 1116a29, on the other hand, *aischron*

son, like all excellent people, must do excellent acts from choice (*prohairesis*) and for their own sake (*EN* 1105a31–32, 1111b4–6) Political courage, on the other hand, is due to an "excellence" that has very different sources. *aidōs* and the desire for the (apparent) good of honor Aristotle is careful to explain this in 1116a27–29. "Excellence" in 1116a28 is explained by the phrase "for [it comes to be] because of *aidōs* and because of desire for the fine" δι' αἰδῶ γὰρ καὶ διὰ καλοῦ ὄρεξιν This latter phrase is in turn explained by the parenthetical phrase in my translation "that is from [desire for] honor and from avoidance of blame, which is shameful" (τιμῆς γὰρ καὶ φυγὴν ὀνείδους, αἰσχροῦ ὄντος) This parenthetical phrase further defines the two causes of excellence mentioned in 1116a28 "*aidōs* and desire for the fine," by substituting "honor" for "desire for the fine," and "avoidance of blame" (φυγὴν ὀνείδους) for *aidōs* That is, political courage is an "excellence" that comes from (1) *aidōs*, defined as "avoidance of blame, which is shameful," and (2) desire for (what some people take to be) the good, that is, honor [51] The definition of *aidōs* as "avoidance of blame" in this passage is prepared by the mention of "blame" in 1116a19, along with the related negative sanctions of "penalties" (ἐπιτίμια 1116a19) and "dishonor" (ἄτιμοι 1116a21) Aristotle's readers would also have known that, after *Iliad* 22 100, quoted at 1116a23, Hector's famous speech mentions *aidōs* "I feel *aidōs* before the Trojans and the long-gowned Trojan women" (*Il* 22 105)

Thus, when Aristotle writes of "excellence" in *Nicomachean Ethics* 3 8, he makes it clear that he is referring to the excellence of popular, and especially Homeric, thought. Political courage is not a true excellence, but one that is closely associated with honor [52] It does not choose to do courageous acts for their own sake, that is, for the sake of the fine, but for the sake of an apparent good honor Nor does it choose to avoid cowardly actions because they are truly base, but because of *aidōs*, avoidance of an apparent evil. blame To endure because of the kind of courage that comes from *aidōs*, however, is superior to standing one's ground merely from fear of physical pain (*phobos* 1116a29–32), a fear that leads people to endure when compelled. *Nicomachean Ethics* 1125b11–12 makes a similar point We sometimes praise the lover of honor, Aristotle writes, as "courageous

means shameful,' because it causes avoidance in the person with *aidōs*, and (1116a32) is opposed to the painful

[51] This interpretation was suggested to me by David Charles

[52] Note the many occurrences of τιμή (honor) and related words in this passage ἐπιτίμια (1116a19), τιμάς (1116a19), ἄτιμοι (1116a21), ἔντιμοι (1116a21), and τιμῆς (1116a28)

and a lover of the fine." This person is praiseworthy because he loves honor more than the many (1125b16).

The interpretation just argued for makes *Nicomachean Ethics* 3.8 consistent with 4.9, where *aidōs* is a "fear of disgrace" that prevents people from acting on base desires. While the 3.8 passage does not explicitly state that *aidōs* prevents people from acting on base desires, the definition of *aidōs* as "avoidance of blame" strongly suggests this. The Homeric quotations also support this view. Diomedes speaks when he is in great danger and has been urged to flee by Nestor. Hector makes his speech after his parents have begged him to flee (*Il.* 22.38–89), and immediately before he actually runs, overcome by fear (131–37). *Nicomachean Ethics* 10.9, as I argue below ("*Aidōs*, Excellence, and Habituation"), holds the same view of *aidōs* and its relative value as do 3.8 and 4.9.[53] Here also, obedience to *aidōs* is superior to obedience because of fear of physical pain, but inferior to true excellence.

Eudemian Ethics

The account of *aidōs* given in the *Eudemian Ethics* agrees in most respects with that of the *Nicomachean Ethics*.[54] A few differences may be noted. Unlike the *Nicomachean Ethics*, the *Eudemian Ethics* does not define *aidōs* as a kind of *phobos*. It is, however, more specific about the dependence of *aidōs* on opinion: "The person who has no regard for any opinion is shameless; the person regarding every opinion equally is *kataplēx*, the person who [holds in regard] the [opinion] of those who appear decent is *aidēmōn*" (*EE* 3.7.1233b27–29). Also, while in the *Nicomachean Ethics* the term *aidōs* always refers only to the occurrent *pathos*, and never to the emotional mean state, in the *Eudemian Ethics*, *aidōs* itself is sometimes said (e g., at 3.7.1233b26) to be one of the emotional mean states (*mesotētes pathētikai*: 1233b18). This is of little philosophical significance, however, for the *Eudemian Ethics* does not consistently classify *aidōs* as an emotional mean state; Aristotle's terminology in this work is notoriously confusing.[55] His

---

[53] Pace Stark, *Aristotelesstudien*, 76–77, who believes that *EN* 10 9 is an earlier passage than the others, and that *aidōs* here is an excellence, as it is in the "earlier" theory of the *Eudemian Ethics*

[54] Like the *Nicomachean Ethics*, the *Eudemian Ethics* is more concerned with *aidōs* than with *aischunē* Susemihl's index lists only two occurrences of *aischunē* and its cognates in the *EE* 1220b17 and 1229a39

[55] Some relevant difficulties are discussed by Dirlmeier, *Eudemische Ethik*, 349–51, Woods, *Eudemian Ethics*, 115–16, and Fortenbaugh, "Mean-Dispositions," esp 206–7

usage reflects the ambiguity in ordinary Greek noted above ("Aristotle and the Greek Tradition"): *aidōs* is an occurrent *pathos*, or a dispositional state. It should be noted, however, that while this dispositional state can be blameworthy in ordinary Greek, in the *Eudemian Ethics* it is always praiseworthy.

Another difference between the two works is more important. The *Eudemian Ethics*, unlike the *Nicomachean Ethics*, explicitly states that *aidōs* differs from excellence in the strict sense in being without *phronēsis* (practical reason) and *prohairesis* (choice).[56] The idea that *aidōs* is without choice is most clearly expressed in *Eudemian Ethics* 3.7.

> All these mean states are praiseworthy, but they are not excellences, nor are their opposites vices, for they are without choice All these are in the division of the *pathē*, for each of them is a *pathos* Because they are natural, they contribute to the natural excellences For, as will be said later, each excellence is somehow both by nature and in another way, with *phronēsis* Now envy contributes to injustice (for the actions that result from it are done to another), and indignation to justice, *aidōs* to *sōphrosunē*, for which reason they even define *sōphrosunē* as being within this kind. (1234a24–33)[57]

Aristotle also indicates that *aidōs* is without choice in *Eudemian Ethics* 3.1. Here, at 1229a12–1230a36, he gives an account of "political courage" that is in many ways remarkably similar to that of *Nicomachean Ethics* 3.8. Both, for example, quote *Iliad* 22 100 (*EN* 1116a23, *EE* 1230a20) Moreover, in the *Eudemian Ethics*, as in the *Nicomachean Ethics*, political courage is said to be due to *aidōs* (1229a13–14, 1230a16–21). In the former, however, Aristotle states that political courage is not "the true [kind of courage]" (1230a21), because "every excellence is characterized by choice [*prohairetikē*]" (1230a27). This differs significantly from the account of *Nicomachean Ethics* 3.8, where political courage is said to be due to the "excellence" of *aidōs* (1116a27–28).

The view that *aidōs* is without choice has important implications If actions done because of *aidōs* lack choice, they differ from truly excellent actions in a specific and essential way. Moreover, if *aidōs* is without choice, it is inferior in this respect not only to excellence but also to self-control

[56] Irwin translates *prohairesis* as "decision," and explains that this is "a desire to do something here and now, the action that deliberation has shown to be the action required to achieve the end" (*Ethics*, 392–93)

[57] On the difficulties presented by this passage, see Dirlmeier, *Eudemische Ethik*, 357–358 A good account of "natural excellence" in the *Nicomachean Ethics* is given by Dahl, *Reason*, 87–89

(*egkrateia*). Self-control, incontinence (*akrasia*), and licentiousness (*akolasia*) all involve choice. The licentious person, like the excellent person, acts with choice, believing that one should always follow pleasure (*EN* 1146b22–23).[58] In contrast to the licentious person, the incontinent person acts against choice (*EN* 1151a5–7) because of a contrary desire or *pathos* (*EN* 1145b12–13). The self-controlled person resembles the incontinent person in having a desire that conflicts with choice, but this person acts in accord with choice (*EN* 1111b13–15)[59] In both incontinence and self-control, then, "choice opposes appetite, but appetite does not oppose appetite" (*EN* 1111b15–16) Unlike choice, Aristotle goes on to say, appetite is concerned with the pleasant and the painful (*EN* 1111b17–18) If *aidōs* lacks choice, then, acting because of *aidōs* would be similar to a case in which appetite, and not choice, opposes appetite. *Aidōs* is itself a *pathos*, and *pathos*, like appetite, is concerned with pleasure and pain When *aidōs* opposes a *pathos* such as *phobos*, *pathos* opposes *pathos*, and action is neither in accord with nor against choice. there is no choice involved.[60]

This would appear to be Aristotle's view of *aidōs* in the *Eudemian Ethics*. In the *Nicomachean Ethics*, however, his views are more complex. Like the *Eudemian Ethics*, *Nicomachean Ethics* 4.9 holds that *aidōs* is without choice, for the young of 4.9 who "live by *pathos*" and are prevented from wrongdoing by the opposing *pathos* of *aidōs* would appear to lack choice On the other hand, *Nicomachean Ethics* 3.8 appears to leave open the possibility that *aidōs* can be with choice. The account of political courage in 3.8 does not deny that *aidōs* lacks choice, and it even calls *aidōs* an "excellence." While "excellence" here is not something chosen for the sake of the (true) good, it might nevertheless be chosen for the sake of the apparent good of honor. Honor as well as *aidōs* is said to be a cause of political courage in 3.8 (1116a28–29).

Support for this view of *Nicomachean Ethics* 3 8 is provided by *Nicomachean Ethics* 1 5, where Aristotle states that honor can be *chosen* as the end of a life. In *Nicomachean Ethics* 1.5.1095b14–1096a10, Aristotle discusses three kinds of lives. the life of pleasure, the "political life," and the life of contemplation. People choose (1095b20) each of these lives for the sake of a different end (1095b23)—for the sake of the good or the apparent good (*EN* 1113a15–16; cf. *DA* 433a28–29). Honor is said to be the end of the political life at 1095b23. There is good reason to hold that the political

---

[58] This view of *akolasia* is defended by Dahl, *Reason*, 83 See also Charles, *Action*, 190

[59] See Charles, *Action*, 133 and n 32

[60] *Pathos* and choice are opposed at *EN* 5 6 1134a20–21 "not because of choice but because of *pathos*"

courage of 3.8 is an excellence within this political life. If someone with political courage chooses to stand his ground for the sake of the (apparent) good of honor and for the sake of avoiding the (apparent) evil of blame, he, like the truly excellent person, acts from choice and for the sake of an end. Even though his end is the apparent good and not the true good, if it is an end in the strict sense—something for the sake of which all else is chosen—his desires, like those of the truly excellent person, will be caused and directed by choice. Thus, *Nicomachean Ethics* 1.5, taken together with 3.8, gives us reason to believe that *aidōs*, as a cause of political courage, involves choice and is an excellence within the political life whose end is honor.

This concept of political courage is very different from that of *Eudemian Ethics* 3.1, where political courage is explicitly said to be without choice. If the political courage in question in *Eudemian Ethics* 3.1 is not a true excellence in absolute terms, neither is it, like the political courage of *Nicomachean Ethics* 3.8, an excellence within a political life. The political life discussed in *Eudemian Ethics* 1.4–5 is concerned with "actions coming from excellence" (1216a21), and the true political person, Aristotle writes, "chooses fine actions for their own sake" (1216a24–26). He chooses these acts not only for the sake of reputation, but also even if he will not get a good reputation (1216a21–22).[61]

It is possible that Aristotle is simply inconsistent in sometimes denying that *aidōs* is with choice and at other times leaving open the possibility that it can be with choice. It is also possible, however, that he recognizes two different roles played by *aidōs*. An immature kind of *aidōs* is appropriate to the young, who do not yet have choice, but who respect the opinions of others without mature reflection. In the truly excellent life, one that chooses truly excellent acts for their own sake, *aidōs* helps the young person acquire choice and an end and then ceases to exist. The person who is excellent in the strict sense will not choose to do excellent acts through fear of others' opinions, but because these acts are excellent. On the other hand, within the political life discussed in *Nicomachean Ethics* 1.5 and perhaps alluded to in 3.8, *aidōs* is compatible with the *prohairesis* that chooses to do excellent acts not for their own sake but for the sake of honor, for the good opinion of others. *Aidōs*, then, might be "with choice" at a mature stage of the political life, and "without choice," though necessary to

[61] Cf. *EE* 1215a30 and 1215b3–4, where concern for reputation is also contrasted with the concern for fine deeds that characterizes the political life. Although *EE* 1.2.1214b6–14 lists honor and reputation among the possible goals of life, it is not concerned with a political life.

its acquisition, at early stages of both the political life and the life of excellence. This hypothesis is supported by Aristotle's view that *aidōs* plays an important role in early education and in habituation throughout life.

Aidōs, *Excellence, and Habituation*

If Aristotle says little about the specific role of *aidōs* in education, what he does say about *aidōs* and about ethical education generally allows us to infer with some confidence that the "semivirtue of the learner"[62] has an important role in the acquisition of excellence. Moreover, the nature of *aidōs* as a conflict emotion responsive to the opinions of others gives it a necessary explanatory role in Aristotle's elliptical account of the acquisition of excellence. *Aidōs* provides a specific psychic mechanism that can account for the development of the affective and cognitive aspects of excellence.

Aristotle is not more explicit about *aidōs*, and about habituation generally, because his main philosophical interests lie elsewhere. He does not share Plato's interest in childhood and the early stages of education. In the *Nicomachean Ethics*, moreover, he tells us explicitly that his concern is with mature adults. At the beginning of the work he says that it is addressed to the person who is experienced in the affairs of life and who is sufficiently mature in character to have "desires in accord with reason." The young person, and the older person who is immature in character, because they live "according to *pathos*," will not profit from this study (1.1095a3–11).[63] Because *aidōs* is praiseworthy only in young people, who live according to *pathos* (4.9.1128b17–19), we should not expect to find much about *aidōs* or the earlier stages of education in the *Nicomachean Ethics*. That the *Eudemian Ethics* has concerns similar to those of the *Nicomachean Ethics* is shown, for one thing, by the existence of the three "common books" shared by the two works. While Aristotle discusses education more fully in books 7 and 8 of the *Politics*, he says disappointingly little about either *aidōs* or interpersonal relationships. In only one passage does he briefly indicate the importance of *aidōs* in a well-regulated state. He writes that magistrates should attend the gymnasia of both young and old, for their presence "produces true *aidōs*, the free man's fear" (1331a40–41). This characterization of *aidōs* is very similar to that of Plato in *Laws* 1 and 2, where *aidōs* is

---

[62] Burnyeat, "Learning," 78.

[63] Pace Burnyeat (ibid., 75), these statements clearly indicate that the student of ethics in *EN* 1 is more advanced ethically than the person in 10.9 who, because he obeys the conflict emotion of *aidōs*, must have desires that are not in accord with reason.

extremely important [64] The *Politics* gives equally cursory attention to some important areas of early education in which *aidōs* might be expected to play a significant role For example, Aristotle does not elaborate on the idea that the "supervisors of education" must allow children to associate with slaves as little as possible (1336a39–b3), and he touches only "in passing" (παραδρομῇ 1336b24) on such related questions as the effect on the young of the illiberal and indecent speech of comedy The absence of a full treatment may, in part, be due to the fact that the discussion of education in the *Politics* is incomplete [65] It may also be due, however, to Aristotle's lack of interest in early education, and to his reliance on Plato in this area Certainly the *Politics* is heavily indebted to Plato s fuller account of early education in the *Laws* [66] Whatever its cause, the absence of a detailed account, in the *Politics* and elsewhere, forces us to rely heavily on a few brief statements, chiefly in the *Nicomachean Ethics*, in attempting to understand Aristotle's views on *aidōs* and early education

The most important passage for this understanding is *Nicomachean Ethics* 10 9 [67] This chapter indicates that people who are 'decent (*epieikeis*), but not fully excellent, are like the young or the immature in character who live according to *pathos*, and that ethical habituation, in which *aidōs* plays an essential role, is useful to them throughout life, as it is in youth to those who are going to become fully excellent Near the beginning of the chapter, Aristotle contrasts those who obey *aidōs* with 'the many," who obey only fear

> Now if arguments were sufficient to make people *epieikeis*, they would rightly get many and great wages, as Theognis says, and it would have been necessary to provide these [wages] But as it is, arguments appear to have the power to urge on and encourage those young people with freeborn characters, and could cause a character that is noble and that truly loves the fine to be possessed by excellence, but [arguments appear] to be unable to urge on the many toward nobility For by nature they do not obey *aidōs* but fear, and do not keep from base acts because of the shameful but because of punishments For living by *pathos* they pursue the pleasures proper to it and the means to

[64] The similarity is noted by Newman, *Politics*, ad loc
[65] See ibid , 1 369–70
[66] See E Barker, *Theory*, 381 The scheme of education in Book VII of the *Politics* is propounded with constant reference to the *Laws*
[67] *EN* 10 9 has received very little attention from scholars The best discussion is that of Burnyeat, Learning

these pleasures, and they avoid the opposite pains, but have no notion of the fine and of true pleasure, not having tasted it (*EN* 10 9 1179b4–16)

This passage gives us important information about the relative value of *aidōs*. On the lowest ethical level, that of "the many," are people who live "by *pathos*" alone—by *pathos* that, unlike the *pathos* of *aidōs*, is not responsive to the opinions of others. They pursue only physical pleasure, and can be restrained from this pursuit only by *phobos*, fear of physical pain. These are the same people who, according to *Nicomachean Ethics* 3.8 (1116a29–32), do not endure dangers in order to avoid the base, but because of fear of physical pain. At a higher level are those who, while still under the influence of *pathos*, obey *aidōs*, a *pathos* responsive to the opinions of others, and refrain from base deeds because they are shameful. These people are like the young of *Nicomachean Ethics* 4.9, and those with political courage in *Nicomachean Ethics* 3.8. They are not truly excellent, since they do not avoid the base because it is base. Nevertheless, they have a "notion of the fine and of true pleasure" (1179b15), and *aidōs* makes them capable of being persuaded and urged toward nobility and excellence in the strict sense.

Shortly afterward, Aristotle restates, in a slightly different form, the ideas expressed in the passage just quoted (1179b4–16).[68] He writes that, of the three things that lead people to become good—nature, habit, and teaching (1179b20–21)—habit (*ethos*) is the most important.

Argument and teaching can never be powerful among all people, but it is necessary for the soul of the learner to have been prepared beforehand by habits to take pleasure and to hate nobly, like earth that will nourish the seed For he who lives according to *pathos* would not be able to hear or to understand argument that turns him away How would it be possible to persuade such a person to change? For in general, *pathos* does not obey argument but force A necessary prerequisite, then, is a character [*ēthos*] that is somehow proper to excellence, loving the fine and hating the base (*EN* 10 9 1179b23–31)

This second argument is a valuable restatement of the first, because it indicates that *aidōs* plays an essential role in habituation. In the second

---

[68] Rassow, "Zu Aristoteles," 594–96, first called attention to repetition in 1179b20–1180a5 of the argument given in 1179b4–20 There is no need, however, to agree with him (and with Gauthier and Jolif, ad loc) that these are two drafts, only one of which is authentic Burnyeat correctly notes that Aristotle repeats this material because he thought it was so important (' Learning," 89 n 9)

passage (1179b23–31), habits (*ethesi* 1179b25) have exactly the same effect *aidōs* (1179b11) does in the first passage (1179b4–16) Arguments are able to urge people toward nobility (1179b10, 1179b20) only when they obey *aidōs* (1179b11) or have souls cultivated by habits (1179b25) Both *aidōs* and habits help turn people away from (ἀπεχεσθαι 1179b11, ἀπο-τρεπovτoς 1179b27) the pleasures and pains pursued and avoided by those who live by *pathos* (1179b13–14, 1179b27–28) *Aidōs* and habits are favorably contrasted with the use of fear (1179b11) and force (1179b29) to keep people in order In 1179b15–16, those who obey *phobos* alone are said to lack a notion and a taste of the fine and of true pleasure, which, Aristotle implies, people who obey *aidōs* do have Similarly, in 1179b29–30, habit is said to give someone a character that "is somehow proper to excellence "

The parallels between these two passages make it reasonable to infer that the preparation of the soul by habit that is a necessary prerequisite for the production of excellence (1179b29–30) results in consistent obedience to the emotional mean state of *aidōs* rather than to fear and force We can also infer that it is the occurrent *pathos* of *aidōs* that makes preparation by habit possible in the first place Force cannot lead people to become habituated, nor is argument effective before habituation occurs *Aidōs*, on the other hand, is a *pathos* responsive to the opinions of others that can, by opposing *pathos*, help produce correct habituation in pleasure and pain If the occurrent *pathos* of *aidōs* makes preparation by habit possible, and, in turn, habituation produces the emotional mean state of *aidōs*, we can learn a great deal about *aidōs* by studying Aristotle's views on habituation [69]

Habituation accomplishes two important tasks in 10 9 First, it leads people to "love the fine and hate the shameful" (1179b30–31, cf 1179b25–26) In *Nicomachean Ethics* 2 2–3, Aristotle states that habituation (*ethizomenoi* 1104b1) helps produce the ethical excellence that is concerned with pleasures and pains (1104b8–9), and he agrees with Plato that people "should be led straight from childhood   to be pleased and pained by the right things, for this is correct education" (1104b11–13) Second, while Aristotle is less explicit about this, he clearly believes that habituation helps us acquire the cognitive abilities needed by true excellence, which requires knowledge of what excellent acts are, and the ability to choose them for their own sake (*EN* 1105a31–32) This is clear from

[69] On the cognitive and affective aspects of habituation, see Sherman, *Fabric*, chap 5, Burnyeat, Learning , and Sorabji, Role Also very helpful is Dahl s account (*Reason*, esp chaps 3–6) of the role of experience in the apprehension and acquisition of ends

10.9.1179b26–28, where correct habituation is said to be necessary for an understanding (συνείη) of argument or reason (λόγου).

These two aspects of habituation, affective and cognitive, are both aspects of *aidōs*. As *phobos adoxias* (EN 4.9.1128b16–17), "fear of bad opinion" (or of disgrace), *aidōs* has an affective aspect (fear) and a cognitive aspect (responsiveness to opinion). To experience *aidōs* one must both understand the opinions of others and feel pleasure or pain in response to them. Through its affective aspects, as fear of disgrace, *aidōs* helps provide the training in pleasure and pain that is the most important foundation for excellence. Its cognitive aspects, as a *pathos* conditioned by the opinions of others, also give *aidōs* an important role in leading young people to acquire the intellectual abilities required by excellence in the strict sense.

Aidōs, the occurrent *pathos*, helps provide correct habituation in pleasure and pain partly because it is a painful emotion. Young people who feel *aidōs* feel pain at the thought of the disgrace that doing shameful acts will incur, and this pain is sufficient to outweigh the pleasure that doing these acts would give them. This pain provides a kind of emotional conditioning that leads young people eventually to acquire the mean state of *aidōs*, consistently hating the acts that incur disgrace. The production of the mean state of *aidōs* by pain in this way is an allopathic treatment for the soul, in which pain and punishment are used to oppose and correct shameless desires to pursue pleasure inappropriately.[70] At *Nicomachean Ethics* 1119a33–b16, Aristotle writes that, because the child, who lives by appetite, tends to be licentious (*akolastos*: literally, unpunished), he requires punishment to make him "persuadable and chastened [*kekolasmenon*]," living according to the command of the tutor (1119a12–14). The chastened child does not yet act according to an internal principle of excellence, but he has the next best thing in the habit of obedience to the tutor, who does have this internal principle. The punishment given this child might include the temporary production of *kataplēxis* (excessive shame) by scolding and shaming. This would help bring the individual soul to an intermediate state between shamelessness and *kataplēxis*, just as two friends with opposite emotional characteristics are brought by each other to an intermediate state (*EE* 1239b25–1240a4).

However, *aidōs* is not purely painful, as is physical punishment, for the young person who obeys *aidōs* is praised (EN 1128b19), and this is pleasant. To refrain from shameful acts is pleasant as well as painful, because of

---

[70] On treatment by means of opposites, see EN 1104b16–18 and EE 1220a34–37, discussed in chap. 9 ("Psychic and Physical Excellence").

the praise and honor that reward refraining. Eventually, this pleasure in refraining from base acts also helps young people become *aidēmones*, consistently taking pleasure in refraining for the sake of praise. *Aidōs* is the more effective in providing habituation in pleasure and pain because young people feel *aidōs* for their fathers, whom, as Aristotle tells us at *Nicomachean Ethics* 10.9 1180b3–7, they love and obey by nature because of kinship and benefits conferred.[71]

Aidōs is particularly well suited to provide the correct habituation in pleasure and pain necessary to the acquisition of excellence because it is, in part, a proportionate blend (*summetria*) of emotional opposites. While Aristotle nowhere explicitly says this, it is a reasonable inference from his statements about the nature of *aidōs*, and about the emotions in general.

In the *Nicomachean Ethics* (1108a30–35) and the *Eudemian Ethics* (1239b27–29), *aidōs* (or the *aidēmōn*) is intermediate between the extremes of shamelessness and extreme shame (*kataplēxis*). The author of the *Magna moralia* is more specific.

> *Aidōs* is a mean state of shamelessness and *kataplēxis*, and it concerns actions and words. The shameless person is one who on all occasions and to everyone says and does whatever occurs to him. The *kataplēx* is the opposite of this one, someone who is cautious about doing and saying everything and to everyone. (This kind of person does not act at all, the person who is *kataplēx* in every way.) *Aidōs* and the *aidēmōn* are a mean state of these. For this person will not say and do everything in every way, like the shameless person, nor, like the *kataplēx*, will he be cautious on every occasion and in every way, but he will do and say the right things, on the right occasions, and at the right times. (*MM* 1193a1–10)[72]

In their physical aspects (their matter), the emotions are either hot and pleasurable or cold and painful. It seems likely, then, that the emotional extremes are excessively hot or cold, while the emotional mean states are intermediate with respect to hot and cold. Since the pursuit of pleasure is associated with hot emotions and the avoidance of pain with cold emotions, shamelessness would appear to be too hot, leading a person to pursue pleasure inappropriately ("saying and doing whatever occurs to him"), and *kataplēxis* to be too cold, leading, in extreme cases, to paralysis from excessive fear of disgrace ("this kind of person does not act at all"). In its

---

[71] On this point, see Sherman, *Fabric*, 152

[72] At 1193a5 I read πρὸς, bracketed by Susemihl. On the question of the authenticity of the *Magna moralia*, see chap. 2, n. 80

physical aspects, *aidōs* would appear to be a mean state that is neither too hot nor too cold, but something intermediate.[73]

Analogies in the *Eudemian Ethics* and *Magna moralia* suggest that emotional mean states are not merely intermediate between two physical extremes. They are also, in their physical aspects, proportionate blends of opposites. In *Eudemian Ethics* 7.5.1239b25–1240a4, Aristotle writes that friends who have opposite emotional characteristics, for example, the "austere" (*austeroi*: 1240a2) and the witty,[74] are brought to the intermediate by each other, just as physical opposites are: "The opposites desire one another because of the intermediate. They desire one another like two halves of a token, because in this way one intermediate comes to be from both. . . . For being excessively cold, if they are heated, they are restored to the intermediate, and being excessively hot, [they are restored] if they are cooled" (*EE* 1239b30–36). In a similar physical analogy, *Magna moralia* 1210a6–22 compares the friendship of unequals to a relationship between the opposites wet and dry (1210a14), and to one between fire and water: water is useful to fire if present in due proportion (*summetron*: 1210a21).

These physical analogies are likely to be more than mere metaphor because Aristotle believes that the emotions have physical aspects. Moreover, Aristotle holds that a *summetria* of the opposites hot, cold, moist, and dry is necessary to a healthy body. (See, in chapter 9, "Medical Katharsis.") Aristotle's analogy suggests that, in their physical aspects, emotional mean states, like physical intermediates, consist of a proportionate blend of opposites, and that, like physical intermediates, they can be produced by using one opposite to counterbalance the other.

While it is not at all clear that the same account could be given of the

[73] The physical manifestations of *aidōs* and *aischunē*, according to "Aristotle," *Prob.* 961a8–15, include a combination of hot (reddening of the ears) and cold (chilling in the eyes)

[74] I take the character traits listed in this passage to be emotional extremes, although they do not correspond to those listed in Aristotle's other accounts of emotional mean states and extremes. In fact, wittiness (εὐτραπελία) is said to be an emotional mean state at *EE* 1234a4. The other pair of opposites listed in *EE* 7 5, people who are quick-tempered (ὀξεῖς) and those who are easygoing (ῥαθύμοις. 1240a2) is a more obvious example of emotional extremes. Dirlmeier, *Eudemische Ethik*, 421, explains that Aristotle uses the term *austeroi* (austere; literally, dry) instead of the more usual *agroikos* (boorish) because of the physical analogy in this passage. Cf. *Laws* 666b6, where Plato uses the cognate noun, *austerotētos*, to refer to the dry and austere nature of old people, who need the drug of hot, moist wine

other emotional mean states,[75] *aidōs*, at least, does appear to consist in part of a proportionate blend of opposites. This emotion opposes both pleasure and pain. In *Nicomachean Ethics* 4.9, *aidōs* involves a conflict between shameless desires and emotions on the one hand, and on the other, the fear of disgrace that prevents people from acting on these emotions. On each occasion, it would appear, occurrent *aidōs*, fear of disgrace, must be proportionate to the shameless desires it opposes. However, *aidōs* opposes not only the (hot) desire for shameless pleasures but also, in its role as a cause of political courage, the (cold) fear of physical dangers. In the latter case, *aidōs* could be produced by adding to preexisting excessively cold fear of physical danger a proportionate amount of hot, aggressive desires that have much in common with shamelessness. *Aidōs* is produced in this way in the old people of Plato's *Laws*, as we saw in chapter 1. The dispositional state of *aidōs* makes the proportion of hot and cold correct on each occasion; it recreates the occurrent *pathos* of *aidōs* by blending emotional extremes in a proportion in which one intermediate comes to be from both. Because the dispositional state of *aidōs* is only an emotional mean state, however, it is not so stable and enduring as excellence, but will require periodic renewal and recreation through a blending of opposites.

Because *aidōs* opposes and is a proportionate blend of the opposite emotional extremes of *kataplēxis* and shamelessness, it has a uniquely important role in producing the intermediate state with respect to pleasure and pain that is a necessary precondition for the acquisition of excellence. Aristotle's account of habituation in *Nicomachean Ethics* 2.2, although it does not mention *aidōs*, allows us to make reasonable inferences about what the role of this emotion might be:

> Both excessive and deficient exercise destroy strength, and similarly drink and food that is more or less [than the right amount] destroy health, but proportionate amounts [*ta summetra*] produce, and augment, and preserve [health and strength]. Now the same thing is true in the case of temperance, and courage, and the other excellences. For the person who runs from and fears everything and endures nothing becomes a coward, while the person who fears nothing at all but encounters everything [becomes] rash. Similarly, the person who enjoys every pleasure and refrains from none [becomes] licentious, while the person avoiding all [pleasure], like boorish people, [becomes] insensible. Temperance and courage are destroyed by excess and deficiency, and are preserved by the mean state [*EN* 1104a15–27]. . . . For by

---

[75] See Fortenbaugh, "Mean-Dispositions," for a discussion of some of the problems in Aristotle's account of emotional mean states.

refraining from pleasures we become temperate. . . . Similarly in the case of courage: having become habituated to despise fearful things and to endure them we become courageous. (*EN* 2.2.1104a33–b2)[76]

In this passage, Aristotle indicates that correct habituation in *pathē* (fears, enjoys) and actions (runs from, refrains from) helps produce, augment, and preserve excellence, just as a *summetria* of food, drink, and exercise helps produce, augment, and preserve health. He clearly does not hold the absurd belief that health *is* a *summetria* of food, drink, and exercise, but believes instead that a *summetria* of these is a necessary but not sufficient condition for the production, increase, and preservation of health. Similarly, Aristotle does not believe, as some have argued, that ethical, like physical, excellence is a proportion of opposites, in a literal sense.[77] This erroneous view of excellence tends to equate it with a simple mixture of hot and cold *pathē*, while ignoring the fact that it involves *prohairesis*, while the *pathē* do not. Excellence is not itself a *pathos*, but is concerned with (*peri*) *pathē* and actions (*EN* 1106b24–25), and it "aims at the intermediate" (1106b28) in these. Habituation in *pathē* and actions is necessary but not sufficient to produce excellence.[78] This is clear from the comparison of excellence with health in the passage just quoted, and from the distinction between doing excellent actions and acting excellently made in *Nicomachean Ethics* 1105a28–33. While habituation can accustom us to doing excellent actions, it alone is not sufficient to allow us to acquire knowledge, *prohairesis*, and a stable character, which are necessary if we are to act excellently.

While Aristotle does not mention *aidōs* in the account of habituation just discussed (*EN* 2.2), *aidōs* is closely connected with habituation in *Nicomachean Ethics* 10.9. Moreover, *aidōs* provides a psychic mechanism that explains how habituation is possible. Because it is, in part, a *summetria* of emotional extremes that opposes both pleasure and pain, *aidōs* provides affective motivation for the correct pursuit and avoidance of pleasure and pain.

Partly because of these affective aspects of *aidōs*, it is reasonable to suppose that it also has an important role in the acquisition of *prohairesis*, a

---

[76] See also *MM* 1185b14–31, esp. 1185b29: *metrioi phoboi* (moderate fears).

[77] See, for example, Burnet, *Ethics*, esp. 69–73, criticized by Hardie, *Theory*, 143–51. See also Tracy, *Mean*, 227–37, and Clark, *Man*, 88–97. I am indebted to Charles Young for helpful discussions of this topic.

[78] Sorabji, "Role" (esp. 211–12 and 216–17), correctly notes that when Aristotle states, at *EN* 1103a17, that ethical excellence comes "from habit," he does not mean that habituation is sufficient for the production of excellence.

deliberative desire (*orexis bouleutikē. EE* 1226b17) to do something for the sake of an end. *Aidōs*, fear of *adoxia* (bad opinion), helps in the acquisition of true excellence by leading young people to attempt to understand what ends their ethical guides aim at, and what specific acts of their own will best achieve these ends and avoid the opposite. Only in this way will they be able in a reliable way to avoid incurring reproach. The pleasure they get in so acting will also help them understand which acts are fine. "Those who do an activity with pleasure judge better and are more accurate about each thing" (*EN* 1175a31–32).[79] *Aidōs, fear* of disgrace, will also lead young people to *desire* to avoid disgrace by avoiding the acts their intellects tell them will incur disgrace. For these reasons, *aidōs* is instrumental in the acquisition of excellence, which requires *prohairesis* and an end (e.g., *EN* 1117a4–5).

Aristotle also tells us (e.g., *EN* 6.1144b12–17) that excellence requires the intellectual abilities of comprehension (*nous*) and practical reason (*phronēsis*). Aristotle's comments on *nous* in *Nicomachean Ethics* 6 are of particular interest in connection with *aidōs*. *Nous*, he writes, comes only at a certain age (1143b7–9), through experience. It helps us perceive particulars as instances of universals (1143b4–5). For example, Aristotle explains in *Posterior Analytics* 2.19, *nous* allows us to perceive Callias as a human being (100a16–b1).[80] In ethical cases, *nous* allows us to understand that particular actions are fine or base because they are actions of a certain kind. For example, *nous* might allow us to understand that striking one's father is a base act, like stealing from a temple or breaking an oath.[81] *Aidōs* helps people understand this because, in leading them to generalize about particular acts that incur disgrace, it encourages them to understand that all these acts are base. *Nicomachean Ethics* 6 also gives us the important information that the experience required by *nous* need not be our own, but can be acquired by paying attention to the opinions (*doxais*) and undemonstrated sayings of experienced older people, or of the practically wise (1143b11–13).[82] One emotion that is highly effective in leading us to pay heedful attention to others' opinions is *aidōs*, fear of bad opinion. This emotion both quickens our perception of these opinions and motivates us to act in accord with them. In this way also, *aidōs* can help us acquire *nous*.

[79] On this idea, see Charles, *Action*, 182, and Sherman, *Fabric*, 184–90

[80] Modrak, *Perception*, 168, explains "We perceive a particular man (i e , a token of a certain type or species), but the perception is of man (i e , the type is the ultimate determinant of the content of the perception) "

[81] On *nous* in ethical cases, see Dahl, *Reason*, 41–45

[82] See ibid , 43 and 230

Habituation and *aidōs* are useful in the development of the affective and cognitive aspects of excellence in general, and they have a more specific relevance for two of the excellences. *sōphrosunē* and courage. Immediately after 1179b23–31 (quoted above), *Nicomachean Ethics* 10.9 states that habituation helps produce *sōphrosunē* and *karteria* (resistance) "It is difficult for someone to get from youth correct guidance toward excellence if he is not brought up under laws of this kind. For it is not pleasant for the many, especially if they are young, to live temperately and with resistance For which reason their upbringing and pursuits should be ordered by the laws. For these things will not be painful if they become habitual" (*EN* 10.9.1179b31–1180a1). Resistance is the ability to endure pain (*EN* 1150a14) While it is not an excellence, it is a praiseworthy state (1145b8–9) and thus conducive to the development of the excellence of courage *Sōphrosunē*, on the other hand, is "a mean state concerning pleasures" (*EN* 1117b25). Thus, in stating that habituation allows young people to live without pain temperately (*sōphronōs*) and with resistance, Aristotle must mean that habituation provides the practice in overcoming pleasures and pains that is conducive to the development of *sōphrosunē* and courage (*EN* 1104a33–b3).

Because *aidōs*, like habituation, helps people resist pleasure and pain, it also helps in the development of *sōphrosunē* and courage. This function of *aidōs* depends on its nature as a conflict emotion, one that prevents people from acting according to the *pathē* that desire to pursue pleasure and avoid pain.[83] *Aidōs* opposes both pleasure and pain, as is evident from its broad role in *Nicomachean Ethics* 4 9 in preventing young people from doing base actions. That it is specifically connected with courage is apparent from its role as a cause of "political courage" in the *Nicomachean Ethics* and *Eudemian Ethics*.[84] The practice of this kind of courage by the young could help provide the habituation in enduring fearful things that is conducive to the development of true courage. The connection of *aidōs* with *sōphrosunē* is brought out in *Eudemian Ethics* 3.7 (1234a24–33), where Aristotle writes that *aidōs* "contributes to" the "natural excellence" of *sōphrosunē*, which lacks *phronēsis* and *prohairesis*. Although Aristotle's views on "natural excellence" are obscure,[85] he appears to mean that *aidōs* contributes to "nat-

---

[83] This dual role of the conflict emotion of *aidōs* is of interest in view of the theoretical difficulties presented by the excellences of courage and *sōphrosunē* It is harder to account for these than for the other excellences in terms of lack of conflict between desire and reason Charles calls them "conflict virtues" *Action*, 170–77

[84] Cf *MM* 1191a5–7, where *aischunē* is said to be the cause of political courage

[85] On this topic, see Dahl, *Reason*, 87–91

ural *sōphrosunē* by leading people to refrain from pleasures without actually being temperate in the strict sense. In this way, *aidōs* provides the kind of practice in refraining from pleasures and in enjoying this very thing that leads people to attain *sōphrosunē* in the strict sense, which does have *phronēsis* and *prohairesis* (EN 1104a33–b16).

Some remarks about *sōphrosunē* in *Politics* 3 are helpful. At 1277b17–18, Aristotle states that the *sōphrosunē* of ruler and ruled are different in kind. Because he goes on to say that the ruler has *phronēsis*, while the ruled has only true opinion (1277b25–29), the *sōphrosunē* of the ruled, in this passage, is like "natural *sōphrosunē*" in *Eudemian Ethics* 3.7, which also lacks *phronēsis*.[86] Moreover, the *sōphrosunē* of the ruled, which lacks *phronēsis*, is a prerequisite for the *sōphrosunē* of the ruler, which does have *phronēsis*. As *Politics* 3 states, "It is necessary for the ruler to learn [political rule] by being ruled" (1277b9–10), and "It is not possible to rule well without having been ruled" (1277b12–13). *Politics* 3, then, like Aristotle's ethical works, holds that the habit of obedience to another has an essential role in the acquisition of excellence. While the *Politics* passage does not mention *aidōs*, we may reasonably infer that here also it is *aidōs*, or something much like it, that "contributes to" the *sōphrosunē* of the ruled by making the right kind of obedience possible in the first place.

Nicomachean Ethics 10.9 makes still another point about habituation that is helpful for an understanding of *aidōs*. Aristotle writes that habituation is useful not only in youth but throughout life: "But surely it is not sufficient for them to get correct upbringing and care when they are young, but also when they have become men they must pursue and be habituated in these things, and we would need laws concerning these things also, and in general concerning all of life" (EN 10.9.1180a1–4). R. A. Gauthier and J. Y. Jolif object that "Aristotle certainly can't mean that mature men should follow the same rules that young people follow, and if it were a question of those rules, they would have no further need to accustom themselves to them."[87] This however, is exactly what Aristotle does mean: the same habituation must continue throughout life.[88] This statement does not appear strange if we pay closer attention to the context.

As the last chapter of the last book of the *Nicomachean Ethics*, 10.9 serves

[86] I owe this observation to Eugene Garver, in conversation. On the interpretation of 1277b17–20, with its many condensations of expression, see Newman, *Politics*, ad loc.

[87] Gauthier and Jolif, 2.2:902. They adopt Susemihl's emendation ἄττα (certain things) for αὐτά (these things) at 1180a3.

[88] Sherman, *Fabric*, 20, correctly notes, in connection with this passage: "Civic law . . . forms a continuing part of the education of character begun in earlier years at home."

as a transition to the *Politics*, referred to explicitly in the concluding words. This chapter deals with the "decent people" (the *epieikeis*: 1179b5, 1179b19, 1180a8, 1180a10) for whom the legislator makes laws. "The many" in a city obey only force and physical punishment (1180a4–5; 1179a11–14). The "decent people," while superior to the many, are not excellent in the strict sense, even when they "become men." Writing from the point of view of these "decent people," Aristotle says that "we must perhaps be content if, when we have everything by means of which we are thought to become decent, we have some share in excellence" (1179b18–20). That the adult "decent people" have not yet attained excellence in the strict sense is also indicated by Aristotle's statement that "we would need laws for these things also" (1180a3)—that is, for the pursuits and habits of people throughout life. Moreover, he compares the laws to a father at 1180b3–7. The person who has attained excellence in the strict sense pursues it for its own sake, without need of laws or of the exhortations of legislators.

Thus, the adult "decent people" are in many ways the same, ethically, as those who obey *aidōs*: the young of 4.9 and the correctly habituated young people of 10.9. This view is consistent with *Politics* 1331a37–b1, where *aidōs* is said to be desirable for both young and old. In *Nicomachean Ethics* 10.9, Aristotle writes that the legislators should exhort these adult "decent people" and "urge" (προτρέπεσθαι) them for the sake of the fine (1180a6–7), while punishing the many. This is the same idea as that expressed at 1179b7–15, where the many who obey only force are contrasted with young people who, because they obey *aidōs* and refrain from base deeds because they are shameful, can be "urged" (προτρέψασθαι: 1179b7, 1179b10) toward nobility. Adults who are "decently brought up in habits" are said to be able to listen to (ἐπακουσομένων) the exhortations of the legislators (1180a7–8). Similarly, young people are said to have souls prepared beforehand by habits so as to be able to listen to (ἀκούσειε) argument or reason (1179b24–28).

The "decent people" who obey *aidōs* would seem to be the same as the "better class of people" (1095b22) of *Nicomachean Ethics* 1.5, who choose the political life (1095b23), the end of which is honor, and within which *aidōs* plays an important role. The people who choose the political life in *Nicomachean Ethics* 1.5 are contrasted, like the "decent people" of 10.9, with the vulgar, who pursue only pleasure. In *Nicomachean Ethics* 3.8, at least, the "political" people are capable of acquiring *prohairesis* and excellence of a kind within the political life. Aristotle appears to hold similar views in *Nicomachean Ethics* 10.9, where he writes that the people who live "in decent pursuits" (1180a16) live "according to a certain *nous* [κατα τινα νοῦν] and correct order' (1180a18), given by law, which is "reason proceeding from a certain *phronēsis* and *nous*" (1180a21–22) Habituation, then, gives the "decent people" the intellectual abilities proper to the kind of excellence of which they are capable, under the rule of law Only a few people will be able to progress beyond this stage to attain excellence in the strict sense

Within the political context of the conclusion of the *Nicomachean Ethics*, habituation is very important It is useful not only for the young, but throughout life, to the class of "decent people "[89] Moreover, it is *aidōs* that makes habituation possible in the first place *Aidōs* is an essentially educable emotion In its affective and cognitive aspects, *aidōs*, "fear of bad opinion," leads us to pay heedful attention to the opinions of others and to desire to act in accord with them *Aidōs*, in sum, is what makes possible the ethical education of the whole person as an individual human being who exists, first and primarily, as a member of a human community

These conclusions are not without relevance for an understanding of the *Poetics* The audience for tragedy does not consist primarily of the *phauloi*, the inferior "many," but of "decent" people, the *epieikeis* This is the clear implication of Aristotle's defense of tragedy against those who claim that it appeals to the *phauloi* rather than to the *epieikeis* (*Po* 26 1462a2–4) These "decent people," it is reasonable to suppose, are the better class of ordinary citizens who, according to *Nicomachean Ethics* 10 9, obey *aidōs* rather than *phobos* and who are "decently" advanced in habits (1180a8) Tragedy, as I will argue in chapter 10, can help provide these people, who are responsive to *aidōs*, with an affective and cognitive ethical education from childhood on

KATAPLĒXIS AND EKPLĒXIS

Two particular fear and shame emotions, *kataplēxis* and *ekplēxis*, have an especially direct relevance to the *Poetics* Aristotle uses *ekplēxis* as other Greek writers do, to refer to emotion aroused by poetry and rhetoric This term is related, linguistically and conceptually, to *kataplēxis*, a term that

[89] It is possible that more ethically advanced people could also benefit from habituation throughout life In *EN* 2 2, Aristotle compares habituation to food and exercise that pro duce, increase, and *preserve* physical health (1104a18) He does not pursue this line of thought, however

refers to excessive shame in Aristotle's ethical works, and in his other works to fear of pain and death (*phobos*).

Kataplēxis is, in Aristotle's ethical works, excessive shame, an emotional extreme of which *aidōs* (or the *aidēmōn*) is the mean state. The most complete account of *kataplēxis* is given in *Magna moralia* 1193a4–6 (quoted above). This account, like those of the *Eudemian Ethics* and the *Nicomachean Ethics*, states that the *kataplēx* is someone who fears the opinion of others to excess.[90] However, according to the *Magna moralia* alone, the *kataplēx* may in extreme cases be literally paralyzed with emotion.

In nonethical contexts also, Aristotle uses *kataplēxis* to refer to fear that is associated with disgrace. This is apparent in three passages in the *Athenian Constitution*. At 25.3–4, Ephialtes, who has been attacking the Council, is led to believe he is in danger of arrest. This causes him to feel *kataplēxis* (25.4.2), and leads him to take refuge, in his shirt, at an altar. Again, at 38.2, the Ten, "being afraid of losing their office, and wishing to cause *kataplēxis* [38.2.3] in the others (which in fact happened)," arrest Demaretus and put him to death. In these two passages, *kataplēxis* is fear of a disgraceful death. In the other passage in which *kataplēxis* and cognates occur (34.3.11), Lysander's siding with the oligarchical party is said to cause *kataplēxis* in the people, who had been in control previously, and forces them to vote for the oligarchy. Here, *kataplēxis* is fear of the destructive and painful reprisals and penalties that would result from an unavailing assertion of rights. It is caused by a loss of social power that was thought by the Greeks to be disgraceful in itself. Like *kataplēxis* and *aidōs* in the ethical works, *kataplēxis* in the *Athenian Constitution* prevents people from acting. In 34.3.11, the people are prevented from asserting their rights; in 38.2.3, those who are opposed to the Ten are prevented from acting, and, in 25.4.2, Ephialtes, like the *kataplēx* of the *Magna moralia*, is prevented by *kataplēxis* from saying or doing anything: instead he sits helpless at an altar.

At *Rhetoric* 1408a25, *kataplēxis*, like *ekplēxis* elsewhere in Greek literature, is used to refer to strong emotion aroused by speech. When the orator speaks emotionally, Aristotle writes, the audience also experiences emotion, even if the speaker says nothing at all of substance. That is why, Aristotle continues, many orators cause *kataplēxis* in the audience when they make a noise (1408a23–25).

In the other relevant occurrence of *kataplēxis* and its cognates in a non-

---

[90] See *EN* 1108a34 and *EE* 1233b28.

ethical context,[91] this term refers to panic in battle. In a tantalizingly brief fragment (153), the Gorgon's head is said to produce *kataplēxis*. Commenting on *Iliad* 5.741, which concerns Athena's *aigis*, ornamented with a Gorgon's head and other terrifying devices, the scholiast writes. "Aristotle says that she never had the Gorgon's head itself on her shield, just as she never had Strife or chilling rout, but [that she had] the kataplectic emotion that is produced by the Gorgon in those seeing it" (12–15). The "kataplectic emotion" (*pathos kataplēktikon*) mentioned here is closely related to *phobos*, fear of physical danger. In *Iliad* 5.738–41, *Phobos* figures prominently on Athena's *aigis*, along with the Gorgon, and the "chilling rout" (*Il.* 5.740) to which Aristotle refers is clearly the panic in battle that Gorgias calls *ekplēxis* (*Encomium of Helen*, 16). This fear not only causes flight, it can also paralyze, an effect traditionally associated with the Gorgon. *Kataplēxis* in fragment 153 is conceptually related to *aidōs* as well as *phobos*, however, for to be overcome by *kataplēxis* in battle is to fail to stand by a comrade—to fail to have *aidōs* for him.[92] Here also, *kataplēxis* refers to fear that is associated with disgrace.

The term *kataplēxis*, then, has three interrelated senses in Aristotle. It refers to excessive shame, fear associated with disgrace, and strong emotion aroused by rhetoric. In other Greek writers also, *kataplēxis* is associated with fear and with rhetoric. Segal cites Thrasymachus (DK A4), where the term *kataplēxis* is said to be used by rhetoricians.[93] Metrodoros of Chios (fourth century B.C.E.) was reported to have said that the Dioscuri produce *kataplēxis* and fear in those who see them.[94] A particularly interesting occurrence of *kataplēxis* is in Thucydides 2.65.9.[95] Pericles, when the people became too hubristic and bold, would strike them with *kataplēxis* by speaking, and thus cause them to fear. λέγων κατέπλησσεν ἐπὶ τὸ φοβεῖσθαι Here, *kataplēxis* is an intense fear emotion aroused by rhetoric

The term *ekplēxis* is very similar in meaning to *kataplēxis* in Aristotle and in Greek literature generally.[96] *Ekplēxis*, however, has stronger aes-

[91] The other occurrence of *kataplēxis*, *On Respiration* 474a15, is connected with respiration, and has nothing to do with emotion In any case, the text is doubtful
[92] See above, n 33
[93] Aristophanes, *Daitales* frag 198, cited by Segal, "Gorgias," 150 n 99 For this fragment, see Hall and Geldart, *Aristophanis Comoediae*, who print τὸ καταπλαγήσει τοῦτο παρὰ τῶν ῥητόρων, noting that καταπλαγήσει is Porson's correction of the MSS reading καταπληγήσῃ Segal fails to note that DK follows Dindorf's emendation καταπλιγήσει, said to be "dubious" by LSJ, s v καταπλίσσομαι
[94] DK A10 Aetius 11 18 2
[95] This passage is cited (incorrectly, as 2 65 8) by Segal, "Gorgias," 130
[96] The similarity is noted by Dirlmeier, *Eudemische Ethik*, 352

thetic and rhetorical associations. This term is used by writers other than Aristotle to refer to strong emotions, especially pity and fear, aroused by poetry and rhetoric. Gorgias (ca. 483–385 B.C E.) was the first, as far as we know, to use *ekplēxis* in connection with poetry. In the *Encomium of Helen* (DK B11), Gorgias states that poetry arouses "fearful shuddering and much-weeping pity" (9), and he compares its effects to the *ekplēxis* that causes soldiers to flee in panic (16).[97] *Ekplēxis* also refers to the emotional effects of drama in Aristophanes' *Frogs*, where Euripides uses it to refer to the effects of Aeschylus's poetry.[98] *Ekplēxis* is also used of intense emotion, especially fear, in the tragedies, and of the effects of poetry by Longinus, Plutarch, Demetrius, and the scholia.[99]

In Plato also, *ekplēxis* can refer to strong emotion, especially pity and fear, aroused by poetry and other kinds of speech. Ion uses *ekplēxis* of the emotional effects of poetry (*Ion* 535b2),[100] in particular those of pity, fear, weeping, and pounding of the heart (535c4–8). The *Symposium* uses *ekplēxis* of the effects of Gorgianic rhetoric. After hearing Agathon's speech, Socrates remarks.

> Who would not have experienced *ekplēxis* on hearing it? For my part, thinking that I would have nothing anywhere near as fine as this to say, I would almost have run away in shame [*aischunēs*], if I had had anywhere to go Indeed, the speech reminded me of Gorgias, so that I simply had the experience recounted by Homer I feared that at last Agathon, sending against my speech this head of Gorgias, who is so astonishing at speaking in speech, should turn me to stone in speechlessness (*Sym.* 198b5–c5)

The "head of Gorgias" is a punning allusion to *Odyssey* 11.633–35, where Odysseus fears that Persephone will send a Gorgon's head from Hades. Plato compares the power of rhetoric to strike people dumb to the Gorgon's power to paralyze with fear Significantly, *ekplēxis* in this passage involves shame (198b7) as well as fear. In several respects, the *ekplēxis* produced by Agathon's speech is like *kataplēxis* in Aristotle, which can also make people speechless with shame, and which is associated with the Gorgon's head and with the emotional effects of speech.

---

[97] On *ekplēxis* in Gorgias, see Segal, ' Gorgias '

[98] *Frogs* 961–62, cited ibid , 130 See also chap 1, n 42

[99] For example, Aeschylus, *Persians* 606, Euripides, *Trojan Women* 183, Longinus 15 2, Plutarch, *Moralia* 16a–17e, 25d, Demetrius, *On Style* 100–101, scholia on Sophocles, *Ajax* 346, 815, Hypothesis to Aeschylus, *Agamemnon* These and other references are given by Heath, *Poetics*, 15–16

[100] This passage is cited ibid , 8

Ekplēxıs also refers to the effects of Socrates' own words ın Plato's *Symposium* These words produce tears and a poundıng heart ın his audıence (215e2), and they paralyze Alcıbıades so that he ıs afraıd of growıng old whıle sıttıng and lıstenıng to the philosopher (216a8), whose arguments he ıs unable to answer (216b3–4) Alcıbıades calls thıs experience "enchantment" (215c1, 215c5), "philosophıcal madness and Bacchıc frenzy" (218b3–4), and *ekplēxıs* "We experience *ekplēxıs* and are possessed" (215d5–6) Thıs "philosophıcal" *ekplēxıs* also ınvolves shame Alcıbıades says that Socrates' philosophıcal words cause hım to feel shame (216b2) and make hım run away (215b5–6), just as Socrates ıs tempted to do ın response to the "head of Gorgıas" Other Platonıc dıalogues, even when they do not use the term *ekplēxıs*, gıve sımılar accounts of the emotıonal effects of the elenchus (the Socratıc cross-examınatıon) Meno suffers just as Alcıbıades does, for he says that Socrates paralyzes hım lıke a stıngray and enchants hım, so that he ıs unable to say anythıng (*Meno* 80b4) Even Thrasymachus blushes (*Rep* 350d3) In the *Sophıst* also, the Socratıc elenchus produces *aıschunē* ın ıts "patient" (230d1) [101]

Plato's "philosophıcal" *ekplēxıs*, then, like *kataplēxıs* ın Arıstotle's ethıcal works, ıs the opposite of shamelessness Before beıng paralyzed by the Socratıc elenchus and brought to the state of beıng unable to say anythıng at all (80b4), Meno was accustomed "to say very many words about excellence on many occasıons, and before many people" (80b2–3) He was lıke the shameless person of the *Magna moralıa* "who on all occasıons and to everyone, says and does whatever occurs to hım" (1193a2–4) Immedıately after the elenchus, however, Meno closely resembles (temporarıly) the *kataplēx* of the *Magna moralıa*, "who ıs cautious about doıng and sayıng everythıng and to everyone," and who, ın extreme cases, does not act or speak at all (1193a4–6) Alcıbıades ın the *Symposıum* was also shameless before hearıng Socrates, who alone makes hım feel shame "Before hım alone of all people, I experienced somethıng that no one would have thought was ın me shame [*aıschunesthaı*] before anyone at all" (216a8–b2)

Arıstotle's concept of *ekplēxıs* ıs rooted ın thıs lıterary and philosophıcal tradıtıon In his works also, *ekplēxıs* refers to strong emotıon, especıally fear and wonder, and ıt ıs often used of the effects of poetry and rhetorıc

In Arıstotle's works other than the *Poetıcs*, *ekplēxıs* sometımes appears to be a synonym for *phobos*, fear of destructıve or paınful evils In *Rhetorıc* 2 8 1385b32–34, people who experience *ekplēxıs* (*ekpeplēgmenoı*) are those

---

[101] On the emotıonal effects of the elenchus, see further below, chap 9

who feel the extreme fear (*phoboumenoi sphodra*) of physical danger that is incompatible with pity. [102] In *Topics* 126b17, on the other hand, *ekplēxis* is defined as "excessive wonder " *Ekplēxis* also appears to mean "wonder" in "Aristotle," *On the Universe* 391a23. The author condemns the small-mindedness of those who experience *ekplēxis* at any chance things and take pride in "unimportant spectacles " If, he writes, they paid attention to what is greatest, the universe, they would never wonder (391b1) at lesser things (391a18–b3). [103] In one passage in Aristotle's genuine works, *History of Animals* 496b27, *ekplēxis* appears to refer to a combination of fear and wonder. In Naxos, Aristotle writes, animals have very large gallbladders People who are ignorant of this fact experience *ekplēxis* when they sacrifice these animals, believing the large gallbladders to be particular signs rather than natural occurrences.

In the *Poetics*, *ekplēxis* and cognates are used of the emotional effects of tragedy in three passages. 1454a4, 1455a17, and 1460b25 Two of these passages concern recognition. At 1454a4, Aristotle writes that, in a plot in which *philos* harms *philos* in ignorance of *philia*, and recognition then follows, recognition is "ekplectic," and at 1455a17 he writes that "the best recognition of all is that which [comes about] from the events themselves, the *ekplēxis* coming by means of plausible things." While recognition is said to cause *ekplēxis* in these two passages, it is said to arouse pity and fear at 1452a38–b1 This suggests that *ekplēxis* and "pity and fear" refer to the same emotional effects of tragedy Aristotle's use of *ekplēxis* in connection with recognition is also of interest because it suggests that *ekplēxis* is aroused by shameful events. In the best plots, recognition takes place before or after a shameful *pathos*, harm of *philos* by *philos*. Only this kind of *pathos* properly arouses pity and fear (1453b17–22) and *ekplēxis* (1454a4).

The third occurrence of *ekplēxis* in the *Poetics* is the most informative. In *Poetics* 25, Aristotle writes that it is sometimes defensible to put impossibilities into a tragedy or epic "But it will be correctly made, if it accomplishes its own end (what the end is has been stated), [that is], if in this way it makes either this or some other part more productive of *ekplēxis*. An

---

[102] The *Rhetoric* differs in this respect from the *Poetics*, where *ekplēxis* is compatible with pity and fear see chap 7 ("Pity and Fear in the *Poetics*") *Ekplēxis* and its cognates also occur in close association with *phobos* and its cognates in *EN* 1115b11, and in "Aristotle," *Virtues and Vices* 1250a7, 1250a19, 1250a44, and *Divisions* 61 27

[103] Cf the association of philosophy (or wisdom) with wonder in *Meta* 982b17–19, *Rhet* 1371a27–28, and *EN* 1177a25

example is the pursuit of Hector" (1460b24–26)[104] This passage tells us that the production of *ekplēxis* is the *telos* of tragedy and epic Elsewhere, the end of tragedy is said to be the production of pleasure and katharsis from pity and fear Does *ekplēxis*, then, refer to still another emotional effect of poetry, as Bywater argues,[105] or is it another term for these same effects?

We have already examined evidence in favor of the second view *Ekplēxis* is traditionally used to refer to the effects of poetry, and Plato and Gorgias closely connect pity and fear with *ekplēxis* In the *Poetics*, recognition is sometimes said to arouse pity and fear and at other times to arouse *ekplēxis* Additional reason to believe that *ekplēxis* is not an emotional effect separate from pity and fear is given by the close connection of *ekplēxis* and wonder in the *Poetics*, the *History of Animals*, and *On the Universe* Bywater notes that the pursuit of Hector in the *Iliad* is called *ekplēktikon* (productive of *ekplēxis*) at 25 1460b25, and *thaumaston* (wonderful) at 1460a14 This, he writes, shows that there is an "affinity of sense" between the two words[106] Wonder, moreover, is closely connected with pity and fear in *Poetics* 9 "Since it [sc, tragedy] is not only imitation of a complete action but also of pitiable and fearful things, these occur most of all when things take place contrary to expectation by means of one another For in this way they will have the wonderful more than if they [occur] of themselves and by chance" (1452a1–6) The logical connection (γαϱ for) made here between events that are "pitiable and fearful" and events that have "the wonderful" implies that tragic pity and fear include an element of wonder In fact, this passage suggests that "the wonderful" is equivalent to "pitiable and fearful" here, just as in *Poetics* 25 "productive of *ekplēxis*" is closely related to "wonderful " If this is so, "wonder" is closely related in sense to both "pity and fear" and *ekplēxis*, which are in turn closely related in sense to each other The evidence, then, favors the view that the term *ekplēxis* does not refer to a separate emotional effect of tragedy, but to pity and fear, which include an element of wonder

SUMMARY

In this chapter I have studied a broad range of fear, pity, and shame emotions, concentrating on Aristotle's works other than the *Poetics* The first

---

[104] I follow Bywater, *Aristotle on the Art*, on 1460b25, in taking if in this way *ekplēxis* in apposition to if it accomplishes its own end
[105] Ibid , on 1460b25
[106] Ibid , on 1454a4

section ("Pity, Fear, and Physical Danger") discussed Aristotle's view that emotion involves the interaction of physiological and cognitive responses. The term *phobos* usually refers to fear of physical pain or death, a cold emotion, the physical matter of which is a chilling and contraction in the region of the heart. In the *Rhetoric*, *phobos* is defined as "pain or disturbance [resulting] from the *phantasia* of imminent destructive or painful evil." *Phobos* can, however, also refer to fear of other kinds of evils, such as disgrace. Pity is a cold emotion causally and conceptually dependent on *phobos*. It is defined in the *Rhetoric* as "pain at an apparent destructive or painful evil of someone who does not deserve to get it, that one could expect oneself, or someone belonging to oneself, to suffer, and this, when it appears near." Pity thus involves more complex judgments and a greater understanding of universals than does fear.

In "Fear of Disgrace," I explored Aristotle's views on the shame emotions, *aidōs* and *aischunē*, in the context of traditional Greek views. Aristotle's concepts of *aidōs* and *aischunē* are derived from and heavily dependent on the Greek, and especially the Homeric, tradition. Within that tradition, *aidōs* is "respect" for fellow humans that preserves the social order and distinguishes humans from animals. It is especially appropriate to young people, and for this reason has an important role in education. Aristotle departs from this tradition in one particularly important respect, however, for he distinguishes sharply between *aidōs* and excellence in the strict sense.

In the *Rhetoric*, Aristotle is concerned less with *aidōs* than with *aischunē*, defined as "pain and disturbance concerning those evils that appear to bring disgrace, whether they are present, or past, or future." *Aischunē* is felt for involuntary as well as for voluntary things, and it is an emotion characteristic of the young.

In Aristotle's ethical works, *aidōs* is more important than *aischunē*. In all three of the ethical works attributed to Aristotle, *aidōs* is intermediate between the extremes of *kataplēxis* and shamelessness. *Kataplēxis* is fear of disgrace that can be so intense as to prevent one from saying or doing anything at all. Shamelessness, on the other hand, leads people to say and do anything that occurs to them, on any occasion. *Aidōs* leads one to say and do the right things, on the right occasions, and at the right time. *Aidōs* can be either an occurrent *pathos* or a dispositional state. Unlike excellence, *aidōs* is, in part, a proportionate blend of opposites within a single individual at the same time. It is a conflict emotion that prevents people from doing base acts, typically by overcoming hot, pleasure-seeking desires with a proportionate amount of cold fear of disgrace.

In the *Nicomachean Ethics*, *aidōs* is always an occurrent *pathos*; the praiseworthy state with respect to it is unnamed, though the person with this state is said to be *aidēmōn*. In 4.9, *aidōs* is a *pathos*, defined as "fear of disgrace." It differs from *aischunē* in the *Nicomachean Ethics* in being more concerned with future evils. *Aidōs* in 4.9 also differs from the *aischunē* of the *Rhetoric* in being felt only for voluntary acts and in essentially involving conflict. It is praiseworthy in the young, because they "live by *pathos*" and will be prevented from doing base acts by *aidōs*. *Aidōs* involves a conflict of emotion with emotion, for we do not feel *aidōs* unless we have a desire to do something of which we would be ashamed. Older people outgrow *aidōs* to the extent that they acquire ends and become excellent in the strict sense. Thus, *aidōs* in *Nicomachean Ethics* 4.9 is of the immature kind that is incompatible with a life in which everything is chosen for the sake of a definite end. Certain other passages in the *Nicomachean Ethics*, on the other hand, leave open the possibility that there can be a more mature kind of *aidōs*, one "with *prohairesis*" within the political life, whose chosen end is honor. Within this life, *aidōs* is a cause of political courage, an excellence that leads people to do fine acts for the sake of honor and because of *aidōs*, "avoidance of blame." In the *Eudemian Ethics*, on the other hand, *aidōs* always differs from excellence in the strict sense in being "without *prohairesis*." That is, to act because of *aidōs* is, in the *Eudemian Ethics*, to act because of emotion, and not because one chooses to act in a certain way for the sake of the truly fine.

Aristotle's brief remarks allow us to infer that *aidōs* has an essential role in ethical education. It involves resistance to both pleasure and pain, and for this reason helps provide the habituation that is particularly conducive to the development of the excellences of temperance and courage. *Aidōs* is useful in helping young people develop the affective aspects of excellence, giving them correct habituation in pleasure and pain, love and hate. While *aidōs* itself is (with the exception just noted) "without *prohairesis*," it is nevertheless useful in the development of the cognitive abilities required by excellence. *prohairesis*, *phronēsis*, and *nous*. Because *aidōs* requires young people to try to understand the opinions of older and wiser people, it helps them understand what kinds of acts these people consider base or fine, see particular actions as base or fine, and, eventually, choose to do fine acts for their own sake.

Although the rare person who is fully excellent in the strict sense has outgrown *aidōs*, *Nicomachean Ethics* 10.9 indicates that this emotion is useful in providing the kind of habituation that "decent" citizens, the *epieikeis*, require throughout life. These people never become excellent in the strict sense, but, because they obey *aidōs*, they are responsive to the law and to the opinions of the legislators. These people retain some base desires throughout life, and require the continual recreation of a proportionate blend of fear of disgrace with shamelessness to prevent their acting on these desires. As they mature, however, they can acquire the kind of *prohairesis* and *nous* that are appropriate to the political life. Within society as a whole, then, we can infer that *aidōs* is a powerful and important educational force. These inferences will be of particular interest when the emotional effects of tragedy are studied in the following chapters

Chapter 6 concluded with a study of two important fear and shame emotions, in Aristotle and in other writers. *kataplēxis* and *ekplēxis*. *Kataplēxis* in Aristotle is (1) excessive shame, of which *aidōs* is the mean state; (2) fear associated with disgrace, and (3) strong emotion aroused by rhetoric. The closely related term *ekplēxis* is used by other Greek writers to refer to the emotional effects of poetry, especially pity and fear. In Plato, *ekplēxis* also involves shame. Aristotle follows Gorgias and Plato in using *ekplēxis* in the *Poetics* to refer to the emotional effects of tragedy and epic. In this work, *ekplēxis* is so closely associated with pity, fear, and wonder that it appears to be another expression for tragic emotion, which includes all these elements. While *ekplēxis* in the *Poetics* is not explicitly associated with shame, it is nevertheless aroused by shameful acts

This examination of a number of different fear and shame emotions provides a background essential to an understanding of Aristotle's views on emotional responses to tragedy. In chapter 7 I will study these responses, and discuss the ways in which they differ from responses to real-life situations and to rhetoric.[107]

[107] An earlier version of some of this material was read at the NEH Summer Institute on Aristotle's Metaphysics, Biology, and Ethics, Durham, N H , 1988, where I benefited from much helpful discussion I am also indebted to Norman Dahl for insightful criticisms of an earlier draft of this chapter

Tragic Emotion

Ⅰɴ ꜱᴛᴜᴅʏɪɴɢ the specific nature of the emotions aroused by tragedy, I draw in chapter 7 on the conclusions reached in chapter 6 about a variety of fear and pity emotions. The first section of chapter 7, "Pɪᴛʏ ᴀɴᴅ Fᴇᴀʀ ɪɴ the *Poetics*," examines some of the similarities and differences between emotion aroused by tragedy and emotion aroused in other situations. Another important difference is discussed in "Flight and Pursuit". tragic pity and fear do not lead to action as do emotions in typical, real-life situations. Chapter 7 concludes with a study of the specific ways in which both rhetoric and tragedy arouse emotion.

Pɪᴛʏ ᴀɴᴅ Fᴇᴀʀ ɪɴ ᴛʜᴇ *Poetics*

A study of the emotional effects of tragedy must begin with the understanding that it is the function of tragedy to produce pleasure and katharsis by arousing the specific emotions of pity and fear, and only these emotions Tragedy is defined as "imitation . . . by means of pity and fear accomplishing the katharsis of such emotions" (*Po.* 1449b24–28). It is "peculiar" (*idion*) to tragedy to imitate pitiable and fearful events (1452b33), and the "proper pleasure" of tragedy is that which comes from pity and fear (1453b11–13). *Phobos* and *eleos*, or their cognates, occur frequently in conjunction in the *Poetics*, although Aristotle also uses synonyms for these terms. *deina* . . . *oiktra* ("terrible . . pitiable". 1453b14), *phrittein kai eleein* ("to shudder and to pity". 1453b5). The *ekplēxis* and wonder aroused by tragedy are not emotional effects separate from pity and fear Instead, *ekplēxis* is another term for the emotional effects of tragedy. pity and fear, which include an element of wonder. Nor is it the function of tragedy to arouse such emotions as anger. Aristotle's statement that *dianoia* (thought) arouses emotions "like pity, or fear, or anger, and all that are such as these" (1456a38–b1) appears in the context of a general account of the "rhetorical" (1456b35) uses of *dianoia*, and should not be taken as an indication that it is the *function* of tragedy to arouse anger as well as pity and fear.[1]

---

[1] Pace Janko, *Poetics I*, on 1456a38

Aristotle follows tradition in holding that tragedy arouses pity and fear. Gorgias writes that poetry produces "very fearful [*periphobos*] shuddering and much-weeping pity" (DK B11. *Encomium of Helen*, 9). According to Plato (*Ion* 535c), the rhapsode produces *phobos* in the audience when he recites what is pitiable and fearful (*phoberon*) or terrible (*deinon*), and (*Phaedrus* 268c) the tragedians make pitiable and fearful (*phoberas*) speeches.[2] In *Republic* 10.606b3, Plato criticizes poets for arousing pity inappropriately. In *Republic* 3, he forbids the poets to represent death as terrible (*deina*: 386b4), because this will cause the guardians to fear death (386a7), when they ought to be courageous He also forbids the poets' use of "terrible [*deina*] and fearful [*phobera*] words," such as "Cocytus" and "Styx," which cause people to shudder (387b8–c4, cf. *Po.* 14.1453b5. "to shudder and to pity"). While Aristotle also holds that tragedy arouses pity and fear, he does not agree with Plato that the *phobos* aroused by poetry is the same fear that makes people cowardly in battle. On the contrary, Aristotle is careful to distinguish tragic *phobos* from the fear aroused by what is merely painful and destructive (*Po.* 14). Aristotelian tragic emotion is aroused by actions (harm of *philos* by *philos*) that are shameful as well as painful or destructive

Pity and fear in the *Poetics*, like *phobos* and *eleos* in Aristotle's other works, are cold, painful emotions, or, to use the phrase of the *Rhetoric*, two kinds of "pain and disturbance " Because pity and fear in the *Poetics* are emotions (*pathēmata. Po.* 6.1449b28), they have physical and cognitive aspects matter and form, to use the terminology of the *De anima*. One indication that fear in the *Poetics* has the same cold, painful physical aspects as fear of physical danger is Aristotle's statement that tragedy makes the viewer "shudder and pity" (*phrittein kai eleein.* 1453b5). Here, "shudder" is substituted for the more usual term *phobos*. Shuddering, a common physical manifestation of fear, is closely associated with fear in *De motu animalium* 701b22 *phrittousi kai phobountai* The physical manifestations of tragic pity, it is reasonable to assume, are the same as those of pity in real-life situations. weeping, for example.

An objection might be raised, however, to the view that tragic fear and pity are painful emotions, as are *phobos* and *eleos* in real-life situations. Aristotle has often been said to believe that tragedy transforms emotions that are painful in real-life situations into special, "aesthetic" emotions that are pleasurable and not painful.[3] This view might appear to derive support

---

[2] These passages are cited by Else, *Plato*, 139–40, who notes, however, that while *Rep* 10 frequently mentions weeping and wailing, it says nothing about fear On tragic emotion in Gorgias and Plato, see also Pohlenz, "Anfange ' 2 461–66

[3] This is argued, for example, by Butcher, *Aristotle's Theory*, 254–73, and Schaper, "Ar-

from the differences between the *Poetics'* characterization of fear and pity and that of the *Rhetoric.* In the *Rhetoric,* Aristotle defines fear as a kind of "pain [λύπη] and disturbance [ταραχη]," and pity as a kind of "pain" (2.5.1382a21 and 2.8 1385b13). In his *Poetics,* however, pity and fear help produce pleasure: "The poet must provide the pleasure that comes from pity and fear by means of imitation" (14.1453b12–13) This passage, however, does not state that pity and fear are themselves pleasurable, it makes the very different point that pleasure comes "from pity and fear *by means of imitation.*"[4] Moreover, the view that tragic pity and fear are not painful would involve Aristotle in serious philosophical difficulties In his theory, tragedy arouses pity and fear, and it is an imitation of, and thus similar to,[5] fearful and pitiable events (e.g , 9 1452a2–3). It is not clear what this would mean if "pity" and "fear" had one sense when used in connection with the events imitated, and another when used in connection with the emotions produced by the imitation This problem does not arise, of course, if we take Aristotle literally. tragedy is an imitation of (painfully) pitiable and fearful events, and is recognized as such because it produces (painful) pity and fear in the audience Tragedy makes us weep and shudder; this is why we say it is an imitation of pitiable and fearful events.

Nevertheless, painful pity and fear also have a certain pleasurable element, in real life as in tragedy. Fear, according to the *Rhetoric,* necessarily involves hope of safety (1383a5–6), and hope is pleasant, since it is accompanied by the *phantasia* of that for which we hope (1370a29–32), and thus gives pleasure just as the real thing does (1370b9–10) Aristotle holds that "a certain pleasure accompanies most of our desires, for people enjoy a kind of pleasure remembering how they got something, or hoping that they will get it" (1370b14–17). Since this is so, even painful emotions such as anger have a certain element of pleasure (1370b10–11) because they include a desire for something pleasant.

It is a common Greek view that there is a certain pleasure involved in painful emotions. Aristotle explains Homer's phrase "desire for weeping" (ἵμερον γόοιο) by noting that we feel pain at the absence of a loved one, and pleasure in remembering this person [6] In the *Republic,* Plato associates

---

istotle's Catharsis," esp 139 On the problem of "aesthetic" emotions, see further below, "Flight and Pursuit "

[4] A good discussion of this point is that of Golden, "Epic On pleasure and imitation, see chap 2 ("Similarity"), chap 7 ("Aesthetic and Real-Life Emotion'), and chap 10

[5] See chap 2 ("Similarity")

[6] *Rhet* 1370b25–29, quoting *Il* 23 108, cf similar phrases at *Il* 24 513 and *Od* 4 102

pleasure with painful emotions for a different reason: he believes that the pleasure arises from fulfilling a physical or psychological need, or from relieving a burden. In *Republic* 10.606a–b, the poet is said to provide pleasure by filling and pleasing the part of the soul that is "starved for weeping" (606a4). In the *Philebus* also, Plato holds that tragedy gives us pleasure, writing that the audience feels pleasure and weeps at the same time (48a5–6). Gorgias, too, believes that pain can be mixed with pleasure, especially in aesthetic situations, for he writes in his *Encomium of Helen* (9) that those listening to poetry are filled with "grief-loving longing" (πόθος φιλοπενθής).

Whatever these other writers may have thought, there is no indication that Aristotle believed that the pleasurable element in these painful emotions is qualitatively different in aesthetic and real-life situations. It seems likely that, in his view, painful emotions aroused by tragedy have only a greater quantity of attendant pleasure in the form of hope than these emotions have in real-life situations. Tragic fear, like fear in other situations, leads us to deliberate about safety. Tragedy, however, also gives us a greater hope of safety by helping us understand fearful things. What tragedy does not do is "transform" a painful, real-life emotion into a pleasurable, "aesthetic" emotion.

If pity and fear in the *Poetics* have the same painful physical aspects that these emotions have in Aristotle's other works, the cognitive aspects of pity and fear in the *Poetics* are also the same, in many respects, as those of pity and fear in Aristotle's other works. It is reasonable to suppose that the desires (final causes) involved in tragic fear and pity are the same, in most respects, as the desires involved in pity and fear in other situations: the desire to avoid painful and destructive evils (fear), and the desire to help those who suffer them (pity). It is also reasonable to suppose that the efficient cause of tragic fear, as of *phobos* in the *Rhetoric*, is a *phantasia* of future evils. The evils that arouse pity and fear in the *Poetics* are painful and destructive, just like the evils that arouse pity and fear in the *Rhetoric*. The *pathos*, a destructive or painful action, is one of the three parts of the tragic plot (*Po.* 11), and *pathē* arouse pity and fear (*Po.* 14).

The cognitive aspects of pity in the *Poetics* are also similar in other ways to these aspects of pity in the *Rhetoric*. In the *Poetics*, we feel pity for the person who does not deserve to suffer (1453a4), but we do not pity an evil person who goes either from bad to good fortune, or from good to bad fortune (1452b36–1453a4). The *Rhetoric* agrees with this account, stating that pity is felt for those who do not deserve to suffer (1385b14), and that the good fortune of someone who does not deserve it produces indignation (νεμεσᾶν), the opposite of pity (1386b9–12) The two works also agree in holding that we pity those who suffer unexpectedly In the *Rhetoric*, Aristotle writes that it is pitiable for "some evil to come whence it was fitting for one to get something good" (1386a11–12) At *Poetics* 1452a3–4, things that occur "contrary to expectation" are said to arouse pity and fear, and at 1453b19–22 we are said to pity people who suffer at the hands of a *philos*, that is, someone from whom this would not be expected [7] Harm by a *philos* is also pitiable because it separates us from *philoi* (*Rhet* 1386a9–11) The parallels between the accounts of pity in the two works are brought out by Aristotle's statement that rhetoricians who use "the actor's art generally are more pitiable For they make the evil appear near by placing it before our eyes" (*Rhet* 1386a32–34) Thus, pity is more easily aroused by drama than it is in real-life situations

There are, however, a number of ways in which the account of pity and fear in the *Poetics* differs from that of the *Rhetoric* One difference is more apparent than real The *Rhetoric* states that people feel pity "if they think that some people are *epieikeis* For someone who thinks that no one is [*epieikēs*] will think that everyone deserves evil" (1385b34–1386a1) But *Poetics* 13 states that the change from good to bad fortune of the *epieikēs* does not arouse pity (1452b34–36) As noted above, *epieikēs* is a slippery word, it means "outstanding in excellence" in *Poetics* 13, but in *Poetics* 15 it has a broader, more social sense In the *Rhetoric* passage, also, this term may simply mean "good" or "decent," but not exceptionally so In that case, there would be no conceptual inconsistency between *Poetics* 13 and the *Rhetoric* In both works, we pity those who are good enough so as not to deserve evil, but not exceptionally excellent Moreover, it is important to note that *Rhetoric* 1385b34–1386a1 does not say that people pity the *epieikēs* [8] It makes the very different point that people with the generally cynical belief that no one is *epieikēs* will think that all people deserve what they get

Another difficulty concerns the different accounts given in the two works of the people for whom pity and fear are felt According to the *Rhetoric*, fear is felt for ourselves "those things that people fear for themselves" (1386a27–28), and pity, not fear, is felt for those who are like us in age, character, disposition, social status, and family (1386a24–25) The *Poetics*, on the other hand, states that 'fear is felt *peri* the person like [us]"

---

[7] On pity, fear, and the unexpected, see the introduction to chap 5

[8] Cope, *Rhetoric*, ad loc , mistranslates this passage, Grimaldi, *Rhetoric II*, correctly interprets it

(1453a5–6). This statement is often taken to mean that we feel fear, of an unusual kind *for* someone (e.g., Oedipus).[9] This interpretation not only makes the *Poetics* conceptually inconsistent with the *Rhetoric*; it also tends to remove the distinction between pity and fear. Following this account, it is hard to explain how fear for Oedipus is different from pity for him. A better way of reading *Poetics* 1453a5–6 is to take *peri* to mean "concerning" or "in the case of," rather than "for":[10] we feel fear (for ourselves) in the case of the sufferings of someone who is like us. When we see someone like us suffering, we reason that we ourselves are also such as to suffer, and then come to feel fear for ourselves.[11] This interpretation is in accord with the views on the arousal of fear expressed in the *Rhetoric*, I argue below.

Another difference between the *Poetics* and the *Rhetoric* is that pity and fear in the *Poetics* are more closely correlated than they are in the *Rhetoric*. This difference, however, is due to the different concerns of the two works rather than to conceptual inconsistencies.

In the *Poetics*, tragedy is often said to arouse both pity and fear.[12] When Aristotle mentions one emotion without the other, or writes "either . . . or" or "neither . . . nor,"[13] on the other hand, his usage might appear to suggest that the two emotions may be separable. But this occasional disjunction is in most cases only a stylistic variant, without real significance.[14] In only one passage does Aristotle make an explicit distinction between the two emotions. Here (1453a4–6), he states that pity is felt for the person who is undeserving of bad fortune, while fear is felt concerning the person "like" us. This very distinction shows how closely interrelated the two emotions are, for in the best tragedy, the person who moves between good and bad fortune is both like us and undeserving of bad fortune. Moreover, if pity is felt only by those who believe they can themselves suffer evils, and who therefore view these evils as fearful, in tragedy, as in

---

[9] See Else, *Argument*, 372, and Bywater, *Aristotle on the Art*, 215.

[10] For *peri* with the accusative in this broader sense ("about, in the case of"), see LSJ C.I.5 and Bonitz, 3c.

[11] Dupont-Roc and Lallot, *Poétique*, 239, mention a "raisonnement d'analogie" of this kind, which Bywater's criticisms (*Aristotle on the Art*, 211–12) of Lessing (*Hamb Dram. St*, 75) fail to take into account.

[12] Pity and fear. 1449b27, 1452a2–3, 1452b32, 1453b1, 1453b5 (*phrittein* substituted for *phobeisthai*), and 1453b12.

[13] This occurs at 1452a38–b1, 1452b36, 1453a1–6, 1453b9, 1453b14 (*deina ē oiktra*), 1453b17, 1456b1, and 1456b3.

[14] Pace Gudeman, *Aristoteles*, 163, and Bywater, *Aristotle on the Art*, 212. An exception (the monstrous· 1453b9) that proves the rule is discussed below.

the real-life situations dealt with in the *Rhetoric*, pity cannot be aroused without fear.[15]

There are reasons to believe that in bad tragedies, and in certain real-life situations, fear can be aroused without pity In real life, fear is typically aroused by the appearance of a particular, perceptible danger to ourselves. A bad tragedy, like a horror film, might arouse fear of this kind by its use of such visual effects as terrifying masks. Aristotle condemns this kind of effect at 1453b8–10: "Those who produce only the monstrous [τερατῶδες] by means of spectacle, and not the fearful, have no share in tragedy." "The monstrous" is a kind of horror very different from the true tragic quality, "the fearful," that accompanies the pitiable A bad tragedy might also arouse fear without pity by representing a particular danger that immediately threatens the audience for example, the Spartans attacking Athens. Such a play would be more like history than poetry because it would "speak of the particular" instead of "the universal" (1451b6–7). Again, a bad tragedy might arouse grief and sorrow for one's own past sufferings, and fear of suffering such things again, without arousing pity. Phrynichus's *Capture of Miletus* was a play of this sort. Herodotus (6 21) writes that when it was presented the audience fell to weeping and the poet was fined "for reminding them of their own evils" (ὡς ἀναμνήσαντα οἰκήια κακά).[16] Phrynichus not only offended the Athenians, he was, according to Aristotle's views, guilty of writing bad tragedy. By representing a particular event he was writing history. Moreover, by representing something too close to the experience of those in the audience, he aroused in them extreme sorrow for themselves, which, like the kind of extreme fear for oneself mentioned in *Rhetoric* 1386a17–24, is incompatible with pity.

Because rhetoric often deals with situations that are not admissible in a good tragedy, we find more examples of the arousal of fear without pity in the *Rhetoric* than in the *Poetics*. Three passages are of particular interest

1. 1375a7–8 That crime is greater "at which the hearers experience fear rather than [μᾶλλον ἤ][17] pity."

[15] On this point in connection with the *Rhetoric*, see Grimaldi, *Rhetoric II*, 146

[16] Contrast Plato's statement that poetry arouses emotion by leading us ἀπὸ τῶν ἀλλοτρίων εἰς τὰ οἰκεῖα, "from others' [pathē] to our own' (*Rep* 10 606b6–7) Cf Gorgias, *Encomium of Helen* 9 ἐπ' ἀλλοτρίων ἴδιόν τι πάθημα, 'from others [to] a *pathos* of our own "

[17] Cope, *Rhetoric*, ad loc , correctly translates the phrase in this way, W Rhys Roberts in Barnes, *Oxford Translation*, incorrectly translates it as "more than "

2. 1385b32–34 People who do not pity include "those who feel extreme fear, for those who experience *ekplēxis* do not pity because they are absorbed in their own suffering."[18]

3. 1386a17–24 People feel terror and not pity when those suffering are "very closely related to them They feel about these people as if they themselves were about to suffer. For this reason Amasis, as they say, did not weep over his son being led away to death, but he did do so over his friend begging. For the latter is pitiable, the former terrible [*deinon*]. The terrible is different from the pitiable, and drives out pity and is often useful for the opposite ⟨For⟩ they ⟨do not⟩ pity any longer when the terrible is near themselves "[19]

The first of these three passages deals with a situation excluded (*Po.* 1453a8–9) from a well-constructed tragedy: a great crime, committed as a result of vice. In the *Rhetoric* passage, Aristotle is discussing crimes that are "injustices" (1374b24), defined as "things not contrary to reasonable expectation, and that result from vice" (1374b8–9). The pity in question in the first passage must be an emotion that would, in the case of a lesser crime, be felt for the victim (rather than for the perpetrator about to be punished, since we do not pity someone who deserves to suffer). The fear, on the other hand, must be that of suffering from a similar injustice ourselves.[20] This first passage deals with the same case as the second passage. that in which people in extreme fear for themselves do not pity others.

In the second and third passages, Aristotle gives two reasons why, in some cases, we fear for ourselves and do not pity others. First, we do not pity those who are very closely related to us because in their case we feel as if we ourselves were about to suffer (1386a18–19). This is because our *philoi* belong to and are part of ourselves (1385b28–29), and fear is felt for ourselves and for what belongs to us (1385b15). That this kind of fear is

---

[18] μήτ' αὖ φοβούμενοι σφόδρα (οὐ γὰρ ἐλεοῦσιν οἱ ἐκπεπληγμένοι διὰ τὸ εἶναι πρὸς τῷ οἰκείῳ πάθει) On πρὸς τῷ οἰκείῳ πάθει as "absorbed in" their own sufferings, see Cope, *Rhetoric*, ad loc

[19] I translate Kassel's text *Ars rhetorica* It should be noted, however, that there are serious textual difficulties The last sentence as it appears in the MSS, "Again, they pity when the terrible is near themselves," seems to contradict the previous sentence "For the terrible is different from pity and drives out pity For this reason, Kassel follows J Vahlen (*Gesammelte philologische Schriften*, 73ff), who added οὐ γὰρ before ἔτι, negating this last sentence On the problems of text and interpretation of this passage, see Grimaldi, *Rhetoric II*, 145–47

[20] See Cope, *Rhetoric*, 1 266

not only compatible with, but also conducive to, pity for someone who is not a close relative is shown by Aristotle's example in the third passage quoted above. Amasis wept at his friend's misfortune soon after he failed to weep at his son's.

The second reason is given in the second passage. Extreme fear or *ekplēxis*[21] in the face of one's own immediate danger prevents pity for anyone else. Aristotle has in mind such cases as those of soldiers deserting their weaker friends as they flee in panic, and people trampling others as they attempt to escape from a fire. In these cases, those who feel extreme fear are so absorbed in their own, immediate, particular dangers that they cannot reflect on anything else. This fear is so extreme that it leaves no room for any other emotion. Moreover, it often requires immediate practical action, such as flight, which is incompatible with any kind of reflection. While a rhetorician may, in some circumstances, want to arouse extreme fear of this sort, a good tragedy will avoid this.

In many respects, then, the *Poetics* and Aristotle's other works, especially the *Rhetoric*, hold the same views about the physical and cognitive aspects of pity and fear, and about the relationship between these emotions. In the *Poetics* and in Aristotle's other works, pity and fear are cold, painful emotions, aroused by (a *phantasia* of) painful and destructive future evils, and in the *Poetics*, as in the *Rhetoric*, pity is felt for someone who does not deserve to suffer. The main differences I have discussed thus far are that pity and fear are more closely linked in the *Poetics* than in the *Rhetoric*, and that tragic fear is felt "concerning" someone similar to us, while in the *Rhetoric* fear is felt "for ourselves." Another difference between the two works is that pity in the *Rhetoric* is felt for past and present as well as future evils (1386a28–34), while tragic pity is more closely connected with future evils. This is clear from passages such as *Poetics* 14.1453b21, where pity is said to be aroused when someone "kills or is about to kill" someone else. The close connection of pity with fear in the *Poetics* also indicates that tragic pity is best aroused by future evils.

Another difference between the accounts of pity and fear in the *Poetics* and in the *Rhetoric* is highly significant. While *phobos* and *eleos* in the *Rhetoric* are aroused at the *phantasia* of evils that are merely physically painful or destructive, the evils that arouse tragic pity and fear are those that appear to be shameful and disgraceful as well as painful or destructive. *Phobos*

---

[21] The term *ekplēxis*, used here to refer to an emotion incompatible with pity, cannot have the same meaning it does in the *Poetics*, where *ekplēxis* is compatible with pity. On *ekplēxis*, see chap. 6

in the *Poetics* has the broader sense the term has in *EN*1115a9–14, where it refers to fear of disgrace as well as to fear of physical pain and death

That the tragic emotions are concerned with evils that bring disgrace is clear from a number of passages in the *Poetics* The best plot, writes Aristotle, concerns the downfall of someone "with great good reputation and good fortune" (*Po.* 1453a10). This downfall necessarily includes disgrace and loss of good reputation More telling, Aristotle writes that an action in which an enemy kills an enemy does not excite pity [and fear] "except in respect to the *pathos* itself" (1453b18) Tragic pity and fear are properly aroused only when *philos* harms, or is about to harm, *philos* (1453b19–22). Thus, while a painful or destructive event is enough to arouse *phobos* in the restrictive sense of the *Rhetoric* (fear of physical danger), and pity for others who suffer this kind of evil, it is not enough to arouse tragic fear and pity. Like *aischunē* and *aidōs*, tragic fear and pity are concerned with evils, such as harm to *philoi*, that bring disgrace We pity Oedipus less because he suffers physical pain at his blinding (a painful *pathos*) than because he has suffered the greatest disgrace a human being can suffer. his acts of parricide and incest have cut him off completely from the human community. Aristotle also makes it clear that tragic fear and pity differ from the fear and pity that are concerned only with physical danger when he writes in *Poetics* 14 that pity and fear should come from the structure of events and not from "spectacle." Spectacle, he explains, may be "monstrous," but it does not produce the "proper pleasure" of tragedy (1453b8–11). Tragedy should not merely produce the fear of physical danger that is aroused, for example, by terrifying masks.

Thus, tragic fear resembles the shame emotions (fear of disgrace) in that it is concerned, in part, with disgraceful evils To give an account of tragic fear, we can adapt the definition of *phobos* in *Rhetoric* 2.5 in order to take disgrace into account. Tragic fear can be characterized as "pain and disturbance at the *phantasia* of imminent evils that are destructive or painful, and disgraceful." Similarly, tragic pity can be characterized, by adapting the definition of pity in *Rhetoric* 2.8, as "pain at an apparent destructive, painful, and disgraceful evil, of someone who does not deserve to get it, that one could expect oneself, or someone belonging to oneself, to suffer, and this, when it appears near."

Because it is concerned with disgrace, tragic *phobos* has much in common with *kataplēxis*, excessive fear of disgrace, in Aristotle's ethical works. Like *kataplēxis*, tragic *phobos* is, in part, an intense emotional reaction to evils that appear to bring disgrace. While viewing a tragedy, however, we do not fear these evils directly for ourselves, but "concerning the person like us." When we see Oedipus, for example, suffering painful and disgraceful evils, we reason that we also are such as to suffer these evils, and then come to fear for ourselves. While we pity rather than blame Oedipus, whose suffering is undeserved, for ourselves we simply fear suffering the pain and disgrace, whether deserved or undeserved, that result from doing disgraceful actions. It is a mistake to view Aristotelian tragic emotion as simply "a violent non-moral *frisson*" aroused by pollution.[22] Because tragic fear involves a fear of pollution and disgrace, it includes a desire to avoid them, and, like *kataplēxis*, it has definite "moral" elements. Aristotle's use of the term *ekplēxis* to refer to tragic emotion is of particular interest in view of the similarities between tragic fear and *kataplēxis*. *Ekplēxis* is closely related to *kataplēxis* linguistically and conceptually. Moreover, *ekplēxis* is connected with shame in Plato. As noted in chapter 6, the *ekplēxis* produced by Socrates' words resembles Aristotelian *kataplēxis* in many respects.

The association of shame with tragic emotion, as I will argue in detail in chapter 10, helps explain the benefits of tragic emotion. The usual view is that tragic fear is a kind of *phobos*, in the restrictive sense of fear of physical danger. However, it is hard to see how the arousal of this kind of fear can be beneficial. It would instead appear to be conducive to cowardice. On the other hand, it is easy to understand why the arousal of intense fear of painful and disgraceful evils can be beneficial. This emotional extreme can counterbalance a preexisting emotional extreme of shamelessness, thereby helping produce the proportionate blend of shame with shamelessness that constitutes, in part, the praiseworthy mean state of *aidōs*. Just as two friends with opposite emotional characteristics correct and bring each other to the intermediate state (*EE* 1239b25–1240a4), so, within the individual, tragic fear can be an antidote for shamelessness, and help produce *aidōs*.

The idea that tragic pity and fear help produce *aidōs* finds support in Greek literature. Pity was traditionally associated with *aidōs*. Moreover, the representation of fearful things in art and literature was traditionally thought to be beneficial in producing the good kind of shame: reverence and fear of wrongdoing (*aidōs*, *sebas*). In the *Oresteia* in particular, fear that results from pollution and wrongdoing is transformed into fear that prevents wrongdoing. At *Agamemnon* 1164, the Chorus, in response to Cassandra's prophecies about kin-murder, uses the uncompounded form of *ekplēxis*: "I am stricken" (*peplēgmai*). According to the Hypothesis of the

---

[22] Adkins, *Merit*, 98, uses this phrase to characterize emotion aroused by pollution.

Agamemnon, this very part of the drama "is wondered at [*thaumazetai*] as having *ekplēxis* and sufficient pity."[23] These same elements—pity, fear (or *ekplēxis*), and wonder—are combined in Aristotelian tragic emotion, which is also aroused by kin-murder. In the *Eumenides*, the fear that results from pollution and wrongdoing is transformed into the fear of wrongdoing that prevents kin-murder This fear is what Aristotle calls *aidōs*. While he does not explicitly say that tragedy produces *aidōs*, this view is not only in accord with Greek traditional views, it also best explains his theory of katharsis of pity and fear

If tragedy helps produce *aidōs*, it helps provide the kind of habituation *aidōs* provides in Aristotle's ethical works. By leading us to feel fear in response to actions that are shameful as well as destructive or painful, tragedy helps us feel pain and pleasure, love and hate, correctly. Tragedy also helps in the development of the intellectual abilities of *phronēsis*, *prohairesis*, and *nous* for which *aidōs* and habituation are prerequisites. It does this by leading us to pay attention to the opinions and undemonstrated sayings of experienced older people, and of the wise. the poets. The tragic poets, with their vivid examples, help us understand what kinds of acts are painful, destructive, and shameful, and helps us want to avoid doing them.[24]

That tragedy can be of some use even to philosophers is shown by the numerous examples from tragedy given in Aristotle's ethical works It is of more use, however, to the better class of ordinary citizens, those with whom Aristotle is concerned in *Nicomachean Ethics* 10.9. These are the *epieikeis*, those "decently advanced in habits" (1180a8) who are not, however, excellent in the strict sense. At *Poetics* 1462a2, Aristotle uses the term *epieikēs* when he defends tragedy against those who claim that it appeals to the *phauloi* rather than to the *epieikeis* (1462a2–4). He also requires in *Poetics* 13 that the tragic agent be "like" us (1453a5–6), and neither exceptionally excellent and just, nor evil and depraved (1453a7–9). It would seem that the audience for tragedy is obedient to *aidōs* and requires habituation throughout life, like the "decent people" of *Nicomachean Ethics* 10.9. Part of this habituation is given by tragedy.

Although tragic pity and fear differ in some ways from the pity and fear aroused in typical real-life situations, it is misleading to call them different *emotions*. Rather, just as the real-life emotions of fear and pity are aroused

---

[23] Lines 13–14 in Page, *Aeschyli*

[24] See chap 6 ("*Aidōs*, Excellence, and Habituation") On the way in which poetry helps produce *phronēsis*, see Carnes Lord, *Education*, 177–79

in different ways in different circumstances, so these same emotions of pity and fear are aroused in one way by, for example, a production of *The Trojan Women*, and in another way by actual war. Because emotions are responses to external circumstances, they will naturally vary as these circumstances vary. Moreover, Aristotle does not hold one uniform view of particular emotions in real-life situations. For example, *phobos* is sometimes said to include expectation of disgraceful evils (*EN* 1115a9–14), and sometimes to exclude this object of fear (*Rhet.* 2.5). Tragic *phobos*, then, does not differ from real-life *phobos* in including expectation of disgraceful evils. Nor do the particular circumstances in which it is aroused mark it as a special, "aesthetic" emotion, qualitatively different from real-life emotion. The next section discusses other important differences in the circumstances in which emotion is aroused, in aesthetic and real-life contexts.

Aesthetic and Real-Life Emotion

Flight and Pursuit

One important difference between emotional responses in aesthetic situations and those in real life is that, while in real life emotion typically leads to action, this is obviously not true of emotional responses in aesthetic situations.[25] Aristotle's reaction to this is significantly different from that of many modern philosophers. While modern aestheticians are usually puzzled that we can be moved (emotionally) by fictions,[26] for Aristotle, the most interesting question is why we are not moved to act in aesthetic situations. That is, he finds it much harder to understand why we do not run screaming from a stage villain or rush to help a victim than why we weep and feel pity at the theater in the first place. For Aristotle, the latter response is unproblematic.

Before considering emotional reactions in aesthetic situations, it will be helpful to examine Aristotle's views on the more typical, real-life cases. I have examined Aristotle's views on the arousal of emotion: I now consider how emotion typically leads to limb motion. flight or pursuit. Aristotle

---

[25] Some of the material in this section was previously published in Belfiore, "Pleasure " Many of the ideas expressed here, however, differ substantially from my earlier views An earlier version of "Flight and Pursuit" was read as "Aristotle on Not Being Moved by Fictions" at the annual meeting of the Pacific Division of the American Society for Aesthetics, Asilomar, Calif , April 1989, where I benefited from helpful discussions

[26] Some recent discussions of this topic are those of Charleton, "Feeling", Eaton, "Sadness", Mannison, "Fiction", and Radford and Weston, "Anna Karenina "

describes the process by which perception leads to limb motion in the *De motu animalium*: "That is why it is pretty much at the same time that the creature thinks it should move forward and moves, unless something else impedes it. For the affections [*pathē*] suitably prepare the organic parts, desire the affections, and *phantasia* the desire; and *phantasia* comes about either through thought or through sense-perception" (*DMA* 702a15–19).[27]

In Aristotle's view, thought and perception are the efficient causes of our seeing something as an object of avoidance or pursuit (*phantasia*); this leads to a desire to flee or pursue. These cognitive responses constitute the form of an emotion. In turn, desire leads to heating or chilling (the matter of an emotion).[28] In the passage just quoted, Aristotle merely says that "desire [prepares] the affections [*pathē*]." What he must mean, however, is that desire prepares *the rest of* the emotion in question—its physical aspects, or matter, the heating and expansion or chilling and contraction that characterize pleasurable and painful emotions respectively. After both the matter and the form of the emotion are "prepared," another step is necessary before limb motion can take place: "the creature thinks [νοεῖ] it should move." Unlike heating and chilling, and the involuntary movements of bodily parts that are consequent on heating or chilling, limb motion requires "thought" or "the command of thought" (*DMA* 703b7–8: κελεύσαντος τοῦ νοῦ). Finally, "unless something else impedes it," Aristotle writes, "the affections [*pathē*] suitably prepare the organic parts" so that limb motion takes place.[29]

A specific example of an angry action illustrates the process Aristotle has in mind. I perceive that Alcibiades is making an obscene gesture in my direction (perception). I see this as a slight (*phantasia*), and because of this (ὑπὸ τοῦδε: the efficient cause of *DA* 403a) I come to have a desire to give pain in return (ἕνεκα τοῦδε: the final cause of the *De anima*). These cognitive aspects of anger, its form, then produce the physical reactions that constitute its matter: the boiling of the blood around my heart, so that I experience the complete *pathos*. Finally, I think that I should move or give a command, and move my hand, hitting Alcibiades in the nose.

The process that, according to *De motu animalium* 702a15–19, leads from perception to limb motion can be expressed schematically in the following simplified explanatory model:

---

[27] Here and in the rest of chap. 7, I quote Nussbaum's translations in *De motu animalium*.

[28] On this process and related topics, see chap. 6 ("Pity, Fear, and Physical Danger").

[29] Nussbaum, *De motu animalium*, 356, argues cogently that the "organic parts" are the limbs.

I.

1. thought or sense-perception
2. *phantasia*
3. desire
4. matter
5. command
6. flight or pursuit

The *De motu animalium* account, and my schema of it, are of course over-simplifications. The specific details would vary from case to case and emotion to emotion. Moreover, even in typical cases the sequence is not strictly temporal. Nevertheless, this schema can serve as a model to explain the process by which perception leads to limb motion.

The typical, real-life sequence, from perception to flight or pursuit, is unproblematic in Aristotle's view. Nor does he believe that our feeling real emotions in aesthetic situations needs to be explained. For Aristotle, emotion aroused in aesthetic situations is not a peculiar, unusual kind of emotion. Instead, because it is caused by a *phantasia* of something as, for example, fearful or pitiable, it is paradigmatic, and in fact less in need of explanation than real-life emotion.[30] In real life, our response is mixed with a great many other factors that may prevent our seeing something as fearful and pitiable: other emotions, physical discomfort, preoccupation with daily cares, distracting noises and sights. In aesthetic situations it is easier to put aside these things that obscure and blunt our emotional response. What needs explanation, in Aristotle's view, is not the power of this response, but its lack of real-life consequences.

In the *De motu animalium*, Aristotle asks: "But how does it happen that thinking is sometimes accompanied by action and sometimes not, sometimes by motion and sometimes not?" (701a7–8). This is a significant question in ethical situations, and it is of primary importance in aesthetic cases, where thought and emotion typically do not lead to limb motion. *De motu animalium* 701a discusses how a practical syllogism leads to action: "For example, whenever someone thinks that every man should take walks, and that he is a man, at once he takes a walk . . . if nothing prevents or compels him" (701a13–16). There is no need to enter into the

---

[30] Compare Charlton, "Feeling," 215: "All imagining, even that of purely imaginary things, involves desire or feeling. It follows, then, that unless we are very expert at imagining in real life we shall be more easily moved by represented situations than by real ones." See also Easterling, "Character," 89, and S. K. Langer, *Feeling and Form*, 310, quoted by Easterling.

modern controversies about the practical syllogism in Aristotle's ethical works in order to gain some understanding of how, in the simpler, aesthetic cases, we can be prevented from acting after we experience an emotion [31] Aristotle's theory that a ' command" ([5] in schema I, above) to pursue or flee is needed before the occurrence of voluntary limb motion (6) goes a long way toward answering the question about how thinking sometimes fails to lead to limb motion

The command in question is a command to pursue or flee, an assertion that something is, in this particular case, to be fled or pursued This command or assertion is different from the *phantasia* of something as an object of avoidance or pursuit [32] The physical reactions of heating and chilling can occur in the absence of an actual object, as a result of *phantasia* and thought (*DMA* 701b16–22) Not only heating and chilling, but also involuntary movements of bodily parts consequent on heating or chilling occur in the absence of a "command" "[Animals] also display involuntary movements in some of their parts   By involuntary I mean such movements as those of the heart and the penis, for often these are moved when something appears, but without the command of thought" (*DMA* 703b4–8) However, a command is necessary for limb motion, as opposed to these involuntary movements, to occur The *De anima*, like the *De motu animalium*, holds that a command or "assertion' is needed for limb motion "For the thinking soul *phantasmata* are like sensations When it asserts or denies that they are good or bad, it flees or pursues" (431a14–16) The distinction between emotion (including desire and involuntary movements consequent on heating or chilling) and limb motion, for which a command is needed, is particularly clear in another passage in the *De anima*

> The theoretical mind contemplates nothing that is to be acted on, nor does
> it say anything about what is to be fled or pursued, while motion is always
> {motion} of something fleeing or pursuing something But not even when

[31] It should be noted, however, that my account of the aesthetic case was influenced by Dahl s view that the practical syllogism [is] at least in part a model for explaining action on the basis of desire (*Reason*, 27) Dahl opposes (29) J M Cooper s more restrictive view of the practical syllogism *Reason and Human Good*, chap 1, sec 2, and appendix

[32] Of course, this command may involve an additional *phantasia* a perception of this object as something to be fled here and now For the other animals, *phantasia* takes the place of the beliefs and thoughts that lead to the actions of human beings (*DA* 428a21–22, 433a11–12) However, the *phantasia* that leads to limb motion is not the same *phantasia* that causes involuntary movements consequent on the matter of fear pounding of the heart and shuddering My account of *phantasia* is an oversimplification, for explanatory purposes, of a complex and controversial subject See chap 6, n 1

the mind contemplates something of this kind does it at once give a command to take flight [χελεύει φεύγειν] or pursue For example, it often thinks of something fearful or pleasant, but it does not give a command to flee [χελεύει δὲ φοβεῖσθαι], though the heart is moved, or if [it thinks of] something pleasant, some other part (*DA* 432b27–433a1)

In this passage, χελεύει δὲ φοβεῖσθαι ("give a command to flee") is equivalent to χελεύει φεύγειν ("give a command to take flight") immediately preceding, so φοβεῖσθαι should be translated "to flee " To translate it "to be afraid," as is usually done, obscures Aristotle's point that we may feel emotion, complete with, for example, the pounding of the heart that is consequent on cognitive responses, *without necessarily moving our limbs* [33] As *De anima* 431a14–16 makes clear, the command to flee or pursue is (at least in the case of rational beings) an assertion or denial that something is good or bad It is an assertion that this thing before us is indeed, in the present case, an object to be fled or pursued Only after this assertion will flight or pursuit take place, unless, as the *De motu animalium* notes, "something else impedes" (702a16–17, cf 701a16)

The cases when something does prevent action are of particular interest in aesthetic cases, for, clearly, emotion experienced at the theater or when viewing pictures differs from emotion felt in other situations in that it does not normally lead to limb motion Aristotle discusses one case in which something impedes action in the *De anima*

> Opining is not up to us For [the opinion] is necessarily either true or false Again, when we have the opinion that something is terrible or fearful, we are at once affected in correspondence [with this opinion] [*sumpaschomen*], and similarly if [we have the opinion that something is] cheering But with respect to *phantasia* we are just as if we were contemplating terrible or cheering things in a picture (*DA* 427b20–24)

Exactly what is it that Aristotle thinks we do experience in the picture-viewing case? A common misunderstanding of this passage, going back to Themistius, is that we experience *no* reactions in the picture-viewing

---

[33] In this passage, φοβεῖσθαι is translated as to be afraid by Furley, Voluntary 2 57, and as fear by Hamlyn, *De anima*, and Hicks, *De anima* It is translated as the emotion of fear' by J A Smith in Barnes, *Oxford Translation* An exception is Rodier, *Traité*, who correctly translates this verb as fuir (to flee) and defends this interpretation in his note ad loc Following the incorrect translation and interpretation, in Belfiore, Pleasure, 355–58, I confused the command to flee with a command to be afraid, to experience the *pathos* in the sense of desire and involuntary physical reactions

case.[34] Following this interpretation, we experience an emotion when we have an opinion that something is frightening, but when we view pictures we do not experience any emotion at all. This interpretation, however, goes against the evidence of many passages examined above in chapters 6 and 7, which assert quite clearly that *phantasia* (the efficient cause of an emotion), to which picture-viewing is compared in *De anima* 427b20–24, produces desire (the final cause of an emotion), which in turn produces heating, chilling, and involuntary movements of bodily parts.

A better interpretation of *De anima* 427b20–24 takes into account Aristotle's views expressed in other passages. For example, in 432b27–433a1, quoted above, Aristotle states that theoretical thinking can be of something terrible or pleasant, and can cause us to have the involuntary movements of bodily parts that are consequent on the matter of emotion, without in itself leading to limb motion. Theoretical thinking in this passage is different from "practical thought" (*DA* 433a18). The latter leads to action because, unlike theoretical thinking, it is concerned with what is *to be fled* or pursued (φευκτοῦ καὶ διωκτοῦ: *DA* 432b28), and because it gives a command to flee. Aristotle's views in *De anima* 427b20–24 are based on a similar distinction between the practical opinion that something is to be fled in this particular case and a more theoretical *phantasia* that does not make this assertion. Opinion (*doxa*) that something is fearful implies the belief (*pistis*: *DA* 428a20–21) that it is a practical object to be fled in the present instance. It thus leads us to have reactions that correspond to this belief (*sumpaschomen*).[35] In the picture-viewing case, however, we experience a *phantasia* of something as fearful or pleasant without a belief that it is to be fled in the present instance. That is why, in the aesthetic case, we experience emotional reactions and involuntary movements without actually fleeing or pursuing.

What impedes flight in the picture-viewing case is a judgment that the frightening thing in the picture is not to be fled. This is clear from an informative passage in *On Dreams*:

[34] "We do not experience the corresponding emotions at all [οὐ συμπάσχομεν οὐδ' ὁτιοῦν], but like those contemplating things drawn in pictures, we do not experience any reactions at all [πάσχομεν οὐδεν]": Themistius, 89.18–19. This passage is quoted with approval by Rodier, *Traité*, on 427b23, and by Hicks, on *DA* 427b23, who states that those viewing pictures are "wholly unaffected."

[35] *Sumpaschein* does not necessarily mean "to sympathize." Instead, this word and its cognates indicate a correspondence between two things, one of which may affect the other. While this may be an emotional correspondence (*Pol.* 1340a13), it can also be one between two physical entities (*PA* 653b6, 690b5, *On Sleep* 455a34), or between psychological and physical characteristics (*Pr An* 70b16)

In anger and in every kind of desire, all are easily deceived, and the more so the more they experience the *pathē*. For this reason also, to people in a fever there sometimes appear [*phainetai*] to be animals on the walls, because of the slight similarity of combinations of lines. And these [effects] sometimes agree in intensity with the *pathē* [emotions and illnesses], so that if they are not very ill, they realize that this is false, but if the *pathos* is greater, they may even move in accordance with these things [that appear to them]. The cause of this is that the authoritative sense and that to which the appearances [*phantasmata*] come do not judge with the same faculty. (*On Dreams* 460b9–18)[36]

In this example, combinations of lines (wall-paintings) appear (*phainetai*) to be animals to those in the delirium of fever. Since this *phantasia* can lead to limb movement, it is clear that it must have emotional content: people in delirium see the lines as frightening animals, and are frightened. That this *phantasia* has emotional content is also clear from Aristotle's comparison of those in fever to people who experience such emotions as anger. In both cases, *phantasia* does not lead to limb motion if it is opposed by a judgment of the authoritative sense. In that case, people are frightened or angry because of their *phantasia*, but they are restrained by judgment from fleeing or pursuing in accord with their emotions.

Aristotle also opposes *phantasia* and judgment in another passage in *On Dreams*: "In general, the ruling sense asserts what comes from each [particular] sense, unless something else more authoritative contradicts it. For in every case something appears [*phainetai*], but we do not in every case have the opinion that what appears is [true]; but [we do so only when] the judging part of the soul is restrained, or is not moving with its proper movement" (*On Dreams* 461b3–7). The reports of the senses involve *phantasiai* that are then confirmed or contradicted by judgment. Aristotle's example of dreaming makes the same point more graphically:

If one perceives that one is asleep, and [perceives] the sleepy state [*pathos*] in which the perception [occurs], it appears [*phainetai*], but something in oneself says that Coriscus appears, but [that] it is not Coriscus. For often when one is asleep something in the soul says that what appears is a dream. But if it escapes one's knowledge that one is sleeping, nothing contradicts the *phantasia*. (*On Dreams* 462a2–8)

[36] Modrak, *Perception*, 149, cites *On Dreams* 460b11–16 and 461b1–8 in connection with *DA* 427b20–24. She identifies the "authoritative sense" mentioned in the *On Dreams* passages with the "common sense" (discussed in her chap. 3, 55–80).

All these passages help us interpret *De anima* 427b20–24. In the case of picture-viewing, we do not assert that the terrible thing in the picture is really to be fled now, and no flight results, because a judgment that this is just a picture impedes assent to the report of perception and *phantasia*. We will nevertheless experience an emotion, and, if our emotion is intense enough, we might, like those in fever, assent and actually flee, being incapable of making the judgment that contradicts the evidence of the senses.

The foregoing discussion allows us to conclude that aesthetic cases, according to Aristotle, differ in very specific ways from simple, real-life cases in which emotional arousal leads to limb motion. Schema II outlines the sequence that leads from emotional arousal to response in these special cases. Like schema I, this is a simplified explanatory model, based on the account in *De motu animalium* 702a15–19 of emotional arousal, and not a description of a real temporal sequence that invariably occurs.

II

1. thought or sense-perception
2. *phantasia*
3. desire
4. matter and involuntary movements
5. judgment that impedes a command to flee or pursue

In the aesthetic case, of course, the judgment is that this thing that appears frightening, for example, is a lion in a picture, or a murder in a play. Only after we make this judgment will we be able to experience the aesthetic pleasure of learning that is so important in the *Poetics*. This aesthetic pleasure is only possible, in Aristotle's view, because we are at the same time moved emotionally by fiction, and *not* moved by it to act.

This account of emotional reactions in aesthetic cases is plausible. In aesthetic cases we experience the same emotions that we do in real-life situations, but because we do not normally have the opinion that the things before us are real, we do not run screaming from a lion in a picture. While normal people are emotionally aroused by drama, only a madman like Don Quixote rushes onto the stage to attack the villain and rescue the victim.[37] Modern science supports this view. Psychological studies have shown that people asked to imagine frightening situations report feeling fear, and experience increased heart rates and other physiological reactions,

[37] See Cervantes' *Don Quixote*, part 2, chap 26, where Don Quixote attacks the Moors in a puppet show, believing that they are real people I owe this example to Peter Belfiore

without, of course, actually running away This is why imagery is an important tool in the treatment of phobias [38]

Tragedy and Rhetoric

The arousal of pity and fear by tragedy is more complex than the simple explanatory model just outlined suggests In typical real-life situations, fear is aroused very directly by, for example, the perception of a lion and the *phantasia* that it is a fearful object Tragic fear, in contrast, is aroused more indirectly by a kind of reasoning process Tragedy, like rhetoric, arouses fear by leading us to understand that we, like others, are "such as to suffer" we are members of the class of those who suffer In the *Rhetoric*, Aristotle tells the rhetorician how to arouse fear in this way

> When it is better for people to be afraid, it is necessary [sc , for the rhetorician] to put them in such a state [as to believe] that they are such as to suffer [τοιοῦτοί εἰσιν οἷοι παθεῖν], for others who are greater have also suffered And [it is necessary] to show people who are like [those in the audience] suffering or having suffered, and by means of those from whom they did not think [to suffer] this, and things they did not think to suffer, and at a time when they did not think to suffer (1383a8–12)

The rhetorician arouses fear by leading the audience to engage in a reasoning process that resembles a practical syllogism whose conclusion is an emotion [39] Because fear is aroused by "the *phantasia* of an imminent destructive or painful evil" (*Rhet* 1382a21–22), it can be aroused by persuading people that, because they are "such as to suffer" this evil, it is likely and imminent In *Rhetoric* 1383a8–12, just quoted, Aristotle tells the rhetorician that when he wants to produce fear in his audience he must show them that "they are such as to suffer" by demonstrating the following points

    1 Others *greater than* themselves have suffered
    2 Others *like* themselves have suffered or are suffering
    3 Others have suffered by means of those from whom they did *not expect to suffer*

---

[38] See, for example, Lang et al , 'Emotional Imagery, and Lang, Imagery in Therapy
[39] An account, different from mine, of the similarity between the arousal of emotion by tragedy and the practical syllogism is given by Packer, Conditions While Packer does not discuss *Rhet* 1383a8–12, the importance of this passage for an understanding of the *Poetics* is noted by many others Dupont-Roc and Lallot, *Poétique*, 239, Laín Entralgo, *Therapy*, 227, Halliwell, *Aristotle's Poetics*, 176–77, and Kokolakis, Greek Drama, 174

4. Others have suffered things they *did not expect to suffer* and at times when they *did not expect to suffer*.

The reasoning process involved in the arousal of fear in the "syllogism" at *Rhetoric* 1383a8–12 may be schematized as follows (step 2 is bracketed because it does not correspond to an explicit statement in this passage):

1. X suffered when this was not expected.
{2. Therefore, X is such as to suffer.]
3. X is greater than we are.
4. X is like us.
5. Therefore, we also are such as to suffer.
6. Fear.

In this case, fear is aroused by the use of a rhetorical example. In the schema above, X is an example of ourselves, because X and we are "under the same universal" (we are both "such as to suffer"); however, X is better known (in the relevant respects) than we are to ourselves.[40] We first see that, because X suffered when this was not expected, X is such as to suffer. We then see that, because we ourselves are like X, but even more likely to suffer (since X is "greater" than we are), we also are such as to suffer. This realization makes us believe danger to be imminent, because it is likely, and so leads us to feel fear.

This is the method Aristotle recommends for arousing fear in those who do not believe they could suffer anything from anyone, at any time (*Rhet.* 1382b31–33). These fearless people include those who "are or are thought to be in great good fortune, for which reason they are hubristic, and contemptuous, and bold" (1383a1–2). To arouse fear in these people, the rhetorician must show that, because even those who do not expect to suffer are in fact such as to suffer, this confidence is based on a false belief. The sufferings of the great (the rich and powerful) are particularly good examples, for these people might least of all expect to suffer. From these examples, people reason that "if what is less likely to occur by nature has occurred, then what is more {likely to occur]" will also occur (*Rhet.* 1392b15–16).[41]

This is exactly the way in which the poet best arouses fear, according to the *Poetics*. The poet should represent the sufferings of a particular kind of person:

[40] On the rhetorical example, see chap. 2 ("Representation" and "*Theōria*").
[41] The arousal of fear by an argument a fortiori is noted by Kokolakis, "Greek Drama," 174.

1. Someone *greater* than the people in the audience, that is, someone with "great good reputation and good fortune" (1453a10)

2. Someone *like* the audience (1453a5–6)

3 Someone who suffers at the hands of a *philos* (1453b19–22), from whom this *is not expected*.

4. Someone who suffers things that occur *contrary to expectation* (1452a3)

5. Someone who suffers things that happen according to what is *probable or necessary* (1451a38).

In hearing the story of fearful events in a tragedy, we go through the same reasoning process we go through in hearing the rhetorician who arouses fear. We first understand that because Oedipus, for example, suffered when he could least have been expected to suffer, Oedipus is such as to suffer. We then see that, because we ourselves are like Oedipus, but even more likely to suffer (since Oedipus is "greater" than we are), we also are such as to suffer. Just as the rhetorician can arouse fear in people who are "hubristic, and contemptuous, and bold," thinking that they can suffer nothing (1382b31–1383a2), so tragedy can arouse fear in an overconfident and hubristic audience. Tragedy, however, is more effective than rhetoric in leading us to see someone like Oedipus as a person who is such as to suffer, for the tragic plot is a *probable or necessary* sequence of events ([5] above). Tragedy thus leads us to see that even unexpected suffering is probable or necessary.[42]

The previous analysis provides a better understanding of what Aristotle means when he writes that tragic fear is felt "in the case of [*peri*] the person who is like" us (1453a5).[43] Oedipus arouses in us fear for ourselves, just as the examples used by the rhetorician arouse fear for ourselves. What we feel, in watching Oedipus, is an extreme fear (*phobos, ekplēxis*) of suffering, as Oedipus does, pain and disgrace, even when this is least to be expected. The fear aroused by tragedy and rhetoric involves an understanding of universals rather than a reaction to a perceptible danger, like that presented by a lion about to spring. This kind of fear depends on a realization of our own vulnerability and mortality that is all the more powerful for being less dependent on the presence of a perceptible danger.

Only after fear is aroused in this way can a second, similar kind of reasoning process lead us to feel pity in response to both tragedy and rhetoric. Pity is causally and conceptually dependent on fear, being "pain at an apparent destructive or painful evil of someone who does not deserve to get it, that one could expect oneself, or someone belonging to oneself, to

[42] On "contrary to expectation" in the *Poetics*, see the introduction to chap 5
[43] On this statement, see above, "Pity and Fear in the *Poetics*"

suffer, and this, when it appears near" (*Rhet.* 1385b13–16). We pity others, Aristotle writes, when we remember that similar things have happened to us, or expect them to happen (1386a1–2)—when we realize that we are "such as to suffer" what someone else is in fact suffering. After we arrive at this kind of universal understanding and feel fear for ourselves, we can feel pity for someone else, by another reasoning process.

1 X suffers what we are such as to suffer
2 X does not deserve to suffer
3 Therefore, we pity X

Pity is aroused by a kind of education in fear. *Rhetoric* 1385b27–28, significantly, tells us that among those inclined to pity are "the educated, for they reason well."

In the *Poetics* as in the *Rhetoric*, pity is said to be felt for someone who does not deserve to suffer (*Po* 1453a5). This person is someone who does not deserve punishment for vicious acts, and whose social position, wealth, and other external goods make suffering objectively unlikely. Such a person, like the person concerning whom fear is felt, can least *expect to* suffer, and is also *greater than* we are. The person pitied is also, of course, *like* us in suffering what we also are such as to suffer. In the *Poetics*, then, we pity the same person concerning whom we feel fear, and the interdependence of the two emotions increases the intensity of each. The dramatic and visual effects of tragedy also contribute to the arousal of pity (*Rhet.* 1386a31–34).

Of course, we do not consciously go through all the logical steps listed above before we experience fear and pity at the theater. However, the syllogistic process spelled out in *Rhetoric* 1383a8–12 provides a useful explanatory model that has practical applications for rhetorician and poet. Although the foregoing explanation may seem unduly abstract and overly logical, Aristotle's ideas about the arousal of fear and pity are in fact clear and simple, and they were shared by many in the ancient world.[44] A specific example from Greek literature can give us a better understanding of how the rhetorician and the poet arouse fear and pity in practice. While this example is drawn from epic, it is also applicable to tragedy, for these genres are closely related in Aristotle's view. both have the same end (*Po.* 1462b12–15), and excellence is the same in both (1449b17–20).[45]

In *Iliad* 24 486–516, Priam arouses fear and pity in Achilles just as

[44] On the rhetorical commonplaces shared by Aristotle and other ancient writers, see Stevens, ' Commonplaces," and Macleod, *Iliad*, 4–6 and 5 n 1

[45] Cf Plato, *Rep* 10 595b9–c2, who calls Homer the "first teacher and leader' of tragedy

Aristotle's rhetorician and poet arouse these emotions in the audience [46]
Priam, who has come to ransom Hector's body from Achilles, supplicates
his son's murderer, and asks him to have *aidōs* (αἰδεῖο) for the gods and to
pity (ἐλέησον) Priam himself (503) In this speech, Priam's first words
are "Remember your father, godlike Achilles" (486) Achilles' father Peleus, he says, is *like* Priam in age (487) and in absence from and love for
his son (488–92) Next, Priam makes the point that he, Priam, does not
deserve to suffer, in the social sense of this phrase He had a great many
excellent sons, including Hector, the finest of all, who defended the city
and the Trojans Now, however, Priam is forced to give a limitless ransom
for him (493–502) These remarks call attention to Priam's great wealth
and power he was *greater* than Achilles and Peleus Moreover, because of
his great power and wealth, and the excellence and number of his children,
Priam, had *least expected* to suffer what he has suffered Priam has all this
time been visibly pitiable, in a suppliant's position, with torn clothes and
the dirt of mourning covering his head His last lines (505–6) call attention to this Aristotle advises the rhetorician to use the same techniques
Priam employs in this speech According to the *Rhetoric*, we fear for ourselves when we see the sufferings of someone who is *greater* than we are,
but also *like* us, and who did not *expect to suffer* We pity the person who
does not *deserve to suffer*, who suffers what we or one of our own might
expect to suffer, when this suffering appears near We also pity others
when we ourselves have parents, wives, or children, "for these belong to
oneself and are such as to suffer" (*Rhet* 1385b28–29) People also pity
others for misfortunes such as old age and physical suffering (1386a8), and
they pity others when they place these sufferings "before the eyes,' by
using pitiable gestures, voice, and appearance (1386a31–32)

Priam's appeal is successful, making Achilles experience in succession
fear and pity First, Achilles feels *fear* for his father "He aroused in him
[sc , Achilles] a desire to bewail his father" (507, cf 511–12) [47] Next,
Achilles feels *pity* for Priam (οἰκτίρων 516) This passage from the *Iliad*
shows us exactly how fear and pity are aroused by a reasoning process in
which we are led to see ourselves and others as instances of the same uni-

[46] On this passage, see Burkert, *Mitleidsbegriff*, 104–7 Kennedy, *Persuasion*, 93, discusses it as an example of emotional appeal in rhetoric On the significance of the passage
within the *Iliad* as a whole, see the insightful comments of Macleod, *Iliad*, Introduction,
(sections 1–3, esp 26–27) I discuss *Il* 24 further in chap 10

[47] While Homer does not explicitly say that Achilles feels *fear*, rather than pity, for
Peleus, he certainly feels a more personal grief for this close *philos* than he feels for Priam,
whom he pities (516) In Homer, as in Aristotle (*Rhet* 1385b28–29), one s close *philoi* are
a part of oneself

versal. Priam, like an Aristotelian rhetorician, causes Achilles to feel fear by showing that his father, like Priam, is such as to suffer. Priam then leads Achilles to feel pity by showing that he, Priam, who does not deserve to suffer, has suffered what Peleus also might expect to suffer.

While Priam arouses fear and pity just as Aristotle's rhetorician and poet do, Priam is more like the rhetorician than the poet in arousing emotion for a specific, practical purpose. Priam states this goal as he mentions his son:

> Hektor; for whose sake I come now to the ships of the Achaians
> to win him back from you, and I bring you gifts beyond number.
>
> (*Il.* 24.501–2: Lattimore)

Priam's next line, "Then have *aidōs* for the gods, Achilles, and pity for me" (503), seeks to persuade Achilles to show pity by returning Hector's body and taking the ransom. After both men weep, Achilles indicates that he will indeed take the action Priam desires:

> he rose from his chair, and took the old man by the hand, and set him
> on his feet again, in pity for the grey head and the grey beard.
>
> (*Il.* 24.515–16: Lattimore)

To take Priam by the hand and raise him is to accept him as a suppliant, to promise to grant his request.[48] In arousing fear and pity in order to persuade Achilles to take specific action, Priam resembles Stesichorus in the *Rhetoric*, who, after using the story of the horse and the stag as an example of Phalaris the dictator, draws the practical conclusion, the "moral" of the story: "So you also see that in wishing to punish your enemies you do not suffer what the horse did."[49] Because rhetoric has a practical goal, the emotion it arouses (if the speaker is successful) is followed, just as it is in typical real-life situations, by a "command," an opinion or assertion that what appears to us to be, for example, pitiable really is to be pitied, and by specific action like that taken by Achilles. In rhetorical situations, emotional arousal and action occur just as they do in schema I above ("Flight and Pursuit").

Unlike rhetoric, poetry is not limited by specific, practical goals; it arouses emotion in order to lead us to contemplate.[50] *Iliad* 24 also clarifies this difference between poetry and rhetoric.

Priam cannot see beyond his own immediate circumstances. As Colin

---

[48] See Gould, "Hiketeia," 79–80, on the ritual acceptance of suppliants in general, and on the Priam-Achilles passage in particular.

[49] *Rhet.* 1393b8–23, discussed in chap. 2 ("Representation").

[50] On this point, see chap. 2 ("*Theōria*").

Macleod points out, Priam's statement that he has borne "things such as no other man on earth has ever yet endured" (505) shows that "he has yet to learn to bear his suffering through the knowledge that it is typically human."[51] It is Achilles who attains this understanding of the human condition that the *Iliad* itself, as tragic poetry, gives its audience.[52] After acknowledging Priam as a suppliant, Achilles considers Priam's pitiable condition (543–48) and that of Peleus (534–42) as part of the human condition as a whole.

> Such is the way the gods spun life for unfortunate mortals,
> that we live in unhappiness, but the gods themselves have no sorrows
>
> (*Il* 24 525–26 Lattimore)

Achilles' reaction to pitiable and fearful events goes beyond practical considerations. It is a more philosophical, "theoretical" response that looks beyond the sufferings of particular individuals who are "such as to suffer," to attain a tragic understanding that suffering is the universal condition of all humans, because they are mortals and not gods. Homer's juxtaposition of Priam's and Achilles' speeches shows us the differences between them, and leads us also to an understanding of the more philosophical, poetic point of view.

If we are philosophers, we can, like Achilles, have this response even in real-life situations. Even if we are not, however, we can have a philosophical experience of this kind when we enjoy epic and tragedy as imitations of things we have seen before Once fear and pity have been aroused by tragedy we do not go on to take action, by, for example, giving aid to Oedipus, whom we pity. Instead, a judgment impedes a command to flee or give aid, as it does in schema II above. Like the dreamer who perceives that he is asleep (*On Dreams* 462a2–8, quoted above, "Flight and Pursuit"), we realize that this is an imitation and not a situation in which it is appropriate to give aid or take some other action. At this point, we are able to view the imitation in the theoretical way Aristotle discusses in *Poetics* 4: "People take pleasure seeing images, because it happens that while they contemplate they learn and reason what each thing is for example, that this is that. For if someone has not happened to see something previously, the imitation will not give pleasure as an imitation" (1448b15–18).

---

[51] Macleod, *Iliad*, 127, on 486–506

[52] Macleod makes these points ibid , 27 (Achilles' insight), and 7–8 (the *Iliad* as tragic poetry)

When we contemplate the tragedy an an imitation, we recollect the things we have seen previously of which it is an imitation. We reason and learn that *this* plot, a probable or necessary sequence of events that arouses pity and fear, is an imitation of *that* sequence of fearful and pitiable events that we have seen before. In this way, we come to understand that the probable or necessary sequence of events that we see, for example, in Sophocles' *Oedipus* also occurs in real life. We learn not only that we and Oedipus are such as to suffer but, like Achilles, we learn that all humans are such as to suffer, because they are mortals and not gods. In this tragic response, the arousal of fear is necessary to the arousal of pity, just as it is in rhetoric. However, because of the imitative context of tragedy, emotion is followed by a judgment that impedes a command to flee or pursue, and then by *theōria*. The poet, unlike the rhetorician, has no immediate, practical goal, but instead leads us to contemplate an imitation as an imitation, for its own sake. *Theōria* is accompanied by the complex intellectual and emotional responses involved in katharsis.

In chapter 7 I have examined Aristotle's views on the emotions aroused by tragedy in light of the views on emotion expressed in his other works. The first section noted the similarities and differences between the accounts of pity and fear in the *Rhetoric* and in the *Poetics*. Many differences are due to the different concerns of these two works rather than to real conceptual inconsistencies. One important conceptual difference, however, is that pity and fear in the *Poetics* are aroused by evils that are disgraceful as well as painful or destructive, while in the *Rhetoric* these emotions are aroused by evils that are merely painful or destructive. "Flight and Pursuit" discussed another important way in which emotions aroused in aesthetic situations differ from emotions aroused in other circumstances. In real-life situations, emotion typically leads to action: flight or pursuit. In aesthetic situations, however, a command to flee or pursue is impeded by a judgment that this is not a situation that requires action. Nevertheless, in aesthetic situations we experience the cognitive and physical aspects of an emotion (e.g., pounding of the heart), just as we do in real-life cases. Chapter 7 concluded with a study of the "practical syllogism" by means of which fear and pity are aroused by rhetoric and tragedy. While both arouse these emotions in similar ways, tragedy, unlike rhetoric, does not have an immediate, practical goal, but leads us to contemplate imitations for their own sake. For this reason, tragedy gives us a deeper understanding of the human condition as a whole.

PART IV
KATHARSIS

*

Katharsis and the Critical Tradition

ARISTOTLE'S ethical and rhetorical works provide us with a great deal of information about pity and the various fear emotions, his biological works are particularly important for an understanding of his concept of katharsis. In chapter 9, I discuss Aristotle's views on biological and psychic katharsis, and in chapter 10 I argue that these views illuminate Aristotelian tragic katharsis. Before we study Aristotle's concepts of biological and psychic katharsis, however, it is essential to review the evidence about tragic katharsis provided by the *Poetics* itself in the context of a long and complex critical tradition. This is the task of chapter 8.[1]

THE DEFINITION OF TRAGEDY

While Aristotle does not explain katharsis in the *Poetics*, he does give us some definite, relevant information in *Poetics* 6. At the beginning of this chapter, Aristotle turns from a discussion of the poetic art in general to introduce the subject of tragedy. "Let us speak concerning tragedy, separating off the definition of its being that results from what has been said" (1449b22–24).[2] Aristotle then defines tragedy. "Tragedy is imitation of a noble-and-serious and complete action, having magnitude, in sweetened speech, with each of the kinds separate in the parts, enacted and not narrated, by means of pity and fear accomplishing the katharsis of such emotions" (1449b24–28). While most of the other elements of the definition of tragedy have been mentioned in "what has been said" previously, this

---

[1] Research on katharsis is hampered by the lack of a comprehensive recent bibliography The latest bibliographies on the *Poetics* are now very much out of date Cooper and Gudeman, *Bibliography*, Herrick, "Supplement', and Else, "Survey " Some recent selective bibliographies and surveys on katharsis can be found in Bennett, "Purging", Halliwell, *Aristotle's Poetics*, app 5 "Interpretations of *Katharsis*," 350–56, Keesey, 'Interpretations", and White, *Sourcebook*

[2] The MSS reading, ἀπολαβόντες (separating off), at 1449b23, defended by Dupont-Roc and Lallot, *Poétique*, 186, is preferable to Bernays s emendation, ἀναλαβόντες (taking up), followed by Kassel

is notoriously not true of katharsis.[3] Nevertheless, the introductory statement at 1449b22–24 is some indication that all the elements of the definition, including katharsis, can be connected in some way with "what has been said."[4] A parallel introductory statement at the beginning of *Metaphysics* 8, where Aristotle sums up the discussion in the previous book, helps us understand the way in which he introduces the definition of tragedy: "We must reckon up the results out of what has been said, and drawing together the main points, add the completion [*telos*]" (1042a3–4).[5] This is exactly what Aristotle does in the definition of tragedy. He gathers together the most important points of what has been said, draws conclusions, and adds a *telos*. Thus, while katharsis is a new element, it nevertheless follows, as a conclusion and *telos*, from what has been said in *Poetics* 1–5. We would expect the definition of tragedy, the conclusion and *telos* of "what has been said," to include the final cause (*telos*) of tragedy, and Aristotle's phrasing, "accomplishing   katharsis," suggests that katharsis is this final cause.[6]

What can we learn from "what has been said" in chapters 1 through 5 of the *Poetics*? In the first place, these chapters tell us something about the way in which katharsis is accomplished. The definition in *Poetics* 6 states that imitation produces katharsis. "Tragedy is imitation   by means of pity and fear accomplishing katharsis." Because imitation is associated with learning in *Poetics* 4, we would expect tragic katharsis to involve learning. We would also expect tragic katharsis to be pleasurable, for, in *Poetics* 4, Aristotle says that learning is pleasurable, and he states in *Poetics* 14 that the poet should produce "the pleasure that comes from pity and fear by means of imitation" (1453b12).

The view that katharsis is to be connected with pleasure and with the *telos* of tragedy is confirmed by Aristotle's later statements that pleasure is the *telos* of tragedy. Aristotle believes that the plot, the *telos* of tragedy (1450a22–23), is analogous to the soul of a living thing (1450a38). The activity of the soul is the *ergon* and *telos* of a living thing. Similarly, the functioning of the plot in producing the "proper pleasure" of tragedy, the "pleasure that comes from pity and fear by means of imitation" (1453b10–

[3] On this point see Else, *Argument*, 221–25, Dupont-Roc and Lallot, *Poétique*, 187–88.

[4] I agree with Golden that katharsis should be connected, in particular, with the discussion of learning in *Po* 4 "Clarification," 443–47, and "Catharsis."

[5] Furth's translation, *Metaphysics*

[6] The view that katharsis is the *telos* of tragedy is held by many, including D W Lucas, *Poetics*, 96, 273, Golden, "Clarification," 443, Janko, *Poetics I*, on 1449b27, and glossary, s v "end." It was challenged by Else, *Argument*, 439–40

13), is the *telos* and *ergon* of this kind of imitation (1462b13–15). Thus, when Aristotle writes in *Poetics* 6 that "tragedy is imitation . . . accomplishing . . . katharsis," he is using "katharsis" where he uses "pleasure" elsewhere, to refer to the *telos* and *ergon* of tragedy.

The definition in *Poetics* 6 also tells us that pity and fear are necessary to the production of katharsis. "What has been said" (chapters 1–5 of the *Poetics*) does not discuss pity and fear as such. Chapter 5, however, distinguishes tragedy and epic from comedy, which deals with what is not destructive or painful, but laughable (1449a34–37). This tells us, indirectly, that tragedy and epic do deal with what is painful and destructive. These kinds of things, according to the *Rhetoric*, arouse pity and fear. Moreover, pity and fear, like all emotions, have physical as well as cognitive aspects in Aristotle's view, and they have an essential connection with the excellences.[7] We would, then, expect tragic katharsis, produced by means of these emotions, to have physical, cognitive, and ethical aspects.

Poetics 1–5, "what has been said," indicates that an interpretation of katharsis must take into account a variety of different things: pleasure, learning, and the physical, cognitive and ethical aspects of the emotions Many scholars, however, have erred in interpreting katharsis too narrowly, in terms of only one of these many aspects. G. E. Lessing characterized katharsis in exclusively ethical terms. "This purification consists in nothing other than the metamorphosis of the passions into virtues "[8] He was criticized by Jacob Bernays, who, however, held an equally narrow view, writing that "*katharsis* . . . must mean one of two things: *either* the absolving from guilt by way of certain priestly ceremonies—a lustration, *or* the removing or alleviating of sickness by some medical method of relief."[9] In arguing for an exclusively medical interpretation of katharsis, Bernays failed to take into account Aristotle's view that the emotions have cognitive as well as physical aspects. On the other hand, Leon Golden's earlier works overemphasized the intellectual aspects of katharsis, arguing that katharsis is "the process of 'clarification' by means of which something that is intellectually obscure is made clear to an observer," and that the "relief of emotions has nothing to do with the term 'catharsis.' "[10] Now, however, broader interpretations of tragic katharsis have been gaining wide acceptance. Golden helped support and disseminate Pedro Laín Entralgo's view

---

[7] On emotion in general, and pity and fear in particular, see chap 6

[8] Lessing, *Hamburgische Dramaturgie* no 78, 332–33, quoted by Bernays, "Effect," 155

[9] Bernays, "Effect," 158, emphasis added by translators

[10] Golden, "Catharsis," 57 and 59 Golden no longer holds an exclusively intellectual view, however, see following note

that "tragic catharsis was pleasurable because it was suitable to the *whole* nature of man."[11] Other recent discussions of katharsis also favor a more inclusive approach.[12]

Poetics 1–5, then, helps us understand Aristotle's puzzling statement in *Poetics* 6 that tragedy, by means of pity and fear, accomplishes "katharsis of such *pathēmatōn*" (τὴν τῶν τοιούτων παθημάτων κάθαρσιν). Nevertheless, this phrase presents notorious difficulties concerning the meanings of the terms *pathēmatōn* (a word I have translated as "emotions") and τοιούτων (such), and concerning the reference of the latter. These problems are discussed below. First, however, I examine one of the critical biases of modern scholarship.

THE HOMEOPATHIC PREJUDICE

Even though Aristotle's statement about katharsis is notoriously controversial, there has been, at least since Bernays, almost universal agreement on one point: if tragic katharsis operates on the emotions at all, it must, in the opinion of most scholars, be a homeopathic process. That is, pity and fear accomplish a "purgation" or "purification" or "clarification" of emotions like themselves. This homeopathic theory of katharsis is one of the unexamined prejudices of modern scholarship.[13] Because it is assumed rather than argued for, texts are sometimes distorted to accommodate this theory, while the evidence in favor of alternative views may be ignored. Seen in this biased way, Aristotelian tragic katharsis appears to be something new and mysterious rather than an integral part of a commonly accepted view of poetry. I argue in the rest of this book that we would benefit

[11] Laín Entralgo, *Therapy*, 235–36, quoted by Golden, "Clarification," 452. Golden is sometimes said to hold an exclusively intellectual view of katharsis, and it is true that he does not emphasize the physical and ethical aspects of the emotions, or attempt to explain the relationship between the intellectual aspects of the emotions and their physical or ethical aspects However, it is clear from "Clarification" and other articles that Golden does not now believe katharsis to be exclusively intellectual. he recognizes that cognitive changes are necessarily accompanied by physical changes. What he correctly insists on is that cognition precedes physical changes.

[12] For example. Halliwell, *Aristotle's Poetics*, 198–201, Janko, *Comedy*, 140, Nussbaum, *Fragility*, 390–91, and Reckford, *Aristophanes*, 56–57, 378–79.

[13] The homeopathic view of katharsis is held, for example, by Butcher, *Aristotle's Theory* 248–73, Bywater, *Aristotle on the Art*, 157, Dupont-Roc and Lallot, *Poétique*, 191–92, Halliwell, *Aristotle's Poetics*, 192–94, Hardy, *Poétique*, 22, House, *Poetics*, 107, Janko, *Comedy*, 142, D. W. Lucas, *Poetics*, 283.

from giving serious consideration once more to an alternative view of tragic katharsis that was widely accepted from the Renaissance through the eighteenth century. In this view, katharsis is allopathic rather than homeopathic, pity and fear affect emotions unlike themselves.[14] While some twentieth-century scholars glance at the possibility of allopathy, none, so far as I know, gives it serious consideration as an alternative to the homeopathic view

The neglect of allopathy by students of the *Poetics* is a comparatively recent phenomenon. In the Renaissance, the allopathic was one of three common views of tragic katharsis. One view, the homeopathic, held that pity and fear produce katharsis (however it was interpreted) of similar emotions. Under the allopathic interpretation, pity and fear were thought to produce katharsis (however it was interpreted) of emotions unlike pity and fear (for example, anger, insolence, and lack of compassion). A third Renaissance view was a mixture of the homeopathic and the allopathic, holding that pity and fear produce katharsis of pity and fear *and* of unlike emotions.[15]

The quarrel between the homeopaths and the allopaths, so to speak, began in Italy in the sixteenth century, shortly after the rediscovery of Aristotle's *Poetics*. It may be described, rather simplistically, as a quarrel between the supporters of Vincenzo Maggi on the allopathic side and of Francesco Robortello on the homeopathic side. In 1550, Maggi took issue with the homeopathic view, writing that it is more reasonable to believe that tragedy uses pity and fear to purge the soul of emotions unlike themselves.

Therefore it is much better, by the intervention of pity and terror, to purge [*expurgare*] the soul of wrath, through which so many violent deaths come about, of avarice, which is the cause of almost an infinity of ills, of lust, thanks to which the most harmful of wicked deeds must frequently be suf-

[14] More accurately, I argue that the emotions affected are like pity and fear in kind (*genos*), but unlike them in form (*eidos*), and that they are affected because they are unlike

[15] Discussions of the katharsis controversy in the Italian Renaissance can be found in Hathaway, *Age*, 205–300 See, in particular, his discussion (251–53) of Lorenzo Giacomini's criticisms of the homeopathic, allopathic, and mixed views See also Weinberg, *History*, and Ryan, "Robortello and Maggi ' Hathaway, "Dryden," discusses a related controversy in the seventeenth and eighteenth centuries Other works are listed in Keesey, "Interpretations,' 193–94 n 1 The details of the history of this controversy and the views of individual writers are in many cases highly controversial The passages quoted below are merely intended to draw attention to the prevalence of an allopathic view in the critical tradition

fered For these reasons I have no doubt whatever that Aristotle was unwilling to make the purgation of terror and pity from the human soul the end of tragedy, but rather, to use these for the removal of other disorders from the soul, through which removal the soul comes to be adorned with the virtues For once wrath is driven out, for example, kindness takes its place [16]

In Maggi's view, tragedy uses pity and fear to produce a katharsis of "other disorders" wrath, greed, lust An allopathic view was also expressed by Antonio Minturno, writing in 1559

What is there indeed which to the same extent as pity or fear breaks the violence of anger, extinguishes the thirst for money, diminishes the desire for honors, represses the eagerness to dominate, restrains the desire for harmful pleasures, holds in check any indomitable fury of the mind? For who is there so possessed by an unbridled desire to avenge, or rule, or own, who, if he is aroused to pity and terror by the calamities of others, does not have his soul purged and purified [*purget, expietque*] of the disorder which brought him that unhappiness? [17]

Another supporter of the allopathic view, Vincenzio Buonamici (1597), wrote that "the soul is purged [*si purga*] by removing the excessive passions and correcting them with their contraries melancholy, with music, with laughter, arrogance in the prosperous events of fortune, with fear and with pity "[18]

There were also many seventeenth- and eighteenth-century expressions of an allopathic view of emotional treatment Edward Reynolds's statements are of particular interest, although they do not directly concern poetry

And therefore we wil here a little observe, what course may be taken for the allaying of this *vehemencie* of our *Affections*, whereby they disturbe the *quiet*, and darken the serenitie of mans *Mind* And this is done, either by *opposing contrary Passions to contrary*, which is *Aristotles* rule, who adviseth, in the bringing of *Passions* from an *extreame* to a *mediocritie*, to incline and bend them towards the other *extreame*, as Husbandmen use to doe those Trees which are crooked, or as dim and weak eyes doe see the light best, when it is broken in a shadow [19]

[16] Maggi, *Explanationes*, 98 I quote Weinberg s translation in *History*, 408

[17] Minturno, *De poeta*, 63–64 I quote Weinberg s translation in *History*, 739

[18] Buonamici, *Discorsi*, 34 I quote Weinberg s translation in *History*, 691

[19] Reynolds, *Treatise*, 52 Emphasis and spelling is that of the original This passage was called to my attention by Hathaway, *Age*, 210–11 n 8 As Reynolds s marginal notes

Reynolds gives as an example of the principle of opposing contrary passions to contrary the suppression of "the *feare* of *Death* by the *shame* of *Baseness*," quoting *Iliad* 13.121–22: "But each of you put in your minds / shame [*aidōs*] and retribution" (*Treatise*, 53–54).

A final example of the allopathic view of tragic katharsis is provided by John Dryden: "Rapin, a judicious critic, has observed from Aristotle, that pride and want of commiseration are the most prominent vices in mankind; therefore, to cure us of these two, the inventors of Tragedy have chosen to work upon two other passions, which are, fear and pity."[20]

One reason the allopathic view of katharsis has been neglected since the late nineteenth century is undoubtedly that Bernays's homeopathic medical views have been so influential, among his attackers as well as his defenders. Another reason is that modern methods of classifying theories of katharsis differ from those of the Renaissance. Theories about katharsis are today commonly classified as (1) medical (purgation), (2) religious-moral (purification), (3) structural (purification of events in the plot), and (4) intellectual (clarification).[21] While this classification is useful in many ways, it has tended to blur the older, Renaissance classification. Through the influence of Bernays, medical and "enthusiastic" theories of katharsis have been identified with the homeopathic interpretation, even though this does not accurately reflect ancient medical and religious views. Moral "purification" theories of katharsis have also been identified with homeopathic theories, though the process of purification can be thought of as allopathic, homeopathic, or mixed. This blurring of the Renaissance distinctions is reflected, for example, in Bywater's list of kinds of purification theories. First on this list, which includes no allopathic theory, is Lessing's ethical, homeopathic theory, which is said to be "the only view that calls for serious consideration."[22] Lessing, according to Bywater, holds that "tragedy is said to purify pity and fear, because the frequent excitement of these emotions in the theatre has a tendency to weaken their force, and thus moderate and reduce them to just measure" (*Aristotle on the Art*, 159).

The structural view and some versions of the intellectual view are today

---

indicate, his sources for "Aristotle's rule" are *EN* 2.9 (1109b5–7), where the "crooked tree" metaphor appears, and 10.1 (1172a32–33). On this metaphor, see chap. 9 ("Iron and Wood").

[20] Dryden, "Preface," quoted by Hathaway, "Dryden," 667.

[21] These broad categories are followed in the main by, for example, Golden, "Clarification"; Halliwell, *Aristotle's Poetics*, app. 5, 350–56 (who lists three varieties of the moral interpretation); and Keesey, "Interpretations."

[22] Bywater, *Aristotle on the Art*, 160.

usually assumed to be the only alternatives to the homeopathic interpretation. This is particularly evident in the work of Else, who, in arguing for his own structural interpretation, criticizes the homeopathic view. He writes: "Almost all of them [sc., writers on the subject of katharsis] understand Aristotle to say that . . . the pity and fear aroused in the spectator somehow purge or purify themselves,"[23] and he notes that "many unprejudiced observers have questioned how pity and fear can be purged or purified—whichever it is—by themselves. Some critics have *therefore* tended to reinterpret 'pity and fear' as 'pathetic and fearful incidents.' "[24] *According to the structural view favored by Else, the term pathēmatōn in* Aristotle's definition of tragedy refers to events in the plot. As Else himself admits, however, this term is most naturally taken to mean "emotions," since "pity and fear" immediately precede it: "It is natural to refer *pathēmatōn* to *eleou kai phobou*, since the latter stand so near" (*Argument*, 228). According to Else, he and other scholars accept the structural interpretation, even though it involves an unnatural reading of the Greek, mainly because they assume that the only alternative is the even more implausible homeopathic interpretation. Thus, Else's arguments, like those of the scholars he criticizes, are weakened by a failure to consider the allopathic alternative.

Other modern scholars also fail to give serious consideration to the allopathic view, even when they are troubled by theoretical problems connected with homeopathy, or fail to find sufficient evidence for Greek homeopathic beliefs. Some examples are instructive. D. W. Lucas remarks: "As Aristotle himself said 'medicines work naturally by means of opposites' (*EN* 1104b18), and it was recognized as paradoxical that this form of *katharsis* [sc., that of *Pol.* 8 and the *Poetics*] worked homoeopathically."[25] Roger Bley argues that musical katharsis works by contraries, but then writes, "The originality of Aristotle is to have discovered and advocated a catharsis not by contraries, *but by similars*."[26] Friedrich Solmsen says there is no evidence for a Pythagorean katharsis in which the arousal of an emotion is the best katharsis for that same emotion. He then states, however, that this homeopathic process is the one Aristotle has in mind.[27] In support of his view Solmsen cites Adolf Busse, who also finds no evidence for a homeopathic Pythagorean katharsis, and who concludes that

[23] Else, *Argument*, 227.
[24] Ibid., 228; emphasis added.
[25] D. W. Lucas, *Poetics*, 283. He does not say *who* recognized this as paradoxical.
[26] Bley, "Aristote," 97; emphasis in original.
[27] Solmsen, review of Rostagni, *Poetica*, 408.

Aristotle must be an exception "It seems, therefore, that we are not unentitled to call the Pythagorean katharsis allopathic, in contrast to the homeopathic katharsis of Aristotle."[28] Again, Carnes Lord's discussion of "Catharsis and Spiritedness" concludes that "catharsis . . serve[s] to purify the spirited passions of their dangerous excesses." Lord notes, correctly, that, in this view, "tragic catharsis can no longer be understood . . as simply homoeopathic the catharsis of anger will be brought about, not by anger, but by pity and fear." Nevertheless, Lord does not seriously consider the allopathic alternative, for he continues. "Yet tragic catharsis can be regarded as loosely analogous to a homoeopathic catharsis by the fact that passion is cured by passion . Aristotle himself so regarded it."[29] Finally, Halliwell correctly notes that neither Pythagorean nor Greek medical katharsis was homeopathic.[30] He nevertheless writes, without argument, that because Aristotle's statement about katharsis in the definition of tragedy "directly expresses an identity of means and object," tragic katharsis is homeopathic (*Aristotle's Poetics*, 192).

Interpretations of the views of Olympiodorus (sixth century c.e) show particularly well the extraordinary persistence of the homeopathic view. Olympiodorus writes that the "Aristotelian" katharsis is that in which "evil cures evil, and by the combat of opposites [τῇ διαμάχῃ τῶν ἐναντίων] brings it to due proportion" (*Alcibiades* 146 3–4) We could not have a clearer statement of the allopathic principle than "the combat of opposites." Yet Alexandre Ničev manages to reconcile this statement with the principle of homeopathy. The opposites, he explains, are not emotions, but opinions by which the emotions are "determined "[31] The actual katharsis is a "purgation" or "liquidation" of emotions that are similar to pity and fear (*Catharsis*, 38). He does not give consideration to an allopathic view Janko also cites Olympiodorus's statement that Aristotelian katharsis "cures evil with evil" as evidence for a homeopathic interpretation, explaining that this phrase means that katharsis "cures the emotions by stimulating them This humorous proverbial phrase confirms the homeopathic nature of catharsis, comparable to curing a fever by piling on blankets." This view requires Janko to explain away Olympiodorus's state-

---

[28] Busse, "Musikasthetik," 50 Solmsen cites him in his review of Rostagni, *Poetica*, n 1

[29] Carnes Lord, *Education*, 164 and n 31 On anger and tragic katharsis, see further below, chap 10

[30] Halliwell, *Aristotle's Poetics*, 186–93, esp n 37

[31] Ničev, *Catharsis*, 186

ment that this kind of katharsis works by "the conflict of opposites": "This is apparently an error based on the Stoics' concept of catharsis."[32]

The arguments of these scholars, whatever their merits in other respects, are seriously weakened by their failure to consider the allopathic interpretation. If there is, as many of them admit, much evidence for allopathy elsewhere in ancient thought, and little evidence for homeopathy, the view that Aristotelian katharsis was homeopathic should at least be questioned, examined, and defended. Once the homeopathic view is examined critically instead of being taken for granted, it is apparent that it faces serious difficulties. It is inherently implausible, and its proponents are unable to describe the process involved in a clear and meaningful way. Moreover, the statements of certain ancient writers who have been cited as evidence that Aristotle held a homeopathic theory of tragic katharsis do not unequivocally support this view.

HOMEOPATHY: THEORETICAL PROBLEMS

Among the weaknesses of modern interpretations of tragic katharsis is a lack of conceptual clarity. In part because of the unexamined assumption that katharsis is homeopathic, scholars are too little conscious of possible ambiguities. It is important, then, to begin by clarifying terms and concepts in order to avoid misunderstandings.

In the first place, ambiguity can arise if we fail to specify what is involved in a kathartic process. In many cases the same phenomenon may be classified as homeopathic when one aspect of it is emphasized, and as allopathic when another aspect is emphasized. For example, katharsis of (painful) anger by means of (painful) fear can be called "homeopathic" if the essential idea is that painful emotion affects painful emotion, or that emotion affects emotion. However, this same process can be called "allopathic" if the differences between anger and fear are thought to be more important.

We must also be extremely cautious in using the terms "homeopathy" and "allopathy," with their modern medical connotations, to characterize the theories of ancient writers whose views on medicine were very different from ours. Ancient writers did not generally use the Greek equivalents of

---

[32] Janko, *Poetics I*, 187; cf. *Comedy*, 147. Although Olympiodorus calls this kind of katharsis "Stoic" (*Alcibiades* 54.18) as well as "Aristotelian" (*Alcibiades* 146.3), there are good Aristotelian parallels for "the cure of evil with evil." See further below, chap. 9 ("Psychic Katharsis").

these terms, but instead wrote of like (or similar) acting on like, or of unlike (or opposite) acting on unlike. In particular, Greek medical treatises frequently mention cures by means of opposites or by means of similars, as do Aristotle's works. The distinction between these two kinds of cures is based on important theoretical principles concerning the ways in which the powers of hot, cold, moist, and dry, in the body and in the environment, produce health, and cause and cure disease. In the field of ethics also, statements that opposites treat opposites are more than mere metaphor.

Nevertheless, we can for convenience use the modern terms "homeopathy" and "allopathy" in characterizing ancient views, provided we do not use these terms loosely, but in a way that reflects these important theoretical distinctions. A katharsis should be called "homeopathic" only if it is a process in which like acts on like *because* it is like, and a katharsis should be called "allopathic" only if it is produced *by means of* things with different or opposite qualities. Moreover, because any two things are like in some respects and unlike in others, it is essential to specify exactly how the kathartic agent and the thing on which it acts are like and how they are unlike. In the specific case of tragic katharsis, for example, it is important to try to determine how, in Aristotle's view, pity and fear are like and unlike the other emotions on which they produce katharsis, and whether or not they affect these other emotions because they are like or because they are unlike. Only then will the labels "homeopathy" and "allopathy" be truly meaningful.

Aristotle was well aware of the possible ambiguities involved in expressions of (homeopathic) views that like affects like, and in (allopathic) views that unlike affects unlike. He writes in *Generation and Corruption* that most philosophers have believed that "like is entirely unaffected by like" (323b3–4). These philosophers, according to Aristotle (323b8–10), say that even cases that might appear to be counterexamples—for example, that of a greater fire putting out a smaller—are really cases of unlike (the greater) affecting unlike (the smaller). Democritus alone, writes Aristotle, believed that like is affected by like (323b10–15). Thus the same phenomenon, a greater fire putting out a smaller, would be characterized by Democritus in homeopathic terms as fire putting out fire, but by other philosophers in allopathic terms as the greater affecting the smaller. Aristotle himself was an allopath in that he believed that one thing affects another, to which it is similar in some ways, not because it is similar but because it is unlike.

Modern scholars, unfortunately, are not so careful as Aristotle was to make relevant distinctions. Auguste Diès, for example, does not consider how Plato viewed the arousal of shamelessness to produce shame he advocated in the *Laws*. Diès simply describes this process in homeopathic terms as the use of similar to expel similar: "The mastery of pleasure by the very experience of pleasure."[33] While such a characterization of this process is possible, Plato's text makes it clear that he viewed it allopathically, as a combat between the opposites shame and shamelessness (e.g., *Laws* 647a–d).

Modern homeopathic medical theories are also less clear about the conceptual distinction between homeopathy and allopathy than is desirable. For example, vaccination is often said to be an application of the homeopathic principle: "When homeopathy is discussed at meetings introducing the subject the comment is often made that this is also the basis of vaccination [in which] a minute dose given to us of modified agents that can produce diseases such as diptheria [sic] or tetanus have effectively increased our resistance to such infections."[34] This treatment is most accurately characterized as homeopathic if the conceptual focus is on certain visible effects: "The disease, and the agent that can treat it, both produce a *similar* effect."[35] However, vaccination is more accurately characterized as an allopathic treatment if the focus is instead on the physical process involved. In vaccination a small dose of the disease makes us immune because it leads us to produce *antibodies* that combat the disease. Seen in this light, what "treats" the disease is really its opposite, the antibodies, not the disease itself.

Because of these possible ambiguities, it is essential for a homeopathic or allopathic theory of katharsis to define "homeopathy" and "allopathy" in clear, unambiguous terms and to distinguish them from each other. The unexamined prejudice in favor of homeopathy and the neglect of allopathy, however, have prevented scholars from seeing the need to make this conceptual distinction.

A second problem for the homeopathic view concerns the meaning of the phrase τοιούτων παθημάτων in Aristotle's definition of tragedy: δι' ἐλέου καὶ φόβου περαίνουσα τὴν τῶν τοιούτων παθημάτων κάθαρσιν ("by means of pity and fear accomplishing the katharsis of such *pathēmata*"). Most scholars take these *pathēmata* to be emotions, and this is the most natural reading of the Greek. The "pity and fear" (ἐλέου καὶ φόβου)

---

[33] Diès, "Introduction," xii.
[34] Clover, *Homeopathy*, 15.
[35] Ibid.; emphasis in original.

mentioned at the beginning of the statement about katharsis are most naturally taken to be *pathē*, "emotions," not "events." We expect, then, that *pathēmata* in the same statement will have this meaning also. If so, however, Aristotle's statement about katharsis presents great difficulties for any interpretation. If Aristotle had written that pity and fear produce katharsis of "these" (τούτων) emotions, or of "other" or "opposite" (ἑτέρων or ἐναντίων) emotions, interpretation would have been much easier. Instead, he writes that pity and fear produce katharsis of τοιούτων ("such") emotions. The homeopathic interpretation must explain why, if pity and fear effect a katharsis of pity and fear, Aristotle does not write "these" (τούτων) emotions instead of "such" (τοιούτων) emotions.[36]

Some proponents of homeopathy have tried to get around the difficulty by arguing that τοιούτων (these kinds, such as these) in the definition of tragedy is equivalent to τούτων (these, meaning those just mentioned).[37] This view, however, is unacceptable for linguistic reasons. John Beare shows that "τὰ τοιαῦτα [these kinds] in Aristotle, with or without substantive, never loses its implication that the individuals referred to fall under a class, and is never exactly equivalent in sense to ταῦτα τά or ταῦτα [these]."[38] Of the many examples Beare cites in support of his contention, *Nicomachean Ethics* 1107a12 is of particular interest. πάντα γὰρ ταῦτα καὶ τὰ τοιαῦτα ("All these and such as these". 130). Beare has demonstrated that the *pathēmata* that are acted on by pity and fear cannot themselves be restricted to pity and fear, but must include other emotions that are "such as" pity and fear in that they are in the same class.

Difficulties arise, however, when proponents of homeopathy attempt to say what this class is. Beare suggests ("Anaphoric," 120) that this class is that of fear and pity emotions, and he cites Bywater's view that it includes the "whole group of disturbing emotions."[39] Richard Janko also argues that the class of emotions referred to by τῶν τοιούτων is that of "painful

[36] The allopathic interpretation, on the other hand, must explain why Aristotle does not write "other" or "opposite' emotions In chap 10 I give reasons for preferring the allopathic interpretation, in spite of this difficulty

[37] Bernays was one of the most influential advocates of the view that τοιούτων is equivalent to τούτων "Effect," 164–65 He was followed by Rostagni, *Poetica*, 33 This view is opposed by Beare, "Anaphoric", Gudeman, *Aristoteles*, 166, Else, *Argument*, 227, and D W Lucas, *Poetics*, 98 Butcher, *Aristotle's Theory*, seems to want to have it both ways, writing that τῶν τοιούτων refers to " 'the aforesaid emotions,' namely, pity and fear," but that Aristotle does not write τούτων in order to avoid suggesting "that the feelings were identically the same" (240–41 n 3)

[38] Beare, "Anaphoric," 123 He cites Kuhner-Gerth, 1 630

[39] Bywater, *Aristotle on the Art*, 152, quoted by Beare, "Anaphoric," 134–35 n

and disturbing emotions."[40] This interpretation, however, gives τῶν τοιούτων too broad a reference. If tragedy is a universal panacea it lacks a specific function and goal. Moreover, it is counterintuitive to see tragedy as a banisher of all painful emotions. If any genre has this characteristic, we would expect it to be comedy. There are, moreover, numerous indications in Aristotle's works that he thought of different kinds of painful emotions in terms of difference and opposition rather than in terms of similarity. Aristotelian emotions can differ in either quality or quantity. Aristotle explicitly states that emotions that differ in degree or quantity are opposites. In *Eudemian Ethics* 1220b31–32, just before giving a table (1220b38–1221a12) listing extremes and intermediates of *pathē* (1221a13) and excellences, Aristotle writes that "the extremes are opposite {*enantia*} both to one another and to the intermediate." For example, in the table at 1221a1, excess fear of the opinions of others (*kataplēxis*) is the opposite of deficiency of fear of these opinions (shamelessness), and of *aidōs*, the intermediate. Many painful emotions that differ in quality from pity and fear are also opposed to or incompatible with pity and fear, in Aristotle's view. In *Rhetoric* 2.9, indignation is said to be opposed to (ἀντί-κειται) pity (1386b9–10), as is envy (1386b16–18). The incompatibility of fear and anger is shown by Aristotle's statement that "it is impossible to fear and be angry at the same time" (*Rhet.* 2.3.1380a33). Pity is also incompatible with anger, for Aristotle writes that people are mild (the opposite of being angry: 1380a5) if they pity (1380b14).[41]

Thus, the view that τοιούτων, "these kinds," in the definition of tragedy refers to a broad spectrum of emotions that are alike in being painful does not unproblematically support the homeopathic interpretation. The evidence suggests, rather, that a katharsis by means of pity and fear that is produced on, for example, anger and the spirited emotions would be allopathic, in Aristotle's view, though modern scholars (e.g., Carnes Lord, quoted above) often think of it as homeopathic.

Some proponents of homeopathy give a different account of how the emotions affected in tragic katharsis can be "such as," but not identical with, kathartic pity and fear. They argue that "aesthetic" pity and fear differ from the "real-life" pity and fear that are "purged" or "purified." Butcher, for example, writes: "Pity and fear are purged of the impure element which clings to them in life." He argues that "The *eleos* and *phobos* of the definition [of tragedy] are the aesthetic emotions of pity and fear,

[40] Janko, *Poetics I*, on 1449b28, cf *Comedy*, 160–61
[41] Reading ἐλεῶσιν with Cope, *Rhetoric*, and Grimaldi, *Rhetoric II*, ad loc

those which are awakened by the tragic representation τῶν τοιούτων παθημάτων [such emotions] are the emotions of pity and fear which belong to real life "[42] There have been many versions of this view Items 3 through 5 in Bywater's list of different accounts of katharsis concern ways in which "aesthetic" emotions have been thought to differ qualitatively from "real-life" emotions

(3) The tragic pity and fear are regarded as pure, because they are aroused not by real suffering, but only by the imaginary woes of the theatre, so that there is no admixture of pain in them

(4) They are regarded as pure, because, as aroused by Tragedy, they are disinterested emotions, with no self-regarding element in them

(5) They are pure, because the sublimity of Tragedy exalts pity and fear into high and noble forms of feeling [43]

However, the view that there are "aesthetic" emotions that differ qualitatively from "real-life" emotions is not Aristotelian [44] Aristotle believed that pity and fear are painful emotions, in tragedy as in real life, and that tragedy gives pleasure not because the pity and fear it arouses are of a special, "aesthetic" kind, but because the *contemplation* in which we engage in aesthetic situations is pleasurable Nor is there any evidence that Aristotle believed pity and fear in aesthetic situations to be more "high and noble," whatever that might mean, than they are anywhere else And far from regarding the tragic emotions as "disinterested," Aristotle believed that we cannot experience pity for another who is "like" us unless we first experience fear for ourselves Moreover, even if kathartic, "aesthetic" emotions differed qualitatively from "real-life" emotions, it would beg the question to assume without argument that katharsis is homeopathic rather than allopathic This is what Butcher does, for example, when he stresses difference in his statement that "the emotion stirred by a fictitious representation must divest itself of its purely selfish and material elements, and become part of a new order of things" but nevertheless assumes that "tragedy is a form of homoeopathic treatment, curing emotion by means of an emotion like in kind but not identical"[45] (248)

Some proponents of homeopathy hold that kathartic pity and fear differ from the pity and fear that they affect in being experienced by different

[42] Butcher, *Aristotle's Theory*, 267, 240–41 n 3

[43] Bywater, *Aristotle on the Art*, 159–60

[44] Discussed above, chap 7 (Pity and Fear in the *Poetics*) See also D W Lucas s criticisms of Butcher (*Poetics*, 98)

[45] Butcher, *Aristotle s Theory*, 271, 248

people. Janko finds support for such a view in Iamblichus's statement that
"by observing others' emotions [ἀλλότρια πάθη] in both comedy and
tragedy, we can check our own emotions [οἰκεῖα πάθη] "[46] The definition
of tragedy in the *Poetics*, however, does not distinguish between our own
and others' emotions, and the view that such a distinction is implicit in
Aristotle's theory is not consistent with the rest of the *Poetics* While some
other imitative arts imitate emotion (*Po* 1447a28), tragedy imitates the
actions of other people, and it arouses pity and fear because it is an imitation of action. Moreover, in the *Poetics*, the pity and fear by means of which
katharsis is accomplished are always emotions aroused in the audience, and
not in the agents of the dramatic action.

Another problem faced by many versions of the homeopathic interpretation is the implausibility of the view that katharsis removes a harmful
excess of pity and fear. The idea that we go around with an excess of pity
and fear that needs to be relieved is not consistent with ordinary experience. Ross's objection is still well taken. "Do most men in fact go about
with an excessive tendency to pity and fear? [Or does tragedy benefit us
instead because] people *deficient* in pity and fear because their lives give
little occasion for such feelings are for once taken out of themselves and
made to realise the heights and depths of human experience?"[47] Most people would agree that, in their own experience, tragedy seems not so much
to relieve a preexisting excess of pity and fear as to arouse these emotions
in which we are usually deficient. A similar point is made by James Gunn,
in a modern novel.

> Some people like to be frightened, you know It gives them the sense of
> being alive, stimulates their adrenals, tones up their whole system Mostly
> they aren't—alive, that is Not in any meaningful sense. They exist at a
> minimum level. If they can achieve the exhilaration of danger while clinging
> to a subconscious realization that they are completely protected, they have
> gained worlds without expense [48]

The view that tragedy relieves people of a harmful excess of pity and
fear is, moreover, Platonic rather than Aristotelian. Plato believed that
poetry satisfies the part of the soul that is "starved for weeping" (*Rep.*

[46] Iamblichus, *On the Mysteries* 1 11 Janko's translation, *Poetics I*, 59 Janko comments
on this idea (186–88, xvi–xx), although he once writes of the representation of "painful
events" rather than of "emotions" (xix) I discuss Iamblichus below, in "Homeopathy The
Ancient Evidence "

[47] W D Ross, *Aristotle*, 284–85, quoted by Golden, "Clarification, ' 448–49

[48] Gunn, *Joy Makers*, 162

10.606a4), and he identified the kind of fear aroused by poetry with the fear of pain and death that makes people cowardly (*Rep.* 3.386–87). In Aristotle's view, however, *tragic* fear is not the same as fear of pain and death; it is more closely connected with shame and fear of wrongdoing. Tragic pity and fear are aroused not at the representation of an event that is merely painful and destructive, but at harm of *philos* by *philos*. If, then, tragic katharsis relieves people of a fear that prevents them from harming kin, it is hard to see how it can be beneficial. Maggi argued forcefully against this view of tragedy: "If tragedy freed the spectators from terror when terror concerns criminals, tragedy would make men more ready to commit crimes. . . . Would it not be astonishing to want to have tragedy purge the human mind of pity and terror if trouble were the result should the human race be deprived of them? For if it were deprived of pity, how would we perform work for the needy?"[49]

Far from being harmful, Aristotelian tragic pity and fear are beneficial as antidotes to shamelessness. Moreover, Aristotle believed that most people do not have an excess of this kind of pity and fear, but instead tend naturally toward the opposite extreme of shameless pursuit of pleasure. He writes in *Nicomachean Ethics* 1119a5–7: "Hardly any are deficient in regard to pleasures and enjoy them less than they should. This kind of insensibility is not human." Insensibility to pleasures is also said in the *Eudemian Ethics* to be uncommon: "For all err more on the other side, and to feel and to be overcome by such pleasures is natural to everyone" (*EE* 1230b16–18). In *Rhetoric* 1382b4–9, Aristotle expresses a similarly pessimistic view of human nature: "The many are inferior, and overcome by desire for gain, and are cowards in dangers. . . . For the most part human beings do injustice, when they are able." Aristotle sums up this view in *Politics* 1267b1: "Human evil is insatiable."

Another problem for proponents of the homeopathetic view is the difficulty of specifying the exact nature of the process that is supposed to be involved. Milton's analogy is unusually clear and unambiguous: "So in Physic things of melancholic hue and quality are us'd against melancholy, sowr against sowr, salt to remove salt humours." Nevertheless, he does not attempt to describe either the medical process ("Physic") or the supposedly analogous psychic process by means of which tragedy has the "power by raising pity and fear, or terror, to purge the mind of those and such like passions."[50]

---

[49] Maggi, *Explanationes*, 97 and 98. I quote Hathaway's translation in *Age*, 222.
[50] Milton, preface to *Samson Agonistes* (1671), quoted by Sellin, "Sources," 713.

One way of explaining how the homeopathic process works is to say that tragedy provides a kind of "inoculation" against pain, just as taking poison in small doses helps people build up an immunity to it F Robortello gave a good account of this homeopathic view in 1548 "When men are present at tragedies and hear and perceive characters saying and doing those things that happen to themselves in reality, they become accustomed to grieving, fearing, and pitying, for which reason it happens that when something befalls them as a result of their human condition, they grieve and fear less "[51] This theory continues into the twentieth century, in this statement by Lionel Trilling, for example "The Aristotelian theory does not deny another function for tragedy   which is suggested by Freud's theory of the traumatic neurosis—which might be called the mithradatic function, by which tragedy is used as the homeopathic administration of pain to inure ourselves to the greater pain which life will force upon us "[52] Trilling's account, unfortunately, gives no details

The most famous, and perhaps the most detailed, account of this "Mithridatic" theory is that expressed in A E Housman's "Terence, this is stupid stuff" (A Shropshire Lad 62, 1886) In the last two stanzas of this poem, Housman compares his own poetry to poison taken in small doses

> Therefore, since the world has still
> Much good, but much less good than ill,
> And while the sun and moon endure
> Luck's a chance, but trouble's sure,
> I'd face it as a wise man would,
> And train for ill and not for good
> 'Tis true, the stuff I bring for sale
> Is not so brisk a brew as ale
> Out of a stem that scored the hand
> I wring it in a weary land
> But take it if the smack is sour,

[51] Robortello, Explicationes, 53 I quote Hathaway s translation in Age, 215 Hathaway attributes this view of poetry to many other Renaissance scholars, including Speroni, Varchi, Minturno, Lapini, Castelvetro, Piccolomini, and Denores (207 n 2) He claims (238) that Lapini credited Plutarch (Moralia 1 15, How to Study Poetry) with the view that, in Hathaway s words, poison taken in small doses guards us against poison and that poetry has this utility While Plutarch compares the mixture of falsehood in poetry to a mixture of poison in food at Moralia 1 17b–c, I find no expression of the view Hathaway attributes to him

[52] Trilling, Freud and Literature, 181 This passage was brought to my attention by Hathaway, Age, 207 n 2

The better for the embittered hour;
It should do good to heart and head
When your soul is in my soul's stead;
And I will friend you, if I may,
In the dark and cloudy day.

There was a king reigned in the East:
There, when kings will sit to feast,
They get their fill before they think
With poisoned meat and poisoned drink.
He gathered all that springs to birth
From the many-venomed earth;
First a little, thence to more,
He sampled all her killing store;
And easy, smiling, seasoned sound,
Sate the king when healths went round.
They put arsenic in his meat
And stared aghast to watch him eat;
They poured strychnine in his cup
And shook to see him drink it up:
They shook, they stared as white's their shirt:
Them it was their poison hurt.
—I tell the tale that I heard told.
Mithridates, he died old.

The view that tragic katharsis is a homeopathic inoculation involves a number of difficulties, however. For one thing, inoculation is not obviously kathartic except in a very vague and metaphorical sense. The "inoculation" theory emphasizes habituation and the building up of resistance. The Greeks, however, did not in most cases call this a "katharsis." Military training, for example, builds up resistance to pain and privation of all sorts, but was not thought to be kathartic. Moreover, when a building up of resistance is called a "katharsis," the process may well be thought of as allopathic. In Plato's *Laws*, for example, the use of a "fear drug" helps build resistance to fear and is compared to a medical katharsis. This process is very carefully described, and it is clearly allopathic, brought about by means of the combat of two opposite kinds of fear. The modern practice of vaccination, as we have just seen, can also be characterized as an allopathic treatment in which *anti*bodies are produced to combat a disease. Nor does Housman's account of the "Mithridatic" function of poetry support the view that tragic katharsis is homeopathic. It does not mention

275

katharsis, nor does it describe the process of building resistance in homeopathic terms. In the Mithridates story, the king is never said to suffer ill effects from the small doses of poison he takes

> And easy, smiling, seasoned sound,
> Sate the king when healths went round

Moreover, when poison is taken in small doses, "the smack is sour," but not even slight symptoms of sickness appear to be produced.

If accounts of the "inoculation" theory are often vague and imprecise, other versions of the homeopathic view are often even less clear. Halliwell, for example, characterizes homeopathic katharsis as "the arousal of the emotions to change the emotions."[53] This characterization could be applied equally well to an allopathic katharsis, in which an emotion is aroused in order to counterbalance its opposite. Bywater writes that katharsis is "a working-off of emotion brought about by something that excites emotion,"[54] and Bernays states that katharsis "seeks not to alter or to subjugate the oppressive element but to arouse it [aufregen] and to draw it out [hervortreiben], and thus to achieve some sort of relief for the oppressed."[55] Without a detailed account of the process involved in "working off" or "drawing out" the emotions, however, these statements might just as well serve to characterize an allopathic process. A more specific explanation has been sought in the detailed psychological theories of Freud, who wrote that "our actual enjoyment of an imaginative work proceeds from a liberation of tensions in our minds."[56] Freud's views, however, must be judged on their own merits, along with a whole complex of ideas Aristotle certainly did not hold. sublimation, the subconscious, wish fulfillment, and the specific stages of childhood development.

D. W. Lucas's account of homeopathic tragic katharsis is somewhat more precise. He writes that in homeopathic musical katharsis, "a further stimulus in the same direction was given, like was cured by like " Tragic katharsis, Lucas writes, involves a similar homeopathic process of "the release of accumulated pity and fear by pity and fear experienced in the theatre." This is an emotional katharsis analogous to a medical katharsis. "An emotional orgy brings release in the same way as blood-letting relieves the over-sanguine."[57]

---

[53] Halliwell, *Aristotle's Poetics*, 194
[54] Bywater, *Aristotle on the Art*, 157
[55] Bernays, "Effect," 160
[56] Freud, "Creative Writers," 153
[57] D W Lucas, *Poetics*, 283, 285

At first, this view appears clear enough: a preexisting excess of pity and fear is relieved by the experience of the same emotions, just as an excess of some humor was thought to be relieved by bloodletting. Bloodletting is more properly called "katharsis" than is inoculation, and it is a simple and readily understandable process. However, I find no evidence that Aristotle ever used "katharsis" or its cognates to refer to bloodletting.[58] Moreover, bloodletting is a mechanical process that is not obviously homeopathic. In fact, Samuel Hahnemann, the founder of "modern" homeopathy, vigorously attacked "the *allopathic* physician with his venesections."[59] Unless the bloodletting analogy can be integrated in a meaningful way into a homeopathic theory, all "katharsis by bloodletting" means is "the release of blood by bloodletting." This is tautological, and cannot be used to explain what might be meant by "the release of accumulated pity and fear by pity and fear experienced in the theatre."

Lucas changes from one metaphor to another when he compares tragic katharsis to an "emotional orgy" in which a "further stimulus in the same direction" is given. Using this analogy, katharsis would seem to be increase followed by relief, and not the simple relief involved in bloodletting. However, an orgy is no more obviously homeopathic than is bloodletting. The same process of arousal and release occurs, in less excessive form, in ordinary real-life situations, where we do not normally call it "homeopathic."[60]

A clearer explanation of homeopathy is given by Janko.

> By representing pitiable, terrifying and other painful events, tragedy arouses pity, terror and other painful emotions in the audience, for each according to his own emotional capacity, and so stimulates these emotions as to relieve them by giving them moderate and harmless exercise, thereby bringing the audience nearer to the mean in their emotional responses, and so nearer to virtue in their characters, and with this relief comes pleasure [61]

According to Janko, tragedy first arouses and stimulates emotion homeopathically, "just as we treat a fever by piling on blankets." This stimulation then leads to a "relief" consisting of "moderate exercise." This exercise "reduces" the emotions so that they are nearer to the mean.[62]

---

[58] On Aristotle's use of "katharsis" and its cognates, see chap 9

[59] Hahnemann, *Organon*, 8 n , emphasis added

[60] The kind of orgy Lucas has in mind is one of "enthusiasm " This topic is discussed in chap 9

[61] Janko, *Poetics I*, xix–xx

[62] Ibid , xix

Although this formulation has the advantages of precision and clarity, and of being based on an interpretation of specific ancient texts, I do not believe the theory it describes is Aristotelian. This observation, however, takes us to the next section, and to an examination of some of these ancient texts concerning katharsis.

HOMEOPATHY: THE ANCIENT EVIDENCE

Much of the ancient evidence concerning katharsis is extremely difficult to assess. Texts are fragmentary and obscure, the influence of a source on or by Aristotle is often impossible to prove, and much important information has been lost entirely. Although a detailed examination of the sources we do have is beyond the scope of this book, in the following limited study I argue that many of the texts that have been cited as sources or evidence for an Aristotelian homeopathic katharsis do not unequivocally support a homeopathic interpretation of the *Poetics*.

Scholars today generally agree that Greek medicine is a poor source for homeopathic tragic katharsis.[63] Antoine Thivel's authoritative study confirms this view. He shows that the (allopathic) principle of opposites dominated Greek medicine until around 430–420 B.C.E., when a new medical theory, based on the (homeopathic) principle of similars, began to be adopted in part.[64] There is abundant evidence for the allopathic "principle of opposites" throughout the Hippocratic corpus.[65] The new "principle of

[63] For example, D. W. Lucas, *Poetics*, 283; Carnes Lord, *Education*, 122; Halliwell, *Aristotle's Poetics*, 193 and n. 37.

[64] Thivel, *Cnide et Cos?* esp. 254–55. On the principle of similars and the principle of opposites, see also 252–71. It should be noted that Thivel places Aristotelian biology in the Empedoclean, or Sicilian, camp associated with the principle of similars, instead of in the older, Ionian camp associated with the principle of opposites (357–73). This view, however, depends largely on an analysis of "Anonymous of London," a work derived in part from a history of medicine written by Menon, a student of Aristotle (358). Because Thivel nowhere gives the kind of detailed analysis of passages in Aristotle's works that he provides for the Hippocratic corpus, his views on Aristotle are considerably less authoritative than are his views on the Hippocratic corpus. There is a good deal of evidence that Aristotle adhered to the principle of opposites.

[65] Some examples are: *Aphorisms* 22 (Littré 4:476): "Diseases that come from repletion are cured by emptying, and those that come from emptying [are cured by] repletion, and in other cases also, [by] opposition"; *Breaths* 1 (Littré 6:92): "Opposites are cures for opposites"; *Regimen* 40 (Littré 6:538): "Hot by nature attracts cold, and cold hot"; *On the Nature of Man* 9 (Littré 6:52): "To sum up, the doctor should oppose the established character of diseases . . . and loosen what is tight, and tighten what is loose"; *On the Nature of*

similars," however, is found in only a few Hippocratic treatises.[66] One of these, *On the Nature of Man*, contains a detailed account of homeopathic katharsis:

> For when the drug enters the body, it first withdraws that constituent of the body which is most akin to itself, and then it draws and purges [*kathairei*] the other constituents. For just as things that are sown and grow in the earth, when they enter it, draw each that constituent of the earth which is nearest akin to it—these are the acid, the bitter, the sweet, the salt and so on—first the plant draws to itself mostly that element which is most akin to it, and then it draws the other constituents also. Such too is the action of drugs in the body.[67]

This passage, however, gives no explanation of the nature of the kathartic process, and it is far from typical of Hippocratic medicine. In fact, the same treatise (*On the Nature of Man* 9 and 13) also contains clear statements of the allopathic principle.[68] Moreover, there are explicit statements in Aristotle's works that medical treatment is by means of opposites. The view that ancient medical theory served as a model for Aristotelian homeopathic katharsis is not supported by the evidence.

If ancient medical katharsis was primarily allopathic, the same appears to have been true of musical katharsis. The view, held by Augusto Rostagni in particular, that Aristotelian tragic katharsis had its source in a Pythagorean homeopathic musical katharsis has now been discredited.[69]

Man 13 (Littré 6.64) "One must cure by opposing the cause of the disease"; *Epidemics* 6.4 (Littré 5 316). "The cure [should] oppose, not agree with, the affliction", *Epidemics* 6.24 (Littré 5.352). "opposite regimes in disease", *Regimen in Health* 1 (Littré 6:74) "By opposing opposites prepare [to go] from summer to winter " For a more popular expression of the principle of opposites, see the statement of the physician Eryximachus in Plato, *Sym.* 186b6–7. "The unlike desires and loves the unlike", cf. 186d5–e1

[66] Thivel, *Cnide et Cos?* 292, lists *On the Nature of Man, Generation, Diseases IV, Eighth Month Child, Flesh,* and *Weeks,* but notes (254) that the new principle is always found mixed with the old.

[67] *On the Nature of Man* 6, W.H.S. Jones's translation, *Hippocrates,* 17 (Littré 6:44) This passage is discussed by Thivel, *Cnide et Cos?* 290–92, and Muller, *Gleiches,* 146. Muller, it should be noted, denies that the kind of katharsis in question here should be connected with katharsis in the *Poetics.* Like others, he believes that the origin of tragic katharsis should be sought in orgiastic ritual rather than in medicine (145 n. 127).

[68] See above, n 65

[69] The homeopathic view was argued for by Rostagni in "Aristotele" (e.g., 143. "magia omeopatico"), cf Koller, *Mimesis* (e.g., 100. "Homoiopathie"). A brief but informative and convincing refutation of the views of Rostagni and Koller is given by Carnes Lord, *Education,* 123 n. 33 Among others who have argued that Pythagorean katharsis was

Nevertheless, Rostagni's ideas are still of interest in two important respects. First, the view for which he argues, that Aristotelian katharsis is homeopathic in that it holds that "others' emotions" affect "our own emotions" by a sort of "sympathic imitation," has a good deal of inherent plausibility, and is still held today.[70] It is important to look closely at this idea, as it is expressed in some ancient sources. Second, Rostagni connects katharsis with a psychic *summetria* (proportion), mentioned in many ancient texts. This is also worth noting, for Aristotle's tragic katharsis does involve a *summetria*, though it is one produced by opposites rather than by similars.[71]

Religious enthusiasm is now taken to be the chief ancient parallel and model for homeopathic tragic katharsis. The primary evidence for this view is a passage in Aristotle's *Politics* 8, which, as I argue in chapter 9, can instead be interpreted allopathically. Another kind of religious katharsis has also been thought to provide a homeopathic source for Aristotelian katharsis: the use of sacrificial blood to cleanse pollution by blood.[72] Heraclitus notes and ridicules the homeopathic principle involved: "They are purified in vain with blood, those polluted with blood, as if someone who stepped in mud should try to wash himself with mud. Anyone who noticed him doing this would think he was mad."[73] This kind of purifi-

---

allopathic are Busse "Musikasthetik", Solmsen, review of Rostagni, *Poetica* (see above, "The Homeopathic Prejudice"), and Tate, review of Koller, *Mimesis*, 258–59. Stefanini, "Catarsi," 9, points out that, in contrast to Aristotle's ideal of emotional equilibrium, the Pythagoreans believed the emotions to be purely negative elements.

[70] Rostagni, "Aristotele," writes of "simpatia imitativa" (143), and of "others' emotions" (148). Janko, in arguing for the homeopathic interpretation, also relies heavily on statements in ancient sources that "others' emotions" affect our own See above, "Homeopathy. Theoretical Problems."

[71] In arguing that *summetria* is produced homeopathically, Rostagni, "Aristotele," cites (109) the *Tractatus Coislinianus*, and (107) Iamblichus, *On the Mysteries* 1 11 I argue below that these texts do not unequivocally support a homeopathic view of Aristotelian tragic katharsis In addition, Rostagni cites (149) a passage in Iamblichus, *Life of Pythagoras* 224, which, according to Carnes Lord (*Education*, 123 n. 33), "refers not to the homoeopathic effect of one kind of music, but to the allopathic effect of different kinds of music " Rostagni also cites (143) Aristoxenus, in Plutarch, *On Music* 43. This passage, as Busse points out ("Musikasthetik," 50 n 1), is, contrary to Rostagni's view, to be taken as evidence that Pythagorean musical theory was allopathic On *summetria*, see further below, chap 9

[72] Halliwell, *Aristotle's Poetics*, 193 n. 37, is one scholar who suggests this, citing Heraclitus, frag. 5 DK, and Plato, *Laws* 873a1 "like murder for like murder " See also Iphigenia's remark about the ritual purification of Orestes in Euripides, *IT* 1223–24 "so that I might wash out polluted blood with blood "

[73] Heraclitus, frag 5 DK (= 117 Kahn) I quote Kahn's translation in *Heraclitus*

cation, however, is not unequivocally homeopathic. While Heraclitus draws attention to the paradoxical, homeopathic aspects of purifying blood with blood, the ritual also has allopathic aspects, as a use of *sacred* blood to cleanse *profane* blood. Parker argues that "the homoeopathic idea of 'washing blood with blood' is a secondary development" in purification by animal sacrifice.[74] This is because "it was not the defiling power of blood in itself that made the ceremony effective," but the ritual context: "The original blood, profanely shed, clung to his [sc., the murderer's] hands, the animal blood, shed in ritual, may be wiped off or washed away."[75] Viewed in this way, purification by blood is allopathic. the sacred purifies the profane. In any case, this kind of purification is a poor source for Aristotelian tragic katharsis. Aristotle was, in general, little concerned with ritual purification of murder.[76] Moreover, ritual katharsis by means of sacrifice has little in common with emotional katharsis. There is, for example, no connection between the katharsis of pity and fear in *Poetics* 6 and the ritual katharsis of Orestes, said in *Poetics* 17 to be merely an episode in Euripides' *Iphigenia in Tauris* (1455b13–15).

Other scholars have claimed to find evidence that Aristotle held a homeopathic view of tragic katharsis in some later texts believed to have been influenced by his ideas. These texts include some passages in Iamblichus, Proclus, Olympiodorus, and the *Tractatus Coislinianus*.[77] While these sources provide us with some important information about ancient concepts of katharsis, they do not provide unequivocal evidence that Aristotelian katharsis was homeopathic.

Iamblichus gives the following account of a kathartic process.

> The potentialities of the human emotions that are in us become more violent if they are hemmed in on every side But if they are briefly put into activity and brought to the point of due proportion [*summetrou*], they give delight in moderation, are satisfied and, purified [*apokathairomenai*] by this means, are stopped by persuasion and not by force For this reason, by observing others'

---

[74] Parker, *Miasma*, 373

[75] Ibid , 234 In note 18, Parker cites Vickers, *Tragedy*, 142ff Vickers writes that "the sacred blood absorbs, decontaminates the profane blood" (143)

[76] For example, *Pol* 1262a32 merely mentions the "customary expiations" for kin-murder Contrast Plato's lengthy treatment of murder in *Laws* 9

[77] These texts are all relatively late Iamblichus, fourth century C E , Olympiodorus, sixth century C E , Proclus, fifth century C E , *Tractatus*, sixth century C E Another text concerning katharsis is papyrus 1581, found at Herculaneum and attributed to Philodemus On this document, see Janko, *Poetics I*, Sutton, "*P Herc* 1581," and Nardelli, "Catarsi "

emotions in both comedy and tragedy, we can check our own emotions, make them more moderate and purify them. (*On the Mysteries* 1 11)[78]

While this statement is unfortunately vague about the precise nature of the kathartic process involved,[79] it does give us some important information. Iamblichus seems to accept the view that ritual and dramatic katharsis are a kind of evacuation of emotion.[80] Like a dammed-up stream, the emotions grow more powerful when "hemmed in." But when small quantities are evacuated and drained off from time to time, the emotions become amenable to persuasion. The phrases "hemmed in" (εἰργόμεναι) and "put into activity" (εἰς ἐνέργειαν) suggest that katharsis is simply an evacuation, and give no suggestion of a homeopathic principle.

On the Mysteries 3.9 sheds further light on Iamblichus's concept of psychic katharsis. At 119.15–120.2, he vehemently denies that music produces a katharsis. Our response to music, Iamblichus writes, "should by no means be called a vomiting [ἀπέρασιν], or katharsis [ἀποκάθαρσιν], or cure. For this state does not originate in us like a disease or an excess or a superfluity." While Iamblichus denies that music produces a katharsis, he holds that psychic katharsis itself is like a vomiting or a medical purge (katharsis). Thus, 3.9 supports the view that the katharsis of 1.11 is also like evacuation or vomiting. This does not however, imply that Iamblichus's katharsis is homeopathic. Katharsis as evacuation (or bloodletting) is in itself neither homeopathic nor allopathic, but a simple mechanical operation that removes noxious material.

It is only the last sentence of *On the Mysteries* 1.11 (quoted above) that might seem to provide some evidence in favor of a homeopathic interpretation. Here, "others' emotions" (ἀλλότρια πάθη) are said to affect "our own emotions" (οἰκεῖα πάθη). According to Iamblichus, the observation of others' emotions at the theater leads us to experience similar emotions of our own, to put them into activity briefly and so to moderate them. If Iamblichus's source is Aristotelian, this homeopathic principle might help explain what Aristotle has in mind in *Poetics* 6: pity and fear aroused at the theater moderate and purify pity and fear.

There are, however, some serious objections to this view of Iamblichus's

[78] 39 14–40 5, Places I quote Janko's translation in *Poetics I* This passage is printed by Kassel, *De arte poetica*, among the "Fragmenta" of the *Poetics*

[79] As Sutton remarks, "this statement is more than somewhat obscure the precise nature of the passions thus to be purged, and the mechanism by which purgation is achieved, are scarcely specified" ("*P Herc* 1581," 275)

[80] In the previous paragraph, at least, Iamblichus is reporting his own views "we say' (38 14), "we think" (38 15), "we believe" (39 5)

statement. First, the connection between Iamblichus and the *Poetics* is doubtful, for Aristotle himself does not contrast "others' emotions" with "our own emotions" in the way Iamblichus does. Again, as Dana Sutton points out, Iamblichus is concerned with the attainment of a kind of "spiritual imperturbability" (*apathia*: 1.11.38.13),[81] which is certainly not Aristotle's ideal. Moreover, Iamblichus is concerned in this passage not with pity and fear, but with something very different: shameless emotions and shameful actions. Our passage occurs within the context of a discussion of the usefulness of obscenities in religious rituals. Iamblichus continues, immediately after the 1.11 passage, "And in sacred rites, by the sight and sound of shameful things, we are freed from the harm that comes from doing them" (1.11.40.5–8). In this context, Iamblichus may mean that tragedy, like comedy, represents shameful deeds (e.g., parricide and incest) and thus purifies our shameless emotions. This, however, tells us nothing about the role of pity and fear in tragic katharsis.

Another objection to using Iamblichus as evidence for a homeopathic Aristotelian theory of katharsis is that he does not describe the kathartic process clearly enough for us to be certain that he viewed it as either homeopathic or allopathic. In *On the Mysteries* 3.10, Iamblichus makes another statement about katharsis that has been thought to provide the relevant details. In writing about the Corybantes, Iamblichus opposes the view that states of possession are diseases:

> We will not say that certain bodily excesses, or those of the soul, require katharsis [*apokathairesthai*] when accumulated, nor that the cycles of the seasons are the causes of these kinds of affections [τῶν τοιούτων παθημάτων], nor will we say that the reception of the similar and the removal of the opposite [τὴν τοῦ ὁμοίου καταδοχὴν καὶ τὴν τοῦ ἐναντίου ἀφαίρεσιν] bring a healing of this kind of surplus. (3.10.122.12–17)

This passage is unusually obscure, and the commentators are of little help. Maria Luisa Nardelli takes it as evidence for a Pythagorean "duplice processo omeopatico-allopatico," and suggests that Aristotelian katharsis may also have been both homeopathic and allopathic. Unfortunately, she does not give a detailed account of her views.[82] Rostagni's more detailed explanation, on the other hand, is unclear and requires us to read a great deal into this passage. He cites it in arguing that Aristotelian katharsis "is not only, like many kinds of medical treatments, a 'removal of the oppo-

---

[81] Sutton, "*P. Herc.* 1581," 275.
[82] Nardelli, "Catarsi," 98 and n. 18.

site,' or a 'bringing around to the opposites'. but it is first of all a 'reception of the similar,' which means an absorption of emotions that are not real, but similar to the real ('likenesses,' Aristotle called them in the *Politics*)."[83] Rostagni probably intends to connect this passage with the 1.11 passage quoted above, which specifically mentions tragedy and comedy In that case, what he may mean is that others' emotions affect our own, because at the theater we experience a "reception of the similar"—that is, of the imitated emotions of others, which are likenesses of our own real emotions. It is doubtful, however, that the kathartic process used to cure possession in 3.10 is the same as the ritual and dramatic katharsis of 1 11. The contexts of the two passages are very different, and, indeed, Iamblichus rejects ("we will not say") the views expressed in 3.10, while he accepts the value of the kind of katharsis in question in 1.11 Moreover, 3.10 mentions an allopathic as well as a homeopathic process "removal of the opposite." It is not clear how both "reception of the similar" and "removal of the opposite" can be applicable to the dramatic katharsis in question in 1.11, and even if it were, there is no reason to give priority to "reception of the similar," as Rostagni's homeopathic interpretation requires.[84]

There are further objections to the view that Iamblichus's ideas on katharsis in *On the Mysteries* had an Aristotelian source. In the first place, Aristotle is not mentioned in the passages cited above Bywater argues that the language of 3.9, in which psychic katharsis is compared to a medical purge and vomiting, "completely . . harmonizes" with that of Aristotle's *Politics* 8, in which katharsis is also compared to a medical cure [85] However, I do not see more than a superficial similarity between these two expressions of the commonplace idea that katharsis is like a medical treatment. Moreover, Iamblichus's language in 1 11 is Platonic rather than Aristotelian The phrasing used by Iamblichus—ἀποπληροῦνται (are satisfied), ἀλλότρια πάθη θεωροῦντες (observing others' emotions), οἰκεῖα πάθη (our own emotions)—recalls that of *Republic* 10 606a–b, where Plato condemns the poet for satisfying the part of the soul that yearns "to be satisfied" (ἀποπλησθῆναι), when we "observe the emotions of others" (ἀλλότρια πάθη θεωροῦν), without realizing that others' emotions affect our own (τὰ οἰκεῖα).[86] Iamblichus seems to be setting up an argument that opposes Plato by stating that it is possible to produce a beneficial katharsis

[83] Rostagni, "Aristotele," 148–49 I translate the Greek phrases quoted by Rostagni
[84] On Rostagni's homeopathic views, see also above, nn 69–71
[85] Bywater, *Aristotle on the Art*, 157–58, discussing 3 9 119 15–120 2, quoted above
[86] Janko, *Poetics I*, 186, notes that Iamblichus echoes Plato

by relieving an excess Emotional satisfactions, the argument goes, provide an evacuation or draining of the emotions, instead of being the literal "filling" or increase that Plato's theory of poetry suggests While the theory Iamblichus presents may well be a reply to Plato, further evidence would be needed to show that it had a source in Aristotle's very different aesthetic views

It might, however, be argued that Proclus, who was in general much influenced by Iamblichus,[87] provides some indirect evidence that Iamblichus's view of katharsis as evacuation and vomiting had an Aristotelian source A kathartic theory of drama much like that discussed by Iamblichus is set out by Proclus

> *Commentary on Plato's Republic I*, p 42 Why does he [i e , Plato] not accept tragedy and the comic art in particular, when these conduce to the expiation [ἀφοσίωσιν] of the emotions? For it is neither possible to shut these out entirely, nor again safe to indulge [ἐμπιμπλάναι] them The emotions need some timely exercise, if this is provided by listening to these [kinds of poetry], it frees us from being troubled by them in the future   p 49 It has been objected that tragedy and comedy are expelled [from Plato's "Republic"] illogically, if by means of these [kinds of poetry] it is possible to satisfy [ἀποπιμπλάναι] the emotions in due measure, and, by satisfying them, to keep them tractable for education, by treating the ache in them Anyway, it was this that gave Aristotle, and the defenders of these [kinds of] poetry in their arguments against Plato,[88] most of the grounds for their accusation [against him] We will refute this [objection], in accord with what preceded, as follows   p 50 We too will say that the statesman should arrange for some vomitings of the emotions we mentioned, but not so that we intensify our clinging to them, but the opposite, so that we bridle them and restrain their stirrings fittingly Those kinds of poetry, then, with their immoderation in calling forth the emotions we mentioned, as well as their diversity, are far from being useful for the expiation [of the emotions] For expiations [of things] consist not in excesses [of them], but in restrained activities—which bear little resemblance to the things which they expiate [89]

[87] See Places, *Jamblique*, Notice, 23–26

[88] In translating in their arguments against Plato I depart from Janko, who translates in his dialogue against Plato See further below

[89] Janko s translation, *Poetics I*, 60, adapted as indicated in the previous note The bracketed English words are Janko s, I have added the bracketed Greek words In quoting Greek phrases I follow Kroll s text, as printed by Kassel, *De arte poetica*, with the Fragmenta of the *Poetics*

Proclus's view of "expiation" ("we too will say") seems similar to that of "Aristotle and the defenders of poetry," although unlike these people and Iamblichus (1.11), Proclus does not believe drama can provide this kind of katharsis (50). Proclus believes that emotional "expiation" involves moderate "exercise," and "satisfaction" (ἐμπιμπλάναι) a treatment of "the ache" in the emotions and "vomitings" (ἀπεράσεις) of them. His phrasing reminds us of Iamblichus's comparison of katharsis to a "vomiting" (ἀπέρασιν) and a cure in *On the Mysteries* 3.9, and of Iamblichus's account of katharsis as involving brief "activity" and moderate satisfaction (ἀποπληροῦνται) of the emotions in 1.11. Proclus, however, differs from Iamblichus in explicitly mentioning an educational goal of "expiation": "to keep them tractable for education" (49). As Janko points out, this idea is thoroughly Aristotelian.[90]

The similarities between the accounts of Proclus and Iamblichus, and the fact that Proclus was in general much influenced by Iamblichus, make it likely that Proclus's theory of "expiation" owes much to Iamblichus's theory of katharsis, or that they had a common source. Proclus's specific mention of Aristotle in this passage, then, gives us some reason to believe that both he and Iamblichus were influenced in some way by an Aristotelian source. Specifically, Janko believes, Proclus is referring to Aristotle's *On Poets*, and "the defenders of poetry" are the characters in this dialogue.[91] Proclus's statement, however, need not be read in this way. The reference on page 49, τοῖς ὑπὲρ τῶν ποιήσεων τούτων ἀγωνισταῖς τῶν πρὸς Πλάτωνα λόγων (literally, "to those in the speeches against Plato [who are] pleading on behalf of these {kinds of} poetry"), might be to *other* defenders of poetry who produced arguments against Plato. This appears to be Bywater's view.[92] It is possible that Proclus is including Aristotle with non-Aristotelian attackers of Plato without distinguishing among different views, or, as Bywater suggests, that he is reporting at second or third hand the views of Aristotle's followers.[93] The value of Proclus as evidence for an Aristotelian evacuative-education theory of katharsis is questionable.

[90] Janko, *Poetics I*, xviii–xix.
[91] Ibid., 186, "Testimonium C." Janko's translation of Proclus, p. 49, "in his dialogue against Plato," reflects this interpretation.
[92] Bywater, *Aristotle on the Art*, 158: "His reference, however, to other apologists for the Drama may make one hesitate to believe him to have found it for himself in the now lost Second Book of the Poetics." See also Gudeman's arguments (*Aristoteles*, 170) against taking Proclus's statement to reflect Aristotle's own views in our *Poetics* or in Aristotle's *On Poets*.
[93] Bywater, *Aristotle on the Art*, 158.

In any case, whether or not Proclus had an Aristotelian source, his statements provide no evidence that he held a homeopathic view of "expiation " Unlike Iamblichus, Proclus does not contrast "others' emotions" with "our own emotions " Moreover, Proclus explicitly denies that "expiations" of the emotions are homeopathic, for the last sentence in the passage quoted above states that expiations consist in restrained activities that have "little resemblance [σμικρὰν ὁμοιότητα] to the things which they expiate "[94]

The foregoing analysis allows us to arrive at some tentative conclusions about the views of Iamblichus and Proclus Iamblichus connects the process by means of which others' emotions affect our own in drama with an evacuation theory of katharsis (*On the Mysteries* 1 11), and in 3 9 he compares katharsis to a ' vomiting " This kind of katharsis is not clearly homeopathic or allopathic Some support for the theory that Iamblichus held a homeopathic view of katharsis might be sought in his distinction between "others' emotions" and "our own emotions" in 1 11, and in his mention of "the reception of the similar" in 3 10 On the other hand, Iamblichus also mentions an allopathic "removal of the opposite" in 3 10, and his views on how others' emotions affect our own are not clearly stated Proclus's views are somewhat clearer This philosopher, in a work that may well have been influenced by Iamblichus, calls "expiation" a "vomiting," and he denies that the "expiation" of the emotions is homeopathic It is possible, then, that both Iamblichus and Proclus are discussing a theory of dramatic katharsis in which others' emotions affect our own in a process of evacuation or "vomiting" that is not homeopathic Linguistic similarities between Proclus and Plato, as well as Proclus's explicit mention of attackers of Plato, point to a response to Plato as the source for this theory Although Proclus mentions Aristotle, his views on this philosopher are not specific or detailed enough to provide reliable evidence for Aristotle's actual views

Olympiodorus provides some indication that the kathartic theory found in Proclus and Iamblichus was neither homeopathic nor allopathic, and that it may have had its source in a non-Aristotelian opponent of Plato Olympiodorus lists three kinds of katharseis an allopathic "Stoic" or "Aristotelian" katharsis that "cures evil with evil,"[95] a "Socratic" homeopathic

---

[94] I owe this observation to Richard Janko The view that Proclus did not have a homeo pathic theory of expiation accords well with Moutsopoulos s claim that Proclus followed Plato in holding an allopathic theory of katharsis Nausee, 77

[95] Olympiodorus, *Alcibiades* 54 18 While Olympiodorus does not call the Stoic katharsis Aristotelian in this passage, it is clear from the close parallel at 146 3–4 that the two are identical See further below, chap 9 (Iron and Wood)

katharsıs that "derıves sımılars from sımılars" (ἀπὸ τῶν ὁμοίων ἐπὶ τὰ ὅμοια μετάγει: 55.8–9), and a "Pythagorean" katharsıs. Thıs last kınd of katharsıs "bıds us gıve ın to the emotıons a lıttle, and to taste them wıth a fingertıp; whıch the doctors call 'less than a lıttle.' For they saıd that those ınflamed wıth some emotıon wıll not get rıd of ıt before they act ın accord wıth ıt."[96] Olympıodorus would appear to have thıs "Pythagorean" katharsıs ın mınd when he wrıtes that those who defend tragedy agaınst Plato say that "ıt does not allow ınflamed emotıons to remaın ın us, but calls them forth and casts them out" (*Gorgıas* 157.12–14). Thıs "Pythagorean" katharsıs, whıch Olympıodorus contrasts wıth "Arıstotelıan" katharsıs, ıs very sımılar to the evacuatıve katharsıs of Proclus and Iamblıchus: both provıde "moderate actıvıty" of the emotıons. Olympıodorus, lıke Proclus, attrıbutes thıs vıew to the defenders of poetry agaınst Plato, and they use the same term to refer to the "callıng forth" of the emotıons προκαλεῖται (Olympıodorus, *Gorgıas* 157 13), προκλήσεσι (Proclus, *Commentary on Plato's Republıc I*, p. 50, Kroll). Accordıng to Olympıodorus, "Pythagorean" katharsıs ıs sımply an evacuatıon Olympıodorus, moreover, contrasts ıt wıth both homeopathıc "Socratıc" katharsıs and allopathıc "Arıstotelıan" katharsıs. All of thıs gıves us some reason to belıeve that ıt ıs not Arıstotle, but Olympıodorus's Pythagorean defenders of poetry agaınst Plato, who are the common source for Iamblıchus and Proclus.

Janko, ın *Arıstotle on Comedy*, has recently called attentıon to another possıble source of ınformatıon about Arıstotelıan katharsıs the *Tractatus Coıslınıanus*, whıch, Janko claıms, gıves us a summary of Arıstotle's *Poetıcs II*. *Tractatus III*, ın Janko's translatıon (23), states. "Tragedy removes the mınd's emotıons of fear [ὑφαιρεῖ τὰ φοβερὰ παθήματα] by means of pıty and terror. . . It aıms to have a due proportıon of fear." Janko wrıtes that thıs passage "puts ınto clear relıef the stark and ınescapable fact of homoeopathy, that pıty and fear do cast out the devıls of pıty and fear ın theır own name" (144). Thıs ınterpretatıon and thıs translatıon requıre us to take τὰ φοβερὰ παθήματα ın the passıve sense, as Janko poınts out. " 'feelıngs of fear,' not 'feelıngs ınspırıng fear' "[97] Certaınly the actıve sense would be odd here, and φοβερός can have a passıve sense [98] Arıstotle, however, always uses the term ın the actıve sense ın the *Poetıcs*, of

---

[96] 55 1–5 See also 145 20–146 2 for a repetıtıon of thıs ıdea ın sımılar words

[97] Janko, *Comedy*, 136 The ambıguıty of L Cooper's translatıon, 'fearful emotıons,' ıs preferable (*Comedy*, 224)

[98] See LSJ, s v φοβερός, II Janko mıstakenly cıtes (*Comedy*, 136) *Rhet* 2 5 1382b7 as a parallel for thıs passıve sense

events that cause fear.[99] His view is that "imitation of fearful [φοβερῶν] and pitiable events" (1452a2–3) produces the pity and fear of the audience that accomplish katharsis. The phrasing of the *Tractatus*, then, while it does suggest a homeopathic view of tragic katharsis, is significantly different from that of the *Poetics*.[100] On the other hand, the "due proportion [*summetria*] of fear" mentioned by the *Tractatus* is likely to have an Aristotelian source. Janko calls attention to Olympiodorus's mention of a *summetria* in connection with an "Aristotelian" katharsis in which evil cures evil "by means of the strife of opposites."[101] However, in dismissing the "strife of opposites" as a "new and unparalleled element, probably imported from Stoic theory" (147), Janko fails to take into account the numerous Aristotelian parallels. The concept of *summetria* is important in Aristotle's biological and ethical works, where it is connected with a balance of *opposing* qualities; that is, *summetria* is associated with an allopathic rather than a homeopathic principle. While Janko's arguments are ingenious, he has not demonstrated that the *Tractatus* provides reliable evidence for a homeopathic tragic katharsis in Aristotle's *Poetics*.

I have argued that the homeopathic interpretation of Aristotelian tragic katharsis should be much more closely examined and questioned before it is assumed to be correct. This view is implausible in itself, and has difficulty giving a clear and detailed account of the kathartic process involved. Moreover, much of the ancient evidence cited in favor of this view does not unequivocally support it. Ancient medical and musical katharsis were entirely or primarily allopathic, not homeopathic, and ritual katharsis by means of sacrifice has little in common with emotional katharsis. Nor do passages in Proclus, Iamblichus, Olympiodorus, and the *Tractatus Coislinianus* provide clear and reliable evidence for an Aristotelian theory of homeopathic tragic katharsis. It would seem, in fact, that scholars already biased in favor of homeopathy have been too ready to find support for their views where the evidence is unclear or ambiguous. Until more conclusive evidence, based on a more objective appraisal of sources, is brought forward, the case for homeopathy remains unproved.

[99] The term φοβερός and its cognates occur in the *Poetics* in this sense at 1452a2, 1452b32, 1452b36, 1453a1, 1453a6, and 1453b1 They also occur frequently in this sense in the discussion of fear in *Rhet* 2 5, see esp 1382b26–27

[100] In other respects also, the *Tractatus* is less Aristotelian than Janko believes See Belfiore, review of *Comedy*

[101] Janko, *Comedy*, 147, citing *Alcibiades* 146 3 *Summetria* is also mentioned by other ancient writers see above, n 71

The allopathic interpretation also presents difficulties, particularly in connection with Aristotle's statement about katharsis in *Poetics* 6, a difficulty shared, as noted above, by the homeopathic reading However, the evidence for an allopathic principle of opposites is much more abundant, both in Aristotle and in other ancient writers, than is the evidence for a homeopathic principle of similars Ancient writers more frequently held the (allopathic) view that unlike acts on unlike because it is unlike than the (homeopathic) view that like acts on like because it is like An allopathic reading of *Poetics* 6 is also plausible in itself There are, moreover, definite parallels to an allopathic tragic katharsis in other clearly described allopathic processes In chapter 9, I examine the evidence in favor of allopathy by studying Aristotle's concepts of physical and psychic katharsis I also examine some significant connections between Aristotle's views and those of other ancient writers This more general study will put us in a better position to understand tragic katharsis [102]

[102] I am indebted to Richard Janko for criticisms of an earlier draft of this chapter, and for helpful discussions of the issues involved

Katharsis in Aristotle's Philosophy

O NE OF THE CHIEF OBSTACLES to a study of Aristotle's views on tragic katharsis is the lack of information about this subject. Aristotle gives no explanation of tragic katharsis in the *Poetics*, nor do his other works contain detailed accounts of emotional katharsis. The clearest account of a process of psychic katharsis in Aristotle's works is a discussion of musical katharsis in *Politics* 8 (1341b32–1342a16). This passage, however, instead of giving a detailed explanation of katharsis, refers us, frustratingly, to an account (now lost) in "the works on poetry" (1341b39–40).

In spite of this lack of direct information, however, we can learn a great deal from more indirect sources, such as passages in other writers and related material in Aristotle's own works. "Katharsis" and its cognates occur with great frequency in Aristotle's works, and computer searches now allow us to examine with ease all these occurrences, giving us some important information, especially concerning biological katharsis, that was not available to earlier scholars. We can also learn much from passages in Aristotle's works about "pure" (*kathara*) states of soul, and about psychic treatments generally. The philosophical tradition of which Aristotle was a part provides additional relevant information. I argue in this chapter that an examination of all this material allows us to draw some plausible inferences. First, when Aristotelian physical katharsis is an interactive process, instead of a simple evacuation or drainage, it is effected by means of opposites rather than by means of similars. Because it works according to the "principle of opposites," it should be called allopathic rather than homeopathic, even though it may also have certain aspects that moderns might call homeopathic.[1] Second, Aristotelian psychic katharsis is analogous to an allopathic medical katharsis that removes material harmful to the body. Passages in a number of ancient works suggest that this analogy was widely accepted by other philosophers as well as by Aristotle.

---

[1] This point is discussed in chap. 8 ("Homeopathy. Theoretical Problems").

OVERVIEW

This chapter begins with a brief survey of the concept of katharsis in Aristotle and other Greek writers, especially Plato, and of Aristotle's use of "katharsis" and its cognates

Some statistics provide illuminating background information A computer search shows that "katharsis" and its cognates occur 161 times in Aristotle's unquestionably authentic works [2] The vast majority, 128, are in the biological works, if not always in biological contexts 50 are in the *Generation of Animals*, 51 in the *History of Animals*, 14 in the *Parts of Animals*, and 13 in the *Parva naturalia* An additional 45 occurrences are in the medical *Problems*, a work of doubtful authenticity that nevertheless contains many Aristotelian ideas [3] These statistics indicate that Aristotelian katharsis is primarily a biological and medical concept 'Katharsis" words occur especially frequently in connection with reproduction In 59 occurrences (29 in the *Generation of Animals*, and 30 in the *History of Animals*), "katharsis" and its cognates are used to refer to, or in close connection with, the evacuation of the menstrual fluid (*katamēnia*) or of other female reproductive material [4] These fifty-nine occurrences comprise more than one-third of all the occurrences of "katharsis' and its cognates in Aristotle's genuine works In contrast, while the semen is itself "pure" (*GA* 737a29, 765b36, *HA* 635b29), the emission of semen is never, with one possible exception (noted below, in ' Katharsis of the *Katamēnia* '), called a "katharsis" in Aristotle's unquestionably authentic works "Katharsis" is also used of medical purges (e g , in *Meta* 1013b1, *Phy* 194b36, *Prob* 864a34, and *HA* 594a29, where it is used of sick dogs purging themselves by eating grass and vomiting) However, ' katharsis" is never used in Aristotle's works of the natural evacuation, unaided by

---

[2] This includes all the occurrences of the lemmata -καθαιρ-, -καθαρ-, -καθηρ- (exclusive of those derived from αἱρέω) given by Ibycus I adopt Barnes s classification, in the *Oxford Translation*, of genuine, doubtful, and spurious works, ignoring, unless otherwise noted, the occurrences in the fragments and in the spurious works (*On the Universe, On Breath, On Things Heard, Physiognomonics, On Marvelous Things Heard, On Virtues and Vices*) I do, however, take into account occurrences in the doubtful *Problems*, because of the intrinsic interest of this work, and because it often reflects Aristotelian ideas

[3] One of these passages, *Prob* 888a17, presents textual difficulties Bekker s text, followed by Ibycus, reads ἀποκάθαρσις, while Ruelle and other editors read ἀποκατάστασις On this textual problem, see Flashar, *Problemata*, 494

[4] Lear, *Katharsis*, 298, asks why no one has suggested the model of menstruation for tragic katharsis This idea deserves more serious consideration than Lear gives it

drugs, of excrement or urine.[5] This distinction between katharsis and natural evacuation is apparent at *History of Animals* 578a3, where Aristotle notes that the mule, according to some, "menstruates [*kathairetai*] while urinating."

A survey of Aristotle's use of "katharsis" and its cognates can also help settle a long-standing dispute about the nature of the genitive in Aristotle's definition of tragedy: περαίνουσα τὴν τῶν τοιούτων παθημάτων κάθαρσιν ("accomplishing the katharsis of such emotions": *Po.* 1449b27–28). In the few parallels in Aristotle's works, nouns in the genitive governed by "katharsis" and cognates refer to what is separated from something else. Uncompounded nominal forms of "katharsis" govern the genitive in only three passages other than *Poetics* 1449b27–28: καθάρσεως τῶν περιττωμάτων ("katharsis of the residues": *GA* 738a29); ἡ τῶν καταμηνίων κάθαρσις ("katharsis of the *katamēnia*": *GA* 774a1); καθάρσεις . . . καταμηνίων ("katharseis . . . of the *katamēnia*": *HA* 572b29). In all these occurrences, a word for the material that is separated from something else is put in the genitive case (i.e., "katharsis of [that is, consisting in the removal of] the *katamēnia* [from the body]"). These parallels suggest that in the *Poetics* also, "katharsis of such emotions" is likely to mean "katharsis consisting in the removal of such emotions."[6]

Additional important background information is provided by a survey of the concept of katharsis in Greek writers other than Aristotle. Many scholars have explored the meaning of "katharsis" in the Greek language generally.[7] Golden has shown that the adjective *katharos* means "clean" or

---

[5] Aristotelian usage differs in this respect from that of the Hippocratic corpus, if Moulinier is correct. He cites *Epidemics* 5, no. 34, and *Prenotations of Cos* 15, no 297, and 19, no 371, for instances of "katharsis" referring to "natural defecation" (*Pur*, 159 n. 3). While it is true that excretion is not drug-induced, these passages, like most of the Hippocratic corpus, deal with diseased states, more research would be required to determine whether "katharsis" is indeed used of *healthy* excretion by "Hippocrates."

[6] Aristotle's use of ἀπο- compounds proves the rule that "katharsis" in its uncompounded form does not take a genitive of the subject from which something is removed. See *HA* 568b9 ἀπὸ δὲ τῶν γονίμων ᾠῶν, αὐξανομένων τῶν ἰχθυδίων, ἀποκαθαίρεται οἷον κέλυφος ("From the fertile eggs, as the small fishes grow, a sort of sheath is thrown off". Peck), and *HA* 624a15· mitys (a substance used by bees) is "a by-product [separated] from wax" (ἀποκάθαρμ[α] . . . τοῦ κηροῦ). It is best to avoid applying the terms "subjective," "objective," or "separative" to the genitive governed by "katharsis," since these terms are used confusingly and inconsistently in the literature, where it is not always clear exactly what is being "separated" or "purged" or "purified" from what. Bywater's characterization is unusually clear and accurate. "the genitive after κάθαρσις, denoting the object purged away or removed" (*Aristotle on the Art*, 156)

[7] The most valuable and comprehensive word and concept study is still that of Mouli-

"clear" in a physical or intellectual sense, while "katharsis" refers to an act of making clear or to the process of clarification.[8] Daniel White finds three groups of "literal" meanings of "katharsis" and its cognates. "physical cleanliness," "freedom from admixture," and "spatial clarity or freedom from obstruction."[9] Nussbaum follows Golden in holding that the "central meaning" of katharsis is that of " 'clearing up' or 'clarification', i.e. of the removal of some obstacle (dirt, or blot, or obscurity, or admixture) that makes the item in question less *clear* than it is in its proper state."[10] Nussbaum's phrasing, "less *clear* than it is in its proper state," suggests that the concept of katharsis involves not only the idea of the removal of an obstacle, but also that of the "proper state" of something. These ideas are interdependent, for what is taken to be an obstacle depends on what one believes the "proper state" of something to be Other scholars have had similar insights. Harvey Goldstein writes that katharsis is not only "a taking-away process," but also "a concomitant shaping process."[11] According to Halliwell, "Aristotle's notion of psychological *katharsis* combines an element of release with a sense of the improved or refined state of what remains."[12] Stephen Salkever, who notes the importance of Plato's *Sophist* for an understanding of Aristotelian katharsis, writes that Platonic katharsis is "a process of restoring or transforming a thing so that it becomes properly or naturally itself," and that "the process . . is not one of removal, but of giving the soul its proper form or order "[13] Finally, Louis Moulinier argues, on the basis of an extensive study of "katharsis" and its cognates in Aristotle and other Greek writers, that "katharsis" in medicine and elsewhere means either "evacuation of harmful or excess material" or the "reestablishment of an order and harmony." "Katharsis" in the *Poetics*, he believes, has the latter sense.[14]

---

nier, *Pur*, especially chap 3, 149–76, and chap 5 See also Lain Entralgo, *Therapy*, 127–38, and White, "Sourcebook," who attempts to give ' an account of all of the forms and meanings of the *kathar-* root from Homer through Aristotle" (v)

[8] Golden, "Catharsis," 55–57, "Clarification," 444–45

[9] White, "Sourcebook," 1

[10] Nussbaum, *Fragility*, 389, emphasis in original

[11] Goldstein, "Mimesis," 575 Goldstein, however, bases his view on the argument that "catharsis comes from the verb *kathaira* [sic] which refers to the pruning of trees and vines," and that "pruning is both a taking-away and a shaping, a way of making material usable " In connecting tragic katharsis with pruning in this way, Goldstein follows DeWitt, "Katharsis," who relies heavily (110) on evidence from the New Testament John 15 2

[12] Halliwell, *Aristotle's Poetics*, 198

[13] Salkever, "Tragedy," 283, 284

[14] Moulinier, *Pur*, 411, cf esp 166–67

Modern scholarship, then, has demonstrated that "katharsis" in Greek thought generally involves not only a removal but also a "reestablishment of order," a "shaping" process, or one that removes obstacles to a thing's "proper state." A study of individual passages, especially those in the Platonic corpus, can help us be more specific about the Greek concept of katharsis.

The process of katharsis in Greek thought is, in the first place, one of separating. For example, "Plato," *Definitions* 415d4, defines "katharsis" as "a separation [*apokrisis*] of the worse from the better." This passage and Plato's *Sophist* show that the concepts of katharsis and separation were closely associated in Greek thought generally. This is true even though a computer search reveals that an association between the terms "katharsis" and *krisis* (separation, judgment) and their respective cognates is rare in Greek writers, at least through the fourth century B.C.E., except in the works of Plato and Aristotle and in the Hippocratic corpus.[15]

Definitions 415d4 also supports the view, discussed above, that katharsis involves more than mere removal. To separate "worse" from "better" is to clear something up, to remove an obstacle, to distinguish good from bad. In many cases, the idea of separation of bad from good involves a very specific concept of what the good for something is. In the typical Aristotelian biological cases, what is good for something depends on what its *phusis* is. In these cases, when the bad has been separated from the good, something is not merely "clear," it is, to use Plato's expression, "purest *by nature*" (*Philebus* 55c7).[16]

That katharsis involves separation of worse from better is also clear from Plato's *Sophist* 226–31. Plato begins by pointing out that a number of processes, such as sifting, straining, winnowing, threshing, carding, and spinning, all involve division (*diairetika.* 226c3), and that all are included within "the separative craft" (*technēn . . . diakritikēn.* c6–8). He then distinguishes two kinds of separation. one that separates like from like and has no name (226d2–5), and one that separates worse from better, "leaving behind the better . . . and casting out the worse" (226d5–6) The latter process, Plato writes, "is said by everyone to be a kind of purification [*katharmos*]" (226d9–10). This account of purification as a kind of separa-

---

[15] Two exceptions, in which the two terms are associated in the works of other writers, are Gorgias s *Defense of Palamedes* (DK B11a 35), where judgment is said to be easy when the truth of the facts is "pure," and Xenophon, *Education of Cyrus* 8 7 20 3, where the intelligence is said to be "pure" when separated from the body On *krisis* and its cognates in Greek medicine, see Thivel, *Cnide et Cos* 180–81

[16] Plato, of course, does not share Aristotle s biologically based concept of *phusis*

tion is clearly intended to be noncontroversial, a reflection of ordinary usage: this "is said by everyone " Finally, at 231b3, Plato writes of "the kathartic [craft that is a subdivision] of the separative [craft]" (cf. 227a1 *diakrinomena kathairetai*).

Katharsis is also a kind of separation in *Timaeus* 52e–53a Here, the separation (*diakrimonena*. 52e6) of the elements in cosmogony is compared to the purification (*katharsis* 52e7) of grain, and both processes are said to separate like from unlike (53a4–6). Again, in *Statesman* 303d6–10, Plato writes that those who purify (*kathairousin*) gold separate (*apokrinousi*) earth and stones from it. That katharsis involves separation is also apparent in a number of passages in Plato where forms of the adjective *katharos* or the noun *katharotēs* (purity) are closely associated with *eilikrinēs* (unmixed).[17]

Two other points about Plato's concept of katharsis should be noted First, in several passages, Plato makes a connection between an intellectual discrimination (*krisis*) and katharsis It is easier to judge something when it is pure (*katharon*), he writes at *Philebus* 52d10–e4 and 55c6–9 Again, at *Republic* 361d4–6, Socrates jokes that Glaucon has been "cleaning up [*ekkathaireis*] for the judging" each of the two kinds of people being discussed, as though they were statues. The psychic katharsis of *Sophist* 230b–d also involves intellectual discrimination, although Plato uses words other than *krisis*.[18] Second, in Plato and in other writers, as scholars have pointed out, katharsis often implies not only a separation of bad from good, but also a *restoration* of a natural, good state This concept of a restoration of order is particularly important in the treatment of disease with medical katharsis. In *Laws* 1.628d, for example, Plato writes of the absurdity of believing that a sick body that has gotten medical katharsis is in the best possible state, while paying no attention to a body that needs no katharsis in the first place.

The idea of separation is central to Aristotle's concept of katharsis, as it is to Plato's. In Aristotle's works, "katharsis" and *krinō* (to separate, to discriminate) and their cognates and compounds (including *eilikrinēs*) occur frequently in close association.[19] In some passages, no conceptual dis-

---

[17] *Phaedo* 67a6–b2, *Philebus* 52d6–7, 53a5–8, 59c3, *Sym* 211e1 The word *eilikrinēs* is derived etymologically from *krino* and (probably) from *eilē* (sunlight or sun heat) see Frisk, **Worterbuch**, and Chantraine, *Dictionnaire*

[18] Golden calls attention to the importance of this passage as evidence for an intellectual sense of "katharsis" in "Clarification, 444

[19] They are closely associated at *GA* 727a5–18, 728b2–3, 738a27–29, 744a9, 765b35–36, 773b35–774a1, 775b5–8, 781a18–20, 781b2–3, 783b29–30, *HA* 583a2–4,

tinction can be made between the two terms. In *Meteorology* 340b8–9 and *Problems* 907a39–b1, the *katharon* cannot be distinguished from the *eilikrinēs*. At *Metaphysics* 989b14–16, the *katharon* is indistinguishable from the unmixed (*amigē*, cf. *DA* 405a17), and what is unmixed appears to be what is separated (*apekekrito*). In *Problems* 883b34–36, bodily katharsis cannot be distinguished from the separation (*apokekritai*) of the residues. At *Generation of Animals* 775b5–8, the katharsis of the *katamēnia* is indistinguishable from their *ekkrisis*. However, other passages make it clear that the relationship between the two terms is not simply one of synonymy. *History of Animals* 583a1–4 shows that *ekkrisis*, referring to the evacuation of urine, is a more inclusive term than *katharsis*, which refers specifically to menstruation in this passage, and which, as we have seen, is never used by Aristotle to refer to the natural evacuation of urine and excrement.

Aristotle also resembles Plato in viewing katharsis as a separation of what is bad or harmful from what is good or beneficial. Aristotelian katharsis, like Greek katharsis generally, always benefits that from which something is separated.[20] In the most common kind of Aristotelian katharsis, the *katamēnia* is evacuated, and this consists of residues that can cause disease, as Aristotle tells us at *Generation of Animals* 738a27–30 and 775b5–17. In medical purges, disease-causing material is evacuated. In another kind of katharsis, undesirable people are separated from the city (*Ath. Pol* 1.1.4), in refining metals, dross is separated from pure iron (*Meteor.* 383a34–b1).

That katharsis is a separation of bad from good is also evident from an examination of Aristotle's use of adjectival and adverbial forms of "katharsis." The process of katharsis renders something *katharon*,[21] and what is *katharon* has no admixture of harmful or obstructing material. The adjectival forms of "katharsis" are used of clean clothing (*GA* 780b31), clear sight (*GA* 780b32–33), clean water (*HA* 595b30), clean beehives (*HA* 623b27), and, by transference, the cleanliness of bees, who clean their hives (*HA* 626a25). They are also used of a clear mirror (*On Dreams* 459b28), a marketplace clear of merchandise (*Pol.* 1331a33), and bare rocks (*Prob.* 935a14). Water mixed with mud is not *kathara* (*Prob.* 935b25). Intellectual katharsis also involves the idea of separation of ob-

---

587b33–588a1, *Meta* 989b14–16, *Meteor* 340b8–9, *Prob* 878a7–8, 883b34–36, 907a39–b1, 933b27–28, 941a1–4, *Rhet* 1414a14, *On Sleep* 458a12–13, and 458a21–23

[20] Moulinier, *Pur*, 165–67, makes this point about Greek katharsis

[21] As Golden notes *Katharsis*, like other nouns in Greek ending in -*sis*, signifies an activity and means the process of making something *katharos* ("Catharsis," 55) Of course, something may also be *katharon* without having first undergone katharsis

structive material. This is apparent in the three instances in which the adjectival or adverbial forms of "katharsis" are used of intellectual matters in Aristotle's works. In *Prior Analytics* 50a40, arguments are examined and marked out *katharōs* (clearly); in *Rhetoric* 1356b27, distinctions are defined and drawn *katharōs* (clearly), and in *Rhetoric* 1414a12–14, a judgment (*krisis*) is *kathara* (clear) when relevant is distinguished from irrelevant material.

Aristotle's concept of katharsis resembles that of Plato and other Greek writers in other respects. First, it often involves the idea of restoration of a good, healthy state. This is particularly true of medical katharsis, discussed, for example, in *Problems* 1.41–43 and 47. Second, just as in other Greek writers the idea of separation of bad from good can involve a very specific concept of what the good for something is, so in Aristotle the idea of katharsis often involves a specific concept of what belongs to a particular thing, and of what is foreign to it. This is apparent in *Rhetoric* 1414a12–14. The style of oratory used when arguing before a single judge, Aristotle writes, is more "exact" than other styles, for in this case "what belongs to the matter and what is foreign to it are more easily seen together, and there is no debate, so that judgment is *kathara*." That is, judgment is *kathara* when what is irrelevant to a particular subject matter is easily separated, intellectually, from what is relevant to it.

Aristotle differs significantly from other writers in one way, however. His concept of katharsis is sometimes closely connected with a specific concept of what belongs to a *phusis* of a particular kind. This is especially true in medical and other biological contexts, where "katharsis" and its cognates occur most often. Medical katharsis, as I argue below, helps restore the healthy state proper to the *phusis* of the body by removing material that is foreign and harmful to this nature. A passage in *Problems* illuminates this Aristotelian idea:

> Why is it that, if a living thing comes to be from our seed, this is our offspring, but if from some other part, or from an excretion [*apokriseōs*], it is not ours? For many things [come to be] from decaying things and from the seed. Why, then, if it is such as we are, is it ours, but if it is foreign [*allotrion*], not? For [it would seem that] either everything or nothing [that comes from us] belongs to us. Is it because, first, in this way it comes to be from what is ours, but in that way from what is foreign, as when things come to be from what is purged [*apokatharmatos*] or excreted [*ekkriseōs*]? And in general, nothing of a living thing generates a living thing, except the seed And what is harmful and bad is proper [*oikeion*] to nothing, nor is what is foreign.

For it is not the same thing to be [a part] of something and to be foreign to it, or other than it, or bad And excretions and putrefactions are not our own, but other and foreign to our nature For not everything that comes to be in the body should be set down as [part] of the body, since even tumors come to be [in it], which people remove and cast out And in general, all that is contrary to nature is foreign (*Prob* 878a1–16)

The author of this passage distinguishes between what is purged {*apokatharmatos*} or excreted as foreign to the body, and what is also expelled from the body but nevertheless "belongs to" it the seed Significantly, in this passage, matter that is "foreign" is matter that is "foreign to our nature" or "contrary to nature " In physical katharsis, then, matter foreign and harmful to the biological nature of something is removed

The emphasis in this passage on the idea of the biological nature of something is thoroughly Aristotelian According to *Nicomachean Ethics* 1104a18, proportionate amounts of food and drink "produce, increase, and preserve" the physical excellence of health In other words, they contribute to the "completion" or "perfection" (*teleiōsis*) of the body, for, according to *Physics* 246a13–15, excellence is a kind of *teleiōsis* in which something is most what it is in accordance with its nature Just as the consumption of proportionate amounts of food and drink contributes to physical excellence, so biological katharsis, by removing what is harmful to the nature of something, helps preserve or restore the excellence that is in accord with this nature This concept of katharsis is apparent in *Generation of Animals* 738a27–30, where Aristotle writes that, in menstruation and "whites"[22] "the secretions [*apokriseis*] of residues preserve bodies, for they are a katharsis of residues that cause sickness in bodies " Aristotelian biological katharsis not only helps make the body "pure" and "unmixed" with material harmful to its nature, it also helps preserve the body in the "complete" or "perfect" state that is most in accord with its nature, or to restore it to this state

It appears that biological katharsis in Aristotle involves a combination of the two processes that are separated in Moulinier's account of the "two senses" of physiological katharsis "evacuation" of something harmful, and the "maintenance" or "reestablishment of an equilibrium "[23] Aristotelian

---

[22] Whites are leukorrhea, according to Balme, *De partibus animalium*, on *GA* 727b33–728a14 This is a pathological condition, apparently confused by Aristotle with a normal discharge

[23] Moulinier, *Pur*, 165 Moulinier sometimes writes, as here, of a *maintenance* or *reestablishment* of order, sometimes of a *production* or *reestablishment* of order (167), and sometimes

biological katharsis is a process of removing what prevents something from preserving or regaining the excellence, the completion, that is in accord with its nature. In the next section, I argue that this account of katharsis is most in accord with Aristotle's biological views. Then, in "Psychic Katharsis," I argue that this biological concept of katharsis can also help us understand Aristotle's elusive concept of psychic katharsis. In psychic as in physical katharsis, the idea of the preservation or restoration of the excellence proper to the nature of the soul is as important as that of evacuation of what is harmful. Physical and psychic katharsis help preserve or restore a *summetria* proper to the nature of body and soul. In psychic katharsis, however, katharsis can also contribute to the production of excellence in the first place, by means of habituation.

Physical Katharsis

Katharsis of the Katamēnia

Aristotle uses "katharsis" and its cognates most often to refer to, or in close connection with, the evacuation of the *katamēnia* (menstrual fluid) or of other female reproductive material. If this is not merely an accident, we need to ask what is typical or paradigmatic about the kind of katharsis involved in the discharge of the *katamēnia*. At first, this kind of katharsis might appear to have little in common with the katharsis of sick bodies effected by medical treatments. Unlike these medical katharseis, the katharsis of the *katamēnia* is a natural (*phusikē*. *GA* 728a25) occurrence that takes place in a normal female body. However, a study of Aristotle's views on the sexes and reproduction indicates that the katharsis of the *katamēnia* is indeed like a medical katharsis in some significant respects.

After nourishment is "concocted" into blood by means of natural heat in the stomach and heart, some of the blood undergoes a further stage of concoction into "residues," such as semen and *katamēnia*. The female, however, does not have sufficient natural heat to be able to carry out the final stage of concoction, which produces semen.[24] Thus, the *katamēnia*, the female generative residue, is "less concocted" than semen (*GA* 726b31–32); it is "impure" semen:

only of a *reestablishment* of order (411) I argue below that both maintenance and reestablishment of order are involved in Aristotelian biological katharsis, but that production of order in the first place is not

[24] I follow the account of concoction given by Peck, *Generation of Animals*, lxiii–lxvii

For the menses [*katamēnia*] are seed that is not pure [*katharon*] but needs working on, similarly in the production connected with crops, when the nutriment has not yet been sifted, although it is present within it needs working on to purify it [*pros tēn katharsin*] That is why, when the former is mixed with semen and the latter with pure nutriment, the one generates and the other nourishes (*GA* 728a26–30 Balme)

Here, "katharsis" is used not of the evacuation of the impure *katamēnia* from the body, but of the process that would be required to make the *katamēnia* itself pure. Unfortunately, however, Aristotle's comparison in this passage is obscured by a corrupt text [25] Moreover, it is hard to say whether the nutriment that needs "working on" is unripe (unconcocted) or ripe but unprocessed by humans [26] Parallel passages in the *Generation of Animals*, however, make it clear that the general idea of this passage is that the *katamēnia* contributes to generation by promoting growth because of its bulk (744b32–745a4), just as residues like *phlegma* nourish when mixed with pure nourishment (725a15–17) [27]

According to Aristotle, the relative coldness of the female, which is the cause of her inability fully to concoct generative residue, is like a "natural deformity". "Females are weaker and colder [than males] in their nature, and we should look upon the female state as being as it were a deformity, though one which occurs in the ordinary course of nature" (*GA* 775a14–16. Peck). The same point is made at 737a27–29 "The female is as it were a deformed male, and the *katamēnia* is impure semen." In a deformity, Peck explains, "*phusis* has not succeeded in achieving her proper *telos*." According to Peck, Aristotle says that the female state is like a natural deformity because he believes "(1) that the male represents the full development of which Nature is capable, it is hotter than the female, and more 'able' to effect concoction, etc., but at the same time (2) the female is so universal and regular an occurrence that it cannot be dismissed out of hand as 'unnatural', besides, the female is essential for generation, which is a typically 'natural' process."[28]

[25] At 728a28, Drossaart Lulofs, *De generatione animalium*, and Balme, *De partibus animalium* (to judge from his translation) read διηττημένη (sifted, from διαττάω) Peck, *Generation of Animals*, however, reads διηθημένη (strained off), following Bonitz, and Bekker reads διητημένη There is another textual problem at 728a29, where one MS has ἀποκάθαρσιν, instead of κάθαρσιν, read by Drossaart Lulofs

[26] See Balme, *De partibus animalium*, on GA 728a26–30

[27] Peck, *Generation of Animals*, note a on 728a31, cites these passages, as well as *Pol* 1281b37

[28] Peck, *Generation of Animals*, xlv–xlvi

This inability and "deformity" of the female not only causes her to produce *katamēnia* rather than semen, it also causes katharsis of the *katamēnia* to occur "When these [sc., the blood vessels] are overfull of nourishment (which owing to its own coldness the female system is unable to concoct), it passes through these extremely fine blood-vessels into the uterus, but owing to their being so narrow they cannot hold the excessive quantity of it, and so a sort of haemorrhage takes place" (*GA* 738a12–16 Peck) [29] For the body to remain healthy, the unconcocted *katamēnia* must be expelled.

> Just as lack of concoction produces in the bowels diarrhoea, so in the blood-vessels it produces discharges of blood of various sorts, and especially the menstrual discharge (which has to be classed as a discharge of blood, though it is a natural discharge, and the rest are morbid ones) (*GA* 728a21–25 Peck)

> These two secretions of residues [sc , menstruation and "whites"], if moderate in amount, keep the body in a sound condition, because they constitute an evacuation of the residues which cause disease If they fail to occur, or occur too plenteously, they are injurious, producing either diseases or a lowering of the body. (*GA* 738a27–31 Peck)

Aristotle's comparison of the menstrual discharge to diarrhea in 728a21–25 is instructive Both discharges, he says, are due to a lack of concoction. This is in accord with Aristotle's biological theories, for concoction preserves health, while lack of concoction causes disease.

Aristotle defines concoction in *Meteorology* 4 "Concoction is a completion [*teleōsis*] by the natural and proper heat of something from the opposing qualities" (379b18–19) "Concoction" can refer to the cooking of food, the ripening of fruit, the digestion of food and its transformation into residues, and the maturing of the embryo (*Meteor* 379b12–14, *GA* 719a33–34, 768b27).[30] The connection between health and concoction is made explicit in *Meteorology* 4

> Everything happens to undergo this [sc , concoction] when its matter and *moisture are mastered, for this [matter] is made determinate by the heat belonging to its nature* For so long as a proportion is in it [sc , the matter],

---

[29] Cf 738a33–37

[30] Furley, "Mechanics," defends the authenticity of *Meteor* 4, and argues cogently that it is "Aristotle's prolegomenon to his biological works ' (93) This book is also held to be authentic by During, *Meteorologica*, and Lee, *Meteorologica* On the other hand, its authenticity has been questioned by Gottschalk, "Authorship," Solmsen, 'Citations,' and Strohm, "Beobachtungen "

this is its nature. And so things like urine, excrement, and the residues in general are a sign of health, and are said to have been concocted, because they show that the natural heat [of the body] masters the indeterminate [matter]. (379b32–380a2)[31]

The connections between concoction and health, and lack of concoction and disease, are also clear from many other passages. For example, at *Generation of Animals* 768b25–36, Aristotle writes that lack of concoction causes deformity in the growth of embryos, in the bodies of athletes, and in the disease of satyriasis, in which the face is deformed. *Problems* 959b23 states, "In general, all weakness results from lack of concoction."[32]

Aristotle's discussion of how lack of concoction causes hair to turn grey in old age (*GA* 5.4) is of particular interest, for it clarifies his views on the female and her katharsis of the *katamēnia*. According to Aristotle, grey hair in old age is due to "weakness and lack of heat" (*GA* 784a30–32). Because old age is cold and dry (784a33–34), its ability to concoct is impaired: "We must bear in mind that the nourishment which reaches each part of the body is concocted by the heat in each part proper to it; and if this heat is unable to do its work the part suffers damage, and deformity or disease is the result" (784a34–b1: Peck). In old age, the heat proper to the hair is unable to concoct the fluid that enters the hair, and putrefaction results (784b3–6). The putrefied nourishment in the hair is white, just as mold is white (784b11–14). Deficiency of heat can also cause hair to turn grey in sickness, but after health is restored the hair can regain its dark color. Aristotle explains this phenomenon:

> The reason is that during a period of infirmity just as the whole body is afflicted by a deficiency of natural heat, so the parts,[33] including even the very small ones, share in this infirmity; also, a great deal of residue is formed in the body and in its parts: hence the lack of concoction in the flesh produces

[31] The statement that excrement and urine "have been concocted" might seem puzzling in view of the statement at 380b5 that they are "raw," that is, as 380a27–28 makes clear, unconcocted. During, *Meteorologica*, 69–70, on 380a1, gives a good explanation of the apparent inconsistency. "The excrements are themselves of course products of apepsia ["inconcoction," indigestion] (380b5 and elsewhere), but in a certain sense they are also products of concoction, reliable symptoms of good indigestion" [sic: obviously an error for "digestion"]. I am indebted to Allan Gotthelf for helpful discussions of these passages.

[32] In many other passages concoction is said to be healthful, or lack of concoction is said to cause disease· *GA* 726a4–6, *PA* 670b4–7; *Meteor.* 4.384a31–33; *Prob.* 859b11–14, 861a5–6, 861b15–17, 861b33–35, 862a34–b6, 862b19, 869b32–870a5, 898a38–b3, 909a35–40, 959b20–30, 962b2.

[33] Peck, unlike Drossaart Lulofs, brackets ἄλλων at 784b27.

grey hairs. But when health and strength is restored, people accomplish a change, as it might be old men renewing their youth, and, in consequence, the conditions also accomplish a corresponding change. In fact, we might justifiably go so far as to describe disease as "adventitious old age" and old age as "natural disease"; at any rate, some diseases produce the same effects as old age does. (784b25–34: Peck)

This account of old age helps us understand Aristotle's views on the female. The production of the *katamēnia* by the female is in some respects like the production of grey hair in old age. Just as old age might be called a "natural disease" because it lacks natural heat, so the female state might be called a "natural deformity" (*GA* 775a15–16) because of its lack of natural heat. The *katamēnia*, like grey hair, is produced because of an inability to concoct. However, while putrefaction of the hair is not harmful in itself, unconcocted *katamēnia* causes disease unless expelled. For this reason, Aristotle compares the "natural discharge" of the *katamēnia* to the "morbid" discharge of diarrhea (*GA* 728a21–25). We might also (although Aristotle himself does not do so) compare the discharge of the *katamēnia* to the medical process of bloodletting, which removes harmful, unconcocted material from the body. Like bloodletting, katharsis of the *katamēnia* is neither homeopathic nor allopathic; it is a simple drainage. It serves as a periodic natural treatment for potentially harmful conditions resulting from the natural deficiency of the female state. Because the female needs this treatment in order to remain healthy, she is in a more precarious state of health than the male, who does not need this periodic discharge. Thus, if the female state is like a "natural deformity," it also resembles old age in being, in some respects, like a "natural disease."

If Aristotle views katharsis of the *katamēnia* as a natural treatment for a condition that resembles a "natural deformity," it is understandable that he should frequently call the expulsion of the female generative residue a "katharsis," although he uses different terms to refer to the emission of the male generative residue.

The semen, unlike the *katamēnia*, is a residue fully concocted from "the final form of nourishment," blood. The loss of semen usually weakens the body (*GA* 725b4–8, 726b1–13) because it is "a separation of pure and natural heat [from the body]" (783b29–30). Only when the semen is overabundant or mixed with disease-causing residue does its emission give relief rather than weakening: *GA* 725b8–15, 726a11–13 (a passage bracketed by H. J. Drossaart Lulofs); *Prob.* 880a22–29. These characteristics of the semen help explain why (again, with one possible exception) "katharsis" is never used of the emission of semen in Aristotle's unquestionably authentic works. At *Generation of Animals* 773b35–774a2, for example, Aristotle compares the male and female reproductive emissions, writing that "the katharsis of the *katamēnia* is an emission (*exodos*) of seed." However, instead of "katharsis" he uses the term *apokrinomenon* (separated) of the male's emission of semen. At *Generation of Animals* 726a13, *apokatharsis* refers to the evacuation not of the semen itself but of the disease-causing residues mixed with it. An exception in the doubtful *Problems* proves the rule. At *Problems* 880a33, melancholic men are said to want to be purged (*apokathairesthai*) of semen that contains too much breath. The one possible exception in the unquestionably genuine works is *Generation of Animals* 747a19–20, where Aristotle writes that "the seminal *katharseis* are from the diaphragm." While it is possible that "katharsis" is used here generically, of the reproductive discharges of both sexes, it should be noted that this passage occurs in the context of a discussion of tests for infertility in women (747a7).

Aristotle does not call the emission of the semen a "katharsis" because he believes that the semen, unlike the *katamēnia*, is fully concocted by the naturally complete male, and that it is not, except in unusual cases, mixed with the disease-causing waste products that result from lack of concoction. Moreover, the emission of semen is essentially different from the evacuation of a waste product, for it is necessary for generation in the female. In contrast, the *katamēnia* that is evacuated in katharsis is useless both to the female and for generation: to generate, the *katamēnia* must remain within the female.

If Aristotle has good philosophical reasons for calling the female, but not the male, reproductive discharge a "katharsis," it is less clear why he does not use "katharsis" of the natural evacuation, unaided by drugs, of excrement and urine. Surely excrement, like the *katamēnia*, is a residue that must be evacuated for the body to remain healthy. It is possible, however, that the difference in use is due to the conceptual connection of katharsis with disease, and to a tendency to use "katharsis" of a process that is similar to but less "healthy" than another process. As we have seen, Aristotle compares the female to a "deformed" male, and believes that her reproductive discharge has closer associations with disease than does the male discharge. He is therefore more likely to use the term "katharsis" to refer to the female discharge because of this term's association with disease. Similarly, in the case of excretion, it is possible that Aristotle reserves the term "katharsis" for medical purges, and uses other terms to refer to natural evacuation in health.

Medical Katharsis

While katharsis of the *katamēnia* is neither homeopathic nor allopathic, but a simple drainage, medical katharsis, for Aristotle as for most of the Hippocratic corpus, works according to the allopathic principle of opposites. Katharsis is a process in which opposite acts on opposite because it is opposite.[34] In order to understand Aristotle's views on medical katharsis, however, we must consider his views on health.

Aristotle gives an informative theoretical account of health in the *Physics*. He first states the general principle that all excellence, including health, is a "completion" or "perfection" (*teleiōsis*). "Excellence is a completion, for when each thing gets its own excellence, then it is said to be complete. For then it is most [what it is] according to [its] nature" (*Phy.* 7.3.246a13–15).[35] Aristotle then contrasts completion with qualitative change (*alloiōsis*). He explains that while health consists in a relation of one thing to another, and is not itself a qualitative change, qualitative changes in the hot, cold, moist, and dry are necessary to its coming-to-be (*genesis*) or destruction.

> And again, we say that all the excellences depend on a particular relation For the excellences of the body, for example health and good condition, we set down as consisting in a mixture and proportion of hot and cold, either of the internal qualities in relation to themselves or to what surrounds them . Since the relatives themselves are not qualitative changes, nor is there qualitative change, or coming-into-being, or in general any change of them, it is clear that neither the dispositions, nor the losses and acquisitions of the dispositions, are qualitative changes, though it may be that they come to be and perish of necessity when other things change . for example, the hot and the cold, or the dry and the moist (*Phy* 246b3–17)

This account tells us that health is a "mixture [*krasis*] and proportion [*summetria*]" of the opposing powers of hot and cold [36] The important prin-

[34] See chap 8 ("Homeopathy Theoretical Problems")

[35] Cf the definition of excellence as *teleiōsis* in *Meta* 4 1021b20, cited by W D Ross, *Physics*, on 246a13–16 The connection between "nature" and *teleiōsis* is made clear in *Phy* 2 8, where Aristotle argues that nature is a final cause (*telos*) See esp 199a30–32 and 199b15–17 I am indebted to Allan Gotthelf for these references

[36] On *summetria* in Aristotle's biology, see Peck, *Generation of Animals*, Introduction, nos 39–40 Tracy, *Mean*, 157–222, gives a valuable, detailed analysis of the principle of *summetria* in Aristotle's physiology He argues convincingly that "the notion of properly proportionate or symmetrical opposites blending in a mean is fundamental to Aristotle's

ciple that a good physical condition depends on the *summetria* of opposites is frequently expressed in Aristotle's other works also. In a number of passages, he mentions the common view that health is "the *summetria* of hot and cold" (*Topics* 139b21, 145b8; *Post. An.* 78b18–20). A *summetria* of hot and cold is needed for generation (*GA* 777b27–28).[37] The healthy condition of particular components of the body also depends on a proper mixture and *summetria*. For example, the brain cools the blood, which the heart heats and boils, so as to make it "well mixed" (*PA* 652b26–27). Again, a proportion (*logos*) of opposites, in both the sense object and the sense organ, is the basis for perception.[38]

Physics 246b3–17 tells us that health is produced or destroyed when the opposing powers change. Because health is a proportion of these powers, the changes in them that destroy health must be changes in this proportion, which occur when one or another of the powers is excessive or deficient. To destroy health, then, is to bring about this deficiency or excess, and to restore it is to correct the imbalance. Other passages in the Aristotelian corpus confirm this view. For example, *Posterior Analytics* 78b18–19 expresses the common view that "lack of *summetria* of the hot and the cold is [the cause] of not being healthy." *Problems* holds a similar view: "Why are great changes unhealthful? Is it because they produce excess or deficiency? And this is disease" (859a1–2). Great changes of the seasons produce diseases because the seasons are "hot and cold and moist and dry, and diseases are excesses of these things, while health is equality [of them]" (*Prob.* 859a11–12).

Health is a *teleiōsis* in which the body is most what it is in accord with its nature. This state consists in a relation, a *summetria* and mixture of opposites. Disease, on the other hand, is a state lacking "completion," in which there is no proportion of opposites because one or more of the opposing powers is in excess. Health can be restored by producing qualitative changes in the powers of hot, cold, moist, and dry.

The medical treatments that produce these qualitative changes in the

---

analysis of man's physical or bodily aspect at every level" (194–95). On *krasis* in Greek medical theory, see also chap. 1, n. 80.

[37] While Aristotle does not specify what process is involved here, he is clearly appealing to the principle of *summetria* of opposing powers. Peck, *Generation of Animals*, ad loc., cites *Phy.* 246b4. Moreover, at *GA* 767a15–23, Aristotle compares the *summetria* of male and female to that required for cooking. Sexual reproduction involves concoction (*GA* 719a33–34, 768b27), as does cooking (*Meteor* 379b12–14), and concoction involves the action of heat on "the opposing qualities" (*Meteor.* 379b18–19).

[38] On this theory, see Modrak, *Perception*, 56–62.

opposing powers would, it is reasonable to suppose, be allopathic Treatments of this kind would be in accord with the general principle Aristotle states at *Parts of Animals* 2.652b16–18, namely, that a proportion of extremes is needed to produce the mean: "Everything needs a counterweight in order to arrive at the measure and the intermediate " Two passages in Aristotle's ethical works clearly show that he adhered to the principle of opposites that dominated Hippocratic medicine In *Nicomachean Ethics* 1104b17–18, he writes that "medical cures are of such a nature as to come about by means of opposites." *Eudemian Ethics* 1220a35–36 expresses the same idea. "Punishments are medical cures, and come about by means of opposites." In both passages, Aristotle states this principle of opposites as an obvious fact, one that requires neither argument nor explanation Aristotle, the son of a physician who himself was greatly interested in medicine, would have been fully aware of the medical implications of such statements.[39]

The discussion of allopathic medical treatments in *Problems* 1.2–3 is consistent with these Aristotelian ideas about *summetria* and health

> Why do they often cure diseases when someone changes greatly? This kind of thing is the art of some doctors. They cure by excess of wine or water or salt or food or starvation Is it because things opposite to each other produce the disease? Each [opposite], then, brings the other to the intermediate Why do changes of the seasons and winds increase or stop and bring to a crisis and produce diseases? Is it because [the seasons] are hot and cold and moist and dry, and diseases are excesses of these, while health is equality [of them]? If, then, [disease] is due to moisture or chill, the opposite season stops it (*Prob* 859a4–13)

One important medical treatment is katharsis. Unfortunately, Aristotle tells us little about this process. The only detailed account of medical katharsis in the Aristotelian corpus occurs in the *Problems* (1.42.864a23–b11), a work of doubtful authenticity.[40] Nevertheless, this passage is a valuable source for Aristotelian ideas, for in many respects it is in accord with views expressed in the genuine works. *Problems* 1.42 gives the following account.

[39] On Aristotle and medicine, see Jaeger, "Medicine," esp 55–56
[40] On the problem of the authorship of the *Problems*, see Flashar, *Problemata*, 303–58, who concludes that the conception and composition of this work as a whole were influenced by Aristotle (356) *Prob* 1 42 presents particular difficulties because it is our most important and detailed explanation of ancient medical katharsis, see Flashar, 327 and 415 My reasons for believing that it contains Aristotelian ideas are given below

Why do drugs purge [*kathairei*], but other things that are more bitter and more sour, or that have an excess of other such qualities, do not purge? Is it because [drugs] do not purge by means of such powers but because they are not concoctable? [41] For things that are small in bulk, and, because of excess of heat or cold are unconcoctable and have the ability to master, but cannot be mastered by the heat of living things, and that are easily dissoluble by the two guts, these things are drugs For when they enter the gut and are dissolved, they are carried into the veins by the same pores as food, not being concocted but mastering, they depart, carrying impediments with them This is called katharsis Bronze and silver and such things are not concoctable by the heat of living things, but are not easily dissoluble in the guts Oil and honey and milk and such foods purge, not by means of their qualities but by means of their quantity For when these things are not concoctable because of their amount, then they purge, if they purge For they are unconcoctable for two causes because of their qualities and because of their quantity And so none of the things mentioned is a drug For none purges because of its power Sourness and bitterness and a bad smell are accidental properties of drugs, because a drug is the opposite of food For what has been concocted by nature becomes part of the body and is called food But what cannot naturally be mastered, and entering into the veins, causes disturbance because of excess heat or cold, this is the nature of a drug (*Prob* 1 42 864a23–b11)

Whether or not *Problems* 1 is authentic, this passage contains Aristotelian ideas *Generation of Animals* 768b25–27 and *Meteorology* 380a34–b2 give the same account of lack of concoction as due either to insufficient power of the concocting and moving agent or to the excessive bulk and coldness of that which is being concocted Even the little detail of the "two guts" (δύο κοιλιῶν 864a29) is Aristotelian, having parallels in several authentic passages [42] Because *Problems* 1 42 is Aristotelian in many respects, it provides some evidence, valuable even if not of unquestionable authenticity, for Aristotle's views on medical katharsis It is also significant in its own right, because it explains, as Hellmut Flashar states, the fundamental principles of katharsis better than any other passage in ancient medical literature [43]

[41] At 864a26 I follow Flashar, *Problemata*, who translates ἄπεπτα as nicht aufkochbar (= unverdaubar)

[42] The upper and lower intestines are meant, as is clear from the parallels in *GA* 725b1–2, 728a15–17, and 728a21–22 I owe these references to James Lennox

[43] Flashar, *Problemata*, 415

Nevertheless, few scholars have given *Problems* 1.42 much attention.[44] Unfortunately, Jeanne Croissant, one of the most influential scholars to have discussed this passage, seriously misunderstood it.[45] Largely through her influence, it has often been taken as evidence for a homeopathic theory of katharsis. Although Croissant correctly notes (*Mystères*, 93, 95) that a purgative drug is said, in *Problems* 1.42, to have an excess of hot *or* cold, she nevertheless believes that "purgation . . . makes use of the mutual reactions of two different quantities of heat" (93). In the treatment of melancholy, for example, "the purgative dominated by its heat the excessive heat of melancholics, and reduced it to a due measure" (104). She thus sees *Problems* 1.42 as support for the view that katharsis is a process like that in which fire is extinguished "by the similar," that is, by a greater heat, and not "by opposites."[46] Croissant's interpretation, however, is inconsistent with the principle of opposites expressed in *Problems* 859a4–13 (quoted above), and it cannot adequately account for the explicit statement by "Aristotle" that a drug works "because of excess of heat *or cold*."

Problems 1.42 is, instead, best understood as an account of an allopathic katharsis, one that is effected by means of opposites. A two-stage process is in question here. When "Aristotle" writes that the drug masters the natural heat and is not concocted, he is not discussing katharsis itself, as Croissant appears to believe, but a precondition for katharsis. What he means is that the drug is unaffected, unchanged by the natural, healthy heat in the guts. Because the drug is not changed by concoction, it retains its excess power (heat or cold) and so is able to act on the harmful excessive power in the body once it enters the veins. Drugs, as "Aristotle" explains further in *Problems* 1.47, must be both unconcoctable and productive of change.[47] While *Problems* 1.42 does not explicitly state that medical katharsis works according to the principle of opposites, the author's insistence that drugs work by their powers of heat and cold, and not by mere quantity, makes it probable that this is his view. In fact, the most com-

---

[44] This is true of the *Problems* generally, as Flashar notes, ibid., 295. Two scholars who discuss, very briefly, the relevance of 1.42 for an understanding of tragic katharsis are Flashar, "Grundlagen," 42–43, and Spiegel, "Nature," 29–30.

[45] Croissant, *Mystères*, 93–96, mentions *Prob.* 1.42 in the context of a discussion of *Prob.* 30.1, arguing that musical (and tragic) katharsis is a cure for the melancholia discussed in the latter passage.

[46] Croissant, *Mystères*, 83; cf. 85: "A determinate quantity of heat is extinguished by the action of a more powerful heat."

[47] *Prob.* 865a15–16. The connection of 1.47 with 1.42 is noted by Flashar, *Problemata*, 415, 417.

mon examples of hot and cold drinks are wine and water, and these are used, as *Problems* 1.2 explicitly states, in treatments by means of opposites.

The best interpretation of *Problems* 1.42 is that it describes an allopathic katharsis in which there are several steps:

1. There is a preexisting unhealthful condition due to excess heat or cold.

2. A drug with the opposing excess power of hot or cold is administered, and is not concocted (changed) in the guts.

3. The drug is carried unchanged through the veins where it causes disturbance because of its excess heat or cold; it reacts with the opposing excess in the body.

4. The drug itself passes out of the body (along with the excess that characterizes the drug), carrying with it the preexisting, opposing excess heat or cold that impedes a healthful mixture and proportion in the body.

5. This removal (katharsis) helps restore a healthful *summetria* of the opposing powers of hot and cold that is proper to the body's nature.

Because kathartic drugs help produce the qualitative change necessary to the restoration of the physical excellence of health, medical katharsis is a process of removing what prevents the body from regaining the *teleiōsis* that is in accord with its nature.

This allopathic interpretation of *Problems* 1.42 is consistent with Aristotle's views on change generally. He clearly believes that change can only be effected by the interaction of certain kinds of opposites. This theoretical principle is explained in Aristotle's discussion of "acting" (ποιεῖν) and "being affected" (πάσχειν) in *Generation and Corruption* 1.7.[48] Here, Aristotle argues that something can only be changed by what is unlike it in form. According to Aristotle, most philosophers have believed that like cannot be affected by like (323b3–4). These philosophers hold that even cases that might appear to be counterexamples—for example, that of a greater fire putting out a smaller—are really cases of unlike (the greater) affecting unlike (the smaller) (323b8–10).[49] Democritus alone, writes Aristotle, held a different view (323b10–15). Aristotle argues against the view that like can affect what is completely like: "For why will one be

---

[48] On this passage, see Joachim, *Coming-to-Be*, 148–56, Williams, *De generatione*, 119–23; and Mourelatos, "Interaction." Mourelatos calls attention (15 n. 20) to Plato's statement that like cannot affect like (*Tim* 57a), and to Solmsen's discussion (*System*, 356–57). Taylor, *Timaeus*, 389, also discusses GC 1 7 in connection with *Tim*. 57a. See also Plato, *Lysis* 214e5–215a1, and compare with GC 323b20–24, quoted below.

[49] Croissant's statement that this process is produced "par le semblable" (*Mystères*, 83) fails to take into account Aristotle's discussion in GC 1 7.

active rather than the other? And if it is possible for something to be affected by its like, [it is] also [possible for it to be affected] by itself. And indeed, if things were like this, nothing would be either indestructible or unchangeable, if like were active as like, for everything will move itself" (323b20–24). On the other hand, writes Aristotle, things that are completely different, such as line and whiteness, cannot affect each other either (323b24–28). The correct account, he believes, is that agent and patient must be alike in kind (*genos*) but unlike in form (*eidos*).[50]

> For things that are neither contraries nor from contraries do not change one another from their nature But since not just any chance thing is of such a nature as to be affected and to act, but only those things that have contrariety or are contraries, it is necessary for the agent and the patient to be like and the same in kind, but unlike and contrary in form (For body is of such a nature as to be affected by body, flavor by flavor, color by color, and in general that which is like in kind by that which is like in kind And the cause of this is that all the contraries are in the same kind, and the contraries act and are affected by one other) Thus, it is necessary for the agent and patient to be the same in one way, and different and unlike each other in another way And since the patient and the agent are the same and like in kind, but unlike in form, and the contraries are of this sort, it is clear that the contraries and the intermediates are affected by and act upon each other For destruction and coming to be consist entirely in these [processes] (323b28–324a9)[51]

The general principle is summed up at *De anima* 417a18–20 "It is possible in one way for something to be affected by like, and in another way by unlike, as we have said. For it is affected by unlike, but when it has been affected it is like."[52]

Harold Joachim explains in *Coming-to-Be* that, according to Aristotle,

[50] In translating *genos* and *eidos* as "kind" and "form" respectively (and not as 'genus' and "species"), I follow Lennox, "Kinds," 339 n I owe this reference to Allan Gotthelf

[51] I translate *enantia* as "contraries" rather than "opposites" in this passage because Aristotle uses this term in a specific technical sense to refer to contrary forms within the same kind For his views on contrariety in *Generation and Corruption*, see Joachim, *Coming-to-Be*, esp 198–203 In many other passages in Aristotle, however, *enantios* has its ordinary Greek sense, as Bonitz notes We cannot assume, for example, that the *enantia* by means of which medicine is said to work in *EN* 1104b18 are contraries in the technical sense of *Generation and Corruption* Thus, in most other cases I use the more general English term 'opposite' to translate *enantios*, and I refer to agent and patient as ' opposites '

[52] Joachim, *Coming-to-Be*, 152, calls attention to this parallel passage and notes that at 417a1–2 there is an explicit reference to *GC* 323b29–324a9

"the true doctrine is that action-passion takes place between things which are contrary forms of the same matter, differentiations of an identical *substratum*, contrasted species within the same genus. Agent and patient, therefore, are both 'like' and 'unlike'. The result of action-passion is to assimilate the patient to the agent" (151–52). Confusions arise, however, because "linguistic usage attributes action and passion now to the *substratum* and now to the *contraries*, and the false theories arose from exclusive attention to the one or the other of these subjects, of which action and passion are commonly predicated" (148).

According to Aristotle, the unqualified statement that "like affects like" and the unqualified statement that "unlike affects unlike" are both potentially misleading. The true account, in his view, is that one thing can affect another only when it is the same in kind but opposite in form. According to this theory, things that differ in degree (for example, greater and lesser fires) affect one another not because they are like, but because they are unlike. "it is affected by the unlike" (*DA* 417a20). While what is like (in kind) is affected by what is like (in kind), it can only be affected because it is unlike and opposite (in form), and never because it is like ("as like". *GC* 323b23). In other words, action and passion are always *allo*pathic and never *homeo*pathic.

To understand particular cases of acting and being affected, we need to determine in what specific respects agent and patient are like and unlike. For example, in *Generation of Animals*, the semen is said to "set" the female's *katamēnia* just as rennet "sets" milk. "The secretion of the female in the uterus is set by the male seed, which latter has an effect on it like that of rennet on milk. For rennet is milk having vital heat, which draws together what is like into one and sets it, and the seed has the same effect on the nature of the *katamēnia*. For milk and the *katamēnia* have the same nature" (*GA* 739b20–25). This passage makes it clear that rennet and milk are like, but also unlike, in just the way *Generation and Corruption* requires: "Rennet is milk having vital heat." Rennet and milk, that is, are the same in kind (both are milk), but unlike and opposite in form. one is hot and the other cold.[53] Similarly, in the case of the restoration of health produced by medical katharsis, the drug must also be like (in kind) that which it affects in the body, but unlike and opposite in being hot, cold, moist, or dry. This theory helps explain *Problems* 1.42. Because bronze and silver are not like food, which can be assimilated and made part of the body, they cannot act on the body and produce katharsis. Being unlike nourishment, they are not dissolved by the guts. Drugs, however, are like the food that is assimilated by the body, and therefore they can be dissolved in the guts and carried into the veins. They are, however, unlike the disease-causing material in respect to the powers of hot, cold, moist, and dry, and so are able to act on this material. They can then produce an allopathic katharsis.

The view that Aristotle adhered to the allopathic principle of opposites, then, is supported by the ideas on health in his biological works, by Aristotle's statements in the ethical works that medical treatments work by means of opposites, by the theoretical discussion of acting and being affected in the *Generation and Corruption*, and by Aristotelian ideas in the *Problems*. The *Problems* also supports the view that katharsis, like other medical treatments, works according to the principle of opposites. Aristotle's views on biology and medicine illuminate his ideas about psychic excellence and katharsis. In this area also, a principle of opposites is extremely important.

PSYCHIC KATHARSIS

Although Aristotle frequently refers to biological katharsis, he very seldom mentions psychic katharsis. In trying to determine what his views on the latter are, we are forced to rely on more indirect information. Accordingly, this section draws some probable inferences from information provided by a variety of sources. It begins ("Purity") with a study of some of the material related to psychic katharsis: the references scattered throughout Aristotle's works to a pure (*katharon*) state of the soul and its various activities, such as sensation, understanding, and contemplation. A study of these passages indicates that the adjective *katharon* and the noun *kathareiotēs* (purity) are used of things that are most closely connected with the rational part of the soul, that which is most proper to the nature and excellence of a human being. While these passages do not give us explicit information about a process by means of which the soul might be made pure (katharsis), the parallels Aristotle draws between physical and psychic excellence allow us to make some inferences about what such a process might be. These parallels are discussed in "Psychic and Physical Excellence." Next, "*Politics* 8" examines the account of psychic katharsis given in that book, arguing that religious-musical katharsis is best interpreted, contrary to the usual view, as analogous to a medical katharsis by means of opposites. After this, two other analogies are studied ("Iron and Wood"). Aristotle compares treatments of the soul by means of opposites to two physical processes that also work by means of opposites: straightening bent wood and tempering iron. Although he does not call these psychic treatments "katharseis," they certainly resemble allopathic medical katharseis. Further evidence that these psychic treatments would have been called "katharseis" in antiquity is provided by other writers. Seen from this broader perspective, Aristotle's analogies provide some evidence that he was working in a tradition that generally accepted the idea of an allopathic katharsis of the soul. The section on psychic katharsis concludes ("The Platonic Elenchus") with a study of an important philosophical document that may well have influenced Aristotle: *Sophist* 230, where Plato discusses a "katharsis concerning the soul." This kathartic process is similar in many ways to the medical katharsis of *Problems* 1.42 examined above. The *Sophist* passage is also significant because it shows us some specific ways in which psychic katharsis differs from physical katharsis. This background material will help us, in the next chapter, understand Aristotelian tragic katharsis.

Purity

In a number of passages in the Aristotelian corpus the adjective *katharon* and the noun *kathareiotēs* are used of the soul or of what is closely connected to it. Aristotle twice quotes Anaxagoras, who held that mind is "simple, and unmixed, and *katharon*" (*De anima* 405a16–17), and that mind alone is "unmixed and *katharon*" (*Meta.* 989b15–16). The spurious work *On Breath* also connects the soul with purity. "What is naturally united with the soul is purer" (481a17). These passages provide some evidence that the soul was traditionally thought to be pure.

According to Aristotle himself, a *katharon* state is specifically connected with the rational part of the soul. On the physiological level, intelligence is associated with pure blood, as opposed to blood mixed with earthy elements.[54] Humans, Aristotle believes, have the purest blood of all living things (*HA* 521a2–3). Moreover, the senses of sight, sound, and smell are purer than those of taste and touch (*EN* 1175b36–1176a1) because they

---

[54] PA 648a2–13, 650b18–24; cf. *On Sleep* 458a10–25, where sleep is said to be caused by impurities in the blood that incapacitate the primary sense-organ. Peck, *Parts of Animals*, 136 n., compares these *Parts of Animals* passages with "Hippocrates," *Regimen* 1.35, on which see Hüffmeier, "Phronesis," esp. 77–84.

aie more closely connected with the rational part of the soul The pleasures connected with sight, sound, and smell resemble, according to Aristotle, the intellectual pleasures of learning, remembering, and hoping in that they are unmixed with pain (EN 1173b16–19) Physical pleasures like those of eating, on the other hand, are preceded by a painful lack (1173b13–15)

Aristotle's discussion (EN 3 10) of the pleasures with which *sōphrosunē* is concerned clarifies why sight, sound, and smell are more closely connected with the rational part of the soul than are taste and touch Aristotle begins by distinguishing psychic pleasures, such as love of honor and love of learning, from bodily pleasures He believes that *sōphrosunē* is concerned with only some of the latter (1117b28–1118a3) We are, he writes, neither temperate nor licentious with respect to the pleasures of sight, smell, and sound (1118a3–12), but only with respect to those of touch and taste (1118a23–26) Because touch and taste are the pleasures we share with other animals, they appear "slavish and bestial" (1118a24–26) Aristotle's distinction among the physical pleasures is made on the basis of whether or not they have some connection with the intellectual capacities He says licentiousness is, strictly speaking, concerned only with touch, because taste has to do with discrimination (*krisis*) of flavors (1118a26–32) Thus, the pleasures of taste are more closely associated with the intellect than are those of touch, such as eating, drinking, and sex (1118a31) [55] Aristotle remarks, significantly, that licentiousness, the excessive enjoyment of the pleasures of touch, "belongs to us not as human beings, but as animals" (1118b2–3) This remark allows us to infer that the purer pleasures of sight, sound, and smell, and of taste insofar as it involves discrimination, are pleasures more closely connected with our natures as (rational) human beings

The point that pure pleasure is associated with the rational part of the soul is made more explicitly in connection with philosophy and contemplation (*theōria*) Philosophy, Aristotle writes, "is thought to have marvelous pleasures, for purity [*katharciotēti*] and stability" (EN 1177a25–26) It is "the most pleasant of all activities in accord with excellence" (1177a23–24) The contemplative life is the most divine (1177b26–31), and theoretical comprehension (*nous*) is least bound up with the "compound" of body and soul (1178a19–22) *Theōria* has these characteristics because it is the activity most proper to the nature of human beings "That which is

[55] For a good discussion of this rather puzzling account of *sōphrosunē*, see Young, Temperance

proper to each thing is by nature best and most pleasant for it. And for a human being [this is] the life in accord with [theoretical] *nous*, since this is most of all a human being. And this life is therefore also most happy" (1178a5–8). The pleasure of contemplation is also pure because it is un-mixed with pain: "There are also pleasures without pain and desire, for example, those of contemplation, when our nature lacks nothing" (1152b36–1153a2).

Pure pleasures in Aristotle's view are those most proper to our nature as rational beings. Such pleasures are also most "complete" (or "perfect"), and belong to the most "complete" human being: "Whether the [activi-ties] of the complete [*teleiou*] and blessed man are one or more than one, the pleasures that complete [*teleiousai*] these activities should be said in the strict sense to be the pleasures of a human being" (*EN* 1176a26–28).[56]

A study of passages in which *katharon* and *kathareiotēs* are used in con-nection with the soul indicates that purity is closely associated with the rational part of the soul, the activity of which is proper to the nature of a human being. While these passages do not give us any information about a process by means of which the soul might be made pure (katharsis), some inferences about what such a process might be can be drawn from Aristot-le's statements about the similarities between physical and psychic excel-lence.

Psychic and Physical Excellence

In *Physics* 7.3, Aristotle states that excellence is a *teleiōsis* in which some-thing is most what it is in accord with its nature (246a13–15). This gen-eral principle is first applied to excellence of the body: health and good condition (246b4–20). It is then applied to psychic excellence: "And sim-ilarly in the case of the dispositions of the soul. All of these depend on a certain relation, and the excellences are *teleiōseis*, the vices departures [from this relation]" (*Phy.* 246b20–247a3). Just as health is a "completion" or "perfection" of the physical nature of a living thing, so psychic excellence is a "completion" or "perfection" of the psychic nature of a human being.

---

[56] The question of the relationships in the *Nicomachean Ethics* among nature, completion, pleasure, and *theōria* involves too many controversial issues to repay study here. *Phy.* 7.3, discussed below, makes it clear without raising these difficulties that psychic, like physical, excellence is a *teleiōsis* in which the nature of something is realized. Some recent discussions of these controversial issues in the *Nicomachean Ethics* are those of Owen, "Aristotelian Pleasures"; Gosling and Taylor, *Pleasure*, 204–24, Ackrill, "*Eudaimonia*"; J. M. Cooper, "Contemplation", and Kraut, *Aristotle*.

Physical excellence is a relation consisting in "a mixture and proportion of hot and cold, either of the internal qualities in relation to themselves or to what surrounds them" (*Phy.* 246b5–6). One kind of psychic excellence, "ethical excellence," according to the *Physics*, is a relation "concerned with bodily pleasures and pains" (247a7–8). Just as health comes to be or perishes when qualitative changes in the hot, cold, moist, or dry take place (246b14–17), so ethical excellence comes to be or perishes when changes concerning pleasures and pains take place, for these are qualitative changes in the perceptive part of the soul (247a4–19).

The parallel between physical and psychic excellence does not, it should be noted, hold in one respect. Physical excellence consists in a *summetria* of the opposites hot and cold. In the *Physics*, as in the ethical works, however, psychic excellence does not consist in, but is "concerned with," a *summetria* of pleasure and pain. As *Nicomachean Ethics* 1104a11–b2 tells us, the mean state concerning pleasure and pain helps produce and maintain excellence, while excess and deficiency destroy it. A correct mixture and proportion of the opposites pleasure and pain can, according to Aristotle's ethical works, help provide the habituation that is a necessary condition for the development of psychic excellence It is, however, a mistake to identify psychic excellence with this kind of proportion.[57] Aristotle avoids making this identification when he writes, in *Nicomachean Ethics* 2.3 1104b8–9 "For ethical excellence is concerned with {περί} pleasures and pains." Aristotle's language in *Physics* 7.3 also reflects this conceptual distinction between physical and psychic excellence. He writes, "We set down {physical excellence} as consisting in {ἐν} a mixture and proportion of hot and cold" (246b5–6) He states, however, that ethical excellence is "concerned with {περί} bodily pleasures and pains" (247a7–8, cf 247a15–16 περὶ ταύτας).

If, with the exception just noted, ethical excellence is analogous to physical excellence, psychic treatment is also analogous to medical treatment. Aristotle's ethical works frequently draw parallels between medical and psychic treatments. As Werner Jaeger has shown, these parallels have real philosophical significance "The medical example, far from being a casual analogy, is present to the philosopher's mind throughout It belongs to the very foundation of his ethical science."[58] We are justified in drawing some substantive conclusions about ethics from what Aristotle says about medicine.

[57] On psychic excellence and habituation, see chap 6
[58] Jaeger, "Medicine,' 56–57 See also Lloyd, "Analogies '

Of particular interest are a number of passages in which Aristotle calls punishment, the infliction of physical or emotional pain, a "medical treatment" for vice. The term for licentiousness, *akolasia*, means, literally, "unpunished," and Aristotle states that the *akolastos* is "someone who has not been punished [*kekolasmenos*] in some way, or medically treated [ἰα-τρευμένος]" (*EE* 1230a38–39). Aristotle rejected the idea, held by some people, that we should call *all* pleasure base in order to control the many. According to these people, "the many are inclined toward it [sc., pleasure], and are enslaved to pleasures, so that it is necessary to lead them to the opposite direction, for in this way they would arrive at the intermediate" (*EN* 1172a31–33). Nevertheless, Aristotle clearly believed in a more selective and judicial application of the principle of treatment by opposites. For example, at *Nicomachean Ethics* 1104b16–18, he writes that it is an indication that excellence is concerned with pleasures and pains that "punishments come by means of these [sc., deprivation of pleasures and infliction of pains].[59] For they are medical treatments [ἰατρεῖαι] and medical treatments by nature take place by means of opposites." *Eudemian Ethics* 1220a34–37 expresses the same idea: "A sign that excellence and vice are concerned with pleasant and painful things is that punishments are medical treatments and come about by means of opposites, just as is true in other cases."

If psychic treatments are like allopathic medical treatments, we can infer that psychic katharsis, like physical katharsis, would use opposites to remove impediments to the completion and excellence of the soul, and thus help it realize its nature. A medical katharsis helps restore the excellence of the body that consists in a proportion of hot and cold, and it does so by using opposite to treat opposite. Similarly, an emotional katharsis could help restore the excellence of the soul by opposing (cold) pain to (hot) pleasure.[60] An allopathic theory of this kind, according to which emotional heat is opposed to cold fear, is implicit in *Problems* 954b14–15: "If it [sc., the melancholic temperament] is inclined to be hot, fear restores it to the measure, and [makes the person] self-possessed and unemotional."

An emotional katharsis, of course, could produce only "ethical excellence" (*Phy.* 247a7–8), and not the very different excellence of the intel-

---

[59] My explanation in the bracketed passages follows the interpretation of Gauthier and Jolif, ad loc.

[60] See chap. 6 ("Pity, Fear, and Physical Danger") for a discussion of Aristotle's view that pleasure is hot while pain is cold.

lectual part of the soul (247b1) [61] This kind of psychic katharsis could not, then, in itself produce the purity that is associated with contemplation, which is a "divine" rather than a human excellence, an ideal toward which we strive (EN 1177b26–1178a2) Ethical or "human excellences," those connected with the "compound" of body and soul (1178a20–21), can, however, help us develop the intellectual excellences An emotional katharsis that helps us develop ethical excellence could, then, also help us strive toward divine purity of soul, to the extent of our ability Thus, it is a reasonable inference that emotional katharsis, in Aristotle's view, is a process that strives toward, but never fully attains, the purity of soul that is the full completion and perfection of our nature as rational beings

Politics 8

While Aristotle does not specifically mention a katharsis of the soul in the ethical works or in the *Physics*, in *Politics* 8 he gives a detailed account of a psychic katharsis produced by "enthusiastic" music

> For an emotion that occurs strongly in some souls exists in all of them, but differs in being less or more [intense], for example pity and fear, and again enthusiasm For some people are inclined to be possessed by this motion, but we see them, when they make use of tunes that put the soul into a state of religious excitement, restored by the sacred tunes as though they had received medical treatment and katharsis This same experience necessarily happens to people who are inclined to pity or fear, and to those who are in general inclined to be emotional, and to others, to the extent that a share of these kinds of things falls to each person, and all get a certain katharsis and relief with pleasure Similarly, kathartic tunes give harmless pleasure to people (1342a4–16)

Because katharsis is not a simple drainage in this passage, but involves an interaction between emotion and music, we may ask whether it can be characterized as homeopathic or allopathic Most scholars assume that the homeopathic interpretation is correct For example, although Carnes Lord notes that the psychic katharsis of *Politics* 8 is "in some sense a medical cure," and that "it is more than doubtful whether catharsis in the medical sense is homoeopathic," he nevertheless writes "The catharsis of which

---

[61] The distinction between ethical and intellectual excellence is also made in the ethical works See, for example, EN 1103a3–10, where Aristotle writes that the intellectual excellences include wisdom, understanding, and practical reason, while the ethical excellences include liberality and *sōphrosunē*

Aristotle speaks is manifestly a homoeopathic cure."[62] In this katharsis, according to Lord, "enthusiastic music . . . effects a catharsis of enthusiasm," for the "sacred tunes" mentioned here are to be identified with the tunes of Olympos that are said to "make souls enthusiastic" in *Politics* 1340a9–11, or with Phrygian enthusiastic music (1340b4–5).[63] Viewed in this way, katharsis is a process in which motion cures motion homeopathically. The people who are "possessed" suffer from a strong internal (e)motion that is cured by an external motion: music (and, we may assume, dance) that moves the soul as well as the body: the tunes "put the soul into a state of religious excitement" (ἐξοργιάζουσι τὴν ψυχήν).

The homeopathic interpretation of *Politics* 1342a, however, faces a number of difficulties. The medical analogy tells against it. Again, as Lord himself points out, the tunes that make normal people enthusiastic do not effect a katharsis of enthusiasm in them (*Education*, 127). This means that the enthusiasm produced by the tunes is not the same as the enthusiasm cured by them. The process is not so "manifestly" homeopathic as Lord believes. Moreover, attempts to find a source for Aristotelian katharsis in a homeopathic musical katharsis have not been successful.

Another objection to the homeopathic interpretation is that there is no clear evidence that cures produced by the "religious excitement" to which Aristotle refers were commonly thought to be homeopathic.[64] In nonphilosophical literature, enthusiastic religious rites are not usually said to work either by similars or by opposites. For example, in Euripides' *Bacchae*, Dionysus, the god of wine, is simply "a medicine for labor" (283), in whose "holy purification rites" (77) his followers participate. In this play, our best single source of information about enthusiastic Bacchic rites, there is no suggestion of a specifically homeopathic or allopathic process. Again, in Aristophanes' *Wasps* (115–24), Bdelucleon makes various attempts to cure his father of madness, including katharsis and the use of the Corybantic rites. As Kenneth Reckford notes, however, the precise nature of these different curative processes is not specified. Instead, the cures "shade off into each other; they share various elements of purifi-

[62] Carnes Lord, *Education*, 122. Other recent scholars who hold a homeopathic view of this passage are Halliwell, *Aristotle's Poetics*, 192, and Janko, *Poetics I*, xix.

[63] Lord, *Education*, 127

[64] Lord, who argues for a religious origin of homeopathic katharsis, notes some of the difficulties for this view ibid., 124–26. I argued in chap. 8 ("Homeopathy: The Ancient Evidence") that one kind of religious katharsis, the use of blood to cleanse blood, is a poor source for Aristotelian tragic katharsis.

cation, purgation, and emotional release; and they belong together as 'therapy' and 'catharsis.' "[65]

Nor do philosophical texts dealing with religious enthusiasm provide clear evidence for homeopathic enthusiastic rites. In *Laws* 7.790–91, for example, Plato gives a detailed account of "the curative processes of the wild Bacchic rites" (790e2–3)[66] used to treat people who suffer from a mad terror:

> These emotions are fear, and fears result from a bad disposition of the soul. But when someone applies a shaking from outside to these kinds of emotions, the motion applied from outside masters the internal fearful and mad motion. When it has mastered, having made a peaceful calm appear in the hard pounding of the heart of each person, something that is entirely desirable, [then, when we are] made to dance and play the flute with the gods to whom each person sacrifices with good omens, it makes us have sane dispositions instead of mad. (*Laws* 7.790e8–791b1)

Scholars have held various and often confusing views about the nature of the process described by Plato. Georg Finsler characterizes these Corybantic cures as homeopathic, finding the homeopathic principle in the application of external motion to internal motion.[67] Carl Müller, on the other hand, believes that Plato's account is based on the principle of allopathy: "agitation [is cured] by means of a (counter) motion," and "the motions . . . are opposites of one another."[68] Ivan Linforth's views are less clear. He appears to hold a homeopathic view when he writes, "The cure is homeopathic in that it produces symptoms identical or nearly identical with those of the disorder to be cured."[69] However, Linforth appears to acknowledge that the cures also have allopathic aspects when he writes that "the inner tumult is cured by outer activity; unwholesome mania is driven out by beneficent mania; and in the end both kinds of mania are gone. We should not overlook that the mania which was cured is not said to have been produced by Corybantic possession" ("Rites," 134). Linforth, moreover, argues against Rohde's "theory . . . that the Corybantic disease was cured homeopathically by the Corybantic rites," and concludes that "there is no instance on record in which any kind of disorder whatsoever that was

[65] Reckford, "Catharsis," 284.

[66] Linforth's translation in "Rites," 132, reading αἱ.

[67] Finsler, *Platon*, 113: "The shaking applied from without has a homeopathic character."

[68] Müller, *Gleiches*, 145 n. 127.

[69] Linforth, "Rites," 158.

produced by the Corybantes was cured by their rites."[70] Evanghélos Moutsopoulos's statements are also somewhat confusing. He holds an allopathic
view of *Laws* 790–91,[71] yet he admits that the rites have homeopathic
aspects when he states that "this therapeutic method reach[es] the limits
of a homeopathic treatment" (*Musique*, 108 n. 2).

This confusion in the literature is understandable. In Plato's Corybantic
rites, ordered movement imposes order on disordered movement.[72] Thus,
the rites should be classified as homeopathic if the essential idea is that
movement acts on movement, but as allopathic if order is thought to act
on disorder. In this passage, unfortunately, Plato does not explicitly state
whether the rites work by means of similars or by means of opposites.

Plato's use of medical terminology and concepts in *Laws* 7.790–91,
however, provides some evidence for the allopathic view. The medical theory of the *Laws* is an allopathic one, based on the concept of *isonomia* (equilibrium) of opposing powers. The rites of *Laws* 7 are analogous to (or, more
properly, an integral part of) a medical treatment in which motion is used
to produce excellence of both soul and body (790c–d). The rites are said
to be "medical treatments" (ἰάσεις: 790e3, ἰάματα: 790d4), in which
someone "applies" (προσφέρῃ: 791a1, 791a2) an external "motion" to a
preexisting internal "mad motion" (κίνησις: 791a2, 791a3). The external
motion "masters" (κρατεῖ: 791a2) the internal motion.[73] The term "masters" has a technical, medical sense earlier in *Laws* 7, where Plato advocates the use of continual motion to produce health, beauty, and strength
in young children, and as an aid to the "mastery" (digestion) of food (κατα-
κρατοῦντα: 789d5–6).

The allopathic interpretation of *Laws* 7 makes sense for other reasons
also. On this view, the Corybantic rites cure by applying a "drug" of orderly, rhythmic motion that "masters" preexisting disorderly motion.
When the orderly motion has "mastered" and produced peace in the soul,
the sufferer participates in the rhythmical motion of the cure by dancing

[70] Ibid., 151. His reference (cited on 146) is to E. Rohde, *Psyche*, 9th and 10th eds.,
2:47ff.

[71] Moutsopoulos, *Musique*, 109 and 106 n. 1.

[72] This essential feature of Plato's account is brought out by Boyancé, *Culte*, 198, and
Moulinier, *Pur*, 418.

[73] That these terms belong to medical vocabulary is shown by LSJ and by Maloney and
Frohn, *Concordance*. See, on προσφέρῃ, LSJ, s.v. προσφέρω, 3.b: "esp. of food, drink, or
medicine"; Maloney and Frohn list 208 occurrences of the lemma προσφέρω. For κίνησις,
see LSJ, s.v. κινέω, A.II.3, which lists a medical sense; Maloney and Frohn list 197 occurrences of the lemma κινέω and 58 of κίνησις. On κρατεῖ, see LSJ, s.v. κρατέω, 3.b: "of
food, *digest, assimilate*"; Maloney and Frohn list 145 occurrences of the lemma κρατέω.

along with the flute music. Thus, musical motion cures because it is itself, and produces in the sufferer, motion that is completely different from the motion that characterizes the disease. This view of music and dance in *Laws* 790–91 is supported by Plato's theory in *Laws* 2 that music and dance originated in the imposition of orderly motion (rhythm and harmony) on disorderly cries and leaps, such as those made by young children (653d7–654a5, 672b–d).[74]

Aristotle's use of medical terms in *Politics* 1342a suggests that he, like Plato, thinks that enthusiastic rites are analogous to a medical treatment by means of opposites. Aristotle compares music to medicine when he writes that sufferers are "restored by the sacred tunes as though they had received medical treatment and katharsis" (καθισταμένους ὥσπερ ἰατρείας τυχόντας καὶ καθάρσεως: 1342a10–11). As Newman points out, "and" (καί) in this phrase is explanatory.[75] That is, the medical treatment *is* a katharsis, and the effect of the "sacred tunes" on the soul is like (ὥσπερ) this medical katharsis. This analogy is significant, for in other passages Aristotle compares a treatment of the soul to a medical treatment, and states that medical treatments work by means of opposites (*EN* 1104b16–18, *EE* 1220a34–37). Earlier in *Politics* 8 itself, Aristotle makes a similar comparison, writing that "relaxation is necessarily pleasant, for it is a medical treatment [ἰατρεία] for the pain that comes from labor" (1339b16–17).[76] Aristotle's use of a number of other medical terms in *Politics* 8.1342a4–16 reinforces the explicit medical analogy: χρήσωνται (make use of: 1342a10), κινήσεως (motion: 1342a8), καθισταμένους (restore: 1342a10), and κουφίζεσθαι (relief: 1342a14).[77]

---

[74] See chap. 1 ("A Medicine to Produce *Aidōs*"). In *Tim.* 88c–e also, regular motion gives order to disordered motion. Moutsopoulos, *Musique*, 98–111, calls attention to the remarkable parallels between this passage and *Laws* 790–91, noting that both describe an allopathic process.

[75] Newman, *Politics* 3.564.

[76] Ibid., on 1339b15, notes that this passage alludes to the principle of treatment by opposites.

[77] Ibid., on 1342a8, notes that Susemihl calls attention to these medical terms, see Susemihl and Hicks, *Politics*, on 1342a9, 1342a10, 1342a14, and 641 n 2, who attribute (641) the observation about medical terminology to Doring, *Aristotelishche Kunsttheorie*, 319ff. Information in LSJ and in Maloney and Frohn, *Concordance*, confirms the view that these terms belong to medical vocabulary. On χρήσωνται, see Maloney and Frohn, who list 677 occurrences under the lemma χράω For κινήσεως, see above, n 73. On καθισταμένους, see LSJ, s.v. καθίστημι, A I.2 "*restore* the general health" (Hippocrates, *Mul.* 2.133); B.5: "*recover*" (Hippocrates, *Coac.* 160), Maloney and Frohn list 189 occurrences under the lemma καθίστημι. On κουφίζεσθαι, see LSJ, s.v. κουφίζω, 2.b: Euripides, *Orestes* 43. "when the body is relieved [κουφίσθη] from sickness", Maloney and Frohn list

The term καθίστημι (restore 1342a10) is of particular interest because of its association in other passages with emotional states intermediate between extremes. At *Politics* 1340b3, Aristotle uses the cognate adverb when he says that people listen to Dorian tunes μέσως καὶ καθεστηκότως. "in a midway state of collectedness and composure."[78] The effect of Dorian tunes is "midway" between that of Mixolydian tunes, to which people listen in a "mournful and contracted [συνεστηκότως]" state, and that of other tunes that are "relaxed" (ἀνειμένας). 1340a42–b3 Contraction and relaxation are associated with the emotional opposites grief and joy, which are produced by these tunes.[79] Again, at 1342b14–16, Dorian harmony is said to be intermediate between extremes The verb καθίστημι (restore) is also associated with an emotional intermediate state in two other passages, where it refers specifically to a process effected by means of opposites. At *Eudemian Ethics* 1239b33–36, Aristotle writes: "For the opposites do not desire one another, but the intermediate. For being excessively cold, if they are heated, they are restored [καθίστανται] to the intermediate, and being excessively hot, [they are restored] if they are cooled." After this passage, Aristotle compares the friendship of people with unlike emotional qualities to the "desire" of these physical extremes for one another. In both cases, opposite "restores" opposite to an intermediate state.[80] The verb καθίστημι (restore) is also associated with physical and emotional temperature at *Problems* 954b14–15. "If it [sc., the melancholic temperament] is inclined to be hot, fear restores [κατέστησεν] it to the measure, and [makes the person] self-possessed and unemotional." Taken together, all of these uses of καθίστημι (restore) suggest that, in *Politics* 1342a10 also, this term might be used to refer to a state between two opposites, produced by means of allopathic treatment.

While Aristotle's medical analogy and his use of medical terminology give us good reason to favor an allopathic interpretation of *Politics* 8.1342a, Aristotle does not give us any detailed information about the

---

31 occurrences under the lemma κουφίζω For the association of katharsis and "relief," see "Aristotle," *Prob* 880a33 "Of necessity, these people often wish to experience a katharsis [ἀποκαθαίρεσθαι], for [then] they are relieved [κουφίζονται]" (cited by Bonitz, s v κουφίζειν)

[78] This is Newman's translation, *Politics*, ad loc , where he compares Aristotle's use of the verb at *Pol* 1342a10 and at *EE* 1239b35

[79] See Newman, *Politics*, on 1340a42, and compare *Prob* 11 13, where laughter, relaxation, hot breath, and high-pitched sounds are all associated with one another, while weeping, tension, cold breath, and low-pitched sounds are also closely associated

[80] This passage is discussed in chap 6 ("*Aidōs*, Excellence, and Habituation")

specific nature of the kathartic process in question. It is possible that he believed, like Plato in the *Laws*, that musical treatment cures strong, internal, disordered, and abnormal (e)motion by means of an opposite external, orderly motion: music and dance. On the other hand, Aristotle may have had in mind some other cure that was traditionally thought to be effected by musical modes and harmonies. Aristides, according to Carnes Lord, held that music can effect "a 'therapeutic' education operating 'by way of opposition' (*kat' enantiotēta*) on those who suffer from an excess of passion."[81] Aristotle's failure to explain katharsis, however, and our imperfect knowledge of Greek musical theory make it difficult to draw definite conclusions.[82]

If *Politics* 8 is of interest because it discusses a treatment of the soul analogous to a medical katharsis, in other respects it is of very limited usefulness for an understanding of katharsis in the *Poetics*.[83] *Politics* 8 is concerned with a musical treatment, while tragic katharsis is produced by the plot and not by music, which is merely a "sweetener" (*Po.* 1449b28–29, 1450b16). Moreover, in the *Politics* Aristotle is concerned with abnormal people who experience emotional states more "strongly" than others (1342a5–6). The statement that "an emotion that occurs strongly in some souls exists in all of them" does not imply that all people could benefit from the treatment that is useful for these abnormal cases. Nor, when Aristotle says that "all" (πᾶσι: 1342a14) get a certain katharsis, is he referring to all people: he is only concerned with all those who are inclined to be abnormally emotional (παθητικούς: 1342a12–13).[84] In the *Poetics*, on the other hand, Aristotle is concerned with a normal audience, as is shown by his defense of the superiority of tragedy in chapter 26, and by the complete absence of any suggestion, in the *Poetics*, that the audience is diseased or abnormal. Finally, in the *Politics*, the kathartic use of music is contrasted with an educational use of music (1341b32–1342a4; cf. 1341a23–24), while in *Poetics* 4 imitation is said to be pleasurable because we learn from it.

[81] Carnes Lord, *Education*, 205, summarizing Aristides Quintilianus, *De musica* 2.9 (68.22–69.1 Winnington-Ingram).

[82] On Greek musical theory and Aristotle, see Lord, *Education*, appendix, 203–19. A good sourcebook, with commentary, is A. Barker, *Greek Musical Writings*

[83] Some differences between the two works are noted by Lord, *Education*, 126–38, and Golden, "Purgation."

[84] Lord, *Education*, 130–34, argues that there are two kinds of katharseis in question: one for abnormal and one for normal people. This interpretation does not appear to me to be supported by the text.

Iron and Wood

In addition to making frequent use of medical analogies, Aristotle sometimes compares ethical treatments to two physical processes that are effected by means of opposites: that of straightening warped wood, and that of tempering iron. These two analogies, especially when the broader Aristotelian and Greek philosophical contexts are taken into account, provide further evidence that Aristotle believed that psychic treatment, like medical treatment, works by means of opposites.

The analogy of straightening warped wood occurs first in Plato's *Protagoras* (325d5–7). If the young do not obey persuasion, Plato writes, people correct them with punishments: "They straighten them with threats and blows, like wood that is warped [διαστρεφόμενον] and bent." While Plato does not call this treatment a katharsis in the *Protagoras*, he does call punishment a katharsis in the *Laws*. Here, in writing about "purifications" (*katharmoi*: e.g., 735d1), Plato compares punishment to a medical katharsis: "The best [purification] is painful, just like that [effected by] drugs of this kind: that which brings to punishment by means of justice and retribution" (735d8–e2). And in *Laws* 1, restoration of psychic health is compared to a medical katharsis (628c9–e1).

Aristotle himself uses the warped-wood analogy in *Nicomachean Ethics* 1109a30–b26. In order to attain the praiseworthy intermediate in ethical matters, he writes, it is "necessary to incline at one time to the excess and at another to the deficiency" (1109b24–25). This is because human nature often tends toward one of the vicious extremes, and "it is necessary to drag ourselves in the opposite direction; for by drawing ourselves far away from error, we will arrive at the intermediate, just as those do who straighten warped wood" (1109b4–7). We humans, Aristotle believes, are naturally inclined toward pleasures, and so are likely to be licentious (1109a14–16). He means, for example, that we naturally tend toward gluttony and drunkenness. To correct this tendency so as to arrive at the intermediate state of *sōphrosunē*, we must, according to Aristotle, bend over backward in the direction of deficiency, toward sobriety and fasting. In straightening warped wood, just as in allopathic medical treatments, an opposing extreme is applied so as to bring a preexisting undesirable extreme to an intermediate state. The wood that people straighten by bending it in the opposite direction needs this treatment because it has been warped (διεστραμμένα: *EN* 1109b6) out of its natural, straight position. Similarly, the soul is "warped" by vice: "For vice warps [διαστρέφει] and makes a person mistaken about the practical first principles" (*EN* 1144a34–36). A treatment by opposites that helps restore the soul to a natural, excellent state, then, is analogous to this process of straightening warped wood

Aristotle himself does not use the term "katharsis" in connection with the warped-wood analogy. However, Olympiodorus's use of this analogy in characterizing an "Aristotelian katharsis" provides evidence that Aristotle was associated in antiquity with an allopathic psychic katharsis.[85] Olympiodorus contrasts an allopathic "Aristotelian" or "Stoic" katharsis that "cures evil with evil" with a "Socratic," homeopathic katharsis that "derives similars from similars," and with a "Pythagorean," evacuative katharsis.[86] He writes that in the "Aristotelian" katharsis "evil cures evil, and by the combat of opposites [τῇ διαμάχῃ τῶν ἐναντίων] brings it to a proportion [*summetria*]" (*Alcibiades* 146.3) Olympiodorus also discusses this "Aristotelian" or "Stoic" katharsis earlier in the same work.

> [Katharsis] cures opposites by means of opposites, applying the appetite to the spirit [*thumos*] and thus softening it, and [applying] the spirit to the appetite,[87] and thus strengthening it and training it to be more manly, like crooked twigs that people bend in the opposite direction when they wish to straighten them, so as to produce a proportion [*summetron*] by carrying them over to the opposite side Similarly, they practice the art of producing harmony in the soul by this kind of method (*Alcibiades* 54 18–55 1)

Olympiodorus's language—"the combat of opposites," "cures opposites by means of opposites"—and his crooked-twig analogy leave no doubt that the katharsis he describes is allopathic, effected by means of opposites This same language also suggests a genuine Aristotelian source. Olympiodorus's statement "like crooked twigs that people bend in the opposite direction when they wish to straighten them [δίκην τῶν κεκαμμένων ῥάβδων ἃς οἱ θέλοντες εὐθῦναι πρὸς τὸ ἐναντίον περιλυγίζουσιν]" recalls Aristotle's language in *Nicomachean Ethics* 1109b4–7 "It is necessary to drag ourselves in the opposite direction [εἰς τοὐναντίον δ᾽ ἑαυτοὺς ἀφέλκειν δεῖ], for by drawing ourselves far away from error, we will arrive

[85] Ničev (*Catharsis*, 183–92, and "Olympiodore') and Janko (*Comedy*, 147) both fail to note that Olympiodorus's warped-wood analogy occurs in Aristotle's own work Both also fail to see, as noted in chap 8 ("The Homeopathic Prejudice) that Olympiodorus s "Aristotelian" katharsis is allopathic

[86] Olympiodorus, *Alcibiades* 54 15–55 14, cf 145 12–146 11 The allopathic katharsis, called "Aristotelian' at 146 3, is clearly the same as the Stoic katharsis mentioned at 54 18, as Ničev points out (*Catharsis*, 184) On these kinds of katharseis, see also chap 8 ("Homeopathy The Ancient Evidence')

[87] At 54 19 I read τῇ δὲ ἐπιθυμίᾳ τὸν θυμόν, suggested by Westerink, *Olympiodorus*

at the intermediate, just as those do who straighten warped wood [ὅπερ οἱ τὰ διεστραμμένα τῶν ξύλων ὀρθοῦντες ποιοῦσιν] " Moreover, the idea of opposites curing opposites is frequently expressed in Aristotle's works, as I have shown above.

Aristotle also compares ethical training to the tempering of iron. In *Politics* 7, Aristotle writes that, for military states, peace can be more dangerous than war.

> Most such [warlike] states are preserved when at war, but are destroyed when they have acquired an empire For they lose their tempering [βαφὴν], like iron, when at peace The lawgiver is to blame for not educating them to be able to be at leisure   War compels people to be just and temperate, but the enjoyment of good fortune, and being at leisure in peacetime make them more inclined to be hubristic (*Pol* 1334a6–10, 25–28)

The analogy in this passage is derived from the technique of strengthening (tempering) iron [88] In the ancient process of ironworking, iron ore was first heated to remove impurities and make the metal soft enough to be shaped. The hot iron was forged, and then dipped into cold water in a process called "quenching" (βαφή) to harden it hence the term Aristotle uses in *Politics* 7 for the result of the whole "tempering" process.[89] Thus, the successive application of the opposites hot and cold produces a useful tool. As Aristotle succinctly puts it in *Generation of Animals* 734b37–735a1, "the hot and the cold make the iron hard and soft " The iron-tempering process is allopathic in that it is effected by means of opposites.

While Aristotle does not give details about the analogous process of tempering the soul in *Politics* 7 1334a, a passage in *Politics* 5 suggests that this process might be effected by opposing (cold) pain and fear to (hot) shameless and hubristic tendencies. While in war fear is naturally present, in peace, Aristotle writes, a beneficial fear would have to be artificially supplied.

> Constitutions are preserved not only because destroyers are far off, but sometimes also because they are near For when they are afraid, people keep the constitution more under control So that it is necessary for those concerned about the constitution to provide fears, and to make what is far off [seem]

[88] I use the term "tempering" loosely, to refer to the process of strengthening iron by means of heating and quenching Technically, "tempering" iron is an entirely different process On ancient techniques of ironworking, see Lee, *Meteorologica*, 324–29, and Forbes, *Studies*, 196–210

[89] Newman, *Politics*, on 1334a8, notes that βαφή ha this meaning here

near, so that [the people] might keep guard and not, like a night watch, neglect their guard over the constitution. (*Pol.* 1308a24–30)

Thucydides' Pericles used fear in just the way Aristotle recommends: "When he had any perception that the people were inappropriately hubristic and bold, by speaking he struck them with terror [κατέπλησεν] to make them fear" (2.65.9).

The iron-tempering analogy of Aristotle's *Politics* also occurs in Plato, as does the warped-wood analogy. Within the context of this Platonic background, the significance of Aristotle's brief allusion to tempering in *Politics* 7 can better be appreciated.

In *Republic* 3.410c–412a, Plato advocates a correct mixture of music and gymnastics in education. This mixture, he believes, is necessary to "harmonize" the spirited and rational parts of the soul with each other by properly tensing and relaxing them (411e4–412a2). Music at first softens the spirited part of the soul "just like iron," and "makes it useful instead of useless and hard." Excessive indulgence in music, however, makes it "melt and liquefy" (411a10–b2). On the other hand, too much physical training produces too much "hardness" of soul (410d1). While the primary analogy in this passage is that of musical harmony, Plato is also comparing psychic training to the process of tempering iron by alternately softening it in fire and hardening it in cold water. Physical training is like cold water, and musical education is like fire. In the *Laws*, as we have seen, Plato uses the iron-tempering analogy in his account of the process by means of which the souls of old people are softened and made more "shameless" by wine. Dionysus, Plato writes, provides "the initiation rite and play of the old, which he gave to human beings in the form of wine,[90] a medicine as a remedy for the austerity of old age, so that we might become young again, and so that through forgetfulness of despondency the hard character of our soul might become softer, like iron put into fire, and so made more easy to mold" (*Laws* 2.666b4–c2). The same analogy recurs in *Laws* 2.671b8–10, where Plato writes that the souls of the wine drinkers "like iron" become "fiery" and "softer"—that is, like iron that has been heated in fire as part of the tempering process.

It is possible that the iron-tempering analogy originated with Socrates. At least, it is associated with him in Plutarch's *Life of Alcibiades* (6.4): "Just as iron softened in fire is contracted again by the cold, and its parts are drawn together, so Socrates, whenever he found Alcibiades full of softness and empty conceit, made him humble and bashful by pressing and reducing him with speech." Here, as in *Laws* 2, the "fire" that softens the

---

[90] Reading τὸν οἶνον at 666b6, with Burnet, *Platonis opera*.

soul is associated with shamelessness, and excess is corrected by means of the opposite extreme.[91]

The old people of Plato's *Laws*, who are too cold and timid, are unlike the people in Aristotle's *Politics* 7, who have lost their "tempering" and become hubristic Nevertheless, the principle of treatment would be the same in both cases. excessive psychic heat or cold can be corrected by the application of the opposite extreme. The iron-tempering analogy is apt in both cases because this process involves both heating and chilling. Although Aristotle does not call this psychic tempering a katharsis, Plato calls wine, which softens and heats the soul, "a drug for the attainment of *aidōs* in the soul" (672d7–8), and he clearly believes that its effect is analogous to that of the medical katharsis mentioned in *Laws* 1 628d2.

Aristotle's warped-wood and iron-tempering analogies, then, provide further circumstantial evidence that Aristotelian psychic katharsis resembles allopathic medical katharsis The analogies themselves are based on allopathic principles. Moreover, Olympiodorus uses the warped-wood analogy in writing about a process he calls "Aristotelian katharsis," and Plato uses the iron-tempering analogy in discussing an allopathic psychic treatment that resembles a medical katharsis. This gives us reason to place Aristotle's analogies in the broader context of a philosophical tradition that generally accepted katharsis by means of opposites If Aristotle himself generally avoids the term "katharsis" in discussing psychic treatments, this may be because the expression "katharsis of the soul" had acquired too many Platonic, Pythagorean, and Orphic connotations. In the *Phaedo*, for example, psychic katharsis is a process of separation of the soul from the body.[92] Aristotle, however, believes that a treatment of the soul must take into account the appetites and desires, pleasures and pains of the body; it cannot simply eliminate these physical elements It is perhaps significant that in the *Laws*, a late dialogue with a radically different psychology from that of the *Phaedo*, Plato generally avoids the term "katharsis," even though he makes it clear that the psychic treatment he describes is analogous to a medical katharsis

The Platonic Elenchus

In the *Sophist*, Plato uses the term "katharsis" to refer to a specific psychic treatment. At *Sophist* 230d7–8, the elenchus is said to be "the greatest and

---

[91] For other metaphorical uses of the iron-tempering process in Plutarch, see two of the passages listed by Lee, *Meteorologica*, 327–28 *Moralia* 73c–d and 943e

[92] See especially *Phaedo* 66d8–67b2, where "katharsis' and its cognates occur five times

most powerful katharsis" for the soul, because psychic katharsis removes from the soul the opinions that impede learning, just as a medical katharsis removes from the body impediments to health (230c3–d4) This psychic katharsis is of particular interest because it does not necessitate the complete separation of the soul from the body, but takes into account the emotional as well as the intellectual aspects of the human personality [93]

As I argued in chapter 6 ("*Kataplēxis* and *Ekplēxis*"), Socrates often produces shame in his interlocutors In *Sophist* 230b–d, Plato discusses in detail the kathartic process that uses shame as a psychic drug Socrates says of the practitioners of the elenchus

> They ask questions concerning those things about which people think they have something to say, while actually saying nothing Then, since people wander [in their views], they easily examine their opinions, and gathering together these opinions in their arguments, they put them in the same place beside each other, and putting them there, they show that these opinions are opposite to one another at the same time, concerning the same things, in relation to the same things, and with respect to the same things And seeing this, the others [sc , the people examined] are angry with themselves and mild toward others, and in this way, they are freed from conceited and stubborn opinions about themselves,[94] the most pleasant of all releases for the audience, and the most lasting for the patient For, dear child, just as doctors of the body believe that the body cannot benefit from the nourishment applied to it before one casts out the impediments within, so those purifying [*kathairontes*] these people believe the same thing about the soul that it will not get any benefit from the learning applied to it before someone by cross-examining brings the person examined to shame [*aischunē*], and taking away the opinions that impede learning, makes him pure [*katharon*], thinking that he knows only those things that he does know, but not more (*Soph* 230b4–d4)

The psychic katharsis produced by the elenchus is much like the physical katharsis produced by drugs in *Problems* 1 42 A medical analogy is fundamental to Plato's account The practitioners of the elenchus are compared to "doctors of the body," and the elenchus, which removes impeding opinions (230d2), is compared to a medical katharsis, which casts out

---

[93] Scholars usually stress the intellectual effects of the elenchus See, for example, Vlastos, "Elenchus" and "Afterthoughts," and Kraut, 'Comments ' However, the elenchus also has important emotional effects, as is noted by Gooch, "Vice ' See also Belfiore, 'Elenchus "

[94] On the meaning of περὶ αὐτοὺς (230c1), see Kerford, ' Sophistry,' 88 n 3, who calls attention to R Robinson, *Plato's Earlier Dialectic*, 2d ed , 12

physical impediments (230c6–7). The "application" of learning is compared to the "application" (προσφερομένης, 230c5, 230c8 [a medical
term])[95] of food. However, because the soul is more complex than the
body, the administration of the drug that induces katharsis is also a more
complex process than is the administration of a physical drug.

The first step in psychic treatment is a diagnosis designed to bring patients to understand what their own opinions are. They have, in the first
place, opinions obstructive to learning and as harmful to the excellence of
the soul as disease-causing elements in the body are harmful to physical
excellence. These opinions, as is clear from Plato's accounts of the elenchus
in other dialogues, make a person shameless: ready to do and say anything
about anything, because of the belief that one knows what one does not
know. These false opinions are inconsistent with one another and with
more modest, true beliefs the patients must also have if they are capable
of shame and curable. In the *Gorgias*, for example, Polus makes the shameless statement that it is worse to suffer injustice than to do it. He also
agrees with Socrates, however, that it is more shameful to do injustice than
to suffer it (474c–d). These two opinions, as Callicles points out (482c–
483a), are inconsistent and lead to Polus's refutation by Socrates.

Diagnosis in the elenchus has two stages. In the first stage (*Soph.*
230b4–5), the doctors of the soul bring the impeding opinions to light by
asking questions designed to reveal the false, shameless beliefs that will
later be removed, and the true opinions with which they are inconsistent.
For example, in answer to Socrates' opening question, "What do you say
excellence is?" (*Meno* 71d5), Meno makes a speech in which he shamelessly
asserts what he thinks he knows, but does not really know, about excellence (71e1–72a5). On this occasion, as on others, Meno was accustomed
"to say very many words about excellence on many occasions, and before
many people" (80b2–3). He was, like the shameless person of the *Magna
moralia*, someone "who on all occasions and to everyone, says and does
whatever occurs to him" (1193a2–4). This bringing to light of shamelessness is an essential preliminary to the Platonic katharsis of the soul. It
should not, however, be confused with the kathartic process itself. Shamelessness does not cast out shamelessness, any more than the impediments
in the body that are discovered in a medical diagnosis cast themselves out.
After the false, shameless opinions have been brought to light, together
with true, more modest opinions, the second stage of the diagnosis takes
place. At this point, the doctors gather together all of the beliefs that have
been brought to light and show that they are inconsistent (*Soph.* 230b5–8).

[95] See above, n. 73.

The next step in psychic treatment is the production of shame (230b8–d2). This comes about as a natural result of the publicly conducted cross-examination: "And seeing this [they] are angry with themselves" (230b8–9); "by cross-examining [the doctor] brings the person examined to shame" (230d1–2). The use of shame to oppose shamelessness is like the use of a drug to counter disease-causing material that has the opposite qualities. In other Platonic dialogues, the "patient" experiences shame so intense that he is, for the moment, paralyzed and speechless, like the *kataplēx* in the *Magna moralia*, "who is cautious about doing and saying everything and to everyone. This kind of person does not act at all, the person who is *kataplēx* in every way" (1193a4–6). For example, when Alcibiades is afraid of growing old while sitting and listening to Socrates (*Sym.* 216a8), his paralysis is closely connected with *ekplēxis* (215d5) and shame. Alcibiades says, "Before him alone of all people, I experienced something that no one would have thought I had in me: shame before anyone at all" (*Sym.* 216a8–b2). Meno states that Socrates has paralyzed him like a stingray, so he is unable to say anything (*Meno* 80b4).[96] It is this emotional shock of anger with oneself and shame before others that has the effect of a drug. While the intellectual knowledge that one's beliefs are inconsistent is necessary to produce katharsis in those who require the elenchus, it is not in itself sufficient, for the more shameless one is, the less likely one is to be troubled by any such inconsistency. Only shame, a public humiliation of the kind Socrates administers, can counteract the shameless tendencies that make one believe, and confidently assert, that one knows what one does not know.

Shame, like a drug, produces katharsis (230d2–4). In this process, the extreme shame produced by the elenchus departs, together with the extreme preexisting shamelessness it has counterbalanced. This is exactly what happens in the case of drugs, in the account of *Problems* 864a32–34: "Not being concocted but mastering, they depart, carrying impediments with them. This is called katharsis." In the psychic katharsis of the *Sophist*, false, shameless opinions are carried off. As the opposing extreme of shame departs from the soul, one is also freed from the effects produced, temporarily, by the elenchus itself: excessive shame that leads one to believe that one knows nothing at all. The result, at least in theory, is a pure (*katharon:*

---

[96] As these parallels show, the *aischunē* mentioned at *Soph.* 230d1 is not, as Gooch writes, "the resulting emotional state" of "modesty" ("Vice," 130), but excessive shame, a counterweight to preexisting shamelessness; the resulting state is *sōphrosunē* (230d5). The effects of the elenchus are also described at *Gorgias* 482e1–2 (binding and gagging, as well as shame); *Laches* 194b1–4 (inability to speak); *Rep.* 350d3 (blushing); and *Rep.* 358b3 (being charmed as if by a snake).

230d3) state of soul, *sōphrosunē* (230d5), in which one thinks one knows only those things one really knows (230d3–4). The person in this state is like the *aidēmōn* of the *Magna moralia*, who "will do and say the right things, on the right occasions and at the right times" (1193a10).

In sum, the elenchus opposes emotion (shame) to emotion (shamelessness), as well as opinion (that one knows nothing) to opinion (that one knows things one does not know). It thus produces an emotional mean state, as well as intellectual purity. Only after attaining this state can a person learn and benefit from teaching. This kathartic process is allopathic in that it is effected by means of opposites. In outline form, the several steps involved in the psychic katharsis of Plato's *Sophist* are the following:

I. Diagnosis

A. Bringing to light of false, shameless opinions (those based on a belief that one knows what one does not know) and of true, more modest opinions

B. Gathering all these opinions together and showing that they are inconsistent

II. Production of shame, which acts as a drug

III. Katharsis: removal of shameless opinions, which are carried off as the opposing extreme of shame departs from the soul

IV. *Sōphrosunē*: a pure, healthy state of the soul, in which one believes that one knows only what one does know

The detailed account of katharsis in the *Sophist* is completely consistent with what little information we have about Aristotelian psychic katharsis, and with what we know about his views on physical katharsis. Plato, moreover, gives us valuable information not available in Aristotle about how a psychic katharsis can affect beliefs. This information is particularly useful because we would expect Aristotelian tragic katharsis to involve the cognitive as well as the physical aspects of the emotions. In tragedy, as in the elenchus, both beliefs and emotions are important. In viewing an imitation, we "put things together," or "reason" (*sullogizesthai: Po.* 4.1448b16). Moreover, in viewing tragedy, as in undergoing the elenchus, we experience *ekplēxis* in response to events that are shameful. Finally, like the elenchus, tragedy brings to light our shameless tendencies, for we enjoy tragedy in part because, at some level, we like hearing about parricide, incest, and other shameless deeds.

In chapter 9 I have examined much material, in Aristotle and in other ancient writers, relevant to an understanding of Aristotelian katharsis. All this material taken collectively allows us to draw some plausible inferences. First, when Aristotelian physical katharsis is an interactive process, rather than a simple drainage, it works by means of opposites and not by means of similars, and it should properly be called "allopathic" rather than "homeopathic." This inference is supported by passages directly concerning katharsis and by Aristotle's theoretical account of action and passion in *Generation and Corruption*. Second, Aristotelian physical katharsis is a process of removing what prevents something from preserving or regaining the excellence ("completion" or "perfection") that is in accord with its nature. This second inference is supported by a study of biological katharsis in Aristotle's works. Medical katharsis is an obvious example of a process that removes material harmful to the body's physical excellence. However, Aristotle most frequently uses "katharsis" of the evacuation of the menstrual fluid (*katamēnia*), which is also a removal of harmful material. Aristotle thinks that the female is like a deformed male, and that her reproductive discharge has closer connections with disease than does the male's. Katharsis of the *katamēnia* is, then, a natural treatment needed to remove material harmful to the female's physical excellence

While Aristotle's views on psychic katharsis are more elusive, there are numerous indications that he thought of it as analogous to an allopathic medical katharsis. Psychic treatments, he notes, work by means of opposites, just as medical treatments do. In *Politics* 8, moreover, psychic katharsis is explicitly compared to medical katharsis Other analogies in Aristotle also support an allopathic interpretation. Aristotelian psychic katharsis appears to be a process, effected by means of opposites, that removes what prevents the soul from preserving or regaining the excellence that is in accord with its nature. Unlike physical katharsis, however, psychic katharsis helps produce excellence in the first place. This allopathic view of psychic katharsis is also supported by passages in ancient writers other than Aristotle. These texts suggest that Aristotle was part of a tradition within which an allopathic psychic katharsis, analogous to a medical katharsis, was widely accepted. In chapter 10 I will examine how this background information and these plausible inferences aid the interpretation of tragic katharsis.[97]

[97] I am indebted to Allan Gotthelf for criticisms of earlier drafts of the first two sections of this chapter, and to Richard Kraut for comments on an earlier draft of the discussion of the elenchus

Tragic Katharsis

WHEN ARISTOTLE defines tragedy as "imitation . . . by means of pity
and fear accomplishing the katharsis of such emotions" (*Po.* 1449b24–28),
he notoriously fails to explain katharsis and to discuss the tragic emotions.
Nevertheless, the *Poetics* gives us much useful information about the kinds
of plot structures that best arouse pity and fear. There is also much relevant
information about Aristotle's views on pity and the fear emotions, on biological katharsis, and on the similarities between psychic and medical
treatments. The views of other Greek writers concerning the benefits of
fear provide additional important information. Although no interpretation of tragic katharsis is susceptible of proof, the theory argued for in this
chapter is most in accord with all this information. This chapter, like an
Aristotelian definition, "reckon[s] up the results out of what has been said,
and drawing together the main points, add[s] the conclusion [*telos*]."[1] The
conclusions summarized here are based in large part on evidence and arguments presented in detail in earlier chapters.

The absence of a discussion of tragic emotion in the *Poetics* is less puzzling when we consider the nature of this work as a whole. Aristotle's
statements about his goals, and the topics covered in the *Poetics*, show that
it is a treatise on the making of poetic compositions, within which a detailed discussion of the emotional effects of poetry would be out of place.

It is noteworthy that, after defining tragedy, Aristotle explains in detail
much that is obvious to us, while he remains frustratingly silent about
those subjects we would most like him to discuss: fear, pity, and katharsis.
The "definition of the being" (1449b23–24) of tragedy is given at the
beginning of *Poetics* 6: "Tragedy is imitation of a noble-and-serious and
complete action, having magnitude, in sweetened speech, with each of the
forms separate in the parts, enacted and not narrated, by means of pity
and fear accomplishing the katharsis of such emotions" (1449b24–28).
Aristotle gives an exceptionally clear explanation of "sweetened speech"
(1449b28–29) and of "separate in the forms" (1449b29–31); in the rest of
chapter 6, he discusses the consequences that result from the definition of
tragedy as imitation of action, enacted rather than narrated. In chapter 7,

[1] *Meta.* 1042a3–4. I adapt Furth's translation in *Metaphysics*.

he discusses the concepts of "complete" and "magnitude." Pity and fear, on the other hand, are treated only indirectly, for example in *Poetics* 13 and 14, as Aristotle considers the kinds of plots that best arouse these emotions. Katharsis is never explained.

It is possible, of course, that these topics were covered in parts of the *Poetics* that are now lost. A better explanation, however, is that Aristotle had already discussed the emotions at length in other works, and that he wished to concentrate on other matters here, while tacitly accepting traditional beliefs about tragic emotion, for the existence of which there is ample evidence in Greek literature. Moreover, Aristotle believed that once we understand how a plot should be constructed the emotional effects of tragedy are also fully intelligible. Looked at this way, his original contribution to aesthetic philosophy was not a theory of katharsis that is now lost, but the detailed analysis of plot structure that is in fact found in our text of the *Poetics*.

The *Poetics* makes a great deal of sense read as a treatise concerned primarily with the organization of the plot and only incidentally and indirectly with emotion. Aristotle begins the work with a clear statement of his goals: "Concerning the poetic art itself and its forms, what sort of power each one has, and how one should organize plots if the poetic composition is going to be good, and again of how many and what kinds of parts [it consists], and similarly concerning the other things belonging to the same method of inquiry, let us speak beginning according to nature, first from first things" (1447a8–13). Our text of the *Poetics* does just this. It considers the poetic art as a whole, and its forms (*eidē*) or genres; it distinguishes the different (emotional) effects produced by different genres of poetry; it emphasizes the organization of the plot, and discusses the number and nature of the "parts" of tragedy.[2] The *Poetics* ends with the statement that the discussion of tragedy and epic, proceeding along the lines laid out at the beginning of the work, has been concluded: "Concerning tragedy and epic, themselves and their forms and parts, how many they are and how they differ, and what are the causes of their being well or not well [made], and concerning criticisms and solutions, let so much have been said" (1462b16–19). The *Poetics* concludes with the same clear statement of goals with which it began. The work as a whole, moreover, consistently aims at these goals, and it fully achieves what it explicitly sets

[2] These are the six qualitative parts of tragedy (plot, character, speech, thought, spectacle, and song) listed in *Po.* 6 (1450a9–10). Epic shares all but two of these parts (1459b9–10).

out to do, with one exception. The statement of goals in the first sentence of the *Poetics* (1447a8–13, quoted above) leads us to expect an examination of comedy, which is also explicitly promised in *Poetics* 6: "Concerning the art of imitation in hexameters and concerning comedy we will speak later" (1449b21–22). "Imitation in hexameters" (epic) is covered in chapters 23 through 26, but the promise to discuss comedy is never kept. Manuscripts and translations of the end of the *Poetics* provide some further indication that a study of comedy originally followed, in book 2, and has been lost. After the conclusion quoted above (1462b16–19), the Latin translation of William of Moerbeke continues: "[Here] ends the first book of Aristotle's *On the Art of Poetry*." Manuscript B also continues, perhaps mentioning iambic and comedy.[3]

In contrast, there are no such clear indications in the *Poetics* itself that discussions of emotion and katharsis are missing from our text. Aristotle's statements of his goals at the beginning and end of the work do not suggest this, nor does anything in the rest of the work or in any manuscript. Although the statement in *Politics* 8 that katharsis will be examined "in the works on poetry" (1341b39–40) is often taken to be a reference to our *Poetics*, the reference may instead be to Aristotle's lost work *On Poets*, or to some other lost text.[4] The promise at the beginning of the *Poetics* that the work will consider "what power each one [of the forms of poetry] has" is kept in the discussions of *what* emotions are aroused by tragedy, epic, and (briefly) comedy, *how* they are aroused by specific plot structures, and *in what respects* tragedy arouses them better than epic. A lengthy examination of psychological effects would be out of place in a study of this sort, focused as it is on the craft of making poetry.

Since our *Poetics* does not deal directly with katharsis and tragic emotion, I have of necessity made extensive use of the literary and philosophical texts of other writers, and of Aristotle's works other than the *Poetics*. This external material, together with indications in the *Poetics* itself, suggests that tragic fear is not merely *phobos*, fear of physical pain, but that it also has much in common with "social" fears, the shame emotions of *aidōs*,

---

[3] The reading of these words is "very difficult," according to Kassel, *De arte poetica*, whose apparatus also quotes the Latin translation See also Gallavotti, *Aristotele*, apparatus, ad loc., and commentary, 222–23. For a discussion of this and other evidence for a lost second book of the *Poetics*, see Janko, *Comedy*, 63–66.

[4] Carnes Lord, *Education*, 148–49, suggests, following Finsler, *Platon*, 3–8, that the *Pol.* 8 reference may be to a lost discussion within the *Politics* itself. Lord argues convincingly that this discussion would be relevant in the context of an examination of music, and that there are difficulties in supposing that it occurred in the *Poetics*.

aischunē, and *kataplēxis*. Tragic fear and pity, unlike their real-life counterparts discussed in the *Rhetoric*, are aroused only in part by a destructive or painful *pathos*. When enemy harms enemy, or neutral harms neutral, Aristotle writes, this is not pitiable (or fearful) "except as regards the *pathos* itself" (1453b17–19). Instead, tragic emotion is best aroused by the shameful actions that violate *philia* relationships. "When the *pathē* occur within *philia* relationships . . . this is to be sought" (1453b19–22). Tragic pity and fear resemble the shame emotions in being concerned, in part, with evils that appear to bring disgrace. Tragic fear can be defined as "pain or disturbance at the *phantasia* of imminent evils that are destructive or painful, and disgraceful." The *Poetics'* use of the traditional term *ekplēxis* to refer to tragic emotion also suggests that it has much in common with the shame emotions. *Ekplēxis* has connotations of shame, particularly in Plato, and in Aristotle, it is conceptually and linguistically related to *kataplēxis*, extreme shame. The view that tragic emotion in the *Poetics* is closely related to the shame emotions is also in accord with traditional Greek views about the primary importance of *philia*. These views are particularly evident in the tragedies, many of which are centrally concerned with the violation of *philia* relationships.

For an understanding of Aristotle's concept of katharsis we must look to his biological and ethical works. In biological and ethical contexts, Aristotelian katharsis is a process of removing what prevents something from preserving or regaining the excellence, the *teleiōsis*, that is in accord with its nature. Moreover, psychic katharsis is analogous to a medical katharsis effected by means of opposites. Aristotle frequently compares psychic to medical treatment, and in Aristotle, as in most of the treatises of the Hippocratic corpus, medical treatment is allopathic, in that it works according to the principle of opposites, and not homeopathic, working according to the principle of similars. This is not to deny that Aristotelian katharsis also has certain aspects that moderns might call "homeopathic". emotion treats emotion, and disturbance caused by drugs cures disturbance caused by disease. In Aristotle's view, however, drugs do not cure because they are like, but because they are unlike, the diseases they cure. To call this process "homeopathic" is to misrepresent Aristotle's medical views, implying that he adhered to the principle of similars. The allopathic view of katharsis is amply supported by evidence in Aristotle's own works, and in the broader philosophical context. It now remains to be seen how these general conclusions can be applied most plausibly to the specific case of tragic katharsis.

The view most in accord with the evidence we have is that tragic katharsis is an allopathic process of removing the shameless emotions that prevent the soul from acquiring, preserving, or regaining the emotional excellence that is in accord with its nature. In this process, an opposing extreme of tragic emotion is applied, like a drug, to a preexisting, opposite emotional extreme of shamelessness. Tragedy accomplishes a katharsis of these opposite, shameless emotions, carrying them with it as it departs from the soul. The result is a healthy emotional state called *aidōs*, *aischunē*, or *sebas* in Greek thought generally, and *aidōs* in Aristotle's ethical works. In the rest of this chapter, I discuss this hypothesis and examine the evidence that supports it.

I have argued that the allopathic interpretation of tragic katharsis is consistent with Aristotle's ethical theories, for Aristotle believed a treatment by means of opposites to be effective in producing and restoring a healthy, natural balance to the soul. He also held that shameless desires may be corrected and opposed by shame. One particularly important kind of shamelessness requires further discussion here.

Aristotle believed that the soul is especially liable to be "warped" or "perverted" by the shameless, aggressive emotions and desires associated with excessive *thumos* (spirit).[5] For Aristotle, the *thumos* is, in Carnes Lord's characterization, a "social passion," an excess of which can lead to socially destructive acts caused by anger, jealousy, hatred, hubris, and arrogance. Aristotle writes that "the *thumos* perverts [or warps διαστρέφει] rulers and the best men" (*Pol* 1287a31–32).[6] The same word is used in *Nicomachean Ethics* 1109b4–6, where ethical treatment by means of opposites is compared to the straightening of warped (διεστραμμένα) wood. The *thumetic* emotions and desires are hot, for "the *thumos* produces heat" (*PA* 650b35). They are associated with young people, who are "spirited [*thumikoi*], and quick-tempered [*oxuthumoi*], and of such a nature as to follow the commands of anger" (*Rhet.* 2.12.1389a9–10). Young people are "passionate" (*thumōdeis*: 1389a26) and "thoroughly heated," like people drunk with wine (1389a19–20). The dangers of excessive spirited are summed up by Stobaeus, in a passage quoted by Lord: "Spiritedness is a passion that is bestial in its disposition, unrelenting in its hold, harsh and violent in its power, a cause of murders, ally of misfortune, companion of injury, instigator of dishonor and waste of substance, and finally of destruction."[7]

---

[5] I am indebted to Lord's excellent discussion of spirit in *Education*, 159–64 and 192–96 Janko, *Comedy*, 148 and 161, also calls attention to the importance of spirit and anger for an understanding of katharsis, though I do not agree with all his conclusions

[6] Carnes Lord, *Education*, 162–63

[7] Stobaeus 3 553 9 Henze, translated by Carnes Lord, *Education*, 163 Lord argues (n 29) that this passage should be included among the fragments of Aristotle

On the other hand, a good blend of spirit and intelligence is essential to a well-ordered city The people who are going to be easily guided toward excellence, Aristotle writes, must have a nature that is "well-blended," so that they are both intelligent and spirited (*Pol* 1327b35–38) Spirit is necessary to a city because it produces friendliness (*to philētikon* 1327b40–1328a1), but it is also a danger to a city and to friendship because it is aroused most against *philoi* (*Pol* 1328a1–5, cf *Rhet* 1379a4–8) Spirit, in short, is like wine its natural heat makes it socially dangerous when unmixed, but healthful and conducive to *aidōs* and *philia* when properly blended

One way of regulating and blending spirit is by means of its opposites fear and the closely related emotion of pity In the *Rhetoric*, Aristotle considers ways in which fear may be produced in those who are hubristic, contemptuous, and bold [8] In the *Politics* also, Aristotle advises those who are concerned about the constitution "to provide fears" and "to make what is far off [seem] near" in order to correct the tendency people have to become hubristic in peacetime, when the fear of danger does not force them to be temperate [9] Tragic fear and pity would be particularly well suited to oppose and correct the hubristic tendencies associated with excessive *thumos*, because both *thumos* and tragic emotion are concerned with *philia* relationships If excess spirit, like unmixed wine, threatens *philia*, tragic emotion, like the addition of cold water to wine, could moderate and oppose excessive spirit to produce a blend conducive to *philia*

If tragic emotion can oppose excessive *thumos*, it is particularly useful for the young, who are both *thumetic* and responsive to shame (*Rhet* 2 12 1389a9–10, 1389a29–31) This function of tragedy is most important, and will be taken as paradigmatic in the following discussion It should be noted, however, that tragic emotion might oppose not only excessive spirit, but also shamelessness caused by other things *Rhetoric* 2 13 tells us that the old have qualities opposite to those of the young, for they are characterized by cold, fearful emotions, and they lack the *thumetic* desires of the young However, Aristotle's old people, unlike the excessively timid old men of Plato's *Laws*, tend to be shameless, because they do not care what people think (*Rhet* 2 13 1390a1–4) Because the emotions involve beliefs, this colder, more intellectual kind of shamelessness could also be treated allopathically with tragic pity and fear

[8] *Rhet* 1383a1–2 and 8–12, discussed in chap 7 (Tragedy and Rhetoric)
[9] *Pol* 5 1308a24–30, with 7 1334a6–10 and 1334a25–28, discussed in chap 9 (Iron and Wood)

The allopathic interpretation of tragic katharsis is consistent with Aristotelian medical as well as ethical theory. In the medical katharsis of "Aristotle," *Problems* 1.42, a disease-causing extreme of hot or cold is treated by means of a drug with the opposing extreme. For example, a cold drug is used to treat a fever. This drug, too excessively cold to be concocted and made part of the body, passes into the veins and masters the opposing excessively hot, disease-causing extreme. It then passes out, carrying with it both excessive heat and its own excessive cold. The result is a healthy *summetria* of hot and cold. Because the emotions are "form *in* matter" (λόγοι ἔνυλοι: *DA* 403a25), having physical aspects and being, in part, hot and cold bodily states, emotional katharsis closely resembles allopathic medical katharsis in some respects. In emotional katharsis, a hot emotional extreme of shamelessness is treated by the application of a cold "drug," tragic pity and fear, which is too excessive to be "concocted," or made part of the soul. Instead, it masters its opposite, shamelessness. It then passes out, carrying with it the obstructions to a healthy, natural emotional state: preexisting, excessive, hot shamelessness, and its own extreme of cold fear and pity. The result is a *summetria* of emotional extremes, the emotional mean state of *aidōs*, which is healthy and natural to the human soul. Emotional katharsis is in part a physical purgation, a pleasurable relief from excess emotional extremes.

Because the emotions are not purely physical, however, tragic katharsis cannot be solely, or even primarily, physical. Aristotle holds in his psychological works that cognitive responses cause the physical responses that are one aspect of emotional reactions: perception and *phantasia* lead to desire, which in turn leads to heating or chilling.[10] In the *Poetics* also, cognitive responses are primary, for pity and fear are aroused by imitation: "Tragedy is *imitation* . . . by means of pity and fear accomplishing . . . katharsis" (1449b24–28). The importance of imitation in the arousal of tragic emotion is also clear from 1453b11–13: "The poet should produce the pleasure that comes from pity and fear by means of imitation." To view something as an imitation, *Poetics* 4 tells us, is to experience the cognitive response of learning that *this* is *that*, and imitation is pleasurable because it leads us to reason and learn. Thus, the cognitive responses involved in viewing an imitation as an imitation are necessary to produce katharsis and the pleasure proper to tragedy. In the case of the old people of *Rhetoric* 2.13, who are physically cold, but who do not pay attention to the opin-

---

[10] See chap. 6 ("Pity, Fear, and Physical Danger").

ions of others, these cognitive responses would be even more important than they are in the case of the *thumetic* young.

Although Aristotle provides few details about the cognitive aspects of psychic katharsis, Plato's account in *Sophist* 230 of the elenchus, "the greatest and most powerful katharsis" for the soul, illuminates the cognitive aspects of emotional katharsis in the *Poetics*. Allopathic Aristotelian tragic katharsis by means of pity and fear involves the same steps that were outlined in chapter 9 ("The Platonic Elenchus") Tragedy begins (stage I[A]) by bringing to the audience's attention, in a kind of diagnosis, the shameless emotions it will eventually cast out. Like the elenchus, tragedy brings to our consciousness the shameless desires even the best of us have to pursue any and every kind of pleasure and to believe that all pleasure is good.[11] Tragedy, by representing shameful deeds—parricide, incest, child-murder—has a certain appeal to our baser instincts. We enjoy watching tragedies in large part because we too, at some level, desire to do anything and everything, and to see these things done by others. The insight was Plato's before it was Freud's In drunken sleep, Plato writes, the bestial part of the soul "dares . . to do everything, since it is released and freed from all shame and wisdom. For it does not shrink from attempting to have intercourse with a mother, as it thinks, or from any murder, or keep from any food. And in a word it lacks no folly or shamelessness" (*Rep.* 9.571c7–d4). The tragedies themselves often play on these desires, as when, for example, the Chorus in Sophocles' *Oedipus at Colonus* reflects the curiosity of the audience as it questions Oedipus. "It is terrible to awaken long-sleeping evil, stranger. Nevertheless, I long to hear" (510–12). The strong word ἔραμαι, "I long," used by this Chorus is cognate with that used by Dionysus in Euripides' *Bacchae* to refer to Pentheus's "lust" to see his mother's supposed orgies. ἔρωτα (813) The desires tragedy brings to the audience's consciousness are not, however, Oedipal desires in a narrow sense, although they are desires connected with shamelessness (*anaischuntia, anaideia*) against *philoi* They include the *thumetic*, pleasure-seeking desires that make us generally overconfident and aggressive, especially against *philoi*, and other shameless tendencies to scorn the opinions of others. Parricide and incest in tragedy represent the extremes to which shamelessness can lead.

Tragedy not only brings our shameless tendencies to our consciousness, it also makes us realize that these desires and beliefs are inconsistent with other beliefs and desires we have (stage I[B] in the outline) Unless we are

[11] I am indebted to David Charles for some good discussions of this point

hopelessly licentious, we also believe that unrestrained pursuit of pleasure is shameful, and we desire to avoid shame. In this way, tragedy makes us realize that we, like Pentheus, would take pleasure in seeing what is bitter to us (Euripides, *Bacchae* 815).

After bringing our shameful desires to our consciousness and making us aware of our own inconsistencies, tragedy administers a drug of fear and shame: tragic fear and pity, that is, *ekplēxis* (stage II). Tragedy arouses this emotion by representing the most painful and shameful consequences of the most shameless acts: violations of *philia* relationships. Good tragedy, moreover, represents these acts in a way that arouses pity and fear rather than the alienation and revulsion produced by the *miaron*. Tragedy shows us that we, like the person on the stage, are such as to suffer bad fortune that is painful, destructive, and shameful. Tragedy thus gives us an emotional shock of *ekplēxis*: fear concerning painful, destructive, and shameful things that could happen to us, and pity for those who suffer these things. This shock of tragic emotion opposes and counterbalances our shameless desires and beliefs. It draws us over to the opposite extreme, so that, temporarily, we fear everything and believe that every pleasure is to be avoided.

After the initial shock, during which we are overcome by emotion, tragic katharsis occurs (stage III). At this stage, the contemplation and understanding that occur as a result of the imitative aspects of tragedy lead us to recognize and despise our shameless desires and beliefs, and to cast them out of our souls. We also recognize and reject the excessively fearful desires and beliefs that tragic emotion at first produces. In allopathic medical katharsis, after drugs have mastered the opposing, disease-causing powers, the drugs "depart, carrying impediments with them. This is called katharsis" (*Prob.* 864a33–34). In tragic katharsis, also, the initial shock of extreme pity and fear passes off, along with the shameless emotions they have "mastered." This is tragic katharsis: the removal, by means of pity and fear, of emotions opposite to themselves—shameless emotions that are impediments to the emotional excellence of the soul. It is a purification of the soul, and an intellectual clarification much like that effected by the Platonic elenchus.

In the elenchus, katharsis results in a pure, healthy state of the soul (stage IV). Similarly, tragic katharsis results in the healthy, emotional mean state of *aidōs*. This state is not itself true excellence, but is conducive to excellence. As the conflict emotion "avoidance of blame" (*EN* 1116a29), *aidōs* is an awareness and active rejection of one's desires to pursue any and every pleasure, and of the accompanying belief that any and every pleasure is to be pursued. Thus, tragic katharsis produces, like the elenchus, a casting out (ἐκβολή *Soph.* 230b1) of false beliefs Only after this process are people ready to accept the true beliefs required by true excellence.

While the Platonic elenchus provides a model for Aristotelian tragic katharsis that is useful in many respects, there are also significant differences between Platonic and Aristotelian katharsis. For one thing, Plato's katharsis is produced by means of philosophical dialogue, Aristotle's tragic katharsis is produced by means of poetic imitation In chapter 2 I considered Aristotle's concept of imitation as a whole, but the specific role of imitation in producing tragic katharsis requires further discussion.

In Aristotle's view, context and function help determine our different responses to a story used as an imitation and to the same story used as a rhetorical example The story used by the rhetorician has the practical purpose of inducing action of a certain kind, while the story used as an imitation by the poet has a purely theoretical function. True, the rhetorician, like the poet, is concerned with the universal, with what a certain kind of person says or does "for the most part." The rhetorician and the poet produce pity and fear in the same way. by leading us to see ourselves and others as instances of a universal For example, rhetoric and poetry lead us to fear for ourselves because we realize that we, like Oedipus, are such as to suffer. Then, because we see that Oedipus suffers the kinds of things that we also are such as to suffer, we pity him Unlike the rhetorician, however, the poet does not have a particular, practical goal In aesthetic situations, fear is not followed by flight or self-defense. Instead, after we understand that this is an imitation and not a situation requiring practical action, we view a particular plot that "speaks of the universal" (*Po.* 1451b6–7) as an imitation of things we have seen before We learn, as *Poetics* 4 states, that *this* is *that*, that the actions of Oedipus reflect the structure of events we have previously perceived with our senses In this way, imitation teaches us about the intelligible structure of the real world. This learning process is part of the activity of *theōria*, "contemplation". Aristotle uses the cognate participle in *Poetics* 4 1448b11 Contemplation is an activity engaged in for its own sake. It is pleasurable in itself, and it also, according to *Parts of Animals* 1.5, leads us to "love" rather than despising such painful objects of perception as corpses [12]

If all imitation leads us to contemplate, tragedy, as the imitation of

[12] The points discussed briefly in this paragraph are covered in more detail in chap 2 ("*Theōria*") and chap 7 ("Tragedy and Rhetoric ')

346

pitiable and fearful actions, leads us to contemplate our condition as mortals. We learn that the painful, destructive, and shameful events we have perceived in the real world have the same kind of intelligible structure the tragic plot has, and we take an intellectual pleasure in contemplating this structure At this point we conclude, by an inductive reasoning process, that not only Oedipus and ourselves but all humans, because they are mortal, are such as to suffer. This new understanding transforms the way in which we respond to things in the world.[13] Instead of perceiving pitiable and fearful events with pain alone, we come to understand them as intelligible structures, reflecting the human condition This poetical, theoretical understanding given by imitation of pitiable and fearful events produces the pleasure proper to tragedy, that which comes "from pity and fear by means of imitation," and it leads us to accept, emotionally and intellectually, that suffering is the human condition While the perception of terrible events continues to give pain, the understanding tragedy gives is deeply consoling Throughout Greek literature, individual sorrows are consoled by appeal to a common human destiny, as in the Chorus's statements in Euripides' *Alcestis*.

> Admetus, it is necessary to bear these misfortunes
> For you are not the first or the last of mortals
> to lose an excellent wife Know
> that all of us must die

$$(416-19)^{14}$$

Because tragedy imitates the most significant and painful of terrible actions—those within *philia* relationships—it arouses pity and fear (*ekplēxis*) most effectively. It also teaches us to respond in the right way, emotionally and intellectually, to our *philoi*, without shamelessness or excessive timidity, but with a proper understanding of their importance to us, and a proper respect for their opinions This psychic condition is called *aidōs* in Greek literature It involves respect not only for our *philoi*, but also for the gods, in that it acknowledges and accepts our condition as mortals. *Aidōs* is the good fear that preserves society, or, in Parker's words, the "self-restraint expressed through respect for recognized values," both social and religious[15] In Aristotle's philosophy, the term *aidōs* retains

[13] Reckford, *Aristophanes*, 11–12, discusses a parallel kind of changed perspective produced by comic recognition and katharsis

[14] On this means of consolation, see Macleod, *Iliad*, 7–8, and Burkert, *Mitleidsbegriff*, 105–6, who cites Pindar, *Pythian* 3 81–84, and *Il* 24 525ff , discussed below

[15] Parker, *Miasma*, 189

much of its traditional meaning, although the religious dimension is less important.[16] *Aidōs* also acquires a more technical sense in Aristotle, referring to a praiseworthy emotional mean state of shamelessness (*anaischuntia*) and excessive fear of the opinions of others (*kataplēxis*). If tragedy helps us respond to our *philoi* in the right way, it also helps produce *aidōs* in this technical sense. Thus, while Aristotle does not use the term *aidōs* in the *Poetics*, the beneficial emotional effect of tragedy is most plausibly taken to be *aidōs*.

Specifically, in tragic katharsis, imitation uses extreme pity and fear (*ekplēxis*) to oppose shamelessness and to produce at last the emotional mean state of *aidōs*. Like biological and ethical katharsis, tragic katharsis is an allopathic process of removing that which prevents something from attaining the *teleiōsis* that is in accord with its nature. Tragic katharsis not only contributes in this way to the *teleiōsis* of the soul, it is itself the *telos* of tragedy: "Tragedy is imitation . . . accomplishing . . . katharsis" (*Po.* 6.1449b24–28). Katharsis, however, is the end of tragedy not in the way in which the last in a series of events is their end, but in the way in which the functioning of a living thing is its end. Aristotle frequently compares tragedy to a living thing, with a soul, an *ergon*, a *telos*, and a nature of its own. The plot, as the "soul" of tragedy, is its *telos* (1450a22–23). Because the plot is itself a process, an activity, the functioning of the plot in producing the "proper pleasure" of tragedy, the "pleasure that comes from pity and fear by means of imitation" (1453b10–12), is the *telos* and *ergon* of tragedy.[17] This pleasure is the pleasure of contemplating, for its own sake, the relationship between imitation and objects imitated—the terrible and pitiable perceptible objects we have seen before—and of coming in this way to understand the human condition. Katharsis as well as the pleasure of contemplation is the end of tragedy, for understanding produces a katharsis of emotional extremes that results in an emotional mean state. As a natural result of contemplation, or, rather, as an integral part of it, katharsis is a part of the "pleasure that comes from pity and fear."

Tragic katharsis involves the whole of human nature. It is a "purgation" of the physical matter of the emotions. It can also be called an emotional "purification" in that it corrects and opposes our shameless tendencies.

---

[16] While I am not aware of any passages in which Aristotle writes of *aidōs* for the gods, he does accept many traditional beliefs about the gods, piety, and ethics. See, for example, *EN* 1179a23–30, quoted by Verdenius, "Aristotle's Religion," 60.

[17] The *ergon* of tragedy (or of imitation) is mentioned at 1450a31, 1452b29–30, and 1462b12–14, where it is clearly identified with the *telos* and the proper pleasure of tragedy. On this topic, and on tragedy as a living thing, see chap 2 ("Production").

Most important, however, tragic katharsis, like the katharsis produced by Plato's elenchus, is an intellectual "clarification." In *Poetics* 4, Aristotle writes that to enjoy an imitation as an imitation is to engage in the philosophical pleasure of contemplation (*theōria*): "For we take pleasure contemplating the most accurately made images of things that themselves give us pain to see, such as the shapes of the most despised animals and of corpses. The cause of this is that learning is most pleasant not only to philosophers, but to others in the same way, though they have only a small share in this" (*Po.* 1448b10–15). This is the same philosophical pleasure that we get from contemplating, for their own sake, "the more despised animals": "For even in those [sc., animals] that are not pleasing to the senses, when contemplated, the nature that crafted them gives immeasurable pleasure in the same way to those who are able to gain knowledge of the causes and are philosophers by nature" (*PA* 1.5.645a7–10). Since philosophy and contemplation are "pure" (*katharai*) pleasures,[18] it is not surprising that the "pure" pleasure of philosophical contemplation should, in the *Poetics*, be closely connected with "purification" (katharsis). Imitation gives all human beings, whose nature it is to imitate and learn, a share in the pure pleasure of philosophical contemplation, to the extent that each individual is capable of sharing in it.

To sum up, the entire process by means of which imitation uses pity and fear to accomplish pleasure and katharsis can be represented in the following explanatory schema:[19]

I. Bringing to light of shameless beliefs and desires, together with the realization that these are inconsistent with the more modest beliefs and desires we also have.

II. Reasoning process:

A. X suffered destructive, painful, and shameful things when this was not expected.

B. Therefore, X is such as to suffer.

C. X is greater than we are.

D. X is like us.

E. Therefore, we also are such as to suffer.

F. Fear of suffering destructive, painful, and shameful things.

III. Reasoning process:

A. X suffers destructive, painful, and shameful things that we also are such as to suffer.

---

[18] See *EN* 1177a25–26, and chap. 9 ("Purity").

[19] See chap. 7 ("Aesthetic and Real-Life Emotion") for an explanation of steps II–IV.

B. X does not deserve to suffer.

C We pity X.

IV. Judgment that impedes command to flee or give aid, this is an imitation and not a real-life situation

V. Contemplation. *this* plot is an imitation of *that* suffering we have seen before: all mortals are such as to suffer destructive, painful, and shameful things.

VI. Pleasure of learning

VII. Katharsis: removal of shameless emotional extremes, which are carried off as the opposing extremes of tragic fear and pity depart from the soul

VIII. *Aidōs*.

Steps IV through VIII do not, of course, actually occur sequentially, but more or less simultaneously. Viewing a tragedy as an imitation leads to contemplation and understanding, which are pleasurable, and which involve an emotional and intellectual acceptance of the human condition that is incompatible with extreme pity and fear and with shamelessness. However, the emotional sequence of fear, pity, and katharsis is a temporal one, for we cannot experience pity until we fear for ourselves, and the katharsis produced by means of pity and fear must come after the emotions that produce it.

The sequence of events in the tragic plot corresponds in some respects to this emotional sequence in the audience. In the *desis* of the tragic plot, fear and pity are first aroused by the representation of harm, or threat of harm, to the *philia* relationship, which is the basis for social order. Then, in the *lusis* of the plot, the social order sanctioned by *aidōs* is reaffirmed, either through the avoidance of threatened harm to *philoi* (good fortune) or through a representation of the terrible consequences of actual violence among *philoi* (bad fortune).[20] Thus, katharsis is an emotional "solution" that is the counterpart of the "solution" of the plot.[21]

In chapter 1, I studied the sequence of fear and *aidōs* reflected in the plot of Aeschylus's *Oresteia*. In the first part of this trilogy, we are aware of the negative aspects of fear caused by polluting kin-murder. This fear, inspired by the anger of the Erinyes and of their human agents, maddens and paralyzes, "binding the wits" (*Eum.* 332). The end of the *Eumenides*,

[20] On the role of Greek festivals and rituals generally in reaffirming the social order, see Burkert, *Greek Religion*, esp 258–59, 264–68

[21] It is a curious coincidence that the Greek term *lusis*, "solution," has the same range of meanings that the word "katharsis" does, referring to a religious purification, a physical evacuation, and an intellectual solution See LSJ, s v λυσις, I 3, II 2, and II 4a

however, reflects the positive aspects of the fear of wrongdoing that prevents pollution and wrath. Fear, in its positive aspects, is the "reverence" (*sebas*, *aidōs*) that preserves *philia* in family and state. *Aidōs* in the *Eumenides* resembles Aristotelian *aidōs* in this respect, as it does in being opposed to each of two complementary extremes: anger, and the maddening fear caused by anger.

Another excellent literary example of the sequence of fear, pity, and *aidōs* is the Priam-Achilles scene in *Iliad* 24. In this passage, as noted in chapter 7, Priam supplicates Achilles, asking him to return Hector's body, and arouses in Achilles first fear for himself and his father (507) and then pity for Priam (516). Moreover, after experiencing fear and pity, Achilles contemplates the human condition as a whole (525–51). What Achilles experiences in this scene, I will now argue, is an emotional katharsis culminating in *aidōs*.

In the "urns of Zeus" passage, Achilles relates the particular instances before him, those of Priam and Peleus, to the human condition generally:

> Such is the way the gods spun life for unfortunate mortals,
> that we live in unhappiness, but the gods themselves have no sorrows.
> There are two urns that stand on the door-sill of Zeus. They are unlike
> for the gifts they bestow: an urn of evils, an urn of blessings.
> If Zeus who delights in thunder mingles these and bestows them
> on man, he shifts, and moves now in evil, again in good fortune.
> But when Zeus bestows from the urn of sorrows, he makes a failure
> of man, and the evil hunger drives him over the shining
> earth, and he wanders respected neither of gods nor mortals.
> Such were the shining gifts given by the gods to Peleus
> from his birth, who outshone all men beside for his riches
> and pride of possession, and was lord over the Myrmidons. Thereto
> the gods bestowed an immortal wife on him, who was mortal.
> But even on him the god piled evil also. . . .
>
> . . . .
>
> And you, old sir, we are told you prospered once. . . .
>
> . . . .
>
> But now the Uranian gods brought us, an affliction upon you.
>
> (*Il*. 24.525–47: Lattimore)

Priam's speech at 486–506 had the practical purpose of arousing fear and pity so as to persuade Achilles to act in a definite way, by giving back Hector's body. In this respect it resembled rhetorical speeches. Achilles' response, however, is more philosophical and poetic, in that he goes beyond practical considerations to contemplate the instances of Priam and Peleus as they reflect the human condition generally.[22] As he contemplates, Achilles learns to endure his own sorrow. Before and after the passage just quoted, framing it, Achilles tells Priam to stop lamenting.

> . . Come, then,
> and sit down upon this chair, and you and I will even let
> our sorrows lie still in the heart for all our grieving There is not
> any advantage to be won from grim lamentation
>
> (521–24 Lattimore)

> But bear up, nor mourn endlessly in your heart, for there is not
> anything to be gained from grief for your son, you will never
> bring him back, sooner must you go through yet another sorrow
>
> (548–51. Lattimore)

As Burkert remarks, this is what others, Thetis in particular, have been trying to get Achilles to do for a long time. Achilles' words show that he has at last fully accepted his mortal condition.[23] Achilles goes from fear for himself and pity for another individual to the intellectual recognition and emotional acceptance of a universal law governing all mortals. This recognition allows him to cease his own excessive mourning, to return Hector's corpse, and to take part in the human community again, in a way that better suits his condition as a mortal. Achilles has learned something higher than pity: *aidōs*.[24] Priam's supplication mentioned *aidōs*. "But have *aidōs* for the gods, Achilles, and pity for me" (503), and Apollo stated at 24.44–45 that "Achilles has lost and destroyed pity, nor does *aidōs* belong to him."[25] While Achilles does not use the word *aidōs*, his speech about the urns of Zeus, and his subsequent actions, in which he gives back Hector's body, dines with Priam, and fully resumes normal life by sleeping with Briseis, show that he has in fact learned *aidōs* for higher things.[26]

When Achilles learns *aidōs* and ceases to grieve excessively, he has experienced an emotional katharsis of wrath, produced by means of pity and

[22] On this aspect of Achilles' speech, see Macleod, *Iliad*, ad loc

[23] Burkert, *Mitleidsbegriff*, 106–7 My account of this scene is much indebted to the illuminating analyses of Burkert, 99–107, and Macleod, *Iliad*, introduction and commentary These scholars, however, stress the effects of pity and do not specifically discuss *aidōs*

[24] On pity and *aidōs*, see chap 6 ("Pity, Fear, and Physical Danger") esp n 20

[25] On this idea, and on the ambivalence of ἀπώλεσεν in line 44, see Burkert, *Mitleidsbegriff*, 101

[26] On the significance of the meal, see Macleod, *Iliad*, on 596–620 Macleod (on 673–76) also notes that Achilles has refused sex since Patroclus's death

fear. Since the death of Patroclus, Achilles has been angry, insolent, piti-
less, and shameless, offending gods and mortals by outraging a corpse and
by refusing to accept his mortal condition, which requires the normal,
human activities of eating, drinking, and sleeping.[27] While the words of
his divine mother Thetis (24.126–37) set in motion Achilles' return to
normality, it is above all the appeal of a fellow mortal, Priam, that effects
this change.[28] Priam's speech arouses in Achilles the fear and pity that
counterbalance his previous shameless state of soul. Achilles' contemplation then allows him to use the particular instances before him to understand the human condition as a whole. He thus acquires the Homeric
excellence of *aidōs*, as he endures sorrow and reenters the human community.[29]

Achilles' experience is in many respects a paradigm of the katharsis produced by tragedy and epic Epic, of course, has the same end (pleasure and
katharsis) as tragedy (*Po.* 1462b12–15). Some indication that epic was
thought to produce a katharsis of excessive spirit or anger is provided by a
Homeric scholion. "They ask why he began from the wrath [of Achilles]
. . . in the first place, in order that the part of the soul that is of this sort
may be purified [ἀποκαθαριεύσῃ] of the passion "[30] Achilles' anger is
purged by his pity, and by the deeper understanding of the human condition to which it leads him. Similarly, through epic and tragedy we too
attain a philosophical understanding of human suffering that tempers anger and unites us in sympathy with our fellow mortals.[31]

While I have argued that the allopathic interpretation of tragic katharsis is supported by evidence in the *Poetics* and elsewhere, it remains to be
shown how this interpretation is consistent with Aristotle's statement in
Poetics 6. "Tragedy is imitation . by means of pity and fear accomplishing the katharsis of such emotions [δι' ἐλέου καὶ φόβου περαίνουσα τὴν

[27] Macleod argues convincingly (ibid , 21–28) that Achilles desire to avenge Patroclus
is an extension of the theme of his wrath

[28] Ibid , on 460–67, notes "Fellow-feeling, like suffering is peculiar to men '

[29] See ibid , 27 "[Achilles' pity] is not only an emotion, but an insight because he sees
that suffering is unavoidable and common to all men, he can keep back, not without a
struggle, his own pride, rage and grief The result is that he acquires a new form of honour
from Zeus (24 110), through neither inaction nor violence, but restraint, not to the det-
riment of comrades or of enemies, but to the benefit of a fellow-man, and not by persuading
or almost coercing, but by obeying the supreme god "

[30] Schol A on *Il* 1 1, translated by Carnes Lord, *Education*, 160 n 22 Cf Janko,
Comedy, 148 It should be noted, however, that there is a textual problem involved, for
ἀποκαθαριεύσῃ is not found in all MSS see the apparatus given by Erbst, *Scolia*

[31] See Macleod, *Iliad*, introduction, 7–8, on the *Iliad* as a tragic poem

τῶν τοιούτων παθημάτων κάθαρσιν]" (1449b24–28). Two conclusions about this definition have already been drawn. First, we saw above (chapter 8, "Theoretical Problems") that *pathēmatōn* here means "emotions," not "events." Thus, katharsis is an interactive process in which emotion acts on emotion. Second, a study of Aristotle's use of "katharsis" and cognates (chapter 9, "Overview") showed that a genitive governed by these words always refers to that which is separated off from something else and never to the subject from which something else is separated. Thus, the phrase τὴν τῶν τοιούτων παθημάτων κάθαρσιν most likely means "katharsis of [consisting in the removal of] such emotions," and not "katharsis of [something else from] such emotions."

A more intractable difficulty concerns the reference of τοιούτων in the definition of tragedy. Those favoring a homeopathic interpretation must explain why Aristotle writes τοιούτων (such) and not τούτων (the same). On the other hand, an allopathic interpretation must explain why Aristotle does not write ἑτέρων (other) or ἐναντίων (opposite) emotions. A solution to this difficulty must take into account both the meaning of τοιούτων and Aristotle's views on the emotions. τοιούτων does not mean either "the same" or "the opposite"; as Beare has shown, it refers instead to emotions that are "such as" pity and fear in that they are in the same class.[32] While some scholars have suggested that this is the class of all painful and disturbing emotions, such a category is too broad and general. What is required instead is a class of emotions all of which are "such as" pity and fear in a more specific way.

Suggestions about what such a class might be can be found in Aristotle's ethical works. Aristotle writes that each of the excellences is "concerned with" (περί) emotions of a certain kind. For example, courage is the mean state "concerning fears" (περὶ φόβους: *EE* 1228a27; *EN* 1117a29–30; *MM* 1185b28–29), and mildness is the mean state "concerning angers" (περὶ ὀργάς: *EN* 1125b26). In *Eudemian Ethics* 2.3, Aristotle writes that what he calls at one time "ethical excellences" (1220b34–35) and at another "emotions" (τὰ μὲν πάθη ταῦτα καὶ τοιαῦτα: 1221a13) are parts of a divisible continuum (συνεχεῖ καὶ διαιρετῷ: 1220b21–22), going from vicious excess to vicious deficiency. Thus, while the courageous person has a mean state concerning fears, both the coward and the rash person fear the wrong things, at the wrong times, and in the wrong way (1221a17–19). Aristotle sums up this theory in *Nicomachean Ethics* 3.7: "The coward, the rash person, and the courageous person are concerned with the same

[32] Beare, "Anaphoric," 123.

things {περι ταυτὰ}, but they differ with respect to these things The ones [sc , the coward and the rash person] exceed and fall short, while the other [sc , the courageous person] is in the intermediate and appropriate state" (1116a4–7)

This account of the relationship between the emotions and the excellences suggests that, in Aristotle's view, there are various kinds (*genera*) of emotions—for example, that of the emotions concerned with *phobos*, fear of physical danger, and that concerned with anger Each of these kinds is a continuum, going from excess to deficiency, with different forms (*eidē*) of emotions occupying different positions on the continuum [33] All these forms are "like" or "such as" (τοιαῦτα) the emotion that characterizes the continuum as a whole, even though the extremes are also opposite in form to one another and to the intermediate [34] For example, the coward experiences an emotion "such as" that experienced by the rash person, for both emotions belong to the same kind, that of the emotions concerned with fear The coward's fear, however, is the excessive extreme, opposite in form to the deficient extreme of fear experienced by the rash person

If the emotions in general have kinds and forms of this sort, tragic emotion is one form of the kind that is "concerned with" (tragic) pity and fear This kind is a continuum going from excess to deficiency, and having different forms, all of which are "such as" the emotion that characterizes the continuum as a whole Tragic emotion (*ekplēxis*) is the excessive extreme of fear of painful and disgraceful evils, and pity for others who suffer them The opposite, deficient extreme is a lack of pity and fear, while *aidōs* is intermediate with respect to both extremes These emotions concerned with tragic pity and fear are similar in some respects to those that constitute the trio listed in the table of extremes and intermediates at *Eudemian Ethics* 2 3 1221a1 shamelessness, *kataplēxis*, and *aidōs* [35] All of these are forms of the kind that is concerned with fear of disgrace, and shamelessness can be said to be "such as" *kataplēxis* in belonging to the same kind Similarly, the shameless emotions opposite to tragic *ekplēxis* are "such as" it because they belong to the same kind

Following this account, the phrase τῶν τοιούτων παθημάτων, "such emotions," refers to fearless and shameless, *thumetic* emotions that are

[33] Aristotle refers to *eidē* of *pathēmata* concerning anger at *EE* 2 3 1221b10

[34] The extremes are opposite {*enantia*} both to one another and to the intermediate (*EE* 1220b31–32), cf *EN* 1108b13–15, and Dirlmeier, *Eudemische Ethik*, on 1220b29 See also chap 8 (Homeopathy Theoretical Problems)

[35] On *ekplēxis*, *kataplēxis*, and *aidōs*, see chap 6 and chap 7 (Pity and Fear in the *Poetics*)

"such as" tragic pity and fear because they belong to the kind that is concerned with the *fearful and shameful events represented in tragedy* These shameless emotions are opposite in form to the tragic emotions by means of which katharsis is accomplished It is precisely this kind of similarity and difference that makes katharsis possible According to *Generation and Corruption*, one thing can act on another only if it is the same and like in kind (*genos*), but different and opposite in form (*eidos*) "The patient and the agent are the same and like in kind, but unlike in form, and the contraries are of this sort [τοιαῦτα]" (324a5–7)

In my view, then, the phrase τῶν τοιουτων παθηματων, 'such emotions," in Aristotle's definition of tragedy refers to emotions that are the same as pity and fear, and like them in kind, but opposite in form In tragic katharsis, the preexisting emotional extreme of fearlessness and shamelessness is treated allopathically with the opposing extreme of tragic emotion *ekplēxis* The pity and fear aroused by tragedy effect a removal (katharsis) of the opposite emotions "concerning (tragic) pity and fear" fearless, shameless, aggressive, *thumetic* emotions

This interpretation is consistent with Greek usage, and it has the advantage of making Aristotle's theory of tragic katharsis consistent with his views on action and passion, and on the emotions generally It is also inherently plausible People are not, in Aristotle's view, usually filled with a disturbing excess of pity and fear concerning shameful and painful events, but are more inclined to be shameless and *thumetic* What they need to fear and to guard against is not excessive timidity, but the aggressive impulses that lead to injury to *philoi*, in family and state On the other hand, a homeopathic interpretation is in itself implausible, and is inconsistent with Aristotle's explicit statements that, in action and passion generally, and in medical treatment in particular, one thing acts on another because it is opposite Thus, while neither interpretation falls easily and naturally out of the Greek, the allopathic theory for which I have argued is the most plausible in itself, and the most consistent with the evidence of Aristotle's other works

Although tragedy is an allopathic treatment for shamelessness, it is useful not only for abnormal or vicious or immature audiences, but also for people at every stage of ethical and intellectual development For those at the lowest level of ethical development, tragedy can provide the fear of physical pain that is alone efficacious in controlling "the many," who "by nature do not obey *aidōs* but fear" (*EN* 1179b11) Tragic fear is, in part, fear of physically painful and destructive events, and the representation of the painful and destructive sufferings of those who commit shameful deeds may arouse this inferior but beneficial fear in those at the lowest stage of development. However, the primary audience for tragedy, according to the *Poetics*, is not the *phauloi*, the inferior "many," but the "decent" people, the *epieikeis*, mentioned at *Poetics* 1462a2–4. These "decent people" are the better class of ordinary citizens who, according to *Nicomachean Ethics* 10.9, obey *aidōs* rather than *phobos*, and are "decently" advanced in habits (1180a8). Tragedy can help this class acquire, preserve, or regain the emotional mean state of *aidōs*, and it can provide them with the training that "urges them toward nobility" (1179b10).[36] Tragedy contributes throughout life to their "perfection" and "completion" (*teleiōsis*) by means of habit. "The excellences come to be neither by nature nor against nature, but [they come to be] in us who are by nature able to acquire them, when we are perfected by means of habit" (*EN* 1103a23–26)

First, tragedy provides the "decent" class of people with an affective and cognitive ethical education, from childhood through youth. Tragedy provides an education in pleasure and pain that is useful for the training in early childhood of people who are going to become "decent." It leads children to hate the shameful deeds that result, in the tragedies, in disgrace, pain, and death, and encourages them to love fine deeds that result in good fortune. It thus helps give children the correct upbringing that leads them "straight from youth . . . to take pleasure in and to feel pain at the right things" (*EN* 1104b11–12). The young person who will become decent must first have been prepared by habits "to feel pleasure and to hate correctly" (1179b24–26), "loving the fine and being disgusted at the shameful" (1179b30–31). This emotional training helps produce and increase *aidōs*, respect for the opinions of others. As training in *aidōs*, tragedy also helps young people acquire the intellectual abilities of *phronēsis* and *nous*. It leads them to see the particular events represented in tragedy as instances of universals, and to contemplate them as imitations of things they have already seen. Tragic imitation helps young people understand the human condition by attending to the fearful and pitiable events in real life that tragedy imitates, and by paying attention to the opinions of experienced older people and of practically wise people (*EN* 1143b11–13). Thus, watching tragedy is one way in which young people can make ethical lessons a part of themselves. "When people first learn something, they string words together, but they do not yet know [what they are saying.]

---

[36] On *EN* 10 9, the role of *aidōs* in habituation, and the audience for tragedy, see chap 6 ("*Aidōs*, Excellence, and Habituation ')

For [knowledge] must become part of their nature [συμφυῆναι], and this requires time" (*EN* 1147a21–22).

The ethical habituation of "decent" people does not stop in youth, but continues throughout life. Even old people need (re)habituation in *aidōs*, for, according to *Rhetoric* 2.13, they are inclined to be shameless, though for different reasons than the young. At *Nicomachean Ethics* 10.9.1180a1– 4, Aristotle states that habituation for adults must continue throughout life, and that laws are needed for this purpose. While this passage does not mention drama, there were in fact important laws concerning dramatic festivals in Athens.[37] Significantly, Aristotle includes overseers of "Dionysiac contests" and of similar "spectacles" among the essential officials of a city that has acquired leisure and prosperity (*Pol.* 1322b37–1323a3). There is no reason to doubt that he shared the traditional view that poetry is a continued education for adults: "Small children have a teacher to counsel them; adults have the poets" (Aristophanes, *Frogs* 1054–55). Tragedy teaches the class of "decent" people throughout life emotional and intellectual lessons that they, like the older people of Plato's Chorus of Dionysus, need to keep relearning. Like wine in Plato's *Laws*, tragedy, another gift of Dionysus, is for Aristotle a drug to produce and renew *aidōs* in the soul.

Even the perfectly excellent person, who does not experience tragic katharsis, can enjoy the philosophical pleasures given to all humans by tragic imitation. When people enjoy tragedy as an imitation, they all share as much as they are able in the essentially human, pure, and rational pleasures of learning and contemplation (*Po.* 4.1448b10–15). Moreover, because tragedy imitates events within *philia* relationships, it teaches us about what is essential to our nature as political animals. Aristotle's own frequent use of examples from tragedy in his ethical works demonstrates that tragedy can be of use to philosophers. Indeed, the varied, extreme, and salient examples given by tragedy can often teach us more than reallife experience. Tragedy can also teach us about some things better than abstract philosophy can because it, unlike philosophy, arouses emotion. Tragic imitation leads us to contemplate, for their own sake, objects that also arouse the emotions of pity and fear. In this way, tragedy teaches us about the objects of perception that arouse emotion, and leads us to understand them intellectually and emotionally. As Nelson Goodman states: "In aesthetic experience the *emotions function cognitively*. The work of art is

---

[37] See chap. 1, esp. n. 6.

apprehended through the feelings as well as through the senses."[38] We cannot really understand human suffering intellectually unless we also feel it. In all these ways, tragedy helps us know ourselves as human beings.

This book began with a brief survey of traditional views about the need for a beneficial fear of wrongdoing within the aggressive, competitive Greek society, within which *philoi* could so easily quarrel. This need was especially great at gatherings of *philoi*, at symposia, at feasts, and at festivals of Dionysus, the wine god who destroys *philia* when excessive and unmixed, but who produces and increases *aidōs* and *philia* when mixed with restraint. I have argued that tragedy is a verbal analogue of the drinking cup reproduced in the frontispiece, in which a terrifying gorgoneion glares in the midst of reveling wine drinkers. The tragedies aroused fear and pity in the Greek audience as antidotes to the shameless emotions that tragedy itself brought to its awareness. Within the City Dionysia also, tragedy was a kind of gorgoneion in the drinking cup. Preceded by reveling, accompanied by wine drinking, and followed by a satyr play, tragedy provided a salutary lesson, cognitive and affective, about the terrible dangers of unmixed wine and revelry. In this way, tragedy helped preserve the polis and produce *aidōs* in the soul. Aristotle fully agreed with Aeschylus:

> There is a place where the terrible is good,
> and must remain established
> an overseer of thoughts.
>
> (*Eum.* 517–19)

Aristotle's views on tragic plots and tragic katharsis are closely bound up with the norms of this Greek society. Many of the specific details of his views, then, cannot be applied to modern literary works, or even to modern viewers or readers of Greek tragedies. For example, kinship does not have the significance today that it had in ancient Greek society, and modern literature is much less concerned with kin-murder than were the ancient tragedies. Morever, the peculiarly Greek emotional state of *aidōs* cannot exist in our very different modern societies.

In many respects, however, Aristotle's theories are more generally relevant. Greek tragedy can still give us a philosophical education. Viewing, or merely reading,[39] a tragedy is in itself a philosophical activity that clar-

---

[38] Goodman, *Languages*, 248; emphasis in original. See further above, chap. 2 ("*Theōria*").

[39] Merely "hearing" a tragic plot produces the emotional effects of tragedy, according to *Po.* 1453b6.

ifies the structure of pitiable and fearful human events in the world around us To the extent that the human suffering represented in the tragedies is universal to human beings, Greek tragedy can help all of us understand the human condition. Other literary genres that deal with human suffering can teach us similar lessons. Moreover, Aristotle's view that tragedy provides an emotional therapy that has both physical and cognitive aspects anticipated the discoveries of modern psychologists Oliver Sachs, for example, writes that art helps people "evoke a self," and that it has a "therapeutic power . . . as strong as any drug."[40] Tragedy can give us today something resembling an Aristotelian katharsis. It teaches us important intellectual and emotional lessons about human suffering, and it provides a therapeutic experience that is physiological as well as psychological In these ways, tragedy can help us achieve our own kind of emotional balance, and acknowledge and accept our mortal condition. it can help us "know ourselves," in the Greek sense.[41]

[40] Sachs, "Neurology," 46

[41] An earlier version of some of the material in this chapter was read at the Princeton Colloquium on Ancient Philosophy in December 1989, where I benefited from much helpful discussion

* Glossary *

NOTE: This list includes only the most relevant words; others are defined in the text. As a general rule, words ending in *-os* have plurals in *-oi*; those ending in *-a* or *-ē* have plurals in *-ai*, those ending in *-is* or *-ēs* have plurals in *-eis*. Other variants occur.

aidōs — shame, respect, reverence
aidēmōn (pl. *aidēmones*) — person characterized by *aidōs*
aischros — shameful, base
aischunē — shame
anagkaion — necessary, *to anagkaion* — necessity
anagnōrisis — recognition
archē — beginning, first principle
aretē — excellence
desis — complication
eikōn — image
eikos — probable, plausible, *to eikos* — probability, plausibility
ekplēxis — fear, wonder, tragic emotion
eleos — pity
enantios — opposite
epieikēs — good, decent person
ergon — function, product
ēthos (pl. *ēthē*) — character
eudaimōn — happy
eudaimonia — happiness
eutuchia — good fortune
hamartia — error
hubris — violence, insult
kakia — baseness, vice
katamēnia — menses, female generative residue
katharos — pure
katharsis — purgation, purification, clarification
kataplēxis — extreme shame or fear
kataplēx — person characterized by *kataplēxis*
kinēsis — movement, process
krasis — mixture
krisis — separation, judgment

361

mellōn — imminent

miaros — shameful, polluted, revolting

mimēsis — imitation

muthos — plot, story

lusis — solution

nous — comprehension

pathos (pl. *pathē*) — (1) emotion; (2) destructive or painful event; (3) affection; something that happens to something

peripeteia — reversal

phantasia — appearance, expectation

phaulos — inferior

philanthropon — "philanthropic"

philia — kinship, friendship, love

philos — kin, friend, loved one

phobos — fear

phronēsis — wisdom, practical reason

phusis — nature

praxis — action

prohairesis — choice

sōphrōn (pl. *sōphrones*) — temperate person

sōphrosunē — temperance

spoudaios — noble, serious

summetria — proportion

sustasis — organization, structure

teleiōsis — completion, perfection

telos — end, result

technē — craft

theōria — contemplation

thumos — spirit, anger

* *Aristotelian Texts Used* *

De anima. Ross, W. D. *Aristotelis De anima*. Oxford, 1956.

De motu animalium: Nussbaum, M. C. *Aristotle's De motu animalium*. Princeton, 1978.

De caelo: Allan, D. J. *Aristotelis De caelo*. Oxford, 1936.

Generation and Corruption: Joachim, H. H. *Aristotle on Coming-to-Be and Passing-Away*. Oxford, 1922.

Eudemian Ethics. Susemihl, F. *Aristotelis Ethica Eudemia*. Leipzig, 1884.

Fragments (other than *Protrepticus*): Rose, V. *Aristotelis Qui ferebantur librorum fragmenta*. Leipzig, 1886.

Generation of Animals: Drossaart Lulofs, H. J. *Aristotelis De generatione animalium*. Oxford, 1965.

History of Animals. Peck, A. L. *Aristotle: Historia animalium*. Books 1–3, Cambridge, Mass., 1979. Books 4–6, Cambridge, Mass., 1984

Magna moralia. Susemihl, F. *Aristotelis Quae feruntur magna moralia*. Leipzig, 1883.

Meteorologica: Fobes, F. H. *Aristotelis Meteorologicorum libri quattuor*. Cambridge, Mass., 1919.

Metaphysics. Ross, W. D. *Aristotle's Metaphysics: A Revised Text with Introduction and Commentary*. 2 vols. Oxford, 1953.

Nicomachean Ethics. Bywater, I. *Aristotelis Ethica Nicomachea*. Oxford, 1894.

Parva naturalia. Ross, W. D. *Aristotle: Parva naturalia*. Oxford, 1955.

Parts of Animals: Peck, A. L. *Aristotle: Parts of Animals*. Cambridge, Mass., 1983.

Physics. Ross, W. D. *Aristotelis Physica*. Oxford, 1956.

Poetics: Kassel, R. *Aristotelis De arte poetica liber*. Oxford, 1966.

Politics. Dreizehnter, A. *Aristoteles' Politik*. Munich, 1970.

Problems. Ruelle, C A., H. Knoellinger, and J Klek. *Aristotelis. Problemata physica*. Leipzig, 1922.

Protrepticus. Pistelli, H. *Iamblichi protrepticus ad fidem codicis Florentini*. Leipzig, 1888.

Rhetoric. Kassel, R. *Aristotelis Ars rhetorica*. Berlin, 1976.

Topics. Ross, W. D. *Aristotelis Topica et Sophistici elenchi*. Oxford, 1958.

Other works: Bekker, I. *Aristotelis opera*. Berlin, 1831.

* Bibliography *

Ackrill, J. L. "Aristotle on *Eudaimonia*." *Proceedings of the British Academy* 60 (1974). 339–59. Reprinted in Rorty, *Ethics*, 15–33.

———, trans. *Aristotle's Categories and De interpretatione*. Oxford, 1963.

Adam, J., ed. *The Republic of Plato*. 2d ed. Cambridge, 1902.

Adkins, A.W.H. "Aristotle and the Best Kind of Tragedy." *CQ* 16 (1966): 78–102.

———. " 'Friendship' and 'Self-Sufficiency' in Homer and Aristotle." *CQ* 13 (1963). 30–45.

———. *Merit and Responsiblity*. Oxford, 1960.

Allan, D. J "Peripeteia quid sit, Caesar occisus ostendit " *Mnemosyne* 29 (1976): 337–50.

Annas, J. "Plato and Aristotle on Friendship and Altruism." *Mind* 86 (1977): 532–54.

———, ed. *Oxford Studies in Ancient Philosophy*. Vol. 1. Oxford, 1983. Vol. 8. Oxford, 1990.

Bain, D. "Audience Address in Greek Tragedy." *CQ* 25 (1975) 13–25.

Baldry, H. C. "The Interpretation of *Poetics* ix." *Phronesis* 2 (1957): 41–45.

Balme, D. M. "Teleology and Necessity." In Gotthelf and Lennox, *Issues*, 275–85.

———, trans. *Aristotle's De partibus animalium I and De generatione animalium I*. Oxford, 1972.

Barker, A., ed. *Greek Musical Writings*. Vol. 2, *Harmonic and Acoustic Theory*. Cambridge, 1989.

Barker, E. *Greek Political Theory*. 3d ed. London, 1947.

Barkhuizen, J. H. "Structural Text Analysis and the Problem of Unity in the Odes of Pindar." *Acta Classica* 19 (1976): 1–19.

Barnes, J., ed. *The Complete Works of Aristotle: The Revised Oxford Translation*. Princeton, 1984.

Barnes, J., M. Schofield, and R Sorabji, eds. *Articles on Aristotle*. Vol. 2, *Ethics and Politics*. New York, 1977. Vol 4, *Psychology and Aesthetics*. New York, 1979.

Barrett, W. S., ed. *Euripides: Hippolytos*. Oxford, 1966.

Bassett, S. E. "*Hē de Odusseian . . . ēthikon (Aristotle, Poetics, xxiv, 1459b, 15)*." In *Classical Studies Presented to Edward Capps*, 3–13. Princeton, 1936.

Beare, J. I. "Anaphoric ὁ τοιοῦτος in Aristotle." *Hermathena* 18 (1914–1919): 116–35.

Bekker, I., ed. *Aristotelis opera*. Berlin, 1831.

Belfiore, E. "Aristotle and Iphigenia." In Rorty, *Poetics*.

Belfiore, E. "Aristotle's Concept of *Praxis* in the *Poetics*." *CJ* 79 (1983–1984). 110–24.

———. "*Elenchus, Epode*, and Magic: Socrates as Silenus." *Phoenix* 34 (1980): 128–37.

———. "*Peripeteia* as Discontinuous Action. Aristotle, *Poetics* 11.1452a22–29." *CP* 83 (1988): 183–94.

———. "Plato's Greatest Accusation against Poetry." *CJP*, suppl. vol 9 (1983): 39–62.

———. "Pleasure, Tragedy, and Aristotelian Psychology." *CQ* 35 (1985): 349–61.

———. Review of Janko, *Comedy. Ancient Philosophy* 7 (1988). 236–39.

———. "A Theory of Imitation in Plato's *Republic*." *TAPA* 114 (1984): 121–46.

———. "Wine and *Catharsis* of the Emotions in Plato's *Laws*." *CQ* 36 (1986). 421–37

Bennett, K. C. "The Purging of Catharsis." *BJA* 21 (1981): 204–13.

Benveniste, E. *Le vocabulaire des institutions indo-européennes*. Vol. 1. Paris, 1969.

Bernays, J. "Aristotle on the Effect of Tragedy." Trans. Jonathon Barnes and Jennifer Barnes from *Zwei Abhandlungen uber die aristotelische Theorie des Drama*. Berlin, 1880. In Barnes, Schofield, and Sorabji, *Articles*, 4.154–65.

Bertier, J. *Mnésithée et Dieuchès*. Leiden, 1972.

Bessig, H. "Gorgund Gorgoneion in der archaischen griechischen Kunst " Ph.D. diss., Berlin, 1937.

Betts, J. H., J. T. Hooker, and J. R. Green, eds. *Studies in Honour of T.B.L. Webster*. Bristol, 1986.

Bley, R. "D'Aristote à Freinet. Problèmes d'une certaine pédagogie curative." *Revue philosophique* 161 (1971) 95–110

Blundell, M. W. *Helping Friends and Harming Enemies* Cambridge, 1989.

Boardman, J. *Athenian Black Figure Vases*. New York, 1974.

———. "A Curious Eye Cup." *Archäologischer Anzeiger* 3 (1976). 281–90.

Bonitz, H. *Index Aristotelicus*. 2d ed. Berlin, 1870.

Bowra, C. M. *Pindar*. Oxford, 1964.

———, ed *Pindari carmina*. 2d ed. Oxford, 1947.

Boyancé, P. *Le culte des Muses chez les philosophes grecs*. Paris, 1937.

Bremer, J. M. *Hamartia*. Amsterdam, 1969.

Brown, A. L. "Eumenides in Greek Tragedy." *CQ* 34 (1984). 260–81.

Buonamici, F. *Discorsi poetici nella Accademia Fiorentina in difesa d'Aristotile*. Florence, 1597.

Burkert, W. *Greek Religion*. Trans. J. Raffan. Cambridge, Mass., 1985.

———. "Zum altgriechischen Mitleidsbegriff." Ph D. diss., Erlangen, 1955.

Burnet, J. *The Ethics of Aristotle*. London, 1900.

———. *Platonis opera*. 5 vols. Oxford, 1900–1907.

Burnett, A. P. *Catastrophe Survived: Euripides' Plays of Mixed Reversal*. Oxford, 1971.

Burnyeat, M. F. "Aristotle on Learning to be Good." In Rorty, *Ethics*, 69–92.

Burton, R.W.B. *Pindar's Pythian Odes*. Oxford, 1962.

Busse, A. "Zur Musikasthetik des Aristoteles." *RhM* 77 (1928). 34–50.

Butcher, S. H *Aristotle's Theory of Poetry and Fine Art*. 4th ed. New York, 1911. Reprint. New York, 1951.

Bywater, I. *Aristotle on the Art of Poetry* Oxford, 1909. Reprint. New York and London, 1980.

Campbell, A., trans. *Greek Lyric* Vol. 1. Cambridge, Mass., 1982.

Carey, C. " 'Philanthropy' in Aristotle's *Poetics*." *Eranos* 86 (1988). 131–39.

Cave, T. *Recognitions*. Oxford, 1988.

Chantraine, P. *Dictionnaire étymologique de la langue grecque*. Paris, 1970.

Charles, D. "Aristotle on Hypothetical Necessity and Irreducibility." *Pacific Philosophical Quarterly* 69 (1988) 1–53.

———— *Aristotle's Philosophy of Action*. Ithaca, 1984.

Charlton, W. "Feeling for the Fictitious." *BJA* 24 (1984). 206–16.

————, trans. *Aristotle's Physics, Books I and II*. Oxford, 1970.

Chase, G. H. *The Shield Devices of the Greeks*. Cambridge, Mass., 1902.

Clark, S.R.L. *Aristotle's Man*. Oxford, 1975

Clover, A. M *Homeopathy*. New York, 1984.

Code, A. "The Aporematic Approach to Primary Being in *Metaphysics Z*." *CJP*, suppl. vol. 10 (1985). 1–20.

Cook, A B. *Zeus*. 3 vols. Cambridge, 1940.

Cooper, J M. "Aristotle on the Forms of Friendship." *Review of Metaphysics* 30 (1977). 619–48.

————. "Aristotle on the Goods of Fortune." *PR* 94 (1985). 173–96.

————. "Contemplation and Happiness. A Reconsideration." *Synthese* 72 (1987). 187–216.

————. "Friendship and the Good in Aristotle." *PR* 86 (1977). 290–315.

————. "Hypothetical Necessity and Natural Teleology." In Gotthelf and Lennox, *Issues*, 243–74.

————. "The *Magna moralia* and Aristotle's Moral Philosophy." *AJP* 94 (1973) 327–49.

————. "Political Animals and Civic Friendship." In *Aristoteles' "Politik,"* ed. G. Patzig, 220–41. Gottingen, 1990.

————. *Reason and Human Good in Aristotle*. Cambridge, Mass., 1975

Cooper, L. *An Aristotelian Theory of Comedy*. New York, 1922.

Cooper, L., and A. Gudeman. *A Bibliography of the Poetics of Aristotle*. New Haven, 1928.

Cope, E. M. *An Introduction to Aristotle's Rhetoric*. London and Cambridge, 1867.

————. *The Rhetoric of Aristotle*. 3 vols. Revised by J. E. Sandys. Cambridge, 1877.

Croissant, J. *Aristote et les mystères*. Paris, 1932

Croon, J. H. "*The Mask of the Underworld Daemon*—Some Remarks on the Perseus-Gorgon Story." *JHS* 75 (1955): 9–16.

Crotty, K. *Song and Action: The Victory Odes of Pindar*. Baltimore, 1982.

Dahl, N. O. *Practical Reason, Aristotle, and Weakness of the Will*. Minneapolis, 1984.

Dawe, R. D. "Some Reflections on Ate and Hamartia " *HSCP* 72 (1967). 84–123.

Deonna, W. *Le symbolisme de l'oeil*. Paris, 1965

Depew, D. J. "Does Aristotle's Political Philosophy Rest on a Contradiction?" Paper presented at meeting of the Society for Ancient Greek Philosophy, Oakland, Calif., March 1989. References are to the written version distributed to members.

————. "Politics, Music, and Contemplation in Aristotle's Ideal State." In Keyt and Miller, *Companion*, 346–80.

DeWitt, N W. "The Meaning of Katharsis in Aristotle's Definition of Tragedy " *Transactions of the Royal Society of Canada*, ser. 3, vol. 28, sec. 2 (1934). 109–15.

Dickie, M. W. "*Hēsychia* and *Hybris* in Pindar." In *Greek Poetry and Philosophy. Studies in Honour of Leonard Woodbury*, ed. D. Gerber, 83–109. Chico, Calif , 1984.

Diehl, E., ed. *Anthologia lyrica Graeca*. 3d ed. Leipzig, 1949–1952.

Diels, H., and W. Kranz, eds. *Die Fragmente der Vorsokratiker*. 3 vols 5th ed Berlin, 1935–1937.

Diès, A. "Introduction, première partie." In *Platon, oeuvres complètes. Les lois*, ed. and trans É. des Places, 11 1 v–xciii. Paris, 1951.

Dietrich, B. C. *Death, Fate and the Gods*. London, 1965

Dirlmeier, F. "*Philos* und *Philia* im vorhellenistischen Griechentum " Ph.D. diss., Munich, 1931.

Dirlmeier, F., trans. *Aristoteles. Eudemische Ethik*. 3d ed. Berlin, 1979.

————. *Aristoteles. Magna moralia*. 2d ed. Berlin, 1966.

Dodds, E. R. *The Greeks and the Irrational*. Berkeley and Los Angeles, 1951

————. "On Misunderstanding the *Oedipus Rex*." *G&R* 13 (1966). 37–49. Reprinted in *Twentieth-Century Interpretations of Oedipus Rex*, ed. M J. O'Brien, 17–29. Englewood Cliffs, N.J., 1968. References are to the reprint edition.

Dolin, E "Interpretations of Pindar's Isthmian 6 and Pythian 12." Ph.D. diss , Harvard, 1965.

Dover, K. J. *Greek Popular Morality in the Time of Plato and Aristotle*. Oxford, 1974.

————, ed. *Aristophanes. Clouds* Oxford, 1968.

Dryden, J. "Preface containing the Grounds of Criticism in Tragedy" to *Troilus and Cressida* (1679). In *Essays of John Dryden*, ed. W. P. Ker, 1.202–29. Oxford, 1926.

Dupont-Roc, R. "Mimesis et énonciation." In *Écriture*, 6–14.

Dupont-Roc, R., and J. Lallot *Aristote: La poétique.* Paris, 1980.

During, I. *Aristotle's Chemical Treatise: Meteorologica, Book IV.* Goteborg, 1944.

Dworacki, S. "Anagnorismos in Greek Drama." *Eos* 66 (1978): 41–54.

Easterling, P. E "Constructing Character in Greek Tragedy." In Pelling, *Characterization*, 83–99.

———. "Presentation of Character in Aeschylus." *G&R* 20 (1973): 3–19.

——— "Tragedy and Ritual." *Metis* 3, no. 1–2 (1988): 87–109.

Eaton, M. M. "A Strange Kind of Sadness." *JAAC* 41 (1982). 51–63.

Écriture et théorie poétique. Paris, 1976.

Eden, K. *Poetic and Legal Fiction in the Aristotelian Tradition.* Princeton, 1986.

Else, G. F. *Aristotle's Poetics: The Argument.* Cambridge, Mass., 1967.

———. " 'Imitation' in the Fifth Century." *CP* 53 (1958): 73–90, and addendum, 245.

———. *Plato and Aristotle on Poetry.* Ed. P Burian. Chapel Hill and London, 1986.

———. "A Survey of Work on Aristotle's *Poetics*, 1940–1954." *Classical Weekly* 48 (1955). 73–82.

Engberg-Pedersen, T. *Aristotle's Theory of Moral Insight* Oxford, 1983.

England, E., ed. *The Laws of Plato.* 2 vols. Manchester and London, 1921.

Erbst, H , ed. *Scolia Graeca in Homeri Iliadem.* Berlin, 1969.

Erffa, C.E.F. von. *Aidos und verwandte Begriffe in ihrer Entwicklung von Homer bis Demokrit. Philologus* suppl. vol 30 2. Leipzig, 1937.

Feldman, T. "Gorgo and the Origins of Fear." *Arion* 4 (1965): 484–94. See also Howe.

Finsler, G "Die medizinischen Grundlagen der Lehre von der Wirkung der Dichtung in der griechischen Poetik." *Hermes* 84 (1956): 12–48.

———. *Platon und die aristotelische Poetik.* Leipzig, 1900.

Flashar, H. *Aristoteles. Problemata physica.* Berlin, 1962.

Floren, J. *Studien zur Typologie des Gorgoneion.* Munster, 1977.

Foley, H P. "The Masque of Dionysus." *TAPA* 110 (1980). 107–33.

Forbes, R. J. *Studies in Ancient Technology.* 2d ed. Vol. 9. Leiden, 1972.

Fortenbaugh, W W. "Aristotle and the Questionable Mean-Dispositions." *TAPA* 99 (1968). 203–31.

———. "Aristotle. Animals, Emotion, and Moral Virtue." *Arethusa* 4 (1971). 137–65.

———. "Aristotle Emotion and Moral Virtue." *Arethusa* 2 (1969). 163–85.

———. *Aristotle on Emotion.* London, 1975.

———. "Aristotle's Analysis of Friendship." *Phronesis* 20 (1975). 51–62.

——— "Un modo di affrontare la distinzione fra virtù etica e saggezza in Aristotele." *Museum Patavinum* 5 (1987). 243–58.

Fraenkel, E., ed. *Aeschylus. Agamemnon.* 3 vols. Oxford, 1962.

Fraisse, J.-C. "*Autarkeia* et *Philia* en EE VII 12, 1244b1–1245b19." In *Peripatoi,*

Bd 1, Untersuchungen zur eudemischen Ethik: Akten des 5. Symposium aristotelicum, ed. P. Moraux and D. Harlfinger, 245–51. Berlin, 1971

Freud, S. "Creative Writers and Daydreaming" (1908). In *The Standard Edition of the Complete Psychological Works of Sigmund Freud,* trans. and ed. J. Strachey, 9:143–53. London, 1959.

Friedrich, R. "*Epeisodion* in Drama and Epic." *Hermes* 11 (1983): 34–52.

Frisk, H. *Griechisches etymologisches Worterbuch.* Heidelberg, 1973.

Furley, D. J. "Aristotle on the Voluntary." In Barnes, Schofield, and Sorabji, *Articles* 2.47–60.

———. "The Mechanics of *Meteorologica* IV " In Moraux and Wiesner, *Zweifelhaftes,* 73–93.

Furth, M., trans. *Aristotle: Metaphysics, Books VII–X* Indianapolis, 1985

Gallavotti, C. "Paralogismi di Ulisse nella Poetica di Aristotele." *La parola del passato* 23 (1968). 241–61.

———, ed. *Aristotele: Dell' arte poetica.* Milan, 1974.

Gallop, D. "Animals in the *Poetics* " In Annas, *Oxford Studies,* 8·145–71

Garvie, A. "Aeschylus' Simple Plots." In *Dionysiaca,* ed R. D. Dawe, J. Diggle, and P. E Easterling, 63–86 Cambridge, 1978.

Gauthier, R. A., and J. Y. Jolif *Aristote. L'éthique à Nicomaque.* 2d ed. 4 vols. Paris and Louvain, 1970.

Gellrich, M. *Tragedy and Theory.* Princeton, 1988.

Gentili, B. *Poesia e pubblico nella Grecia antica.* Rome and Bari, 1985.

Gilbert, A. H. "The Word *Epeisodion* in Aristotle's *Poetics.*" *AJP* 70 (1949). 56–64.

Glanville, I. "Note on *Peripeteia.*" *CQ* 41 (1947) 73–78.

Glotz, G. *La solidarité de la famille dans le droit criminel en Grèce.* Paris, 1904.

Goheen, R. F. "Aspects of Dramatic Symbolism " *AJP* 76 (1955) 113–37.

Golden, L. "Catharsis." *TAPA* 93 (1962). 51–60.

———. "The Clarification Theory of *Katharsis.*" *Hermes* 104 (1976) 437–52.

———. "Epic, Tragedy, and Catharsis " *CP* 71 (1976). 77–85.

———. "Is Tragedy the 'Imitation of a *Serious* Action'?" *GRBS* 6 (1965). 283–89.

———. "The Purgation Theory of Catharsis " *JAAC* 31 (1973). 473–79.

———. Review of Schutrumpf, *Bedeutung CP* 66 (1971): 286–87

Golden, L., trans., and O B. Hardison, Jr., commentator. *Aristotle's Poetics* Englewood Cliffs, N.J., 1968 Reprint, with addendum to bibliography. Tallahassee, Fla., 1981.

Goldhill, S. "Character and Action." In Pelling, *Characterization,* 100–27.

———. "The Great Dionysia and Civic Ideology." *JHS* 107 (1987) 58–76. Revised and reprinted in Winkler and Zeitlin, *Dionysos,* 97–129; references are to the *Dionysos* volume.

———. *Reading Greek Tragedy.* Cambridge, 1986.

Goldschmidt, V. *Temps physique et temps tragique chez Aristote.* Paris, 1982

Goldstein, H. D. "Mimesis and Catharsis Reëxamined." *JAAC* 24 (1966): 567–77.

Gombrich, E. H. *Art and Illusion.* 2d ed. Princeton, 1961.

———. "Meditations on a Hobby Horse" (1951). Reprinted in *Meditations on a Hobby Horse,* 1–11. 2d ed. London and New York, 1971.

Gooch, P. W. " 'Vice Is Ignorance': The Interpretation of Sophist 226a–231b." *Phoenix* 25 (1971): 124–33.

Goodman, N. *Languages of Art.* Indianapolis, 1976.

Gosling, J.C.B., and C.C.W. Taylor. *The Greeks on Pleasure.* Oxford, 1982.

Gotthelf, A. "Aristotle's Conception of Final Causality." In Gotthelf and Lennox, *Issues,* 204–42.

Gotthelf, A., and J. G. Lennox, eds. *Philosophical Issues in Aristotle's Biology.* Cambridge, 1987.

Gottschalk, H. B. "The Authorship of *Meteorologica,* Book IV." *CQ* 11 (1962): 67–79.

Gould, J. "Hiketeia." *JHS* 93 (1973): 74–103.

Grimaldi, W.M.A. *Aristotle, Rhetoric I: A Commentary.* New York, 1980. *Aristotle, Rhetoric II: A Commentary.* New York, 1988.

Gudeman, A. *Aristoteles: Peri Poiētikēs.* Berlin and Leipzig, 1934.

Gunn, J. *The Joy Makers.* Reprinted in *Classics of Modern Science Fiction,* ed. G. Zebrowski. Vol. 2. New York, 1984.

Hahnemann, S. *Organon of Medicine.* Trans. R. E. Dudgeon. Chicago, 1896.

Hall, F. W., and W. M. Geldart, eds. *Aristophanis comoediae.* 2d ed. Oxford, 1907.

Hall, R. *Plato and the Individual.* The Hague, 1963.

Halliwell, S. *Aristotle's Poetics.* London, 1986.

———, trans. *The Poetics of Aristotle.* London, 1987.

Hamlyn, D. W., trans. *Aristotle's De anima, Books II and III.* Oxford, 1968.

Hardie, W.F.R. *Aristotle's Ethical Theory.* 2d ed. Oxford, 1968.

Hardy, J. *Aristote: Poétique.* Paris, 1952.

Hathaway, B. *The Age of Criticism.* Ithaca, 1962.

———. "John Dryden and the Function of Tragedy." *PMLA* 58 (1943): 665–73.

Headlam, W. "The Last Scene of the *Eumenides.*" *JHS* 26 (1906): 268–77.

———. "Notes on Euripides." *CR* 15 (1901): 15–25, 98–108.

Heath, M. "Aristotelian Comedy." *CQ* 39 (1989): 344–54.

———. *The Poetics of Greek Tragedy.* Stanford, 1987.

———. *Unity in Greek Poetics.* Oxford, 1989.

Heer, C. de. *Makar-Eudaimon-Olbios.* Amsterdam, 1969.

Held, G. F. "*Spoudaios* and Teleology in the *Poetics.*" *TAPA* 114 (1984): 59–176.

Herman, G. *Ritualised Friendship and the Greek City.* Cambridge, 1987.

Herrick, M. T. "A Supplement to Cooper and Gudeman's Bibliography of the *Poetics* of Aristotle." *AJP* 52 (1931): 168–74.

Hicks, R. D , trans. *Aristotle. De anima.* London, 1907. Reprint Amsterdam, 1965.

Horn, H.-J "Zur Begrundung des Vorrangs der *praxis* vor dem *ēthos* in der aristotelischen Tragodientheorie " *Hermes* 103 (1975) 292–99

House, H. *Aristotle's Poetics* Revised by C Hardie London, 1956.

Howe [Feldman], T. P. "The Origin and Function of the Gorgon-Head " *American Journal of Archaeology* 58 (1954): 209–21 See also Feldman

Howell, W S. "Aristotle and Horace on Rhetoric and Poetics." *Quarterly Journal of Speech* 54 (1968). 325–39.

———. "Rhetoric and Poetics: A Plea for the Recognition of the Two Literatures." In *The Classical Tradition. Literary and Historical Studies in Honor of Harry Caplan*, ed. L. Wallach, 374–90. Ithaca, 1966.

Huffmeier, F. "Phronesis in den Schriften des Corpus Hippocraticum." *Hermes* 89 (1961): 51–84.

Iamblichus *Jamblique Les mystères d'Égypte* Ed and trans É des Places Paris, 1966.

Ibycus Scholarly Computer. TLG CD-ROM, 3/10/88 version.

Irwin, T. *Aristotle's First Principles.* Oxford, 1988.

———, trans. *Aristotle. Nicomachean Ethics.* Indianapolis, 1985

Jaeger, W. "Aristotle's Use of Medicine as Model of Method in His Ethics." *JHS* 77 (1957). 54–61.

Janko, R. *Aristotle on Comedy.* London, 1984.

———, trans. *Aristotle: Poetics I.* Indianapolis and Cambridge, 1987

Joachim, H. H., ed. *Aristotle on Coming-to-Be and Passing-Away* Oxford, 1922

Jones, J. *On Aristotle and Greek Tragedy.* Stanford, 1962.

Jones, W.H.S., trans. *Hippocrates* Vol. 4. Cambridge, Mass., 1979

Kahn, C. H. *The Art and Thought of Heraclitus.* Cambridge, 1979.

Kamerbeek, W. J. "A Note on Arist. *Poet* C. xi, 1452A22–26, 29–33." *Mnemosyne* 18 (1965): 279–81.

Kassel, R. ed. *Aristotelis De arte poetica liber.* Oxford, 1966

Keesey, D. "On Some Recent Interpretations of Catharsis." *The Classical World* 72 (1979). 193–205.

Kennedy, G. *The Art of Persuasion in Greece.* Princeton, 1963

Kerford, G. B. "Plato's Noble Art of Sophistry." *CQ*, n s. 4 (1954). 84–90

Keuls, E. C. *Plato and Greek Painting.* Leiden, 1978

Keyt, D. "Three Fundamental Theorems in Aristotle's *Politics* " *Phronesis* 32 (1987): 54–79.

Keyt, D., and F. D. Miller, Jr., eds. *A Companion to Aristotle's Politics.* Oxford, 1991.

Kohnken, A. *Die Funktion des Mythos bei Pindar.* Berlin, 1971.

Kokolakis, M. "Greek Drama: The Stirring of Pity " In Betts, Hooker, and Green, *Studies*, 1.170–78.

Koller, H. *Die Mimesis in der Antike.* Bern, 1954.

Krauskopf, I , and S -C Dahlinger "Gorgo, Gorgones " In *Lexicon Iconographicum*, 284–330

Kraut, R *Aristotle on the Human Good* Princeton, 1989

——— "Comments on Gregory Vlastos, 'The Socratic Elenchus ' " In Annas, *Oxford Studies*, 1 59–70

Kuhner, R , and B Gerth *Ausfuhrliche Grammatik der griechischen Sprache* (1890–1904) Reprint Leverkusen, 1955

Kullmann, W "Der Mensch als politisches Lebewesen bei Aristoteles " *Hermes* 108 (1980) 419–43 Translated as "Man as a Political Animal " In Keyt and Miller, *Companion*, 94–117 References are to the original

Laín Entralgo, P *The Therapy of the Word* Ed and trans L J Rather and J M Sharp New Haven, 1970

Lallot, J "La *mimesis* selon Aristote et l'excellence d'Homere " In *Ecriture*, 15–25

Lamberton, R D "*Philanthropia* and the Evolution of Dramatic Taste " *Phoenix* 37 (1983) 95–103

Lang, P "Imagery in Therapy An Information Processing Analysis of Fear " *Behavior Therapy* 8 (1977) 862–86

Lang, P , et al "Emotional Imagery Conceptual Structure and Pattern of Somato-Visceral Response ' *Psychophysiology* 17 (1980) 179–92

Lattimore, R "The Legend in Greek Tragedy " In *Literature and Western Civilization*, ed D Daiches and A Thorlby, 1 173–91 London, 1972

———, trans *The Iliad of Homer* Chicago, 1951

Lear, J "*Katharsis* " *Phronesis* 33 (1988) 297–326

Lee, H D P , trans *Aristotle Meteorologica* Cambridge, Mass , 1952

Leighton, S R "Aristotle and the Emotions " *Phronesis* 27 (1982) 144–74

——— "*Eudemian Ethics* 1220b11–13 " *CQ* 34 (1984) 135–38

Lennox, J G "Kinds, Forms of Kinds, and the More and the Less in Aristotle's Biology " In Gotthelf and Lennox, *Issues*, 339–59

Levine, D B "Symposium and the Polis " In *Theognis of Megara*, ed T J Figueira and G Nagy, 176–96 Baltimore, 1985

Lexicon Iconographicum Mythologiae Classicae Zurich and Munich, 1986

Liddell, H G , and R Scott, *A Greek-English Lexicon* 9th ed Rev H S Jones Oxford, 1968

Linforth, I M "The Corybantic Rites in Plato " *University of California Publications in Classical Philology* 13 (1946) 121–62

Lissarrague, F *The Aesthetics of the Greek Banquet* Trans A Szegedy-Maszak Princeton, 1990

Littré, E , ed *Oeuvres completes d'Hippocrate* 10 vols Paris, 1839–1861

Lloyd, G E R "The Role of Medical and Biological Analogies in Aristotle's Ethics " *Phronesis* 13 (1968) 68–83

Lobel, E , and D L Page *Poetarum Lesbiorum fragmenta* Oxford, 1955

Lock, W "The Use of *Peripeteia* in Aristotle's *Poetics* " *CR* 9 (1895) 251–53

Lord, Carnes. *Education and Culture in the Political Thought of Aristotle.* Ithaca, 1982.

Lord, Catherine. "Tragedy without Character. *Poetics* VI.1450a24." *JAAC* 28 (1969–1970): 55–62.

Louis, P., ed. *Aristote. Histoire des animaux.* Paris, 1964–1969.

Lucas, D. W. "Pity, Terror, and *Peripeteia.*" *CQ* 12 (1962): 52–60.

—, ed. *Aristotle: Poetics.* Oxford, 1972.

Lucas, F. L. "The Reverse of Aristotle." *CR* 37 (1923). 98–104.

Lyons, W. *Emotion.* Cambridge, 1980.

MacKinney, L. "The Concept of Isonomia in Greek Medicine." In *Isonomia. Studien zur Gleichheitsvorstellung im griechischen Denken,* ed. J. Mau and E. Schmidt, 79–88. Berlin, 1964.

Macleod, C. W. "Clothing in the *Oresteia.*" *Maia* 27 (1975). 201–3. Reprinted in *Collected Essays,* 41–43. Oxford, 1983. References are to the reprint edition.

—. "Politics and the *Oresteia.*" *JHS* 102 (1982) 124–44. Reprinted in *Collected Essays,* 20–40. Oxford, 1983. References are to the reprint edition.

—, ed. *Homer: Iliad, Book XXIV.* Cambridge, 1982.

Maggi, V., and B. Lombardi. *In Aristotelis librum de poetica communes explanationes.* Venice, 1550.

Maloney, G., and W. Frohn, eds. *Concordance des oeuvres hippocratiques.* Quebec, 1984.

Mannison, D. "On Being Moved by Fiction." *Philosophy* 60 (1985). 71–87.

Maxwell-Stuart, P. G. "The Appearance of Aeschylus' Erinyes." *G&R* 20 (1973). 81–84.

Minturno, A. S. *Antonii Sebastiani Minturni De poeta* Venice, 1559.

Modrak, D.K.W. *Aristotle· The Power of Perception.* Chicago, 1987.

Moles, J. "Notes on Aristotle, *Poetics* 13 and 14." *CQ* 29 (1979). 77–94.

—. "*Philanthropia* in the Poetics." *Phoenix* 38 (1984): 325–35.

Moraux, P., and J. Wiesner, eds. *Zweifelhaftes im Corpus Aristotelicum: Akten des 9. Symposium Aristotelicum (Berlin, 7.–16. September 1981).* Berlin and New York, 1983.

Moreau, A. "L'oeil maléfique dans l'oeuvre d'Eschyle." *Revue des études anciennes* 78–79 (1976–1977). 50–64.

Morrow, G. "Aristotle's Comments on Plato's *Laws.*" In *Aristotle and Plato in the Mid-Fourth Century,* ed. I. During and G.E.L Owen, 145–62. Goteborg, 1960.

Moulinier, L. *Le pur et l'impur dans la pensée des Grecs* Paris, 1952.

Mourelatos, A.P.D. "Aristotle's Rationalist Account of Qualitative Interaction." *Phronesis* 29 (1984): 1–16.

Moutsopoulos, E. *La musique dans l'oeuvre de Platon.* Paris, 1959.

—. "Nausée et 'Catharsis des Passions.' " *Diotima* 10 (1982): 76–80.

Mulgan, R. G. "Aristotle's Doctrine that Man Is a Political Animal." *Hermes* 102 (1974): 438–45.

Müller, C. W. *Gleiches zu Gleichem: Ein Prinzip frühgriechischen Denkens*. Wiesbaden, 1965.

Murray, O., ed. *Sympotica*. Oxford, 1990.

Nagy, G. *The Best of the Achaeans*. Baltimore, 1979.

———. *Pindar's Homer*. Baltimore, 1990.

Napier, A. D. *Masks, Transformation, and Paradox*. Berkeley and Los Angeles, 1986.

Nardelli, M. L. "La catarsi poetica nel PHerc. 1581." *Cronache Ercolanesi* 8 (1978): 96–103.

Nauck, A., ed. *Tragicorum Graecorum fragmenta*. 2d ed. Leipzig, 1889. Reprint. Hildesheim, 1964.

Newman, W. L. *The Politics of Aristotle*. 4 vols. Oxford, 1887–1902.

Ničev, A. *L'énigme de la catharsis tragique dans Aristote*. Sofia, 1970.

———. "Olympiodore et la catharsis tragique d'Aristote." In *Studi in onore de A. Ardizzoni*, ed. E. Livrea and G. A. Privitera, 641–59. Rome, 1978.

Nickau, K. "Epeisodion und Episode." *MH* 23 (1966): 155–71.

Niese, B. "Gorgo." In *Paulys Realencyclopädie der classischen Altertumswissenschaft*, revised by G. Wissowa, 8.2:1630–55. Stuttgart, 1893.

North, H. *Sophrosyne*. Ithaca, 1966.

Nussbaum, M. C. "Fictions of the Soul." *Philosophy and Literature* 7 (1983): 145–61.

———. *The Fragility of Goodness*. Cambridge, 1986.

———, ed. and trans. *Aristotle's De motu animalium*. Princeton, 1978.

O'Brien, M. J. "Orestes and the Gorgon: Euripides' *Electra*." *AJP* 85 (1964): 13–39.

———. *The Socratic Paradoxes and the Greek Mind*. Chapel Hill, 1967.

Olympiodorus. *Olympiodorus: Commentary on the First Alcibiades of Plato*. Ed. L. G. Westerink. Amsterdam, 1956.

———. *Olympiodorus: In Platonis Gorgiam Commentaria*. Ed. L. G. Westerink. Leipzig, 1970.

Ostwald, M. *Anagkē in Thucydides*. Atlanta, 1988.

Owen, G.E.L. "Aristotelian Pleasures." *Proceedings of the Aristotelian Society* 72 (1971–1972): 135–52. Reprinted in Barnes, Schofield, and Sorabji, *Articles*, 2:92–103.

Packer, M. "The Conditions of Aesthetic Feeling in Aristotle's *Poetics*." *BJA* 24 (1984): 138–48.

Page, D., ed. *Aeschyli septem quae supersunt tragoedias*. Oxford, 1972.

Parker, R. *Miasma: Pollution and Purification in Early Greek Religion*. Oxford, 1983.

Pearson, L. "Characterization in Drama and Oratory—*Poetics* 1450a20." *CQ* 18 (1968): 76–83.

Peck, A. L., ed. and trans. *Aristotle: Generation of Animals*. Cambridge, Mass., 1942.

Peck, A L *Aristotle Historia Animalium Books I–III* Cambridge, Mass , 1979 *Books IV–VI* Cambridge, Mass , 1984

——— *Aristotle Parts of Animals* Cambridge, Mass , 1983

Pelling, C B R , ed *Characterization and Individuality in Greek Literature* Oxford, 1990

Pellizer, E "Della zuffa simpotica " In Vetta, *Poesia*, 31–41

Perrin, B "Recognition Scenes in Greek Literature " *AJP* 30 (1909) 371–404

Philippart, H "La theorie aristotelicienne de l anagnorisis " *REG* 38 (1925) 171–204

Phinney, E , Jr "Perseus' Battle with the Gorgons " *TAPA* 102 (1971) 445–63

Pickard-Cambridge, A *The Dramatic Festivals of Athens* 2d ed Revised by J Gould and D M Adams, with supplement and corrections Oxford, 1988

Places, E des, ed and trans *Jamblique Les mysteres d'Egypte* Paris, 1966

Pohlenz, M "Die Anfange der griechischen Poetik " *Nachrichten der Gesellschaft der Wissenschaften zu Gottingen, Philologisch-historische Klasse* (1920) 142–78 Reprinted in *Kleine Schriften*, ed H Dorrie, 2 436–72 Hildesheim, 1965 References are to the reprint edition

——— "Furcht und Mitleid? Ein Nachwort " *Hermes* 84 (1956) 49–74

Pollitt, J *The Ancient View of Greek Art* New Haven, 1974

Prag, A J N W *The Oresteia Iconographic and Narrative Tradition* Chicago, 1985

Price, A W *Love and Friendship in Plato and Aristotle* Oxford, 1989

Radford, C , and M Weston "How Can We Be Moved by the Fate of Anna Karenina?" *Proceedings of the Aristotelian Society*, suppl vol 49 (1975) 67–93

Radt, S L "Zum 13 Kapitel von Aristoteles' Poetik " In *Miscellanea Tragica in Honorem J C Kamerbeek*, ed J M Bremer, S L Radt, and C J Ruijgh, 271–84 Amsterdam, 1976

Raphael, D D *The Paradox of Tragedy* Bloomington, 1960

Rassow, H "Zu Aristoteles " *RhM* 43 (1888) 583–96

Reckford, K *Aristophanes' Old-and-New Comedy* Chapel Hill, 1987

——— "Catharsis and Dream-Interpretation in Aristophanes' *Wasps* " *TAPA* 107 (1977) 284–312

Rees, B R *"Pathos* in the *Poetics* of Aristotle " *G&R* 19 (1972) 1–11

——— "Plot, Character, and Thought " In *Le monde grec Pensee, litterature, histoire, documents Homages a Claire Préaux*, 188–96 Brussels, 1975

——— Review of Schutrumpf, *Bedeutung CR* 23 (1973) 50–52

Reynolds, E *A Treatise of the Passions* London, 1640

Riccioni, G "Origine e sviluppo del gorgoneion " *Rivista dell' istituto nazionale di archeologia e storia dell' arte*, n s 9 (1960) 127–206

Roberts, J "Political Animals in the *Nicomachean Ethics* " *Phronesis* 34 (1989) 185–204

Robortello, F *In librum Aristotelis de arte poetica explicationes* Florence, 1548

Rodier, G , trans *Aristote Traité de l'âme* 2 vols Paris, 1900

Romilly, J de *La crainte et l'angoisse dans le théâtre d'Eschyle* Paris, 1958

Rorty, A. O. "Aristotle on the Metaphysical Status of *Pathe*." *Review of Metaphysics* 37 (1984). 521–46

———. "The Psychology of Aristotelian Tragedy." In Rorty, *Poetics*.

———, ed. *Essays on Aristotle's Ethics*. Berkeley and Los Angeles, 1980.

——— *Essays on Aristotle's Poetics* Princeton, 1992.

Rose, H. J. *A Commentary on the Surviving Plays of Aeschylus*. Amsterdam, 1958.

Rosenmeyer, T. G. *The Art of Aeschylus* Berkeley and Los Angeles, 1982.

———. "Design and Execution in Aristotle, *Poetics* ch xxv." *California Studies in Classical Antiquity* 6 (1974). 231–52.

Ross, G.R.T. *Aristotle: De sensu and De memoria*. Cambridge, 1906.

Ross, W D., ed. *Aristotle's Metaphysics: A Revised Text with Introduction and Commentary*. 2 vols. Oxford, 1953

———. *Aristotle's Physics: A Revised Text with Introduction and Commentary*. Oxford, 1936.

Rostagni, A. "Aristotele e l'aristotelismo nella storia dell'estetica antica." *Studi italiani di filologia classica*, n.s. 2 (1922). 1–147. Reprinted in *Scritti minori I*, 76–237. Turin, 1955. References are to the reprint edition.

———, ed. *Aristotele: Poetica*. 2d ed. Turin, 1945.

Ryan, E. E "Robortello and Maggi on Aristotle's Theory of Catharsis " *Rinascimento*, ser. 2, vol. 22 (1982). 263–73.

Sachs, O. "Neurology and the Soul." *New York Review of Books*, 22 November 1990, 44–50.

Said, S. "Concorde et civilisation dans les *Euménides*." In *Théâtre et spectacles dans l'antiquité: Actes du colloque de Strasbourg, 5–7 novembre, 1981*, 97–121. Leiden, 1983.

———. *La faute tragique*. Paris, 1978.

Sainte-Croix, G.E.M. de. "Aristotle on History and Poetry (*Poetics* 9, 1451a36–b11)." In *The Ancient Historian and His Materials: Essays in Honour of C. E. Stevens on His Seventieth Birthday*, ed. B. Levick, 45–58. Farnborough, England, 1975.

Salkever, S. G. "Tragedy and the Education of the *Dēmos*. Aristotle's Response to Plato." In *Greek Tragedy and Political Theory*, ed. J. P. Euben, 274–303. Berkeley and Los Angeles, 1986.

Sarian, H. "Erinys." In *Lexicon Iconographicum*, 825–43.

Schadewaldt, W. "Furcht und Mitleid?" *Hermes* 83 (1955): 129–71.

Schaper, E. "Aristotle's Catharsis and Aesthetic Pleasure." *Philosophical Quarterly* 18 (1968): 131–43.

Schauenburg, K. "Zu attisch-schwarzfigurigen Schalen mit Innenfriesen." *Antike Kunst* 7 (1970): 33–46.

Schlesinger, E. "Pindar, Pyth. 12." *Hermes* 96 (1968). 275–86.

Schofield, M. "Aristotle on the Imagination." In *Aristotle on Mind and the Senses*, ed. G.E.R. Lloyd and G.E.L. Owen, 99–129. Cambridge, 1978. Reprinted in Barnes, Schofield, and Sorabji, *Articles* 4.103–32 References are to the reprint edition.

Schopsdau, K. "Tapferkeit, Aidos, und Sophrosyne im ersten Buch der platonischen Nomoi." *RhM* 129 (1986) 97–123.

Schrier, O. J. "A Simple View of *Peripeteia*." *Mnemosyne* 33 (1980) 96–118.

Schutrumpf, E. *Die Bedeutung des Wortes ēthos in der Poetik des Aristoteles* Munich, 1970.

Seaford, R. "Homeric and Tragic Sacrifice." *TAPA* 119 (1989) 87–88.

Segal, C. P. "Gorgias and the Psychology of the Logos." *HSCP* 66 (1962). 99–155.

Sellin, P. R. "Sources of Milton's Catharsis. A Reconsideration." *Journal of English and Germanic Philology* 60 (1961): 712–30.

Sheppard, J. T. "The Electra of Euripides." *CR* 32 (1918). 137–41

———, trans. *The Oedipus Tyrannus of Sophocles*. Cambridge, 1920.

Sherman, N. *The Fabric of Character: Aristotle's Theory of Virtue* Oxford, 1989.

Sider, D. "Stagecraft in the *Oresteia*." *AJP* 99 (1978). 12–27

Sifakis, G. M. "Learning from Art and Pleasure in Learning. An Interpretation of Aristotle, *Poetics* 4 1448b8–19." In Betts, Hooker, and Green, *Studies* 1 211–22.

Slater, W. J "Doubts about Pindaric Interpretation " *CJ* 72 (1977). 193–208.

———. "Peace, the Symposium, and the Poet." *Illinois Classical Studies* 6 (1981) 205–14.

Smyth, H. W. *Greek Grammar*. Rev. G. M. Messing. Cambridge, Mass., 1956

Solmsen, F. *Aristotle's System of the Physical World*. Ithaca, 1960.

———. "Citations in Their Bearing on the Origin of 'Aristotle,' *Meteorologica* iv." *Hermes* 113 (1985): 448–59.

———. *Hesiod and Aeschylus*. Ithaca, 1949.

———. "Leisure and Play in Aristotle's Ideal State." *RhM* 107 (1964). 193–220.

———. Review of Rostagni, *La Poetica di Aristotele. Gnomon* 5 (1929). 400–14.

Sommerstein, A. H., ed. *Aeschylus. Eumenides.* Cambridge, 1989

Sorabji, R. *Aristotle on Memory*. London, 1972

———. "Aristotle on the Role of Intellect in Virtue " *Proceedings of the Aristotelian Society*, n.s. 74 (1973–1974). 107–29. Reprinted in Rorty, *Ethics*, 201–19. References are to the reprint edition.

———. *Necessity, Cause, and Blame*. Ithaca, 1980

Sörbom, G. *Mimesis and Art*. Stockholm, 1966.

Spiegel, N. "The Nature of Katharsis According to Aristotle." *Revue belge de philologie et d'histoire* 43 (1965). 22–39.

Stalley, R. *An Introduction to Plato's Laws*. Indianapolis, 1983.

Stanford, W. B. *Greek Tragedy and the Emotions*. London and Boston, 1983.

Stark, R. *Aristotelesstudien*. Munich, 1954.

Stefanini, L. "La catarsi musicale dei pitagorici " *Rivista di storia della filosofia* 4 (1949). 1–10

Stevens, E. B. "Some Attic Commonplaces of Pity." *AJP* 65 (1944): 1–25.

Stinton, T.C.W. "*Hamartia* in Aristotle and Greek Tragedy." *CQ* 25 (1975): 221–54.

Stocks, J. L. "*Scholē*." *CQ* 30 (1936): 177–87.

Strohm, H. "Beobachtungen zum vierten Buch der aristotelischen Meteorologie." In Moraux and Wiesner, *Zweifelhaftes*, 94–115.

Susemihl, F., and R. D. Hicks, eds. *The Politics of Aristotle*. London and New York, 1894.

Sutton, D. F. "*P. Herc.* 1581: The Argument." *Philosophia* 12 (1982): 270–76.

Taplin, O. *Greek Tragedy in Action*. Berkeley and Los Angeles, 1978.

———. *The Stagecraft of Aeschylus*. Oxford, 1977.

Tarkow, T. A. "Thematic Implications of Costuming in the *Oresteia*." *Maia* 32 (1980): 153–65.

Tate, J. Review of Koller, *Mimesis*. *CR*, n.s. 5 (1955): 258–60.

Taylor, A. E. *A Commentary on Plato's Timaeus*. Oxford, 1928.

Tecuşan, M. "*Logos Sympotikos*: Patterns of the Irrational in Philosophical Drinking." In Murray, *Sympotica*, 238–60.

Teichmüller, G. *Aristotelische Forschungen*. Halle, 1869.

Themistius. *Themistii in libros Aristotelis De anima paraphrasis*. Ed. R. Heinze. Berlin, 1899.

Thivel, A. *Cnide et Cos? Essai sur les doctrines medicales dans la collection hippocratique*. Paris, 1981.

Tracy, T. *Physiological Theory and the Doctrine of the Mean in Plato and Aristotle*. The Hague and Paris, 1969.

Trendall, A. D., and T.B.L. Webster. *Illustrations of Greek Drama*. London, 1971.

Trilling, L. "Freud and Literature." In *Criticism*, ed. M. Schorer, J. Miles, and G. McKenzie, 172–82. New York, 1948.

Tsagarakis, O. "*Katachrēsis* of the Aristotelian Term *Epeisodion* as Applied to Homer." *REG* 86 (1973): 294–307.

Turner, P. "The Reverse of Vahlen." *CR* 9 (1959): 207–15.

Vahlen, J. *Beiträge zu Aristoteles' Poetik*. Berlin and Leipzig, 1914.

Verdenius, W. J. "Arist. *Poet*. 1452a25." *Mnemosyne* 18 (1965): 281.

———. "Traditional and Personal Elements in Aristotle's Religion." *Phronesis* 5 (1960): 56–70.

Vernant, J.-P. "Ambiguity and Reversal." In *Tragedy and Myth in Ancient Greece*, by J.-P. Vernant and P. Vidal-Naquet, trans. J. Lloyd, 87–119. Sussex, 1981.

Vetta, M., ed. *Poesia e simposio nella Grecia antica: Guida storica e critica*. Rome and Bari, 1983.

Vickers, B. *Towards Greek Tragedy*. London, 1973.

Vlastos, G. "Afterthoughts on the Socratic Elenchus." In Annas, *Oxford Studies* 1:71–74.

Vlastos, G "Equality and Justice in Early Greek Cosmologies " CP 42 (1947) 156–78

———— "The Socratic Elenchus " In Annas, Oxford Studies 1 27–58

Voelke, A -J Les rapports avec autrui dans la philosophie grecque d'Aristote a Panétius Paris, 1961

Vondeling, J "Eranos " Ph D diss , Utrecht, 1961

Vourveris, K "ΘΕΙΟΣ ΦΟΒΟΣ " Ἐπιστημονικὴ ἐπετηρὶς τῆς φιλοσοφικῆς σχολῆς τοῦ πανεπιστημίου Ἀθηνῶν (University of Athens) 10 (1953–1954) 122–31

Vuillemin, J "Le paralogisme du bain " REG 94 (1981) 287–94

———— "La reconnaissance dans l'épopée et dans la tragedie " Archiv fur Geschichte der Philosophie 66 (1984) 243–80

Wagner, C " 'Katharsis' in der aristotelischen Tragodiendefinition " Grazer Beitrage 11 (1984) 67–87

Walsh, G B The Varieties of Enchantment Chapel Hill, 1984

Waterlow, S Nature, Change, and Agency in Aristotle's Physics Oxford, 1982

Wedin, M V Mind and Imagination in Aristotle New Haven, 1988

Weinberg, B "Formal Analysis in Poetry and Rhetoric " In Papers in Rhetoric and Poetic, ed D Bryant, 36–45 Iowa City, 1965

———— A History of Literary Criticism in the Italian Renaissance 2 vols Chicago, 1961

Westerink, L G , ed Olympiodorus Commentary on the First Alcibiades of Plato Amsterdam, 1956

White, D R "A Sourcebook on the Catharsis Controversy Ph D diss , Florida State University, 1984

Williams, C J F , trans Aristotle's De generatione et corruptione Oxford, 1982

Winkler, J J 'The Ephebes' Song Tragōidia and Polis ' Representations 11 (1985) 26–62 Reprinted in Winkler and Zeitlin, Dionysos, 20–62, references are to the Dionysos volume

———— "An Oscar for Iphigeneia " Martin Classical Lecture no 4, Stanford, Calif , September 1988 In Rehearsals of Manhood Princeton, forthcoming

Winkler, J J , and Froma I Zeitlin, eds Nothing to Do with Dionysos ? Athenian Drama in Its Social Context Princeton, 1990

Wollheim, R Painting as an Art Princeton, 1987

Woods, M , trans Aristotle's Eudemian Ethics Books I, II, and VIII Oxford, 1982

Wordsworth, W "Preface to Lyrical Ballads ' (1850) In The Prose Works of William Wordsworth, ed W J B Owen and J W Smyser Oxford, 1974

Xanthakis-Karamanos, G Studies in Fourth-Century Tragedy Athens, 1980

Young, C "Aristotle on Temperance " PR 97 (1988) 521–42

* Index of Passages Cited *

Libation Bearers
16 158
35 25
46. 25
55–59 25
84–151 158
164–211 158
212ff 158
219 158n 75
283 25
288 24n 54, 25
297–305 109
523–25 25
535 25
547 25
831–37 20n 35
887 159
889 159
893 159
899–904 109
929 25
1024 25
1048–50 20
1052 25
1056 24n 54, 25
1058 20, 21n 40

Persians
606 219n 99
931–33 159

Seven against Thebes
791 20

ARISTIDES QUINTILIANUS

De musica
2 9 326

ARISTOPHANES

Clouds
309–12 10

Daitales
frag 198 Kock 218n 93

Frogs
961–62 219
962 21n 42

1054–55 358
1182 100n 50
1187 100n 50

Wasps
115–24 321

ARISTOTLE

Categories
6a36–37 50n 17
6b28–30 50n 17
10b5–9 105n 61
14b6 68n 54

De interpretatione
16a19–20 50n 16
16a26–28 50n 16

Prior Analytics
I 25b14 115n 12
32b4–13 115n 12
32b5–6 115n 11
32b5–10 116
50a40 298
II 70a5 112n 3
70b16 243n 35

Posterior Analytics
I 78b18–20 307
78b18–19 307
II 94a22 113n 5
100a15–b1 63
100a16–b1 212

Topics
IV 126b17 221
VI 139b21 307
140a14–15 53
145b8 307
VIII 156a30–33 181n 3

Physics
II 192b8–15 59
192b13–14 56
192b16–19 59
193b3–5 59
193b8–12 59
194a21–22 53n 24

* General Index *

Ackrill, J L , 50n 16

action in drama and real life, 88–91, and *hamartia*, 168–70, as object of imitation, 45–46, 80, 81, 272, and passion (*poiein, paschein*), 311–14, 356, and *peripeteia*, 142–53, and *philia*, 70–71, 157–60 See also *praxis*

Adkins, A W H , 70–71, 103, 107n 65, 158, 165n 89, 236n

Aeschylus, 191, *Oresteia*, 19–30, 72–73, 108–9, 155, 158–59, 236–37, 297–98, 350–51, *Persians*, 159, 169, *Prometheus Bound*, 161–62, 169 See also audience

aidôs See shame

Alcmaeon, 35

allopathy in Aristotle's philosophy, 207, 267, 289, 291, 304, 306, 307–14, 319, 324–31, 336, 340, 343, distinguished from homeopathy, 266–68, in Greek medicine, 30, 35–38, 264, 278–79, 306, 340, in Greek philosophy, 30, 35–39, 264–68, 275, 279nn 65 and 69, 280n 71, 281, 283–84, 287–88, 323–24, 326–35, and tragic katharsis, chap 8, passim, 261–63, 270, 290, 340–60

Anaxagoras, 315

anaxios dustuchein See bad fortune

anger and *thumos* (spirit) in Aristotle's philosophy, 181–84, 228, 239, 270, 341–42, 354, 355n 33, in Greek literature and philosophy, 23, 26, 28, 328, 330, 350–51, 352–53, and *philia*, 342, and pity and fear, 342, and *Poetics*, 226, 261–62, 265, 355–56

audience and Aeschylus, 21, 26–30, 219, for tragedy, in *Poetics*, 216, 237, 326, 356–59

bad fortune, undeserved concept of, in *Poetics*, 106–7, and "contrary to expectation," 133, and *hamartia*, 166–67, and pity and fear, 85–86, 163, 229, 231, 234, 249, 250 *See also* good fortune

Bain, D , 27n 61

Baldry, H C , 68n 52

Balme, D , 56n 29, 58, 152–53

Barker, E , 204n 66

Bassett, S E , 98

Beare, J I , 269, 354

beauty, 60

Belfiore, E , 88n 12, 89n 16, 90n 19, 150n 46, 242n 33

Benveniste, E , 71nn 58 and 60

Bernays, J , 259, 260, 263, 269n 37, 276

Bley, R , 264

Blundell, M W , 118n 16

Bowra, C M , 15n 19

Brown, A L , 22n 48

Buonamici, F , 262

Burkert, W , 186nn 16 and 20–22, 191, 352

Burnett, A P , 137n 17

Burnyeat, M , 203nn 62 and 63, 205n

Burton, R W B , 18n 28

Busse, A , 264–65, 280n 71

Butcher, S H , 158, 269n 37, 270–71

Bywater, I , 130n 40, 133n 3, 150n 48, 153, 222, 231n 11, 263, 269, 271, 276, 284, 286, 293n 6

Carey, C , 163, 164n 88

character See *êthos*

Charles, D , 145n 35, 146, 198n 51, 201n 58, 213n 83

Charlton, W , 240n 30

choice in Aristotle's ethical works, 85, 197–99, 200–203, 206–7, 211–12, 213–14, 215–16, 237, in *Poetics*, 85–86, 88, 94–100, 101, 104–5, 108, 145

Clark, S R L , 112n 2

Code, A , 69

CPSIA information can be obtained
at www.ICGtesting.com
Printed in the USA
LVOW13s1202130418
573315LV00007B/39/P